LSAT*

ENDURANCE PRACTICE

KAPLAN

TEST PREP

*LSAT is a registered trademark of the Law School Admission Council.

Special thanks to the Kaplan teams who made this LSAT course possible:

Contributing Developers: Misha Alexeef, M.F.A., Joshua Allen, M.F.A. (exp. '11), Krista Ammons, Deborah Baker, J.D., Jennifer Barta, Chris Bauer, Ph.D. (exp. '13), Kevin Bedeau, Matthew Belinkie, Howard Bell, J.D., Jeff Boudreau, Richard Boutcher, J.D., Aaron Brown, Robert Brown, J.D., Juliet Brownell, Zarina Burbacki, Geri Burgert, Matthew Burke, M.Div., Jack Chase, J.D., Ahn Chi, Natasha Chua Tan, J.D. (exp. '12), Christopher Combs, Gerard Cortinez, Christopher Cosci, Emily Cripe, Ph.D. (exp. '12), John Cummins, Jeffrey Cunningham, Erin Decker, M.A., Zach Denver, J.D. (exp. '13), Michael Durante, J.D.(exp. '12), Ian Edelson, Scott Emerson, Cailin Emmett, Jesse Evans, Ben Fierce, Paula Fleming, Joe Freimuth, John Fritschie, J.D., Darcy Galane, J.D., Devu Gandhi, M.B.A., Megan Gendell, Christopher Gomes, Joanna Graham, Raul Grau, Aaron Hammes, William Havemann, J.D., Christian Hertzog, J.D., Jeannie Ho, Gar Hong, Jonathan Hopkins, Rebecca Houck, J.D., Cinzia Iacono, Sasha Kahn, Deborah Katz, J.D., Heather M. Kenney-Nield, J.D., Stuart Kovinsky, L.L.B., Sarah Kramer, Michael Kermmoade, Ph.D. (exp. '11), Joanne L'Abbate, Dianne Lake, Julie Lamberth, J.D., Lisa Lamming, J.D., Devin Landin, Matthew Landin, Carolyn Landis, J.D., Elizabeth Ledkovsky, J.D. (exp. '13), Farrah Lehman, Jay Libou, J.D. (exp. '13), Kristin Longley, Adam Loren, Keith Lubeley, Andrew Lucas, Wesley Madison, Kalee Magnani, J.D., Eric May, Danielle Mazza, Amy McClish, Shana McCullough, Sheryl McNamee, Jason Moss, M.B.A., Maria Nicholas, Walt Niedner, M.B.A., Josh Newville, J.D. (exp. '12), Deborah Osborn, J.D., Anne Pennick, Glenn Phillips, Lisa Plante, M.B.A., Lindsey Plyler, Kate Rawsthorne, J.D., Scott Reed, J.D., Andrew Royal, J.D., Helen Sabo, J.D., Stephanie Schrauth, Eric Sepe, Rebecca Shansky, Ph.D., Jessica Smith, Murl Smith, J.D., Stephen Snyder, Richard Spoonts, J.D. (exp. '13), Jennifer Steiger, J.D., M.B.A. (exp. '10), J. Ethan Sterling, M.A., Glen Stohr, J.D., Caroline Sykes, J.D., Bruce Symaka, L.L.B., Jeff Thomas, J.D., Anthony Todd, Shaunagh Tomlin, Barry Tonoff, Martha P. Torres, Michael Vandenbrooks, Bob Verini, M.F.A., Thomas Volo, Missy Wanstall, M.S., Bryce Warwick, J.D., Shane Wesley, Emily West, M.A., Andrew Whang, J.D., Wayne Wilden, Matthew Williamson, J.D., Dan Wittich, James Yeh, Matthew Zaller, Elizabeth Zeanah, Ph.D. (exp. '12), and Heather Zezeck.

Additional Support: Advisory Panel and Brain Trust, Customer Service, Corporate Marketing, Creative Services, Production Development, Kaplan Publishing, Catalyst, Corporate Research, Territory and Regional Staff, eLearning, Live Online, Graduate Programs, Scheduling, Mailroom, Technical Support, Midwest and Canada Territory, Philadelphia, Orange County, and Washington, DC Centers.

TABLE OF CONTENTS

Welcome to Endurance Practice

As you know, one of the most difficult aspects of the LSAT is its length—a full 3.5 hours of testing time (and much more when you count breaks and delays). Building your test-taking stamina is critical to performing well on Test Day.

As you work through the Kaplan program, you will be doing a good deal of work with full-length exams to build this endurance. Multiple additional full-length exams are provided in this book, should you have the opportunity to complete them. The Endurance Practice tests reflect a broad range of administration dates. We recommend starting with the most recent tests, which are closer to the front of the book; these are more likely to reflect what will be on your LSAT.

If you are an LSAT Advanced student, do not take Endurance Practice Tests 1 and 2. They will be taken as part of your class: Tests 6 and 5, respectively.

On Test Day, you will see five multiple-choice sections, including the "Experimental" section. Since only the four multiple-choice sections that count toward a score are released by the LSAC, a full section from an earlier exam has been added to function as an "Experimental" section and increase the realism of the Endurance Practice tests. The answer key at the end of each exam and the index at the back of the book will tell you which section has been added. **Do not look at this information until after you have completed the test.** Because you will ultimately see a test with five multiple-choice sections, it makes little sense to practice your endurance against only 80% of the test by doing just the original four released sections. When you are ready for endurance practice, complete all five sections under timed conditions (also include the Writing Sample as the 6th timed section if you have the opportunity). Answer grids for each exam are provided at the back of the book. After you've completed the test, enter your answers in Smart Reports™ to see your test score and receive personalized guidance and recommendations based on your performance.

This book contains PrepTests 55, 54, 53, 52, 51, 50, 48, 46, 42, 40, and sections of PrepTests 32, 31, 7, 5, 4, 3, and 1.

Note: If needed, material from these full-length tests can be used for additional mastery practice. Specific question types and difficulties can be located by referencing the Q-Rater on your online syllabus.

Endurance Practice

Endurance Practice Test 1

PrepTest 55 plus experimental from PrepTest 31, Section II

SCAN CODE: LL9001

1 **1** **1**

SECTION I

Time—35 minutes

25 Questions

Directions: The questions in this section are based on the reasoning contained in brief statements or passages. For some questions, more than one of the choices could conceivably answer the question. However, you are to choose the best answer; that is, the response that most accurately and completely answers the question. You should not make assumptions that are by commonsense standards implausible, superfluous, or incompatible with the passage. After you have chosen the best answer, blacken the corresponding space on your answer sheet.

1. The editor of a magazine has pointed out several errors of spelling and grammar committed on a recent TV program. But she can hardly be trusted to pass judgment on such matters: similar errors have been found in her own magazine.

The flawed reasoning in the argument above is most similar to that in which one of the following?

(A) Your newspaper cannot be trusted with the prerogative to criticize the ethics of our company: you misspelled our president's name.

(B) Your news program cannot be trusted to judge our hiring practices as unfair: you yourselves unfairly discriminate in hiring and promotion decisions.

(C) Your regulatory agency cannot condemn our product as unsafe: selling it is allowed under an existing-product clause.

(D) Your coach cannot be trusted to judge our swimming practices: he accepted a lucrative promotional deal from a soft-drink company.

(E) Your teen magazine should not run this feature on problems afflicting modern high schools: your revenue depends on not alienating the high school audience.

2. Soaking dried beans overnight before cooking them reduces cooking time. However, cooking without presoaking yields plumper beans. Therefore, when a bean dish's quality is more important than the need to cook that dish quickly, beans should not be presoaked.

Which one of the following is an assumption required by the argument?

(A) Plumper beans enhance the quality of a dish.

(B) There are no dishes whose quality improves with faster cooking.

(C) A dish's appearance is as important as its taste.

(D) None of the other ingredients in the dish need to be presoaked.

(E) The plumper the bean, the better it tastes.

3. Durth: Increasingly, businesses use direct mail advertising instead of paying for advertising space in newspapers, in magazines, or on billboards. This practice is annoying and also immoral. Most direct mail advertisements are thrown out without ever being read, and the paper on which they are printed is wasted. If anyone else wasted this much paper, it would be considered unconscionable.

Which one of the following most accurately describes Durth's method of reasoning?

(A) presenting a specific counterexample to the contention that direct mail advertising is not immoral

(B) asserting that there would be very undesirable consequences if direct mail advertising became a more widespread practice than it is now

(C) claiming that direct mail advertising is immoral because one of its results would be deemed immoral in other contexts

(D) basing a conclusion on the claim that direct mail advertising is annoying to those who receive it

(E) asserting that other advertising methods do not have the negative effects of direct mail advertising

GO ON TO THE NEXT PAGE.

4. Among the various models of Delta vacuum cleaners, one cannot accurately predict how effectively a particular model cleans simply by determining how powerful its motor is. The efficiency of dust filtration systems varies significantly, even between models of Delta vacuum cleaners equipped with identically powerful motors.

The argument's conclusion is properly drawn if which one of the following is assumed?

(A) For each Delta vacuum cleaner, the efficiency of its dust filtration system has a significant impact on how effectively it cleans.

(B) One can accurately infer how powerful a Delta vacuum cleaner's motor is from the efficiency of the vacuum cleaner's dust filtration system.

(C) All Delta vacuum cleaners that clean equally effectively have identically powerful motors.

(D) For any two Delta vacuum cleaners with equally efficient dust filtration systems, the one with the more powerful motor cleans more effectively.

(E) One cannot accurately assess how effectively any Delta vacuum cleaner cleans without knowing how powerful that vacuum cleaner's motor is.

5. Many scientists believe that bipedal locomotion (walking on two feet) evolved in early hominids in response to the move from life in dense forests to life in open grasslands. Bipedalism would have allowed early hominids to see over tall grasses, helping them to locate food and to detect and avoid predators. However, because bipedalism also would have conferred substantial advantages upon early hominids who never left the forest—in gathering food found within standing reach of the forest floor, for example—debate continues concerning its origins. It may even have evolved, like the upright threat displays of many large apes, because it bettered an individual's odds of finding a mate.

Which one of the following statements is most supported by the information above?

(A) For early hominids, forest environments were generally more hospitable than grassland environments.

(B) Bipedal locomotion would have helped early hominids gather food.

(C) Bipedal locomotion actually would not be advantageous to hominids living in open grassland environments.

(D) Bipedal locomotion probably evolved among early hominids who exclusively inhabited forest environments.

(E) For early hominids, gathering food was more relevant to survival than was detecting and avoiding predators.

6. Mathematics teacher: Teaching students calculus before they attend university may significantly benefit them. Yet if students are taught calculus before they are ready for the level of abstraction involved, they may abandon the study of mathematics altogether. So if we are going to teach pre-university students calculus, we must make sure they can handle the level of abstraction involved.

Which one of the following principles most helps to justify the mathematics teacher's argument?

(A) Only those who, without losing motivation, can meet the cognitive challenges that new intellectual work involves should be introduced to it.

(B) Only those parts of university-level mathematics that are the most concrete should be taught to pre-university students.

(C) Cognitive tasks that require exceptional effort tend to undermine the motivation of those who attempt them.

(D) Teachers who teach university-level mathematics to pre-university students should be aware that students are likely to learn effectively only when the application of mathematics to concrete problems is shown.

(E) The level of abstraction involved in a topic should not be considered in determining whether that topic is appropriate for pre-university students.

GO ON TO THE NEXT PAGE.

LSAT ADVANCED STUDENTS: THIS TEST IS TAKEN AS TEST 6 OF YOUR CLASS. DO NOT USE THIS TEST FOR PRACTICE.

1   1   1

7. In 1955, legislation in a certain country gave the government increased control over industrial workplace safety conditions. Among the high-risk industries in that country, the likelihood that a worker will suffer a serious injury has decreased since 1955. The legislation, therefore, has increased overall worker safety within high-risk industries.

Which one of the following, if true, most weakens the argument above?

(A) Because of technological innovation, most workplaces in the high-risk industries do not require as much unprotected interaction between workers and heavy machinery as they did in 1955.

(B) Most of the work-related injuries that occurred before 1955 were the result of worker carelessness.

→ (C) The annual number of work-related injuries has increased since the legislation took effect.

(D) The number of work-related injuries occurring within industries not considered high-risk has increased annually since 1955.

(E) Workplace safety conditions in all industries have improved steadily since 1955.

8. Economist: Historically, sunflower seed was one of the largest production crops in Kalotopia, and it continues to be a major source of income for several countries. The renewed growing of sunflowers would provide relief to Kalotopia's farming industry, which is quite unstable. Further, sunflower oil can provide a variety of products, both industrial and consumer, at little cost to Kalotopia's already fragile environment.

The economist's statements, if true, most strongly support which one of the following?

(A) Kalotopia's farming industry will deteriorate if sunflowers are not grown there.

(B) Stabilizing Kalotopia's farming industry would improve the economy without damaging the environment.

(C) Kalotopia's farming industry would be better off now if it had never ceased to grow any of the crops that historically were large production crops.

(D) A crop that was once a large production crop in Kalotopia would, if it were grown there again, benefit that country's farmers and general economy.

(E) Sunflower seed is a better crop for Kalotopia from both the environmental and the economic viewpoints than are most crops that could be grown there.

9. Several major earthquakes have occurred in a certain region over the last ten years. But a new earthquake prediction method promises to aid local civil defense officials in deciding exactly when to evacuate various towns. Detected before each of these major quakes were certain changes in the electric current in the earth's crust.

Which one of the following, if true, most weakens the argument?

(A) Scientists do not fully understand what brought about the changes in the electric current in the earth's crust that preceded each of the major quakes in the region over the last ten years.

(B) Most other earthquake prediction methods have been based on a weaker correlation than that found between the changes in the electric current in the earth's crust and the subsequent earthquakes.

(C) The frequency of major earthquakes in the region has increased over the last ten years.

(D) There is considerable variation in the length of time between the changes in the electric current and the subsequent earthquakes.

(E) There is presently only one station in the region that is capable of detecting the electric current in the earth's crust.

10. Unlike many machines that are perfectly useful in isolation from others, fax machines must work with other fax machines. Thus, in the fax industry, the proliferation of incompatible formats, which resulted from the large number of competing manufacturers, severely limited the usefulness—and hence the commercial viability—of fax technology until the manufacturers agreed to adopt a common format for their machines.

The information above provides the most support for which one of the following propositions?

(A) Whenever machines are dependent on other machines of the same type, competition among manufacturers is damaging to the industry.

(B) In some industries it is in the interest of competitors to cooperate to some extent with one another.

(C) The more competitors there are in a high-tech industry, the more they will have to cooperate in determining the basic design of their product.

(D) Some cooperation among manufacturers in the same industry is more beneficial than is pure competition.

(E) Cooperation is beneficial only in industries whose products depend on other products of the same type.

GO ON TO THE NEXT PAGE.

LSAT ADVANCED STUDENTS: THIS TEST IS TAKEN AS TEST 6 OF YOUR CLASS. DO NOT USE THIS TEST FOR PRACTICE.

1   1   1

11. In comparing different methods by which a teacher's performance can be evaluated and educational outcomes improved, researchers found that a critique of teacher performance leads to enhanced educational outcomes if the critique is accompanied by the information that teacher performance is merely one of several factors that, in concert with other factors, determines the educational outcomes.

[handwritten: just 1 factor]

Which one of the following best illustrates the principle illustrated by the finding of the researchers?

(A) Children can usually be taught to master subject matter in which they have no interest if they believe that successfully mastering it will earn the respect of their peers.

(B) People are generally more willing to accept a negative characterization of a small group of people if they do not see themselves as members of the group being so characterized.

(C) An actor can more effectively evaluate the merits of her own performance if she can successfully convince herself that she is really evaluating the performance of another actor.

(D) The opinions reached by a social scientist in the study of a society can be considered as more reliable and objective if that social scientist is not a member of that society.

(E) It is easier to correct the mistakes of an athlete if it is made clear to him that the criticism is part of an overarching effort to rectify the shortcomings of the entire team on which he plays.

12. Critic: A novel cannot be of the highest quality unless most readers become emotionally engaged with the imaginary world it describes. Thus shifts of narrative point of view within a novel, either between first and third person or of some other sort, detract from the merit of the work, since such shifts tend to make most readers focus on the author.

Which one of the following is an assumption necessary for the critic's conclusion to be properly drawn?

(A) Most readers become emotionally engaged with the imaginary world described by a novel only if the novel is of the highest quality.

(B) A novel is generally not considered to be of high quality unless it successfully engages the imagination of most readers.

(C) Most readers cannot become emotionally involved with a novel's imaginary world if they focus on the author.

(D) Most readers regard a novel's narrative point of view as representing the perspective of the novel's author.

(E) Shifts in narrative point of view serve no literary purpose.

13. People aged 46 to 55 spend more money per capita than people of any other age group. So it is puzzling that when companies advertise consumer products on television, they focus almost exclusively on people aged 25 and under. Indeed, those who make decisions about television advertising think that the value of a television advertising slot depends entirely on the number of people aged 25 and under who can be expected to be watching at that time.

Which one of the following, if true, most helps to explain the puzzling facts stated above?

(A) The expense of television advertising slots makes it crucial for companies to target people who are most likely to purchase their products.

(B) Advertising slots during news programs almost always cost far less than advertising slots during popular sitcoms whose leading characters are young adults.

(C) When television executives decide which shows to renew, they do so primarily in terms of the shows' ratings among people aged 25 and under.

(D) Those who make decisions about television advertising believe that people older than 25 almost never change their buying habits.

(E) When companies advertise consumer products in print media, they focus primarily on people aged 26 and over.

14. Eighteenth-century moralist: You should never make an effort to acquire expensive new tastes, since they are a drain on your purse and in the course of acquiring them you may expose yourself to sensations that are obnoxious to you. Furthermore, the very effort that must be expended in their acquisition attests their superfluity.

The moralist's reasoning is most vulnerable to criticism on the grounds that the moralist

(A) draws a conclusion that simply restates a claim presented in support of that conclusion

(B) takes for granted that the acquisition of expensive tastes will lead to financial irresponsibility

(C) uses the inherently vague term "sensations" without providing a definition of that term

(D) mistakes a cause of acquisition of expensive tastes for an effect of acquisition of such tastes

(E) rejects trying to achieve a goal because of the cost of achieving it, without considering the benefits of achieving it

GO ON TO THE NEXT PAGE.

KAPLAN

LSAT ADVANCED STUDENTS: THIS TEST IS TAKEN AS TEST 6 OF YOUR CLASS. DO NOT USE THIS TEST FOR PRACTICE.

1   1   1

15. Zack's Coffeehouse schedules free poetry readings almost every Wednesday. Zack's offers half-priced coffee all day on every day that a poetry reading is scheduled.

Which one of the following can be properly inferred from the information above?

(A) Wednesday is the most common day on which Zack's offers half-priced coffee all day.

(B) Most free poetry readings given at Zack's are scheduled for Wednesdays.

(C) Free poetry readings are scheduled on almost every day that Zack's offers half-priced coffee all day.

(D) Zack's offers half-priced coffee all day on most if not all Wednesdays.

(E) On some Wednesdays Zack's does not offer half-priced coffee all day.

16. Philosopher: An event is intentional if it is a human action performed on the basis of a specific motivation. An event is random if it is not performed on the basis of a specific motivation and it is not explainable by normal physical processes.

Which one of the following inferences conforms most closely to the philosopher's position?

(A) Tarik left the keys untouched on the kitchen counter, but he did not do so on the basis of a specific motivation. Therefore, the keys' remaining on the kitchen counter was a random event.

(B) Ellis tore the envelope open in order to read its contents, but the envelope was empty. Nevertheless, because Ellis acted on the basis of a specific motivation, tearing the envelope open was an intentional event.

(C) Judith's hailing a cab distracted a driver in the left lane. She performed the action of hailing the cab on the basis of a specific motivation, so the driver's becoming distracted was an intentional event.

(D) Yasuko continued to breathe regularly throughout the time that she was asleep. This was a human action, but it was not performed on the basis of a specific motivation. Therefore, her breathing was a random event.

(E) Henry lost his hold on the wrench and dropped it because the handle was slippery. This was a human action and is explainable by normal physical processes, so it was an intentional event.

17. It is a mistake to conclude, as some have, that ancient people did not know what moral rights were simply because no known ancient language has an expression correctly translatable as "a moral right." This would be like saying that a person who discovers a wild fruit tree and returns repeatedly to harvest from it and study it has no idea what the fruit is until naming it or learning its name.

Which one of the following is an assumption required by the argument?

(A) To know the name of something is to know what that thing is.

(B) People who first discover what something is know it better than do people who merely know the name of the thing.

(C) The name or expression that is used to identify something cannot provide any information about the nature of the thing that is identified.

(D) A person who repeatedly harvests from a wild fruit tree and studies it has some idea of what the fruit is even before knowing a name for the fruit.

(E) One need not know what something is before one can name it.

18. There is little plausibility to the claim that it is absurd to criticize anyone for being critical. Obviously, people must assess one another and not all assessments will be positive. However, there is wisdom behind the injunction against being judgmental. To be judgmental is not merely to assess someone negatively, but to do so prior to a serious effort at understanding.

Which one of the following most accurately expresses the main conclusion drawn in the argument?

(A) To be judgmental is to assess someone negatively prior to making a serious effort at understanding.

(B) It is absurd to criticize anyone for being critical.

(C) There is some plausibility to the claim that it is absurd to criticize anyone for being critical.

(D) Not all assessments people make of one another will be positive.

(E) There is wisdom behind the injunction against being judgmental.

GO ON TO THE NEXT PAGE.

LSAT ADVANCED STUDENTS: THIS TEST IS TAKEN AS TEST 6 OF YOUR CLASS. DO NOT USE THIS TEST FOR PRACTICE.

1   1   1

19. Even those who believe that the art of each age and culture has its own standards of beauty must admit that some painters are simply superior to others in the execution of their artistic visions. But this superiority must be measured in light of the artist's purposes, since the high merits, for example, of Jose Rey Toledo's work and his extraordinary artistic skills are not in doubt, despite the fact that his paintings do not literally resemble what they represent.

The claim that some painters are superior to others in the execution of their artistic visions plays which one of the following roles in the argument?

(A) It is a hypothesis that the argument attempts to refute.

(B) It is a generalization, one sort of objection to which the argument illustrates by giving an example.

(C) It is a claim that, according to the argument, is to be understood in a manner specified by the conclusion.

(D) It is a claim that the argument derives from another claim and that it uses to support its conclusion.

(E) It is a generalization that the argument uses to justify the relevance of the specific example it cites.

20. A study of rabbits in the 1940s convinced many biologists that parthenogenesis—reproduction without fertilization of an egg—sometimes occurs in mammals. However, the study's methods have since been shown to be flawed, and no other studies have succeeded in demonstrating mammalian parthenogenesis. Thus, since parthenogenesis is known to occur in a wide variety of nonmammalian vertebrates, there must be something about mammalian chromosomes that precludes the possibility of parthenogenesis.

A flaw in the reasoning of the argument is that the argument

(A) takes for granted that something that has not been proven to be true is for that reason shown to be false

(B) infers that a characteristic is shared by all nonmammalian vertebrate species merely because it is shared by some nonmammalian vertebrate species

(C) rules out an explanation of a phenomenon merely on the grounds that there is another explanation that can account for the phenomenon

(D) confuses a necessary condition for parthenogenesis with a sufficient condition for it

(E) assumes that the methods used in a study of one mammalian species were flawed merely because the study's findings cannot be generalized to all other mammalian species

21. Advertiser: Most TV shows depend on funding from advertisers and would be canceled without such funding. However, advertisers will not pay to have their commercials aired during a TV show unless many people watching the show buy the advertised products as a result. So if people generally fail to buy the products advertised during their favorite shows, these shows will soon be canceled. Thus, anyone who feels that a TV show is worth preserving ought to buy the products advertised during that show.

The advertiser's reasoning most closely conforms to which one of the following principles?

(A) If a TV show that one feels to be worth preserving would be canceled unless one took certain actions, then one ought to take those actions.

(B) If a TV show would be canceled unless many people took certain actions, then everyone who feels that the show is worth preserving ought to take those actions.

(C) If a TV show is worth preserving, then everyone should take whatever actions are necessary to prevent that show from being canceled.

(D) If one feels that a TV show is worth preserving, then one should take at least some actions to reduce the likelihood that the show will be canceled.

(E) If a TV show would be canceled unless many people took certain actions, then those who feel most strongly that it is worth preserving should take those actions.

GO ON TO THE NEXT PAGE.

LSAT ADVANCED STUDENTS: THIS TEST IS TAKEN AS TEST 6 OF YOUR CLASS. DO NOT USE THIS TEST FOR PRACTICE.

1

1

1

22. Psychologist: It is well known that becoming angry often induces temporary incidents of high blood pressure. A recent study further showed, however, that people who are easily angered are significantly more likely to have permanently high blood pressure than are people who have more tranquil personalities. Coupled with the long-established fact that those with permanently high blood pressure are especially likely to have heart disease, the recent findings indicate that heart disease can result from psychological factors.

Which one of the following would, if true, most weaken the psychologist's argument?

(A) Those who are easily angered are less likely to recover fully from episodes of heart disease than are other people.

(B) Medication designed to control high blood pressure can greatly affect the moods of those who use it.

(C) People with permanently high blood pressure who have tranquil personalities virtually never develop heart disease.

(D) Those who discover that they have heart disease tend to become more easily frustrated by small difficulties.

(E) The physiological factors that cause permanently high blood pressure generally make people quick to anger.

23. A professor of business placed a case-study assignment for her class on her university's computer network. She later found out that instead of reading the assignment on the computer screen, 50 out of the 70 students printed it out on paper. Thus, it is not the case that books delivered via computer will make printed books obsolete.

Which one of the following, if true, most strengthens the argument?

(A) Several colleagues of the professor have found that, in their non-business courses, several of their students behave similarly in relation to assignments placed on the computer network.

(B) Studies consistently show that most computer users will print reading material that is more than a few pages in length rather than read it on the computer screen.

(C) Some people get impaired vision from long periods of reading printed matter on computer screens, even if they use high quality computer screens.

(D) Scanning technology is very poor, causing books delivered via computer to be full of errors unless editors carefully read the scanned versions.

(E) Books on cassette tape have only a small fraction of the sales of printed versions of the same books, though sales of videos of books that have been turned into movies remain strong.

GO ON TO THE NEXT PAGE.

LSAT ADVANCED STUDENTS: THIS TEST IS TAKEN AS TEST 6 OF YOUR CLASS. DO NOT USE THIS TEST FOR PRACTICE.

1 1

24. Advertisement: Researchers studied a group of people trying to lose weight and discovered that those in the group who lost the most weight got more calories from protein than from carbohydrates and ate their biggest meal early in the day. So anyone who follows our diet, which provides more calories from protein than from anything else and which requires that breakfast be the biggest meal of the day, is sure to lose weight.

The reasoning in the advertisement is most vulnerable to criticism on the grounds that the advertisement overlooks the possibility that

(A) eating foods that derive a majority of their calories from carbohydrates tends to make one feel fuller than does eating foods that derive a majority of their calories from protein

(B) a few of the people in the group studied who lost significant amounts of weight got nearly all of their calories from carbohydrates and ate their biggest meal at night

(C) the people in the group studied who increased their activity levels lost more weight, on average, than those who did not, regardless of whether they got more calories from protein or from carbohydrates

(D) some people in the group studied lost no weight yet got more calories from protein than from carbohydrates and ate their biggest meal early in the day

(E) people who eat their biggest meal at night tend to snack more during the day and so tend to take in more total calories than do people who eat their biggest meal earlier in the day

25. Some twentieth-century art is great art. All great art involves original ideas, and any art that is not influential cannot be great art.

Each of the following statements follows logically from the set of statements above EXCEPT:

(A) Some influential art involves original ideas.

(B) Some twentieth-century art involves original ideas.

(C) Only art that involves original ideas is influential.

(D) Only art that is influential and involves original ideas is great art.

(E) Some twentieth-century art is influential and involves original ideas.

S T O P

IF YOU FINISH BEFORE TIME IS CALLED, YOU MAY CHECK YOUR WORK ON THIS SECTION ONLY.
DO NOT WORK ON ANY OTHER SECTION IN THE TEST.

2   **2**   **2**   **2**

SECTION II

Time—35 minutes

24 Questions

Directions: The questions in this section are based on the reasoning contained in brief statements or passages. For some questions, more than one of the choices could conceivably answer the question. However, you are to choose the best answer; that is, the response that most accurately and completely answers the question. You should not make assumptions that are by commonsense standards implausible, superfluous, or incompatible with the passage. After you have chosen the best answer, blacken the corresponding space on your answer sheet.

1. Moralist: TV talk shows are contributing to the moral decline in our country. By constantly being shown the least moral people in our society, viewers begin to think that such people are the norm, and that there is something wrong with being morally upright.

   TV talk show host: Well, if there is such a decline, it's not because of TV talk shows: we simply show people what they want to see. What can be wrong with letting the viewers decide? Furthermore, if restrictions were put on my show, that would amount to censorship, which is wrong.

   The moralist's and the TV talk show host's statements provide the most support for holding that they disagree about whether

   (A) TV talk shows should be censored
   (B) people's moral standards have changed
   (C) TV talk shows influence people's conception of what is the norm
   (D) TV talk shows, by presenting immoral guests, are causing a moral decline
   (E) it is wrong not to let the viewers decide what they want to see

2. For the last three years, entomologists have been searching for a parasite to help control a whitefly that has recently become a serious crop pest. Believing this new pest to be a variety of sweet-potato whitefly, the entomologists confined their search to parasites of the sweet-potato whitefly. Genetic research now shows the new pest to be a distinct species, the silverleaf whitefly. Therefore, the search for a parasite has so far been wasted effort.

   Which one of the following is an assumption on which the argument relies?

   (A) All varieties of the sweet-potato whitefly are serious crop pests.
   (B) If a crop pest has a parasite, that parasite can always be used to control that pest.
   (C) The chances of successfully identifying a useful parasite of the new pest have increased since the proper identification of the pest.
   (D) No parasite of the sweet-potato whitefly is also a parasite of the silverleaf whitefly.
   (E) In the last three years, the entomologists found no parasites of the sweet-potato whitefly.

3. Announcement for a television program: Are female physicians more sensitive than male physicians to the needs of women patients? To get the answer, we'll ask physicians of both sexes this question. Tune in tomorrow.

   Which one of the following, if true, identifies a flaw in the plan for the program?

   (A) Physicians are in general unwilling to describe the treatment style of other physicians.
   (B) There still are fewer women than men who are physicians, so a patient might not have the opportunity to choose a woman as a physician.
   (C) Those who are best able to provide answers to the question are patients, rather than physicians.
   (D) Since medical research is often performed on men, not all results are fully applicable to women as patients.
   (E) Women as patients are now beginning to take a more active role in managing their care and making sure that they understand the medical alternatives.

GO ON TO THE NEXT PAGE.

LSAT ADVANCED STUDENTS: THIS TEST IS TAKEN AS TEST 6 OF YOUR CLASS. DO NOT USE THIS TEST FOR PRACTICE.

2   2

4. Doctor: The practice of using this therapy to treat the illness cannot be adequately supported by the claim that any therapy for treating the illness is more effective than no therapy at all. What must also be taken into account is that this therapy is expensive and complicated.

Which one of the following most accurately expresses the main point of the doctor's argument?

(A) The therapy is more effective than no treatment at all for the illness.

(B) The therapy is more effective than other forms of treatment for the illness.

(C) The therapy is more expensive and complicated than other forms of treatment for the illness.

(D) The therapy should not be used to treat the illness unless it is either effective or inexpensive.

(E) The therapy's possible effectiveness in treating the illness is not sufficient justification for using it.

5. Television executives recently announced that advertising time on television will cost 10 to 15 percent more next fall than it cost last fall. The executives argued that in spite of this increase, advertisers will continue to profit from television advertising, and so advertising time will be no harder to sell next fall than it was last fall.

Which one of the following, if true, would most support the television executives' argument?

(A) Most costs of production and distribution of products typically advertised on television are expected to rise 3 to 7 percent in the next year.

(B) The system for rating the size of the audience watching any given television advertisement will change next fall.

(C) Next fall advertising time on television will no longer be available in blocks smaller than 30 seconds.

(D) The amount of television advertising time purchased by providers of services is increasing, while the amount of such time purchased by providers of products is decreasing.

(E) A recent survey has shown that the average number of hours people spend watching television is increasing at the rate of 2 percent every two months.

6. It is proposed to allow the sale, without prescription, of a medication that physicians currently prescribe to treat the common ear inflammation called "swimmer's ear." The principal objection is that most people lack the expertise for proper self-diagnosis and might not seek medical help for more serious conditions in the mistaken belief that they have swimmer's ear. Yet in a recent study, of 1,000 people who suspected that they had swimmer's ear, 84 percent had made a correct diagnosis—a slightly better accuracy rate than physicians have in diagnosing swimmer's ear. Thus, clearly, most people can diagnose swimmer's ear in themselves without ever having to consult a physician.

Which one of the following, if true, most undermines the conclusion?

(A) Cases in which swimmer's ear progresses to more serious infections are very rare.

(B) Most of those who suspected incorrectly that they had swimmer's ear also believed that they had other ailments that in fact they did not have.

(C) Most of the people who diagnosed themselves correctly had been treated by a physician for prior occurrence of swimmer's ear.

(D) Physicians who specialize in ear diseases are generally able to provide more accurate diagnoses than those provided by general practitioners.

(E) For many people who develop swimmer's ear, the condition disappears without medical or pharmaceutical intervention.

GO ON TO THE NEXT PAGE.

LSAT ADVANCED STUDENTS: THIS TEST IS TAKEN AS TEST 6 OF YOUR CLASS. DO NOT USE THIS TEST FOR PRACTICE.

2　　　2　　　2　　　2

7. Social critic: The whole debate over the legal right of rock singers to utter violent lyrics misses the point. Legally, there is very little that may not be said. But not everything that may legally be said, ought to be said. Granted, violence predates the rise in popularity of such music. Yet words also have the power to change the way we see and the way we act.

Which one of the following is most strongly supported by the passage?

(A) If rock music that contains violent lyrics is morally wrong, then it should be illegal.

(B) The law should be changed so that the government is mandated to censor rock music that contains violent lyrics.

(C) Violent rock song lyrics do not incite violence, they merely reflect the violence in society.

(D) If rock musicians voluntarily censor their violent lyrics, this may help to reduce violence in society.

(E) Stopping the production of rock music that contains violent lyrics would eliminate much of the violence within society.

8. For all species of higher animals, reproduction requires the production of eggs but not necessarily the production of sperm. There are some species whose members are all female; the eggs produced by a rare female-only species of salamander hatch without fertilization. This has the drawback that all offspring have genetic codes nearly identical to that of the single parent, making the species less adaptive than species containing both male and female members.

If the statements above are true, each of the following could be true EXCEPT:

(A) There are some species of salamanders that have both male and female members.

(B) There are some species of higher animals none of whose members produce eggs.

(C) There is a significant number of female-only species of higher animals.

(D) Some species of higher animals containing both female and male members are not very adaptive.

(E) Some offspring of species of higher animals containing both female and male members have genetic codes more similar to one parent than to the other parent.

9. As part of a survey, approximately 10,000 randomly selected individuals were telephoned and asked a number of questions about their income and savings. Those conducting the survey observed that the older the person being queried, the more likely it was that he or she would refuse to answer any of the questions. This finding clearly demonstrates that, in general, people are more willing when they are younger than when they are older to reveal personal financial information to strangers over the telephone.

The argument above is vulnerable to criticism on the grounds that the argument

(A) offers no evidence that the individuals queried would have responded differently had they been asked the same questions in years prior to the survey

(B) fails to specify the exact number of people who were telephoned as part of the survey

(C) assumes without warrant that age is the main determinant of personal income and savings levels

(D) assumes from the outset what it purports to establish on the basis of a body of statistical evidence

(E) provides no reason to believe that what is true of a given age group in general is also true of all individuals within that age group

GO ON TO THE NEXT PAGE.

LSAT ADVANCED STUDENTS: THIS TEST IS TAKEN AS TEST 6 OF YOUR CLASS. DO NOT USE THIS TEST FOR PRACTICE.

2   2   2   2

10. If something would have been justifiably regretted if it had occurred, then it is something that one should not have desired in the first place. It follows that many forgone pleasures should not have been desired in the first place.

The conclusion above follows logically if which one of the following is assumed?

(A) One should never regret one's pleasures.
(B) Forgone pleasures that were not desired would not have been justifiably regretted.
(C) Everything that one desires and then regrets not having is a forgone pleasure.
(D) Many forgone pleasures would have been justifiably regretted.
(E) Nothing that one should not have desired in the first place fails to be a pleasure.

11. Several thousand years ago, people in what is now North America began to grow corn, which grows faster and produces more food per unit of land than do the grains these people had grown previously. Corn is less nutritious than those other grains, however, and soon after these people established corn as their staple grain crop, they began having nutrition-related health problems. Yet the people continued to grow corn as their staple grain, although they could have returned to growing the more nutritious grains.

Which one of the following, if true, most helps to explain why the people mentioned continued to grow corn as their staple grain crop?

(A) The variety of corn that the people relied on as their staple grain produced more food than did the ancestors of that variety.
(B) Modern varieties of corn are more nutritious than were the varieties grown by people in North America several thousand years ago.
(C) The people did not domesticate large animals for meat or milk, either of which could supply nutrients not provided by corn.
(D) Some grain crops that could have been planted instead of corn required less fertile soil in order to flourish than corn required.
(E) The people discovered some years after adopting corn as their staple grain that a diet that supplemented corn with certain readily available nongrain foods significantly improved their health.

12. Some biologists believe that the capacity for flight first developed in marine reptiles, claiming that feathers are clearly developed from scales. Other biologists rightly reject this suggestion, pointing out that bats have no scales and that nonmarine reptiles also have scales. Those who believe that flight first developed in tree-dwelling reptiles reject the claim that the limbs of land-dwelling reptiles might have developed into wings. They insist that it is more likely that tree-dwelling reptiles developed wings to assist their leaps from branch to branch.

Which one of the following most accurately describes the role played in the passage by the claim that nonmarine reptiles have scales?

(A) It is cited as evidence against the claim that the capacity for flight first developed in marine reptiles.
(B) It is cited as evidence against the claim that the capacity for flight first developed in land-dwelling animals.
(C) It is cited as evidence against the claim that the capacity for flight first developed in tree-dwelling reptiles.
(D) It weakens the claim that tree-dwelling reptiles were the first kind of reptile to develop the capacity for flight.
(E) It corroborates the observation that some mammals without scales, such as bats, developed the capacity to fly.

GO ON TO THE NEXT PAGE.

2 **2**   **2**

13. Studies have shown that, contrary to popular belief, middle-aged people have more fear of dying than do elderly people.

Each of the following, if true, contributes to an explanation of the phenomenon shown by the studies EXCEPT:

(A) The longer one lives, the more likely it is that one has come to terms with dying.

(B) Middle-aged people have more people dependent upon them than people of any other age group.

(C) Many people who suffer from depression first become depressed in middle age.

(D) The longer one lives, the more imperturbable one becomes.

(E) Middle-aged people have a more acute sense of their own mortality than do people of any other age group.

14. Historian: Leibniz, the seventeenth-century philosopher, published his version of calculus before Newton did. But then Newton revealed his private notebooks, which showed he had been using these ideas for at least a decade before Leibniz's publication. Newton also claimed that he had disclosed these ideas to Leibniz in a letter shortly before Leibniz's publication. Yet close examination of the letter shows that Newton's few cryptic remarks did not reveal anything important about calculus. Thus, Leibniz and Newton each independently discovered calculus.

Which one of the following is an assumption required by the historian's argument?

(A) Leibniz did not tell anyone about calculus prior to publishing his version of it.

(B) No third person independently discovered calculus prior to Newton and Leibniz.

(C) Newton believed that Leibniz was able to learn something important about calculus from his letter to him.

(D) Neither Newton or Leibniz knew that the other had developed a version of calculus prior to Leibniz's publication.

(E) Neither Newton nor Leibniz learned crucial details about calculus from some third source.

15. For a ten-month period, the total monthly sales of new cars within the country of Calistan remained constant. During this period the monthly sales of new cars manufactured by Marvel Automobile Company doubled, and its share of the new car market within Calistan increased correspondingly. At the end of this period, emission standards were imposed on new cars sold within Calistan. During the three months following this imposition, Marvel Automobile Company's share of the Calistan market declined substantially even though its monthly sales within Calistan remained constant at the level reached in the last month of the ten-month period.

If the statements above are true, which one of the following CANNOT be true?

(A) The total monthly sales within Calistan of new cars by companies other than Marvel Automobile Company decreased over the three months following the imposition of the emission standards.

(B) Over the three months before the imposition of the emission standards, the combined market share of companies other than Marvel Automobile Company selling new cars in Calistan decreased.

(C) If the emission standards had not been imposed, Marvel Automobile Company would have lost an even larger share of the number of new cars sold in Calistan than, in fact, it did.

(D) A decrease in the total monthly sales of new cars within Calistan will occur if the emission standards remain in effect.

(E) Since the imposition of the emission standards, Marvel Automobile Company's average profit on each new car sold within Calistan has increased.

GO ON TO THE NEXT PAGE.

LSAT ADVANCED STUDENTS: THIS TEST IS TAKEN AS TEST 6 OF YOUR CLASS. DO NOT USE THIS TEST FOR PRACTICE.

2   2   2   2

Questions 16–17

Because addictive drugs are physically harmful, their use by athletes is never justified. Purists, however, claim that taking massive doses of even such nonaddictive drugs as aspirin and vitamins before competing should also be prohibited because they are unnatural. This is ridiculous; almost everything in sports is unnatural, from high-tech running shoes to padded boxing gloves to highly-specialized bodybuilding machines. Yet, none of these is prohibited on the basis of its being unnatural. Furthermore, we should be attending to far more serious problems that plague modern sports and result in unnecessary deaths and injuries. Therefore, the use of nonaddictive drugs by athletes should not be prohibited.

16. Which one of the following statements, if true, would be the strongest challenge to the author's conclusion?

  (A) Massive doses of aspirin and vitamins enhance athletic performance.
  (B) Addictive drugs are just as unnatural as nonaddictive drugs like aspirin and vitamins.
  (C) Unnecessary deaths and injuries occur in other walks of life besides modern sports.
  (D) There would be more unnecessary deaths and injuries if it were not for running shoes, boxing gloves, and bodybuilding machines.
  (E) Taking massive doses of aspirin or vitamins can be physically harmful.

17. Which one of the following can be inferred from the passage above?

  (A) The fact that something is unnatural is not a sufficient reason for banning it.
  (B) There is nothing unnatural about the use of nonaddictive drugs by athletes.
  (C) The use of addictive drugs by athletes should be prohibited because addictive drugs are unnatural.
  (D) Some of the unnecessary deaths and injuries in modern sports are caused by the use of addictive drugs by athletes.
  (E) The use of addictive drugs by athletes is a less serious problem than are unnecessary injuries.

18. Not all works of art represent something, but some do, and their doing so is relevant to our aesthetic experience of them; representation is therefore an aesthetically relevant property. Whether a work of art possesses this property is dependent upon context. Yet there are no clear criteria for determining whether context-dependent properties are present in an object, so there cannot be any clear criteria for determining whether an object qualifies as art.

The reasoning above is questionable because it fails to exclude the possibility that

  (A) because some works of art are nonrepresentational, there is no way of judging our aesthetic experience of them
  (B) an object may have some aesthetic properties and not be a work of art
  (C) aesthetically relevant properties other than representation can determine whether an object is a work of art
  (D) some works of art may have properties that are not relevant to our aesthetic experience of them
  (E) some objects that represent things other than themselves are not works of art

19. If the flowers Drew received today had been sent by someone who knows Drew well, that person would have known that Drew prefers violets to roses. Yet Drew received roses. On the other hand, if the flowers had been sent by someone who does not know Drew well, then that person would have sent a signed card with the flowers. Yet Drew received no card. Therefore, the florist must have made some sort of mistake: either Drew was supposed to receive violets, or a card, or these flowers were intended for someone else.

Which one of the following statements, if true, most weakens the argument?

  (A) Most people send roses when they send flowers.
  (B) Some people send flowers for a reason other than the desire to please.
  (C) Someone who does not know Drew well would be unlikely to send Drew flowers.
  (D) The florist has never delivered the wrong flowers to Drew before.
  (E) Some people who know Drew well have sent Drew cards along with flowers.

GO ON TO THE NEXT PAGE.

LSAT ADVANCED STUDENTS: THIS TEST IS TAKEN AS TEST 6 OF YOUR CLASS. DO NOT USE THIS TEST FOR PRACTICE.

2   2   2   2

20. One of the most vexing problems in historiography is dating an event when the usual sources offer conflicting chronologies of the event. Historians should attempt to minimize the number of competing sources, perhaps by eliminating the less credible ones. Once this is achieved and several sources are left, as often happens, historians may try, though on occasion unsuccessfully, to determine independently of the usual sources which date is more likely to be right.

Which one of the following inferences is most strongly supported by the information above?

(A) We have no plausible chronology of most of the events for which attempts have been made by historians to determine the right date.

(B) Some of the events for which there are conflicting chronologies and for which attempts have been made by historians to determine the right date cannot be dated reliably by historians.

(C) Attaching a reliable date to any event requires determining which of several conflicting chronologies is most likely to be true.

(D) Determining independently of the usual sources which of several conflicting chronologies is more likely to be right is an ineffective way of dating events.

(E) The soundest approach to dating an event for which the usual sources give conflicting chronologies is to undermine the credibility of as many of these sources as possible.

21. Bank deposits are credited on the date of the transaction only when they are made before 3 P.M. Alicia knows that the bank deposit was made before 3 P.M. So, Alicia knows that the bank deposit was credited on the date of the transaction.

Which one of the following exhibits both of the logical flaws exhibited by the argument above?

(A) Journalists are the only ones who will be permitted to ask questions at the press conference. Since Marjorie is a journalist, she will be permitted to ask questions.

(B) We know that Patrice works only on Thursday. Today is Thursday, so it follows that Patrice is working today.

(C) It is clear that George knows he will be promoted to shift supervisor, because George will be promoted to shift supervisor only if Helen resigns, and George knows Helen will resign.

(D) John believes that 4 is a prime number and that 4 is divisible by 2. Hence John believes that there is a prime number divisible by 2.

(E) Pat wants to become a social worker. It is well known that social workers are poorly paid. Pat apparently wants to be poorly paid.

22. On the surface, Melville's *Billy Budd* is a simple story with a simple theme. However, if one views the novel as a religious allegory, then it assumes a richness and profundity that place it among the great novels of the nineteenth century. However, the central question remains: Did Melville intend an allegorical reading? Since there is no textual or historical evidence that he did, we should be content with reading *Billy Budd* as a simple tragedy.

Which one of the following most accurately expresses the principle underlying the argument?

(A) Given a choice between an allegorical and a nonallegorical reading of a novel, one should choose the latter.

(B) The only relevant evidence in deciding in which genre to place a novel is the author's stated intention.

(C) In deciding between rival readings of a novel, one should choose the one that is most favorable to the work.

(D) Without relevant evidence as to a novel's intended reading, one should avoid viewing the work allegorically.

(E) The only relevant evidence in deciding the appropriate interpretation of a text is the text itself.

GO ON TO THE NEXT PAGE.

3 **3** **3** **3**

2. Given the passage's content and tone, which one of the following statements would most likely be found elsewhere in a work from which this passage is an excerpt?

(A) Given the law as it stands, corporations concerned about preserving trade secrets might be best served by giving their employees strong incentives to stay in their current jobs.

(B) While difficult to enforce and interpret, injunctions are probably the most effective means of halting the inadvertent transfer of trade secrets while simultaneously protecting the rights of employees.

(C) Means of redress must be made available to companies that suspect, but cannot prove, that former employees are revealing protected information to competitors.

(D) Even concrete materials such as computer disks are so easy to copy and conceal that it will be a waste of time for courts to try to prevent the spread of information through physical theft.

(E) The psychological barriers that an injunction can place on an employee in a new workplace are inevitably so subtle that they have no effect on the employee.

3. The author's primary purpose in the passage is to

(A) suggest that injunctions against the disclosure of trade secrets not only create problems for employees in the workplace, but also are unable to halt the illicit spread of proprietary information

(B) suggest that the information contained in "documents and other concrete embodiments" is usually so trivial that injunctions do little good in protecting intellectual property

(C) argue that new methods must be found to address the delicate balance between corporate and individual rights

(D) support the position that the concept of protecting trade secrets is no longer viable in an age of increasing access to information

(E) argue that injunctions are not necessary for the protection of trade secrets

4. The passage provides the most support for which one of the following assertions?

(A) Injunctions should be imposed by the courts only when there is strong reason to believe that an employee will reveal proprietary information.

(B) There is apparently no reliable way to protect both the rights of companies to protect trade secrets and the rights of employees to seek new employment.

(C) Employees should not be allowed to take jobs with their former employers' competitors when their new job could compromise trade secrets of their former employers.

(D) The multiplicity of means for transferring information in the workplace only increases the need for injunctions.

(E) Some companies seek injunctions as a means of punishing employees who take jobs with their competitors.

5. With which one of the following statements regarding documents and other concrete embodiments mentioned in line 58 would the author be most likely to agree?

(A) While the transfer of such materials would be damaging, even the seemingly innocuous contributions of an employee to a competitor can do more harm in the long run.

(B) Such materials are usually less informative than what the employee may recollect about a previous job.

(C) Injunctions against the disclosure of trade secrets should carefully specify which materials are included in order to focus on the most damaging ones.

(D) Large-scale transfer of documents and other materials cannot be controlled by injunctions.

(E) Such concrete materials lend themselves to control and identification more readily than do subtler means of transferring information.

6. In the passage, the author makes which one of the following claims?

(A) Injunctions against the disclosure of trade secrets limit an employee's chances of being hired by a competitor.

(B) Measures against the disclosure of trade secrets are unnecessary except in the case of documents and other concrete embodiments of the secrets.

(C) Employees who switch jobs to work for a competitor usually unintentionally violate the law by doing so.

(D) Employers are not restricted in the tactics they can use when seeking to secure protected information from new employees.

(E) What may seem like intellectual theft may in fact be an example of independent innovation.

GO ON TO TH

22

KAPLA

LSAT ADVANCED STUDENTS: THIS TEST IS TAKEN AS TEST 6 OF YOUR CLASS. DO NOT USE THIS TEST FOR PRACTICE.

3 3 3 3

The following passages concern a plant called purple loosestrife. Passage A is excerpted from a report issued by a prairie research council; passage B from a journal of sociology.

Passage A

Purple loosestrife (*Lythrum salicaria*), an aggressive and invasive perennial of Eurasian origin, arrived with settlers in eastern North America in the early 1800s and has spread across the continent's
(5) midlatitude wetlands. The impact of purple loosestrife on native vegetation has been disastrous, with more than 50 percent of the biomass of some wetland communities displaced. Monospecific blocks of this weed have maintained themselves for at least 20 years.
(10) Impacts on wildlife have not been well studied, but serious reductions in waterfowl and aquatic furbearer productivity have been observed. In addition, several endangered species of vertebrates are threatened with further degradation of their
(15) breeding habitats. Although purple loosestrife can invade relatively undisturbed habitats, the spread and dominance of this weed have been greatly accelerated in disturbed habitats. While digging out the plants can temporarily halt their spread, there has been little
(20) research on long-term purple loosestrife control. Glyphosate has been used successfully, but no measure of the impact of this herbicide on native plant communities has been made.
    With the spread of purple loosestrife growing
(25) exponentially, some form of integrated control is needed. At present, coping with purple loosestrife hinges on early detection of the weed's arrival in areas, which allows local eradication to be carried out with minimum damage to the native plant community.

Passage B

(30)   The war on purple loosestrife is apparently conducted on behalf of nature, an attempt to liberate the biotic community from the tyrannical influence of a life-destroying invasive weed. Indeed, purple loosestrife control is portrayed by its practitioners as
(35) an environmental initiative intended to save nature rather than control it. Accordingly, the purple loosestrife literature, scientific and otherwise, dutifully discusses the impacts of the weed on endangered species—and on threatened biodiversity
(40) more generally. Purple loosestrife is a pollution, according to the scientific community, and all of nature suffers under its pervasive influence.
    Regardless of the perceived and actual ecological effects of the purple invader, it is apparent that
(45) popular pollution ideologies have been extended into the wetlands of North America. Consequently, the scientific effort to liberate nature from purple loosestrife has failed to decouple itself from its philosophical origin as an instrument to control nature
(50) to the satisfaction of human desires. Birds, particularly game birds and waterfowl, provide the bulk of the justification for loosestrife management.

However, no bird species other than the canvasback has been identified in the literature as endangered by
(55) purple loosestrife. The impact of purple loosestrife on furbearing mammals is discussed at great length, though none of the species highlighted (muskrat, mink) can be considered threatened in North America. What is threatened by purple loosestrife is the
(60) economics of exploiting such preferred species and the millions of dollars that will be lost to the economies of the United States and Canada from reduced hunting, trapping, and recreation revenues due to a decline in the production of the wetland
(65) resource.

7. Both passages explicitly mention which one of the following?

    (A) furbearing animals
    (B) glyphosate
    (C) the threat purple loosestrife poses to economies
    (D) popular pollution ideologies
    (E) literature on purple loosestrife control

8. Each of the passages contains information sufficient to answer which one of the following questions?

    (A) Approximately how long ago did purple loosestrife arrive in North America?
    (B) Is there much literature discussing the potential benefit that hunters might derive from purple loosestrife management?
    (C) What is an issue regarding purple loosestrife management on which both hunters and farmers agree?
    (D) Is the canvasback threatened with extinction due to the spread of purple loosestrife?
    (E) What is a type of terrain that is affected in at least some parts of North America by the presence of purple loosestrife?

9. It can be inferred that the authors would be most likely to disagree about which one of the following?

    (A) Purple loosestrife spreads more quickly in disturbed habitats than in undisturbed habitats.
    (B) The threat posed by purple loosestrife to local aquatic furbearer populations is serious.
    (C) Most people who advocate that eradication measures be taken to control purple loosestrife are not genuine in their concern for the environment.
    (D) The size of the biomass that has been displaced by purple loosestrife is larger than is generally thought.
    (E) Measures should be taken to prevent other non-native plant species from invading North America.

GO ON TO THE NEXT PAGE.

3 **3** **3** **3**

16. It can be inferred from the passage that the author uses the phrase "personally remembered stories" (line 32) primarily to refer to

    (A) a literary genre of first-person storytelling
    (B) a thematically organized personal narrative of one's own past
    (C) partially idiosyncratic memories of narratives
    (D) the retention in memory of precise sequences of words
    (E) easily identifiable thematic issues in literature

17. In which one of the following is the use of cotton fibers or cotton cloth most analogous to Kingston's use of the English language as described in lines 51–55?

    (A) Scraps of plain cotton cloth are used to create a multicolored quilt.
    (B) The surface texture of woolen cloth is simulated in a piece of cotton cloth by a special process of weaving.
    (C) Because of its texture, cotton cloth is used for a certain type of clothes for which linen is inappropriate.
    (D) In making a piece of cloth, cotton fiber is substituted for linen because of the roughly similar texture of the two materials.
    (E) Because of their somewhat similar textures, cotton and linen fibers are woven together in a piece of cloth to achieve a savings in price over a pure linen cloth.

18. The passage most clearly suggests that Kingston believes which one of the following about at least some of the stories contained in her writings?

    (A) Since they are intimately tied to the nature of the Chinese language, they can be approximated, but not adequately expressed, in English.
    (B) They should be thought of primarily as ethnic literature and evaluated accordingly by critics.
    (C) They will likely be retold and altered to some extent in the process.
    (D) Chinese American history is best chronicled by traditional talk-story.
    (E) Their significance and beauty cannot be captured at all in written texts.

19. The author's argument in the passage would be most weakened if which one of the following were true?

    (A) Numerous writers in the United States have been influenced by oral traditions.
    (B) Most Chinese American writers' work is very different from Kingston's.
    (C) Native American storytellers use narrative devices similar to those used in talk-story.
    (D) *China Men* is for the most part atypical of Kingston's literary works.
    (E) Literary critics generally appreciate the authenticity of Kingston's work.

20. The author's specific purpose in detailing typical talk-story forms (lines 43–51) is to

    (A) show why Kingston's book *China Men* establishes her as a major literary figure
    (B) support the claim that Kingston's use of typically oral techniques makes her work a part of the talk-story tradition
    (C) dispute the critics' view that Chinese American literature lacks literary antecedents
    (D) argue for Kingston's view that the literary artist is at best a "privileged keeper" of stories
    (E) provide an alternative to certain critics' view that Kingston's work should be judged primarily as literature

21. Which one of the following most accurately identifies the attitude shown by the author in the passage toward talk-story?

    (A) scholarly appreciation for its longstanding artistic sophistication
    (B) mild disappointment that it has not distinguished itself from other oral traditions
    (C) tentative approval of its resistance to critical evaluations
    (D) clear respect for the diversity of its ancient sources and cultural derivations
    (E) open admiration for the way it uses song to express narrative

GO ON TO THE NEXT PAGE.

KAPLAN

LSAT ADVANCED STUDENTS: THIS TEST IS TAKEN AS TEST 6 OF YOUR CLASS. DO NOT USE THIS TEST FOR PRACTICE.

3   3   3   3   3

In economics, the term "speculative bubble"
refers to a large upward move in an asset's price
driven not by the asset's fundamentals—that is, by
the earnings derivable from the asset—but rather by
(5) mere speculation that someone else will be willing to
pay a higher price for it. The price increase is then
followed by a dramatic decline in price, due to a loss
in confidence that the price will continue to rise, and
the "bubble" is said to have burst. According to
(10) Charles Mackay's classic nineteenth-century account,
the seventeenth-century Dutch tulip market provides
an example of a speculative bubble. But the
economist Peter Garber challenges Mackay's view,
arguing that there is no evidence that the Dutch tulip
(15) market really involved a speculative bubble.

By the seventeenth century, the Netherlands had
become a center of cultivation and development of
new tulip varieties, and a market had developed in
which rare varieties of bulbs sold at high prices. For
(20) example, a Semper Augustus bulb sold in 1625 for an
amount of gold worth about U.S.$11,000 in 1999.
Common bulb varieties, on the other hand, sold for
very low prices. According to Mackay, by 1636 rapid
price rises attracted speculators, and prices of many
(25) varieties surged upward from November 1636 through
January 1637. Mackay further states that in February
1637 prices suddenly collapsed; bulbs could not be
sold at 10 percent of their peak values. By 1739, the
prices of all the most prized kinds of bulbs had fallen
(30) to no more than one two-hundredth of 1 percent of
Semper Augustus's peak price.

Garber acknowledges that bulb prices increased
dramatically from 1636 to 1637 and eventually
reached very low levels. But he argues that this
(35) episode should not be described as a speculative
bubble, for the increase and eventual decline in bulb
prices can be explained in terms of the fundamentals.
Garber argues that a standard pricing pattern occurs
for new varieties of flowers. When a particularly
(40) prized variety is developed, its original bulb sells for
a high price. Thus, the dramatic rise in the price of
some original tulip bulbs could have resulted as tulips
in general, and certain varieties in particular, became
fashionable. However, as the prized bulbs become
(45) more readily available through reproduction from the
original bulb, their price falls rapidly; after less than
30 years, bulbs sell at reproduction cost. But this
does not mean that the high prices of original bulbs
are irrational, for earnings derivable from the millions
(50) of bulbs descendent from the original bulbs can be
very high, even if each individual descendent bulb
commands a very low price. Given that an original
bulb can generate a reasonable return on investment
even if the price of descendent bulbs decreases
(55) dramatically, a rapid rise and eventual fall of tulip
bulb prices need not indicate a speculative bubble.

22. Which one of the following most accurately expresses
the main point of the passage?

(A) The seventeenth-century Dutch tulip market is
widely but mistakenly believed by economists to
provide an example of a speculative bubble.

(B) Mackay did not accurately assess the earnings
that could be derived from rare and expensive
seventeenth-century Dutch tulip bulbs.

(C) A speculative bubble occurs whenever the price
of an asset increases substantially followed by a
rapid and dramatic decline.

(D) Garber argues that Mackay's classic account of
the seventeenth-century Dutch tulip market as
a speculative bubble is not supported by the
evidence.

(E) A tulip bulb can generate a reasonable return on
investment even if the price starts very high and
decreases dramatically.

23. Given Garber's account of the seventeenth-century
Dutch tulip market, which one of the following is most
analogous to someone who bought a tulip bulb of a
certain variety in that market at a very high price, only
to sell a bulb of that variety at a much lower price?

(A) someone who, after learning that many others had
withdrawn their applications for a particular job,
applied for the job in the belief that there would
be less competition for it

(B) an art dealer who, after paying a very high price
for a new painting, sells it at a very low price
because it is now considered to be an inferior
work

(C) someone who, after buying a box of rare
motorcycle parts at a very high price, is forced
to sell them at a much lower price because of the
sudden availability of cheap substitute parts

(D) a publisher who pays an extremely high price
for a new novel only to sell copies at a price
affordable to nearly everyone

(E) an airline that, after selling most of the tickets for
seats on a plane at a very high price, must sell
the remaining tickets at a very low price

GO ON TO THE NEXT PAGE.

LSAT ADVANCED STUDENTS: THIS TEST IS TAKEN AS TEST 6 OF YOUR CLASS. DO NOT USE THIS TEST FOR PRACTICE.

3 **3** **3** **3**

24. The passage most strongly supports the inference that Garber would agree with which one of the following statements?

    (A) If speculative bubbles occur at all, they occur very rarely.

    (B) Many of the owners of high-priced original tulip bulbs could have expected to at least recoup their original investments from sales of the many bulbs propagated from the original bulbs.

    (C) If there is not a speculative bubble in a market, then the level of prices in that market is not irrational.

    (D) Most people who invested in Dutch tulip bulbs in the seventeenth century were generally rational in all their investments.

    (E) Mackay mistakenly infers from the fact that tulip prices dropped rapidly that the very low prices that the bulbs eventually sold for were irrational.

25. The passage states that Mackay claimed which one of the following?

    (A) The rapid rise in price of Dutch tulip bulbs was not due to the fashionability of the flowers they produced.

    (B) The prices of certain varieties of Dutch tulip bulbs during the seventeenth century were, at least for a time, determined by speculation.

    (C) The Netherlands was the only center of cultivation and development of new tulip varieties in the seventeenth century.

    (D) The very high prices of bulbs in the seventeenth-century Dutch tulip market were not irrational.

    (E) Buyers of rare and very expensive Dutch tulip bulbs were ultimately able to derive earnings from bulbs descendent from the original bulbs.

26. The main purpose of the second paragraph is to

    (A) present the facts that are accepted by all experts in the field

    (B) identify the mistake that one scholar alleges another scholar made

    (C) explain the basis on which one scholar makes an inference with which another scholar disagrees

    (D) undermine the case that one scholar makes for the claim with which another scholar disagrees

    (E) outline the factual errors that led one scholar to draw the inference that he drew

27. The phrase "standard pricing pattern" as used in line 38 most nearly means a pricing pattern

    (A) against which other pricing patterns are to be measured

    (B) that conforms to a commonly agreed-upon criterion

    (C) that is merely acceptable

    (D) that regularly recurs in certain types of cases

    (E) that serves as an exemplar

S T O P

IF YOU FINISH BEFORE TIME IS CALLED, YOU MAY CHECK YOUR WORK ON THIS SECTION ONLY. DO NOT WORK ON ANY OTHER SECTION IN THE TEST.

LSAT ADVANCED STUDENTS: THIS TEST IS TAKEN AS TEST 6 OF YOUR CLASS. DO NOT USE THIS TEST FOR PRACTICE.

4 4 4 4 4 4

SECTION IV

Time—35 minutes

25 Questions

Directions: The questions in this section are based on the reasoning contained in brief statements or passages. For some questions, more than one of the choices could conceivably answer the question. However, you are to choose the best answer; that is, the response that most accurately and completely answers the question. You should not make assumptions that are by commonsense standards implausible, superfluous, or incompatible with the passage. After you have chosen the best answer, blacken the corresponding space on your answer sheet.

1. Aristophanes' play *The Clouds*, which was written when the philosopher Socrates was in his mid-forties, portrays Socrates as an atheistic philosopher primarily concerned with issues in natural science. The only other surviving portrayals of Socrates were written after Socrates' death at age 70. They portrayed Socrates as having a religious dimension and a strong focus on ethical issues.

Which one of the following, if true, would most help to resolve the apparent discrepancy between Aristophanes' portrayal of Socrates and the other surviving portrayals?

(A) Aristophanes' portrayal of Socrates in *The Clouds* was unflattering, whereas the other portrayals were very flattering.

(B) Socrates' philosophical views and interests changed sometime after his mid-forties.

(C) Most of the philosophers who lived before Socrates were primarily concerned with natural science.

(D) Socrates was a much more controversial figure in the years before his death than he was in his mid-forties.

(E) Socrates had an influence on many subsequent philosophers who were primarily concerned with natural science.

2. Board member: The J Foundation, a philanthropic organization, gave you this grant on the condition that your resulting work not contain any material detrimental to the J Foundation's reputation. But your resulting work never mentions any of the laudable achievements of our foundation. Hence your work fails to meet the conditions under which the grant was made.

The reasoning in the board member's argument is vulnerable to criticism on the grounds that the argument

(A) takes for granted that a work that never mentions any laudable achievements cannot be of high intellectual value

(B) confuses a condition necessary for the receipt of a grant with a condition sufficient for the receipt of a grant

(C) presumes, without providing justification, that a work that does not mention a foundation's laudable achievements is harmful to that foundation's reputation

(D) fails to consider that recipients of a grant usually strive to meet a foundation's conditions

(E) fails to consider the possibility that the work that was produced with the aid of the grant may have met all conditions other than avoiding detriment to the J Foundation's reputation

3. Psychiatrist: Breaking any habit is difficult, especially when it involves an addictive substance. People who break a habit are more likely to be motivated by immediate concerns than by long-term ones. Therefore, people who succeed in breaking their addiction to smoking cigarettes are more likely to be motivated by the social pressure against smoking—which is an immediate concern—than by health concerns, since _____.

The conclusion of the psychiatrist's argument is most strongly supported if which one of the following completes the argument?

(A) a habit that involves an addictive substance is likely to pose a greater health threat than a habit that does not involve any addictive substance

(B) for most people who successfully quit smoking, smoking does not create an immediate health concern at the time they quit

(C) some courses of action that exacerbate health concerns can also relieve social pressure

(D) most people who succeed in quitting smoking succeed only after several attempts

(E) everyone who succeeds in quitting smoking is motivated either by social pressure or by health concerns

GO ON TO THE NEXT PAGE.

4 **4** **4** **4** **4** **4**

4. Cassie: In order to improve the quality of customer service provided by our real estate agency, we should reduce client loads—the number of clients each agent is expected to serve at one time.

Melvin: Although smaller client loads are desirable, reducing client loads at our agency is simply not feasible. We already find it very difficult to recruit enough qualified agents; recruiting even more agents, which would be necessary in order to reduce client loads, is out of the question.

Of the following, which one, if true, is the logically strongest counter that Cassie can make to Melvin's argument?

(A) Since reducing client loads would improve working conditions for agents, reducing client loads would help recruit additional qualified agents to the real estate agency.

(B) Many of the real estate agency's current clients have expressed strong support for efforts to reduce client loads.

(C) Several recently conducted studies of real estate agencies have shown that small client loads are strongly correlated with high customer satisfaction ratings.

(D) Hiring extra support staff for the real estate agency's main office would have many of the same beneficial effects as reducing client loads.

(E) Over the last several years, it has become increasingly challenging for the real estate agency to recruit enough qualified agents just to maintain current client loads.

5. The star-nosed mole has a nose that ends in a pair of several-pointed stars, or tentacles that are crucial for hunting, as moles are poor-sighted. These tentacles contain receptors that detect electric fields produced by other animals, enabling the moles to detect and catch suitable prey such as worms and insects.

Which one of the following is most strongly supported by the information above?

(A) Both worms and insects produce electric fields.

(B) The star-nosed mole does not rely at all on its eyesight for survival.

(C) The star-nosed mole does not rely at all on its sense of smell when hunting.

(D) Only animals that hunt have noses with tentacles that detect electric fields.

(E) The star-nosed mole does not produce an electric field.

6. In her recent book a psychologist described several cases that exhibit the following pattern: A child, denied something by its parent, initiates problematic behavior such as screaming; the behavior escalates until finally the exasperated parent acquiesces to the child's demand. At this point the child, having obtained the desired goal, stops the problematic behavior, to the parent's relief. This self-reinforcing pattern of misbehavior and accommodation is repeated with steadily increasing levels of misbehavior by the child.

The cases described by the psychologist illustrate each of the following generalizations EXCEPT:

(A) A child can develop problematic behavior patterns as a result of getting what it wants.

(B) A child and parent can mutually influence each other's behavior.

(C) Parents, by their choices, can inadvertently increase their child's level of misbehavior.

(D) A child can unintentionally influence a parent's behavior in ways contrary to the child's intended goals.

(E) A child can get what it wants by doing what its parent doesn't want it to do.

7. Scientist: In our study, chemical R did not cause cancer in laboratory rats. But we cannot conclude from this that chemical R is safe for humans. After all, many substances known to be carcinogenic to humans cause no cancer in rats; this is probably because some carcinogens cause cancer only via long-term exposure and rats are short lived.

Which one of the following most precisely describes the role played in the scientist's argument by the statement that chemical R did not cause cancer in laboratory rats?

(A) It is cited as evidence against the conclusion that chemical R is safe for humans.

(B) It is advanced to support the contention that test results obtained from laboratory rats cannot be extrapolated to humans.

(C) It illustrates the claim that rats are too short lived to be suitable as test subjects for the carcinogenic properties of substances to which humans are chronically exposed.

(D) It is used as evidence to support the hypothesis that chemical R causes cancer in humans via long-term exposure.

(E) It is cited as being insufficient to support the conclusion that chemical R is safe for humans.

GO ON TO THE NEXT PAGE.

4   **4**

8. Department store manager: There is absolutely no reason to offer our customers free gift wrapping again this holiday season. If most customers take the offer, it will be expensive and time-consuming for us. On the other hand, if only a few customers want it, there is no advantage in offering it.

Which one of the following is an assumption required by the department store manager's argument?

(A) Gift wrapping would cost the store more during this holiday season than in previous holiday seasons.

(B) Anything that slows down shoppers during the holiday season costs the store money.

(C) It would be to the store's advantage to charge customers for gift wrapping services.

(D) It would be expensive to inform customers about the free gift wrapping service.

(E) Either few customers would want free gift wrapping or most customers would want it.

9. Among people who have a history of chronic trouble falling asleep, some rely only on sleeping pills to help them fall asleep, and others practice behavior modification techniques and do not take sleeping pills. Those who rely only on behavior modification fall asleep more quickly than do those who rely only on sleeping pills, so behavior modification is more effective than are sleeping pills in helping people to fall asleep.

Which one of the following, if true, most weakens the argument?

(A) People who do not take sleeping pills spend at least as many total hours asleep each night as do the people who take sleeping pills.

(B) Most people who have trouble falling asleep and who use behavior modification techniques fall asleep more slowly than do most people who have no trouble falling asleep.

(C) Many people who use only behavior modification techniques to help them fall asleep have never used sleeping pills.

(D) The people who are the most likely to take sleeping pills rather than practice behavior modification techniques are those who have previously had the most trouble falling asleep.

(E) The people who are the most likely to practice behavior modification techniques rather than take sleeping pills are those who prefer not to use drugs if other treatments are available.

10. Lawyer: This witness acknowledges being present at the restaurant and watching when my client, a famous television personality, was assaulted. Yet the witness claims to recognize the assailant, but not my famous client. Therefore, the witness's testimony should be excluded.

The lawyer's conclusion follows logically if which one of the following is assumed?

(A) If a witness claims to recognize both parties involved in an assault, then the witness's testimony should be included.

(B) There are other witnesses who can identify the lawyer's client as present during the assault.

(C) It is impossible to determine whether the witness actually recognized the assailant.

(D) The testimony of a witness to an assault should be included only if the witness claims to recognize both parties involved in the assault.

(E) It is unlikely that anyone would fail to recognize the lawyer's client.

11. Biologist: Many paleontologists have suggested that the difficulty of adapting to ice ages was responsible for the evolution of the human brain. But this suggestion must be rejected, for most other animal species adapted to ice ages with no evolutionary changes to their brains.

The biologist's argument is most vulnerable to criticism on which one of the following grounds?

(A) It fails to address adequately the possibility that even if a condition is sufficient to produce an effect in a species, it may not be necessary to produce that effect in that species.

(B) It fails to address adequately the possibility that a condition can produce a change in a species even if it does not produce that change in other species.

(C) It overlooks the possibility that a condition that is needed to produce a change in one species is not needed to produce a similar change in other species.

(D) It presumes without warrant that human beings were presented with greater difficulties during ice ages than were individuals of most other species.

(E) It takes for granted that, if a condition coincided with the emergence of a certain phenomenon, that condition must have been causally responsible for the phenomenon.

GO ON TO THE NEXT PAGE.

USE ONLY A NO 2. OR HB PENCIL TO COMPLETE THIS ANSWER SHEET. DO NOT USE INK.

● Right Mark   ⊘ ⊗ ⊙ Wrong Marks

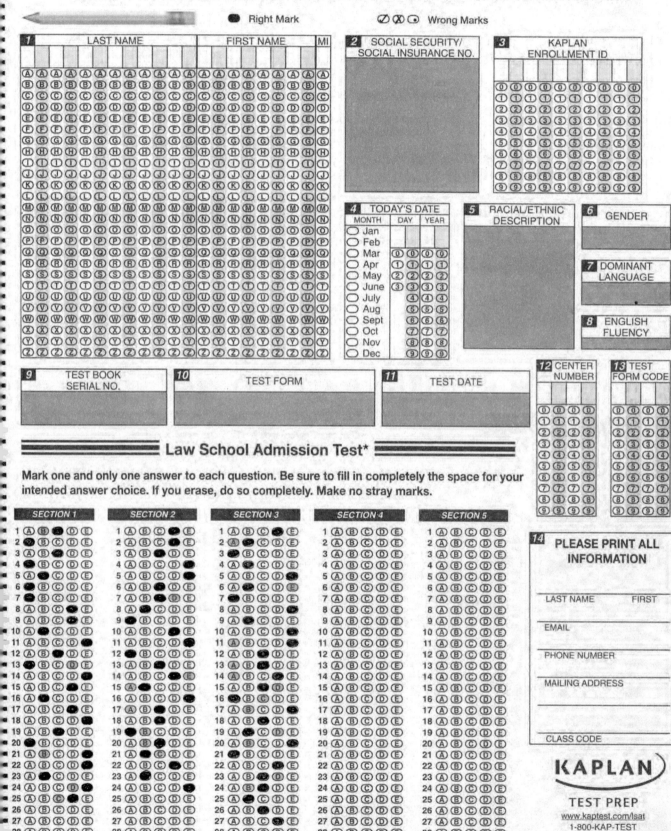

Law School Admission Test*

Mark one and only one answer to each question. Be sure to fill in completely the space for your intended answer choice. If you erase, do so completely. Make no stray marks.

KAPLAN
TEST PREP
www.kaptest.com/lsat
1-800-KAP-TEST

LSAT is a registered trademark of the Law School Admissions Council, Inc.

General Directions for the LSAT* Answer Sheet

The actual testing time for this portion of the test will be 2 hours 55 minutes. There are five sections, each with a time limit of 35 minutes. The supervisor will tell you when to begin and end each section. If you finish a section before time is called, you may check your work on that section only; do not turn to any other section of the test book and do not work on any other section either in the test book or on the answer sheet.

There are several different types of questions on the test, and each question type has its own directions. Be sure you understand the directions for each question type before attempting to answer any questions in that section.

Not everyone will finish all the questions in the time allowed. Do not hurry, but work steadily and as quickly as you can without sacrificing accuracy. You are advised to use your time effectively. If a question seems too difficult, go on to the next one and return to the difficult question after completing the section. MARK THE BEST ANSWER YOU CAN FOR EVERY QUESTION. NO DEDUCTIONS WILL BE MADE FOR WRONG ANSWERS. YOUR SCORE WILL BE BASED ONLY ON THE NUMBER OF QUESTIONS YOU ANSWER CORRECTLY.

ALL YOUR ANSWERS MUST BE MARKED ON THE ANSWER SHEET. Answer spaces for each question are lettered to correspond with the letters of the potential answers to each question in the test book. After you have decided which of the answers is correct, blacken the corresponding space on the answer sheet. BE SURE THAT EACH MARK IS BLACK AND COMPLETELY FILLS THE ANSWER SPACE. Give only one answer to each question. If you change an answer, be sure that all previous marks are erased completely. Since the answer sheet is machine scored, incomplete erasures may be interpreted as intended answers. ANSWERS RECORDED IN THE TEST BOOK WILL NOT BE SCORED.

There may be more questions noted on this answer sheet than there are questions in a section. Do not be concerned but be certain that the section and number of the question you are answering matches the answer sheet section and question number. Additional answer spaces in any answer sheet section should be left blank. Begin your next section in the number one answer space for that section.

Kaplan takes various steps to ensure that answer sheets are returned from test centers in a timely manner for processing. In the unlikely event that an answer sheet(s) is not received, Kaplan will permit the examinee to either retest at no additional fee or to receive a refund of his or her test fee. THESE REMEDIES ARE THE EXCLUSIVE REMEDIES AVAILABLE IN THE UNLIKELY EVENT THAT AN ANSWER SHEET IS NOT RECEIVED BY KAPLAN.

Score Cancellation

Complete this section only if you are absolutely certain you want to cancel your score. A CANCELLATION REQUEST CANNOT BE RESCINDED. IF YOU ARE AT ALL UNCERTAIN, YOU SHOULD NOT COMPLETE THIS SECTION.

To cancel your score from this administration, you **must**:

A. fill in both ovals here..... ○ ○

B. read the following statement. Then sign your name and enter the date. **YOUR SIGNATURE ALONE IS NOT SUFFICIENT FOR SCORE CANCELLATION. BOTH OVALS MUST BE FILLED IN FOR SCANNING EQUIPMENT TO RECOGNIZE YOUR REQUEST FOR SCORE CANCELLATION.**

I certify that I wish to cancel my test score from this administration. I understand that my request is irreversible and that my score will not be sent to me or to the law schools to which I apply.

_____
Sign your name in full

_____
Date

HOW DID YOU PREPARE FOR THE LSAT*?
(Select all that apply.)

Responses to this item are voluntary and will be used for statistical research purposes only.

○ By attending a Kaplan LSAT* prep course or tutoring program
○ By attending a non-Kaplan prep course or tutoring program (Please specify:_____)
○ By using a Kaplan LSAT* prep book
○ By using a non-Kaplan prep book (Please specify: _____)
○ By working through the sample questions and free sample tests provided by the LSAC
○ By working through official LSAT* PrepTests and/or other LSAC test prep products
○ Other preparation (Please specify: _____)
○ No preparation

CERTIFYING STATEMENT

Please write (DO NOT PRINT) the following statement. Sign and date.

I certify that I am the examinee whose name appears on this answer sheet and that I am here to take the LSAT for the sole purpose of being considered for application to law school. I further certify that I will neither assist nor receive assistance from any other candidate, and I agree not to copy or retain examination questions or to transmit them to or discuss them with any other person in any form.

_____
_____
_____
_____
_____
_____
_____

SIGNATURE:_____   TODAY'S DATE: ___/___/___
                                                   MONTH DAY YEAR

*LSAT is a registered trademark of the Law School Admissions Council, Inc.

4 **4** **4** **4** **4** **4**

12. The total number of book titles published annually in North America has approximately quadrupled since television first became available. Retail sales of new titles, as measured in copies, increased rapidly in the early days of television, though the rate of increase has slowed in recent years. Library circulation has been flat or declining in recent years.

Which one of the following is most strongly supported by the information above?

(A) Television has, over the years, brought about a reduction in the amount of per capita reading in North America.

(B) The introduction of television usually brings about a decrease in library use.

(C) Book publishers in North America now sell fewer copies per title than they sold in the early days of television.

(D) The availability of television does not always cause a decline in the annual number of book titles published or in the number of books sold.

(E) The introduction of television expanded the market for books in North America.

13. Botanist: It has long been believed that people with children or pets should keep poinsettia plants out of their homes. Although this belief has been encouraged by child-rearing books, which commonly list poinsettias as poisonous and therefore dangerous, it is mistaken. Our research has shown, conclusively, that poinsettias pose no risk to children or pets.

Which one of the following most accurately expresses the conclusion drawn in the botanist's argument?

(A) Child-rearing books should encourage people with children to put poinsettias in their homes.

(B) Poinsettias are not dangerously poisonous.

(C) According to many child-rearing books, poinsettias are dangerous.

(D) The belief that households with children or pets should not have poinsettias is mistaken.

(E) Poinsettias pose no risk to children or pets.

14. Archaeologist: An ancient stone building at our excavation site was composed of three kinds of stone—quartz, granite, and limestone. Of these, only limestone occurs naturally in the area. Most of the buildings at the site from the same time period had limestone as their only stone component, and most were human dwellings. Therefore, the building we are studying probably was not a dwelling.

Which one of the following, if true, would most strengthen the archaeologist's reasoning?

(A) Most of the buildings that were used as dwellings at the site were made, at least in part, of limestone.

(B) Most of the buildings at the site that were not dwellings were made, at least in part, from types of stone that do not occur naturally in the area.

(C) Most of the buildings that were built from stones not naturally occurring in the area were not built with both quartz and granite.

(D) Most of the buildings at the site were used as dwellings.

(E) No quartz has been discovered on the site other than that found in the building being studied.

GO ON TO THE NEXT PAGE.

KAPLAN

4 4 4 4

15. Theodore will be able to file his tax return on time only in the event that he has an accountant prepare his tax return and the accountant does not ask Theodore for any additional documentation of his business expenses. If he does have an accountant prepare his return, the accountant will necessarily ask Theodore to provide this additional documentation. Therefore, Theodore will not be able to file on time.

The pattern of reasoning in which one of the following arguments most closely parallels the pattern of reasoning in the argument above?

(A) Given the demands of Timothy's job, his next free evening will occur next Friday. Since he spent a lot of money on his last evening out, he will probably decide to spend his next free evening at home. Therefore, Timothy will probably be at home next Friday evening.

(B) Tovah cannot attend the concert next week if she is away on business. If she misses that concert, she will not have another opportunity to attend a concert this month. Since she will be away on business, Tovah will not be able to attend a concert this month.

(C) Mark's children will not be content this weekend unless he lets them play video games some of the time. Mark will let them play video games, but only at times when he has no other activities planned. Therefore, unless Mark and his children take a break from planned activities, Mark's children will not be content this weekend.

(D) If Teresa is not seated in first class on her airline flight, she will be seated in business class. Therefore, since she cannot be seated in first class on that flight, she will necessarily be seated in business class.

(E) Susannah will have a relaxing vacation only if her children behave especially well and she does not start to suspect that they are planning some mischief. Since she will certainly start to suspect that they are planning some mischief if they behave especially well, Susannah's vacation cannot possibly be relaxing.

16. When a threat to life is common, as are automobile and industrial accidents, only unusual instances tend to be prominently reported by the news media. Instances of rare threats, such as product tampering, however, are seen as news by reporters and are universally reported in featured stories. People in general tend to estimate the risk of various threats by how frequently those threats come to their attention.

If the statements above are true, which one of the following is most strongly supported on the basis of them?

(A) Whether governmental action will be taken to lessen a common risk depends primarily on the prominence given to the risk by the news media.

(B) People tend to magnify the risk of a threat if the threat seems particularly dreadful or if those who would be affected have no control over it.

(C) Those who get their information primarily from the news media tend to overestimate the risk of uncommon threats relative to the risk of common threats.

(D) Reporters tend not to seek out information about long-range future threats but to concentrate their attention on the immediate past and future.

(E) The resources that are spent on avoiding product tampering are greater than the resources that are spent on avoiding threats that stem from the weather.

GO ON TO THE NEXT PAGE.

4 **4** **4** **4** **4** 4

17. Real estate agent: Upon selling a home, the sellers are legally entitled to remove any items that are not permanent fixtures. Legally, large appliances like dishwashers are not permanent fixtures. However, since many prospective buyers of the home are likely to assume that large appliances in the home would be included with its purchase, sellers who will be keeping the appliances are morally obliged either to remove them before showing the home or to indicate in some other way that the appliances are not included.

Which one of the following principles, if valid, most helps to justify the real estate agent's argumentation?

(A) If a home's sellers will be keeping any belongings that prospective buyers of the home might assume would be included with the purchase of the home, the sellers are morally obliged to indicate clearly that those belongings are not included.

(B) A home's sellers are morally obliged to ensure that prospective buyers of the home do not assume that any large appliances are permanent fixtures in the home.

(C) A home's sellers are morally obliged to include with the sale of the home at least some of the appliances that are not permanent fixtures but were in the home when it was shown to prospective buyers.

(D) A home's sellers are morally obliged not to deliberately mislead any prospective buyers of their home about which belongings are included with the sale of the home and which are not.

(E) If a home's sellers have indicated in some way that a large appliance is included with the home's purchase, then they are morally obliged not to remove that appliance after showing the home.

18. Many parents rigorously organize their children's activities during playtime, thinking that doing so will enhance their children's cognitive development. But this belief is incorrect. To thoroughly structure a child's playtime and expect this to produce a creative and resourceful child would be like expecting a good novel to be produced by someone who was told exactly what the plot and characters must be.

The argument is most vulnerable to criticism on which one of the following grounds?

(A) It takes for granted that if something is conducive to a certain goal it cannot also be conducive to some other goal.

(B) It overlooks the possibility that many children enjoy rigorously organized playtime.

(C) It takes a necessary condition for something's enhancing a child's creativity and resourcefulness to be a sufficient condition for its doing so.

(D) It fails to consider the possibility that being able to write a good novel requires something more than creativity and resourcefulness.

(E) It fails to consider the possibility that something could enhance a child's overall cognitive development without enhancing the child's creativity and resourcefulness.

19. Bureaucrat: The primary, constant goal of an ideal bureaucracy is to define and classify all possible problems and set out regulations regarding each eventuality. Also, an ideal bureaucracy provides an appeal procedure for any complaint. If a complaint reveals an unanticipated problem, the regulations are expanded to cover the new issue, and for this reason an ideal bureaucracy will have an ever-expanding system of regulations.

Which one of the following is an assumption the bureaucrat's argument requires?

(A) An ideal bureaucracy will provide an appeal procedure for complaints even after it has defined and classified all possible problems and set out regulations regarding each eventuality.

(B) For each problem that an ideal bureaucracy has defined and classified, the bureaucracy has received at least one complaint revealing that problem.

(C) An ideal bureaucracy will never be permanently without complaints about problems that are not covered by that bureaucracy's regulations.

(D) An ideal bureaucracy can reach its primary goal if, but only if, its system of regulations is always expanding to cover problems that had not been anticipated.

(E) Any complaint that an ideal bureaucracy receives will reveal an unanticipated problem that the bureaucracy is capable of defining and classifying.

GO ON TO THE NEXT PAGE

KAPLAN

34

4   4   4   4   4   4

20. Scientists studying a common type of bacteria have discovered that most bacteria of that type are in hibernation at any given time. Some microbiologists have concluded from this that bacteria in general are usually in hibernation. This conclusion would be reasonable if all types of bacteria were rather similar. But, in fact, since bacteria are extremely diverse, it is unlikely that most types of bacteria hibernate regularly.

Which one of the following most accurately expresses the overall conclusion of the argument?

(A) Bacteria of most types are usually in hibernation.
(B) It is probably not true that most types of bacteria hibernate regularly.
(C) If bacteria are extremely diverse, it is unlikely that most types of bacteria hibernate regularly.
(D) The conclusion that bacteria in general are usually in hibernation would be reasonable if all types of bacteria were rather similar.
(E) It is likely that only one type of bacteria hibernates regularly.

21. Any student who is not required to hand in written homework based on the reading assignments in a course will not complete all of the reading assignments. Even highly motivated students will neglect their reading assignments if they are not required to hand in written homework. Therefore, if the students in a course are given several reading assignments and no written assignments, no student in that course will receive a high grade for the course.

The conclusion of the argument follows logically if which one of the following is assumed?

(A) No student who completes anything less than all of the reading assignments for a course will earn a high grade for that course.
(B) Any student who completes all of the reading and written assignments for a course will earn a high grade in that course.
(C) All highly motivated students who complete all of the reading assignments for a course will receive high grades for that course.
(D) If highly motivated students are required to hand in written homework on their reading assignments, then they will complete all of their reading assignments.
(E) Some highly motivated students will earn high grades in a course if they are required to hand in written homework on their reading assignments.

22. In a study, one group of volunteers was fed a high-protein, low-carbohydrate diet; another group was fed a low-protein, high-carbohydrate diet. Both diets contained the same number of calories, and each volunteer's diet prior to the experiment had contained moderate levels of proteins and carbohydrates. After ten days, those on the low-carbohydrate diet had lost more weight than those on the high-carbohydrate diet. Thus, the most effective way to lose body fat is to eat much protein and shun carbohydrates.

Which one of the following, if true, most weakens the argument above?

(A) A low-protein, high-carbohydrate diet causes the human body to retain water, the added weight of which largely compensates for the weight of any body fat lost, whereas a high-protein, low-carbohydrate diet does not.
(B) Many people who consume large quantities of protein nevertheless gain significant amounts of body fat.
(C) A high-protein, low-carbohydrate diet will often enable the human body to convert some body fat into muscle, without causing any significant overall weight loss.
(D) In the experiment, the volunteers on the high-carbohydrate diet engaged in regular exercise of a kind known to produce weight loss, and those on the low-carbohydrate diet did not.
(E) Many of the volunteers who had been on the low-carbohydrate diet eventually regained much of the weight they had lost on the diet after returning to their normal diets.

GO ON TO THE NEXT PAGE.

LSAT ADVANCED STUDENTS: THIS TEST IS TAKEN AS TEST 6 OF YOUR CLASS. DO NOT USE THIS TEST FOR PRACTICE.

4 **4** **4** **4** **4** **4**

23. Essayist: Computers have the capacity to represent and to perform logical transformations on pieces of information. Since exactly the same applies to the human mind, the human mind is a type of computer.

The flawed pattern of reasoning in which one of the following most closely resembles the flawed pattern of reasoning in the essayist's argument?

(A) Often individual animals sacrifice their lives when the survival of their offspring or close relatives is threatened. It is probable, therefore, that there is a biological basis for the fact that human beings are similarly often willing to sacrifice their own well-being for the good of their community.

(B) In the plastic arts, such as sculpture or painting, no work can depend for its effectiveness upon a verbal narrative that explains it. Since the same can be said of poetry, we cannot consider this characteristic as a reasonable criterion for distinguishing the plastic arts from other arts.

(C) In any organism, the proper functioning of each component depends upon the proper functioning of every other component. Thus, communities belong to the category of organisms, since communities are invariably characterized by this same interdependence of components.

(D) Some vitamins require the presence in adequate amounts of some mineral in order to be fully beneficial to the body. Thus, since selenium is needed to make vitamin E fully active, anyone with a selenium deficiency will have a greater risk of contracting those diseases from which vitamin E provides some measure of protection.

(E) Friendship often involves obligations whose fulfillment can be painful or burdensome. The same can be said of various forms of cooperation that cannot strictly be called friendship. Thus cooperation, like friendship, can require that priority be given to goals other than mere self-interest.

24. It is popularly believed that a poem has whatever meaning is assigned to it by the reader. But objective evaluation of poetry is possible only if this popular belief is false; for the aesthetic value of a poem cannot be discussed unless it is possible for at least two readers to agree on the correct interpretation of the poem.

Which one of the following is an assumption required by the argument?

(A) Only if they find the same meaning in a poem can two people each judge that it has aesthetic value.

(B) If two readers agree about the meaning of a given poem, that ensures that an objective evaluation of the poem can be made.

(C) Discussion of a poem is possible only if it is false that a poem has whatever meaning is assigned to it by the reader.

(D) A given poem can be objectively evaluated only if the poem's aesthetic value can be discussed.

(E) Aesthetic evaluation of literature is best accomplished through discussion by more than two readers.

25. Dean: The mathematics department at our university has said that it should be given sole responsibility for teaching the course Statistics for the Social Sciences. But this course has no more mathematics in it than high school algebra does. The fact that a course has mathematics in it does not mean that it needs to be taught by a mathematics professor, any more than a course approaching its subject from a historical perspective must be taught by a history professor. Such demands by the mathematics department are therefore unjustified.

The dean's argument is most vulnerable to criticism on the grounds that it

(A) presumes, without providing justification, that expertise in a subject does not enable one to teach that subject well

(B) purports to refute a view by showing that one possible reason for that view is insufficient

(C) presumes, without providing justification, that most students are as knowledgeable about mathematics as they are about history

(D) fails to establish that mathematics professors are not capable of teaching Statistics for the Social Sciences effectively

(E) presumes, without providing justification, that any policies that apply to history courses must be justified with respect to mathematics courses

S T O P

IF YOU FINISH BEFORE TIME IS CALLED, YOU MAY CHECK YOUR WORK ON THIS SECTION ONLY.
DO NOT WORK ON ANY OTHER SECTION IN THE TEST.

LSAT ADVANCED STUDENTS: THIS TEST IS TAKEN AS TEST 6 OF YOUR CLASS. DO NOT USE THIS TEST FOR PRACTICE.

5   5

SECTION V

Time—35 minutes

23 Questions

Directions: Each group of questions in this section is based on a set of conditions. In answering some of the questions, it may be useful to draw a rough diagram. Choose the response that most accurately and completely answers each question and blacken the corresponding space on your answer sheet.

Questions 1–6

There are exactly six law students—Gambini, Little, Mitchum, Richardson, Saito, and Veracruz—in a trial advocacy class. The class is divided into three trial teams—team 1, team 2, and team 3—of exactly two students each. Each student is on exactly one of the teams. Each student prepares exactly one of either the opening argument or the final argument for his or her team. The teams must be formed according to the following specifications:

Mitchum is on the same team as either Gambini or Veracruz.

Little prepares an opening argument.

Either Gambini or Richardson, but not both, prepares a final argument.

1. Which one of the following could be the composition of each team and the argument each student prepares?

(A) team 1: Little, opening; Gambini, final
team 2: Veracruz, opening; Mitchum, final
team 3: Saito, opening; Richardson, final

(B) team 1: Mitchum, opening; Gambini, final
team 2: Veracruz, opening; Little, final
team 3: Richardson, opening; Saito, final

(C) team 1: Richardson, opening; Gambini, final
team 2: Mitchum, opening; Saito, final
team 3: Little, opening; Veracruz, final

(D) team 1: Gambini, opening; Mitchum, final
team 2: Little, opening; Richardson, final
team 3: Veracruz, opening; Saito, final

(E) team 1: Gambini, opening; Mitchum, final
team 2: Richardson, opening; Saito, final
team 3: Little, opening; Veracruz, final

2. If Gambini is on the same team as Mitchum, and if Gambini prepares the final argument for that team, then which one of the following could be true?

(A) Little is on the same team as Veracruz, who prepares the opening argument for the team.

(B) Richardson is on the same team as Saito, who prepares the opening argument for the team.

(C) Richardson is on the same team as Saito, who prepares the final argument for the team.

(D) Saito is on the same team as Veracruz, who prepares the opening argument for the team.

(E) Saito is on the same team as Veracruz, who prepares the final argument for the team.

3. Which one of the following could be true?

(A) Gambini, who prepares a final argument, is on the same team as Richardson.

(B) Gambini, who prepares a final argument, is on the same team as Veracruz.

(C) Gambini, who prepares an opening argument, is on the same team as Little.

(D) Little, who prepares an opening argument, is on the same team as Mitchum.

(E) Mitchum, who prepares an opening argument, is on the same team as Saito.

4. If Richardson is on the same team as Veracruz, then for exactly how many of the students can it be determined which of the arguments he or she prepares?

(A) one
(B) two
(C) three
(D) four
(E) five

5. If Little is on the same team as Richardson, then which one of the following must be true?

(A) Saito is on the same team as Veracruz.
(B) Gambini is on the same team as Mitchum.
(C) Mitchum prepares a final argument.
(D) Veracruz prepares a final argument.
(E) Gambini prepares an opening argument.

6. If Saito prepares an opening argument, then which one of the following pairs of students could be on the same team as each other?

(A) Gambini and Little
(B) Gambini and Saito
(C) Little and Veracruz
(D) Mitchum and Veracruz
(E) Richardson and Veracruz

GO ON TO THE NEXT PAGE.

5   **5**

Questions 7–12

While on vacation, Sukanya receives several e-mail messages from work, each message from one of three associates: Hilary, Jerome, and Lula. Sukanya receives at least one and no more than two messages from each of them. Sukanya receives each message on the day it is sent. No more than one message is sent each day. The messages are received in a manner consistent with the following:

The first message is not from Lula.
Both the first and last messages are from the same person.
Exactly once Sukanya receives a message from Jerome on the day after receiving one from Hilary.
Of the first three messages, exactly one is from Jerome.

7. Which one of the following could be an accurate list of the e-mail messages Sukanya receives, identified by the person each message is from and listed in the order she receives them?

  (A) Lula, Hilary, Jerome, Hilary, Jerome, Lula
  (B) Jerome, Lula, Hilary, Lula, Jerome
  (C) Jerome, Lula, Hilary, Jerome, Hilary
  (D) Jerome, Lula, Hilary, Hilary, Jerome
  (E) Hilary, Lula, Lula, Jerome, Jerome, Hilary

8. What is the maximum possible number of e-mail messages Sukanya receives after Jerome's first message but before Hilary's first message?

  (A) zero
  (B) one
  (C) two
  (D) three
  (E) four

9. If Sukanya receives exactly four e-mail messages, then which one of the following must be true?

  (A) Exactly one of the messages is from Lula.
  (B) Exactly two of the messages are from Jerome.
  (C) The second message is from Lula.
  (D) The third message is from Hilary.
  (E) The fourth message is from Jerome.

10. Which one of the following e-mail messages CANNOT be from Lula?

  (A) the second message
  (B) the third message
  (C) the fourth message
  (D) the fifth message (if there is a fifth one)
  (E) the sixth message (if there is a sixth one)

11. If Sukanya receives six e-mail messages, the fifth of which is from Lula, which one of the following must be true?

  (A) The first message is from Jerome.
  (B) The second message is from Lula.
  (C) The third message is from Hilary.
  (D) The fourth message is from Jerome.
  (E) The sixth message is from Lula.

12. If Sukanya receives two e-mail messages from Lula, what is the maximum possible number of e-mail messages Sukanya receives after Lula's first message but before Lula's last message?

  (A) zero
  (B) one
  (C) two
  (D) three
  (E) four

GO ON TO THE NEXT PAGE.

Questions 13–18

Mercotek carried out a study to compare the productivity of its night shift with that of its day shift. Every week the company's six crews—F, G, H, R, S, and T—were ranked from first (most productive) to sixth (least productive). There were no ties. For any given week, either G and T were the two night-shift crews or else S and H were—the four other crews were the day-shift crews for that week. The following relationships held for every week of the study:

F is more productive than G.
R is more productive than S.
R is more productive than T.
S is more productive than H.
G is more productive than T.

13. Which one of the following could be an accurate ranking of all the crews, in order from first to sixth, for a given week of the study?

(A) F, G, T, R, S, H
(B) F, R, G, T, H, S
(C) G, R, T, S, H, F
(D) R, F, G, S, H, T
(E) R, S, H, T, F, G

14. If F is ranked third for a given week of the study, then which one of the following could also be true of that week?

(A) G ranks second.
(B) H ranks fourth.
(C) R ranks second.
(D) S ranks fourth.
(E) T ranks fourth.

15. Which one of the following CANNOT be the crew ranked fifth for any given week of the study?

(A) G
(B) H
(C) R
(D) S
(E) T

16. For any given week of the study, the ranking of all the crews is completely determined if which one of the following is true?

(A) F ranks second that week.
(B) G ranks fifth that week.
(C) H ranks third that week.
(D) R ranks third that week.
(E) S ranks third that week.

17. If the night-shift crews rank fifth and sixth for a given week of the study, then which one of the following could also be true of that week?

(A) G ranks fourth.
(B) H ranks fifth.
(C) R ranks third.
(D) S ranks fourth.
(E) T ranks fifth.

18. Which one of the following is a complete and accurate list of the crews that CANNOT be ranked third for any given week of the study?

(A) G, H, S
(B) R, T
(C) F, T
(D) G, T
(E) T

GO ON TO THE NEXT PAGE.

KAPLAN

LSAT ADVANCED STUDENTS: THIS TEST IS TAKEN AS TEST 6 OF YOUR CLASS. DO NOT USE THIS TEST FOR PRACTICE.

5   5

Questions 19–23

A shuttle van stops exactly four times—once at Fundy, once at Los Altos, once at Mineola, and once at Simcoe—not necessarily in that order. The van starts with exactly four passengers on board—Greg, Jasmine, Rosa, and Vijay—each of whom gets off at a different stop. The following conditions hold:

Los Altos is the first or second stop.
Rosa is still on board when the van reaches Mineola.
Jasmine is on board longer than Vijay.
If Jasmine is still on board when the van reaches Fundy, then Greg is still on board when the van reaches Simcoe; otherwise, Greg is not still on board when the van reaches Simcoe.

19. Which one of the following could be a complete and accurate matching of stops, listed in the order in which the van stops at them, to the passengers who get off at them?

(A)   Los Altos: Greg
      Mineola: Vijay
      Fundy: Jasmine
      Simcoe: Rosa
(B)   Simcoe: Vijay
      Mineola: Greg
      Fundy: Rosa
      Los Altos: Jasmine
(C)   Los Altos: Jasmine
      Mineola: Vijay
      Fundy: Greg
      Simcoe: Rosa
(D)   Los Altos: Rosa
      Mineola: Vijay
      Fundy: Jasmine
      Simcoe: Greg
(E)   Los Altos: Vijay
      Fundy: Jasmine
      Mineola: Rosa
      Simcoe: Greg

20. If Mineola is the first stop, which one of the following is a complete and accurate list of the passengers who could possibly get off there?

(A)   Rosa
(B)   Greg, Rosa
(C)   Greg, Vijay
(D)   Greg, Rosa, Vijay
(E)   Jasmine, Rosa, Vijay

21. If Fundy is the first stop, then which one of the following could accurately list the passengers in order from first to last off?

(A)   Greg, Vijay, Jasmine, Rosa
(B)   Rosa, Vijay, Greg, Jasmine
(C)   Vijay, Greg, Rosa, Jasmine
(D)   Vijay, Jasmine, Greg, Rosa
(E)   Vijay, Rosa, Jasmine, Greg

22. Which one of the following must be true if Greg is still on board both when the van reaches Los Altos and when it reaches Simcoe, not necessarily in that order, assuming he is the second one off the van?

(A)   Vijay is on board when the van reaches Simcoe.
(B)   Vijay is on board when the van reaches Los Altos.
(C)   Rosa is on board when the van reaches Simcoe.
(D)   Rosa is on board when the van reaches Fundy.
(E)   Jasmine is on board when the van reaches Mineola.

23. If Greg is not on board when the van reaches Simcoe, then which one of the following must be false?

(A)   Greg is on board when the van reaches Fundy.
(B)   Jasmine is on board when the van reaches Mineola.
(C)   Rosa is on board when the van reaches Fundy.
(D)   Vijay is on board when the van reaches Fundy.
(E)   Vijay is on board when the van reaches Mineola.

S T O P

IF YOU FINISH BEFORE TIME IS CALLED, YOU MAY CHECK YOUR WORK ON THIS SECTION ONLY.
DO NOT WORK ON ANY OTHER SECTION IN THE TEST.

Acknowledgment is made to the following sources from which material has been adapted for use in this test booklet:

Peter M. Garber, *Famous Bubbles: The Fundamentals of Early Manias*. ©2000 by MIT Press.

John Sandlos, "Purple Loosestrife and the 'Bounding' of Nature in North American Wetlands." ©1997 by Electronic Journal of Sociology.

Linda Ching Sledge, "Oral Tradition in Kingston's *China Men*." ©1990 by The Modern Language Association of America.

Daniel Q. Thompson, Ronald L. Stuckey, and Edith B. Thompson, "Spread, Impact, and Control of Purple Loosestrife (*Lythrum salicaria*) in North American Wetlands." ©1987 by US Fish and Wildlife Service.

Wait for the supervisor's instructions before you open the page to the topic.
Please print and sign your name and write the date in the designated spaces below.

Time: 35 Minutes

General Directions

You will have 35 minutes in which to plan and write an essay on the topic inside. Read the topic and the accompanying directions carefully. You will probably find it best to spend a few minutes considering the topic and organizing your thoughts before you begin writing. In your essay, be sure to develop your ideas fully, leaving time, if possible, to review what you have written. **Do not write on a topic other than the one specified. Writing on a topic of your own choice is not acceptable.**

No special knowledge is required or expected for this writing exercise. Law schools are interested in the reasoning, clarity, organization, language usage, and writing mechanics displayed in your essay. How well you write is more important than how much you write.

Confine your essay to the blocked, lined area on the front and back of the separate Writing Sample Response Sheet. Only that area will be reproduced for law schools. Be sure that your writing is legible.

Both this topic sheet and your response sheet must be turned over to the testing staff before you leave the room.

Topic Code	Print Your Full Name Here		
_____	Last	First	M.I.
Date	**Sign Your Name Here**		
/ /			

Scratch Paper
Do not write your essay in this space.

LSAT Writing Sample Topic

Directions: The scenario presented below describes two choices, either one of which can be supported on the basis of the information given. Your essay should consider both choices and argue for one and against the other, based on the two specified criteria and the facts provided. There is no "right" or "wrong" choice: a reasonable argument can be made for either.

Aña Rodriguez is a shy five-year-old girl. The Rodriguez family must send Aña to either Mercer Preschool or Butte Preschool. The Rodriguezes are equally satisfied with the quality of the teachers and the facilities at both schools. Using the facts below, write an essay in which you argue for one preschool over the other based on the following two criteria:

- The preschool must provide a stimulating social environment for Aña.
- The preschool must be conveniently located.

Aña is an only child who lives on a block with no other children her age. Two children Aña occasionally plays with at the local playground would be in her class at Mercer. The class size at Mercer is eight children. Mercer occupies its students' time, for the most part, with activities for the entire class. There is little unstructured time. Mercer is within easy walking distance of the Rodriguez home. Parking near Mercer is nearly impossible. After the infrequent winter snowstorms, snow is typically left to melt rather than shoveled. Walking can be difficult at such times.

Aña's best friend will be attending Butte. Aña knows none of the other children who would be in her class. The class size at Butte is 12 children. Most of the students' time is not formally structured. The children are free to participate in a number of optional activities with or without their classmates. The few structured activities all involve small groups of two or three children. Butte is a 10-minute drive, or 20-minute bus ride, from the Rodriguez house. Parking is always available since Butte has its own lot. Aña's younger cousin Pablo, who lives on her block, will be attending a different class at Butte.

Scratch Paper
Do not write your essay in this space.

LAST NAME (Print)

MI

FIRST NAME (Print)

SIGNATURE

Writing Sample Response Sheet

DO NOT WRITE
IN THIS SPACE

Begin your essay in the lined area below.
Continue on the back if you need more space.

Directions:

1. Use the Answer Key on the next page to check your answers.

2. Use the Scoring Worksheet below to compute your raw score.

3. Use the Score Conversion Chart to convert your raw score into the 120–180 scale.

Scoring Worksheet

1. Enter the number of questions you answered correctly in each section

	Number Correct
SECTION I	_____
SECTION II	_EXP_
SECTION III	_____
SECTION IV	_____
SECTION V	_____

2. Enter the sum here: _____
   This is your Raw Score.

Conversion Chart

For Converting Raw Score to the 120–180 LSAT Scaled Score
LSAT PrepTest 55

Reported Score	Raw Score Lowest	Raw Score Highest
180	99	100
179	98	98
178	97	97
177	96	96
176	—*	—*
175	95	95
174	94	94
173	—*	—*
172	93	93
171	92	92
170	91	91
169	90	90
168	89	89
167	87	88
166	86	86
165	85	85
164	83	84
163	82	82
162	81	81
161	79	80
160	77	78
159	76	76
158	74	75
157	72	73
156	70	71
155	69	69
154	67	68
153	65	66
152	63	64
151	61	62
150	59	60
149	58	58
148	56	57
147	54	55
146	52	53
145	50	51
144	48	49
143	47	47
142	45	46
141	43	44
140	41	42
139	40	40
138	38	39
137	36	37
136	35	35
135	33	34
134	32	32
133	30	31
132	29	29
131	27	28
130	26	26
129	25	25
128	24	24
127	22	23
126	21	21
125	20	20
124	19	19
123	18	18
122	17	17
121	16	16
120	0	15

*There is no raw score that will produce this scaled score for this form

SECTION I

1.	B	8.	D	15.	D	22.	E
2.	A	9.	D	16.	B	23.	B
3.	C	10.	B	17.	D	24.	D
4.	A	11.	E	18.	E	25.	C
5.	B	12.	C	19.	C		
6.	A	13.	D	20.	A		
7.	A	14.	E	21.	B		

SECTION II (experimental)

1.	D	8.	B	15.	A	22.	D
2.	D	9.	A	16.	E	23.	B
3.	C	10.	D	17.	A	24.	E
4.	E	11.	E	18.	C		
5.	E	12.	A	19.	B		
6.	C	13.	C	20.	B		
7.	D	14.	E	21.	C		

SECTION III

1.	D	8.	E	15.	D	22.	D
2.	A	9.	B	16.	C	23.	D
3.	A	10.	E	17.	B	24.	B
4.	B	11.	A	18.	C	25.	B
5.	E	12.	C	19.	D	26.	C
6.	E	13.	A	20.	B	27.	D
7.	A	14.	A	21.	A		

SECTION IV

1.	B	8.	E	15.	E	22.	A
2.	C	9.	D	16.	C	23.	C
3.	B	10.	D	17.	A	24.	D
4.	A	11.	B	18.	E	25.	B
5.	A	12.	D	19.	C		
6.	D	13.	D	20.	B		
7.	E	14.	B	21.	A		

SECTION V

1.	D	8.	C	15.	C	22.	C
2.	C	9.	A	16.	C	23.	D
3.	A	10.	E	17.	C		
4.	B	11.	D	18.	E		
5.	E	12.	B	19.	E		
6.	C	13.	D	20.	D		
7.	D	14.	B	21.	D		

Endurance Practice Test 2

PrepTest 54 plus experimental from PrepTest 32, Section I

SCAN CODE: LL9002

LSAT ADVANCED STUDENTS: THIS TEST IS TAKEN AS TEST 5 OF YOUR CLASS. DO NOT USE THIS TEST FOR PRACTICE.

1   1

SECTION I

Time—35 minutes

25 Questions

Directions: The questions in this section are based on the reasoning contained in brief statements or passages. For some questions, more than one of the choices could conceivably answer the question. However, you are to choose the best answer; that is, the response that most accurately and completely answers the question. You should not make assumptions that are by commonsense standards implausible, superfluous, or incompatible with the passage. After you have chosen the best answer, blacken the corresponding space on your answer sheet.

1. Editorial: The structure of the present school calendar was established to satisfy the requirements of early-twentieth-century agricultural life. In those days, farmers needed their children to have long breaks during which they could remain at home and help with the harvest. The contemporary school year is thus made up of periods of study interspersed with long breaks. But agricultural life no longer occupies most of our citizens, so we can now make changes that serve the interests of children. Therefore, long breaks should be removed from the school calendar.

Which one of the following is an assumption on which the editorial's argument depends?

(A) During long breaks children have a tendency to forget what they have learned.

(B) Children of farmers need to continue observing a school calendar made up of periods of study interspersed with long breaks.

(C) Long breaks in the school calendar should be replaced with breaks that are no longer than workers' average vacations.

(D) A change in the present school calendar that shortened breaks would serve the interests of agricultural life.

(E) A school calendar made up of periods of study without long breaks would serve the interests of children more than a school calendar with long breaks.

2. Leatherbacks, the largest of the sea turtles, when subjected to the conditions of captivity, are susceptible to a wide variety of fatal diseases with which they would never come in contact if they lived in the wild. It is surprising, therefore, that the likelihood that a leatherback will reach its theoretical maximum life expectancy is about the same whether that animal is living in captivity or in the wild.

Which one of the following, if true, most helps to resolve the apparent discrepancy?

(A) Fewer diseases attach leatherbacks than attack other large aquatic reptiles.

(B) The average life expectancy of sea turtles in general is longer than that of almost all other marine animals.

(C) Most leatherbacks that perish in the wild are killed by predators.

(D) Few zoologists have sufficient knowledge to establish an artificial environment that is conducive to the well-being of captive leatherbacks.

(E) The size of a leatherback is an untrustworthy indicator of its age.

GO ON TO THE NEXT PAGE.

LSAT ADVANCED STUDENTS: THIS TEST IS TAKEN AS TEST 5 OF YOUR CLASS. DO NOT USE THIS TEST FOR PRACTICE.

1   1   1

3. Chairperson: The board of directors of our corporation should not allow the incentives being offered by two foreign governments to entice us to expand our operations into their countries without further consideration of the issue. Although there is an opportunity to increase our profits by expanding our operations there, neither of these countries is politically stable.

The chairperson's reasoning most closely conforms to which one of the following principles?

(A) A corporation should never expand operations into countries that are politically unstable.

(B) Corporations should expand operations into countries when there is a chance of increasing profits.

(C) Political stability is the most important consideration in deciding whether to expand operations into a country.

(D) Corporations should always be cautious about expanding operations into politically unstable countries.

(E) Boards of directors should always disregard governmental incentives when considering where to expand corporate operations.

4. Maria: Thomas Edison was one of the most productive inventors of his time, perhaps of all time. His contributions significantly shaped the development of modern lighting and communication systems. Yet he had only a few months of formal schooling. Therefore, you do not need a formal education to make crucial contributions to technological advancement.

Frank: That is definitely not true anymore. Since Edison's day there have been many new developments in technology; to make crucial contributions today you need much more extensive technical knowledge than was needed then.

Frank's reasoning in his response to Maria is most vulnerable to criticism on the grounds that it

(A) fails to address the possibility that technical knowledge may be acquired without formal education

(B) does not consider whether there have been improvements in formal education since Edison's day

(C) relies on using the term "crucial" differently from the way Maria used it

(D) presumes that no other inventor of Edison's time could have been as productive as Edison

(E) fails to criticize or question any of Maria's statements about Edison

5. In some countries, there is a free flow of information about infrastructure, agriculture, and industry, whereas in other countries, this information is controlled by a small elite. In the latter countries, the vast majority of the population is denied vital information about factors that determine their welfare. Thus, these countries are likely to experience more frequent economic crises than other countries do.

The conclusion follows logically if which one of the following is assumed?

(A) It is more likely that people without political power will suffer from economic crises than it is that people in power will.

(B) Economic crises become more frequent as the amount of information available to the population about factors determining its welfare decreases.

(C) In nations in which the government controls access to information about infrastructure, agriculture, and industry, economic crises are common.

(D) The higher the percentage of the population that participates in economic decisions, the better those decisions are.

(E) A small elite that controls information about infrastructure, agriculture, and industry is likely to manipulate that information for its own benefit.

GO ON TO THE NEXT PAGE.

6. Hana said she was not going to invite her brothers to her birthday party. However, among the gifts Hana received at her party was a recording in which she had expressed an interest. Since her brothers had planned to give her that recording, at least some of Hana's brothers must have been among the guests at Hana's birthday party after all.

A reasoning error in the argument is that the argument

(A) disregards the possibility that a change of mind might be justified by a change in circumstances

(B) treats the fact of someone's presence at a given event as a guarantee that that person had a legitimate reason to be at that event

(C) uses a term that is intrinsically evaluative as though that term was purely descriptive

(D) fails to establish that something true of some people is true of only those people

(E) overlooks the possibility that a person's interest in one kind of thing is compatible with that person's interest in a different kind of thing

7. If you have no keyboarding skills at all, you will not be able to use a computer. And if you are not able to use a computer, you will not be able to write your essays using a word processing program.

If the statements above are true, which one of the following must be true?

(A) If you have some keyboarding skills, you will be able to write your essays using a word processing program.

(B) If you are not able to write your essays using a word processing program, you have no keyboarding skills.

(C) If you are able to write your essays using a word processing program, you have at least some keyboarding skills.

(D) If you are able to use a computer, you will probably be able to write your essays using a word processing program.

(E) If you are not able to write your essays using a word processing program, you are not able to use a computer.

Questions 8–9

Rossi: It is undemocratic for people to live under a government in which their interests are not represented. So children should have the right to vote, since sometimes the interests of children are different from those of their parents.

Smith: Granted, children's interests are not always the same as their parents'; governmental deficits incurred by their parents' generation will later affect their own generation's standard of living. But even if children are told about the issues affecting them, which is not generally the case, their conceptions of what can or should be done are too simple, and their time horizons are radically different from those of adults, so we cannot give them the responsibility of voting.

8. Which one of the following most accurately describes Rossi's argument?

(A) It makes an appeal to a general principle.

(B) It denies the good faith of an opponent.

(C) It relies on evaluating the predictable consequences of a proposal.

(D) It substitutes description for giving a rationale for a policy.

(E) It employs a term on two different occasions in different senses.

9. Smith's statements can most directly be used as part of an argument for which one of the following views?

(A) A democratic government does not infringe on the rights of any of its citizens.

(B) Children have rights that must be respected by any political authority that rules over them.

(C) News programs for children would give them enough information to enable them to vote in an informed way.

(D) If there are any limitations on full democracy that result from denying the vote to children, such limitations must be accepted.

(E) If parents do not adequately represent their children's interests in the political sphere, those interests will be adequately represented by someone else.

GO ON TO THE NEXT PAGE.

LSAT ADVANCED STUDENTS: THIS TEST IS TAKEN AS TEST 5 OF YOUR CLASS. DO NOT USE THIS TEST FOR PRACTICE.

1   1   1

10. To accommodate the personal automobile, houses are built on widely scattered lots far from places of work and shopping malls are equipped with immense parking lots that leave little room for wooded areas. Hence, had people generally not used personal automobiles, the result would have to have been a geography of modern cities quite different from the one we have now.

The argument's reasoning is questionable because the argument

(A) infers from the idea that the current geography of modern cities resulted from a particular cause that it could only have resulted from that cause

(B) infers from the idea that the current geography of modern cities resulted from a particular cause that other facets of modern life resulted from that cause

(C) overlooks the fact that many technological innovations other than the personal automobile have had some effect on the way people live

(D) takes for granted that shopping malls do not need large parking lots even given the use of the personal automobile

(E) takes for granted that people ultimately want to live without personal automobiles

11. Many of the presidents and prime ministers who have had the most successful foreign policies had no prior experience in foreign affairs when they assumed office. Although scholars and diplomats in the sacrosanct inner circle of international affairs would have us think otherwise, anyone with an acute political sense, a disciplined temperament, and a highly developed ability to absorb and retain information can quickly learn to conduct a successful foreign policy. In fact, prior experience alone will be of little value to a foreign policymaker who lacks all three of these traits.

If all of the statements above are true, which one of the following must be true?

(A) Scholars and diplomats have more experience in foreign affairs than most presidents and prime ministers bring to office.

(B) Prior experience in foreign affairs is neither a sufficient nor a necessary condition for a president or prime minister to have a successful foreign policy.

(C) Prior experience in foreign affairs is a necessary but not sufficient condition for a president or prime minister to have a successful foreign policy.

(D) An acute political sense, a disciplined temperament, and a highly developed ability to absorb and retain information are each necessary conditions for a president or prime minister to have a successful foreign policy.

(E) A president or prime minister with years of experience in foreign affairs will have a more successful foreign policy than one who does not have experience in foreign affairs.

12. Navigation in animals is defined as the animal's ability to find its way from unfamiliar territory to points familiar to the animal but beyond the immediate range of the animal's senses. Some naturalists claim that polar bears can navigate over considerable distances. As evidence, they cite an instance of a polar bear that returned to its home territory after being released over 500 kilometers (300 miles) away.

Which one of the following, if true, casts the most doubt on the validity of the evidence offered in support of the naturalists' claim?

(A) The polar bear stopped and changed course several times as it moved toward its home territory.

(B) The site at which the polar bear was released was on the bear's annual migration route.

(C) The route along which the polar bear traveled consisted primarily of snow and drifting ice.

(D) Polar bears are only one of many species of mammal whose members have been known to find their way home from considerable distances.

(E) Polar bears often rely on their extreme sensitivity to smell in order to scent out familiar territory.

GO ON TO THE NEXT PAGE.

LSAT ADVANCED STUDENTS: THIS TEST IS TAKEN AS TEST 5 OF YOUR CLASS. DO NOT USE THIS TEST FOR PRACTICE.

1   1   1

Questions 13–14

City council member: Despite the city's desperate need to exploit any available source of revenue, the mayor has repeatedly blocked council members' attempts to pass legislation imposing real estate development fees. It is clear that in doing so the mayor is sacrificing the city's interests to personal interests. The mayor cites figures to show that, in the current market, fees of the size proposed would significantly reduce the number of building starts and thus, on balance, result in a revenue loss to the city. But the important point is that the mayor's family is heavily involved in real estate development and thus has a strong financial interest in the matter.

13. Which one of the following most accurately and completely expresses the main conclusion of the city council member's argument?

(A) Imposing real estate development fees is the best way for the city to exploit the available sources of revenue.

(B) The city would benefit financially from the passage of legislation imposing real estate development fees.

(C) In blocking council members' attempts to impose real estate development fees, the mayor is sacrificing the city's interests to personal interests.

(D) Significantly reducing the number of building starts would not, on balance, result in revenue loss to the city.

(E) The mayor's family has a strong financial interest in preventing the passage of legislation that would impose real estate development fees.

14. The reasoning in the city council member's argument is flawed because

(A) the issue of the mayor's personal interest in the proposed legislation is irrelevant to any assessment of the mayor's action with respect to that legislation

(B) the mayor's course of action being personally advantageous is not inconsistent with the mayor's action being advantageous for the city

(C) the council member's own absence of personal interest in the proposed legislation has not been established

(D) that a person or a municipality has a need for something does not, in itself, establish that that person or that municipality has a right to that thing

(E) the possibility remains open that the mayor's need to avoid loss of family revenue is as desperate as the city's need to increase municipal revenue

15. Seemingly inconsequential changes in sea temperature due to global warming eventually result in declines in fish and seabird populations. A rise of just two degrees prevents the vertical mixing of seawater from different strata. This restricts the availability of upwelling nutrients to phytoplankton. Since zooplankton, which feed upon phytoplankton, feed the rest of the food chain, the declines are inevitable.

Which one of the following most accurately describes the role played in the argument by the statement that zooplankton feed upon phytoplankton?

(A) It is a hypothesis supported by the fact that phytoplankton feed on upwelling nutrients.

(B) It is intended to provide an example of the ways in which the vertical mixing of seawater affects feeding habits.

(C) It helps show how global temperature changes affect larger sea animals indirectly.

(D) It is offered as one reason that global warming must be curtailed.

(E) It is offered in support of the idea that global warming poses a threat to all organisms.

GO ON TO THE NEXT PAGE.

LSAT ADVANCED STUDENTS: THIS TEST IS TAKEN AS TEST 5 OF YOUR CLASS. DO NOT USE THIS TEST FOR PRACTICE.

1 **1** **1**

16. Retailers that excel in neither convenience nor variety of merchandise tend not to be very successful. Yet many successful retailers excel in just one of the areas and meet competitors' standards for the other. Hence, a retailer's success need not depend on excellence in both areas.

The structure of the reasoning in the argument above is most parallel to that in which one of the following?

(A) Runners who have only average speed and endurance are unlikely to win long-distance races. Some long-distance champions, however, win by being above average in speed or endurance only; therefore, being above average in both speed and endurance is not necessary.

(B) Bicyclists who have only average speed are unlikely to win short races, but in a long-distance race such bicyclists can win if they have better-built bicycles than average and better endurance than average. Therefore, most bicycle races are not won by bicyclists with above-average speed.

(C) Excellence in a particular swimming stroke is not always necessary in order for a swimmer to win a race that requires each swimmer to use several different strokes in sequence, and many swimmers win these races without being the best at any of the strokes. Therefore, anyone who does excel at all the strokes is almost certain to win.

(D) Apples that are neither especially firm nor especially flavorful are unsuitable for baking; yet while flavor is essential for both baking and eating, many flavorful apples that are soft are suitable for eating. Hence, the apples that are best for eating need not be both firm and flavorful.

(E) Most plants that are neither ornamental nor edible are useless and are thus classified as weeds; yet many such plants are useful for purposes other than food or ornamentation, and are thus not classified as weeds. Hence, not all inedible and non-ornamental plants are weeds.

17. Detective: Because the embezzler must have had specialized knowledge and access to internal financial records, we can presume that the embezzler worked for XYZ Corporation as either an accountant or an actuary. But an accountant would probably not make the kind of mistakes in ledger entries that led to the discovery of the embezzlement. Thus it is likely that the embezzler is one of the actuaries.

Each of the following weakens the detective's argument EXCEPT:

(A) The actuaries' activities while working for XYZ Corporation were more closely scrutinized by supervisors than were the activities of the accountants.

(B) There is evidence of breaches in computer security at the time of the embezzlement that could have given persons outside XYZ Corporation access to internal financial records.

(C) XYZ Corporation employs eight accountants, whereas it has only two actuaries on its staff.

(D) An independent report released before the crime took place concluded that XYZ Corporation was vulnerable to embezzlement.

(E) Certain security measures at XYZ Corporation made it more difficult for the actuaries to have access to internal financial records than for the accountants.

GO ON TO THE NEXT PAGE.

1   **1**   **1**

18. Until 1985 all commercial airlines completely replenished the cabin air in planes in flight once every 30 minutes. Since then the rate has been once every hour. The less frequently cabin air is replenished in a plane in flight, the higher the level of carbon dioxide in that plane and the easier it is for airborne illnesses to be spread.

Which one of the following is most strongly supported by the information above?

(A) In 1985 there was a loosening of regulations concerning cabin air in commercial airline flights.

(B) People who fly today are more likely to contract airborne illnesses than were people who flew prior to 1985.

(C) Low levels of carbon dioxide in cabin air make it impossible for airborne illnesses to spread.

(D) In 1980 the rate at which the cabin air was replenished in commercial airliners was sufficient to protect passengers from the effects of carbon dioxide buildup.

(E) In 1980 the level of carbon dioxide in the cabin air on a two-hour commercial airline flight was lower than it is today on a similar flight.

19. There is no genuinely altruistic behavior. Everyone needs to have sufficient amount of self-esteem, which crucially depends on believing oneself to be useful and needed. Behavior that appears to be altruistic can be understood as being motivated by the desire to reinforce that belief, a clearly self-interested motivation.

A flaw in the argument is that it

(A) presupposes that anyone who is acting out of self-interest is being altruistic

(B) illicitly infers that behavior is altruistic merely because it seems altruistic

(C) fails to consider that self-esteem also depends on maintaining an awareness of one's own value

(D) presumes, without providing justification, that if one does not hold oneself in sufficient self-esteem one cannot be useful or needed

(E) takes for granted that any behavior that can be interpreted as self-interested is in fact self-interested

20. Current maps showing the North American regions where different types of garden plants will flourish are based on weather data gathered 60 years ago from a few hundred primitive weather stations. New maps are now being compiled using computerized data from several thousand modern weather stations and input from home gardeners across North America. These maps will be far more useful.

Each of the following, if true, helps to support the claim that the new maps will be more useful EXCEPT:

(A) Home gardeners can provide information on plant flourishing not available from weather stations.

(B) Some of the weather stations currently in use are more than 60 years old.

(C) Weather patterns can be described more accurately when more information is available.

(D) Weather conditions are the most important factor in determining where plants will grow.

(E) Weather patterns have changed in the past 60 years.

21. A smoker trying to quit is more likely to succeed if his or her doctor greatly exaggerates the dangers of smoking. Similar strategies can be used to break other habits. But since such strategies involve deception, individuals cannot easily adopt them unless a doctor or some other third party provides the warning.

Which one of the following is an assumption on which the argument depends?

(A) People tend to believe whatever doctors tell them.

(B) Most of the techniques that help people quit smoking can also help people break other habits.

(C) The more the relevant danger is exaggerated, the more likely one is to break one's habit.

(D) People generally do not find it easy to deceive themselves.

(E) A doctor is justified in deceiving a patient whenever doing so is likely to make the patient healthier.

GO ON TO THE NEXT PAGE.

LSAT ADVANCED STUDENTS: THIS TEST IS TAKEN AS TEST 5 OF YOUR CLASS. DO NOT USE THIS TEST FOR PRACTICE.

1   1   1

22. Most people who shop for groceries no more than three times a month buy prepared frozen dinners regularly. In Hallstown most people shop for groceries no more than three times a month. Therefore, in Hallstown most people buy prepared frozen dinners regularly.

Which one of the following arguments has a flawed pattern of reasoning most like the flawed reasoning in the argument above?

(A) It is clear that most drivers in West Ansland are safe drivers since there are very few driving accidents in West Ansland and most accidents there are not serious.

(B) It is clear that John cannot drive, since he does not own a car and no one in his family who does not own a car can drive.

(C) It is clear that Fernando's friends usually drive to school, since all of his friends can drive and all of his friends go to school.

(D) It is clear that most people in Highland County drive sedans, since most people who commute to work drive sedans and most people in Highland County commute to work.

(E) It is clear that most of Janine's friends are good drivers, since she accepts rides only from good drivers and she accepts rides from most of her friends.

23. Editorial: This political party has repeatedly expressed the view that increasing spending on education is a worthy goal. On other occasions, however, the same party has claimed that the government should not increase spending on education. So this party's policy is clearly inconsistent.

The argument in the editorial depends on assuming which one of the following?

(A) It is inconsistent for a legislator both to claim that increasing spending on education is a worthy goal and to vote against increasing spending on education.

(B) A consistent course of action in educational policy is usually the course of action that will reduce spending on education in the long run.

(C) Even if a goal is a morally good one, one should not necessarily try to achieve it.

(D) A consistent political policy does not hold that an action that comprises a worthy goal should not be performed.

(E) Members of one political party never have inconsistent views on how to best approach a political issue.

24. Science journalist: Brown dwarfs are celestial objects with more mass than planets but less mass than stars. They are identified by their mass and whether or not lithium is present in their atmospheres. Stars at least as massive as the Sun have lithium remaining in their atmospheres because the mixing of elements in their internal nuclear furnaces is incomplete. Stars with less mass than the Sun have no lithium because the element has been fully mixed into their nuclear furnaces and consumed. A brown dwarf does not have a fully functional nuclear furnace and so its lithium cannot be consumed.

Which one of the following is most strongly supported by the science journalist's statements?

(A) Any celestial object without lithium in its atmosphere is a star with less mass than the Sun.

(B) Any celestial object with lithium in its atmosphere has a nuclear furnace that has incompletely mixed the object's elements.

(C) No celestial object that has no lithium in its atmosphere is a brown dwarf.

(D) No celestial object with lithium in its atmosphere has less mass than the Sun.

(E) No celestial object less massive than a brown dwarf has lithium in its atmosphere.

25. Native speakers perceive sentences of their own language as sequences of separate words. But this perception is an illusion. This is shown by the fact that travelers who do not know a local language hear an unintelligible, uninterrupted stream of sound, not sentences with distinct words.

Which one of the following is an assumption on which the argument depends?

(A) It is impossible to understand sentences if they are in fact uninterrupted streams of sound.

(B) Those who do not know a language cannot hear the way speech in that language actually sounds.

(C) People pay less close attention to the way their own language sounds than they do to the way an unfamiliar language sounds.

(D) Accomplished non-native speakers of a language do not perceive sentences as streams of sound.

(E) Native speakers' perceptions of their own language are not more accurate than are the perceptions of persons who do not know that language.

S T O P

IF YOU FINISH BEFORE TIME IS CALLED, YOU MAY CHECK YOUR WORK ON THIS SECTION ONLY.
DO NOT WORK ON ANY OTHER SECTION IN THE TEST.

LSAT ADVANCED STUDENTS: THIS TEST IS TAKEN AS TEST 5 OF YOUR CLASS. DO NOT USE THIS TEST FOR PRACTICE.

2   2

SECTION II

Time—35 minutes

27 Questions

Directions: Each set of questions in this section is based on a single passage or a pair of passages. The questions are to be answered on the basis of what is stated or implied in the passage or pair of passages. For some of the questions, more than one of the choices could conceivably answer the question. However, you are to choose the best answer; that is, the response that most accurately and completely answers the question, and blacken the corresponding space on your answer sheet.

This passage was adapted from an article published in 1996.

The Internet is a system of computer networks that allows individuals and organizations to communicate freely with other Internet users throughout the world. As a result, an astonishing

(5) variety of information is able to flow unimpeded across national and other political borders, presenting serious difficulties for traditional approaches to legislation and law enforcement, to which such borders are crucial.

(10) Control over physical space and the objects located in it is a defining attribute of sovereignty. Lawmaking presupposes some mechanism for enforcement, i.e., the ability to control violations. But jurisdictions cannot control the information and

(15) transactions flowing across their borders via the Internet. For example, a government might seek to intercept transmissions that propagate the kinds of consumer fraud that it regulates within its jurisdiction. But the volume of electronic communications

(20) crossing its territorial boundaries is too great to allow for effective control over individual transmissions. In order to deny its citizens access to specific materials, a government would thus have to prevent them from using the Internet altogether. Such a draconian

(25) measure would almost certainly be extremely unpopular, since most affected citizens would probably feel that the benefits of using the Internet decidedly outweigh the risks.

One legal domain that is especially sensitive to

(30) geographical considerations is that governing trademarks. There is no global registration of trademarks; international protection requires registration in each country. Moreover, within a country, the same name can sometimes be used

(35) proprietarily by businesses of different kinds in the same locality, or by businesses of the same kind in different localities, on the grounds that use of the trademark by one such business does not affect the others. But with the advent of the Internet, a business

(40) name can be displayed in such a way as to be accessible from any computer connected to the Internet anywhere in the world. Should such a display advertising a restaurant in Norway be deemed to infringe a trademark in Brazil just because it can be

(45) accessed freely from Brazil? It is not clear that any particular country's trademark authorities possess, or should possess, jurisdiction over such displays. Otherwise, any use of a trademark on the Internet could be subject to the jurisdiction of every country

(50) simultaneously.

The Internet also gives rise to situations in which regulation is needed but cannot be provided within the existing framework. For example, electronic communications, which may pass through many

(55) different territorial jurisdictions, pose perplexing new questions about the nature and adequacy of privacy protections. Should French officials have lawful access to messages traveling via the Internet from Canada to Japan? This is just one among many

(60) questions that collectively challenge the notion that the Internet can be effectively controlled by the existing system of territorial jurisdictions.

1. Which one of the following most accurately expresses the main point of the passage?

(A) The high-volume, global nature of activity on the Internet undermines the feasibility of controlling it through legal frameworks that presuppose geographic boundaries.

(B) The system of Internet communications simultaneously promotes and weakens the power of national governments to control their citizens' speech and financial transactions.

(C) People value the benefits of their participation on the Internet so highly that they would strongly oppose any government efforts to regulate their Internet activity.

(D) Internet communications are responsible for a substantial increase in the volume and severity of global crime.

(E) Current Internet usage and its future expansion pose a clear threat to the internal political stability of many nations.

GO ON TO THE NEXT PAGE.

LSAT ADVANCED STUDENTS: THIS TEST IS TAKEN AS TEST 5 OF YOUR CLASS. DO NOT USE THIS TEST FOR PRACTICE.

2   2   2   2

2. The author mentions French officials in connection with messages traveling between Canada and Japan (lines 57–59) primarily to

(A) emphasize that the Internet allows data to be made available to users worldwide

(B) illustrate the range of languages that might be used on the Internet

(C) provide an example of a regulatory problem arising when an electronic communication intended for a particular destination passes through intermediate jurisdictions

(D) show why any use of a trademark on the Internet could be subject to the jurisdiction of every country simultaneously

(E) highlight the kind of international cooperation that made the Internet possible

3. According to the passage, which one of the following is an essential property of political sovereignty?

(A) control over business enterprises operating across territorial boundaries

(B) authority over communicative exchanges occurring within a specified jurisdiction

(C) power to regulate trademarks throughout a circumscribed geographic region

(D) control over the entities included within a designated physical space

(E) authority over all commercial transactions involving any of its citizens

4. Which one of the following words employed by the author in the second paragraph is most indicative of the author's attitude toward any hypothetical measure a government might enact to deny its citizens access to the Internet?

(A) benefits
(B) decidedly
(C) unpopular
(D) draconian
(E) risks

5. What is the main purpose of the fourth paragraph?

(A) to call into question the relevance of the argument provided in the second paragraph

(B) to provide a practical illustration that questions the general claim made in the first paragraph

(C) to summarize the arguments provided in the second and third paragraphs

(D) to continue the argument that begins in the third paragraph

(E) to provide an additional argument in support of the general claim made in the first paragraph

GO ON TO THE NEXT PAGE.

LSAT ADVANCED STUDENTS: THIS TEST IS TAKEN AS TEST 5 OF YOUR CLASS. DO NOT USE THIS TEST FOR PRACTICE.

2   2   2   2

Passage A

Drilling fluids, including the various mixtures known as drilling muds, play essential roles in oil-well drilling. As they are circulated down through the drill pipe and back up the well itself, they lubricate the
(5) drill bit, bearings, and drill pipe; clean and cool the drill bit as it cuts into the rock; lift rock chips (cuttings) to the surface; provide information about what is happening downhole, allowing the drillers to monitor the behavior, flow rate, pressure, and
(10) composition of the drilling fluid; and maintain well pressure to control cave-ins.

Drilling muds are made of bentonite and other clays and polymers, mixed with a fluid to the desired viscosity. By far the largest ingredient of drilling
(15) muds, by weight, is barite, a very heavy mineral of density 4.3 to 4.6. It is also used as an inert filler in some foods and is more familiar in its medical use as the "barium meal" administered before X-raying the digestive tract.
(20) Over the years individual drilling companies and their expert drillers have devised proprietary formulations, or mud "recipes," to deal with specific types of drilling jobs. One problem in studying the effects of drilling waste discharges is that the drilling
(25) fluids are made from a range of over 1,000, sometimes toxic, ingredients—many of them known, confusingly, by different trade names, generic descriptions, chemical formulae, and regional or industry slang words, and many of them kept secret by companies or individual
(30) formulators.

Passage B

Drilling mud, cuttings, and associated chemicals are normally released only during the drilling phase of a well's existence. These discharges are the main environmental concern in offshore oil production, and
(35) their use is tightly regulated. The discharges are closely monitored by the offshore operator, and releases are controlled as a condition of the operating permit.

One type of mud—water-based mud (WBM)—is a mixture of water, bentonite clay, and chemical
(40) additives, and is used to drill shallow parts of wells. It is not particularly toxic to marine organisms and disperses readily. Under current regulations, it can be dumped directly overboard. Companies typically recycle WBMs until their properties are no longer
(45) suitable and then, over a period of hours, dump the entire batch into the sea.

For drilling deeper wells, oil-based mud (OBM) is normally used. The typical difference from WBM is the high content of mineral oil (typically 30 percent).
(50) OBMs also contain greater concentrations of barite, a powdered heavy mineral, and a number of additives. OBMs have a greater potential for negative environmental impact, partly because they do not disperse as readily. Barite may impact some
(55) organisms, particularly scallops, and the mineral oil may have toxic effects. Currently only the residues of OBMs adhering to cuttings that remain after the cuttings are sieved from the drilling fluids may be discharged overboard, and then only mixtures up to a
(60) specified maximum oil content.

6. A primary purpose of each of the passages is to

    (A) provide causal explanations for a type of environmental pollution
    (B) describe the general composition and properties of drilling muds
    (C) point out possible environmental impacts associated with oil drilling
    (D) explain why oil-well drilling requires the use of drilling muds
    (E) identify difficulties inherent in the regulation of oil-well drilling operations

7. Which one of the following is a characteristic of barite that is mentioned in both of the passages?

    (A) It does not disperse readily in seawater.
    (B) It is not found in drilling muds containing bentonite.
    (C) Its use in drilling muds is tightly regulated.
    (D) It is the most commonly used ingredient in drilling muds.
    (E) It is a heavy mineral.

8. Each of the following is supported by one or both of the passages EXCEPT:

    (A) Clay is an important constituent of many, if not all, drilling muds.
    (B) At least one type of drilling mud is not significantly toxic to marine life.
    (C) There has been some study of the environmental effects of drilling-mud discharges.
    (D) Government regulations allow drilling muds to contain 30 percent mineral oil.
    (E) During the drilling of an oil well, drilling mud is continuously discharged into the sea.

GO ON TO THE NEXT PAGE.

LSAT ADVANCED STUDENTS: THIS TEST IS TAKEN AS TEST 5 OF YOUR CLASS. DO NOT USE THIS TEST FOR PRACTICE.

2 2 2

9. Which one of the following can be most reasonably inferred from the two passages taken together, but not from either one individually?

(A) Barite is the largest ingredient of drilling muds, by weight, and also the most environmentally damaging.

(B) Although barite can be harmful to marine organisms, it can be consumed safely by humans.

(C) Offshore drilling is more damaging to the environment than is land-based drilling.

(D) The use of drilling muds needs to be more tightly controlled by government.

(E) If offshore drilling did not generate cuttings, it would be less harmful to the environment.

10. Each of the following is supported by one or both of the passages EXCEPT:

(A) Drillers monitor the suitability of the mud they are using.

(B) The government requires drilling companies to disclose all ingredients used in their drilling muds.

(C) In certain quantities, barite is not toxic to humans.

(D) Oil reserves can be found within or beneath layers of rock.

(E) Drilling deep oil wells requires the use of different mud recipes than does drilling shallow oil wells.

11. Based on information in the passages, which one of the following, if true, provides the strongest support for a prediction that the proportion of oil-well drilling using OBMs will increase in the future?

(A) The cost of certain ingredients in WBMs is expected to increase steadily over the next several decades.

(B) The deeper an offshore oil well, the greater the concentration of barite that must be used in the drilling mud.

(C) Oil reserves at shallow depths have mostly been tapped, leaving primarily much deeper reserves for future drilling.

(D) It is unlikely that oil drillers will develop more efficient ways of removing OBM residues from cuttings that remain after being sieved from drilling fluids.

(E) Barite is a common mineral, the availability of which is virtually limitless.

12. According to passage B, one reason OBMs are potentially more environmentally damaging than WBMs is that OBMs

(A) are slower to disperse
(B) contain greater concentrations of bentonite
(C) contain a greater number of additives
(D) are used for drilling deeper wells
(E) cannot be recycled

GO ON TO THE NEXT PAGE.

LSAT ADVANCED STUDENTS: THIS TEST IS TAKEN AS TEST 5 OF YOUR CLASS. DO NOT USE THIS TEST FOR PRACTICE.

2　　　　2　　　　2　　　　2

Aida Overton Walker (1880–1914), one of the most widely acclaimed African American performers of the early twentieth century, was known largely for popularizing a dance form known as the cakewalk
(5) through her choreographing, performance, and teaching of the dance. The cakewalk was originally developed prior to the United States Civil War by African Americans, for whom dance was a means of maintaining cultural links within a slave society. It
(10) was based on traditional West African ceremonial dances, and like many other African American dances, it retained features characteristic of African dance forms, such as gliding steps and an emphasis on improvisation.
(15) To this African-derived foundation, the cakewalk added certain elements from European dances: where African dances feature flexible body postures, large groups and separate-sex dancing, the cakewalk developed into a high-kicking walk performed by a
(20) procession of couples. Ironically, while these modifications later enabled the cakewalk to appeal to European Americans and become one of the first cultural forms to cross the racial divide in North America, they were originally introduced with satiric
(25) intent. Slaves performed the grandiloquent walks in order to parody the processional dances performed at slave owners' balls and, in general, the self-important manners of slave owners. To add a further irony, by the end of the nineteenth century, the cakewalk was
(30) itself being parodied by European American stage performers, and these parodies in turn helped shape subsequent versions of the cakewalk.
While this complex evolution meant that the cakewalk was not a simple cultural phenomenon—
(35) one scholar has characterized this layering of parody upon parody with the phrase "mimetic vertigo"—it is in fact what enabled the dance to attract its wide audience. In the cultural and socioeconomic flux of the turn-of-the-century United States, where
(40) industrialization, urbanization, mass immigration, and rapid social mobility all reshaped the cultural landscape, an art form had to be capable of being many things to many people in order to appeal to a large audience.
(45) Walker's remarkable success at popularizing the cakewalk across otherwise relatively rigid racial boundaries rested on her ability to address within her interpretation of it the varying and sometimes conflicting demands placed on the dance. Middle-
(50) class African Americans, for example, often denounced the cakewalk as disreputable, a complaint reinforced by the parodies circulating at the time. Walker won over this audience by refining the cakewalk and emphasizing its fundamental grace.
(55) Meanwhile, because middle- and upper-class European Americans often felt threatened by the tremendous cultural flux around them, they prized what they regarded as authentic art forms as bastions of stability; much of Walker's success with this

(60) audience derived from her distillation of what was widely acclaimed as the most authentic cakewalk. Finally, Walker was able to gain the admiration of many newly rich industrialists and financiers, who found in the grand flourishes of her version of the
(65) cakewalk a fitting vehicle for celebrating their newfound social rank.

13. Which one of the following most accurately expresses the main point of the passage?

(A) Walker, who was especially well known for her success in choreographing, performing, and teaching the cakewalk, was one of the most widely recognized African American performers of the early twentieth century.

(B) In spite of the disparate influences that shaped the cakewalk, Walker was able to give the dance broad appeal because she distilled what was regarded as the most authentic version in an era that valued authenticity highly.

(C) Walker popularized the cakewalk by capitalizing on the complex cultural mix that had developed from the dance's original blend of satire and cultural preservation, together with the effects of later parodies.

(D) Whereas other versions of the cakewalk circulating at the beginning of the twentieth century were primarily parodic in nature, the version popularized by Walker combined both satire and cultural preservation.

(E) Because Walker was able to recognize and preserve the characteristics of the cakewalk as African Americans originally performed it, it became the first popular art form to cross the racial divide in the United States.

14. The author describes the socioeconomic flux of the turn-of-the-century United States in the third paragraph primarily in order to

(A) argue that the cakewalk could have become popular only in such complex social circumstances

(B) detail the social context that prompted performers of the cakewalk to fuse African and European dance forms

(C) identify the target of the overlapping parodic layers that characterized the cakewalk

(D) indicate why a particular cultural environment was especially favorable for the success of the cakewalk

(E) explain why European American parodies of the cakewalk were able to reach wide audiences

GO ON TO THE NEXT PAGE.

2   2   2   2

15. Which one of the following is most analogous to the author's account in the second paragraph of how the cakewalk came to appeal to European Americans?

(A) Satirical versions of popular music songs are frequently more popular than the songs they parody.

(B) A style of popular music grows in popularity among young listeners because it parodies the musical styles admired by older listeners.

(C) A style of music becomes admired among popular music's audience in part because of elements that were introduced in order to parody popular music.

(D) A once popular style of music wins back its audience by incorporating elements of the style of music that is currently most popular.

(E) After popular music begins to appropriate elements of a traditional style of music, interest in that traditional music increases.

16. The passage asserts which one of the following about the cakewalk?

(A) It was largely unknown outside African American culture until Walker popularized it.

(B) It was mainly a folk dance, and Walker became one of only a handful of people to perform it professionally.

(C) Its performance as parody became uncommon as a result of Walker's popularization of its authentic form.

(D) Its West African origins became commonly known as a result of Walker's work.

(E) It was one of the first cultural forms to cross racial lines in the United States.

17. It can be inferred from the passage that the author would be most likely to agree with which one of the following statements?

(A) Because of the broad appeal of humor, satiric art forms are often among the first to cross racial or cultural divisions.

(B) The interactions between African American and European American cultural forms often result in what is appropriately characterized as "mimetic vertigo."

(C) Middle-class European Americans who valued the cakewalk's authenticity subsequently came to admire other African American dances for the same reason.

(D) Because of the influence of African dance forms, some popular dances that later emerged in the United States featured separate-sex dancing.

(E) Some of Walker's admirers were attracted to her version of the cakewalk as a means for bolstering their social identities.

18. The passage most strongly suggests that the author would be likely to agree with which one of the following statements about Walker's significance in the history of the cakewalk?

(A) Walker broadened the cakewalk's appeal by highlighting elements that were already present in the dance.

(B) Walker's version of the cakewalk appealed to larger audiences than previous versions did because she accentuated its satiric dimension.

(C) Walker popularized the cakewalk by choreographing various alternative interpretations of it, each tailored to the interests of a different cultural group.

(D) Walker added a "mimetic vertigo" to the cakewalk by inserting imitations of other performers' cakewalking into her dance routines.

(E) Walker revitalized the cakewalk by disentangling its complex admixture of African and European elements.

19. The passage provides sufficient information to answer which one of the following questions?

(A) What were some of the attributes of African dance forms that were preserved in the cakewalk?

(B) Who was the first performer to dance the cakewalk professionally?

(C) What is an aspect of the cakewalk that was preserved in other North American dance forms?

(D) What features were added to the original cakewalk by the stage parodies circulating at the end of the nineteenth century?

(E) For about how many years into the twentieth century did the cakewalk remain widely popular?

GO ON TO THE NEXT PAGE.

LSAT ADVANCED STUDENTS: THIS TEST IS TAKEN AS TEST 5 OF YOUR CLASS. DO NOT USE THIS TEST FOR PRACTICE.

2　　　2　　　2　　　2

In principle, a cohesive group—one whose members generally agree with one another and support one another's judgments—can do a much better job at decision making than it could if it were
(5) noncohesive. When cohesiveness is low or lacking entirely, compliance out of fear of recrimination is likely to be strongest. To overcome this fear, participants in the group's deliberations need to be confident that they are members in good standing and
(10) that the others will continue to value their role in the group, whether or not they agree about a particular issue under discussion. As members of a group feel more accepted by the others, they acquire greater freedom to say what they really think, becoming less
(15) likely to use deceitful arguments or to play it safe by dancing around the issues with vapid or conventional comments. Typically, then, the more cohesive a group becomes, the less its members will deliberately censor what they say out of fear of being punished socially
(20) for antagonizing their fellow members.

But group cohesiveness can have pitfalls as well: while the members of a highly cohesive group can feel much freer to deviate from the majority, their desire for genuine concurrence on every important
(25) issue often inclines them not to use this freedom. In a highly cohesive group of decision makers, the danger is not that individuals will conceal objections they harbor regarding a proposal favored by the majority, but that they will think the proposal is a good one
(30) without attempting to carry out a critical scrutiny that could reveal grounds for strong objections. Members may then decide that any misgivings they feel are not worth pursuing—that the benefit of any doubt should be given to the group consensus. In this way, they
(35) may fall victim to a syndrome known as "groupthink," which one psychologist concerned with collective decision making has defined as "a deterioration of mental efficiency, reality testing, and moral judgment that results from in-group pressures."
(40) Based on analyses of major fiascoes of international diplomacy and military decision making, researchers have identified groupthink behavior as a recurring pattern that involves several factors: overestimation of the group's power and morality,
(45) manifested, for example, in an illusion of invulnerability, which creates excessive optimism; closed-mindedness to warnings of problems and to alternative viewpoints; and unwarranted pressures toward uniformity, including self-censorship with
(50) respect to doubts about the group's reasoning and a concomitant shared illusion of unanimity concerning group decisions. Cohesiveness of the decision-making group is an essential antecedent condition for this syndrome but not a sufficient one, so it is important
(55) to work toward identifying the additional factors that determine whether group cohesiveness will deteriorate into groupthink or allow for effective decision making.

20. Which one of the following most accurately expresses the main point of the passage?

(A) Despite its value in encouraging frank discussion, high cohesion can lead to a debilitating type of group decision making called groupthink.

(B) Group members can guard against groupthink if they have a good understanding of the critical role played by cohesion.

(C) Groupthink is a dysfunctional collective decision-making pattern that can occur in diplomacy and military affairs.

(D) Low cohesion in groups is sometimes desirable when higher cohesion involves a risk of groupthink behavior.

(E) Future efforts to guard against groupthink will depend on the results of ongoing research into the psychology of collective decision making.

21. A group of closely associated colleagues has made a disastrous diplomatic decision after a series of meetings marked by disagreement over conflicting alternatives. It can be inferred from the passage that the author would be most likely to say that this scenario

(A) provides evidence of chronic indecision, thus indicating a weak level of cohesion in general

(B) indicates that the group's cohesiveness was coupled with some other factor to produce a groupthink fiasco

(C) provides no evidence that groupthink played a role in the group's decision

(D) provides evidence that groupthink can develop even in some groups that do not demonstrate an "illusion of unanimity"

(E) indicates that the group probably could have made its decision-making procedure more efficient by studying the information more thoroughly

GO ON TO THE NEXT PAGE.

LSAT ADVANCED STUDENTS: THIS TEST IS TAKEN AS TEST 5 OF YOUR CLASS. DO NOT USE THIS TEST FOR PRACTICE.

2 2 2

22. Which one of the following, if true, would most support the author's contentions concerning the conditions under which groupthink takes place?

(A) A study of several groups, each made up of members of various professions, found that most fell victim to groupthink.

(B) There is strong evidence that respectful dissent is more likely to occur in cohesive groups than in groups in which there is little internal support.

(C) Extensive analyses of decisions made by a large number of groups found no cases of groupthink in groups whose members generally distrust one another's judgments.

(D) There is substantial evidence that groupthink is especially likely to take place when members of a group develop factions whose intransigence prolongs the group's deliberations.

(E) Ample research demonstrates that voluntary deference to group opinion is not a necessary factor for the formation of groupthink behavior.

23. The passage mentions which one of the following as a component of groupthink?

(A) unjustified suspicions among group members regarding an adversary's intentions

(B) strong belief that the group's decisions are right

(C) group members working under unusually high stress, leading to illusions of invulnerability

(D) the deliberate use of vapid, clichéd arguments

(E) careful consideration of objections to majority positions

24. It can be inferred from the passage that both the author of the passage and the researchers mentioned in the passage would be most likely to agree with which one of the following statements about groupthink?

(A) Groupthink occurs in all strongly cohesive groups, but its contribution to collective decision making is not fully understood.

(B) The causal factors that transform group cohesion into groupthink are unique to each case.

(C) The continued study of cohesiveness of groups is probably fruitless for determining what factors elicit groupthink.

(D) Outside information cannot influence group decisions once they have become determined by groupthink.

(E) On balance, groupthink cannot be expected to have a beneficial effect in a group's decision making.

25. In the passage, the author says which one of the following about conformity in decision-making groups?

(A) Enforced conformity may be appropriate in some group decision situations.

(B) A high degree of conformity is often expected of military decision-making group members.

(C) Inappropriate group conformity can result from inadequate information.

(D) Voluntary conformity occurs much less frequently than enforced conformity.

(E) Members of noncohesive groups may experience psychological pressure to conform.

26. In line 5, the author mentions low group cohesiveness primarily in order to

(A) contribute to a claim that cohesiveness can be conducive to a freer exchange of views in groups

(B) establish a comparison between groupthink symptoms and the attributes of low-cohesion groups

(C) suggest that there may be ways to make both cohesive and noncohesive groups more open to dissent

(D) indicate that both cohesive and noncohesive groups may be susceptible to groupthink dynamics

(E) lay the groundwork for a subsequent proposal for overcoming the debilitating effects of low cohesion

27. Based on the passage, it can be inferred that the author would be most likely to agree with which one of the following?

(A) Highly cohesive groups are more likely to engage in confrontational negotiating styles with adversaries than are those with low cohesion.

(B) It is difficult for a group to examine all relevant options critically in reaching decisions unless it has a fairly high degree of cohesiveness.

(C) A group with varied viewpoints on a given issue is less likely to reach a sound decision regarding that issue than is a group whose members are unified in their outlook.

(D) Intense stress and high expectations are the key factors in the formation of groupthink.

(E) Noncohesive groups can, under certain circumstances, develop all of the symptoms of groupthink.

S T O P

IF YOU FINISH BEFORE TIME IS CALLED, YOU MAY CHECK YOUR WORK ON THIS SECTION ONLY.
DO NOT WORK ON ANY OTHER SECTION IN THE TEST.

3   3

SECTION III

Time—35 minutes

26 Questions

Directions: The questions in this section are based on the reasoning contained in brief statements or passages. For some questions, more than one of the choices could conceivably answer the question. However, you are to choose the best answer; that is, the response that most accurately and completely answers the question. You should not make assumptions that are by commonsense standards implausible, superfluous, or incompatible with the passage. After you have chosen the best answer, blacken the corresponding space on your answer sheet.

1. Executive: Our company is proud of its long history of good relations with its employees. In fact, a recent survey of our retirees proves that we treat our employees fairly, since 95 percent of the respondents reported that they had always been treated fairly during the course of their careers with us.

The executive's argument is flawed in that it

(A) presents as its sole premise a claim that one would accept as true only if one already accepted the truth of the conclusion
(B) relies on evidence that cannot be verified
(C) equivocates on the word "fairly"
(D) bases a generalization on a sample that may not be representative
(E) presumes, without providing justification, that older methods of managing employees are superior to newer ones

2. Many of those who are most opposed to cruelty to animals in the laboratory, in the slaughterhouse, or on the farm are people who truly love animals and who keep pets. The vast majority of domestic pets, however, are dogs and cats, and both of these species are usually fed meat. Therefore, many of those who are most opposed to cruelty to animals do, in fact, contribute to such cruelty.

Which one of the following is an assumption made by the argument?

(A) Loving pets requires loving all forms of animal life.
(B) Many of those who are opposed to keeping dogs and cats as pets are also opposed to cruelty to animals.
(C) Some people who work in laboratories, in slaughterhouses, or on farms are opposed to cruelty to animals.
(D) Many popular pets are not usually fed meat.
(E) Feeding meat to pets contributes to cruelty to animals.

3. Statistics from the National Booksellers Association indicate that during the last five years most bookstores have started to experience declining revenues from the sale of fiction, despite national campaigns to encourage people to read more fiction. Therefore, these reading campaigns have been largely unsuccessful.

Which one of the following statements, if true, most seriously weakens the argument?

(A) Mail order book clubs have enjoyed substantial growth in fiction sales throughout the last five years.
(B) During the last five years the most profitable items in bookstores have been newspapers and periodicals rather than novels.
(C) Fierce competition has forced booksellers to make drastic markdowns on the cover price of best-selling biographies.
(D) Due to the poor economic conditions that have prevailed during the last five years, most libraries report substantial increases in the number of patrons seeking books on changing careers and starting new businesses.
(E) The National Booksellers Association statistics do not include profits from selling novels by mail to overseas customers.

4. People who consume a lot of honey tend to have fewer cavities than others have. Yet, honey is high in sugar, and sugar is one of the leading causes of tooth decay.

Which one of the following, if true, most helps to resolve the apparent paradox described above?

(A) People who eat a lot of honey tend to consume very little sugar from other sources.
(B) Many people who consume a lot of honey consume much of it dissolved in drinks.
(C) People's dental hygiene habits vary greatly.
(D) Refined sugars have been linked to more health problems than have unrefined sugars.
(E) Honey contains bacteria that inhibit the growth of the bacteria that cause tooth decay.

GO ON TO THE NEXT PAGE.

KAPLAN

3 **3** **3** **3** **3**

5. Byrne: One of our club's bylaws specifies that any officer who fails to appear on time for any one of the quarterly board meetings, or who misses two of our monthly general meetings, must be suspended. Thibodeaux, an officer, was recently suspended. But Thibodeaux has never missed a monthly general meeting. Therefore, Thibodeaux must have failed to appear on time for a quarterly board meeting.

The reasoning in Byrne's argument is flawed in that the argument

(A) fails to consider the possibility that Thibodeaux has arrived late for two or more monthly general meetings

(B) presumes, without providing justification, that if certain events each produce a particular result, then no other event is sufficient to produce that result

(C) takes for granted that an assumption required to establish the argument's conclusion is sufficient to establish that conclusion

(D) fails to specify at what point someone arriving at a club meeting is officially deemed late

(E) does not specify how long Thibodeaux has been an officer

6. Manufacturers of writing paper need to add mineral "filler" to paper pulp if the paper made from the pulp is to look white. Without such filler, paper products look grayish. To make writing paper that looks white from recycled paper requires more filler than is required to make such paper from other sources. Therefore, barring the more efficient use of fillers in paper manufacturing or the development of paper-whitening technologies that do not require mineral fillers, if writing paper made from recycled paper comes to replace other types of writing paper, paper manufacturers will have to use more filler than they now use.

Which one of the following is an assumption on which the argument depends?

(A) Certain kinds of paper cannot be manufactured from recycled paper.

(B) The fillers that are used to make paper white are harmful to the environment.

(C) Grayish writing paper will not be a universally acceptable alternative to white writing paper.

(D) Beyond a certain limit, increasing the amount of filler added to paper pulp does not increase the whiteness of the paper made from the pulp.

(E) The total amount of writing paper manufactured worldwide will increase significantly in the future.

7. Environmentalist: The excessive atmospheric buildup of carbon dioxide, which threatens the welfare of everyone in the world, can be stopped only by reducing the burning of fossil fuels. Any country imposing the strict emission standards on the industrial burning of such fuels that this reduction requires, however, would thereby reduce its gross national product. No nation will be willing to bear singlehandedly the costs of an action that will benefit everyone. It is obvious, then, that the catastrophic consequences of excessive atmospheric carbon dioxide are unavoidable unless _____.

Which one of the following most logically completes the argument?

(A) all nations become less concerned with pollution than with the economic burdens of preventing it

(B) multinational corporations agree to voluntary strict emission standards

(C) international agreements produce industrial emission standards

(D) distrust among nations is eliminated

(E) a world government is established

8. A clear advantage of digital technology over traditional printing is that digital documents, being patterns of electronic signals rather than patterns of ink on paper, do not generate waste in the course of their production and use. However, because patterns of electronic signals are necessarily ephemeral, a digital document can easily be destroyed and lost forever.

The statements above best illustrate which one of the following generalizations?

(A) A property of a technology may constitute an advantage in one set of circumstances and a disadvantage in others.

(B) What at first appears to be an advantage of a technology may create more problems than it solves.

(C) It is more important to be able to preserve information than it is for information to be easily accessible.

(D) Innovations in document storage technologies sometimes decrease, but never eliminate, the risk of destroying documents.

(E) Advances in technology can lead to increases in both convenience and environmental soundness.

GO ON TO THE NEXT PAGE.

3 **3** **3** **3**

9. Museum visitor: The national government has mandated a 5 percent increase in the minimum wage paid to all workers. This mandate will adversely affect the museum-going public. The museum's revenue does not currently exceed its expenses, and since the mandate will significantly increase the museum's operating expenses, the museum will be forced either to raise admission fees or to decrease services.

Which one of the following is an assumption required by the museum visitor's argument?

(A) Some of the museum's employees are not paid significantly more than the minimum wage.

(B) The museum's revenue from admission fees has remained constant over the past five years.

(C) Some of the museum's employees are paid more than the current minimum wage.

(D) The annual number of visitors to the museum has increased steadily.

(E) Not all visitors to the museum are required to pay an admission fee.

10. Helen: Reading a book is the intellectual equivalent of investing money: you're investing time, thereby foregoing other ways of spending that time, in the hope that what you learn will later afford you more opportunities than you'd get by spending the time doing something other than reading that book.

Randi: But that applies only to vocational books. Reading fiction is like watching a sitcom: it's just wasted time.

Which one of the following most accurately describes the technique Randi uses in responding to Helen's claims?

(A) questioning how the evidence Helen uses for a claim was gathered

(B) disputing the scope of Helen's analogy by presenting another analogy

(C) arguing that Helen's reasoning ultimately leads to an absurd conclusion

(D) drawing an analogy to an example presented by Helen

(E) denying the relevance of an example presented by Helen

11. Contrary to recent speculations, no hardware store will be opening in the shopping plaza. If somebody were going to open a store there, they would already have started publicizing it. But there has been no such publicity.

Which one of the following most accurately expresses the conclusion drawn in the argument?

(A) Some people have surmised that a hardware store will be opening in the shopping plaza.

(B) A hardware store will not be opening in the shopping plaza.

(C) If somebody were going to open a hardware store in the shopping plaza, that person would already have started publicizing it.

(D) It would be unwise to open a hardware store in the shopping plaza.

(E) There has been no publicity concerning the opening of a hardware store in the shopping plaza.

12. Ethicist: Although science is frequently said to be morally neutral, it has a traditional value system of its own. For example, scientists sometimes foresee that a line of theoretical research they are pursuing will yield applications that could seriously harm people, animals, or the environment. Yet, according to science's traditional value system, such consequences do not have to be considered in deciding whether to pursue that research. Ordinary morality, in contrast, requires that we take the foreseeable consequences of our actions into account whenever we are deciding what to do.

The ethicist's statements, if true, most strongly support which one of the following?

(A) Scientists should not be held responsible for the consequences of their research.

(B) According to the dictates of ordinary morality, scientists doing research that ultimately turns out to yield harmful applications are acting immorally.

(C) Science is morally neutral because it assigns no value to the consequences of theoretical research.

(D) It is possible for scientists to both adhere to the traditional values of their field and violate a principle of ordinary morality.

(E) The uses and effects of scientifically acquired knowledge can never be adequately foreseen.

GO ON TO THE NEXT PAGE.

3 **3** **3** **3** **3**

13. Consumers seek to purchase the highest quality at the lowest prices. Companies that do not offer products that attract consumers eventually go bankrupt. Therefore, companies that offer neither the best quality nor the lowest price will eventually go bankrupt.

The conclusion above follows logically if which one of the following is assumed?

(A) No company succeeds in producing a product that is both highest in quality and lowest in price.

(B) Products that are neither highest in quality nor lowest in price do not attract consumers.

(C) Any company that offers either the highest quality or the lowest price will avoid bankruptcy.

(D) Some consumers will not continue to patronize a company purely out of brand loyalty.

(E) No company is driven from the market for reasons other than failing to meet consumer demands.

14. The number of serious traffic accidents (accidents resulting in hospitalization or death) that occurred on Park Road from 1986 to 1990 was 35 percent lower than the number of serious accidents from 1981 to 1985. The speed limit on Park Road was lowered in 1986. Hence, the reduction of the speed limit led to the decrease in serious accidents.

Which one of the following statements, if true, most weakens the argument?

(A) The number of speeding tickets issued annually on Park Road remained roughly constant from 1981 to 1990.

(B) Beginning in 1986, police patrolled Park Road much less frequently than in 1985 and previous years.

(C) The annual number of vehicles using Park Road decreased significantly and steadily from 1981 to 1990.

(D) The annual number of accidents on Park Road that did not result in hospitalization remained roughly constant from 1981 to 1990.

(E) Until 1986 accidents were classified as "serious" only if they resulted in an extended hospital stay.

15. Humans are supposedly rational: in other words, they have a capacity for well-considered thinking and behavior. This is supposedly the difference that makes them superior to other animals. But humans knowingly pollute the world's precious air and water and, through bad farming practices, deplete the soil that feeds them. Thus, humans are not rational after all, so it is absurd to regard them as superior to other animals.

The reasoning above is flawed in that it

(A) relies crucially on an internally contradictory definition of rationality

(B) takes for granted that humans are aware that their acts are irrational

(C) neglects to show that the irrational acts perpetrated by humans are not also perpetrated by other animals

(D) presumes, without offering justification, that humans are no worse than other animals

(E) fails to recognize that humans may possess a capacity without displaying it in a given activity

16. "Good hunter" and "bad hunter" are standard terms in the study of cats. Good hunters can kill prey that weigh up to half their body weight. All good hunters have a high muscle-to-fat ratio. Most wild cats are good hunters, but some domestic cats are good hunters as well.

If the statements above are true, which one of the following must also be true?

(A) Some cats that have a high muscle-to-fat ratio are not good hunters.

(B) A smaller number of domestic cats than wild cats have a high muscle-to-fat ratio.

(C) All cats that are bad hunters have a low muscle-to-fat ratio.

(D) Some cats that have a high muscle-to-fat ratio are domestic.

(E) All cats that have a high muscle-to-fat ratio can kill prey that weigh up to half their body weight.

GO ON TO THE NEXT PAGE.

17. Ethicist: The penalties for drunk driving are far more severe when the drunk driver accidentally injures people than when no one is injured. Moral responsibility for an action depends solely on the intentions underlying the action and not on the action's results. Therefore, legal responsibility, depending as it does in at least some cases on factors other than the agent's intentions, is different than moral responsibility.

The claim that the penalties for drunk driving are far more severe when the drunk driver accidentally injures people than when no one is injured plays which one of the following roles in the ethicist's argument?

(A) It is a premise offered in support of the claim that legal responsibility for an action is based solely upon features of the action that are generally unintended by the agent.

(B) It is offered as an illustration of the claim that the criteria of legal responsibility for an action include but are not the same as those for moral responsibility.

(C) It is offered as an illustration of the claim that people may be held morally responsible for an action for which they are not legally responsible.

(D) It is a premise offered in support of the claim that legal responsibility depends in at least some cases on factors other than the agent's intentions.

(E) It is a premise offered in support of the claim that moral responsibility depends solely on the intentions underlying the action and not on the action's result.

18. Columnist: Taking a strong position on an issue makes one likely to misinterpret or ignore additional evidence that conflicts with one's stand. But in order to understand an issue fully, it is essential to consider such evidence impartially. Thus, it is best not to take a strong position on an issue unless one has already considered all important evidence conflicting with that position.

The columnist's reasoning most closely conforms to which one of the following principles?

(A) It is reasonable to take a strong position on an issue if one fully understands the issue and has considered the evidence regarding that issue impartially.

(B) To ensure that one has impartially considered the evidence regarding an issue on which one has taken a strong position, one should avoid misinterpreting or ignoring evidence regarding that issue.

(C) Anyone who does not understand an issue fully should avoid taking a strong position on it.

(D) One should try to understand an issue fully if doing so will help one to avoid misinterpreting or ignoring evidence regarding that issue.

(E) It is reasonable to take a strong position on an issue only if there is important evidence conflicting with that position.

GO ON TO THE NEXT PAGE.

3 **3** **3** **3**

19. The coach of the Eagles used a computer analysis to determine the best combinations of players for games. The analysis revealed that the team has lost only when Jennifer was not playing. Although no computer was needed to discover this information, this sort of information is valuable, and in this case it confirms that Jennifer's presence in the game will ensure that the Eagles will win.

The argument above is most vulnerable to criticism on the grounds that it

(A) infers from the fact that a certain factor is sufficient for a result that the absence of that factor is necessary for the opposite result

(B) presumes, without providing justification, that a player's contribution to a team's win or loss can be reliably quantified and analyzed by computer

(C) draws conclusions about applications of computer analyses to sports from the evidence of a single case

(D) presumes, without providing justification, that occurrences that have coincided in the past must continue to coincide

(E) draws a conclusion about the value of computer analyses from a case in which computer analysis provided no facts beyond what was already known

20. Of the various food containers made of recycled Styrofoam, egg cartons are among the easiest to make. Because egg shells keep the actual food to be consumed from touching the Styrofoam, used Styrofoam need not be as thoroughly cleaned when made into egg cartons as when made into other food containers.

Which one of the following is most strongly supported by the information above?

(A) No food containers other than egg cartons can safely be made of recycled Styrofoam that has not been thoroughly cleaned.

(B) There are some foods that cannot be packaged in recycled Styrofoam no matter how the Styrofoam is recycled.

(C) The main reason Styrofoam must be thoroughly cleaned when recycled is to remove any residual food that has come into contact with the Styrofoam.

(D) Because they are among the easiest food containers to make from recycled Styrofoam, most egg cartons are made from recycled Styrofoam.

(E) Not every type of food container made of recycled Styrofoam is effectively prevented from coming into contact with the food it contains.

GO ON TO THE NEXT PAGE.

3 **3** **3** **3** **3**

21. Most people who become migraine sufferers as adults were prone to bouts of depression as children. Hence it stands to reason that a child who is prone to bouts of depression is likely to suffer migraines during adulthood.

The flawed pattern of reasoning in the argument above is most parallel to that in which one of the following?

(A) Most good-tempered dogs were vaccinated against rabies as puppies. Therefore, a puppy that is vaccinated against rabies is likely to become a good-tempered dog.

(B) Most vicious dogs were ill-treated when young. Hence it can be concluded that a pet owner whose dog is vicious is likely to have treated the dog badly when it was young.

(C) Most well-behaved dogs have undergone obedience training. Thus, if a dog has not undergone obedience training, it will not be well behaved.

(D) Most of the pets taken to veterinarians are dogs. Therefore, it stands to reason that dogs are more prone to illness or accident than are other pets.

(E) Most puppies are taken from their mothers at the age of eight weeks. Thus, a puppy that is older than eight weeks is likely to have been taken from its mother.

22. Student: The publications of Professor Vallejo on the origins of glassblowing have reopened the debate among historians over whether glassblowing originated in Egypt or elsewhere. If Professor Vallejo is correct, there is insufficient evidence for claiming, as most historians have done for many years, that glassblowing began in Egypt. So, despite the fact that the traditional view is still maintained by the majority of historians, if Professor Vallejo is correct, we must conclude that glassblowing originated elsewhere.

Which one of the following is an error in the student's reasoning?

(A) It draws a conclusion that conflicts with the majority opinion of experts.

(B) It presupposes the truth of Professor Vallejo's claims.

(C) It fails to provide criteria for determining adequate historical evidence.

(D) It mistakes the majority view for the traditional view.

(E) It confuses inadequate evidence for truth with evidence for falsity.

23. At Southgate Mall, mattresses are sold only at Mattress Madness. Every mattress at Mattress Madness is on sale at a 20 percent discount. So every mattress for sale at Southgate Mall is on sale at a 20 percent discount.

Which one of the following arguments is most similar in its reasoning to the argument above?

(A) The only food in Diane's apartment is in her refrigerator. All the food she purchased within the past week is in her refrigerator. Therefore, she purchased all the food in her apartment within the past week.

(B) Diane's refrigerator, and all the food in it, is in her apartment. Diane purchased all the food in her refrigerator within the past week. Therefore, she purchased all the food in her apartment within the past week.

(C) All the food in Diane's apartment is in her refrigerator. Diane purchased all the food in her refrigerator within the past week. Therefore, she purchased all the food in her apartment within the past week.

(D) The only food in Diane's apartment is in her refrigerator. Diane purchased all the food in her refrigerator within the past week. Therefore, all the food she purchased within the past week is in her apartment.

(E) The only food that Diane has purchased within the past week is in her refrigerator. All the food that she has purchased within the past week is in her apartment. Therefore, all the food in her apartment is in her refrigerator.

GO ON TO THE NEXT PAGE.

LSAT ADVANCED STUDENTS: THIS TEST IS TAKEN AS TEST 5 OF YOUR CLASS. DO NOT USE THIS TEST FOR PRACTICE.

3   3   3   3   3

24. There are 1.3 billion cows worldwide, and this population is growing to keep pace with the demand for meat and milk. These cows produce trillions of liters of methane gas yearly, and this methane contributes to global warming. The majority of the world's cows are given relatively low-quality diets even though cows produce less methane when they receive better-quality diets. Therefore, methane production from cows could be kept in check if cows were given better-quality diets.

Which one of the following, if true, adds the most support for the conclusion of the argument?

(A) Cows given good-quality diets produce much more meat and milk than they would produce otherwise.

(B) Carbon and hydrogen, the elements that make up methane, are found in abundance in the components of all types of cow feed.

(C) Most farmers would be willing to give their cows high-quality feed if the cost of that feed were lower.

(D) Worldwide, more methane is produced by cows raised for meat production than by those raised for milk production.

(E) Per liter, methane contributes more to global warming than does carbon dioxide, a gas that is thought to be the most significant contributor to global warming.

25. To face danger solely because doing so affords one a certain pleasure does not constitute courage. Real courage is manifested only when a person, in acting to attain a goal, perseveres in the face of fear prompted by one or more dangers involved.

Which one of the following statements can be properly inferred from the statements above?

(A) A person who must face danger in order to avoid future pain cannot properly be called courageous for doing so.

(B) A person who experiences fear of some aspects of a dangerous situation cannot be said to act courageously in that situation.

(C) A person who happens to derive pleasure from some dangerous activities is not a courageous person.

(D) A person who faces danger in order to benefit others is acting courageously only if the person is afraid of the danger.

(E) A person who has no fear of the situations that everyone else would fear cannot be said to be courageous in any situation.

26. The government will purchase and install new severe weather sirens for this area next year if replacement parts for the old sirens are difficult to obtain. The newspaper claims that public safety in the event of severe weather would be enhanced if new sirens were to be installed. The local company from which replacement parts were purchased last year has since gone out of business. So, if the newspaper is correct, the public will be safer during severe weather in the future.

The argument's conclusion follows logically from its premises if which one of the following is assumed?

(A) If public safety in the event of severe weather is enhanced next year, it will be because new sirens have been purchased.

(B) The newspaper was correct in claiming that public safety in the event of severe weather would be enhanced if new sirens were purchased.

(C) The local company from which replacement parts for the old sirens were purchased last year was the only company in the area that sold them.

(D) Replacement parts for the old sirens will be difficult to obtain if the government cannot obtain them from the company it purchased them from last year.

(E) Because the local company from which replacement parts had been purchased went out of business, the only available parts are of such inferior quality that use of them would make the sirens less reliable.

S T O P

IF YOU FINISH BEFORE TIME IS CALLED, YOU MAY CHECK YOUR WORK ON THIS SECTION ONLY.
DO NOT WORK ON ANY OTHER SECTION IN THE TEST.

4   4   4   4   4   4

SECTION IV
Time—35 minutes
23 Questions

Directions: Each group of questions in this section is based on a set of conditions. In answering some of the questions, it may be useful to draw a rough diagram. Choose the response that most accurately and completely answers each question and blacken the corresponding space on your answer sheet.

Questions 1–5

A dance is being choreographed for six dancers: three men—Felipe, Grant, and Hassan—and three women—Jaclyn, Keiko, and Lorena. At no time during the dance will anyone other than the dancers be on stage. Who is on stage and who is off stage at any particular time in the dance is determined by the following constraints:

If Jaclyn is on stage, Lorena is off stage.
If Lorena is off stage, Jaclyn is on stage.
If Felipe is off stage, Jaclyn is also off stage.
If any of the women are on stage, Grant is also on stage.

1. Which one of the following is a list of all of the dancers who could be on stage at a particular time?

    (A) Grant
    (B) Keiko, Lorena
    (C) Grant, Hassan, Lorena
    (D) Grant, Hassan, Jaclyn
    (E) Felipe, Grant, Jaclyn, Lorena

2. Which one of the following CANNOT be true at any time during the dance?

    (A) Felipe and Grant are the only men on stage.
    (B) Grant and Hassan are the only men on stage.
    (C) Jaclyn is the only woman on stage.
    (D) Keiko is the only woman on stage.
    (E) Jaclyn and Keiko are the only women on stage.

3. Which one of the following is a complete and accurate list of the dancers any one of whom could be off stage when Jaclyn is on stage?

    (A) Lorena
    (B) Felipe, Lorena
    (C) Hassan, Lorena
    (D) Hassan, Keiko
    (E) Hassan, Keiko, Lorena

4. If there are more women than men on stage, then exactly how many dancers must be on stage?

    (A) five
    (B) four
    (C) three
    (D) two
    (E) one

5. What is the minimum number of dancers that must be on stage at any given time?

    (A) zero
    (B) one
    (C) two
    (D) three
    (E) four

GO ON TO THE NEXT PAGE.

4   4   4   4   4   4

<u>Questions 6–12</u>

A critic has prepared a review of exactly six music CDs—*Headstrong*, *In Flight*, *Nice*, *Quasi*, *Reunion*, and *Sounds Good*. Each CD received a rating of either one, two, three, or four stars, with each CD receiving exactly one rating. Although the ratings were meant to be kept secret until the review was published, the following facts have been leaked to the public:

  For each of the ratings, at least one but no more than two of the CDs received that rating.
  Headstrong received exactly one more star than *Nice* did.
  Either *Headstrong* or *Reunion* received the same number of stars as *In Flight* did.
  At most one CD received more stars than *Quasi* did.

6. Which one of the following could be an accurate matching of ratings to the CDs that received those ratings?

  (A) one star: *In Flight*, *Reunion*; two stars: *Nice*; three stars: *Headstrong*; four stars: *Quasi*, *Sounds Good*
  (B) one star: *In Flight*, *Reunion*; two stars: *Quasi*, *Sounds Good*; three stars: *Nice*; four stars: *Headstrong*
  (C) one star: *Nice*; two stars: *Headstrong*; three stars: *In Flight*, *Sounds Good*; four stars: *Quasi*, *Reunion*
  (D) one star: *Nice*, *Sounds Good*; two stars: *In Flight*, *Reunion*; three stars: *Quasi*; four stars: *Headstrong*
  (E) one star: *Sounds Good*; two stars: *Reunion*; three stars: *Nice*, *Quasi*; four stars: *Headstrong*, *In Flight*

7. If *Headstrong* is the only CD that received a rating of two stars, then which one of the following must be true?

  (A) *In Flight* received a rating of three stars.
  (B) *Nice* received a rating of three stars.
  (C) *Quasi* received a rating of three stars.
  (D) *Reunion* received a rating of one star.
  (E) *Sounds Good* received a rating of one star.

8. If *Reunion* received the same rating as *Sounds Good*, then which one of the following must be true?

  (A) *Headstrong* received a rating of two stars.
  (B) *In Flight* received a rating of three stars.
  (C) *Nice* received a rating of two stars.
  (D) *Quasi* received a rating of four stars.
  (E) *Sounds Good* received a rating of one star.

9. If *Nice* and *Reunion* each received a rating of one star, then which one of the following could be true?

  (A) *Headstrong* received a rating of three stars.
  (B) *Headstrong* received a rating of four stars.
  (C) *In Flight* received a rating of three stars.
  (D) *Sounds Good* received a rating of two stars.
  (E) *Sounds Good* received a rating of three stars.

10. Which one of the following CANNOT be true?

  (A) *Quasi* is the only CD that received a rating of three stars.
  (B) *Quasi* is the only CD that received a rating of four stars.
  (C) *Reunion* is the only CD that received a rating of one star.
  (D) *Reunion* is the only CD that received a rating of two stars.
  (E) *Reunion* is the only CD that received a rating of three stars.

11. If *Reunion* is the only CD that received a rating of one star, then which one of the following could be true?

  (A) *Headstrong* received a rating of four stars.
  (B) *In Flight* received a rating of two stars.
  (C) *Nice* received a rating of three stars.
  (D) *Quasi* received a rating of three stars.
  (E) *Sounds Good* received a rating of two stars.

12. Which one of the following CANNOT have received a rating of four stars?

  (A) *Headstrong*
  (B) *In Flight*
  (C) *Quasi*
  (D) *Reunion*
  (E) *Sounds Good*

GO ON TO THE NEXT PAGE.

4   **4**   **4**   **4**   **4**   **4**

Questions 13–17

A cake has exactly six layers—lemon, marzipan, orange, raspberry, strawberry, and vanilla. There is exactly one bottom layer (the first layer), and each succeeding layer (from second through sixth) completely covers the layer beneath it. The following conditions must apply:

The raspberry layer is neither immediately above nor immediately below the strawberry layer.

The marzipan layer is immediately above the lemon layer.

The orange layer is above the marzipan layer but below the strawberry layer.

13. Which one of the following could be an accurate list of the layers of the cake, from bottom to top?

(A) lemon, marzipan, orange, strawberry, vanilla, raspberry

(B) lemon, marzipan, orange, strawberry, raspberry, vanilla

(C) marzipan, lemon, raspberry, vanilla, orange, strawberry

(D) raspberry, lemon, marzipan, vanilla, strawberry, orange

(E) raspberry, orange, lemon, marzipan, strawberry, vanilla

14. If the strawberry layer is not immediately above the orange layer, then which one of the following could be true?

(A) The raspberry layer is immediately above the vanilla layer.

(B) The raspberry layer is immediately above the orange layer.

(C) The raspberry layer is immediately below the marzipan layer.

(D) The raspberry layer is the second layer.

(E) The raspberry layer is the top layer.

15. If the strawberry layer is not the top layer, then which one of the following is a complete and accurate list of the layers that could be the vanilla layer?

(A) the first, the second, the third, the fourth, the fifth, the sixth

(B) the second, the third, the fourth, the fifth, the sixth

(C) the third, the fourth, the fifth, the sixth

(D) the fourth, the fifth, the sixth

(E) the fifth, the sixth

16. If the lemon layer is third, then which one of the following could be true?

(A) The vanilla layer is fifth.

(B) The vanilla layer is immediately above the raspberry layer.

(C) The orange layer is not immediately above the marzipan layer.

(D) The raspberry layer is above the marzipan layer.

(E) The strawberry layer is not the top layer.

17. Which one of the following could be an accurate list of the two lowest layers of the cake, listed in order from the bottom up?

(A) lemon, raspberry

(B) vanilla, raspberry

(C) marzipan, raspberry

(D) raspberry, marzipan

(E) raspberry, strawberry

GO ON TO THE NEXT PAGE.

4 4 4

Questions 18–23

A panel reviews six contract bids—H, J, K, R, S, and T. No two bids have the same cost. Exactly one of the bids is accepted. The following conditions must hold:

The accepted bid is either K or R and is either the second or the third lowest in cost.

H is lower in cost than each of J and K.

If J is the fourth lowest in cost, then J is lower in cost than each of S and T.

If J is not the fourth lowest in cost, then J is higher in cost than each of S and T.

Either R or S is the fifth lowest in cost.

18. Which one of the following could be an accurate list of the bids in order from lowest to highest in cost?

(A) T, K, H, S, J, R
(B) H, T, K, S, R, J
(C) H, S, T, K, R, J
(D) H, K, S, J, R, T
(E) H, J, K, R, S, T

19. Which one of the following bids CANNOT be the fourth lowest in cost?

(A) H
(B) J
(C) K
(D) R
(E) T

20. Which one of the following bids CANNOT be the second lowest in cost?

(A) H
(B) J
(C) K
(D) R
(E) T

21. If R is the accepted bid, then which one of the following must be true?

(A) T is the lowest in cost.
(B) K is the second lowest in cost.
(C) R is the third lowest in cost.
(D) S is the fifth lowest in cost.
(E) J is the highest in cost.

22. Which one of the following must be true?

(A) H is lower in cost than S.
(B) H is lower in cost than T.
(C) K is lower in cost than J.
(D) S is lower in cost than J.
(E) S is lower in cost than K.

23. If R is the lowest in cost, then which one of the following could be false?

(A) J is the highest in cost.
(B) S is the fifth lowest in cost.
(C) K is the third lowest in cost.
(D) H is the second lowest in cost.
(E) K is the accepted bid.

S T O P

IF YOU FINISH BEFORE TIME IS CALLED, YOU MAY CHECK YOUR WORK ON THIS SECTION ONLY. DO NOT WORK ON ANY OTHER SECTION IN THE TEST.

SECTION V

Time—35 minutes

25 Questions

Directions: The questions in this section are based on the reasoning contained in brief statements or passages. For some questions, more than one of the choices could conceivably answer the question. However, you are to choose the <u>best</u> answer; that is, the response that most accurately and completely answers the question. You should not make assumptions that are by commonsense standards implausible, superfluous, or incompatible with the passage. After you have chosen the best answer, blacken the corresponding space on your answer sheet.

1. Editorialist: Advertisers devote millions of dollars to the attempt to instill attitudes and desires that lead people to purchase particular products, and advertisers' techniques have been adopted by political strategists in democratic countries, who are paid to manipulate public opinion in every political campaign. Thus, the results of elections in democratic countries cannot be viewed as representing the unadulterated preferences of the people.

    Which one of the following, if true, most strengthens the editorialist's argument?

    (A)   Public opinion can be manipulated more easily by officials of nondemocratic governments than by those of democratic governments.

    (B)   Advertisers' techniques are often apparent to the people to whom the advertisements are directed.

    (C)   Many democratic countries have laws limiting the amount that may be spent on political advertisements in any given election.

    (D)   People who neither watch television nor read any print media are more likely to vote than people who do one or both of these activities.

    (E)   Unlike advertisements for consumer products, most of which only reinforce existing beliefs, political advertisements often change voters' beliefs.

2. Kris: Years ago, the chemical industry claimed that technological progress cannot occur without pollution. Today, in the name of technological progress, the cellular phone industry manufactures and promotes a product that causes environmental pollution in the form of ringing phones and loud conversations in public places. Clearly, the cellular industry must be regulated, just as the chemical industry is now regulated.

    Terry: That's absurd. Chemical pollution can cause physical harm, but the worst harm that cellular phones can cause is annoyance.

    Terry responds to Kris's argument by doing which one of the following?

    (A)   questioning the reliability of the source of crucial information in Kris's argument

    (B)   attacking the accuracy of the evidence about the chemical industry that Kris puts forward

    (C)   arguing that an alleged cause of a problem is actually an effect of that problem

    (D)   questioning the strength of the analogy on which Kris's argument is based

    (E)   rejecting Kris's interpretation of the term "technological progress"

GO ON TO THE NEXT PAGE.

KAPLAN

LSAT ADVANCED STUDENTS: THIS TEST IS TAKEN AS TEST 5 OF YOUR CLASS. DO NOT USE THIS TEST FOR PRACTICE.

5   5

3. Researcher: Any country can determine which type of public school system will work best for it by investigating the public school systems of other countries. Nationwide tests could be given in each country and other countries could adopt the system of the country that has the best scores on these tests.

Which one of the following is an assumption required by the researcher's argument?

(A) A type of school system that works well in one country will work well in any other country.

(B) A number of children in each country in the research sample are educated in private schools.

(C) If two countries performed differently on these nationwide tests, further testing could determine what features of the school systems account for the differences.

(D) Most countries in the research sample already administer nationwide tests to their public school students.

(E) The nationwide testing in the research sample will target as closely as possible grade levels that are comparable in the different countries in the research sample.

4. Ray: Cynthia claims that her car's trunk popped open because the car hit a pothole. Yet, she also acknowledged that the trunk in that car had popped open on several other occasions, and that on none of those other occasions had the car hit a pothole. Therefore, Cynthia mistakenly attributed the trunk's popping open to the car's having hit a pothole.

The reasoning in Ray's argument is most vulnerable to criticism in that the argument

(A) fails to consider the possibility that the trunks of other cars may pop open when those cars hit potholes

(B) fails to consider the possibility that potholes can have negative effects on a car's engine

(C) presumes, without providing justification, that if one event causes another, it cannot also cause a third event

(D) fails to consider the possibility that one type of event can be caused in many different ways

(E) presumes the truth of the claim that it is trying to establish

5. Journalists agree universally that lying is absolutely taboo. Yet, while many reporters claim that spoken words ought to be quoted verbatim, many others believe that tightening a quote from a person who is interviewed is legitimate on grounds that the speaker's remarks would have been more concise if the speaker had written them instead. Also, many reporters believe that, to expose wrongdoing, failing to identify oneself as a reporter is permissible, while others condemn such behavior as a type of lying.

Which one of the following is most supported by the information above?

(A) Reporters make little effort to behave ethically.

(B) There is no correct answer to the question of whether lying in a given situation is right or wrong.

(C) Omission of the truth is the same thing as lying.

(D) Since lying is permissible in some situations, reporters are mistaken to think that it is absolutely taboo.

(E) Reporters disagree on what sort of behavior qualifies as lying.

6. Wood-frame houses withstand earthquakes far better than masonry houses do, because wooden frames have some flexibility; their walls can better handle lateral forces. In a recent earthquake, however, a wood-frame house was destroyed, while the masonry house next door was undamaged.

Which one of the following, if true, most helps to explain the results of the earthquake described above?

(A) In earthquake-prone areas, there are many more wood-frame houses than masonry houses.

(B) In earthquake-prone areas, there are many more masonry houses than wood-frame houses.

(C) The walls of the wood-frame house had once been damaged in a flood.

(D) The masonry house was far more expensive than the wood-frame house.

(E) No structure is completely impervious to the destructive lateral forces exerted by earthquakes.

GO ON TO THE NEXT PAGE.

LSAT ADVANCED STUDENTS: THIS TEST IS TAKEN AS TEST 5 OF YOUR CLASS. DO NOT USE THIS TEST FOR PRACTICE.

5   5

7. In an experiment, biologists repeatedly shone a bright light into a tank containing a sea snail and simultaneously shook the tank. The snail invariably responded by tensing its muscular "foot," a typical reaction in sea snails to ocean turbulence. After several repetitions of this procedure, the snail tensed its "foot" whenever the biologists shone the light into its tank, even when the tank was not simultaneously shaken. Therefore, the snail must have learned to associate the shining of the bright light with the shaking of the tank.

Which one of the following is an assumption required by the argument?

(A) All sea snails react to ocean turbulence in the same way as the sea snail in the experiment did.

(B) Sea snails are not ordinarily exposed to bright lights such as the one used in the biologists' experiment.

(C) The sea snail used in the experiment did not differ significantly from other members of its species in its reaction to external stimuli.

(D) The appearance of a bright light alone would ordinarily not result in the sea snail's tensing its "foot."

(E) Tensing of the muscular "foot" in sea snails is an instinctual rather than a learned response to ocean turbulence.

8. The university's purchasing department is highly efficient overall. We must conclude that each of its twelve staff members is highly efficient.

Which one of the following arguments exhibits flawed reasoning most similar to that exhibited by the argument above?

(A) The employees at this fast-food restaurant are the youngest and most inexperienced of any fast-food workers in the city. Given this, it seems obvious that customers will have to wait longer for their food at this restaurant than at others.

(B) The outside audit of our public relations department has exposed serious deficiencies in the competence of each member of that department. We must conclude that the department is inadequate for our needs.

(C) This supercomputer is the most sophisticated—and the most expensive—ever built. It must be that each of its components is the most sophisticated and expensive available.

(D) Literature critics have lavished praise on every chapter of this book. In light of their reviews, one must conclude that the book is excellent.

(E) Passing a driving test is a condition of employment at the city's transportation department. It follows that each of the department's employees has passed the test.

9. The Jacksons regularly receive wrong-number calls for Sara, whose phone number was misprinted in a directory. Sara contacted the Jacksons, informing them of the misprint and her correct number. The Jacksons did not lead Sara to believe that they would pass along the correct number, but it would be helpful to Sara and of no difficulty for them to do so. Thus, although it would not be wrong for the Jacksons to tell callers trying to reach Sara merely that they have dialed the wrong number, it would be laudable if the Jacksons passed along Sara's correct number.

Which one of the following principles, if valid, most helps to justify the reasoning in the argument?

(A) It is always laudable to do something helpful to someone, but not doing so would be wrong only if one has led that person to believe one would do it.

(B) Being helpful to someone is laudable whenever it is not wrong to do so.

(C) If one can do something that would be helpful to someone else and it would be easy to do, then it is laudable and not wrong to do so.

(D) Doing something for someone is laudable only if it is difficult for one to do so and it is wrong for one not to do so.

(E) The only actions that are laudable are those that it would not be wrong to refrain from doing, whether or not it is difficult to do so.

GO ON TO THE NEXT PAGE.

10. Albert: The government has proposed new automobile emissions regulations designed to decrease the amount of polycyclic aromatic hydrocarbons (PAHs) released into the atmosphere by automobile exhaust. I don't see the need for such regulations; although PAHs are suspected of causing cancer, a causal link has never been proven.

Erin: Scientists also blame PAHs for 10,000 premature deaths in this country each year from lung and heart disease. So the proposed regulations would save thousands of lives.

Which one of the following, if true, is the logically strongest counter that Albert can make to Erin's argument?

(A) Most automobile manufacturers are strongly opposed to additional automobile emissions regulations.

(B) It is not known whether PAHs are a causal factor in any diseases other than heart and lung disease and cancer.

(C) Even if no new automobile emissions regulations are enacted, the amount of PAHs released into the atmosphere will decrease if automobile usage declines.

(D) Most of the PAHs released into the atmosphere are the result of wear and tear on automobile tires.

(E) PAHs are one of several components of automobile exhaust that scientists suspect of causing cancer.

11. Australia has considerably fewer species of carnivorous mammals than any other continent does but about as many carnivorous reptile species as other continents do. This is probably a consequence of the unusual sparseness of Australia's ecosystems. To survive, carnivorous mammals must eat much more than carnivorous reptiles need to; thus carnivorous mammals are at a disadvantage in ecosystems in which there is relatively little food.

Which one of the following most accurately expresses the main conclusion of the argument?

(A) Australia has considerably fewer species of carnivorous mammals than any other continent does but about as many carnivorous reptile species as other continents do.

(B) In ecosystems in which there is relatively little food carnivorous mammals are at a disadvantage relative to carnivorous reptiles.

(C) The unusual sparseness of Australia's ecosystems is probably the reason Australia has considerably fewer carnivorous mammal species than other continents do but about as many carnivorous reptile species.

(D) The reason that carnivorous mammals are at a disadvantage in ecosystems in which there is relatively little food is that they must eat much more in order to survive than carnivorous reptiles need to.

(E) Because Australia's ecosystems are unusually sparse, carnivorous mammals there are at a disadvantage relative to carnivorous reptiles.

12. Linguist: The Sapir-Whorf hypothesis states that a society's world view is influenced by the language or languages its members speak. But this hypothesis does not have the verifiability of hypotheses of physical science, since it is not clear that the hypothesis could be tested.

If the linguist's statements are accurate, which one of the following is most supported by them?

(A) The Sapir-Whorf hypothesis is probably false.

(B) Only the hypotheses of physical science are verifiable.

(C) Only verifiable hypotheses should be seriously considered.

(D) We do not know whether the Sapir-Whorf hypothesis is true or false.

(E) Only the hypotheses of physical science should be taken seriously.

GO ON TO THE NEXT PAGE.

5   5

13. The highest mountain ranges are formed by geological forces that raise the earth's crust: two continent-bearing tectonic plates of comparable density collide and crumple upward, causing a thickening of the crust. The erosive forces of wind and precipitation inexorably wear these mountains down. Yet the highest mountain ranges tend to be found in places where these erosive forces are most prevalent.

Which one of the following, if true, most helps to reconcile the apparent conflict described above?

(A) Patterns of extreme wind and precipitation often result from the dramatic differences in elevation commonly found in the highest mountain ranges.

(B) The highest mountain ranges have less erosion-reducing vegetation near their peaks than do other mountain ranges.

(C) Some lower mountain ranges are formed by a different collision process, whereby one tectonic plate simply slides beneath another of lesser density.

(D) The amount of precipitation that a given region of the earth receives may vary considerably over the lifetime of an average mountain range.

(E) The thickening of the earth's crust associated with the formation of the highest mountain ranges tends to cause the thickened portion of the crust to sink over time.

14. Expert: A group of researchers claims to have shown that for an antenna to work equally well at all frequencies, it must be symmetrical in shape and have what is known as a fractal structure. Yet the new antenna developed by these researchers, which satisfies both of these criteria, in fact works better at frequencies below 250 megahertz than at frequencies above 250 megahertz. Hence, their claim is incorrect.

The reasoning in the expert's argument is flawed because the argument

(A) fails to provide a definition of the technical term "fractal"

(B) contradicts itself by denying in its conclusion the claim of scientific authorities that it relies on in its premises

(C) concludes that a claim is false merely on the grounds that there is insufficient evidence that it is true

(D) interprets an assertion that certain conditions are necessary as asserting that those conditions are sufficient

(E) takes for granted that there are only two possible alternatives, either below or above 250 megahertz

15. Singletary: We of Citizens for Cycling Freedom object to the city's new ordinance requiring bicyclists to wear helmets. If the city wanted to become a safer place for cyclists, it would not require helmets. Instead, it would construct more bicycle lanes and educate drivers about bicycle safety. Thus, passage of the ordinance reveals that the city is more concerned with the appearance of safety than with bicyclists' actual safety.

Which one of the following most accurately describes the role played in Singletary's argument by the statement that mentions driver education?

(A) It is cited as evidence for the claim that the city misunderstands the steps necessary for ensuring bicyclists' safety.

(B) It is used as partial support for a claim about the motivation of the city.

(C) It is offered as evidence of the total ineffectiveness of the helmet ordinance.

(D) It is offered as an example of further measures the city will take to ensure bicyclists' safety.

(E) It is presented as an illustration of the city's overriding interest in its public image.

16. Max: Although doing so would be very costly, humans already possess the technology to build colonies on the Moon. As the human population increases and the amount of unoccupied space available for constructing housing on Earth diminishes, there will be a growing economic incentive to construct such colonies to house some of the population. Thus, such colonies will almost certainly be built and severe overcrowding on Earth relieved.

Max's argument is most vulnerable to criticism on which one of the following grounds?

(A) It takes for granted that the economic incentive to construct colonies on the Moon will grow sufficiently to cause such a costly project to be undertaken.

(B) It takes for granted that the only way of relieving severe overcrowding on Earth is the construction of colonies on the Moon.

(C) It overlooks the possibility that colonies will be built on the Moon regardless of any economic incentive to construct such colonies to house some of the population.

(D) It overlooks the possibility that colonies on the Moon might themselves quickly become overcrowded.

(E) It takes for granted that none of the human population would prefer to live on the Moon unless Earth were seriously overcrowded.

GO ON TO THE NEXT PAGE.

17. Ethicist: An action is wrong if it violates a rule of the society in which the action is performed and that rule promotes the general welfare of people in the society. An action is right if it is required by a rule of the society in which the action is performed and the rule promotes the general welfare of the people in that society.

Which one of the following judgments most closely conforms to the principle cited by the ethicist?

(A) Amelia's society has a rule against lying. However, she lies anyway in order to protect an innocent person from being harmed. While the rule against lying promotes the general welfare of people in the society, Amelia's lie is not wrong because she is preventing harm.

(B) Jordan lives in a society that requires its members to eat certain ceremonial foods during festivals. Jordan disobeys this rule. Because the rule is not detrimental to the general welfare of people in her society, Jordan's disobedience is wrong.

(C) Elgin obeys a certain rule of his society. Because Elgin knows that this particular rule is detrimental to the general welfare of the people in his society, his obedience is wrong.

(D) Dahlia always has a cup of coffee before getting dressed in the morning. Dahlia's action is right because it does not violate any rule of the society in which she lives.

(E) Edward's society requires children to take care of their aged parents. Edward's taking care of his aged parents is the right thing for him to do because the rule requiring this action promotes the general welfare of people in the society.

18. Teresa: If their goal is to maximize profits, film studios should concentrate on producing big-budget films rather than small-budget ones. For, unlike big-budget films, small-budget films never attract mass audiences. While small-budget films are less expensive to produce and, hence, involve less risk of unprofitability than big-budget films, low production costs do not guarantee the highest possible profits.

Which one of the following is an assumption required by Teresa's argument?

(A) Each big-budget film is guaranteed to attract a mass audience.

(B) A film studio cannot make both big-budget films and small-budget films.

(C) A film studio will not maximize its profits unless at least some of its films attract mass audiences.

(D) It is impossible to produce a big-budget film in a financially efficient manner.

(E) A film studio's primary goal should be to maximize profits.

19. Cyclists in the Tour de France are extremely physically fit: all of the winners of this race have had abnormal physiological constitutions. Typical of the abnormal physiology of these athletes are exceptional lung capacity and exceptionally powerful hearts. Tests conducted on last year's winner did not reveal an exceptionally powerful heart. That cyclist must, therefore, have exceptional lung capacity.

The reasoning in the argument is most vulnerable to criticism on the grounds that it overlooks the possibility that

(A) having exceptional lung capacity and an exceptionally powerful heart is an advantage in cycling

(B) some winners of the Tour de France have neither exceptional lung capacity nor exceptionally powerful hearts

(C) cyclists with normal lung capacity rarely have exceptionally powerful hearts

(D) the exceptional lung capacity and exceptionally powerful hearts of Tour de France winners are due to training

(E) the notions of exceptional lung capacity and exceptional heart function are relative to the physiology of most cyclists

20. TV meteorologist: Our station's weather forecasts are more useful and reliable than those of the most popular news station in the area. After all, the most important question for viewers in this area is whether it will rain, and on most of the occasions when we have forecast rain for the next day, we have been right. The same cannot be said for either of our competitors.

Which one of the following, if true, most strengthens the meteorologist's argument?

(A) The meteorologist's station forecast rain more often than did the most popular news station in the area.

(B) The less popular of the competing stations does not employ any full-time meteorologists.

(C) The most popular news station in the area is popular because of its investigative news reports.

(D) The meteorologist's station has a policy of not making weather forecasts more than three days in advance.

(E) On most of the occasions when the meteorologist's station forecast that it would not rain, at least one of its competitors also forecast that it would not rain.

GO ON TO THE NEXT PAGE.

LSAT ADVANCED STUDENTS: THIS TEST IS TAKEN AS TEST 5 OF YOUR CLASS. DO NOT USE THIS TEST FOR PRACTICE.

5   5

21. In an experiment, volunteers witnessed a simulated crime. After they witnessed the simulation the volunteers were first questioned by a lawyer whose goal was to get them to testify inaccurately about the event. They were then cross-examined by another lawyer whose goal was to cause them to correct the inaccuracies in their testimony. The witnesses who gave testimony containing fewer inaccurate details than most of the other witnesses during the first lawyer's questioning also gave testimony containing a greater number of inaccurate details than most of the other witnesses during cross-examination.

Which one of the following, if true, most helps to resolve the apparent conflict in the results concerning the witnesses who gave testimony containing fewer inaccurate details during the first lawyer's questioning?

(A) These witnesses were more observant about details than were most of the other witnesses.
(B) These witnesses had better memories than did most of the other witnesses.
(C) These witnesses were less inclined than most of the other witnesses to be influenced in their testimony by the nature of the questioning.
(D) These witnesses were unclear about the details at first but then began to remember more accurately as they answered questions.
(E) These witnesses tended to give testimony containing more details than most of the other witnesses.

22. The short-term and long-term interests of a business often conflict; when they do, the morally preferable act is usually the one that serves the long-term interest. Because of this, businesses often have compelling reasons to execute the morally preferable act.

Which one of the following, if assumed, enables the conclusion of the argument to be properly drawn?

(A) A business's moral interests do not always provide compelling reasons for executing an act.
(B) A business's long-term interests often provide compelling reasons for executing an act.
(C) The morally preferable act for a business to execute and the long-term interests of the business seldom conflict.
(D) The morally preferable act for a business to execute and the short-term interests of the business usually conflict.
(E) When a business's short-term and long-term interests conflict, morality alone is rarely the overriding consideration.

23. Politician: The current crisis in mathematics education must be overcome if we are to remain competitive in the global economy. Alleviating this crisis requires the employment of successful teaching methods. No method of teaching a subject can succeed that does not get students to spend a significant amount of time outside of class studying that subject.

Which one of the following statements follows logically from the statements above?

(A) If students spend a significant amount of time outside of class studying mathematics, the current crisis in mathematics education will be overcome.
(B) The current crisis in mathematics education will not be overcome unless students spend a significant amount of time outside of class studying mathematics.
(C) Few subjects are as important as mathematics to the effort to remain competitive in the global economy.
(D) Only if we succeed in remaining competitive in the global economy will students spend a significant amount of time outside of class studying mathematics.
(E) Students' spending a significant amount of time outside of class studying mathematics would help us to remain competitive in the global economy.

GO ON TO THE NEXT PAGE.

24. Downtown Petropolis boasted over 100 large buildings 5 years ago. Since then, 60 of those buildings have been demolished. Since the number of large buildings in a downtown is an indicator of the economic health of that downtown, it is clear that downtown Petropolis is in a serious state of economic decline.

Which one of the following is an assumption required by the argument?

(A) The demolitions that have taken place during the past 5 years have been evenly spread over that period.

(B) There have never been significantly more than 100 large buildings in downtown Petropolis.

(C) Most of the buildings demolished during the past 5 years were torn down because they were structurally unsound.

(D) The large buildings demolished over the past 5 years have been replaced with small buildings built on the same sites.

(E) Significantly fewer than 60 new large buildings have been built in downtown Petropolis during the past 5 years.

25. To get the free dessert, one must order an entree and a salad. But anyone who orders either an entree or a salad can receive a free soft drink. Thus, anyone who is not eligible for a free soft drink is not eligible for a free dessert.

The reasoning in the argument above is most similar to the reasoning in which one of the following arguments?

(A) To get an executive position at Teltech, one needs a university diploma and sales experience. But anyone who has worked at Teltech for more than six months who does not have sales experience has a university diploma. Thus, one cannot get an executive position at Teltech unless one has worked there for six months.

(B) To be elected class president, one must be well liked and well known. Anyone who is well liked or well known has something better to do than run for class president. Therefore, no one who has something better to do will be elected class president.

(C) To grow good azaleas, one needs soil that is both rich in humus and low in acidity. Anyone who has soil that is rich in humus or low in acidity can grow blueberries. So, anyone who cannot grow blueberries cannot grow good azaleas.

(D) To drive to Weller, one must take the highway or take Old Mill Road. Anyone who drives to Weller on the highway will miss the beautiful scenery. Thus, one cannot see the beautiful scenery without taking Old Mill Road to Weller.

(E) To get a discount on ice cream, one must buy frozen raspberries and ice cream together. Anyone who buys ice cream or raspberries will get a coupon for a later purchase. So, anyone who does not get the discount on ice cream will not get a coupon for a later purchase.

S T O P

IF YOU FINISH BEFORE TIME IS CALLED, YOU MAY CHECK YOUR WORK ON THIS SECTION ONLY.
DO NOT WORK ON ANY OTHER SECTION IN THE TEST.

Acknowledgment is made to the following sources from which material has been adapted for use in this test booklet:

Irving L. Janis, *Groupthink: Psychological Studies of Policy Decisions and Fiascoes*. ©1982 by Houghton Mifflin Co.

David R. Johnson and David Post, "Law and Borders—The Rise of Law in Cyberspace."
   ©1996 by the Board of Trustees of the Leland Stanford Jr. University.

David Krasner, "Rewriting the Body: Aida Overton Walker and the Social Formation of Cakewalking."
   ©1996 by the American Society for Theatre Research.

Wait for the supervisor's instructions before you open the page to the topic.
Please print and sign your name and write the date in the designated spaces below.

Time: 35 Minutes

General Directions

You will have 35 minutes in which to plan and write an essay on the topic inside. Read the topic and the accompanying directions carefully. You will probably find it best to spend a few minutes considering the topic and organizing your thoughts before you begin writing. In your essay, be sure to develop your ideas fully, leaving time, if possible, to review what you have written. **Do not write on a topic other than the one specified. Writing on a topic of your own choice is not acceptable.**

No special knowledge is required or expected for this writing exercise. Law schools are interested in the reasoning, clarity, organization, language usage, and writing mechanics displayed in your essay. How well you write is more important than how much you write.

Confine your essay to the blocked, lined area on the front and back of the separate Writing Sample Response Sheet. Only that area will be reproduced for law schools. Be sure that your writing is legible.

Both this topic sheet and your response sheet must be turned over to the testing staff before you leave the room.

Topic Code	Print Your Full Name Here		
_____	Last	First	M.I.

Date	Sign Your Name Here
/ /	

Scratch Paper
Do not write your essay in this space.

LSAT Writing Sample Topic

Directions: The scenario presented below describes two choices, either one of which can be supported on the basis of the information given. Your essay should consider both choices and argue <u>for</u> one and <u>against</u> the other, based on the two specified criteria and the facts provided. There is no "right" or "wrong" choice: a reasonable argument can be made for either.

Carol Hudson, the concert coordinator for Jordan Arena, a very large entertainment venue, must schedule one of two musical groups to perform on an open date in the arena's schedule. Using the facts below, write an essay in which you argue for one group over the other based on the following two criteria:

• Carol wants to continue Jordan Arena's long-standing record of sold-out concerts.
• Carol wants to attract an audience at least a third of whom are aged 14 to 24.

The first group, The Mustangs, plays cutting-edge music of a sort popular with the 14- to 24-year-old demographic. The Mustangs, gradually growing in popularity, have filled steadily larger venues. The group recently sold out in record time its largest venue ever, the Midvale Arena, located in a large metropolitan area. Jorden Arena, which is located in a different large metropolitan area, has twice the seating capacity of Midvale Arena. The Mustangs' video of the cover song for their debut album is scheduled for release a few weeks before the Jordan Arena concert date. If the music video is a success, as many expect, The Mustangs' popularity will rapidly soar.

The second group, Radar Love, is an aging but well-established hard rock band, which has consistently appealed to a wide-ranging audience. It has sold out all appearances for the past 20 years, including venues considerably larger than Jordan Arena. A song on the group's latest album quickly became a runaway hit among the 14- to 24-year-old demographic, the first time the group has appealed to this extent to this audience. Twenty percent of the audience at the group's most recent concert, which featured songs from the group's latest album, constituted 14- to 24-year-olds, a significant increase from prior concerts.

Scratch Paper
Do not write your essay in this space.

LAST NAME (Print)　　　　　　　　　　MI　　FIRST NAME (Print)

SIGNATURE

Writing Sample Response Sheet

DO NOT WRITE
IN THIS SPACE

**Begin your essay in the lined area below.
Continue on the back if you need more space.**

Computing Your Score

Directions:

1. Use the Answer Key on the next page to check your answers.

2. Use the Scoring Worksheet below to compute your raw score.

3. Use the Score Conversion Chart to convert your raw score into the 120–180 scale.

Scoring Worksheet

1. Enter the number of questions you answered correctly in each section

	Number Correct
SECTION I	__EXP__
SECTION II	_____
SECTION III	_____
SECTION IV	_____
SECTION V	_____

2. Enter the sum here: _____

This is your Raw Score.

Conversion Chart

For Converting Raw Score to the 120–180 LSAT Scaled Score
LSAT PrepTest 54

Reported Score	Raw Score Lowest	Raw Score Highest
180	99	101
179	98	98
178	—*	—*
177	97	97
176	96	96
175	95	95
174	—*	—*
173	94	94
172	93	93
171	92	92
170	91	91
169	90	90
168	89	89
167	88	88
166	87	87
165	85	86
164	84	84
163	83	83
162	81	82
161	80	80
160	78	79
159	76	77
158	75	75
157	73	74
156	71	72
155	69	70
154	67	68
153	66	66
152	64	65
151	62	63
150	60	61
149	58	59
148	56	57
147	54	55
146	52	53
145	50	51
144	49	49
143	47	48
142	45	46
141	43	44
140	42	42
139	40	41
138	38	39
137	37	37
136	35	36
135	33	34
134	32	32
133	30	31
132	29	29
131	28	28
130	26	27
129	25	25
128	24	24
127	23	23
126	21	22
125	20	20
124	19	19
123	18	18
122	16	17
121	—*	—*
120	0	15

*There is no raw score that will produce this scaled score for this test.

KAPLAN

Answer Key

SECTION I (experimental)

1.	E	8.	A	15.	C	22.	D
2.	C	9.	D	16.	A	23.	D
3.	D	10.	A	17.	D	24.	C
4.	A	11.	B	18.	E	25.	E
5.	B	12.	B	19.	E		
6.	D	13.	C	20.	B		
7.	C	14.	B	21.	D		

SECTION II

1.	A	8.	E	15.	C	22.	C
2.	C	9.	B	16.	E	23.	B
3.	D	10.	B	17.	E	24.	E
4.	D	11.	C	18.	A	25.	E
5.	E	12.	A	19.	A	26.	A
6.	B	13.	C	20.	A	27.	B
7.	E	14.	D	21.	C		

SECTION III

1.	D	8.	A	15.	E	22.	E
2.	E	9.	A	16.	D	23.	C
3.	A	10.	B	17.	D	24.	A
4.	E	11.	B	18.	C	25.	D
5.	B	12.	D	19.	D	26.	D
6.	C	13.	B	20.	E		
7.	C	14.	C	21.	A		

SECTION IV

1.	C	8.	D	15.	E	22.	C
2.	D	9.	E	16.	B	23.	A
3.	E	10.	D	17.	B		
4.	C	11.	E	18.	B		
5.	C	12.	B	19.	A		
6.	A	13.	A	20.	B		
7.	A	14.	B	21.	D		

SECTION V

1.	E	8.	C	15.	B	22.	B
2.	D	9.	A	16.	A	23.	B
3.	A	10.	D	17.	E	24.	E
4.	D	11.	C	18.	C	25.	C
5.	E	12.	D	19.	B		
6.	C	13.	A	20.	A		
7.	D	14.	D	21.	C		

Endurance Practice Test 3

PrepTest 53 plus experimental from PrepTest 32, Section IV

SCAN CODE: LL9003

SECTION I

Time—35 minutes

25 Questions

Directions: The questions in this section are based on the reasoning contained in brief statements or passages. For some questions, more than one of the choices could conceivably answer the question. However, you are to choose the best answer; that is, the response that most accurately and completely answers the question. You should not make assumptions that are by commonsense standards implausible, superfluous, or incompatible with the passage. After you have chosen the best answer, blacken the corresponding space on your answer sheet.

1. Consumer advocate: Businesses are typically motivated primarily by the desire to make as great a profit as possible, and advertising helps businesses to achieve this goal. But it is clear that the motive of maximizing profits does not impel businesses to present accurate information in their advertisements. It follows that consumers should be skeptical of the claims made in advertisements.

    Each of the following, if true, would strengthen the consumer advocate's argument EXCEPT:

    (A) Businesses know that they can usually maximize their profits by using inaccurate information in their advertisements.
    (B) Businesses have often included inaccurate information in their advertisements.
    (C) Many consumers have a cynical attitude toward advertising.
    (D) Those who create advertisements are less concerned with the accuracy than with the creativity of advertisements.
    (E) The laws regulating truth in advertising are not applicable to many of the most common forms of inaccurate advertising.

2. Elaine: The purpose of art museums is to preserve artworks and make them available to the public. Museums, therefore, should seek to acquire and display the best examples of artworks from each artistic period and genre, even if some of these works are not recognized by experts as masterpieces.

    Frederick: Art museums ought to devote their limited resources to acquiring the works of recognized masters in order to ensure the preservation of the greatest artworks.

    Elaine's and Frederick's statements provide the most support for the claim that they would disagree about whether

    (A) many artistic masterpieces are not recognized as such by art experts
    (B) museums should seek to represent all genres of art in their collections
    (C) art museums should seek to preserve works of art
    (D) an art museum ought to acquire an unusual example of a period or genre if more characteristic examples are prohibitively expensive
    (E) all of the artworks that experts identify as masterpieces are actually masterpieces

3. Science columnist: It is clear why humans have so many diseases in common with cats. Many human diseases are genetically based, and cats are genetically closer to humans than are any other mammals except nonhuman primates. Each of the genes identified so far in cats has an exact counterpart in humans.

    Which one of the following, if true, most weakens the science columnist's explanation for the claim that humans have so many diseases in common with cats?

    (A) Cats have built up resistance to many of the diseases they have in common with humans.
    (B) Most diseases that humans have in common with cats have no genetic basis.
    (C) Cats have more diseases in common with nonhuman primates than with humans.
    (D) Many of the diseases humans have in common with cats are mild and are rarely diagnosed.
    (E) Humans have more genes in common with nonhuman primates than with cats.

4. This region must find new ways to help business grow. After all, shoe manufacturing used to be a major local industry, but recently has experienced severe setbacks due to overseas competition, so there is a need for expansion into new manufacturing areas. Moreover, our outdated public policy generally inhibits business growth.

    Which one of the following most accurately expresses the main conclusion drawn in the argument?

    (A) The region needs to find new ways to enhance business growth.
    (B) Shoe manufacturing is no longer a major source of income in the region.
    (C) Shoe manufacturing in the region has dramatically declined due to overseas competition.
    (D) Business in the region must expand into new areas of manufacturing.
    (E) Outdated public policy inhibits business growth in the region.

GO ON TO THE NEXT PAGE.

5. As a result of modern medicine, more people have been able to enjoy long and pain-free lives. But the resulting increase in life expectancy has contributed to a steady increase in the proportion of the population that is of advanced age. This population shift is creating potentially devastating financial problems for some social welfare programs.

    Which one of the following propositions is most precisely exemplified by the situation presented above?

    (A) Technical or scientific innovation cannot be the solution to all problems.
    (B) Implementing technological innovations should be delayed until the resulting social changes can be managed.
    (C) Every enhancement of the quality of life has unavoidable negative consequences.
    (D) All social institutions are affected by a preoccupation with prolonging life.
    (E) Solving one set of problems can create a different set of problems.

6. Since Jackie is such a big fan of Moral Vacuum's music, she will probably like The Cruel Herd's new album. Like Moral Vacuum, The Cruel Herd on this album plays complex rock music that employs the acoustic instrumentation and harmonic sophistication of early sixties jazz. The Cruel Herd also has very witty lyrics, full of puns and sardonic humor, like some of Moral Vacuum's best lyrics.

    Which one of the following, if true, most strengthens the argument?

    (A) Jackie has not previously cared for The Cruel Herd, but on the new album The Cruel Herd's previous musical arranger has been replaced by Moral Vacuum's musical arranger.
    (B) Though The Cruel Herd's previous albums' production quality was not great, the new album is produced by one of the most widely employed producers in the music industry.
    (C) Like Moral Vacuum, The Cruel Herd regularly performs in clubs popular with many students at the university that Jackie attends.
    (D) All of the music that Jackie prefers to listen to on a regular basis is rock music.
    (E) Jackie's favorite Moral Vacuum songs have lyrics that are somber and marked by a strong political awareness.

7. Superconductors are substances that conduct electricity without resistance at low temperatures. Their use, however, will never be economically feasible, unless there is a substance that superconducts at a temperature above minus 148 degrees Celsius. If there is such a substance, that substance must be an alloy of niobium and germanium. Unfortunately, such alloys superconduct at temperatures no higher than minus 160 degrees Celsius.

    If the statements above are true, which one of the following must also be true?

    (A) The use of superconductors will never be economically feasible.
    (B) If the alloys of niobium and germanium do not superconduct at temperatures above minus 148 degrees Celsius, then there are other substances that will do so.
    (C) The use of superconductors could be economically feasible if there is a substance that superconducts at temperatures below minus 148 degrees Celsius.
    (D) Alloys of niobium and germanium do not superconduct at temperatures below minus 160 degrees Celsius.
    (E) No use of alloys of niobium and germanium will ever be economically feasible.

8. Doctor: In three separate studies, researchers compared children who had slept with night-lights in their rooms as infants to children who had not. In the first study, the children who had slept with night-lights proved more likely to be nearsighted, but the later studies found no correlation between night-lights and nearsightedness. However, the children in the first study were younger than those in the later studies. This suggests that if night-lights cause nearsightedness, the effect disappears with age.

    Which one of the following, if true, would most weaken the doctor's argument?

    (A) A fourth study comparing infants who were currently sleeping with night-lights to infants who were not did not find any correlation between night-lights and nearsightedness.
    (B) On average, young children who are already very nearsighted are no more likely to sleep with night-lights than young children who are not already nearsighted.
    (C) In a study involving children who had not slept with night-lights as infants but had slept with night-lights when they were older, most of the children studied were not nearsighted.
    (D) The two studies in which no correlation was found did not examine enough children to provide significant support for any conclusion regarding a causal relationship between night-lights and nearsightedness.
    (E) In a fourth study involving 100 children who were older than those in any of the first three studies, several of the children who had slept with night-lights as infants were nearsighted.

GO ON TO THE NEXT PAGE.

9. Global surveys estimate the earth's population of nesting female leatherback turtles has fallen by more than two-thirds in the past 15 years. Any species whose population declines by more than two-thirds in 15 years is in grave danger of extinction, so the leatherback turtle is clearly in danger of extinction.

Which one of the following is an assumption that the argument requires?

(A) The decline in the population of nesting female leatherback turtles is proportional to the decline in the leatherback turtle population as a whole.

(B) If the global population of leatherback turtles falls by more than two-thirds over the next 15 years, the species will eventually become extinct.

(C) The global population of leatherback turtles consists in roughly equal numbers of females and males.

(D) Very few leatherback turtles exist in captivity.

(E) The only way to ensure the continued survival of leatherback turtles in the wild is to breed them in captivity.

10. Public health experts have waged a long-standing educational campaign to get people to eat more vegetables, which are known to help prevent cancer. Unfortunately, the campaign has had little impact on people's diets. The reason is probably that many people simply dislike the taste of most vegetables. Thus, the campaign would probably be more effective if it included information on ways to make vegetables more appetizing.

Which one of the following, if true, most strengthens the argument?

(A) The campaign to get people to eat more vegetables has had little impact on the diets of most people who love the taste of vegetables.

(B) Some ways of making vegetables more appetizing diminish vegetables' ability to help prevent cancer.

(C) People who find a few vegetables appetizing typically do not eat substantially more vegetables than do people who dislike the taste of most vegetables.

(D) People who dislike the taste of most vegetables would eat many more vegetables if they knew how to make them more appetizing.

(E) The only way to make the campaign to get people to eat more vegetables more effective would be to ensure that anyone who at present dislikes the taste of certain vegetables learns to find those vegetables appetizing.

11. Pure science—research with no immediate commercial or technological application—is a public good. Such research requires a great amount of financial support and does not yield profits in the short term. Since private corporations will not undertake to support activities that do not yield short-term profits, a society that wants to reap the benefits of pure science ought to use public funds to support such research.

The claim about private corporations serves which one of the following functions in the argument?

(A) It expresses the conclusion of the argument.

(B) It explains what is meant by the expression "pure research" in the context of the argument.

(C) It distracts attention from the point at issue by introducing a different but related goal.

(D) It supports the conclusion by ruling out an alternative way of achieving the benefits mentioned.

(E) It illustrates a case where unfortunate consequences result from a failure to accept the recommendation offered.

12. Melinda: Hazard insurance decreases an individual's risk by judiciously spreading the risk among many policyholders.

Jack: I disagree. It makes sense for me to buy fire insurance for my house, but I don't see how doing so lessens the chances that my house will burn down.

Jack's response most clearly trades on an ambiguity in which one of the following expressions used by Melinda?

(A) judiciously spreading

(B) many policyholders

(C) risk

(D) decreases

(E) hazard insurance

GO ON TO THE NEXT PAGE.

13. Some doctors believe that a certain drug reduces the duration of episodes of vertigo, claiming that the average duration of vertigo for people who suffer from it has decreased since the drug was introduced. However, during a recent three-month shortage of the drug, there was no significant change in the average duration of vertigo. Thus, we can conclude that the drug has no effect on the duration of vertigo.

Which one of the following is an assumption required by the argument?

(A) If a drug made a difference in the duration of vertigo, a three-month shortage of that drug would have caused a significant change in the average duration of vertigo.

(B) If there were any change in the average duration of vertigo since the introduction of the drug, it would have demonstrated that the drug has an effect on the duration of vertigo.

(C) A period of time greater than three months would not have been better to use in judging whether the drug has an effect on the duration of vertigo.

(D) Changes in diet and smoking habits are not responsible for any change in the average duration of vertigo since the introduction of the drug.

(E) There are various significant factors other than drugs that decrease the duration of vertigo for many people who suffer from it.

14. It has been suggested that a television set should be thought of as nothing more than "a toaster with pictures" and that since we let market forces determine the design of kitchen appliances we can let them determine what is seen on television. But that approach is too simple. Some governmental control is needed, since television is so important politically and culturally. It is a major source of commercial entertainment. It plays an important political role because it is the primary medium through which many voters obtain information about current affairs. It is a significant cultural force in that in the average home it is on for more than five hours a day.

Which one of the following most accurately expresses the role played in the argument by the claim that television is so important politically and culturally?

(A) It states a view that the argument as a whole is designed to discredit.

(B) It is an intermediate conclusion that is offered in support of the claim that a television set should be thought of as nothing more than "a toaster with pictures" and for which the claim that we can let market forces determine what is seen on television is offered as support.

(C) It is a premise that is offered in support of the claim that we let market forces determine the design of kitchen appliances.

(D) It is an intermediate conclusion that is offered in support of the claim that some governmental control of television is needed and for which the claim that the television is on for more than five hours a day in the average home is offered as partial support.

(E) It is a premise that is offered in support of the claim that television is the primary medium through which many voters obtain information about current affairs.

GO ON TO THE NEXT PAGE.

15. Earthworms, vital to the health of soil, prefer soil that is approximately neutral on the acid-to-alkaline scale. Since decomposition of dead plants makes the top layer of soil highly acidic, application of crushed limestone, which is highly alkaline, to the soil's surface should make the soil more attractive to earthworms.

Which one of the following is an assumption on which the argument depends?

(A) As far as soil health is concerned, aiding the decomposition of dead plants is the most important function performed by earthworms.

(B) After its application to the soil's surface, crushed limestone stays in the soil's top layer long enough to neutralize some of the top layer's acidity.

(C) Crushed limestone contains available calcium and magnesium, both of which are just as vital as earthworms to healthy soil.

(D) By itself, acidity of soil does nothing to hasten decomposition of dead plants.

(E) Alkaline soil is significantly more likely to benefit from an increased earthworm population than is highly acidic soil.

16. Jurist: A nation's laws must be viewed as expressions of a moral code that transcends those laws and serves as a measure of their adequacy. Otherwise, a society can have no sound basis for preferring any given set of laws to all others. Thus, any moral prohibition against the violation of statutes must leave room for exceptions.

Which one of the following can be properly inferred from the jurist's statements?

(A) Those who formulate statutes are not primarily concerned with morality when they do so.

(B) Sometimes criteria other than the criteria derived from a moral code should be used in choosing one set of laws over another.

(C) Unless it is legally forbidden ever to violate some moral rules, moral behavior and compliance with laws are indistinguishable.

(D) There is no statute that a nation's citizens have a moral obligation to obey.

(E) A nation's laws can sometimes come into conflict with the moral code they express.

17. An association between two types of conditions does not establish that conditions of one type cause conditions of the other type. Even persistent and inviolable association is inconclusive; such association is often due to conditions of both types being effects of the same kind of cause.

Which one of the following judgments most closely conforms to the principle stated above?

(A) Some people claim that rapid growth of the money supply is what causes inflation. But this is a naive view. What these people do not realize is that growth in the money supply and inflation are actually one and the same phenomenon.

(B) People who have high blood pressure tend to be overweight. But before we draw any inferences, we should consider that an unhealthy lifestyle can cause high blood pressure, and weight gain can result from living unhealthily.

(C) In some areas, there is a high correlation between ice cream consumption and the crime rate. Some researchers have proposed related third factors, but we cannot rule out that the correlation is purely coincidental.

(D) People's moods seem to vary with the color of the clothes they wear. Dark colors are associated with gloomy moods, and bright colors are associated with cheerful moods. This correlation resolves nothing, however. We cannot say whether it is the colors that cause the moods or the converse.

(E) Linguists propose that the similarities between Greek and Latin are due to their common descent from an earlier language. But how are we to know that the similarities are not actually due to the two languages having borrowed structures from one another, as with the languages Marathi and Telegu?

GO ON TO THE NEXT PAGE.

18. Salesperson: When a salesperson is successful, it is certain that that person has been in sales for at least three years. This is because to succeed as a salesperson, one must first establish a strong client base, and studies have shown that anyone who spends at least three years developing a client base can eventually make a comfortable living in sales.

The reasoning in the salesperson's argument is vulnerable to criticism on the grounds that it fails to consider the possibility that

(A) salespeople who have spent three years developing a client base might not yet be successful in sales

(B) some salespeople require fewer than three years in which to develop a strong client base

(C) a salesperson who has not spent three years developing a client base may not succeed in sales

(D) it takes longer than three years for a salesperson to develop a strong client base

(E) few salespeople can afford to spend three years building a client base

19. People who have habitually slept less than six hours a night and then begin sleeping eight or more hours a night typically begin to feel much less anxious. Therefore, most people who sleep less than six hours a night can probably cause their anxiety levels to fall by beginning to sleep at least eight hours a night.

The reasoning in which one of the following arguments is most similar to that in the argument above?

(A) When a small company first begins to advertise on the Internet, its financial situation generally improves. This shows that most small companies that have never advertised on the Internet can probably improve their financial situation by doing so.

(B) Certain small companies that had never previously advertised on the Internet have found that their financial situations began to improve after they started to do so. So most small companies can probably improve their financial situations by starting to advertise on the Internet.

(C) It must be true that any small company that increases its Internet advertising will improve its financial situation, since most small companies that advertise on the Internet improved their financial situations soon after they first began to do so.

(D) Usually, the financial situation of a small company that has never advertised on the Internet will improve only if that company starts to advertise on the Internet. Therefore, a typical small company that has never advertised on the Internet can probably improve its financial situation by doing so.

(E) A small company's financial situation usually improves soon after that company first begins to advertise on the Internet. Thus, most small companies that have never advertised on the Internet could probably become financially strong.

GO ON TO THE NEXT PAGE.

20. Biologist: Lions and tigers are so similar to each other anatomically that their skeletons are virtually indistinguishable. But their behaviors are known to be quite different: tigers hunt only as solitary individuals, whereas lions hunt in packs. Thus, paleontologists cannot reasonably infer solely on the basis of skeletal anatomy that extinct predatory animals, such as certain dinosaurs, hunted in packs.

The conclusion is properly drawn if which one of the following is assumed?

(A) The skeletons of lions and tigers are at least somewhat similar in structure in certain key respects to the skeletons of at least some extinct predatory animals.

(B) There have existed at least two species of extinct predatory dinosaurs that were so similar to each other that their skeletal anatomy is virtually indistinguishable.

(C) If skeletal anatomy alone is ever an inadequate basis for inferring a particular species' hunting behavior, then it is never reasonable to infer, based on skeletal anatomy alone, that a species of animals hunted in packs.

(D) If any two animal species with virtually indistinguishable skeletal anatomy exhibit quite different hunting behaviors, then it is never reasonable to infer, based solely on the hunting behavior of those species, that the two species have the same skeletal anatomy.

(E) If it is unreasonable to infer, solely on the basis of differences in skeletal anatomy, that extinct animals of two distinct species differed in their hunting behavior, then the skeletal remains of those two species are virtually indistinguishable.

21. The trees always blossom in May if April rainfall exceeds 5 centimeters. If April rainfall exceeds 5 centimeters, then the reservoirs are always full on May 1. The reservoirs were not full this May 1 and thus the trees will not blossom this May.

Which one of the following exhibits a flawed pattern of reasoning most similar to the flawed pattern of reasoning in the argument above?

(A) If the garlic is in the pantry, then it is still fresh. And the potatoes are on the basement stairs if the garlic is in the pantry. The potatoes are not on the basement stairs, so the garlic is not still fresh.

(B) The jar reaches optimal temperature if it is held over the burner for 2 minutes. The contents of the jar liquefy immediately if the jar is at optimal temperature. The jar was held over the burner for 2 minutes, so the contents of the jar must have liquefied immediately.

(C) A book is classified "special" if it is more than 200 years old. If a book was set with wooden type, then it is more than 200 years old. This book is not classified "special," so it is not printed with wooden type.

(D) The mower will operate only if the engine is not flooded. The engine is flooded if the foot pedal is depressed. The foot pedal is not depressed, so the mower will operate.

(E) If the kiln is too hot, then the plates will crack. If the plates crack, then the artisan must redo the order. The artisan need not redo the order. Thus, the kiln was not too hot.

22. Doctor: Being overweight has long been linked with a variety of health problems, such as high blood pressure and heart disease. But recent research conclusively shows that people who are slightly overweight are healthier than those who are considerably underweight. Therefore, to be healthy, it suffices to be slightly overweight.

The argument's reasoning is flawed because the argument

(A) ignores medical opinions that tend to lead to a conclusion contrary to the one drawn

(B) never adequately defines what is meant by "healthy"

(C) does not take into account the fact that appropriate weight varies greatly from person to person

(D) holds that if a person lacks a property that would suffice to make the person unhealthy, then that person must be healthy

(E) mistakes a merely relative property for one that is absolute

GO ON TO THE NEXT PAGE.

23. Robust crops not only withstand insect attacks more successfully than other crops, they are also less likely to be attacked in the first place, since insects tend to feed on weaker plants. Killing insects with pesticides does not address the underlying problem of inherent vulnerability to damage caused by insect attacks. Thus, a better way to reduce the vulnerability of agricultural crops to insect pest damage is to grow those crops in good soil—soil with adequate nutrients, organic matter, and microbial activity.

Which one of the following is an assumption on which the argument depends?

(A) The application of nutrients and organic matter to farmland improves the soil's microbial activity.

(B) Insects never attack crops grown in soil containing adequate nutrients, organic matter, and microbial activity.

(C) The application of pesticides to weak crops fails to reduce the extent to which they are damaged by insect pests.

(D) Crops that are grown in good soil tend to be more robust than other crops.

(E) Growing crops without the use of pesticides generally produces less robust plants than when pesticides are used.

24. People perceive color by means of certain photopigments in the retina that are sensitive to certain wavelengths of light. People who are color-blind are unable to distinguish between red and green, for example, due to an absence of certain photopigments. What is difficult to explain, however, is that in a study of people who easily distinguish red from green, 10 to 20 percent failed to report distinctions between many shades of red that the majority of the subjects were able to distinguish.

Each of the following, if true, helps to explain the result of the study cited above EXCEPT:

(A) People with abnormally low concentrations of the photopigments for perceiving red can perceive fewer shades of red than people with normal concentrations.

(B) Questions that ask subjects to distinguish between different shades of the same color are difficult to phrase with complete clarity.

(C) Some people are uninterested in fine gradations of color and fail to notice or report differences they do not care about.

(D) Some people are unable to distinguish red from green due to an absence in the retina of the photopigment sensitive to green.

(E) Some people fail to report distinctions between certain shades of red because they lack the names for those shades.

25. Occultist: The issue of whether astrology is a science is easily settled: it is both an art and a science. The scientific components are the complicated mathematics and the astronomical knowledge needed to create an astrological chart. The art is in the synthesis of a multitude of factors and symbols into a coherent statement of their relevance to an individual.

The reasoning in the occultist's argument is most vulnerable to criticism on the grounds that the argument

(A) presumes, without providing justification, that any science must involve complicated mathematics

(B) incorrectly infers that a practice is a science merely from the fact that the practice has some scientific components

(C) denies the possibility that astrology involves components that are neither artistic nor scientific

(D) incorrectly infers that astronomical knowledge is scientific merely from the fact that such knowledge is needed to create an astrological chart

(E) presumes, without providing justification, that any art must involve the synthesis of a multitude of factors and symbols

S T O P

IF YOU FINISH BEFORE TIME IS CALLED, YOU MAY CHECK YOUR WORK ON THIS SE~ ~NLY.
DO NOT WORK ON ANY OTHER SECTION IN THE TEST.

SECTION II
Time—35 minutes

23 Questions

<u>Directions:</u> Each group of questions in this section is based on a set of conditions. In answering some of the questions, it may be useful to draw a rough diagram. Choose the response that most accurately and completely answers each question and blacken the corresponding space on your answer sheet.

Questions 1–5

Five performers—Traugott, West, Xavier, Young, and Zinser—are recruited by three talent agencies—Fame Agency, Premier Agency, and Star Agency. Each performer signs with exactly one of the agencies and each agency signs at least one of the performers. The performers' signing with the agencies is in accord with the following:

Xavier signs with Fame Agency.
Xavier and Young do not sign with the same agency as each other.
Zinser signs with the same agency as Young.
If Traugott signs with Star Agency, West also signs with Star Agency.

1. Which one of the following could be a complete and accurate list of the performers who sign with each agency?

   (A) Fame Agency: Xavier
   Premier Agency: West
   Star Agency: Traugott, Young, Zinser
   (B) Fame Agency: Xavier
   Premier Agency: Traugott, West
   Star Agency: Young, Zinser
   (C) Fame Agency: Xavier
   Premier Agency: Traugott, Young
   Star Agency: West, Zinser
   (D) Fame Agency: Young, Zinser
   Premier Agency: Xavier
   Star Agency: Traugott, West
   (E) Fame Agency: Xavier, Young, Zinser
   Premier Agency: Traugott
   Star Agency: West

2. Which one of the following could be true?

   (A) West is the only performer who signs with Star Agency.
   (B) West, Young, and Zinser all sign with Premier Agency.
   (C) Xavier signs with the same agency as Zinser.
   (D) Zinser is the only performer who signs with Star Agency.
   (E) Three of the performers sign with Fame Agency.

3. Which one of the following must be true?

   (A) West and Zinser do not sign with the same agency as each other.
   (B) Fame Agency signs at most two of the performers.
   (C) Fame Agency signs the same number of the performers as Star Agency.
   (D) Traugott signs with the same agency as West.
   (E) West does not sign with Fame Agency.

4. The agency with which each of the performers signs is completely determined if which one of the following is true?

   (A) Traugott signs with Fame Agency.
   (B) Traugott signs with Star Agency.
   (C) West signs with Premier Agency.
   (D) Xavier signs with Fame Agency.
   (E) Zinser signs with Premier Agency.

5. If Zinser signs with Star Agency, which one of the following must be false?

   (A) Premier Agency signs exactly one performer.
   (B) Star Agency signs exactly three of the performers.
   (C) Traugott signs with Star Agency.
   (D) West signs with Star Agency.
   (E) None of the other performers signs with the same agency as Xavier.

GO ON TO THE NEXT PAGE.

Questions 6–11

A competition is being held to select a design for Yancy College's new student union building. Each of six architects—Green, Jackson, Liu, Mertz, Peete, and Valdez—has submitted exactly one design. There are exactly six designs, and they are presented one at a time to the panel of judges, each design being presented exactly once, consistent with the following conditions:

Mertz's design is presented at some time before Liu's and after Peete's.

Green's design is presented either at some time before Jackson's or at some time after Liu's, but not both.

Valdez's design is presented either at some time before Green's or at some time after Peete's, but not both.

6. Which one of the following could be the order in which the designs are presented, from first to last?

   (A) Jackson's, Peete's, Mertz's, Green's, Valdez's, Liu's
   (B) Peete's, Jackson's, Liu's, Mertz's, Green's, Valdez's
   (C) Peete's, Mertz's, Jackson's, Liu's, Green's, Valdez's
   (D) Peete's, Mertz's, Valdez's, Green's, Liu's, Jackson's
   (E) Valdez's, Liu's, Jackson's, Peete's, Mertz's, Green's

7. Mertz's design CANNOT be presented

   (A) sixth
   (B) fifth
   (C) fourth
   (D) third
   (E) second

8. If Liu's design is presented sixth, then which one of the following must be true?

   (A) Green's design is presented at some time before Jackson's.
   (B) Jackson's design is presented at some time before Mertz's.
   (C) Peete's design is presented at some time before Green's.
   (D) Peete's design is presented at some time before Valdez's.
   (E) Valdez's design is presented at some time before Green's.

9. If Jackson's design is presented at some time before Mertz's, then each of the following could be true EXCEPT:

   (A) Jackson's design is presented second.
   (B) Peete's design is presented third.
   (C) Peete's design is presented fourth.
   (D) Jackson's design is presented fifth.
   (E) Liu's design is presented fifth.

10. Which one of the following designs CANNOT be the design presented first?

   (A) Green's
   (B) Jackson's
   (C) Liu's
   (D) Peete's
   (E) Valdez's

11. Which one of the following could be an accurate partial list of the architects, each matched with his or her design's place in the order in which the designs are presented?

   (A) first: Mertz; fourth: Liu; fifth: Green
   (B) second: Green; third: Peete; fourth: Jackson
   (C) second: Mertz; fifth: Green; sixth: Jackson
   (D) fourth: Peete; fifth: Liu; sixth: Jackson
   (E) fourth: Valdez; fifth: Green; sixth: Liu

GO ON TO THE NEXT PAGE.

Questions 12–17

Detectives investigating a citywide increase in burglaries questioned exactly seven suspects—S, T, V, W, X, Y, and Z—each on a different one of seven consecutive days. Each suspect was questioned exactly once. Any suspect who confessed did so while being questioned. The investigation conformed to the following:

    T was questioned on day three.
    The suspect questioned on day four did not confess.
    S was questioned after W was questioned.
    Both X and V were questioned after Z was questioned.
    No suspects confessed after W was questioned.
    Exactly two suspects confessed after T was questioned.

12. Which one of the following could be true?

    (A)   X was questioned on day one.
    (B)   V was questioned on day two.
    (C)   Z was questioned on day four.
    (D)   W was questioned on day five.
    (E)   S was questioned on day six.

13. If Z was the second suspect to confess, then each of the following statements could be true EXCEPT:

    (A)   T confessed.
    (B)   T did not confess.
    (C)   V did not confess.
    (D)   X confessed.
    (E)   Y did not confess.

14. If Y was questioned after V but before X, then which one of the following could be true?

    (A)   V did not confess.
    (B)   Y confessed.
    (C)   X did not confess.
    (D)   X was questioned on day four.
    (E)   Z was questioned on day two.

15. Which one of the following suspects must have been questioned before T was questioned?

    (A)   V
    (B)   W
    (C)   X
    (D)   Y
    (E)   Z

16. If X and Y both confessed, then each of the following could be true EXCEPT:

    (A)   V confessed.
    (B)   X was questioned on day five.
    (C)   Y was questioned on day one.
    (D)   Z was questioned on day one.
    (E)   Z did not confess.

17. If neither X nor V confessed, then which one of the following must be true?

    (A)   T confessed.
    (B)   V was questioned on day two.
    (C)   X was questioned on day four.
    (D)   Y confessed.
    (E)   Z did not confess.

GO ON TO THE NEXT PAGE.

Questions 18–23

The three highest-placing teams in a high school debate tournament are the teams from Fairview, Gillom, and Hilltop high schools. Each team has exactly two members. The individuals on these three teams are Mei, Navarro, O'Rourke, Pavlovich, Sethna, and Tsudama. The following is the case:

Sethna is on the team from Gillom High.
Tsudama is on the second-place team.
Mei and Pavlovich are not on the same team.
Pavlovich's team places higher than Navarro's team.
The team from Gillom High places higher than the team from Hilltop High.

18. Which one of the following could be an accurate list of the members of each of the three highest-placing teams?

  (A)   first place: Mei and O'Rourke
          second place: Pavlovich and Sethna
          third place: Navarro and Tsudama
  (B)   first place: Mei and Pavlovich
          second place: Sethna and Tsudama
          third place: Navarro and O'Rourke
  (C)   first place: Navarro and Sethna
          second place: Pavlovich and Tsudama
          third place: Mei and O'Rourke
  (D)   first place: O'Rourke and Pavlovich
          second place: Navarro and Tsudama
          third place: Mei and Sethna
  (E)   first place: Pavlovich and Sethna
          second place: O'Rourke and Tsudama
          third place: Mei and Navarro

19. If Pavlovich is on the team from Hilltop High, then which one of the following could be true?

  (A)   O'Rourke is on the first-place team.
  (B)   Pavlovich is on the first-place team.
  (C)   Mei is on the second-place team.
  (D)   Navarro is on the second-place team.
  (E)   Sethna is on the second-place team.

20. If O'Rourke is on the second-place team, then which one of the following could be true?

  (A)   Mei is on the team from Gillom High.
  (B)   Navarro is on the team from Fairview High.
  (C)   O'Rourke is on the team from Gillom High.
  (D)   Pavlovich is on the team from Hilltop High.
  (E)   Tsudama is on the team from Gillom High.

21. If Pavlovich and Tsudama are teammates, then for how many of the individuals can it be exactly determined where his or her team places?

  (A)   two
  (B)   three
  (C)   four
  (D)   five
  (E)   six

22. If Mei is on a team that places higher than the Hilltop team, then which one of the following could be true?

  (A)   The Fairview team places first.
  (B)   The Gillom team places second.
  (C)   Navarro is on the second-place team.
  (D)   O'Rourke is on the first-place team.
  (E)   Pavlovich is on the first-place team.

23. Sethna's teammate could be any one of the following EXCEPT:

  (A)   Mei
  (B)   Navarro
  (C)   O'Rourke
  (D)   Pavlovich
  (E)   Tsudama

S T O P

**IF YOU FINISH BEFORE TIME IS CALLED, YOU MAY CHECK YOUR WORK ON THIS SECTION ONLY.
DO NOT WORK ON ANY OTHER SECTION IN THE TEST.**

SECTION III
Time—35 minutes
25 Questions

<u>Directions:</u> The questions in this section are based on the reasoning contained in brief statements or passages. For some questions, more than one of the choices could conceivably answer the question. However, you are to choose the <u>best</u> answer; that is, the response that most accurately and completely answers the question. You should not make assumptions that are by commonsense standards implausible, superfluous, or incompatible with the passage. After you have chosen the best answer, blacken the corresponding space on your answer sheet.

1.   Yuriko: Our city's campaign to persuade parents to have their children vaccinated ought to be imitated by your city. In the 16 months since the enactment of legislation authorizing the campaign, vaccinations in our city have increased by 30 percent.

Susan: But the major part of that increase occurred in the first 6 months after that legislation was enacted, right after your city's free neighborhood health clinics opened, and before the vaccination campaign really got going.

In responding to Yuriko, Susan does which one of the following?

(A)   She denies Yuriko's assumption that Susan's city wants to increase the vaccination rate for children.
(B)   She cites facts that tend to weaken the force of the evidence with which Yuriko supports her recommendation.
(C)   She introduces evidence to show that the campaign Yuriko advocates is only effective for a short period to time.
(D)   She advances the claim that a campaign such as Yuriko recommends is not necessary because most parents already choose to have their children vaccinated.
(E)   She presents evidence to suggest that vaccination campaigns are usually ineffective.

2.   The process by which nylon is manufactured releases large amounts of the gas nitrous oxide, which is harmful to the environment. Since the processing of cotton fiber does not release environmentally harmful gases, there would be less environmental damage done if cotton fiber rather than nylon were used to make products such as thread and rope.

Which one of the following, if true, would weaken the argument?

(A)   Even if the quantity of nitrous oxide released into the environment decreased, many environmental problems would remain unsolved.
(B)   Even if only some of the thread and rope that is currently being made from nylon were instead made from cotton fiber, some environmental damage would be avoided.
(C)   If cotton fiber replaced nylon in the production of thread and rope, there would be a resulting increase in the amount of nylon used in other manufactured products.
(D)   If the quantity of nylon manufactured annually decreased substantially, the volume of several pollutants that are released into the environment during its manufacture would be reduced.
(E)   If thread and rope continue to be made from nylon, the production of cotton fiber will not increase as rapidly as it would if all thread and rope were to be made from cotton fiber.

GO ON TO THE NEXT PAGE.

3. John: It was wrong of you to blame me for that traffic accident. You know full well that the accident was due to my poor vision, and I certainly cannot be held responsible for the fact that my vision has deteriorated.

   Michiko: But I can hold you responsible for your hazardous driving, because you know how poor your vision is. People are responsible for the consequences of actions that they voluntarily undertake, if they know that those actions risk such consequences.

   The principle that Michiko invokes, if established, would justify which one of the following judgments?

   (A) Colleen was responsible for missing her flight home from Paris, because she decided to take one more trip to the Eiffel Tower even though she knew she might not have sufficient time to get to the airport if she did so.
   (B) Colleen was responsible for having offended her brother when she reported to him an offensive comment made about his colleague, although she did not know her brother would mistakenly understand the comment to be about himself.
   (C) Colleen was responsible for her automobile's having been stolen two weeks ago, because she did not take any of the precautions that the town police recommended in the antitheft manual they published last week.
   (D) Colleen was responsible for her cat's being frightened, because, even though it was her brother who allowed the door to slam shut, she knew that cats are often frightened by loud noises.
   (E) Colleen was not responsible for losing her job, because, knowing that her position was in danger of being eliminated, she did everything possible to preserve it.

4. Psychiatrist: Take any visceral emotion you care to consider. There are always situations in which it is healthy to try to express that emotion. So, there are always situations in which it is healthy to try to express one's anger.

   The conclusion of the argument follows logically if which one of the following is assumed?

   (A) Anger is always expressible.
   (B) Anger is a visceral emotion.
   (C) Some kinds of emotions are unhealthy to express.
   (D) All emotions that are healthy to express are visceral.
   (E) An emotion is visceral only if it is healthy to express.

5. Cigarette companies claim that manufacturing both low- and high-nicotine cigarettes allows smokers to choose how much nicotine they want. However, a recent study has shown that the levels of nicotine found in the blood of smokers who smoke one pack of cigarettes per day are identical at the end of a day's worth of smoking, whatever the level of nicotine in the cigarettes they smoke.

   Which one of the following, if true, most helps to explain the finding of the nicotine study?

   (A) Blood cannot absorb more nicotine per day than that found in the smoke from a package of the lowest-nicotine cigarettes available.
   (B) Smokers of the lowest-nicotine cigarettes available generally smoke more cigarettes per day than smokers of high-nicotine cigarettes.
   (C) Most nicotine is absorbed into the blood of a smoker even if it is delivered in smaller quantities.
   (D) The level of tar in cigarettes is higher in low-nicotine cigarettes than it is in some high-nicotine cigarettes.
   (E) When taking in nicotine by smoking cigarettes is discontinued, the level of nicotine in the blood decreases steadily.

6. Editorial: The premier's economic advisor assures her that with the elimination of wasteful spending the goal of reducing taxes while not significantly decreasing government services can be met. But the premier should not listen to this advisor, who in his youth was convicted of embezzlement. Surely his economic advice is as untrustworthy as he is himself, and so the premier should discard any hope of reducing taxes without a significant decrease in government services.

   Which one of the following is a questionable argumentative strategy employed in the editorial's argument?

   (A) rejecting a proposal on the grounds that a particular implementation of the proposal is likely to fail
   (B) trying to win support for a proposal by playing on people's fears of what could happen otherwise
   (C) criticizing the source of a claim rather than examining the claim itself
   (D) taking lack of evidence for a claim as evidence undermining that claim
   (E) presupposing what it sets out to establish

GO ON TO THE NEXT PAGE.

Questions 7–8

Figorian Wildlife Commission: The development of wetlands in industrialized nations for residential and commercial uses has endangered many species. To protect wildlife we must regulate such development in Figoria: future wetland development must be offset by the construction of replacement wetland habitats. Thus, development would cause no net reduction of wetlands and pose no threat to the species that inhabit them.

Figorian Development Commission: Other nations have flagrantly developed wetlands at the expense of wildlife. We have conserved. Since Figorian wetland development might not affect wildlife and is necessary for growth, we should allow development. We have as much right to govern our own resources as countries that have already put their natural resources to commercial use.

7. Which one of the following is an assumption on which the argument advanced by the Figorian Wildlife Commission depends?

(A) More species have been endangered by the development of wetlands than have been endangered by any other type of development.
(B) The species indigenous to natural wetland habitats will survive in specially constructed replacement wetlands.
(C) In nations that are primarily agricultural, wetland development does not need to be regulated.
(D) Figorian regulation of development has in the past protected and preserved wildlife.
(E) The species that inhabit Figorian wetlands are among the most severely threatened of the designated endangered species.

8. Which one of the following principles, if accepted, would most strongly support the Figorian Development Commission's position against the Figorian Wildlife Commission's position?

(A) National resources should be regulated by international agreement when wildlife is endangered.
(B) The right of future generations to have wildlife preserved supersedes the economic needs of individual nations.
(C) Only when a reduction of populations of endangered species by commercial development has been found should regulation be implemented to prevent further damage.
(D) Environment regulation must aim at preventing any further environmental damage and cannot allow for the different degrees to which different nations have already harmed the environment.
(E) It is imprudent to allow further depletion of natural resources.

9. High blood cholesterol levels are bad for the heart. Like meat, eggs, and poultry, shellfish contains cholesterol. But shellfish is not necessarily bad for the heart; it is very low in saturated fat, which affects blood cholesterol levels much more than dietary cholesterol does.

Which one of the following, if true, most strengthens the argument?

(A) Meat and eggs are high in saturated fat.
(B) Small quantities of foods high in saturated fat are not bad for the heart
(C) Shellfish has less cholesterol per gram than meat, eggs, and poultry do.
(D) Foods low in saturated fat promote low blood cholesterol.
(E) A serving of meat or poultry is typically larger than a serving of shellfish.

10. Every moral theory developed in the Western tradition purports to tell us what a good life is. However, most people would judge someone who perfectly embodied the ideals of any one of these theories not to be living a good life—the kind of life they would want for themselves and their children.

The statements above, if true, most strongly support which one of the following?

(A) Most people desire a life for themselves and their children that is better than a merely good life.
(B) A person who fits the ideals of one moral theory in the Western tradition would not necessarily fit the ideals of another.
(C) Most people have a conception of a good life that does not match that of any moral theory in the Western tradition.
(D) A good life as described by moral theories in the Western tradition cannot be realized.
(E) It is impossible to develop a theory that accurately describes what a good life is.

GO ON TO THE NEXT PAGE.

11. Biologist: Humans have five fingers because we descended from a fish with five phalanges in its fins. Despite our prejudices to the contrary, our configuration of fingers is no more or less useful than several other possible configurations, e.g., six per hand. So, if humans had descended from a fish with six phalanges in its fins and had six fingers on each hand, then we would be just as content with that configuration.

Which one of the following, if true, most strengthens the biologist's argument?

(A) Everyone is equally content with our present configuration of fingers.
(B) Humans are never equally content with two things of unequal usefulness.
(C) Humans are always equally content with two things of equal usefulness.
(D) The perceived usefulness of our configuration of fingers is an illusory result of our prejudices.
(E) At least one species of fish had six phalanges in its fins.

12. Surrealist: Many artists mistakenly think that models need be taken only from outside the psyche. Although human sensibility can confer beauty upon even the most vulgar external objects, using the power of artistic representation solely to preserve and reinforce objects that would exist even without artists is an ironic waste.

Which one of the following most accurately expresses the conclusion of the surrealist's argument?

(A) An artist's work should not merely represent objects from outside the psyche.
(B) Artistic representation is used solely to preserve and reinforce objects.
(C) Artists should not base all their work on mere representation.
(D) Great art can confer beauty even upon very vulgar external objects.
(E) True works of art rarely represent objects from outside the psyche.

13. Harrold Foods is attempting to dominate the soft-drink market by promoting "Hero," its most popular carbonated drink product, with a costly new advertising campaign. But survey results show that, in the opinion of 72 percent of all consumers, "Hero" already dominates the market. Since any product with more than 50 percent of the sales in a market is, by definition, dominant in that market, Harrold Foods dominates the market now and need only maintain its current market share in order to continue to do so.

The argument commits which one of the following errors in reasoning?

(A) failing to exclude the possibility that what appears to be the result of a given market condition may in fact be the cause of that condition
(B) mistaking a condition required if a certain result is to obtain for a condition that by itself is sufficient to guarantee that result
(C) treating the failure to establish that a certain claim is false as equivalent to a demonstration that that claim is true
(D) taking evidence that a claim is believed to be true to constitute evidence that the claim is in fact true
(E) describing survey results that were obtained in the past as if they are bound to obtain in the future as well

GO ON TO THE NEXT PAGE.

14. Theoretically, analog systems are superior to digital systems. A signal in a pure analog system can be infinitely detailed, while digital systems cannot produce signals that are more precise than their digital units. With this theoretical advantage there is a practical disadvantage, however. Since there is no limit on the potential detail of the signal, the duplication of an analog representation allows tiny variations from the original, which are errors. These errors tend to accumulate as signals are duplicated, until this "noise" obliterates the information embodied in the original signal.

The statements above, if true, most strongly support which one of the following?

(A) Many ideas that work well in theory do not work well in practice.
(B) Analog representation of information is impractical because we do not need infinitely detailed information.
(C) Digital systems are the best information systems because error cannot occur in the emission of digital signals.
(D) Analog systems are inferior to digital systems for most practical purposes.
(E) Digital systems are preferable to analog systems when the signal must be reproduced many times.

15. Psychologist: Doctors should never prescribe sedatives for people with insomnia. Most cases of insomnia that psychologists treat are known to be caused by psychological stress. This suggests that insomniacs do not need drugs that alter their biochemistry, but rather need psychotherapy to help them alleviate the stress causing their insomnia.

Each of the following describes a flaw in the psychologist's reasoning EXCEPT:

(A) It presumes, without providing warrant, that insomnia contributes to an inability to cope with stress.
(B) It fails to consider the possibility that sedatives are the only treatment known to be effective for cases of insomnia not caused by stress.
(C) It neglects the possibility that for some people psychotherapy is a completely ineffective treatment for stress.
(D) It overlooks the possibility that sedatives could help insomniacs cope with stress.
(E) It presumes, without providing justification, that the cases of insomnia psychologists treat are representative of all cases of insomnia.

16. Numerous paintings and engravings representing warfare can be found in remains of all civilizations going back to and including the Neolithic period, when agriculture was first developed. However, no paintings or engravings of warfare are found dating from before the Neolithic period. Therefore, warfare must have first developed as a result of the transition to an agricultural society.

Which one of the following is an assumption required by the argument?

(A) Paintings and engravings were the dominant forms of artistic expression during the Neolithic period.
(B) Warfare in the Neolithic period was always motivated by territorial disputes over agricultural land.
(C) There was no warfare prior to the period in which paintings and engravings of warfare were first created.
(D) Warfare is the inevitable result of the development of a civilization.
(E) Paintings and engravings of agricultural life began to be made at the same time as paintings and engravings of warfare.

17. An antidote for chicken pox has been developed, but researchers warn that its widespread use could be dangerous, despite the fact that this drug has no serious side effects and is currently very effective at limiting the duration and severity of chicken pox.

Which one of the following, if true, helps most to reconcile the apparent discrepancy indicated above?

(A) The drug is extremely expensive and would be difficult to make widely available.
(B) The drug has to be administered several times a day, so patient compliance is likely to be low.
(C) The drug does not prevent the spread of chicken pox from one person to another, even when the drug eventually cures the disease in the first person.
(D) When misused by taking larger-than-prescribed doses, the drug can be fatal.
(E) Use of the drug contributes to the development of deadlier forms of chicken pox that are resistant to the drug.

GO ON TO THE NEXT PAGE.

18. The tendency toward overspecialization in the study of artifacts is unfortunate. Scholars can enhance their understanding of a certain artistic period by studying art from earlier periods that had a significant influence on it. For instance, because of its influence on Spanish artisans, a proper understanding of Arabic porcelain is indispensable for a proper understanding of Spanish porcelain.

Of the following, which one most closely conforms to the principle that the passage as a whole illustrates?

(A) To understand completely the major trends in research on aging, one must understand the influences these trends exert on society's view of aging.

(B) To understand fully the historical events of this century, a historian must have an understanding of similar events in earlier centuries.

(C) To appreciate fully the French language, one must understand the other languages that share its linguistic ancestry.

(D) To understand properly any academic discipline, one must have at least a superficial acquaintance with the practices of the wider academic community.

(E) To understand completely Aristotle's philosophy, one must be well acquainted with the philosophy of his intellectual mentor, Plato.

19. Editorial: Medical schools spend one hour teaching preventive medicine for every ten hours spent teaching curative medicine, even though doctors' use of the techniques of preventive medicine cuts down medical costs greatly. Therefore, if their goal is to make medicine more cost-effective, medical schools spend insufficient time teaching preventive medicine.

Which one of the following is an assumption on which the editorial's argument depends?

(A) Preventive medicine makes use of technologies that are lower in initial cost than the technologies used within the practice of curative medicine.

(B) Every hour devoted to the teaching of preventive medicine reduces medical costs by 10 percent or more.

(C) Medical schools could increase their total number of teaching hours.

(D) Improvements in doctors' use of the techniques of curative medicine would only increase overall medical costs.

(E) The time required to teach preventive medicine thoroughly is greater than one hour for every ten that are now spent teaching curative medicine.

20. Dana: It is wrong to think that the same educational methods should be used with all children. Many children have been raised in more communal environments than others and would therefore learn better through group, rather than individual, activities. A child's accustomed style of learning should always dictate what method is used.

Pat: No, not always. The flexibility of being able to work either on one's own or in a group is invaluable in a world where both skills are in demand.

The conversation lends the most support to the claim that Dana and Pat disagree on which one of the following?

(A) All children can learn valuable skills from individual activities.

(B) All children should learn to adapt to various educational methods.

(C) Many children would learn better through group, rather than individual, activities.

(D) The main purpose of education is to prepare children to meet the demands of the job market as adults.

(E) It is sometimes desirable to tailor educational methods to the way a child learns best.

GO ON TO THE NEXT PAGE.

21. Experimental psychology requires the application of statistics to interpret empirical data and assess their significance. A person will not be able to understand such applications without training in statistics. Therefore, the more training one has in statistics, the better one will be at research in experimental psychology.

Which one of the following arguments exhibits a flawed pattern of reasoning most similar to that exhibited by the argument above?

(A)   Most people need the love and support of others; without it, they become depressed and unhappy. Therefore, in most instances, the more love and support a person receives, the happier that person will be.

(B)   Since in most jobs there are annual wage or salary increases, the longer one has worked, the more raises one will have received. Therefore, in a typical job, the longer one has worked, the greater one's income will be.

(C)   The main cause of heart attacks is arteriosclerosis, the buildup of plaque on the interior wall of the coronary arteries. It develops over an extended period of time. Therefore, if one is at risk for arteriosclerosis, one becomes more likely to suffer a heart attack as one gets older.

(D)   Since many disease processes are biochemical in nature, unless one understands chemistry one will not be able to understand the explanations for many diseases. Therefore, if one has no training in chemistry, one will not be able to master medicine.

(E)   Since most disease processes are biochemical in nature, an understanding of chemistry will enable one to understand most diseases. Therefore, one needs little more than training in chemistry to be able to master medicine.

22. In 1988 the government of Country X began using a new computer program to determine the number of people employed in that country. The program simply tallied the number of paychecks per pay period issued by employers in X, and used that figure as its estimate of employment. The government reported that, compared with the immediately preceding quarter, there was a large increase in the number of people employed for the first quarter for which the program was used.

Which one of the following can be properly concluded from the information above, together with the fact that in the first quarter for which the program was used, some employers in X issued separate paychecks for the regular hours an employee worked, for the employee's overtime, and for bonuses and commissions?

(A)   The government's estimate of growth in the number of people employed was less accurate after the government began using the new program than it had been before.

(B)   The people who designed the new program were unaware of the fact that some workers in X receive more than one paycheck per pay period.

(C)   The government had not reported strong growth in the number of people employed for the quarters just before the new program was used.

(D)   The government overestimated the total number of people employed in X for the first quarter for which the program was used.

(E)   Contrary to the claims of the government of Country X, there was no growth in the number of people employed in X in the first quarter for which the program was used.

GO ON TO THE NEXT PAGE.

23. Some vegetarians have argued that there are two individually sufficient reasons for not eating meat—one based on health considerations, and the other based on the aversion to living at the expense of other conscious creatures. But suppose that eating meat were essential to good health for humans. Then it would be less clear that an aversion to living at the expense of other conscious creatures is enough of a reason to stop eating meat.

Which one of the following most accurately describes the role played in the argument by the supposition that eating meat is essential to good health?

(A) It is used to disprove the vegetarian position that we should not eat meat.
(B) It is used to show that the two types of reasons cited in favor of vegetarianism are independent.
(C) It is used to disprove the claim that a vegetarian diet is healthy.
(D) It is used to weaken the claim that the consciousness of animals is a sufficient reason for not eating meat.
(E) It is used to show that there is no sufficient reason for not eating meat.

24. The increasing complexity of scientific inquiry has led to a proliferation of multiauthored technical articles. Reports of clinical trials involving patients from several hospitals are usually coauthored by physicians from each participating hospital. Likewise, physics papers reporting results from experiments using subsystems developed at various laboratories generally have authors from each laboratory.

If all the statements above are true, which one of the following must be true?

(A) Clinical trials involving patients from several hospitals are never conducted solely by physicians from just one hospital.
(B) Most reports of clinical trials involving patients from several hospitals have multiple authors.
(C) When a technical article has multiple authors, they are usually from several different institutions.
(D) Physics papers authored by researchers from multiple laboratories usually report results from experiments using subsystems developed at each laboratory.
(E) Most technical articles are authored solely by the researchers who conducted the experiments these articles report.

25. Helena: Extroversion, or sociability, is not biologically determined. Children whose biological parents are introverted, when adopted by extroverts, tend to be more sociable than children of introverted parents who are not adopted.

Jay: Your conclusion does not follow. Some of these children adopted by extroverts remain introverted no matter how young they are when adopted.

Jay's response suggests that he interpreted Helena's remarks to mean that

(A) biological factors play only a partial role in a child being extroverted
(B) most but not all children whose biological parents are introverted become extroverted when adopted by extroverts
(C) children whose biological parents are introverted, when adopted by extroverts, tend not to be more sociable than children of introverted parents who are not adopted
(D) biological factors do not play any role in a child being extroverted
(E) environmental factors can sometimes be more influential than biological factors in determining extroversion

S T O P

IF YOU FINISH BEFORE TIME IS CALLED, YOU MAY CHECK YOUR WORK ON THIS SECTION ONLY.
DO NOT WORK ON ANY OTHER SECTION IN THE TEST.

SECTION IV
Time—35 minutes
25 Questions

<u>Directions:</u> The questions in this section are based on the reasoning contained in brief statements or passages. For some questions, more than one of the choices could conceivably answer the question. However, you are to choose the <u>best</u> answer; that is, the response that most accurately and completely answers the question. You should not make assumptions that are by commonsense standards implausible, superfluous, or incompatible with the passage. After you have chosen the best answer, blacken the corresponding space on your answer sheet.

1. At many electronics retail stores, the consumer has the option of purchasing product warranties that extend beyond the manufacturer's warranty. However, consumers are generally better off not buying extended warranties. Most problems with electronic goods occur within the period covered by the manufacturer's warranty.

   Which one of the following, if true, most strengthens the argument?

   (A) Problems with electronic goods that occur after the manufacturer's warranty expires are generally inexpensive to fix in comparison with the cost of an extended warranty.

   (B) Because problems are so infrequent after the manufacturer's warranty expires, extended warranties on electronic goods are generally inexpensive.

   (C) Most of those who buy extended warranties on electronic goods do so because special circumstances make their item more likely to break than is usually the case.

   (D) Some extended warranties on electronic goods cover the product for the period covered by the manufacturer's warranty as well as subsequent years.

   (E) Retail stores sell extended warranties in part because consumers who purchase them are likely to purchase other products from the same store.

2. Since the 1970s, environmentalists have largely succeeded in convincing legislators to enact extensive environmental regulations. Yet, as environmentalists themselves not only admit but insist, the condition of the environment is worsening, not improving. Clearly, more environmental regulations are not the solution to the environment's problems.

   The argument's reasoning is flawed because the argument

   (A) attacks the environmentalists themselves instead of their positions

   (B) presumes, without providing warrant, that only an absence of environmental regulations could prevent environmental degradation

   (C) fails to consider the possibility that the condition of the environment would have worsened even more without environmental regulations

   (D) fails to justify its presumption that reducing excessive regulations is more important than preserving the environment

   (E) fails to consider the views of the environmentalists' opponents

GO ON TO THE NEXT PAGE.

3. Although it is unwise to take a developmental view of an art like music—as if Beethoven were an advance over Josquin, or Miles Davis an advance over Louis Armstrong—there are ways in which it makes sense to talk about musical knowledge growing over time. We certainly know more about certain sounds than was known five centuries ago; that is, we understand how sounds that earlier composers avoided can be used effectively in musical compositions. For example, we now know how the interval of the third, which is considered dissonant, can be used in compositions to create consonant musical phrases.

Which one of the following most accurately expresses the main conclusion of the argument?

(A) Sounds that were never used in past musical compositions are used today.
(B) Sounds that were once considered dissonant are more pleasing to modern listeners.
(C) It is inappropriate to take a developmental view of music.
(D) It is unwise to say that one composer is better than another.
(E) Our understanding of music can improve over the course of time.

4. A recent test of an electric insect control device discovered that, of the more than 300 insects killed during one 24-hour period, only 12 were mosquitoes. Thus this type of device may kill many insects, but will not significantly aid in controlling the potentially dangerous mosquito population.

Which one of the following, if true, most seriously weakens the argument?

(A) A careful search discovered no live mosquitoes in the vicinity of the device after the test.
(B) A very large proportion of the insects that were attracted to the device were not mosquitoes.
(C) The device is more likely to kill beneficial insects than it is to kill harmful insects.
(D) Many of the insects that were killed by the device are mosquito-eating insects.
(E) The device does not succeed in killing all of the insects that it attracts.

5. Brain-scanning technology provides information about processes occurring in the brain. For this information to help researchers understand how the brain enables us to think, however, researchers must be able to rely on the accuracy of the verbal reports given by subjects while their brains are being scanned. Otherwise brain-scan data gathered at a given moment might not contain information about what the subject reports thinking about at that moment, but instead about some different set of thoughts.

Which one of the following most accurately expresses the main conclusion of the argument?

(A) It is unlikely that brain-scanning technology will ever enable researchers to understand how the brain enables us to think.
(B) There is no way that researchers can know for certain that subjects whose brains are being scanned are accurately reporting what they are thinking.
(C) Because subjects whose brains are being scanned may not accurately report what they are thinking, the results of brain-scanning research should be regarded with great skepticism.
(D) Brain scans can provide information about the accuracy of the verbal reports of subjects whose brains are being scanned.
(E) Information from brain scans can help researchers understand how the brain enables us to think only if the verbal reports of those whose brains are being scanned are accurate.

GO ON TO THE NEXT PAGE.

6. Ornithologist: This bird species is widely thought to
subsist primarily on vegetation, but my research
shows that this belief is erroneous. While
concealed in a well-camouflaged blind, I have
observed hundreds of these birds every morning
over a period of months, and I estimate that over
half of what they ate consisted of insects and
other animal food sources.

The reasoning in the ornithologist's argument is most
vulnerable to criticism on the grounds that the argument

(A) assumes, without providing justification, that the
feeding behavior of the birds observed was not
affected by the ornithologist's act of observation
(B) fails to specify the nature of the animal food
sources, other than insects, that were consumed
by the birds
(C) adopts a widespread belief about the birds'
feeding habits without considering the evidence
that led to the belief
(D) neglects the possibility that the birds have
different patterns of food consumption during
different parts of the day and night
(E) fails to consider the possibility that the birds' diet
has changed since the earlier belief about their
diet was formed

7. Educator: Only those students who are genuinely
curious about a topic can successfully learn about
that topic. They find the satisfaction of their
curiosity intrinsically gratifying, and appreciate
the inherent rewards of the learning process itself.
However, almost no child enters the classroom
with sufficient curiosity to learn successfully
all that the teacher must instill. A teacher's job,
therefore, _____.

Which one of the following most logically completes the
educator's argument?

(A) requires for the fulfillment of its goals the
stimulation as well as the satisfaction of
curiosity
(B) necessitates the creative use of rewards that are
not inherent in the learning process itself
(C) is to focus primarily on those topics that do not
initially interest the students
(D) is facilitated by students' taking responsibility for
their own learning
(E) becomes easier if students realize that some
learning is not necessarily enjoyable

8. Environmentalist: When bacteria degrade household
cleaning products, vapors that are toxic to
humans are produced. Unfortunately, household
cleaning products are often found in landfills.
Thus, the common practice of converting landfills
into public parks is damaging human health.

Which one of the following is an assumption the
environmentalist's argument requires?

(A) In at least some landfills that have been converted
into public parks there are bacteria that degrade
household cleaning products.
(B) Converting a landfill into a public park will cause
no damage to human health unless toxic vapors
are produced in that landfill and humans are
exposed to them.
(C) If a practice involves the exposure of humans to
vapors from household cleaning products, then it
causes at least some damage to human health.
(D) When landfills are converted to public parks,
measures could be taken that would prevent
people using the parks from being exposed to
toxic vapors.
(E) If vapors toxic to humans are produced by the
degradation of household cleaning products by
bacteria in any landfill, then the health of at least
some humans will suffer.

9. Tea made from camellia leaves is a popular beverage.
However, studies show that regular drinkers of
camellia tea usually suffer withdrawal symptoms if
they discontinue drinking the tea. Furthermore, regular
drinkers of camellia tea are more likely than people in
general to develop kidney damage. Regular consumption
of this tea, therefore, can result in a heightened risk of
kidney damage.

Which one of the following, if true, most seriously
weakens the argument?

(A) Several other popular beverages contain the same
addictive chemical that is found in camellia tea.
(B) Addictive chemicals are unlikely to cause kidney
damage solely by virtue of their addictive
qualities.
(C) Some people claim that regular consumption of
camellia tea helps alleviate their stress.
(D) Most people who regularly drink camellia tea do
not develop kidney damage.
(E) Many people who regularly consume camellia
tea also regularly consume other beverages
suspected of causing kidney damage.

GO ON TO THE NEXT PAGE.

10. Artist: Avant-garde artists intend their work to challenge a society's mainstream beliefs and initiate change. And some art collectors claim that an avant-garde work that becomes popular in its own time is successful. However, a society's mainstream beliefs do not generally show any significant changes over a short period of time. Therefore, when an avant-garde work becomes popular it is a sign that the work is not successful, since it does not fulfil the intentions of its creator.

The reference to the claim of certain art collectors plays which one of the following roles in the artist's argument?

(A) It serves to bolster the argument's main conclusion.
(B) It identifies a view that is ultimately disputed by the argument.
(C) It identifies a position supported by the initial premise in the argument.
(D) It provides support for the initial premise in the argument.
(E) It provides support for a counterargument to the initial premise.

11. A recent epidemiological study found that businesspeople who travel internationally on business are much more likely to suffer from chronic insomnia than are businesspeople who do not travel on business. International travelers experience the stresses of dramatic changes in climate, frequent disruption of daily routines, and immersion in cultures other than their own, stresses not commonly felt by those who do not travel. Thus, it is likely that these stresses cause the insomnia.

Which one of the following would, if true, most strengthen the reasoning above?

(A) Most international travel for the sake of business occurs between countries with contiguous borders.
(B) Some businesspeople who travel internationally greatly enjoy the changes in climate and immersion in another culture.
(C) Businesspeople who already suffer from chronic insomnia are no more likely than businesspeople who do not to accept assignments from their employers that require international travel.
(D) Experiencing dramatic changes in climate and disruption of daily routines through international travel can be beneficial to some people who suffer from chronic insomnia.
(E) Some businesspeople who once traveled internationally but no longer do so complain of various sleep-related ailments.

12. Many mountain climbers regard climbing Mount Everest as the ultimate achievement. But climbers should not attempt this climb since the risk of death or serious injury in an Everest expedition is very high. Moreover, the romantic notion of gaining "spiritual discovery" atop Everest is dispelled by climbers' reports that the only profound experiences they had at the top were of exhaustion and fear.

Which one of the following principles, if valid, most helps to justify the reasoning above?

(A) Projects undertaken primarily for spiritual reasons ought to be abandoned if the risks are great.
(B) Dangerous activities that are unlikely to result in significant spiritual benefits for those undertaking them should be avoided.
(C) Activities that are extremely dangerous ought to be legally prohibited unless they are necessary to produce spiritual enlightenment.
(D) Profound spiritual experiences can be achieved without undergoing the serious danger involved in mountain climbing.
(E) Mountain climbers and other athletes should carefully examine the underlying reasons they have for participating in their sports.

13. Each of the smallest particles in the universe has an elegantly simple structure. Since these particles compose the universe, we can conclude that the universe itself has an elegantly simple structure.

Each of the following arguments exhibits flawed reasoning similar to that in the argument above EXCEPT:

(A) Each part of this car is nearly perfectly engineered. Therefore this car is nearly perfect, from an engineering point of view.
(B) Each part of this desk is made of metal. Therefore this desk is made of metal.
(C) Each brick in this wall is rectangular. Therefore this wall is rectangular.
(D) Each piece of wood in this chair is sturdy. Therefore this chair is sturdy.
(E) Each sentence in this novel is well constructed. Therefore this is a well-constructed novel.

GO ON TO THE NEXT PAGE.

14. Criminologist: A judicial system that tries and punishes criminals without delay is an effective deterrent to violent crime. Long, drawn-out trials and successful legal maneuvering may add to criminals' feelings of invulnerability. But if potential violent criminals know that being caught means prompt punishment, they will hesitate to break the law.

Which one of the following, if true, would most seriously weaken the criminologist's argument?

(A) It is in the nature of violent crime that it is not premeditated.

(B) About one-fourth of all suspects first arrested for a crime are actually innocent.

(C) Many violent crimes are committed by first-time offenders.

(D) Everyone accused of a crime has the right to a trial.

(E) Countries that promptly punish suspected lawbreakers have lower crime rates than countries that allow long trials.

15. Journalist: Many people object to mandatory retirement at age 65 as being arbitrary, arguing that people over 65 make useful contributions. However, if those who reach 65 are permitted to continue working indefinitely, we will face unacceptable outcomes. First, young people entering the job market will not be able to obtain decent jobs in the professions for which they were trained, resulting in widespread dissatisfaction among the young. Second, it is not fair for those who have worked 40 or more years to deprive others of opportunities. Therefore, mandatory retirement should be retained.

The journalist's argument depends on assuming which one of the following?

(A) Anyone who has worked 40 years is at least 65 years old.

(B) All young people entering the job market are highly trained professionals.

(C) It is unfair for a person not to get a job in the profession for which that person was trained.

(D) If people are forced to retire at age 65, there will be much dissatisfaction among at least some older people.

(E) If retirement ceases to be mandatory at age 65, at least some people will choose to work past age 65.

16. Editorial: Contrary to popular belief, teaching preschoolers is not especially difficult, for they develop strict systems (e.g., for sorting toys by shape), which help them to learn, and they are always intensely curious about something new in their world.

Which one of the following, if true, most seriously weakens the editorial's argument?

(A) Preschoolers have a tendency to imitate adults, and most adults follow strict routines.

(B) Children intensely curious about new things have very short attention spans.

(C) Some older children also develop strict systems that help them learn.

(D) Preschoolers ask as many creative questions as do older children.

(E) Preschool teachers generally report lower levels of stress than do other teachers.

17. Lawyer: A body of circumstantial evidence is like a rope, and each item of evidence is like a strand of that rope. Just as additional pieces of circumstantial evidence strengthen the body of evidence, adding strands to the rope strengthens the rope. And if one strand breaks, the rope is not broken nor is its strength much diminished. Thus, even if a few items of a body of circumstantial evidence are discredited, the overall body of evidence retains its basic strength.

The reasoning in the lawyer's argument is most vulnerable to criticism on the grounds that the argument

(A) takes for granted that no items in a body of circumstantial evidence are significantly more critical to the strength of the evidence than other items in that body

(B) presumes, without providing justification, that the strength of a body of evidence is less than the sum of the strengths of the parts of that body

(C) fails to consider the possibility that if many items in a body of circumstantial evidence were discredited, the overall body of evidence would be discredited

(D) offers an analogy in support of a conclusion without indicating whether the two types of things compared share any similarities

(E) draws a conclusion that simply restates a claim presented in support of that conclusion

GO ON TO THE NEXT PAGE.

18. Ethicist: Many environmentalists hold that the natural environment is morally valuable for its own sake, regardless of any benefits it provides us. However, even if nature has no moral value, nature can be regarded as worth preserving simply on the grounds that people find it beautiful. Moreover, because it is philosophically disputable whether nature is morally valuable but undeniable that it is beautiful, an argument for preserving nature that emphasizes nature's beauty will be less vulnerable to logical objections than one that emphasizes its moral value.

The ethicist's reasoning most closely conforms to which one of the following principles?

(A) An argument in favor of preserving nature will be less open to logical objections if it avoids the issue of what makes nature worth preserving.

(B) If an argument for preserving nature emphasizes a specific characteristic of nature and is vulnerable to logical objections, then that characteristic does not provide a sufficient reason for preserving nature.

(C) If it is philosophically disputable whether nature has a certain characteristic, then nature would be more clearly worth preserving if it did not have that characteristic.

(D) Anything that has moral value is worth preserving regardless of whether people consider it to be beautiful.

(E) An argument for preserving nature will be less open to logical objections if it appeals to a characteristic that can be regarded as a basis for preserving nature and that philosophically indisputably belongs to nature.

19. An editor is compiling a textbook containing essays by several different authors. The book will contain essays by Lind, Knight, or Jones, but it will not contain essays by all three. If the textbook contains an essay by Knight, then it will also contain an essay by Jones.

If the statements above are true, which one of the following must be true?

(A) If the textbook contains an essay by Lind, then it will not contain an essay by Knight.

(B) The textbook will contain an essay by only one of Lind, Knight, and Jones.

(C) The textbook will not contain an essay by Knight.

(D) If the textbook contains an essay by Lind, then it will also contain an essay by Jones.

(E) The textbook will contain an essay by Lind.

20. The ability of mammals to control their internal body temperatures is a factor in the development of their brains and intelligence. This can be seen from the following facts: the brain is a chemical machine, all chemical reactions are temperature dependent, and any organism that can control its body temperature can assure that these reactions occur at the proper temperatures.

Which one of the following is an assumption on which the argument depends?

(A) Organisms unable to control their body temperatures do not have the capacity to generate internal body heat without relying on external factors.

(B) Mammals are the only animals that have the ability to control their internal body temperatures.

(C) The brain cannot support intelligence if the chemical reactions within it are subject to uncontrolled temperatures.

(D) The development of intelligence in mammals is not independent of the chemical reactions in their brains taking place at the proper temperatures.

(E) Organisms incapable of controlling their internal body temperatures are subject to unpredictable chemical processes.

21. People who object to the proposed hazardous waste storage site by appealing to extremely implausible scenarios in which the site fails to contain the waste safely are overlooking the significant risks associated with delays in moving the waste from its present unsafe location. If we wait to remove the waste until we find a site certain to contain it safely, the waste will remain in its current location for many years, since it is currently impossible to guarantee that any site can meet that criterion. Yet keeping the waste at the current location for that long clearly poses unacceptable risks.

The statements above, if true, most strongly support which one of the following?

(A) The waste should never have been stored in its current location.

(B) The waste should be placed in the most secure location that can ever be found.

(C) Moving the waste to the proposed site would reduce the threat posed by the waste.

(D) Whenever waste must be moved, one should limit the amount of time allotted to locating alternative waste storage sites.

(E) Any site to which the waste could be moved will be safer than its present site.

GO ON TO THE NEXT PAGE.

22. A recent survey indicates that the average number of books read annually per capita has declined in each of the last three years. However, it also found that most bookstores reported increased profits during the same period.

Each of the following, if true, helps to resolve the survey's apparently paradoxical results EXCEPT:

(A) Recent cutbacks in government spending have forced public libraries to purchase fewer popular contemporary novels.

(B) Due to the installation of sophisticated new antitheft equipment, the recent increase in shoplifting that has hit most retail businesses has left bookstores largely unaffected.

(C) Over the past few years many bookstores have capitalized on the lucrative coffee industry by installing coffee bars.

(D) Bookstore owners reported a general shift away from the sale of inexpensive paperback novels and toward the sale of lucrative hardback books.

(E) Citing a lack of free time, many survey respondents indicated that they had canceled magazine subscriptions in favor of purchasing individual issues at bookstores when time permits.

23. Naturalist: A species can survive a change in environment, as long as the change is not too rapid. Therefore, the threats we are creating to woodland species arise not from the fact that we are cutting down trees, but rather from the rate at which we are doing so.

The reasoning in which one of the following is most similar to that in the naturalist's argument?

(A) The problem with burning fossil fuels is that the supply is limited; so, the faster we expend these resources, the sooner we will be left without an energy source.

(B) Many people gain more satisfaction from performing a job well—regardless of whether they like the job—than from doing merely adequately a job they like; thus, people who want to be happy should choose jobs they can do well.

(C) Some students who study thoroughly do well in school. Thus, what is most important for success in school is not how much time a student puts into studying, but rather how thoroughly the student studies.

(D) People do not fear change if they know what the change will bring; so, our employees' fear stems not from our company's undergoing change, but from our failing to inform them of what the changes entail.

(E) Until ten years ago, we had good soil and our agriculture flourished. Therefore, the recent decline of our agriculture is a result of our soil rapidly eroding and there being nothing that can replace the good soil we lost.

GO ON TO THE NEXT PAGE.

24. Professor: A person who can select a beverage from among 50 varieties of cola is less free than one who has only these 5 choices: wine, coffee, apple juice, milk, and water. It is clear, then, that meaningful freedom cannot be measured simply by the number of alternatives available; the extent of the differences among the alternatives is also a relevant factor.

The professor's argument proceeds by

(A) supporting a general principle by means of an example
(B) drawing a conclusion about a particular case on the basis of a general principle
(C) supporting its conclusion by means of an analogy
(D) claiming that whatever holds for each member of a group must hold for the whole group
(E) inferring one general principle from another, more general, principle

25. Principle: Meetings should be kept short, addressing only those issues relevant to a majority of those attending. A person should not be required to attend a meeting if none of the issues to be addressed at the meeting are relevant to that person.

Application: Terry should not be required to attend today's two o'clock meeting.

Which one of the following, if true, most justifies the stated application of the principle?

(A) The only issues on which Terry could make a presentation at the meeting are issues irrelevant to at least a majority of those who could attend.
(B) If Terry makes a presentation at the meeting, the meeting will not be kept short.
(C) No issue relevant to Terry could be relevant to a majority of those attending the meeting.
(D) If Terry attends the meeting a different set of issues will be relevant to a majority of those attending than if Terry does not attend.
(E) The majority of the issues to be addressed at the meeting are not relevant to Terry.

S T O P

IF YOU FINISH BEFORE TIME IS CALLED, YOU MAY CHECK YOUR WORK ON THIS SECTION ONLY.
DO NOT WORK ON ANY OTHER SECTION IN THE TEST.

SECTION V

Time—35 minutes

27 Questions

<u>Directions:</u> Each set of questions in this section is based on a single passage or a pair of passages. The questions are to be answered on the basis of what is <u>stated</u> or <u>implied</u> in the passage or pair of passages. For some of the questions, more than one of the choices could conceivably answer the question. However, you are to choose the <u>best</u> answer; that is, the response that most accurately and completely answers the question, and blacken the corresponding space on your answer sheet.

Asian American poetry from Hawaii, the Pacific island state of the United States, is generally characterizable in one of two ways: either as portraying a model multicultural paradise, or as
(5) exemplifying familiar Asian American literary themes such as generational conflict. In this light, the recent work of Wing Tek Lum in *Expounding the Doubtful Points* is striking for its demand to be understood on its own terms. Lum offers no romanticized notions of
(10) multicultural life in Hawaii, and while he does explore themes of family, identity, history, and literary tradition, he does not do so at the expense of attempting to discover and retain a local sensibility. For Lum such a sensibility is informed by the fact
(15) that Hawaii's population, unlike that of the continental U.S., has historically consisted predominantly of people of Asian and Pacific island descent, making the experience of its Asian Americans somewhat different than that of mainland
(20) Asian Americans.

In one poem, Lum meditates on the ways in which a traditional Chinese lunar celebration he is attending at a local beach both connects him to and separates him from the past. In the company of new
(25) Chinese immigrants, the speaker realizes that while ties to the homeland are comforting and necessary, it is equally important to have "a sense of new family" in this new land of Hawaii, and hence a new identity—one that is sensitive to its new environment.
(30) The role of immigrants in this poem is significant in that, through their presence, Lum is able to refer both to the traditional culture of his ancestral homeland as well as to the flux within Hawaiian society that has been integral to its heterogeneity. Even in a laudatory
(35) poem to famous Chinese poet Li Po (701–762 A.D.), which partly serves to place Lum's work within a distinguished literary tradition, Lum refuses to offer a stereotypical nostalgia for the past, instead pointing out the often elitist tendencies inherent in the work of
(40) some traditionally acclaimed Chinese poets.

Lum closes his volume with a poem that further points to the complex relationships between heritage and local culture in determining one's identity. Pulling together images and figures as vastly
(45) disparate as a famous Chinese American literary character and an old woman selling bread, Lum avoids an excessively romantic vision of U.S. culture, while simultaneously acknowledging the dream of this culture held by many newly arrived immigrants.

(50) The central image of a communal pot where each person chooses what she or he wishes to eat but shares with others the "sweet soup / spooned out at the end of the meal" is a hopeful one; however, it also appears to caution that the strong cultural
(55) emphasis in the U.S. on individual drive and success that makes retaining a sense of homeland tradition difficult should be identified and responded to in ways that allow for a healthy new sense of identity to be formed.

1. Which one of the following most accurately expresses the main point of the passage?

(A) The poetry of Lum departs from other Asian American poetry from Hawaii in that it acknowledges its author's heritage but also expresses the poet's search for a new local identity.

(B) Lum's poetry is in part an expression of the conflict between a desire to participate in a community with shared traditions and values and a desire for individual success.

(C) Lum writes poetry that not only rejects features of the older literary tradition in which he participates but also rejects the popular literary traditions of Hawaiian writers.

(D) The poetry of Lum illustrates the extent to which Asian American writers living in Hawaii have a different cultural perspective than those living in the continental U.S.

(E) Lum's poetry is an unsuccessful attempt to manage the psychological burdens of reconciling a sense of tradition with a healthy sense of individual identity.

GO ON TO THE NEXT PAGE.

2. Given the information in the passage, which one of the following is Lum most likely to believe?

   (A) Images in a poem should be explained in that poem so that their meaning will be widely understood.
   (B) The experience of living away from one's homeland is necessary for developing a healthy perspective on one's cultural traditions.
   (C) It is important to reconcile the values of individual achievement and enterprise with the desire to retain one's cultural traditions.
   (D) One's identity is continually in transition and poetry is a way of developing a static identity.
   (E) One cannot both seek a new identity and remain connected to one's cultural traditions.

3. The author of the passage uses the phrase "the flux within Hawaiian society" (line 33) primarily in order to

   (A) describe the social tension created by the mix of attitudes exhibited by citizens of Hawaii
   (B) deny that Hawaiian society is culturally distinct from that of the continental U.S.
   (C) identify the process by which immigrants learn to adapt to their new communities
   (D) refer to the constant change to which the culture in Hawaii is subject due to its diverse population
   (E) emphasize the changing attitudes of many immigrants to Hawaii toward their traditional cultural norms

4. According to the passage, some Asian American literature from Hawaii has been characterized as which one of the following?

   (A) inimical to the process of developing a local sensibility
   (B) centered on the individual's drive to succeed
   (C) concerned with conflicts between different age groups
   (D) focused primarily on retaining ties to one's homeland
   (E) tied to a search for a new sense of family in a new land

5. The author of the passage describes *Expounding the Doubtful Points* as "striking" (lines 7–8) primarily in order to

   (A) underscore the forceful and contentious tone of the work
   (B) indicate that the work has not been properly analyzed by literary critics
   (C) stress the radical difference between this work and Lum's earlier work
   (D) emphasize the differences between this work and that of other Asian American poets from Hawaii
   (E) highlight the innovative nature of Lum's experiments with poetic form

6. With which one of the following statements regarding Lum's poetry would the author of the passage be most likely to agree?

   (A) It cannot be used to support any specific political ideology.
   (B) It is an elegant demonstration of the poet's appreciation of the stylistic contributions of his literary forebears.
   (C) It is most fruitfully understood as a meditation on the choice between new and old that confronts any human being in any culture.
   (D) It conveys thoughtful assessments of both his ancestral homeland tradition and the culture in which he is attempting to build a new identity.
   (E) It conveys Lum's antipathy toward tradition by juxtaposing traditional and nontraditional images.

GO ON TO THE NEXT PAGE.

In England the burden of history weighs heavily on common law, that unwritten code of time-honored laws derived largely from English judicial custom and precedent. Students of contemporary British law are
(5) frequently required to study medieval cases, to interpret archaic Latin maxims, or to confront doctrinal principles whose validity is based solely on their being part of the "timeless reason" of the English legal tradition. Centuries-old custom serves as
(10) the basis both for the divisions of law school subject matter and for much of the terminology of legal redress. Connected not only with legal history but also with the cultural history of the English people, common law cannot properly be understood without
(15) taking a long historical view.

Yet the academic study of jurisprudence has seldom treated common law as a constantly evolving phenomenon rooted in history; those interpretive theories that do acknowledge the antiquity of
(20) common law ignore the practical contemporary significance of its historical forms. The reasons for this omission are partly theoretical and partly political. In theoretical terms, modern jurisprudence has consistently treated law as a unified system of
(25) rules that can be studied at any given moment in time as a logical whole. The notion of jurisprudence as a system of norms or principles deemphasizes history in favor of the coherence of a system. In this view, the past of the system is conceived as no more than
(30) the continuous succession of its states of presence. In political terms, believing in the logic of law is a necessary part of believing in its fairness; even if history shows the legal tradition to be far from unitary and seldom logical, the prestige of the legal
(35) institution requires that jurisprudence treat the tradition as if it were, in essence, the application of known rules to objectively determined facts. To suggest otherwise would be dispiriting for the student and demoralizing for the public.
(40) Legal historian Peter Goodrich has argued, however, that common law is most fruitfully studied as a continually developing tradition rather than as a set of rules. Taking his cue from the study of literature, Goodrich sees common law as a sort of
(45) literary text, with history and tradition serving as the text's narrative development. To study the common law historically, says Goodrich, is to study a text in which fiction is as influential as analysis, perception as significant as rule, and the play of memory as
(50) strong as the logic of argument. The concept of tradition, for Goodrich, implies not only the preservation and transmission of existing forms, but also the continuous rewriting of those forms to adapt them to contemporary legal circumstances.

7. Which one of the following statements best expresses the main idea of the passage?

(A) The residual influences of common law explain not only the divisions of subject matter but also the terminology associated with many legal procedures.

(B) In the academic study of jurisprudence, theoretical interpretations of common law have traditionally been at odds with political interpretations of common law.

(C) Common law, while often treated as an oral history of the English people, would, according to one scholar, be more fruitfully studied as a universally adaptable and constantly changing system of rules.

(D) Although obviously steeped in history and tradition, common law has seldom been studied in relation to its development, as one theorist proposes that it be understood.

(E) Although usually studied as a unitary and logical system of rules and norms, the history of common law shows that body of law to be anything but consistent and fair.

8. It can be inferred that the author of the passage believes which one of the following about the history of law in relation to modern jurisprudence?

(A) Modern jurisprudence misinterprets the nature of the legal tradition.

(B) The history of law proves the original forms of common law to be antiquated and irrelevant to modern jurisprudence.

(C) The history of law, if it is to be made applicable to modern jurisprudence, is best studied as a system of rules rather than as a literary text.

(D) Mainstream theories of modern jurisprudence overlook the order and coherence inherent in legal history.

(E) Mainstream theories of modern jurisprudence, by and large devoid of a sense of legal history, are unnecessarily dispiriting to students and the public alike.

GO ON TO THE NEXT PAGE.

9. Which one of the following would best exemplify the kind of interpretive theory referred to in the first sentence of the second paragraph of the passage?

(A) a theory that traced modern customs involving property ownership to their origins in medieval practice

(B) a theory that relied on a comparison between modern courtroom procedures and medieval theatrical conventions

(C) a theory that analyzed medieval marriage laws without examining their relationship to modern laws

(D) a theory that compared the development of English common law in the twentieth century with simultaneous developments in German common law without examining the social repercussions of either legal system

(E) a theory that compared rules of evidence in civil courts with those in criminal courts

10. It can be inferred from the passage that Peter Goodrich would be most likely to agree with which one of the following statements concerning common law?

(A) Common law is more fruitfully studied as a relic of the history of the English people than as a legal code.

(B) The "text" of common law has degenerated from an early stage of clarity to a current state of incoherence.

(C) Without the public's belief in the justness of common law, the legal system cannot be perpetuated.

(D) While rich in literary significance, the "text" of common law has only a very limited applicability to modern life.

(E) The common law "text" inherited by future generations will differ from the one currently in use.

11. Which one of the following best defines the word "political" as it is used in the second paragraph of the passage?

(A) concerned with the ways by which people seek to advance themselves in a profession

(B) concerned with the covert and possibly unethical methods by which governments achieve their goals

(C) having to do with the maintenance of ethical standards between professions and the citizenry

(D) having to do with the maintenance of an institution's effectiveness

(E) having to do with the manner in which institutions are perceived by radical theorists

12. The passage states that students of British law are frequently required to study

(A) histories of English politics
(B) episodes of litigation from the Middle Ages
(C) treatises on political philosophy
(D) histories of ancient Roman jurisprudence
(E) essays on narrative development

13. Which one of the following best describes the author's opinion of most modern academic theories of common law?

(A) They are overly detailed and thus stultifying to both the student and the public.

(B) They lack an essential dimension that would increase their accuracy.

(C) They overemphasize the practical aspects of the common law at the expense of the theoretical.

(D) They excuse students of the law from the study of important legal disputes of the past.

(E) They routinely treat the study of the law as an art rather than as a science.

14. The primary purpose of the passage is to

(A) explain a paradoxical situation and discuss a new view of the situation

(B) supply a chronological summary of the history of an idea

(C) trace the ideas of an influential theorist and evaluate the theorist's ongoing work

(D) contrast the legal theories of past eras with those of today and suggest how these theories should be studied

(E) advocate a traditional school of thought while criticizing a new trend

GO ON TO THE NEXT PAGE.

The passages discuss relationships between business interests and university research.

Passage A

As university researchers working in a "gift economy" dedicated to collegial sharing of ideas, we have long been insulated from market pressures. The recent tendency to treat research findings as
(5) commodities, tradable for cash, threatens this tradition and the role of research as a public good.

The nurseries for new ideas are traditionally universities, which provide an environment uniquely suited to the painstaking testing and revision of
(10) theories. Unfortunately, the market process and values governing commodity exchange are ill suited to the cultivation and management of new ideas. With their shareholders impatient for quick returns, businesses are averse to wide-ranging experimentation. And, what
(15) is even more important, few commercial enterprises contain the range of expertise needed to handle the replacement of shattered theoretical frameworks.

Further, since entrepreneurs usually have little affinity for adventure of the intellectual sort, they can
(20) buy research and bury its products, hiding knowledge useful to society or to their competitors. The growth of industrial biotechnology, for example, has been accompanied by a reduction in the free sharing of research methods and results—a high price to pay for
(25) the undoubted benefits of new drugs and therapies.

Important new experimental results once led university scientists to rush down the hall and share their excitement with colleagues. When instead the rush is to patent lawyers and venture capitalists, I
(30) worry about the long-term future of scientific discovery.

Passage B

The fruits of pure science were once considered primarily a public good, available for society as a whole. The argument for this view was that most of
(35) these benefits were produced through government support of universities, and thus no individual was entitled to restrict access to them.

Today, however, the critical role of science in the modern "information economy" means that what was
(40) previously seen as a public good is being transformed into a market commodity. For example, by exploiting the information that basic research has accumulated about the detailed structures of cells and genes, the biotechnology industry can derive profitable
(45) pharmaceuticals or medical screening technologies. In this context, assertion of legal claims to "intellectual property"—not just in commercial products but in the underlying scientific knowledge—becomes crucial.

Previously, the distinction between a scientific
(50) "discovery" (which could not be patented) and a technical "invention" (which could) defined the limits of industry's ability to patent something. Today, however, the speed with which scientific discoveries can be turned into products and the large profits
(55) resulting from this transformation have led to a blurring of both the legal distinction between discovery and invention and the moral distinction between what should and should not be patented.

Industry argues that if it has supported—either in
(60) its own laboratories or in a university—the makers of a scientific discovery, then it is entitled to seek a return on its investment, either by charging others for using the discovery or by keeping it for its own exclusive use.

15. Which one of the following is discussed in passage B but not in passage A?

(A) the blurring of the legal distinction between discovery and invention
(B) the general effects of the market on the exchange of scientific knowledge
(C) the role of scientific research in supplying public goods
(D) new pharmaceuticals that result from industrial research
(E) industry's practice of restricting access to research findings

16. Both passages place in opposition the members of which one of the following pairs?

(A) commercially successful research and commercially unsuccessful research
(B) research methods and research results
(C) a marketable commodity and a public good
(D) a discovery and an invention
(E) scientific research and other types of inquiry

GO ON TO THE NEXT PAGE.

17. Both passages refer to which one of the following?

    (A) theoretical frameworks
    (B) venture capitalists
    (C) physics and chemistry
    (D) industrial biotechnology
    (E) shareholders

18. It can be inferred from the passages that the authors believe that the increased constraint on access to scientific information and ideas arises from

    (A) the enormous increase in the volume of scientific knowledge that is being generated
    (B) the desire of individual researchers to receive credit for their discoveries
    (C) the striving of commercial enterprises to gain a competitive advantage in the market
    (D) moral reservations about the social impact of some scientific research
    (E) a drastic reduction in government funding for university research

19. Which one of the following statements is most strongly supported by both passages?

    (A) Many scientific researchers who previously worked in universities have begun to work in the biotechnology industry.
    (B) Private biotechnology companies have invalidly patented the basic research findings of university researchers.
    (C) Because of the nature of current scientific research, patent authorities no longer consider the distinction between discoveries and inventions to be clear-cut.
    (D) In the past, scientists working in industry had free access to the results of basic research conducted in universities.
    (E) Government-funded research in universities has traditionally been motivated by the goals of private industry.

GO ON TO THE NEXT PAGE.

Sometimes there is no more effective means of controlling an agricultural pest than giving free rein to its natural predators. A case in point is the cyclamen mite, a pest whose population can be
(5) effectively controlled by a predatory mite of the genus *Typhlodromus*. Cyclamen mites infest strawberry plants; they typically establish themselves in a strawberry field shortly after planting, but their populations do not reach significantly damaging
(10) levels until the plants' second year. *Typhlodromus* mites usually invade the strawberry fields during the second year, rapidly subdue the cyclamen mite populations, and keep them from reaching significantly damaging levels.

(15)   *Typhlodromus* owes its effectiveness as a predator to several factors in addition to its voracious appetite. Its population can increase as rapidly as that of its prey. Both species reproduce by parthenogenesis—a mode of reproduction in which unfertilized eggs
(20) develop into fertile females. Cyclamen mites lay three eggs per day over the four or five days of their reproductive life span; *Typhlodromus* lay two or three eggs per day for eight to ten days. Seasonal synchrony of *Typhlodromus* reproduction with the
(25) growth of prey populations and ability to survive at low prey densities also contribute to the predatory efficiency of *Typhlodromus*. During winter, when cyclamen mite populations dwindle to a few individuals hidden in the crevices and folds of leaves
(30) in the crowns of the strawberry plants, the predatory mites subsist on the honeydew produced by aphids and white flies. They do not reproduce except when they are feeding on the cyclamen mites. These features, which make *Typhlodromus* well-suited for
(35) exploiting the seasonal rises and falls of its prey, are common among predators that control prey populations.

     Greenhouse experiments have verified the importance of *Typhlodromus* predation for keeping
(40) cyclamen mites in check. One group of strawberry plants was stocked with both predator and prey mites; a second group was kept predator-free by regular application of parathion, an insecticide that kills the predatory species but does not affect the cyclamen
(45) mite. Throughout the study, populations of cyclamen mites remained low in plots shared with *Typhlodromus*, but their infestation attained significantly damaging proportions on predator-free plants.

(50)   Applying parathion in this instance is a clear case in which using a pesticide would do far more harm than good to an agricultural enterprise. The results were similar in field plantings of strawberries, where cyclamen mites also reached damaging levels when
(55) predators were eliminated by parathion, but they did not attain such levels in untreated plots. When cyclamen mite populations began to increase in an untreated planting, the predator populations quickly responded to reduce the outbreak. On average,
(60) cyclamen mites were about 25 times more abundant in the absence of predators than in their presence.

20. Which one of the following most accurately expresses the main point of the passage?

(A)   Control of agricultural pests is most effectively and safely accomplished without the use of pesticides, because these pesticides can kill predators that also control the pests.

(B)   Experimental verification is essential in demonstrating the effectiveness of natural controls of agricultural pests.

(C)   The relationship between *Typhlodromus* and cyclamen mites demonstrates how natural predation can keep a population of agricultural pests in check.

(D)   Predation by *Typhlodromus* is essential for the control of cyclamen mite populations in strawberry fields.

(E)   Similarity in mode and timing of reproduction is what enables *Typhlodromus* effectively to control populations of cyclamen mites in fields of strawberry plants.

21. Based on the passage, the author would probably hold that which one of the following principles is fundamental to long-term predatory control of agricultural pests?

(A)   The reproduction of the predator population should be synchronized with that of the prey population, so that the number of predators surges just prior to a surge in prey numbers.

(B)   The effectiveness of the predatory relationship should be experimentally demonstrable in greenhouse as well as field applications.

(C)   The prey population should be able to survive in times of low crop productivity, so that the predator population will not decrease to very low levels.

(D)   The predator population's level of consumption of the prey species should be responsive to variations in the size of the prey population.

(E)   The predator population should be vulnerable only to pesticides to which the prey population is also vulnerable.

22. Which one of the following is mentioned in the passage as a factor contributing to the effectiveness of *Typhlodromus* as a predator?

(A)   its ability to withstand most insecticides except parathion

(B)   its lack of natural predators in strawberry fields

(C)   its ability to live in different climates in different geographic regions

(D)   its constant food supply in cyclamen mite populations

(E)   its ability to survive when few prey are available

GO ON TO THE NEXT PAGE.

23. Suppose that pesticide X drastically slows the reproductive rate of cyclamen mites and has no other direct effect on cyclamen mites or *Typhlodromus*. Based on the information in the passage, which one of the following would most likely have occurred if, in the experiments mentioned in the passage, pesticide X had been used instead of parathion, with all other conditions affecting the experiments remaining the same?

    (A) In both treated and untreated plots inhabited by both *Typhlodromus* and cyclamen mites, the latter would have been effectively controlled.
    (B) Cyclamen mite populations in all treated plots from which *Typhlodromus* was absent would have been substantially lower than in untreated plots inhabited by both kinds of mites.
    (C) In the treated plots, slowed reproduction in cyclamen mites would have led to a loss of reproductive synchrony between *Typhlodromus* and cyclamen mites.
    (D) In the treated plots, *Typhlodromus* populations would have decreased temporarily and would have eventually increased.
    (E) In the treated plots, cyclamen mite populations would have reached significantly damaging levels more slowly, but would have remained at those levels longer, than in untreated plots.

24. It can be inferred from the passage that the author would be most likely to agree with which one of the following statements about the use of predators to control pest populations?

    (A) If the use of predators to control cyclamen mite populations fails, then parathion should be used to control these populations.
    (B) Until the effects of the predators on beneficial insects that live in strawberry fields are assessed, such predators should be used with caution to control cyclamen mite populations.
    (C) Insecticides should be used to control certain pest populations in fields of crops only if the use of natural predators has proven inadequate.
    (D) If an insecticide can effectively control pest populations as well as predator populations, then it should be used instead of predators to control pest populations.
    (E) Predators generally control pest populations more effectively than pesticides because they do not harm the crops that their prey feed on.

25. The author mentions the egg-laying ability of each kind of mite (lines 20–23) primarily in order to support which one of the following claims?

    (A) Mites that reproduce by parthenogenesis do so at approximately equal rates.
    (B) Predatory mites typically have a longer reproductive life span than do cyclamen mites.
    (C) *Typhlodromus* can lay their eggs in synchrony with cyclamen mites.
    (D) *Typhlodromus* can reproduce at least as quickly as cyclamen mites.
    (E) The egg-laying rate of *Typhlodromus* is slower in the presence of cyclamen mites than it is in their absence.

26. Which one of the following would, if true, most strengthen the author's position regarding the practical applicability of the information about predatory mites presented in the passage?

    (A) The individual *Typhlodromus* mites that have the longest reproductive life spans typically also lay the greatest number of eggs per day.
    (B) The insecticides that are typically used for mite control on strawberry plants kill both predatory and nonpredatory species of mites.
    (C) In areas in which strawberry plants become infested by cyclamen mites, winters tend to be short and relatively mild.
    (D) *Typhlodromus* are sometimes preyed upon by another species of mites that is highly susceptible to parathion.
    (E) *Typhlodromus* easily tolerate the same range of climatic conditions that strawberry plants do.

27. Information in the passage most strongly supports which one of the following statements?

    (A) Strawberry crops can support populations of both cyclamen mites and *Typhlodromus* mites without significant damage to those crops.
    (B) For control of cyclamen mites by another mite species to be effective, it is crucial that the two species have the same mode of reproduction.
    (C) Factors that make *Typhlodromus* effective against cyclamen mites also make it effective against certain other pests of strawberry plants.
    (D) When *Typhlodromus* is relied on to control cyclamen mites in strawberry crops, pesticides may be necessary to prevent significant damage during the first year.
    (E) Strawberry growers have unintentionally caused cyclamen mites to become a serious crop pest by the indiscriminate use of parathion.

S T O P

IF YOU FINISH BEFORE TIME IS CALLED, YOU MAY CHECK YOUR WORK ON THIS SECTION ONLY.
DO NOT WORK ON ANY OTHER SECTION IN THE TEST.

Acknowledgment is made to the following sources from which material has been adapted for use in this test booklet:

Brenda Kwon, review of *Expanding the Doubtful Points* by Wing Tek Lum. ©1995 by the Regents of the University of California.

Robert E. Ricklefs and Gary L. Miller, *Ecology*, Third Edition. ©1990 by W.H. Freeman and Company.

Edward Rothstein, *Emblems of Mind*. ©1995 by Edward Rothstein.

Wait for the supervisor's instructions before you open the page to the topic.
Please print and sign your name and write the date in the designated spaces below.

Time: 35 Minutes

General Directions

You will have 35 minutes in which to plan and write an essay on the topic inside. Read the topic and the accompanying directions carefully. You will probably find it best to spend a few minutes considering the topic and organizing your thoughts before you begin writing. In your essay, be sure to develop your ideas fully, leaving time, if possible, to review what you have written. **Do not write on a topic other than the one specified. Writing on a topic of your own choice is not acceptable.**

No special knowledge is required or expected for this writing exercise. Law schools are interested in the reasoning, clarity, organization, language usage, and writing mechanics displayed in your essay. How well you write is more important than how much you write.

Confine your essay to the blocked, lined area on the front and back of the separate Writing Sample Response Sheet. Only that area will be reproduced for law schools. Be sure that your writing is legible.

Both this topic sheet and your response sheet must be turned over to the testing staff before you leave the room.

Topic Code	Print Your Full Name Here		
_____	Last	First	M.I.

Date	Sign Your Name Here
/ /	

Scratch Paper
Do not write your essay in this space.

LSAT Writing Sample Topic

Dennis, a photographer and local historian, has been commissioned to write a book about the preservation of photographs. He has worked out two different approaches to completing the book, which must be finished in two years. Using the facts below, write an essay in which you argue for one approach over the other based on the following two criteria:

- Dennis would like to improve his knowledge of photographic preservation through practical, hands-on experience.
- Dennis wants to produce a draft of the book as soon as possible.

One approach is for Dennis to take a two-year, part-time position at the photographic archives of a prestigious portrait gallery. He would help people locate visual images for publication, exhibition, research, or personal use from the archives. He would also perform various administrative tasks. Over the two-year period, Dennis would learn a great deal about the methodologies and techniques relating to photographic preservation through routine contact with professional archivists and visiting researchers. He would also enjoy extensive access to the portrait gallery's resources during that time.

Alternatively, Dennis can take a one-year, full-time position with the local public archives, which has a vast collection of photographs from the surrounding region dating back to 1865. Dennis would be helping to complete the cataloging and scanning of those photographs for inclusion in an online system. His extensive responsibilities would include entering historic photographs into a web-based database, determining the street address or location of scenes depicted in the photographs, transferring historic photographic negatives to acid-free storage, and retouching scanned images. He would work alongside skilled archivists and would gain a working knowledge of photographic conservation-preservation procedures.

Scratch Paper
Do not write your essay in this space.

Writing Sample Response Sheet

DO NOT WRITE IN THIS SPACE

**Begin your essay in the lined area below.
Continue on the back if you need more space.**

Directions:

1. Use the Answer Key on the next page to check your answers.

2. Use the Scoring Worksheet below to compute your raw score.

3. Use the Score Conversion Chart to convert your raw score into the 120–180 scale.

Scoring Worksheet

1. Enter the number of questions you answered correctly in each section

	Number Correct
SECTION I	_____
SECTION II	_____
SECTION III	__EXP__
SECTION IV	_____
SECTION V	_____

2. Enter the sum here: _____

   This is your Raw Score.

Conversion Chart

For Converting Raw Score to the 120–180 LSAT Scaled Score
LSAT PrepTest 53

Reported Score	Raw Score Lowest	Raw Score Highest
180	98	100
179	97	97
178	96	96
177	_*	_*
176	95	95
175	94	94
174	93	93
173	92	92
172	91	91
171	90	90
170	89	89
169	88	88
168	87	87
167	86	86
166	84	85
165	83	83
164	81	82
163	80	80
162	78	79
161	77	77
160	75	76
159	73	74
158	71	72
157	70	70
156	68	69
155	66	67
154	64	65
153	62	63
152	61	61
151	59	60
150	57	58
149	55	56
148	53	54
147	52	52
146	50	51
145	48	49
144	46	47
143	45	45
142	43	44
141	41	42
140	40	40
139	38	39
138	36	37
137	35	35
136	33	34
135	32	32
134	30	31
133	29	29
132	28	28
131	26	27
130	25	25
129	24	24
128	22	23
127	21	21
126	20	20
125	19	19
124	18	18
123	17	17
122	16	16
121	15	15
120	0	14

*There is no raw score that will produce this scaled score for this form.

SECTION I

1.	C	8.	D	15.	B	22.	E
2.	B	9.	A	16.	E	23.	D
3.	B	10.	D	17.	B	24.	D
4.	A	11.	D	18.	B	25.	B
5.	E	12.	C	19.	A		
6.	A	13.	A	20.	C		
7.	A	14.	D	21.	A		

SECTION II

1.	B	8.	A	15.	E	22.	E
2.	A	9.	D	16.	A	23.	B
3.	B	10.	C	17.	D		
4.	B	11.	B	18.	E		
5.	C	12.	B	19.	A		
6.	C	13.	E	20.	B		
7.	A	14.	A	21.	C		

SECTION III (experimental)

1.	B	8.	C	15.	A	22.	D
2.	C	9.	D	16.	C	23.	D
3.	A	10.	C	17.	E	24.	B
4.	B	11.	C	18.	E	25.	D
5.	A	12.	A	19.	E		
6.	C	13.	D	20.	B		
7.	B	14.	E	21.	A		

SECTION IV

1.	A	8.	A	15.	E	22.	B
2.	C	9.	E	16.	B	23.	D
3.	E	10.	B	17.	A	24.	A
4.	A	11.	C	18.	E	25.	C
5.	E	12.	B	19.	A		
6.	D	13.	B	20.	D		
7.	A	14.	A	21.	C		

SECTION V

1.	A	8.	A	15.	A	22.	E
2.	C	9.	C	16.	C	23.	A
3.	D	10.	E	17.	D	24.	C
4.	C	11.	D	18.	C	25.	D
5.	D	12.	B	19.	D	26.	E
6.	D	13.	B	20.	C	27.	A
7.	D	14.	A	21.	D		

Endurance Practice Test 4

**PrepTest 52 plus experimental
from PrepTest 32, Section II**

SECTION I

Time—35 minutes

25 Questions

Directions: The questions in this section are based on the reasoning contained in brief statements or passages. For some questions, more than one of the choices could conceivably answer the question. However, you are to choose the best answer; that is, the response that most accurately and completely answers the question. You should not make assumptions that are by commonsense standards implausible, superfluous, or incompatible with the passage. After you have chosen the best answer, blacken the corresponding space on your answer sheet.

1. Certain companies require their managers to rank workers in the groups they supervise from best to worst, giving each worker a unique ranking based on job performance. The top 10 percent of the workers in each group are rewarded and the bottom 10 percent are penalized or fired. But this system is unfair to workers. Good workers could receive low rankings merely because they belong to groups of exceptionally good workers. Furthermore, managers often give the highest rankings to workers who share the manager's interests outside of work.

    Which one of the following most accurately expresses the conclusion drawn in the argument?

    (A) Some companies require their managers to give unique rankings to the workers they supervise.
    (B) Under the ranking system, the top 10 percent of the workers in each group are rewarded and the bottom 10 percent are penalized or fired.
    (C) The ranking system is not a fair way to determine penalties or rewards for workers.
    (D) Workers in exceptionally strong work groups are unfairly penalized under the ranking system.
    (E) Managers often give the highest rankings to workers who share the manager's outside interests.

2. Psychologist: A study of 436 university students found that those who took short naps throughout the day suffered from insomnia more frequently than those who did not. Moreover, people who work on commercial fishing vessels often have irregular sleep patterns that include frequent napping, and they also suffer from insomnia. So it is very likely that napping tends to cause insomnia.

    The reasoning in the psychologist's argument is most vulnerable to criticism on the grounds that the argument

    (A) presumes, without providing justification, that university students suffer from insomnia more frequently than do members of the general population
    (B) presumes that all instances of insomnia have the same cause
    (C) fails to provide a scientifically respectable definition for the term "napping"
    (D) fails to consider the possibility that frequent daytime napping is an effect rather than a cause of insomnia
    (E) presumes, without providing justification, that there is such a thing as a regular sleep pattern for someone working on a commercial fishing vessel

GO ON TO THE NEXT PAGE.

3. Whenever Joe's car is vacuemed, the employees of K & L Auto vacuum it; they are the only people who ever vacuum Joe's car. If the employees of K & L Auto vacuemed Joe's car, then Joe took his car to K & L Auto to be fixed. Joe's car was recently vacuemed. Therefore, Joe took his car to K & L Auto to be fixed.

The pattern of reasoning exhibited by the argument above is most similar to that exhibited by which one of the following?

(A) Emily's water glass is wet and it would be wet only if she drank water from it this morning. Since the only time she drinks water in the morning is when she takes her medication, Emily took her medication this morning.

(B) Lisa went to the hair salon today since either she went to the hair salon today or she went to the bank this morning, but Lisa did not go to the bank this morning.

(C) There are no bills on John's kitchen table. Since John gets at least one bill per day and he always puts his bills on his kitchen table, someone else must have checked John's mail today.

(D) Linda is grumpy only if she does not have her coffee in the morning, and Linda does not have her coffee in the morning only if she runs out of coffee. Therefore, Linda runs out of coffee only on days that she is grumpy.

(E) Jeff had to choose either a grapefruit or cereal for breakfast this morning. Given that Jeff is allergic to grapefruit, Jeff must have had cereal for breakfast this morning.

4. Editorialist: In a large corporation, one of the functions of the corporation's president is to promote the key interests of the shareholders. Therefore, the president has a duty to keep the corporation's profits high.

Which one of the following, if true, would most strengthen the editorialist's argument?

(A) Shareholders sometimes will be satisfied even if dividends paid to them from company profits are not high.

(B) The president and the board of directors of a corporation are jointly responsible for advancing the key interests of the shareholders.

(C) Keeping a corporation's profits high is likely to advance the important interests of the corporation's shareholders.

(D) In considering where to invest, most potential shareholders are interested in more than just the profitability of a corporation.

(E) The president of a corporation has many functions besides advancing the important interests of the corporation's shareholders.

5. Everyone in Biba's neighborhood is permitted to swim at Barton Pool at some time during each day that it is open. No children under the age of 6 are permitted to swim at Barton Pool between noon and 5 P.M. From 5 P.M. until closing, Barton Pool is reserved for adults only.

If all the sentences above are true, then which one of the following must be true?

(A) Few children under the age of 6 live in Biba's neighborhood.

(B) If Biba's next-door neighbor has a child under the age of 6, then Barton Pool is open before noon.

(C) If most children who swim in Barton Pool swim in the afternoon, then the pool is generally less crowded after 5 P.M.

(D) On days when Barton Pool is open, at least some children swim there in the afternoon.

(E) Any child swimming in Barton Pool before 5 P.M. must be breaking Barton Pool rules.

6. Beck: Our computer program estimates municipal automotive use based on weekly data. Some staff question the accuracy of the program's estimates. But because the figures it provides are remarkably consistent from week to week, we can be confident of its accuracy.

The reasoning in Beck's argument is flawed in that it

(A) fails to establish that consistency is a more important consideration than accuracy

(B) fails to consider the program's accuracy in other tasks that it may perform

(C) takes for granted that the program's output would be consistent even if its estimates were inaccurate

(D) regards accuracy as the sole criterion for judging the program's value

(E) fails to consider that the program could produce consistent but inaccurate output

GO ON TO THE NEXT PAGE.

7. Inertia affects the flow of water pumped through a closed system of pipes. When the pump is first switched on, the water, which has mass, takes time to reach full speed. When the pump is switched off, inertia causes the decrease in the water flow to be gradual. The effects of inductance in electrical circuits are similar to the effects of inertia in water pipes.

The information above provides the most support for which one of the following?

(A) The rate at which electrical current flows is affected by inductance.
(B) The flow of electrical current in a circuit requires inertia.
(C) Inertia in the flow of water pumped by an electrically powered pump is caused by inductance in the pump's circuits.
(D) Electrical engineers try to minimize the effects of inductance in electrical circuits.
(E) When a water pump is switched off it continues to pump water for a second or two.

8. Journalist: To reconcile the need for profits sufficient to support new drug research with the moral imperative to provide medicines to those who most need them but cannot afford them, some pharmaceutical companies feel justified in selling a drug in rich nations at one price and in poor nations at a much lower price. But this practice is unjustified. A nation with a low average income may still have a substantial middle class better able to pay for new drugs than are many of the poorer citizens of an overall wealthier nation.

Which one of the following principles, if valid, most helps to justify the journalist's reasoning?

(A) People who are ill deserve more consideration than do healthy people, regardless of their relative socioeconomic positions.
(B) Wealthy institutions have an obligation to expend at least some of their resources to assist those incapable of assisting themselves.
(C) Whether one deserves special consideration depends on one's needs rather than on characteristics of the society to which one belongs.
(D) The people in wealthy nations should not have better access to health care than do the people in poorer nations.
(E) Unequal access to health care is more unfair than an unequal distribution of wealth.

9. Robert: The school board is considering adopting a year-round academic schedule that eliminates the traditional three-month summer vacation. This schedule should be adopted, since teachers need to cover more new material during the school year than they do now.

Samantha: The proposed schedule will not permit teachers to cover more new material. Even though the schedule eliminates summer vacation, it adds six new two-week breaks, so the total number of school days will be about the same as before.

Which one of the following, if true, is a response Robert could make that would counter Samantha's argument?

(A) Teachers would be willing to accept elimination of the traditional three-month summer vacation as long as the total vacation time they are entitled to each year is not reduced.
(B) Most parents who work outside the home find it difficult to arrange adequate supervision for their school-age children over the traditional three-month summer vacation.
(C) In school districts that have adopted a year-round schedule that increases the number of school days per year, students show a deeper understanding and better retention of new material.
(D) Teachers spend no more than a day of class time reviewing old material when students have been away from school for only a few weeks, but have to spend up to a month of class time reviewing after a three-month summer vacation.
(E) Students prefer taking a long vacation from school during the summer to taking more frequent but shorter vacations spread throughout the year.

GO ON TO THE NEXT PAGE.

10. In order to reduce traffic congestion and raise revenue for the city, the mayor plans to implement a charge of $10 per day for driving in the downtown area. Payment of this charge will be enforced using a highly sophisticated system that employs digital cameras and computerized automobile registration. This system will not be ready until the end of next year. Without this system, however, mass evasion of the charge will result. Therefore, when the mayor's plan is first implemented, payment of the charge will not be effectively enforced.

Which one of the following is an assumption on which the argument depends for its conclusion to be properly drawn?

(A) The mayor's plan to charge for driving downtown will be implemented before the end of next year.
(B) The city will incur a budget deficit if it does not receive the revenue it expects to raise from the charge for driving downtown.
(C) The plan to charge for driving downtown should be implemented as soon as payment of the charge can be effectively enforced.
(D) Raising revenue is a more important consideration for the city than is reducing traffic congestion.
(E) A daily charge for driving downtown is the most effective way to reduce traffic congestion.

11. A recent study revealed that the percentage of people treated at large, urban hospitals who recover from their illnesses is lower than the percentage for people treated at smaller, rural hospitals.

Each of the following, if true, contributes to an explanation of the difference in recovery rates EXCEPT:

(A) Because there are fewer patients to feed, nutritionists at small hospitals are better able to tailor meals to the dietary needs of each patient.
(B) The less friendly, more impersonal atmosphere of large hospitals can be a source of stress for patients at those hospitals.
(C) Although large hospitals tend to draw doctors trained at the more prestigious schools, no correlation has been found between the prestige of a doctor's school and patients' recovery rate.
(D) Because space is relatively scarce in large hospitals, doctors are encouraged to minimize the length of time that patients are held for observation following a medical procedure.
(E) Doctors at large hospitals tend to have a greater number of patients and consequently less time to explain to staff and to patients how medications are to be administered.

12. Perry: Worker-owned businesses require workers to spend time on management decision-making and investment strategy, tasks that are not directly productive. Also, such businesses have less extensive divisions of labor than do investor-owned businesses. Such inefficiencies can lead to low profitability, and thus increase the risk for lenders. Therefore, lenders seeking to reduce their risk should not make loans to worker-owned businesses.

Which one of the following, if true, most seriously weakens Perry's argument?

(A) Businesses with the most extensive divisions of labor sometimes fail to make the fullest use of their most versatile employees' potential.
(B) Lenders who specialize in high-risk loans are the largest source of loans for worker-owned businesses.
(C) Investor-owned businesses are more likely than worker-owned businesses are to receive start-up loans.
(D) Worker-owned businesses have traditionally obtained loans from cooperative lending institutions established by coalitions of worker-owned businesses.
(E) In most worker-owned businesses, workers compensate for inefficiencies by working longer hours than do workers in investor-owned businesses.

13. Some paleontologists believe that certain species of dinosaurs guarded their young in protective nests long after the young hatched. As evidence, they cite the discovery of fossilized hadrosaur babies and adolescents in carefully designed nests. But similar nests for hatchlings and adolescents are constructed by modern crocodiles, even though crocodiles guard their young only for a very brief time after they hatch. Hence, _____.

Which one of the following most logically completes the argument?

(A) paleontologists who believe that hadrosaurs guarded their young long after the young hatched have no evidence to support this belief
(B) we will never be able to know the extent to which hadrosaurs guarded their young
(C) hadrosaurs guarded their young for at most very brief periods after hatching
(D) it is unclear whether what we learn about hadrosaurs from their fossilized remains tells us anything about other dinosaurs
(E) the construction of nests for hatchlings and adolescents is not strong evidence for the paleontologists' belief

GO ON TO THE NEXT PAGE.

14. For one academic year all the students at a high school were observed. The aim was to test the hypothesis that studying more increased a student's chances of earning a higher grade. It turned out that the students who spent the most time studying did not earn grades as high as did many students who studied less. Nonetheless, the researchers concluded that the results of the observation supported the initial hypothesis.

Which one of the following, if true, most helps to explain why the researchers drew the conclusion described above?

(A) The students who spent the most time studying earned higher grades than did some students who studied for less time than the average.

(B) The students tended to get slightly lower grades as the academic year progressed.

(C) In each course, the more a student studied, the better his or her grade was in that course.

(D) The students who spent the least time studying tended to be students with no more than average involvement in extracurricular activities.

(E) Students who spent more time studying understood the course material better than other students did.

15. Researchers had three groups of professional cyclists cycle for one hour at different levels of intensity. Members of groups A, B, and C cycled at rates that sustained, for an hour, pulses of about 60 percent, 70 percent, and 85 percent, respectively, of the recommended maximum pulse rate for recreational cyclists. Most members of Group A reported being less depressed and angry afterward. Most members of Group B did not report these benefits. Most members of Group C reported feeling worse in these respects than before the exercise.

Which one of the following is most strongly supported by the information above?

(A) The higher the pulse rate attained in sustained exercise, the less psychological benefit the exercise tends to produce.

(B) The effect that a period of cycling has on the mood of professional cyclists tends to depend at least in part on how intense the cycling is.

(C) For professional cyclists, the best exercise from the point of view of improving mood is cycling that pushes the pulse no higher than 60 percent of the maximum pulse rate.

(D) Physical factors, including pulse rate, contribute as much to depression as do psychological factors.

(E) Moderate cycling tends to benefit professional cyclists physically as much or more than intense cycling.

16. Anyone who believes in extraterrestrials believes in UFOs. But the existence of UFOs has been conclusively refuted. Therefore a belief in extraterrestrials is false as well.

Which one of the following arguments contains flawed reasoning most similar to that in the argument above?

(A) Anyone who believes in unicorns believes in centaurs. But it has been demonstrated that there are no centaurs, so there are no unicorns either.

(B) Anyone who believes in unicorns believes in centaurs. But you do not believe in centaurs, so you do not believe in unicorns either.

(C) Anyone who believes in unicorns believes in centaurs. But you do not believe in unicorns, so you do not believe in centaurs either.

(D) Anyone who believes in unicorns believes in centaurs. But there is no good reason to believe in centaurs, so a belief in unicorns is unjustified as well.

(E) Anyone who believes in unicorns believes in centaurs. But it has been conclusively proven that there is no such thing as a unicorn, so a belief in centaurs is mistaken as well.

17. People want to be instantly and intuitively liked. Those persons who are perceived as forming opinions of others only after cautiously gathering and weighing the evidence are generally resented. Thus, it is imprudent to appear prudent.

Which one of the following, if assumed, enables the argument's conclusion to be properly drawn?

(A) People who act spontaneously are well liked.

(B) Imprudent people act instantly and intuitively.

(C) People resent those less prudent than themselves.

(D) People who are intuitive know instantly when they like someone.

(E) It is imprudent to cause people to resent you.

GO ON TO THE NEXT PAGE.

18. Journalist: Recent studies have demonstrated that a regular smoker who has just smoked a cigarette will typically display significantly better short-term memory skills than a nonsmoker, whether or not the nonsmoker has also just smoked a cigarette for the purposes of the study. Moreover, the majority of those smokers who exhibit this superiority in short-term memory skills will do so for at least eight hours after having last smoked.

If the journalist's statements are true, then each of the following could be true EXCEPT:

(A) The short-term memory skills exhibited by a nonsmoker who has just smoked a cigarette are usually substantially worse than the short-term memory skills exhibited by a nonsmoker who has not recently smoked a cigarette.

(B) The short-term memory skills exhibited by a nonsmoker who has just smoked a cigarette are typically superior to those exhibited by a regular smoker who has just smoked a cigarette.

(C) The short-term memory skills exhibited by a nonsmoker who has just smoked a cigarette are typically superior to those exhibited by a regular smoker who has not smoked for more than eight hours.

(D) A regular smoker who, immediately after smoking a cigarette, exhibits short-term memory skills no better than those typically exhibited by a nonsmoker is nevertheless likely to exhibit superior short-term memory skills in the hours following a period of heavy smoking.

(E) The short-term memory skills exhibited by a regular smoker who last smoked a cigarette five hours ago are typically superior to those exhibited by a regular smoker who has just smoked a cigarette.

19. Educator: It has been argued that our professional organization should make decisions about important issues—such as raising dues and taking political stands—by a direct vote of all members rather than by having members vote for officers who in turn make the decisions. This would not, however, be the right way to decide these matters, for the vote of any given individual is much more likely to determine organizational policy by influencing the election of an officer than by influencing the result of a direct vote on a single issue.

Which one of the following principles would, if valid, most help to justify the educator's reasoning?

(A) No procedure for making organizational decisions should allow one individual's vote to weigh more than that of another.

(B) Outcomes of organizational elections should be evaluated according to their benefit to the organization as a whole, not according to the fairness of the methods by which they are produced.

(C) Important issues facing organizations should be decided by people who can devote their full time to mastering the information relevant to the issues.

(D) An officer of an organization should not make a particular decision on an issue unless a majority of the organization's members would approve of that decision.

(E) An organization's procedures for making organizational decisions should maximize the power of each member of the organization to influence the decisions made.

GO ON TO THE NEXT PAGE.

20. Neural connections carrying signals from the cortex (the brain region responsible for thought) down to the amygdala (a brain region crucial for emotions) are less well developed than connections carrying signals from the amygdala up to the cortex. Thus, the amygdala exerts a greater influence on the cortex than vice versa.

The argument's conclusion follows logically if which one of the following is assumed?

(A) The influence that the amygdala exerts on the rest of the brain is dependent on the influence that the cortex exerts on the rest of the brain.

(B) No other brain region exerts more influence on the cortex than does the amygdala.

(C) The region of the brain that has the most influence on the cortex is the one that has the most highly developed neural connections to the cortex.

(D) The amygdala is not itself controlled by one or more other regions of the brain.

(E) The degree of development of a set of neural connections is directly proportional to the influence transmitted across those connections.

21. The *Iliad* and the *Odyssey* were both attributed to Homer in ancient times. But these two poems differ greatly in tone and vocabulary and in certain details of the fictional world they depict. So they are almost certainly not the work of the same poet.

Which one of the following statements, if true, most weakens the reasoning above?

(A) Several hymns that were also attributed to Homer in ancient times differ more from the *Iliad* in the respects mentioned than does the *Odyssey*.

(B) Both the *Iliad* and the *Odyssey* have come down to us in manuscripts that have suffered from minor copying errors and other textual corruptions.

(C) Works known to have been written by the same modern writer are as different from each other in the respects mentioned as are the *Iliad* and the *Odyssey*.

(D) Neither the *Iliad* nor the *Odyssey* taken by itself is completely consistent in all of the respects mentioned.

(E) Both the *Iliad* and the *Odyssey* were the result of an extended process of oral composition in which many poets were involved.

22. Moralist: A statement is wholly truthful only if it is true and made without intended deception. A statement is a lie if it is intended to deceive or if its speaker, upon learning that the statement was misinterpreted, refrains from clarifying it.

Which one of the following judgments most closely conforms to the principles stated by the moralist?

(A) Ted's statement to the investigator that he had been abducted by extraterrestrial beings was wholly truthful even though no one has ever been abducted by extraterrestrial beings. After all, Ted was not trying to deceive the investigator.

(B) Tony was not lying when he told his granddaughter that he did not wear dentures, for even though Tony meant to deceive his granddaughter, she made it clear to Tony that she did not believe him.

(C) Siobhan did not tell a lie when she told her supervisor that she was ill and hence would not be able to come to work for an important presentation. However, even though her statement was true, it was not wholly truthful.

(D) Walter's claim to a potential employer that he had done volunteer work was a lie. Even though Walter had worked without pay in his father's factory, he used the phrase "volunteer work" in an attempt to deceive the interviewer into thinking he had worked for a socially beneficial cause.

(E) The tour guide intended to deceive the tourists when he told them that the cabin they were looking at was centuries old. Still, his statement about the cabin's age was not a lie, for if he thought that this statement had been misinterpreted, he would have tried to clarify it.

GO ON TO THE NEXT PAGE.

23. Principle: It is healthy for children to engage in an activity that promotes their intellectual development only if engaging in that activity does not detract from their social development.

Application: Although Megan's frequent reading stimulates her intellectually, it reduces the amount of time she spends interacting with other people. Therefore, it is not healthy for her to read as much as she does.

The application of the principle is most vulnerable to criticism on which one of the following grounds?

(A) It misinterprets the principle as a universal claim intended to hold in all cases without exception, rather than as a mere generalization.

(B) It overlooks the possibility that the benefits of a given activity may sometimes be important enough to outweigh the adverse health effects.

(C) It misinterprets the principle to be, at least in part, a claim about what is unhealthy, rather than solely a claim about what is healthy.

(D) It takes for granted that any decrease in the amount of time a child spends interacting with others detracts from that child's social development.

(E) It takes a necessary condition for an activity's being healthy as a sufficient condition for its being so.

24. In response to several bacterial infections traced to its apple juice, McElligott now flash pasteurizes its apple juice by quickly heating and immediately rechilling it. Intensive pasteurization, in which juice is heated for an hour, eliminates bacteria more effectively than does any other method, but is likely to destroy the original flavor. However, because McElligott's citrus juices have not been linked to any bacterial infections, they remain unpasteurized.

The statements above, if true, provide the most support for which one of the following claims?

(A) McElligott's citrus juices contain fewer infectious bacteria than do citrus juices produced by other companies.

(B) McElligott's apple juice is less likely to contain infectious bacteria than are McElligott's citrus juices.

(C) McElligott's citrus juices retain more of the juices' original flavor than do any pasteurized citrus juices.

(D) The most effective method for eliminating bacteria from juice is also the method most likely to destroy flavor.

(E) Apple juice that undergoes intensive pasteurization is less likely than McElligott's apple juice is to contain bacteria.

25. Sociologist: Widespread acceptance of the idea that individuals are incapable of looking after their own welfare is injurious to a democracy. So legislators who value democracy should not propose any law prohibiting behavior that is not harmful to anyone besides the person engaging in it. After all, the assumptions that appear to guide legislators will often become widely accepted.

The sociologist's argument requires the assumption that

(A) democratically elected legislators invariably have favorable attitudes toward the preservation of democracy

(B) people tend to believe what is believed by those who are prominent and powerful

(C) legislators often seem to be guided by the assumption that individuals are incapable of looking after their own welfare, even though these legislators also seem to value democracy

(D) in most cases, behavior that is harmful to the person who engages in it is harmful to no one else

(E) a legislator proposing a law prohibiting an act that can harm only the person performing the act will seem to be assuming that individuals are incapable of looking after their own welfare

S T O P

IF YOU FINISH BEFORE TIME IS CALLED, YOU MAY CHECK YOUR WORK ON THIS SECTION ONLY.
DO NOT WORK ON ANY OTHER SECTION IN THE TEST.

SECTION II

Time—35 minutes

27 Questions

<u>Directions:</u> Each passage in this section is followed by a group of questions to be answered on the basis of what is <u>stated</u> or <u>implied</u> in the passage. For some of the questions, more than one of the choices could conceivably answer the question. However, you are to choose the <u>best</u> answer; that is, the response that most accurately and completely answers the question, and blacken the corresponding space on your answer sheet.

Is it necessary for defense lawyers to believe that the clients they defend are innocent of the charges against them? Some legal scholars hold that lawyers'
sole obligation is to provide the best defense they are
(5) capable of, claiming that in democratic societies all people accused of crimes are entitled to the best possible legal representation. They argue that lawyers have no right to judge defendants because it is the job of the courts to determine guilt or innocence and the
(10) job of the lawyer to represent the defendant before the court. They believe that the lawyer's responsibility is to state those facts that will assist each client's case, construct sound arguments based on these facts, and identify flaws in the arguments of opposing counsel.
(15) According to these scholars, the lawyer's role is not to express or act on personal opinions but to act as an advocate, saying only what defendants would say if they possessed the proper training or resources with which to represent themselves.
(20) But such a position overlooks the fact that the defense lawyer's obligation is twofold: to the defendant, certainly, but no less so to the court and, by extension, to society. For this reason, lawyers, great as their obligation to defendants is, should not, as officers
(25) of the court, present to the court assertions that they know to be false. But by the same principle, lawyers who are convinced that their clients are guilty should not undertake to demonstrate their innocence. Guilty defendants should not be entitled to false or insincere
(30) representation. When lawyers know with certainty that a defendant is guilty, it is their duty not to deny this. Rather, they should appraise the case as much as possible in their client's favor, after giving due consideration to the facts on the other side, and then
(35) present any extenuating circumstances and argue for whatever degree of leniency in sentencing they sincerely believe is warranted. In cases where it is uncertain whether the client is guilty but the lawyer sincerely believes the client may well be innocent, the
(40) lawyer should of course try to prove that the client is innocent.

The lawyer's obligation to the court and to society also ultimately benefits the defendant, because the "best defense" can only truly be provided by an
(45) advocate who, after a careful analysis of the facts, is convinced of the merits of the case. The fact that every client is entitled to a defense does not mean that defense lawyers should take every case they are offered. Lawyers should not be mere mouthpieces for a
(50) defendant but instead advocates for the rights of the defendant given the facts of the case.

1. Which one of the following most accurately expresses the main idea of the passage?

(A) Some legal scholars defend a morally questionable view that defense lawyers' sole obligation to their clients is to provide the best defense, while it is the court's job to determine guilt or innocence.

(B) Defense lawyers should put aside personal judgments about their clients' guilt when determining how best to proceed when representing a client.

(C) In a democracy, all persons accused of crimes have a right to an attorney who will state the facts, construct sound arguments, and identify flaws in the arguments of opposing counsel.

(D) Lawyers should be mindful of their duty to society as well as to their clients and base the decision as to whether, and how, to defend a client on the facts of the case.

(E) Defense attorneys are obligated to defend clients who request their professional services, especially when the attorney is absolutely convinced of the client's innocence.

2. Which one of the following most accurately describes the author's attitude toward the twofold obligation introduced in lines 20–23?

(A) confident that it enables defense lawyers to balance their competing responsibilities to the court and to society

(B) certain that it prevents defense lawyers from representing clients whom they know to be guilty

(C) satisfied that it helps defense lawyers to uncover the relevant facts of a case

(D) pleased that it does not interfere with common defense strategies used by defense lawyers

(E) convinced that it does not represent a conflict of interest for defense lawyers

GO ON TO THE NEXT PAGE.

3. Which one of the following sentences would most
    logically begin a paragraph immediately following the
    end of the passage?

    (A) In keeping with this role, defense lawyers should
        base their cases upon the foundations of honesty,
        substantive accuracy and selectivity.
    (B) Therefore, the practice of law remains morally
        dubious, in that misrepresentation may achieve
        acquittal for an attorney's client.
    (C) Consequently, the defendant's right to legal
        representation varies from case to case,
        depending on the severity of the alleged crime
        and the defense lawyer's personal interpretation
        of the case.
    (D) Thus, the lawyers' obligations are threefold—to
        be faithful to the dictates of the court, society,
        and themselves by proving their professional
        worth in securing acquittal for the clients whom
        they represent.
    (E) Therefore, judges or other officials of the court
        should interrogate defense attorneys regarding
        any prior knowledge they may have of their
        clients' innocence or guilt.

4. According to the passage, the legal scholars mentioned
    in lines 15–19 believe that it is a defense lawyer's role
    to be

    (A) a source of legal information that can help a jury
        to reach decisions that are fair and equitable
    (B) a thorough investigator of all relevant evidence
    (C) a diligent representative of the client's position
    (D) a facilitator and expediter of the cause of justice
    (E) an energetic advocate of the client's right to legal
        representation

5. The relationship of the information contained in the
    two sentences at lines 28–31 to that in the sentence at
    lines 7–11 can most accurately be described as

    (A) no significant relationship because they represent
        two unrelated factual statements
    (B) the author's opinion opposing another opinion
        reported by the author in the earlier lines
    (C) a hypothetical situation supporting a statement
        reported by the author in the earlier lines
    (D) agreement in general with the earlier position but
        disagreement over the particulars
    (E) essentially equivalent assertions arising from
        different perspectives

6. It can be inferred from the passage that the author holds
    that a defense attorney who argues in court that a client
    is innocent

    (A) should sincerely believe that the client may be
        innocent
    (B) would be right to do so even if the attorney
        knows that the client is actually guilty
    (C) is assuming that role of mouthpiece for the client
    (D) has favored the obligation to the client over that
        to society
    (E) has typically not researched the facts of the case
        thoroughly

7. The primary purpose of the passage is to

    (A) show that ethical dilemmas in the legal profession
        can complicate the defense lawyer's role
    (B) argue that the defense lawyer's duty to the
        court and society complements effective legal
        representation for the client
    (C) explain why the actual guilt or innocence of a
        defendant is not an important issue to many
        defense attorneys
    (D) discuss some of the issues that a defense lawyer
        must resolve prior to accepting a case
    (E) reveal how the practice of law strengthens the
        values and principles of democratic societies

GO ON TO THE NEXT PAGE.

Many educators in Canada and the United States advocate multicultural education as a means of achieving multicultural understanding. There are, however, a variety of proposals as to what multicultural
(5) education should consist of. The most modest of these proposals holds that schools and colleges should promote multicultural understanding by teaching about other cultures, teaching which proceeds from within the context of the majority culture. Students should
(10) learn about other cultures, proponents claim, but examination of these cultures should operate with the methods, perspectives, and values of the majority culture. These values are typically those of liberalism: democracy, tolerance, and equality of persons.

(15) Critics of this first proposal have argued that genuine understanding of other cultures is impossible if the study of other cultures is refracted through the distorting lens of the majority culture's perspective. Not all cultures share liberal values. Their value
(20) systems have arisen in often radically different social and historical circumstances, and thus, these critics argue, cannot be understood and adequately appreciated if one insists on approaching them solely from within the majority culture's perspective.

(25) In response to this objection, a second version of multicultural education has developed that differs from the first in holding that multicultural education ought to adopt a neutral stance with respect to the value differences among cultures. The values of one culture
(30) should not be standards by which others are judged; each culture should be taken on its own terms. However, the methods of examination, study, and explanation of cultures in this second version of multicultural education are still identifiably Western.
(35) They are the methods of anthropology, social psychology, political science, and sociology. They are, that is, methods which derive from the Western scientific perspective and heritage.

Critics of this second form of multicultural
(40) education argue as follows: The Western scientific heritage is founded upon an epistemological system that prizes the objective over the subjective, the logical over the intuitive, and the empirically verifiable over the mystical. The methods of social-scientific
(45) examination of cultures are thus already value laden; the choice to examine and understand other cultures by these methods involves a commitment to certain values such as objectivity. Thus, the second version of multicultural education is not essentially different from
(50) the first. Scientific discourse has a privileged place in Western cultures, but the discourses of myth, tradition, religion, and mystical insight are often the dominant forms of thought and language of non-Western cultures. To insist on trying to understand nonscientific
(55) cultures by the methods of Western science is not only distorting, but is also an expression of an attempt to maintain a Eurocentric cultural chauvinism: the chauvinism of science. According to this objection, it is only by adopting the (often nonscientific) perspectives
(60) and methods of the cultures studied that real understanding can be achieved.

8. Which one of the following most accurately states the main point of the passage?

(A) Proponents of two proposals for promoting multicultural understanding disagree about both the goal of multicultural education and the means for achieving this goal.

(B) Proponents of two proposals for promoting multicultural understanding claim that education should be founded upon an epistemological system that recognizes the importance of the subjective, the intuitive, and the mystical.

(C) Proponents of two proposals for promoting multicultural understanding claim that it is not enough to refrain from judging non-Western cultures if the methods used to study these cultures are themselves Western.

(D) Critics of two proposals for promoting multicultural understanding disagree about the extent to which a culture's values are a product of its social and historical circumstances.

(E) Critics of two proposals for promoting multicultural understanding claim these proposals are not value neutral and are therefore unable to yield a genuine understanding of cultures with a different value system.

9. Critics who raise the objection discussed in the second paragraph would be most likely to agree with which one of the following?

(A) The social and historical circumstances that give rise to a culture's values cannot be understood by members of a culture with different values.

(B) The historical and social circumstances of a culture can play an important role in the development of that culture's values.

(C) It is impossible for one culture to successfully study another culture unless it does so from more than one cultural perspective.

(D) Genuine understanding of another culture is impossible unless that culture shares the same cultural values.

(E) The values of liberalism cannot be adequately understood if we approach them solely through the methods of Western science.

GO ON TO THE NEXT PAGE.

10. Which one of the following most accurately describes the organization of the passage as a whole?

  (A) Difficulties in achieving a goal are contrasted with the benefits of obtaining that goal.
  (B) A goal is argued to be unrealizable by raising objections to the means proposed to achieve it.
  (C) Two means for achieving a goal are presented along with an objection to each.
  (D) Difficulties in achieving a goal are used to defend several radical revisions to that goal.
  (E) The desirability of a goal is used to defend against a number of objections to its feasibility.

11. The version of multicultural education discussed in the first paragraph is described as "modest" (line 5) most likely because it

  (A) relies on the least amount of speculation about non-Western cultures
  (B) calls for the least amount of change in the educational system
  (C) involves the least amount of Eurocentric cultural chauvinism
  (D) is the least distorting since it employs several cultural perspectives
  (E) deviates least from a neutral stance with respect to differences in values

12. Given the information in the passage, which one of the following would most likely be considered objectionable by proponents of the version of multicultural education discussed in the third paragraph?

  (A) a study of the differences between the moral codes of several Western and non-Western societies
  (B) a study of a given culture's literature to determine the kinds of personal characteristics the culture admires
  (C) a study that employs the methods of Western science to investigate a nonscientific culture
  (D) a study that uses the literary theories of one society to criticize the literature of a society that has different values
  (E) a study that uses the methods of anthropology and sociology to criticize the values of Western culture

13. Which one of the following, if true, would provide the strongest objection to the criticism in the passage of the second version of multicultural education?

  (A) It is impossible to adopt the perspectives and methods of a culture unless one is a member of that culture.
  (B) Many non-Western societies have value systems that are very similar to one another.
  (C) Some non-Western societies use their own value system when studying cultures that have different values.
  (D) Students in Western societies cannot understand their culture's achievements unless such achievements are treated as the subject of Western scientific investigations.
  (E) Genuine understanding of another culture is necessary for adequately appreciating that culture.

GO ON TO THE NEXT PAGE.

In studying the autobiographies of Native Americans, most scholars have focused on as-told-to life histories that were solicited, translated, recorded, and edited by non-Native American collaborators—that
(5) emerged from "bicultural composite authorship." Limiting their studies to such written documents, these scholars have overlooked traditional, preliterate modes of communicating personal history. In addition, they have failed to address the cultural constructs of the
(10) highly diverse Native American peoples, who prior to contact with nonindigenous cultures did not share with Europeans the same assumptions about self, life, and writing that underlie the concept of an autobiography— that indeed constitute the English word's root meaning.

(15)   The idea of self was, in a number of pre-contact Native American cultures, markedly inclusive: identity was not merely individual, but also relational to a society, a specific landscape, and the cosmos. Within these cultures, the expression of life experiences tended
(20) to be oriented toward current events: with the participation of fellow tribal members, an individual person would articulate, reenact, or record important experiences as the person lived them, a mode of autobiography seemingly more fragmented than the
(25) European custom of writing down the recollections of a lifetime. Moreover, expression itself was not a matter of writing but of language, which can include speech and signs. Oral autobiography comprised songs, chants, stories, and even the process whereby one repeatedly
(30) took on new names to reflect important events and deeds in one's life. Dance and drama could convey personal history; for example, the advent of a vision to one person might require the enactment of that vision in the form of a tribal pageant.

(35)   One can view as autobiographical the elaborate tattoos that symbolized a warrior's valorous deeds, and such artifacts as a decorated shield that communicated the accomplishments and aspirations of its maker, or a robe that was emblazoned with the pictographic history
(40) of the wearer's battles and was sometimes used in reenactments. Also autobiographical, and indicative of high status within the tribe, would have been a tepee painted with symbolic designs to record the achievements and display the dreams or visions of its
(45) owner, who was often assisted in the painting by other tribal members.

    A tribe would, then, have contributed to the individual's narrative not merely passively, by its social codes and expectations, but actively by joining
(50) in the expression of that narrative. Such intercultural collaboration may seem alien to the European style of autobiography, yet any autobiography is shaped by its creator's ideas about the audience for which it is intended; in this sense, autobiography is justly called a
(55) simultaneous individual story and cultural narrative. Autobiographical expressions by early Native Americans may additionally have been shaped by the cultural perspectives of the people who transmitted them.

14. Which one of the following most accurately expresses the main conclusion of the passage?

(A) Scholars have tended to overlook the nuances of concepts about identity that existed in some of the early Native American cultures.

(B) As demonstrated by early Native Americans, autobiography can exist in a variety of media other than written documents.

(C) The Native American life histories collected and recorded by non-Native American writers differ from European-style autobiographies in their depictions of an individual's relation to society.

(D) Early Native Americans created autobiographies with forms and underlying assumptions that frequently differ from those of European-style autobiographies.

(E) The autobiographical forms traditionally used by Native Americans are more fragmented than European forms and thus less easily recognizable as personal history.

15. Which one of the following phrases best conveys the author's attitude toward the earlier scholarship on Native American autobiographies that is mentioned in the passage?

(A) "failed to address" (line 9)
(B) "highly diverse" (line 10)
(C) "markedly inclusive" (line 16)
(D) "seemingly more fragmented" (line 24)
(E) "alien to the European style" (line 51)

GO ON TO THE NEXT PAGE.

16. Which one of the following most accurately conveys the meaning of the phrase "bicultural composite authorship" as it is used in line 5 of the passage?

   (A) written by a member of one culture but based on the artifacts and oral traditions of another culture
   (B) written by two people, each of whom belongs to a different culture but contributes in the same way to the finished product
   (C) compiled from the writings of people who come from different cultures and whose identities cannot be determined
   (D) written originally by a member of one culture but edited and revised by a member of another culture
   (E) written by a member of one culture but based on oral communication by a member of another culture

17. Which one of the following most accurately describes the function of the third paragraph within the passage as a whole?

   (A) to refute traditional interpretations of certain artifacts
   (B) to present evidence that undermines a theory
   (C) to provide examples that support an argument
   (D) to contrast several different modes of expression
   (E) to enumerate specific instances in which a phenomenon recurred

18. The author of the passage refers to "self, life, and writing" (lines 12–13) most probably in order to

   (A) identify concepts about which Europeans and Native Americans had contrasting ideas
   (B) define a word that had a different meaning for early Native Americans than it has for contemporary Native Americans
   (C) illustrate how words can undergo a change in meaning after their introduction into the language
   (D) posit a fundamental similarity in the origins of a concept in both European and Native American cultures
   (E) explain how the assumptions that underlie European-style autobiography arose

19. Which one of the following would be most consistent with the ideas about identity that the author attributes to pre-contact Native American cultures?

   (A) A person who is born into one tribe but is brought up by members of another tribe retains a name given at birth.
   (B) A pictograph that represents a specific person incorporates the symbol for a constellation.
   (C) A similar ritual for assuming a new name is used in diverse communities.
   (D) A name given to one member of a community cannot be given to another member of the same community.
   (E) A decorated shield that belonged to an individual cannot be traced to a particular tribe.

GO ON TO THE NEXT PAGE.

Most scientists who study the physiological effects of alcoholic beverages have assumed that wine, like beer or distilled spirits, is a drink whose only active ingredient is alcohol. Because of this assumption, these
(5) scientists have rarely investigated the effects of wine as distinct from other forms of alcoholic beverages. Nevertheless, unlike other alcoholic beverages, wine has for centuries been thought to have healthful effects that these scientists—who not only make no distinction
(10) among wine, beer, and distilled spirits but also study only the excessive or abusive intake of these beverages— have obscured.

Recently, a small group of researchers has questioned this assumption and investigated the effects
(15) of moderate wine consumption. While alcohol has been shown conclusively to have negative physiological effects—for example, alcohol strongly affects the body's processing of lipids (fats and other substances including cholesterol), causing dangerous increases in
(20) the levels of these substances in the blood, increases that are a large contributing factor in the development of premature heart disease—the researchers found that absorption of alcohol into the bloodstream occurs much more slowly when subjects drink wine than when they
(25) drink distilled spirits. More remarkably, it was discovered that deaths due to premature heart disease in the populations of several European countries decreased dramatically as the incidence of moderate wine consumption increased. One preliminary study
(30) linked this effect to red wine, but subsequent research has shown identical results whether the wine was white or red. What could explain such apparently healthful effects?

For one thing, the studies show increased activity
(35) of a natural clot-breaking compound used by doctors to restore blood flow through blocked vessels in victims of heart disease. In addition, the studies of wine drinkers indicate increased levels of certain compounds that may help to prevent damage from high lipid levels.
(40) And although the link between lipid processing and premature heart disease is one of the most important discoveries in modern medicine, in the past 20 years researchers have found several additional important contributing factors. We now know that endothelial
(45) cell reactivity (which affects the thickness of the innermost walls of blood vessels) and platelet adhesiveness (which influences the degree to which platelets cause blood to clot) are each linked to the development of premature heart disease. Studies show
(50) that wine appears to have ameliorating effects on both of these factors: it decreases the thickness of the innermost walls of blood vessels, and it reduces platelet adhesiveness. One study demonstrated a decrease in platelet adhesiveness among individuals who drank
(55) large amounts of grape juice. This finding may be the first step in confirming speculation that the potentially healthful effects of moderate wine intake may derive from the concentration of certain natural compounds found in grapes and not present in other alcoholic
(60) beverages.

20. Which one of the following most accurately states the author's main point in the passage?

(A) Because of their assumption that alcohol is the only active ingredient in wine, beer, and distilled spirits, scientists have previously studied these beverages in ways that obscure their healthful effects.

(B) A new study of moderate wine consumption calls into question the belief that premature heart disease is caused solely by the presence of high lipid levels in the bloodstream.

(C) Researchers have found that alcohol from moderate wine consumption is absorbed into the bloodstream more slowly than is alcohol from other alcoholic beverages.

(D) Although it has long been held that moderate wine consumption has healthful effects, scientific studies have yet to prove such effects definitively.

(E) Wine, unlike other alcoholic beverages, appears to have a number of significant healthful effects that may be tied to certain natural compounds found in grapes.

21. In the first paragraph, the author most likely refers to the centuries-old belief that wine has healthful effects in order to

(A) demonstrate that discoveries in the realm of science often bear out popular beliefs

(B) provide evidence for the theory that moderate wine consumption ameliorates factors that contribute to premature heart disease

(C) argue that traditional beliefs are no less important than scientific evidence when investigating health matters

(D) suggest that a prevailing scientific assumption might be mistaken

(E) refute the argument that science should take cues from popular beliefs

GO ON TO THE NEXT PAGE.

22. According to the passage, each of the following might help to prevent premature heart disease EXCEPT:

    (A) an increase in the degree to which platelets cause blood to clot
    (B) an increase in the body's ability to remove lipids from the bloodstream
    (C) an increase in the amount of time it takes alcohol to be absorbed into the bloodstream
    (D) increased activity of a natural compound that reduces blood clotting
    (E) increased levels of compounds that prevent damage from high lipid levels

23. Which one of the following, if true, would most strengthen the passage's position concerning the apparently healthful effects of moderate wine consumption?

    (A) Subjects who consumed large amount of grape juice exhibited decreased thickness of the innermost walls of their blood vessels.
    (B) Subjects who were habitual drinkers of wine and subjects who were habitual drinkers of beer exhibited similar lipid levels in their bloodstreams.
    (C) Subjects who drank grape juice exhibited greater platelet adhesiveness than did subjects who drank no grape juice.
    (D) Subjects who drank excessive amounts of wine suffered from premature heart disease at roughly the same rate as moderate wine drinkers.
    (E) Subjects who possess a natural clot-breaking compound were discovered to have a certain gene that is absent from subjects who do not possess the compound.

24. It can be inferred from the passage that the author would most likely agree with which one of the following statements?

    (A) Scientists should not attempt to study the possible healthful effects of moderate consumption of beer and distilled spirits.
    (B) The conclusion that alcohol affects lipid processing should be questioned in light of studies of moderate wine consumption.
    (C) Moderate consumption of wine made from plums or apples rather than grapes would be unlikely to reduce the risk of premature heart disease.
    (D) Red wine consumption has a greater effect on reducing death rates from premature heart disease than does white wine consumption.
    (E) Beer and distilled spirits contain active ingredients other than alcohol whose effects tend to be beneficial.

25. Based on the passage, the author's attitude toward the scientists discussed in the first paragraph can most accurately be described as

    (A) highly enthusiastic
    (B) tacitly approving
    (C) grudgingly accepting
    (D) overtly critical
    (E) clearly outraged

26. In the passage, the author is primarily concerned with doing which one of the following?

    (A) advocating a particular method of treatment
    (B) criticizing popular opinion
    (C) correcting a scientific misconception
    (D) questioning the relevance of newly discovered evidence
    (E) countering a revolutionary hypothesis

27. The author suggests each of the following in the passage EXCEPT:

    (A) Greater platelet adhesiveness increases the risk of premature heart disease.
    (B) The body's ability to process lipids is compromised by the presence of alcohol in the bloodstream.
    (C) Doctors have access to a natural compound that breaks down blood clots.
    (D) High lipid levels are dangerous because they lead to increased endothelial cell reactivity and platelet adhesiveness.
    (E) Moderate wine consumption appears to decrease the thickness of the interior walls of blood vessels.

S T O P

IF YOU FINISH BEFORE TIME IS CALLED, YOU MAY CHECK YOUR WORK ON THIS SECTION ONLY.
DO NOT WORK ON ANY OTHER SECTION IN THE TEST.

SECTION III

Time—35 minutes

23 Questions

Directions: Each group of questions in this section is based on a set of conditions. In answering some of the questions, it may be useful to draw a rough diagram. Choose the response that most accurately and completely answers each question and blacken the corresponding space on your answer sheet.

Questions 1–7

Workers at a water treatment plant open eight valves—G, H, I, K, L, N, O, and P—to flush out a system of pipes that needs emergency repairs. To maximize safety and efficiency, each valve is opened exactly once, and no two valves are opened at the same time. The valves are opened in accordance with the following conditions:

Both K and P are opened before H.
O is opened before L but after H.
L is opened after G.
N is opened before H.
I is opened after K.

1. Which one of the following could be the order, from first to last, in which the valves are opened?

(A) P, I, K, G, N, H, O, L
(B) P, G, K, N, L, H, O, I
(C) G, K, I, P, H, O, N, L
(D) N, K, P, H, O, I, L, G
(E) K, I, N, G, P, H, O, L

2. Each of the following could be the fifth valve opened EXCEPT:

(A) H
(B) I
(C) K
(D) N
(E) O

3. If I is the second valve opened, then each of the following could be true EXCEPT:

(A) G is the third valve opened.
(B) H is the fourth valve opened.
(C) P is the fifth valve opened.
(D) O is the sixth valve opened.
(E) G is the seventh valve opened.

4. If L is the seventh valve opened, then each of the following could be the second valve opened EXCEPT:

(A) G
(B) I
(C) K
(D) N
(E) P

5. Which one of the following must be true?

(A) At least one valve is opened before P is opened.
(B) At least two valves are opened before G is opened.
(C) No more than two valves are opened after O is opened.
(D) No more than three valves are opened after H is opened.
(E) No more than four valves are opened before N is opened.

6. If K is the fourth valve opened, then which one of the following could be true?

(A) I is the second valve opened.
(B) N is the third valve opened.
(C) G is the fifth valve opened.
(D) O is the fifth valve opened.
(E) P is the sixth valve opened.

7. If G is the first valve opened and I is the third valve opened, then each of the following must be true EXCEPT:

(A) K is the second valve opened.
(B) N is the fourth valve opened.
(C) H is the sixth valve opened.
(D) O is the seventh valve opened.
(E) L is the eighth valve opened.

GO ON TO THE NEXT PAGE.

Questions 8–12

On a field trip to the Museum of Natural History, each of six children—Juana, Kyle, Lucita, Salim, Thanh, and Veronica—is accompanied by one of three adults—Ms. Margoles, Mr. O'Connell, and Ms. Podorski. Each adult accompanies exactly two of the children, consistent with the following conditions:

If Ms. Margoles accompanies Juana, then Ms. Podorski accompanies Lucita.

If Kyle is not accompanied by Ms. Margoles, then Veronica is accompanied by Mr. O'Connell.

Either Ms. Margoles or Mr. O'Connell accompanies Thanh.

Juana is not accompanied by the same adult as Kyle; nor is Lucita accompanied by the same adult as Salim; nor is Thanh accompanied by the same adult as Veronica.

8. Which one of the following could be an accurate matching of the adults to the children they accompany?

(A)   Ms. Margoles: Juana, Thanh; Mr. O'Connell: Lucita, Veronica; Ms. Podorski: Kyle, Salim

(B)   Ms. Margoles: Kyle, Thanh; Mr. O'Connell: Juana, Salim; Ms. Podorski: Lucita, Veronica

(C)   Ms. Margoles: Lucita, Thanh; Mr. O'Connell: Juana, Salim; Ms. Podorski: Kyle, Veronica

(D)   Ms. Margoles: Kyle, Veronica; Mr. O'Connell: Juana, Thanh; Ms. Podorski: Lucita, Salim

(E)   Ms. Margoles: Salim, Veronica; Mr. O'Connell: Kyle, Lucita; Ms. Podorski: Juana, Thanh

9. If Ms. Margoles accompanies Lucita and Thanh, then which one of the following must be true?

(A)   Juana is accompanied by the same adult as Veronica.

(B)   Kyle is accompanied by the same adult as Salim.

(C)   Juana is accompanied by Mr. O'Connell.

(D)   Kyle is accompanied by Ms. Podorski.

(E)   Salim is accompanied by Ms. Podorski.

10. If Ms. Podorski accompanies Juana and Veronica, then Ms. Margoles could accompany which one of the following pairs of children?

(A)   Kyle and Salim

(B)   Kyle and Thanh

(C)   Lucita and Salim

(D)   Lucita and Thanh

(E)   Salim and Thanh

11. Ms. Podorski CANNOT accompany which one of the following pairs of children?

(A)   Juana and Lucita

(B)   Juana and Salim

(C)   Kyle and Salim

(D)   Salim and Thanh

(E)   Salim and Veronica

12. Mr. O'Connell CANNOT accompany which one of the following pairs of children?

(A)   Juana and Lucita

(B)   Juana and Veronica

(C)   Kyle and Thanh

(D)   Lucita and Thanh

(E)   Salim and Veronica

GO ON TO THE NEXT PAGE.

Questions 13–17

Three short seminars—Goals, Objections, and Persuasion—and three long seminars—Humor, Negotiating, and Telemarketing—will be scheduled for a three-day sales training conference. On each day, two of the seminars will be given consecutively. Each seminar will be given exactly once. The schedule must conform to the following conditions:

Exactly one short seminar and exactly one long seminar will be given each day.

Telemarketing will not be given until both Goals and Objections have been given.

Negotiating will not be given until Persuasion has been given.

13. Which one of the following could be an accurate schedule for the sales training conference?

(A) first day: Persuasion followed by Negotiating
second day: Objections followed by Telemarketing
third day: Goals followed by Humor

(B) first day: Objections followed by Humor
second day: Goals followed by Telemarketing
third day: Persuasion followed by Negotiating

(C) first day: Objections followed by Negotiating
second day: Persuasion followed by Humor
third day: Goals followed by Telemarketing

(D) first day: Objections followed by Goals
second day: Telemarketing followed by Persuasion
third day: Negotiating followed by Humor

(E) first day: Goals followed by Humor
second day: Persuasion followed by Telemarketing
third day: Objections followed by Negotiating

14. If Goals is given on the first day of the sales training conference, then which one of the following could be true?

(A) Negotiating is given on the first day.
(B) Objections is given on the first day.
(C) Persuasion is given on the first day.
(D) Humor is given on the second day.
(E) Telemarketing is given on the second day.

15. If Negotiating is given at some time before Objections, then which one of the following must be true?

(A) Negotiating is given at some time before Goals.
(B) Persuasion is given at some time before Goals.
(C) Persuasion is given at some time before Objections.
(D) Humor is given at some time before Objections.
(E) Negotiating is given at some time before Humor.

16. Which one of the following CANNOT be the second seminar given on the second day of the sales training conference?

(A) Humor
(B) Persuasion
(C) Objections
(D) Negotiating
(E) Goals

17. If Humor is given on the second day of the sales training conference, then which one of the following could be true?

(A) Telemarketing is given on the first day.
(B) Negotiating is given on the second day.
(C) Telemarketing is given on the second day.
(D) Objections is given on the third day.
(E) Persuasion is given on the third day.

GO ON TO THE NEXT PAGE.

Questions 18–23

A bread truck makes exactly one bread delivery to each of six restaurants in succession—Figueroa's, Ginsberg's, Harris's, Kanzaki's, Leacock's, and Malpighi's—though not necessarily in that order. The following conditions must apply:

Ginsberg's delivery is earlier than Kanzaki's but later than Figueroa's.

Harris's delivery is earlier than Ginsberg's.

If Figueroa's delivery is earlier than Malpighi's, then Leacock's delivery is earlier than Harris's.

Either Malpighi's delivery is earlier than Harris's or it is later than Kanzaki's, but not both.

18. Which one of the following accurately represents an order in which the deliveries could occur, from first to last?

(A) Harris's, Figueroa's, Leacock's, Ginsberg's, Kanzaki's, Malpighi's

(B) Leacock's, Harris's, Figueroa's, Ginsberg's, Malpighi's, Kanzaki's

(C) Malpighi's, Figueroa's, Harris's, Ginsberg's, Leacock's, Kanzaki's

(D) Malpighi's, Figueroa's, Kanzaki's, Harris's, Ginsberg's, Leacock's

(E) Malpighi's, Figueroa's, Ginsberg's, Kanzaki's, Harris's, Leacock's

19. If Figueroa's delivery is fourth, then which one of the following must be true?

(A) Ginsberg's delivery is fifth.
(B) Harris's delivery is second.
(C) Harris's delivery is third.
(D) Leacock's delivery is second.
(E) Malpighi's delivery is first.

20. If Malpighi's delivery is first and Leacock's delivery is third, then which one of the following must be true?

(A) Figueroa's delivery is second.
(B) Harris's delivery is second.
(C) Harris's delivery is fourth.
(D) Kanzaki's delivery is fifth.
(E) Kanzaki's delivery is last.

21. Which one of the following must be true?

(A) Figueroa's delivery is earlier than Leacock's.
(B) Ginsberg's delivery is earlier than Leacock's.
(C) Harris's delivery is earlier than Kanzaki's.
(D) Leacock's delivery is earlier than Ginsberg's.
(E) Malpighi's delivery is earlier than Harris's.

22. If Kanzaki's delivery is earlier than Leacock's, then which one of the following could be true?

(A) Figueroa's delivery is first.
(B) Ginsberg's delivery is third.
(C) Harris's delivery is third.
(D) Leacock's delivery is fifth.
(E) Malpighi's delivery is second.

23. Which one of the following must be false?

(A) Figueroa's delivery is first.
(B) Ginsberg's delivery is fifth.
(C) Harris's delivery is third.
(D) Leacock's delivery is second.
(E) Malpighi's delivery is fourth.

S T O P

IF YOU FINISH BEFORE TIME IS CALLED, YOU MAY CHECK YOUR WORK ON THIS SECTION ONLY.
DO NOT WORK ON ANY OTHER SECTION IN THE TEST.

SECTION IV
Time—35 minutes
25 Questions

Directions: The questions in this section are based on the reasoning contained in brief statements or passages. For some questions, more than one of the choices could conceivably answer the question. However, you are to choose the best answer; that is, the response that most accurately and completely answers the question. You should not make assumptions that are by commonsense standards implausible, superfluous, or incompatible with the passage. After you have chosen the best answer, blacken the corresponding space on your answer sheet.

1. Any museum that owns the rare stamp that features an airplane printed upside down should not display it. Ultraviolet light causes red ink to fade, and a substantial portion of the stamp is red. If the stamp is displayed, it will be damaged. It should be kept safely locked away, even though this will deny the public the chance to see it.

    The reasoning above most closely conforms to which one of the following principles?

    (A) The public should judge the quality of a museum by the rarity of the objects in its collection.
    (B) Museum display cases should protect their contents from damage caused by ultraviolet light.
    (C) Red ink should not be used on items that will not be exposed to ultraviolet light.
    (D) A museum piece that would be damaged by display should not be displayed.
    (E) The primary purpose of a museum is to educate the public.

2. Dietitian: Many diet-conscious consumers are excited about new "fake fat" products designed to give food the flavor and consistency of fatty foods, yet without fat's harmful effects. Consumers who expect the new fat substitute to help them lose weight arc likely to be disappointed, however. Research has shown that when people knowingly or unknowingly eat foods containing "fake fat," they tend to take in at least as many additional calories as are saved by eating "fake fat."

    Which one of the following most accurately expresses the conclusion of the dietitian's argument?

    (A) People tend to take in a certain number of daily calories, no matter what types of food they eat
    (B) Most consumers who think that foods with "fake fat" are more nutritious than fatty foods are destined to be disappointed.
    (C) "Fake fat" products are likely to contribute to obesity more than do other foods.
    (D) "Fake fat" in foods is probably not going to help consumers meet weight loss goals.
    (E) "Fake fat" in foods is indistinguishable from genuine fat by most consumers on the basis of taste alone.

3. Banking analyst: Banks often offer various services to new customers at no charge. But this is not an ideal business practice, since regular, long-term customers, who make up the bulk of the business for most banks, are excluded from these special offers.

    Which one of the following, if true, most strengthens the banking analyst's argument?

    (A) Most banks have similar charges for most services and pay similar interest rates on deposits.
    (B) Banks do best when offering special privileges only to their most loyal customers.
    (C) Offering services at no charge to all of its current customers would be prohibitively expensive for a bank.
    (D) Once they have chosen a bank, people tend to remain loyal to that bank.
    (E) Some banks that offer services at no charge to new customers are very successful.

GO ON TO THE NEXT PAGE.

4. Panelist: Medical research articles cited in popular newspapers or magazines are more likely than other medical research articles to be cited in subsequent medical research. Thus, it appears that medical researchers' judgments of the importance of prior research are strongly influenced by the publicity received by that research and do not strongly correspond to the research's true importance.

The panelist's argument is most vulnerable to criticism on the grounds that it

(A) presents counterarguments to a view that is not actually held by any medical researcher

(B) fails to consider the possibility that popular newspapers and magazines do a good job of identifying the most important medical research articles

(C) takes for granted that coverage of medical research in the popular press is more concerned with the eminence of the scientists involved than with the content of their research

(D) fails to consider the possibility that popular newspapers and magazines are able to review only a minuscule percentage of medical research articles

(E) draws a conclusion that is logically equivalent to its premise

5. Lahar: We must now settle on a procedure for deciding on meeting agendas. Our club's constitution allows three options: unanimous consent, majority vote, or assigning the task to a committee. Unanimous consent is unlikely. Forming a committee has usually led to factionalism and secret deals. Clearly, we should subject meeting agendas to majority vote.

Lahar's argument does which one of the following?

(A) rejects suggested procedures on constitutional grounds

(B) claims that one procedure is the appropriate method for reaching every decision in the club

(C) suggests a change to a constitution on the basis of practical considerations

(D) recommends a choice based on the elimination of alternative options

(E) supports one preference by arguing against those who have advocated alternatives

6. Mayor: Local antitobacco activists are calling for expanded antismoking education programs paid for by revenue from heavily increased taxes on cigarettes sold in the city. Although the effectiveness of such education programs is debatable, there is strong evidence that the taxes themselves would produce the sought-after reduction in smoking. Surveys show that cigarette sales drop substantially in cities that impose stiff tax increases on cigarettes.

Which one of the following, if true, most undermines the reasoning in the argument above?

(A) A city-imposed tax on cigarettes will substantially reduce the amount of smoking in the city if the tax is burdensome to the average cigarette consumer.

(B) Consumers are more likely to continue buying a product if its price increases due to higher taxes than if its price increases for some other reason.

(C) Usually, cigarette sales will increase substantially in the areas surrounding a city after that city imposes stiff taxes on cigarettes.

(D) People who are well informed about the effects of long-term tobacco use are significantly less likely to smoke than are people who are not informed.

(E) Antismoking education programs that are funded by taxes on cigarettes will tend to lose their funding if they are successful.

GO ON TO THE NEXT PAGE.

7. Gotera: Infants lack the motor ability required to voluntarily produce particular sounds, but produce various babbling sounds randomly. Most children are several years old before they can voluntarily produce most of the vowel and consonant sounds of their language. We can conclude that speech acquisition is entirely a motor control process rather than a process that is abstract or mental.

Which one of the following is an assumption required by Gotera's argument?

(A) Speech acquisition is a function only of one's ability to produce the sounds of spoken language.
(B) During the entire initial babbling stage, infants cannot intentionally move their tongues while they are babbling.
(C) The initial babbling stage is completed during infancy.
(D) The initial babbling stage is the first stage of the speech acquisition process.
(E) Control of tongue and mouth movements requires a sophisticated level of mental development.

8. Caldwell: The government recently demolished a former naval base. Among the complex's facilities were a gymnasium, a swimming pool, office buildings, gardens, and housing for hundreds of people. Of course the government was legally permitted to use these facilities as it wished. But clearly, using them for the good of the community would have benefited everyone, and thus the government's actions were not only inefficient but immoral.

Caldwell's argument is most vulnerable to criticism on the grounds that it

(A) fails to consider that an action may be morally permissible even if an alternative course of action is to everyone's advantage
(B) presumes, without providing justification, that the actual consequences of an action are irrelevant to the action's moral permissibility
(C) presumes, without providing justification, that the government never acts in the most efficient manner
(D) presumes, without providing justification, that any action that is efficient is also moral
(E) inappropriately treats two possible courses of action as if they were the only options

9. Reducing stress lessens a person's sensitivity to pain. This is the conclusion reached by researchers who played extended audiotapes to patients before they underwent surgery and afterward while they were recovering. One tape consisted of conversation; the other consisted of music. Those who listened only to the latter tape required less anesthesia during surgery and fewer painkillers afterward than those who listened only to the former tape.

Which one of the following is an assumption on which the researchers' reasoning depends?

(A) All of the patients in the study listened to the same tape before surgery as they listened to after surgery.
(B) Anticipating surgery is no less stressful than recovering from surgery.
(C) Listening to music reduces stress.
(D) The psychological effects of music are not changed by anesthesia or painkillers.
(E) Both anesthesia and painkillers tend to reduce stress.

10. Samuel: Because communication via computer is usually conducted privately and anonymously between people who would otherwise interact in person, it contributes to the dissolution, not the creation, of lasting communal bonds.

Tova: You assume that communication via computer replaces more intimate forms of communication and interaction, when more often it replaces asocial or even antisocial behavior.

On the basis of their statements, Samuel and Tova are committed to disagreeing about which one of the following?

(A) A general trend of modern life is to dissolve the social bonds that formerly connected people.
(B) All purely private behavior contributes to the dissolution of social bonds.
(C) Face-to-face communication is more likely to contribute to the creation of social bonds than is anonymous communication.
(D) It is desirable that new social bonds be created to replace the ones that have dissolved.
(E) If people were not communicating via computer, they would most likely be engaged in activities that create stronger social bonds.

GO ON TO THE NEXT PAGE.

11. Spreading iron particles over the surface of the earth's oceans would lead to an increase in phytoplankton, decreasing the amount of carbon dioxide in the atmosphere and thereby counteracting the greenhouse effect. But while counteracting the greenhouse effect is important, the side effects of an iron-seeding strategy have yet to be studied. Since the oceans represent such an important resource, this response to the greenhouse effect should not be implemented immediately.

The reasoning above most closely conforms to which one of the following principles?

(A) A problem-solving strategy should be implemented if the side effects of the strategy are known.
(B) Implementing a problem-solving strategy that alters an important resource is impermissible if the consequences are not adequately understood.
(C) We should not implement a problem-solving strategy if the consequences of doing so are more serious than the problem itself.
(D) We should not implement a problem-solving strategy if that strategy requires altering an important resource.
(E) As long as there is a possibility that a strategy for solving a problem may instead exacerbate that problem, such a solution should not be adopted.

12. No matter how conscientious they are, historians always have biases that affect their work. Hence, rather than trying to interpret historical events, historians should instead interpret what the people who participated in historical events thought about those events.

The reasoning in the argument is most vulnerable to criticism on the grounds that the argument fails to consider the possibility that

(A) historians who have different biases often agree about many aspects of some historical events
(B) scholars in disciplines other than history also risk having their biases affect their work
(C) many of the ways in which historians' biases affect their work have been identified
(D) not all historians are aware of the effect that their particular biases have on their work
(E) the proposed shift in focus is unlikely to eliminate the effect that historians' biases have on their work

13. Humanitarian considerations aside, sheer economics dictates that country X should institute, as country Y has done, a nationwide system of air and ground transportation for conveying seriously injured persons to specialized trauma centers. Timely access to the kind of medical care that only specialized centers can provide could save the lives of many people. The earnings of these people would result in a substantial increase in country X's gross national product, and the taxes paid on those earnings would substantially augment government revenues.

The argument depends on the assumption that

(A) lifetime per-capita income is roughly the same in country X as it is in country Y
(B) there are no specialized trauma centers in country X at present
(C) the treatment of seriously injured persons in trauma centers is not more costly than treatment elsewhere
(D) there would be a net increase in employment in country X if more persons survived serious injury
(E) most people seriously injured in automobile accidents in country X do not now receive treatment in specialized trauma centers

14. Early urban societies could not have been maintained without large-scale farming nearby. This is because other methods of food acquisition, such as foraging, cannot support populations as dense as urban ones. Large-scale farming requires irrigation, which remained unfeasible in areas far from rivers or lakes until more recent times.

Which one of the following is most strongly supported by the information above?

(A) Most peoples who lived in early times lived in areas near rivers or lakes.
(B) Only if farming is possible in the absence of irrigation can societies be maintained in areas far from rivers or lakes.
(C) In early times it was not possible to maintain urban societies in areas far from rivers or lakes.
(D) Urban societies with farms near rivers or lakes do not have to rely upon irrigation to meet their farming needs.
(E) Early rural societies relied more on foraging than on agriculture for food.

GO ON TO THE NEXT PAGE.

15. Economist: A country's rapid emergence from an economic recession requires substantial new investment in that country's economy. Since people's confidence in the economic policies of their country is a precondition for any new investment, countries that put collective goals before individuals' goals cannot emerge quickly from an economic recession.

Which one of the following, if assumed, enables the economist's conclusion to be properly drawn?

(A) No new investment occurs in any country that does not emerge quickly from an economic recession.

(B) Recessions in countries that put collective goals before individuals' goals tend not to affect the country's people's support for their government's policies.

(C) If the people in a country that puts individuals' goals first are willing to make new investments in their country's economy, their country will emerge quickly from an economic recession.

(D) People in countries that put collective goals before individuals' goals lack confidence in the economic policies of their countries.

(E) A country's economic policies are the most significant factor determining whether that country's economy will experience a recession.

16. The average length of stay for patients at Edgewater Hospital is four days, compared to six days at University Hospital. Since studies show that recovery rates at the two hospitals are similar for patients with similar illnesses, University Hospital could decrease its average length of stay without affecting quality of care.

The reasoning in the argument is most vulnerable to criticism on the grounds that the argument

(A) equates the quality of care at a hospital with patients' average length of stay

(B) treats a condition that will ensure the preservation of quality of care as a condition that is required to preserve quality of care

(C) fails to take into account the possibility that patients at Edgewater Hospital tend to be treated for different illnesses than patients at University Hospital

(D) presumes, without providing justification, that the length of time patients stay in the hospital is never relevant to the recovery rates of these patients

(E) fails to take into account the possibility that patients at University Hospital generally prefer longer hospital stays

17. Philosopher: Graham argues that since a person is truly happy only when doing something, the best life is a life that is full of activity. But we should not be persuaded by Graham's argument. People sleep, and at least sometimes when sleeping, they are truly happy, even though they are not doing anything.

Which one of the following most accurately describes the role played in the philosopher's argument by the claim that at least sometimes when sleeping, people are truly happy, even though they are not doing anything?

(A) It is a premise of Graham's argument.

(B) It is an example intended to show that a premise of Graham's argument is false.

(C) It is an analogy appealed to by Graham but that the philosopher rejects.

(D) It is an example intended to disprove the conclusion of Graham's argument.

(E) It is the main conclusion of the philosopher's argument.

GO ON TO THE NEXT PAGE.

18. Historian: In rebuttal of my claim that West influenced Stuart, some people point out that West's work is mentioned only once in Stuart's diaries. But Stuart's diaries mention several meetings with West, and Stuart's close friend, Abella, studied under West. Furthermore, Stuart's work often uses West's terminology which, though now commonplace, none of Stuart's contemporaries used.

Which one of the following propositions is most supported by the historian's statements, if those statements are true?

(A) Stuart's discussions with Abella were one of the means by which West influenced Stuart.
(B) It is more likely that Stuart influenced West than that West influenced Stuart.
(C) Stuart's contemporaries were not influenced by West.
(D) Stuart's work was not entirely free from West's influence
(E) Because of Stuart's influence on other people, West's terminology is now commonplace.

19. One theory to explain the sudden extinction of all dinosaurs points to "drug overdoses" as the cause. Angiosperms, a certain class of plants, first appeared at the time that dinosaurs became extinct. These plants produce amino-acid-based alkaloids that are psychoactive agents. Most plant-eating mammals avoid these potentially lethal poisons because they taste bitter. Moreover, mammals have livers that help detoxify such drugs. However, dinosaurs could neither taste the bitterness nor detoxify the substance once it was ingested. This theory receives its strongest support from the fact that it helps explain why so many dinosaur fossils are found in unusual and contorted positions.

Which one of the following, if true, would most undermine the theory presented above?

(A) Many fossils of large mammals are found in contorted positions.
(B) Angiosperms provide a great deal of nutrition.
(C) Carnivorous dinosaurs mostly ate other, vegetarian, dinosaurs that fed on angiosperms.
(D) Some poisonous plants do not produce amino-acid-based alkaloids.
(E) Mammals sometimes die of drug overdoses from eating angiosperms.

20. There are two ways to manage an existing transportation infrastructure: continuous maintenance at adequate levels, and periodic radical reconstruction. Continuous maintenance dispenses with the need for radical reconstruction, and radical reconstruction is necessitated by failing to perform continuous maintenance. Over the long run, continuous maintenance is far less expensive; nevertheless, it almost never happens.

Which one of the following, if true, most contributes to an explanation of why the first alternative mentioned is almost never adopted?

(A) Since different parts of the transportation infrastructure are the responsibility of different levels of government, radical reconstruction projects are very difficult to coordinate efficiently.
(B) When funds for transportation infrastructure maintenance are scarce, they are typically distributed in proportion to the amount of traffic that is borne by different elements of the infrastructure.
(C) If continuous maintenance is performed at less-than-adequate levels, the need for radical reconstruction will often arise later than if maintenance had been restricted to responding to emergencies.
(D) Radical reconstruction projects are, in general, too costly to be paid for from current revenue.
(E) For long periods, the task of regular maintenance lacks urgency, since the consequences of neglecting it are very slow to manifest themselves.

GO ON TO THE NEXT PAGE.

21. A good way to get over one's fear of an activity one finds terrifying is to do it repeatedly. For instance, over half of people who have parachuted only once report being extremely frightened by the experience, while less than 1 percent of those who have parachuted ten times or more report being frightened by it.

The reasoning in the argument is most vulnerable to criticism on the grounds that the argument

(A) takes for granted that the greater the number of dangerous activities one engages in the less one is frightened by any one of them

(B) neglects to consider those people who have parachuted more than once but fewer than ten times

(C) takes for granted that people do not know how frightening something is unless they have tried it

(D) fails to take into account the possibility that people would be better off if they did not do things that terrify them

(E) overlooks the possibility that most people who have parachuted many times did not find it frightening initially

22. Most economists believe that reducing the price of any product generally stimulates demand for it. However, most wine merchants have found that reducing the price of domestic wines to make them more competitive with imported wines with which they were previously comparably priced is frequently followed by an increase in sales of those imported wines.

Which one of the following, if true, most helps to reconcile the belief of most economists with the consequences observed by most wine merchants?

(A) Economists' studies of the prices of grocery items and their rates of sales rarely cover alcoholic beverages.

(B) Few merchants of any kind have detailed knowledge of economic theories about the relationship between item prices and sales rates.

(C) Consumers are generally willing to forgo purchasing other items they desire in order to purchase a superior wine.

(D) Imported wines in all price ranges are comparable in quality to domestic wines that cost less.

(E) An increase in the demand for a consumer product is compatible with an increase in demand for a competing product.

23. Certain bacteria that produce hydrogen sulfide as a waste product would die if directly exposed to oxygen. The hydrogen sulfide reacts with oxygen, removing it and so preventing it from harming the bacteria. Furthermore, the hydrogen sulfide tends to kill other organisms in the area, thereby providing the bacteria with a source of food. As a result, a dense colony of these bacteria produces for itself an environment in which it can continue to thrive indefinitely.

Which one of the following is most strongly supported by the information above?

(A) A dense colony of the bacteria can indefinitely continue to produce enough hydrogen sulfide to kill other organisms in the area and to prevent oxygen from harming the bacteria.

(B) The hydrogen sulfide produced by the bacteria kills other organisms in the area by reacting with and removing oxygen.

(C) Most organisms, if killed by the hydrogen sulfide produced by the bacteria, can provide a source of food for the bacteria.

(D) The bacteria can continue to thrive indefinitely only in an environment in which the hydrogen sulfide they produce has removed all oxygen and killed other organisms in the area.

(E) If any colony of bacteria produces hydrogen sulfide as a waste product, it thereby ensures that it is both provided with a source of food and protected from harm by oxygen.

GO ON TO THE NEXT PAGE.

24. Books that present a utopian future in which the inequities and sufferings of the present are replaced by more harmonious and rational social arrangements will always find enthusiastic buyers. Since gloomy books predicting that even more terrifying times await us are clearly not of this genre, they are unlikely to be very popular.

The questionable pattern of reasoning in which one of the following arguments is most similar to that in the argument above?

(A) Art that portrays people as happy and contented has a tranquilizing effect on the viewer, an effect that is appealing to those who are tense or anxious. Thus, people who dislike such art are neither tense nor anxious.

(B) People who enjoy participating in activities such as fishing or hiking may nevertheless enjoy watching such spectator sports as boxing or football. Thus, one cannot infer from someone's participating in vigorous contact sports that he or she is not also fond of less violent forms of recreation.

(C) Action movies that involve complicated and dangerous special-effects scenes are enormously expensive to produce. Hence, since traditional dramatic or comedic films contain no such scenes, it is probable that they are relatively inexpensive to produce.

(D) Adults usually feel a pleasant nostalgia when hearing the music they listened to as adolescents, but since adolescents often like music specifically because they think it annoys their parents, adults rarely appreciate the music that their children will later listen to with nostalgia.

(E) All self-employed businesspeople have salaries that fluctuate with the fortunes of the general economy, but government bureaucrats are not self-employed. Therefore, not everyone with an income that fluctuates with the fortunes of the general economy is a government bureaucrat.

25. Some people mistakenly believe that since we do not have direct access to the distant past we cannot learn much about it. Contemporary historians and archaeologists find current geography, geology, and climate to be rich in clues about a given region's distant history. However, the more distant the period we are studying is, the less useful the study of the present becomes.

Of the following, which one most closely conforms to the principle that the passage illustrates?

(A) Astronomers often draw inferences about the earlier years of our solar system on the basis of recently collected data. Unfortunately, they have been able to infer comparatively little about the origin of our solar system.

(B) Much can be learned about the perpetrator of a crime by applying scientific methods of investigation to the crime scene. But the more the crime scene has been studied the less likely anything will be learned from further study.

(C) To understand a literary text one needs to understand the author's world view. However, the farther that world view gets from one's own the less one will be able to appreciate the text.

(D) We often extrapolate from ordinary sensory experience to things beyond such experience and form a rash judgment, such as the claim that the earth is the center of the universe because it appears that way to us.

(E) One crucial clue to the extent of the ancient Egyptians' mathematical knowledge came from studying the pyramids. The more we studied such structures, the more impressed we were by how much the Egyptians knew.

S T O P

IF YOU FINISH BEFORE TIME IS CALLED, YOU MAY CHECK YOUR WORK ON THIS SECTION ONLY.
DO NOT WORK ON ANY OTHER SECTION IN THE TEST.

SECTION V

Time—35 minutes

27 Questions

<u>Directions:</u> Each set of questions in this section is based on a single passage or a pair of passages. The questions are to be answered on the basis of what is <u>stated</u> or <u>implied</u> in the passage or pair of passages. For some of the questions, more than one of the choices could conceivably answer the question. However, you are to choose the <u>best</u> answer; that is, the response that must accurately and completely answers the question, and blacken the corresponding space on your answer sheet.

Many critics agree that the primary characteristic of Senegalese filmmaker Ousmane Sembène's work is its sociopolitical commitment. Sembène was trained in Moscow in the cinematic methods of socialist
(5) realism, and he asserts that his films are not meant to entertain his compatriots, but rather to raise their awareness of the past and present realities of their society. But his originality as a filmmaker lies most strikingly in his having successfully adapted film,
(10) originally a Western cultural medium, to the needs, pace, and structures of West African culture. In particular, Sembène has found within African oral culture techniques and strategies that enable him to express his views and to reach both literate and
(15) nonliterate Senegalese viewers.

A number of Sembène's characters and motifs can be traced to those found in traditional West African storytelling. The tree, for instance, which in countless West African tales symbolizes knowledge, life, death,
(20) and rebirth, is a salient motif in *Emitaï*. The trickster, usually a dishonest individual who personifies antisocial traits, appears in *Borom Sarret*, *Mandabi*, and *Xala* as a thief, a corrupted civil servant, and a member of the elite, respectively. In fact, most of
(25) Sembène's characters, like those of many oral West African narratives, are types embodying collective ideas or attitudes. And in the oral tradition, these types face archetypal predicaments, as is true, for example, of the protagonist of *Borom Sarret*, who has
(30) no name and is recognizable instead by his trade—he is a street merchant—and by the difficulties he encounters but is unable to overcome.

Moreover, many of Sembène's films derive their structure from West African dilemma tales, the
(35) outcomes of which are debated and decided by their audiences. The open-endedness of most of his plots reveals that Sembène similarly leaves it to his viewers to complete his narratives: in such films as *Borom Sarret*, *Mandabi*, and *Ceddo*, for example, he
(40) provides his spectators with several alternatives as the films end. The openness of his narratives is also evidenced by his frequent use of freeze-frames, which carry the suggestion of continued action.

Finally, like many West African oral tales,
(45) Sembène's narratives take the form of initiatory journeys that bring about a basic change in the worldview of the protagonist and ultimately, Sembène hopes, in that of the viewer. His films denounce social and political injustice. and his protagonists'
(50) social consciousness emerges from an acute self-consciousness brought about by the juxtaposition of opposites within the films' social context: good versus evil, powerlessness versus power, or poverty versus wealth. Such binary oppositions are used analogously
(55) in West African tales, and it seems likely that these dialectical elements are related to African oral storytelling more than, as many critics have supposed, to the Marxist components of his ideology.

1. Which one of the following most accurately states the main point of the passage?

(A) Sembène's originality as a filmmaker lies in his adaptation of traditional archetypal predicaments and open-ended plots, both of which are derived from West African oral tales.

(B) Many of the characters in Sembène's films are variations on character types common to traditional West African storytelling.

(C) Sembène's films derive their distinctive characteristics from oral narrative traditions that had not previously been considered suitable subject matter for films.

(D) Sembène's films give vivid expression to the social and political beliefs held by most of the Senegalese people.

(E) Sembène's films are notable in that they use elements derived from traditional West African storytelling to comment critically on contemporary social and political issues.

GO ON TO THE NEXT PAGE.

2. The author says that Sembène does which one of the following in at least some of his films?

   (A) uses animals as symbols
   (B) uses slow motion for artistic effect
   (C) provides oral narration of the film's story
   (D) juxtaposes West African images and Marxist symbols
   (E) leaves part of the story to be filled in by audiences

3. Which one of the following would, if true, most strengthen the claim made by the author in the last sentence of the passage (lines 54–58)?

   (A) Several African novelists who draw upon the oral traditions of West Africa use binary oppositions as fundamental structures in their narratives, even though they have not read Marxist theory.
   (B) Folklorists who have analyzed oral storytelling traditions from across the world have found that the use of binary oppositions to structure narratives is common to many of these traditions.
   (C) When he trained in Moscow, Sembène read extensively in Marxist political theory and worked to devise ways of synthesizing Marxist theory and the collective ideas expressed in West African storytelling.
   (D) Very few filmmakers in Europe or North America make use of binary oppositions to structure their narratives.
   (E) Binary oppositions do not play an essential structuring role in the narratives of some films produced by other filmmakers who subscribe to Marxist principles.

4. Which one of the following inferences about Sembène is most strongly supported by the passage?

   (A) His films have become popular both in parts of Africa and elsewhere.
   (B) He has not received support from government agencies for his film production.
   (C) His films are widely misunderstood by critics in Senegal.
   (D) His characters are drawn from a broad range of social strata.
   (E) His work has been subjected to government censorship.

5. Which one of the following most closely expresses the author's intended meaning in using the word "initiatory" (line 45)?

   (A) beginning a series
   (B) experimental
   (C) transformative
   (D) unprecedented
   (E) prefatory

6. The passage does NOT provide evidence that Sembène exhibits which one of the following attitudes in one or more of his films?

   (A) disenchantment with attempts to reform Senegalese government
   (B) confidence in the aptness of using traditional motifs to comment on contemporary issues
   (C) concern with social justice
   (D) interest in the vicissitudes of ordinary people's lives
   (E) desire to educate his audience

GO ON TO THE NEXT PAGE.

Passage A

Readers, like writers, need to search for answers. Part of the joy of reading is in being surprised, but academic historians leave little to the imagination. The perniciousness of the historiographic approach became
(5) fully evident to me when I started teaching. Historians require undergraduates to read scholarly monographs that sap the vitality of history; they visit on students what was visited on them in graduate school. They assign books with formulaic arguments that transform
(10) history into an abstract debate that would have been unfathomable to those who lived in the past. Aimed so squarely at the head, such books cannot stimulate students who yearn to connect to history emotionally as well as intellectually.
(15) In an effort to address this problem, some historians have begun to rediscover stories. It has even become something of a fad within the profession. This year, the American Historical Association chose as the theme for its annual conference some putative connection to
(20) storytelling: "Practices of Historical Narrative." Predictably, historians responded by adding the word "narrative" to their titles and presenting papers at sessions on "Oral History and the Narrative of Class Identity," and "Meaning and Time: The Problem of
(25) Historical Narrative." But it was still historiography. intended only for other academics. At meetings of historians, we still encounter very few historians telling stories or moving audiences to smiles, chills, or tears.

Passage B

Writing is at the heart of the lawyer's craft, and so,
(30) like it or not, we who teach the law inevitably teach aspiring lawyers how lawyers write. We do this in a few stand-alone courses and, to a greater extent, through the constraints that we impose on their writing throughout the curriculum. Legal writing, because of the purposes
(35) it serves, is necessarily ruled by linear logic, creating a path without diversions, surprises, or reversals. Conformity is a virtue, creativity suspect, humor forbidden, and voice mute.
Lawyers write as they see other lawyers write, and,
(40) influenced by education, profession, economic constraints, and perceived self-interest, they too often write badly. Perhaps the currently fashionable call for attention to narrative in legal education could have an effect on this. It is not yet exactly clear what role
(45) narrative should play in the law, but it is nonetheless true that every case has at its heart a story—of real events and people, of concerns, misfortunes, conflicts, feelings. But because legal analysis strips the human narrative content from the abstract, canonical legal
(50) form of the case, law students learn to act as if there is no such story.
It may well turn out that some of the terminology and public rhetoric of this potentially subversive movement toward attention to narrative will find its
(55) way into the law curriculum, but without producing corresponding changes in how legal writing is actually taught or in how our future colleagues will write. Still,

even mere awareness of the value of narrative could perhaps serve as an important corrective.

7. Which one of the following does each of the passages display?

(A) a concern with the question of what teaching methods are most effective in developing writing skills
(B) a concern with how a particular discipline tends to represent points of view it does not typically deal with
(C) a conviction that writing in specialized professional disciplines cannot be creatively crafted
(D) a belief that the writing in a particular profession could benefit from more attention to storytelling
(E) a desire to see writing in a particular field purged of elements from other disciplines

8. The passages most strongly support which one of the following inferences regarding the authors' relationships to the professions they discuss?

(A) Neither author is an active member of the profession that he or she discusses.
(B) Each author is an active member of the profession he or she discusses.
(C) The author of passage A is a member of the profession discussed in that passage, but the author of passage B is not a member of either of the professions discussed in the passages.
(D) Both authors are active members of the profession discussed in passage B.
(E) The author of passage B, but not the author of passage A, is an active member of both of the professions discussed in the passages.

GO ON TO THE NEXT PAGE.

9. Which one of the following does each passage indicate is typical of writing in the respective professions discussed in the passages?

   (A) abstraction
   (B) hyperbole
   (C) subversion
   (D) narrative
   (E) imagination

10. In which one of the following ways are the passages NOT parallel?

    (A) Passage A presents and rejects arguments for an opposing position, whereas passage B does not.
    (B) Passage A makes evaluative claims, whereas passage B does not.
    (C) Passage A describes specific examples of a phenomenon it criticizes, whereas passage B does not.
    (D) Passage B offers criticism, whereas passage A does not.
    (E) Passage B outlines a theory, whereas passage A does not.

11. The phrase "scholarly monographs that sap the vitality of history" in passage A (lines 6–7) plays a role in that passage's overall argument that is most analogous to the role played in passage B by which one of the following phrases?

    (A) "Writing is at the heart of the lawyer's craft" (line 29)
    (B) "Conformity is a virtue, creativity suspect, humor forbidden, and voice mute" (lines 37–38)
    (C) "Lawyers write as they see other lawyers write" (line 39)
    (D) "every case has at its heart a story" (line 46)
    (E) "Still, even mere awareness of the value of narrative could perhaps serve as an important corrective" (lines 57–59)

12. Suppose that a lawyer is writing a legal document describing the facts that are at issue in a case. The author of passage B would be most likely to expect which one of the following to be true of the document?

    (A) It will be poorly written because the lawyer who is writing it was not given explicit advice by law professors on how lawyers should write.
    (B) It will be crafted to function like a piece of fiction in its description of the characters and motivations of the people involved in the case.
    (C) It will be a concise, well-crafted piece of writing that summarizes most, if not all, of the facts that are important in the case.
    (D) It will not genuinely convey the human dimension of the case, regardless of how accurate the document may be in its details.
    (E) It will neglect to make appropriate connections between the details of the case and relevant legal doctrines.

GO ON TO THE NEXT PAGE.

Traditional theories of animal behavior assert that animal conflict within a species is highly ritualized and does not vary from contest to contest. This species-specific model assumes that repetitive use of
(5) the same visual and vocal displays and an absence of escalated fighting evolved to prevent injury. The contestant that exhibits the "best" display wins the contested resource. Galápagos tortoises, for instance, settle contests on the basis of height: the ritualized
(10) display consists of two tortoises facing one another and stretching their necks skyward; the tortoise perceived as being "taller" wins.

In populations of the spider *Agelenopsis aperta*, however, fighting behavior varies greatly from contest
(15) to contest. In addition, fighting is not limited to displays: biting and shoving are common. Susan Riechert argues that a recently developed model, evolutionary game theory, provides a closer fit to *A. aperta* territorial disputes than does the species-
(20) specific model, because it explains variations in conflict behavior that may result from varying conditions, such as differences in size, age, and experience of combatants. Evolutionary game theory was adapted from the classical game theory that was
(25) developed by von Neumann and Morganstern to explain human behavior in conflict situations. In both classical and evolutionary game theory, strategies are weighed in terms of maximizing the average payoff against contestants employing both the same and
(30) different strategies. For example, a spider may engage in escalated fighting during a dispute only if the disputed resource is valuable enough to warrant the risk of physical injury. There are, however, two major differences between the classical and evolutionary
(35) theories. First, whereas in classical game theory it is assumed that rational thought is used to determine which action to take, evolutionary game theory assumes that instinct and long-term species advantage ultimately determine the strategies that are exhibited.
(40) The other difference is in the payoffs: in classical game theory, the payoffs are determined by an individual's personal judgment of what constitutes winning; in evolutionary game theory, the payoffs are defined in terms of reproductive success.
(45) In studying populations of *A. aperta* in a grassland habitat and a riparian habitat, Riechert predicts that such factors as the size of the opponents, the potential rate of predation in a habitat, and the probability of winning a subsequent site if the dispute
(50) is lost will all affect the behavior of spiders in territorial disputes. In addition, she predicts that the markedly different levels of competition for web sites in the two habitats will affect the spiders' willingness to engage in escalated fighting. In the grassland,
(55) where 12 percent of the habitat is available for occupation by *A. aperta*, Riechert predicts that spiders will be more willing to engage in escalated fighting than in the riparian habitat, where 90 percent of the habitat is suitable for occupation.

13. Which one of the following best states the main idea of the passage?

(A) Evolutionary game theory and classical game theory can be used to analyze the process of decision-making used by humans and animals in settling disputes.

(B) *A. aperta* in grassland habitats and riparian habitats exhibit an unusually wide variety of fighting behaviors in territorial disputes.

(C) Evolutionary game theory may be useful in explaining the behavior of certain spiders during territorial disputes.

(D) The traditional theory of animal behavior in conflict situations cannot be used to explain the fighting behavior of most species.

(E) Evolutionary game theory, adapted from classical game theory, is currently used by scientists to predict the behavior of spiders in site selection.

14. The author of the passage mentions Galápagos tortoises in the first paragraph most likely in order to

(A) describe a kind of fighting behavior that is used by only a few species

(B) suggest that repetitive use of the same visual and vocal displays is a kind of fighting behavior used by some but not all species

(C) provide evidence to support the claim that fighting behavior does not vary greatly from contest to contest for most species

(D) provide an example of a fighting behavior that is unique to a particular species

(E) provide an example of a ritualized fighting behavior of the kind that traditional theorists assume is the norm for most species

GO ON TO THE NEXT PAGE.

15. Item Removed From Scoring.

16. Which one of the following, if true, is LEAST consistent with Riechert's theory about fighting behavior in spiders?

(A) Spiders in the grassland habitat engage in escalated fighting when a disputed site is highly desirable.

(B) Spiders in the riparian habitat are not willing to engage in escalated fighting for less-than-suitable sites.

(C) Spiders in the riparian habitat confine their fighting to displays more regularly than do spiders in the grassland habitat.

(D) Spiders in the riparian habitat are as willing to engage in escalated fighting as are spiders in the grassland habitat.

(E) Spiders in the riparian habitat are more likely to withdraw when faced with a larger opponent in territorial disputes than are spiders in the grassland habitat.

17. Which one of the following best states the function of the third paragraph of the passage?

(A) It develops a comparison of the two theories that were introduced in the preceding paragraph.

(B) It continues a discussion of a controversial theory described in the first two paragraphs of the passage.

(C) It describes an experiment that provides support for the theory described in the preceding paragraph.

(D) It describes a rare phenomenon that cannot be accounted for by the theory described in the first paragraph.

(E) It describes predictions that can be used to test the validity of a theory described in a preceding paragraph.

18. The passage suggests which one of the following about the behavior of *A. aperta* in conflict situations?

(A) They exhibit variations in fighting behavior from contest to contest primarily because of the different levels of competition for suitable sites in different habitats.

(B) They may confine their fighting behavior to displays if the value of a disputed resource is too low and the risk of physical injury is too great.

(C) They exhibit variations in fighting behavior that are similar to those exhibited by members of most other species of animals.

(D) They are more likely to engage in escalated fighting during disputes than to limit their fighting behavior to visual and vocal displays.

(E) They are more willing to engage in escalated fighting during conflict situations than are members of most other species of animals.

19. The primary purpose of the passage is to

(A) present an alternative to a traditional approach

(B) describe a phenomenon and provide specific examples

(C) evaluate evidence used to support an argument

(D) present data that refutes a controversial theory

(E) suggest that a new theory may be based on inadequate research

GO ON TO THE NEXT PAGE.

Most people acknowledge that not all governments have a moral right to govern and that there are sometimes morally legitimate reasons for disobeying the law, as when a particular law
(5) prescribes behavior that is clearly immoral. It is also commonly supposed that such cases are special exceptions and that, in general, the fact that something is against the law counts as a moral, as well as legal, ground for not doing it; i.e., we
(10) generally have a moral duty to obey a law simply because it is the law. But the theory known as philosophical anarchism denies this view, arguing instead that people who live under the jurisdiction of governments have no moral duty to those
(15) governments to obey their laws. Some commentators have rejected this position because of what they take to be its highly counterintuitive implications: (1) that no existing government is morally better than any other (since all are, in a sense, equally illegitimate),
(20) and (2) that, lacking any moral obligation to obey any laws, people may do as they please without scruple. In fact, however, philosophical anarchism does not entail these claims.

First, the conclusion that no government is
(25) morally better than any other does not follow from the claim that nobody owes moral obedience to any government. Even if one denies that there is a moral obligation to follow the laws of any government, one can still evaluate the morality of the policies and
(30) actions of various governments. Some governments do more good than harm, and others more harm than good, to their subjects. Some violate the moral rights of individuals more regularly, systematically, and seriously than others. In short, it is perfectly
(35) consistent with philosophical anarchism to hold that governments vary widely in their moral stature.

Second, philosophical anarchists maintain that all individuals have basic, nonlegal moral duties to one another—duties not to harm others in their lives,
(40) liberty, health, or goods. Even if governmental laws have no moral force, individuals still have duties to refrain from those actions that constitute crimes in the majority of legal systems (such as murder, assault, theft, and fraud). Moreover, philosophical anarchists
(45) hold that people have a positive moral obligation to care for one another, a moral obligation that they might even choose to discharge by supporting cooperative efforts by governments to help those in need. And where others are abiding by established
(50) laws, even those laws derived from mere conventions, individuals are morally bound not to violate those laws when doing so would endanger others. Thus, if others obey the law and drive their vehicles on the right, one must not endanger them by driving on the
(55) left, for, even though driving on the left is not inherently immoral, it is morally wrong to deliberately harm the innocent.

20. Which one of the following most accurately expresses the main point of the passage?

(A) Some views that certain commentators consider to be implications of philosophical anarchism are highly counterintuitive.

(B) Contrary to what philosophical anarchists claim, some governments are morally superior to others, and citizens under legitimate governments have moral obligations to one another.

(C) It does not follow logically from philosophical anarchism that no government is morally better than any other or that people have no moral duties toward one another.

(D) Even if, as certain philosophical anarchists claim, governmental laws lack moral force, people still have a moral obligation to refrain from harming one another.

(E) Contrary to what some of its opponents have claimed, philosophical anarchism does not conflict with the ordinary view that one should obey the law because it is the law.

21. The author identifies which one of the following as a commonly held belief?

(A) In most cases we are morally obligated to obey the law simply because it is the law.
(B) All governments are in essence morally equal.
(C) We are morally bound to obey only those laws we participate in establishing.
(D) Most crimes are morally neutral, even though they are illegal.
(E) The majority of existing laws are intended to protect others from harm.

22. The author's stance regarding the theory of philosophical anarchism can most accurately be described as one of

(A) ardent approval of most aspects of the theory
(B) apparent acceptance of some of the basic positions of the theory
(C) concerned pessimism about the theory's ability to avoid certain extreme views
(D) hesitant rejection of some of the central features of the theory
(E) resolute antipathy toward both the theory and certain of its logical consequences

GO ON TO THE NEXT PAGE.

23. By attributing to commentators the view that philosophical anarchism has implications that are "counterintuitive" (line 17), the author most likely means that the commentators believe that

    (A) the implications conflict with some commonly held beliefs
    (B) there is little empirical evidence that the implications are actually true
    (C) common sense indicates that philosophical anarchism does not have such implications
    (D) the implications appear to be incompatible with each other
    (E) each of the implications contains an internal logical inconsistency

24. Which one of the following scenarios most completely conforms to the views attributed to philosophical anarchists in lines 37–44?

    (A) A member of a political party that is illegal in a particular country divulges the names of other members because he fears legal penalties.
    (B) A corporate executive chooses to discontinue her company's practice of dumping chemicals illegally when she learns that the chemicals are contaminating the water supply.
    (C) A person who knows that a coworker has stolen funds from their employer decides to do nothing because the coworker is widely admired.
    (D) A person neglects to pay her taxes, even though it is likely that she will suffer severe legal penalties as a consequence, because she wants to use the money to finance a new business.
    (E) A driver determines that it is safe to exceed the posted speed limit, in spite of poor visibility, because there are apparently no other vehicles on the road.

25. It can be inferred that the author would be most likely to agree that

    (A) people are subject to more moral obligations than is generally held to be the case
    (B) governments that are morally superior recognize that their citizens are not morally bound to obey their laws
    (C) one may have good reason to support the efforts of one's government even if one has no moral duty to obey its laws
    (D) there are some sound arguments for claiming that most governments have a moral right to require obedience to their laws
    (E) the theory of philosophical anarchism entails certain fundamental principles regarding how laws should be enacted and enforced

26. The author's discussion of people's positive moral duty to care for one another (lines 44–49) functions primarily to

    (A) demonstrate that governmental efforts to help those in need are superfluous
    (B) suggest that philosophical anarchists maintain that laws that foster the common good are extremely rare
    (C) imply that the theoretical underpinnings of philosophical anarchism are inconsistent with certain widely held moral truths
    (D) indicate that philosophical anarchists recognize that people are subject to substantial moral obligations
    (E) illustrate that people are morally obligated to refrain from those actions that arc crimes in most legal systems

27. In the passage, the author seeks primarily to

    (A) describe the development and theoretical underpinnings of a particular theory
    (B) establish that a particular theory conforms to the dictates of common sense
    (C) argue that two necessary implications of a particular theory are morally acceptable
    (D) defend a particular theory against its critics by showing that their arguments are mistaken
    (E) demonstrate that proponents of a particular theory are aware of the theory's defects

S T O P

IF YOU FINISH BEFORE TIME IS CALLED, YOU MAY CHECK YOUR WORK ON THIS SECTION ONLY.
DO NOT WORK ON ANY OTHER SECTION IN THE TEST.

Acknowledgment is made to the following sources from which material has been adapted for use in this test booklet:

A.S. Cutler, "Lawyers Should Not Accept Unlawful Cases." © 1983 by Greenhaven Press, Inc.

Carl Sagan, "*Cosmos*" © 1980 by Carl Sagan Productions, Inc.

Dinha Kaplan, "When Less Is More." ©1997 by Sussex Publishers, Inc.

Françoise Pfaff, "The Uniqueness of Ousmane Sembène's Cinema." ©1993 by Five Colleges, Inc.

A. John Simmons, *On the Edge of Anarchy: Locke, Consent, and the Limits of Society*. ©1993 by Princeton University Press.

Wait for the supervisor's instructions before you open the page to the topic.
Please print and sign your name and write the date in the designated spaces below.

Time: 35 Minutes

General Directions

You will have 35 minutes in which to plan and write an essay on the topic inside. Read the topic and the accompanying directions carefully. You will probably find it best to spend a few minutes considering the topic and organizing your thoughts before you begin writing. In your essay, be sure to develop your ideas fully, leaving time, if possible, to review what you have written. **Do not write on a topic other than the one specified. Writing on a topic of your own choice is not acceptable.**

No special knowledge is required or expected for this writing exercise. Law schools are interested in the reasoning, clarity, organization, language usage, and writing mechanics displayed in your essay. How well you write is more important than how much you write.

Confine your essay to the blocked, lined area on the front and back of the separate Writing Sample Response Sheet. Only that area will be reproduced for law schools. Be sure that your writing is legible.

Both this topic sheet and your response sheet must be turned over to the testing staff before you leave the room.

Topic Code	Print Your Full Name Here		
_____	Last	First	M.I.

Date	Sign Your Name Here
/ /	

Scratch Paper
Do not write your essay in this space.

LSAT Writing Sample Topic

A neighborhood association is planning to sponsor a public event on the first day of summer—either a walking tour or a 5 kilometer run. Using the facts below, write an essay in which you argue for one event over the other based on the following two criteria:

- The association wants to encourage more neighborhood residents to become association members.
- In order to conduct other activities during the year, the association wants to minimize the time and resources required by the event.

The first event is a free, self-guided walking tour of some of the neighborhood's private homes and historic buildings. The tour would feature the association's promotional table and exhibits of crafts, music, and cooking. Many neighborhood residents have expressed interest in such a tour. Some of the responsibility for organizing the event would be borne by those who own the homes and buildings; the association would be responsible for the remaining details. The costs of this event would consume most of the association's annual budget. Other neighborhood associations that have conducted similar tours report robust neighborhood participation and accompanying increases in membership.

The second event is a 5 kilometer run through the neighborhood. The association has sponsored this yearly event for almost a decade. In recent years, the association has hired a third-party company to manage the race and would do so again. Registration fees collected from race participants would cover administrative costs. In the past the event has led to modest increases in membership for the associating. At its peak, almost 1,000 people participated in the race, most of them from out of town. This year more people are expected to participate, because the course has been professionally certified and the race would serve as a qualifying race for a national championship.

Scratch Paper
Do not write your essay in this space.

LAST NAME (Print)　　　　　　　　　　MI　　FIRST NAME (Print)

SIGNATURE

Writing Sample Response Sheet

DO NOT WRITE
IN THIS SPACE

Begin your essay in the lined area below.
Continue on the back if you need more space.

Directions:

1. Use the Answer Key on the next page to check your answers.

2. Use the Scoring Worksheet below to compute your raw score.

3. Use the Score Conversion Chart to convert your raw score into the 120–180 scale.

Scoring Worksheet

1. Enter the number of questions you answered correctly in each section

	Number Correct
SECTION I	_____
SECTION II	__EXP__
SECTION III	_____
SECTION IV	_____
SECTION V	_____

2. Enter the sum here: _____

This is your Raw Score.

Conversion Chart

For Converting Raw Score to the 120–180 LSAT Scaled Score

LSAT PrepTest 52

Reported Score	Raw Score Lowest	Raw Score Highest
180	97	99
179	—*	—*
178	96	96
177	95	95
176	94	94
175	—*	—*
174	93	93
173	92	92
172	91	91
171	90	90
170	89	89
169	88	88
168	87	87
167	86	86
166	84	85
165	83	83
164	82	82
163	80	81
162	78	79
161	77	77
160	75	76
159	73	74
158	72	72
157	70	71
156	68	69
155	66	67
154	64	65
153	62	63
152	61	61
151	59	60
150	57	58
149	55	56
148	53	54
147	51	52
146	50	50
145	48	49
144	46	47
143	45	45
142	43	44
141	41	42
140	40	40
139	38	39
138	36	37
137	35	35
136	33	34
135	32	32
134	31	31
133	29	30
132	28	28
131	27	27
130	25	26
129	24	24
128	23	23
127	22	22
126	21	21
125	20	20
124	19	19
123	18	18
122	16	17
121	—*	—*
120	0	15

*There is no raw score that will produce this scaled score for this form.

SECTION I

1.	C	8.	C	15.	B	22.	D
2.	D	9.	D	16.	A	23.	D
3.	A	10.	A	17.	E	24.	E
4.	C	11.	C	18.	B	25.	E
5.	B	12.	E	19.	E		
6.	E	13.	E	20.	E		
7.	A	14.	C	21.	C		

SECTION II (experimental)

1.	D	8.	E	15.	A	22.	A
2.	E	9.	B	16.	E	23.	A
3.	A	10.	C	17.	C	24.	C
4.	C	11.	B	18.	A	25.	D
5.	B	12.	D	19.	B	26.	C
6.	A	13.	A	20.	E	27.	D
7.	B	14.	D	21.	D		

SECTION III

1.	E	8.	B	15.	C	22.	C
2.	C	9.	E	16.	B	23.	E
3.	B	10.	A	17.	D		
4.	B	11.	D	18.	C		
5.	E	12.	C	19.	A		
6.	B	13.	B	20.	E		
7.	B	14.	E	21.	C		

SECTION IV

1.	D	8.	A	15.	D	22.	E
2.	D	9.	C	16.	C	23.	A
3.	B	10.	E	17.	B	24.	C
4.	B	11.	B	18.	D	25.	A
5.	D	12.	E	19.	A		
6.	C	13.	D	20.	E		
7.	A	14.	C	21.	E		

SECTION V

1.	E	8.	B	15.	*	22.	B
2.	E	9.	A	16.	D	23.	A
3.	A	10.	C	17.	E	24.	B
4.	D	11.	B	18.	B	25.	C
5.	C	12.	D	19.	A	26.	D
6.	A	13.	C	20.	C	27.	D
7.	D	14.	E	21.	A		

Endurance Practice Test 5

PrepTest 51 plus experimental from PrepTest 7, Section IV

SCAN CODE: LL9005

SECTION I

Time—35 minutes

25 Questions

Directions: The questions in this section are based on the reasoning contained in brief statements or passages. For some questions, more than one of the choices could conceivably answer the question. However, you are to choose the best answer; that is, the response that most accurately and completely answers the question. You should not make assumptions that are by commonsense standards implausible, superfluous, or incompatible with the passage. After you have chosen the best answer, blacken the corresponding space on your answer sheet.

1. Editorial: Almost every year the Smithfield River floods the coastal fishing community of Redhook, which annually spends $3 million on the cleanup. Some residents have proposed damming the river, which would cost $5 million but would prevent the flooding. However, their position is misguided. A dam would prevent nutrients in the river from flowing into the ocean. Fish that now feed on those nutrients would start feeding elsewhere. The loss of these fish would cost Redhook $10 million annually.

Which one of the following most accurately expresses the main conclusion of the editorial's argument?

(A) The Smithfield River should be dammed to prevent flooding.
(B) Nutrients from the Smithfield River are essential to the local fish population.
(C) Damming the Smithfield River is not worth the high construction costs for such a project.
(D) For Redhook to build a dam on the Smithfield River would be a mistake.
(E) The Smithfield River floods cost Redhook $3 million every year.

2. We already knew from thorough investigation that immediately prior to the accident, either the driver of the first vehicle changed lanes without signaling or the driver of the second vehicle was driving with excessive speed. Either of these actions would make a driver liable for the resulting accident. But further evidence has proved that the first vehicle's turn signal was not on, though the driver of that vehicle admits to having changed lanes. So the driver of the second vehicle is not liable for the accident.

Which one of the following would be most important to know in evaluating the conclusion drawn above?

(A) whether the second vehicle was being driven at excessive speed
(B) whether the driver of the first vehicle knew that the turn signal was not on
(C) whether any other vehicles were involved in the accident
(D) whether the driver of the first vehicle was a reliable witness
(E) whether the driver of the second vehicle would have seen the turn signal flashing had it been on

3. In some places, iceberg lilies are the mainstay of grizzly bears' summer diets. The bears forage meadows for the lilies, uprooting them and eating their bulbs. Although the bears annually destroy a large percentage of the lilies, scientists have determined that the bears' feeding habits actually promote the survival of iceberg lilies.

Which one of the following, if true, most helps to resolve the apparent discrepancy in the statements above?

(A) When grizzly bears forage for iceberg lilies, they generally kill many more lilies than they eat.
(B) Iceberg lilies produce so many offspring that, when undisturbed, they quickly deplete the resources necessary for their own survival.
(C) A significantly smaller number of iceberg lily flowers are produced in fields where grizzly bears forage than in fields of undisturbed iceberg lilies.
(D) The geographic regions in which iceberg lilies are most prevalent are those regions populated by grizzly bears.
(E) Iceberg lilies contain plentiful amounts of some nutrients that are necessary for grizzly bears' survival.

GO ON TO THE NEXT PAGE.

4. Advertisement: Seventy-five percent of dermatologists surveyed prefer Dermactin to all other brands of skin cream. Why? We consulted dermatologists during the development of Dermactin to ensure that you have the best skin cream on the market. So if you need a skin cream, use Dermactin.

The reasoning in the advertisement is questionable because the advertisement

(A) overlooks the possibility that other types of doctors have cause to use Dermactin, which would render the sample unrepresentative

(B) fails to state the number of dermatologists surveyed, which leaves open the possibility that the sample of doctors is too small to be reliable

(C) presumes, without providing justification, that some dermatologists are less qualified than others to evaluate skin cream

(D) relies on an inappropriate appeal to the opinions of consumers with no special knowledge of skin care

(E) overlooks the possibility that for a few people, using no skin cream is preferable to using even the best skin cream

5. Landscape architect: If the screen between these two areas is to be a hedge, that hedge must be of either hemlocks or Leyland cypress trees. However, Leyland cypress trees cannot be grown this far north. So if the screen is to be a hedge, it will be a hemlock hedge.

In which one of the following is the pattern of reasoning most similar to that in the landscape architect's argument?

(A) If there is to be an entrance on the north side of the building, it will have to be approached by a ramp. However, a ramp would become impossibly slippery in winter, so there will be no entrance on the north side.

(B) If visitors are to travel to this part of the site by automobile, there will be a need for parking spaces. However, no parking spaces are allowed for in the design. So if visitors are likely to come by automobile, the design will be changed.

(C) The subsoil in these five acres either consists entirely of clay or consists entirely of shale. Therefore, if one test hole in the area reveals shale, it will be clear that the entire five acres has a shale subsoil.

(D) Any path along this embankment must be either concrete or stone. But a concrete path cannot be built in this location. So if there is to be a path on the embankment, it will be a stone path.

(E) A space the size of this meadow would be suitable for a playground or a picnic area. However, a playground would be noisy and a picnic area would create litter. So it will be best for the area to remain a meadow.

6. Deirdre: Many philosophers have argued that the goal of every individual is to achieve happiness—that is, the satisfaction derived from fully living up to one's potential. They have also claimed that happiness is elusive and can be achieved only after years of sustained effort. But these philosophers have been unduly pessimistic, since they have clearly exaggerated the difficulty of being happy. Simply walking along the seashore on a sunny afternoon causes many people to experience feelings of happiness.

Which one of the following most accurately describes a reasoning flaw in Deirdre's argument?

(A) It dismisses a claim because of its source rather than because of its content.

(B) It fails to take into account that what brings someone happiness at one moment may not bring that person happiness at another time.

(C) It allows the key term "happiness" to shift in meaning illicitly in the course of the argument.

(D) It presumes, without providing justification, that happiness is, in fact, the goal of life.

(E) It makes a generalization based on the testimony of a group whose views have not been shown to be representative.

7. Global ecological problems reduce to the problem of balancing supply and demand. Supply is strictly confined by the earth's limitations. Demand, however, is essentially unlimited, as there are no limits on the potential demands made by humans. The natural tendency for there to be an imbalance between demand and sustainable supply is the source of these global problems. Therefore, any solutions require reducing current human demand.

Which one of the following is an assumption on which the argument depends?

(A) Supply and demand tend to balance themselves in the long run.

(B) It is possible to determine the limitations of the earth's sustainable supply.

(C) Actual human demand exceeds the earth's sustainable supply.

(D) It is never possible to achieve a balance between the environmental supply and human demand.

(E) Human consumption does not decrease the environmental supply.

GO ON TO THE NEXT PAGE.

8. We can now dismiss the widely held suspicion that sugar consumption often exacerbates hyperactivity in children with attention deficit disorder. A scientific study of the effects of three common sugars—sucrose, fructose, and glucose—on children who have attention deficit disorder, with experimental groups each receiving a type of sugar in their diets and a control group receiving a sugar substitute instead of sugar, showed no statistically significant difference between the groups in thinking or behavior.

Which one of the following, if true, would most weaken the argument above?

(A) Only one of the three types of sugar used in the study was ever widely suspected of exacerbating hyperactivity.

(B) The consumption of sugar actually has a calming effect on some children.

(C) The consumption of some sugar substitutes exacerbates the symptoms of hyperactivity.

(D) The study included some observations of each group in contexts that generally tend to make children excited and active.

(E) Some children believe that they can tell the difference between the taste of sugar and that of sugar substitutes.

9. Philosopher: An action is morally good if it both achieves the agent's intended goal and benefits someone other than the agent.

Which one of the following judgments most closely conforms to the principle cited by the philosopher?

(A) Colin chose to lie to the authorities questioning him, in an attempt to protect his friends. The authorities discovered his deception and punished Colin and his friends severely. But because he acted out of love for his friends, Colin's action was morally good.

(B) Derek prepared a steak dinner to welcome his new neighbors to the neighborhood. When they arrived for dinner, Derek found out that the newcomers were strict vegetarians. Though the new neighbors were still grateful for Derek's efforts to welcome them, Derek's action was not morally good.

(C) Ellen worked overtime hoping to get a promotion. The extra money she earned allowed her family to take a longer vacation that year, but she failed to get the promotion. Nevertheless, Ellen's action was morally good.

(D) Louisa tried to get Henry into serious trouble by making it appear that he stole some expensive clothes from a store. But the store's detective realized what Louisa did, and so Louisa was punished rather than Henry. Since she intended to harm Henry, Louisa's action was not morally good.

(E) Yolanda took her children to visit their grandfather because she wanted her children to enjoy their vacation and she knew they adored their grandfather. The grandfather and the children all enjoyed the visit. Though Yolanda greatly enjoyed the visit, her action was morally good.

GO ON TO THE NEXT PAGE.

10. Columnist: A recent research report suggests that by exercising vigorously, one significantly lowers one's chances of developing certain cardio-respiratory illnesses. But exercise has this effect, the report concludes, only if the exercise is vigorous. Thus, one should not heed older studies purporting to show that nonstrenuous walking yields the same benefits.

The reasoning in the columnist's argument is most vulnerable to criticism on the grounds that this argument

(A) fails to consider the possibility that the risk of developing certain cardio-respiratory illnesses can be reduced by means other than exercise

(B) fails to consider that those who exercise vigorously are at increased risk of physical injury caused by exercise

(C) overlooks the possibility that vigorous exercise may prevent life-endangering diseases that have little to do with the cardio-respiratory system

(D) fails to consider the possibility that those who engage in vigorous physical exercise are more likely than others to perceive themselves as healthy

(E) fails to show that a certain conclusion of the recent report is better justified than an opposing conclusion reached in older studies

11. Some statisticians believe that the method called extreme value theory (EVT) is a powerful analytical tool. The curves generated by traditional statistical methods to analyze empirical data on human longevity predict that some humans would live beyond 130 years. According to the curves EVT generates, however, the limit on human life spans is probably between 113 and 124 years. To date, no one has lived beyond the upper limits indicated by EVT analysis.

Which one of the following can be properly inferred from the statements above?

(A) EVT is, in general, a more reliable method for projecting future trends based on past observations than are traditional statistical methods.

(B) EVT fits the data about the highest observed human life spans more closely than do traditional statistical methods.

(C) According to the findings derived through the use of EVT, it is physically impossible for any human being to live longer than 124 years.

(D) Given the results generated by EVT, there is no point in conducting research aimed at greatly extending the upper limit on human life spans.

(E) Traditional statistical methods of empirical data analysis should eventually be replaced by some version of EVT.

12. The number of different synthetic chemical compounds that are known to be carcinogenic but are nonetheless used as pesticides, preservatives, or food additives is tiny compared to the number of nonsynthetic carcinogenic compounds widely found in plants and animals. It is therefore absurd to suppose that the rise in the cancer rate in recent decades is due to synthetic carcinogens.

The reasoning above is most vulnerable to criticism on the grounds that it overlooks the possibility that

(A) the rise in the cancer rate in recent decades is due to increased exposure to nonsynthetic pollutants

(B) the rise in the cancer rate in recent decades is due to something other than increased exposure to carcinogens

(C) some synthetic chemical compounds that are not known to be carcinogenic are in other respects toxic

(D) people undergo significantly less exposure to carcinogens that are not synthetic than to those that are synthetic

(E) people can vary greatly in their susceptibility to cancers caused by nonsynthetic carcinogens

13. It is a mistake to think, as ecologists once did, that natural selection will eventually result in organisms that will be perfectly adapted to their environments. After all, perfect adaptation of an individual to its environment is impossible, for an individual's environment can vary tremendously; no single set of attributes could possibly prepare an organism to cope with all the conditions that it could face.

Which one of the following most accurately expresses the main conclusion of the argument?

(A) It is not possible for an individual to be perfectly adapted to its environment.

(B) Natural selection will never result in individuals that will be perfectly adapted to their environments.

(C) No single set of attributes could enable an individual organism to cope with all of the conditions that it might face.

(D) Because an individual's environment can vary tremendously, no individual can be perfectly adapted to its environment.

(E) Ecologists once believed that natural selection would eventually result in individuals that will be perfectly adapted to their environments.

GO ON TO THE NEXT PAGE.

14. It would not be surprising to discover that the trade routes between China and the West were opened many centuries, even millennia, earlier than 200 B.C., contrary to what is currently believed. After all, what made the Great Silk Road so attractive as a trade route linking China and the West—level terrain, easily traversable mountain passes, and desert oases—would also have made it an attractive route for the original emigrants to China from Africa and the Middle East, and this early migration began at least one million years ago.

That a migration from Africa and the Middle East to China occurred at least one million years ago figures in the above reasoning in which one of the following ways?

(A) It is cited as conclusive evidence for the claim that trade links between China and the Middle East were established long before 200 B.C.

(B) It is an intermediate conclusion made plausible by the description of the terrain along which the migration supposedly took place.

(C) It is offered as evidence in support of the claim that trade routes between China and the West could easily have been established much earlier than is currently believed.

(D) It is offered as evidence against the claim that trade routes between China and Africa preceded those eventually established between China and the Middle East.

(E) It is the main conclusion that the argument attempts to establish about intercourse between China and the West.

15. The typological theory of species classification, which has few adherents today, distinguishes species solely on the basis of observable physical characteristics, such as plumage color, adult size, or dental structure. However, there are many so-called "sibling species," which are indistinguishable on the basis of their appearance but cannot interbreed and thus, according to the mainstream biological theory of species classification, are separate species. Since the typological theory does not count sibling species as separate species, it is unacceptable.

The reasoning in the argument is most vulnerable to criticism on the grounds that

(A) the argument does not evaluate all aspects of the typological theory

(B) the argument confuses a necessary condition for species distinction with a sufficient condition for species distinction

(C) the argument, in its attempt to refute one theory of species classification, presupposes the truth of an opposing theory

(D) the argument takes a single fact that is incompatible with a theory as enough to show that theory to be false

(E) the argument does not explain why sibling species cannot interbreed

16. Chiu: The belief that a person is always morally blameworthy for feeling certain emotions, such as unjustifiable anger, jealousy, or resentment, is misguided. Individuals are responsible for only what is under their control, and whether one feels such an emotion is not always under one's control.

Chiu's conclusion follows logically if which one of the following is assumed?

(A) Individuals do not have control over their actions when they feel certain emotions.

(B) If a person is morally blameworthy for something, then that person is responsible for it.

(C) Although a person may sometimes be unjustifiably angry, jealous, or resentful, there are occasions when these emotions are appropriate.

(D) If an emotion is under a person's control, then that person cannot hold others responsible for it.

(E) The emotions for which a person is most commonly blamed are those that are under that person's control.

GO ON TO THE NEXT PAGE.

17. Industrial adviser: If two new processes under consideration are not substantially different in cost, then the less environmentally damaging process should be chosen. If, however, a company already employs an environmentally damaging process and retooling for a less damaging process would involve substantial cost, then that company should retool only if retooling is either legally required or likely to bring long-term savings substantially greater than the cost.

Which one of the following judgments conforms most closely to the principles described by the industrial adviser?

(A) A new law offering companies tax credits for reducing pollution would enable a company to realize a slight long-term savings by changing to a more environmentally sound process for manufacturing dye, despite the substantial cost of retooling. In light of the new law, the company should change its process.

(B) In manufacturing pincushions, a company uses a process that, though legal, has come under heavy public criticism for the environmental damage it causes. The company should change its process to preserve its public image, despite some expected long-term losses from doing so.

(C) A company is considering two new processes for the manufacture of staples. Process A is more expensive than process B but not substantially so. However, process A is substantially less environmentally damaging than process B. The company should implement process A.

(D) Two new processes are being considered for the manufacture of ball bearings. The processes are similar, except that the chemicals used in process A will pollute a nearby river slightly more than will the chemicals for process B. Process A is also slightly cheaper than process B. The company should use process A.

(E) A company is considering changing its process for manufacturing shoelaces. The new process is cheaper and less environmentally damaging than the old. Both are legal. Changing processes would be costly, but the cost would be almost entirely recovered in long-term savings. The company should switch processes.

18. In a poll of a representative sample of a province's residents, the provincial capital was the city most often selected as the best place to live in that province. Since the capital is also the largest of that province's many cities, the poll shows that most residents of that province generally prefer life in large cities to life in small cities.

The argument is most vulnerable to the criticism that it

(A) overlooks the possibility that what is true of the residents of the province may not be true of other people

(B) does not indicate whether most residents of other provinces also prefer life in large cities to life in small cities

(C) takes for granted that when people are polled for their preferences among cities, they tend to vote for the city that they think is the best place to live

(D) overlooks the possibility that the people who preferred small cities over the provincial capital did so not because of their general feelings about the sizes of cities, but because of their general feelings about capital cities

(E) overlooks the possibility that most people may have voted for small cities even though a large city received more votes than any other single city

19. Geneticist: Genes, like viruses, have a strong tendency to self-replicate; this has led some biologists to call genes "selfish." This term is, in this instance, intended to be defined behaviorally: it describes what genes do without ascribing intentions to them. But even given that genes are ascribed no intentions, the label "selfish" as applied to genes is a misnomer. Selfishness only concerns bringing about the best conditions for oneself; creating replicas of oneself is not selfish.

Which one of the following, if assumed, allows the geneticist's conclusion to be properly drawn?

(A) Bringing about the best conditions for oneself is less important than doing this for others.

(B) Creating replicas of oneself does not help bring about the best conditions for oneself.

(C) The behavioral definition of "selfish" is incompatible with its everyday definition.

(D) To ignore the fact that self-replication is not limited to genes is to misunderstand genetic behavior.

(E) Biologists have insufficient evidence about genetic behavior to determine whether it is best described as selfish.

GO ON TO THE NEXT PAGE.

20. Only experienced salespeople will be able to meet the company's selling quota. Thus, I must not count as an experienced salesperson, since I will be able to sell only half the quota.

The pattern of flawed reasoning exhibited by the argument above is most similar to that exhibited by which one of the following?

(A) Only on Fridays are employees allowed to dress casually. Today is Friday but Hector is dressed formally. So he must not be going to work.

(B) Only music lovers take this class. Thus, since Hillary is not taking this class, she apparently does not love music.

(C) Only oceanographers enjoy the Atlantic in midwinter. Thus, we may expect that Gerald does not enjoy the Atlantic in midwinter, since he is not an oceanographer.

(D) As this tree before us is a giant redwood, it follows that we must be in a northern latitude, since it is only in northern latitudes that one finds giant redwoods.

(E) Only accomplished mountain climbers can scale El Capitan. Thus, Michelle must be able to scale El Capitan, since she is an accomplished mountain climber.

21. Designer: Any garden and adjoining living room that are separated from one another by sliding glass doors can visually merge into a single space. If the sliding doors are open, as may happen in summer, this effect will be created if it does not already exist and intensified if it does. The effect remains quite strong during colder months if the garden is well coordinated with the room and contributes strong visual interest of its own.

The designer's statements, if true, most strongly support which one of the following?

(A) A garden separated from an adjoining living room by closed sliding glass doors cannot be well coordinated with the room unless the garden contributes strong visual interest.

(B) In cold weather, a garden and an adjoining living room separated from one another by sliding glass doors will not visually merge into a single space unless the garden is well coordinated with the room.

(C) A garden and an adjoining living room separated by sliding glass doors cannot visually merge in summer unless the doors are open.

(D) A garden can visually merge with an adjoining living room into a single space even if the garden does not contribute strong visual interest of its own.

(E) Except in summer, opening the sliding glass doors that separate a garden from an adjoining living room does not intensify the effect of the garden and room visually merging into a single space.

22. Last summer, after a number of people got sick from eating locally caught anchovies, the coastal city of San Martin advised against eating such anchovies. The anchovies were apparently tainted with domoic acid, a harmful neurotoxin. However, a dramatic drop in the population of *P. australis* plankton to numbers more normal for local coastal waters indicates that it is once again safe to eat locally caught anchovies.

Which one of the following, if true, would most help to explain why it is now safe to lift the advisory?

(A) *P. australis* is one of several varieties of plankton common to the region that, when ingested by anchovies, cause the latter to secrete small amounts of domoic acid.

(B) *P. australis* naturally produces domoic acid, though anchovies consume enough to become toxic only when the population of *P. australis* is extraordinarily large.

(C) Scientists have used *P. australis* plankton to obtain domoic acid in the laboratory.

(D) A sharp decline in the population of *P. australis* is typically mirrored by a corresponding drop in the local anchovy population.

(E) *P. australis* cannot survive in large numbers in seawater that does not contain significant quantities of domoic acid along with numerous other compounds.

23. Constance: The traditional definition of full employment as a 5 percent unemployment rate is correct, because at levels below 5 percent, inflation rises.

Brigita: That traditional definition of full employment was developed before the rise of temporary and part-time work and the fall in benefit levels. When people are juggling several part-time jobs with no benefits, or working in a series of temporary assignments, as is now the case, 5 percent unemployment is not full employment.

The dialogue most strongly supports the claim that Constance and Brigita disagree with each other about which one of the following?

(A) what definition of full employment is applicable under contemporary economic conditions

(B) whether it is a good idea, all things considered, to allow the unemployment level to drop below 5 percent

(C) whether a person with a part-time job should count as fully employed

(D) whether the number of part-time and temporary workers has increased since the traditional definition of full employment was developed

(E) whether unemployment levels above 5 percent can cause inflation levels to rise

GO ON TO THE NEXT PAGE.

24. The supernova event of 1987 is interesting in that there is still no evidence of the neutron star that current theory says should have remained after a supernova of that size. This is in spite of the fact that many of the most sensitive instruments ever developed have searched for the tell-tale pulse of radiation that neutron stars emit. Thus, current theory is wrong in claiming that supernovas of a certain size always produce neutron stars.

Which one of the following, if true, most strengthens the argument?

(A) Most supernova remnants that astronomers have detected have a neutron star nearby.

(B) Sensitive astronomical instruments have detected neutron stars much farther away than the location of the 1987 supernova.

(C) The supernova of 1987 was the first that scientists were able to observe in progress.

(D) Several important features of the 1987 supernova are correctly predicted by the current theory.

(E) Some neutron stars are known to have come into existence by a cause other than a supernova explosion.

25. On average, corporations that encourage frequent social events in the workplace show higher profits than those that rarely do. This suggests that the EZ Corporation could boost its profits by having more staff parties during business hours.

Which one of the following, if true, most weakens the argument above?

(A) The great majority of corporations that encourage frequent social events in the workplace do so at least in part because they are already earning above-average profits.

(B) Corporations that have frequent staff parties after business hours sometimes have higher profits than do corporations that have frequent staff parties during business hours.

(C) The EZ Corporation already earns above-average profits, and it almost never brings play into the workplace.

(D) Frequent social events in a corporate workplace leave employees with less time to perform their assigned duties than they would otherwise have.

(E) At one time the EZ Corporation encouraged social events in the workplace more frequently than it currently does, but it has not always been one of the most profitable corporations of its size.

S T O P

IF YOU FINISH BEFORE TIME IS CALLED, YOU MAY CHECK YOUR WORK ON THIS SECTION ONLY. DO NOT WORK ON ANY OTHER SECTION IN THE TEST.

SECTION II
Time—35 minutes
28 Questions

Directions: Each passage in this section is followed by a group of questions to be answered on the basis of what is stated or implied in the passage. For some of the questions, more than one of the choices could conceivably answer the question. However, you are to choose the best answer; that is, the response that most accurately and completely answers the question, and blacken the corresponding space on your answer sheet.

The work of South African writer Ezekiel Mphahlele has confounded literary critics, especially those who feel compelled to draw a sharp distinction between autobiography and fiction. These critics point
(5) to Mphahlele's best-known works—his 1959 autobiography *Down Second Avenue* and his 1971 novel *The Wanderers*—to illustrate the problem of categorizing his work. While his autobiography traces his life from age five until the beginning of his
(10) self-imposed 20-year exile at age thirty-eight, *The Wanderers* appears to pick up at the beginning of his exile and go on from there. Critics have variously decried the former as too fictionalized and the latter as too autobiographical, but those who focus on
(15) traditional labels inevitably miss the fact that Mphahlele manipulates different prose forms purely in the service of the social message he advances.
        Even where critics give him a favorable reading, all too often their reviews carry a negative subtext.
(20) For example, one critic said of *The Wanderers* that if anger, firsthand experiences, compassion, and topicality were the sole requirements for great literature, the novel might well be one of the masterpieces of this declining part of the twentieth
(25) century. And although this critic may not have meant to question the literary contribution of the novel, there are those who are outright dismissive of *The Wanderers* because it contains an autobiographical framework and is populated with real-world
(30) characters. Mphahlele briefly defends against such charges by pointing out the importance of the fictional father-son relationship that opens and closes the novel. But his greater concern is the social vision that pervades his work, though it too is prone to
(35) misunderstandings and underappreciation. Mphahlele is a humanist and an integrationist, and his writings wonderfully articulate his vision of the future; but critics often balk at this vision because Mphahlele provides no road maps for bringing such a future
(40) about.
        Mphahlele himself shows little interest in establishing guidelines to distinguish autobiography from fiction. Though he does refer to *Down Second Avenue* as an autobiography and *The Wanderers* as a
(45) novel, he asserts that no novelist can write complete fiction or absolute fact. It is the nature of writing, at least the writing he cares about, that the details must be drawn from the writer's experiences, and thus are in some sense fact, but conveyed in such a way as
(50) to maximize the effectiveness of the social message

contained in the work, and thus inevitably fiction. As he claims, the whole point of the exercise of writing has nothing to do with classification; in all forms writing is the transmission of ideas, and important
(55) ideas at that: "Whenever you write prose or poetry or drama you are writing a social criticism of one kind or another. If you don't, you are completely irrelevant—you don't count."

1. Based on the passage, with which one of the following statements would Mphahlele be most likely to agree?

    (A) All works of literature should articulate a vision of the future.
    (B) It is not necessary for a writer to write works to fit predetermined categories.
    (C) Literary categories are worth addressing only when literary works are being unjustifiably dismissed.
    (D) Most works of literature that resemble novels could accurately be classified as autobiographies.
    (E) The most useful categories in literature are those that distinguish prose from poetry and poetry from drama.

2. The passage states that Mphahlele believes which one of the following?

    (A) Writing should provide a guide for achieving social change.
    (B) Writing should have as its goal the transmission of ideas.
    (C) Writing is most effective when it minimizes the use of real people and events to embellish a story.
    (D) Good writing is generally more autobiographical than fictional.
    (E) Fiction and autobiography are clearly identifiable literary forms if the work is composed properly.

GO ON TO THE NEXT PAGE.

3. In lines 18–25, the author uses the phrase "negative subtext" in reference to the critic's comment to claim that

(A) the critic believes that Mphahlele himself shows little interest in establishing guidelines that distinguish fact from fiction in literature

(B) the comment is unfairly one-sided and gives no voice to perspectives that Mphahlele might embrace

(C) the requirement of firsthand experiences mentioned in the comment is in direct contradiction to the requirements of fiction

(D) the requirements for great literature mentioned in the comment are ill conceived, thus the requirements have little bearing on what great literature really is

(E) the requirements for great literature mentioned in the comment are not the sole requirements, thus Mphahlele's work is implied by the critic not to be great literature

4. According to the passage, critics offer which one of the following reasons for their dismissal of *The Wanderers*?

(A) It should not have been populated with real-world characters.

(B) It should have been presented as an autobiography.

(C) It does not clearly display Mphahlele's vision.

(D) It intends to deliver controversial social criticisms.

(E) It places too much emphasis on relationships.

5. The author quotes Mphahlele (lines 55–58) primarily in order to

(A) demonstrate Mphahlele's eloquence as a writer

(B) provide a common goal of writing among novelists

(C) further elaborate the kind of writing Mphahlele values

(D) introduce the three literary forms Mphahlele uses to write social criticism

(E) show that Mphahlele makes no distinction among prose, poetry, and drama

6. Which one of the following aspects of Mphahlele's work does the author of the passage appear to value most highly?

(A) his commitment to communicating social messages

(B) his blending of the categories of fiction and autobiography

(C) his ability to redefine established literary categories

(D) his emphasis on the importance of details

(E) his plan for bringing about the future he envisions

7. Which one of the following is most strongly suggested by the information in the passage?

(A) Mphahlele's stance as a humanist and an integrationist derives from an outlook on writing that recognizes a sharp distinction between fiction and autobiography.

(B) The social vision contained in a work is irrelevant to critics who feel compelled to find distinct categories in which to place literary works.

(C) Critics are concerned with categorizing the works they read not as a means to judge the quality of the works but as a way of discovering tendencies within literary traditions.

(D) If Mphahlele were to provide direction as to how his vision of the future might be realized, more critics might find this vision acceptable.

(E) For a work to be classified as a novel, it must not contain any autobiographical elements.

GO ON TO THE NEXT PAGE.

A vigorous debate in astronomy centers on an epoch in planetary history that was first identified by analysis of rock samples obtained in lunar missions. Scientists discovered that the major craters on the
(5) Moon were created by a vigorous bombardment of debris approximately four billion years ago—the so-called late heavy bombardment (LHB). Projectiles from this bombardment that affected the Moon should also have struck Earth, a likelihood with profound
(10) consequences for the history of Earth since, until the LHB ended, life could not have survived here.

Various theoretical approaches have been developed to account for both the evidence gleaned from samples of Moon rock collected during lunar
(15) explorations and the size and distribution of craters on the Moon. Since the sizes of LHB craters suggest they were formed by large bodies, some astronomers believe that the LHB was linked to the disintegration of an asteroid or comet orbiting the Sun. In this view,
(20) a large body broke apart and peppered the inner solar system with debris. Other scientists disagree and believe that the label "LHB" is in itself a misnomer. These researchers claim that a cataclysm is not necessary to explain the LHB evidence. They claim
(25) that the Moon's evidence merely provides a view of the period concluding billions of years of a continuous, declining heavy bombardment throughout the inner solar system. According to them, the impacts from the latter part of the bombardment were
(30) so intense that they obliterated evidence of earlier impacts. A third group contends that the Moon's evidence supports the view that the LHB was a sharply defined cataclysmic cratering period, but these scientists believe that because of its relatively brief
(35) duration, this cataclysm did not extend throughout the inner solar system. They hold that the LHB involved only the disintegration of a body within the Earth-Moon system, because the debris from such an event would have been swept up relatively quickly.
(40) New support for the hypothesis that a late bombardment extended throughout the inner solar system has been found in evidence from the textural features and chemical makeup of a meteorite that has been found on Earth. It seems to be a rare example of
(45) a Mars rock that made its way to Earth after being knocked from the surface of Mars. The rock has recently been experimentally dated at about four billion years old, which means that, if the rock is indeed from Mars, it was knocked from the planet at
(50) about the same time that the Moon was experiencing the LHB. This tiny piece of evidence suggests that at least two planetary systems in the inner solar system experienced bombardment at the same time. However, to determine the pervasiveness of the LHB, scientists
(55) will need to locate many more such rocks and perhaps obtain surface samples from other planets in the inner solar system.

8. Which one of the following most accurately expresses the main point of the passage?

(A) The LHB is an intense meteorite bombardment that occurred about four billion years ago and is responsible for the cratering on the Moon and perhaps on other members of the inner solar system as well.

(B) Astronomers now believe that they may never collect enough evidence to determine the true nature of the LHB.

(C) If scientists continue to collect new clues at their current rate, the various LHB hypotheses can soon be evaluated and a clear picture will emerge.

(D) The Moon's evidence shows that the LHB was linked to a small body that disintegrated while in solar orbit and sprayed the inner solar system with debris.

(E) New evidence has been found that favors the view that the LHB was widespread, but before competing theories of the LHB can be excluded, more evidence needs to be gathered.

9. The author's attitude toward arguments that might be based on the evidence of the rock mentioned in the passage as being from Mars (lines 44–46) can most accurately be described as

(A) ambivalence because the theory of the rock's migration to Earth is at once both appealing and difficult to believe

(B) caution because even if the claims concerning the rock's origins can be proven, it is unwise to draw general conclusions without copious evidence

(C) skepticism because it seems unlikely that a rock could somehow make its way from Mars to Earth after being dislodged

(D) curiosity because many details of the rock's interplanetary travel, its chemical analysis, and its dating analysis have not yet been published

(E) outright acceptance because the origins of the rock have been sufficiently corroborated

10. The author mentions that the LHB "should also have struck Earth" (lines 8–9) primarily to

(A) support a particular theory of the extent of the LHB

(B) question the lack of LHB evidence found on Earth

(C) advocate certain scientific models for the origins of life on Earth

(D) provide a reason why scientists are interested in studying the LHB

(E) introduce additional support for the dating of the LHB

GO ON TO THE NEXT PAGE.

11. The author implies that all theoretical approaches to the LHB would agree on which one of the following?

(A) the approximate duration of the LHB
(B) the origin of the debris involved in the LHB
(C) the idea that cratering decreased significantly after the LHB
(D) the idea that the LHB destroyed the life that existed on Earth four billion years ago
(E) the approximate amount of debris involved in the LHB

12. According to the passage, the third group of scientists (line 31) believes that the LHB

(A) affected only the Moon
(B) was so brief that its extent had to be fairly localized
(C) consisted of so little debris that it was absorbed quickly by the planets in the inner solar system
(D) occurred more recently than four billion years ago
(E) may have lasted a long time, but all its debris remained within the Earth-Moon system

13. Which one of the following, if true, would lend the most support to the view that the LHB was limited to Earth and the Moon?

(A) An extensive survey of craters on Mars shows very little evidence for an increase in the intensity of projectiles striking Mars during the period from three billion to five billion years ago.
(B) Scientists discover another meteorite on Earth that they conclude had been knocked from the surface of the Moon during the LHB.
(C) A re-analysis of Moon rocks reveals that several originated on Earth during the LHB.
(D) Based on further testing, scientists conclude that the rock believed to have originated on Mars actually originated on the Moon.
(E) Excavations on both Earth and the Moon yield evidence that the LHB concluded billions of years of heavy bombardment.

GO ON TO THE NEXT PAGE.

Specialists in international communications almost unanimously assert that the broadcasting in developing nations of television programs produced by industrialized countries amounts to cultural
(5) imperialism: the phenomenon of one culture's productions overwhelming another's, to the detriment of the flourishing of the latter. This assertion assumes the automatic dominance of the imported productions and their negative effect on the domestic culture. But
(10) the assertion is polemical and abstract, based on little or no research into the place held by imported programs in the economies of importing countries or in the lives of viewers. This is not to deny that dominance is sometimes a risk in relationships
(15) between cultures, but rather to say that the assertion lacks empirical foundation and in some cases goes against fact. For one example, imported programs rarely threaten the economic viability of the importing country's own television industry. For
(20) another, imported programs do not uniformly attract larger audiences than domestically produced programs; viewers are not part of a passive, undifferentiated mass but are individuals with personal tastes, and most of them tend to prefer domestically
(25) produced television over imported television.

The role of television in developing nations is far removed from what the specialists assert. An anthropological study of one community that deals in part with residents' viewing habits where imported
(30) programs are available cites the popularity of domestically produced serial dramas and points out that, because viewers enjoy following the dramas from day to day, television in the community can serve an analogous function to that of oral poetry,
(35) which the residents often use at public gatherings as a daily journal of events of interest.

An empirical approach not unlike that of anthropologists is needed if communications specialists are to understand the impact of external
(40) cultural influences on the lives of people in a society. The first question they must investigate is: Given the evidence suggesting that the primary relationship of imported cultural productions to domestic ones is not dominance, then what model best represents the true
(45) relationship? One possibility is that, rather than one culture's productions dominating another's, the domestic culture absorbs the imported productions and becomes enriched. Another is that the imported productions fuse with domestic culture only where
(50) the two share common aspects, such as the use of themes, situations, or character types that are relevant and interesting to both cultures.

Communications researchers will also need to consider how to assess the position of the individual
(55) viewer in their model of cultural relationships. This model must emphasize the diversity of human responses, and will require engaging with the actual experiences of viewers, taking into account the variable contexts in which productions are
(60) experienced, and the complex manner in which individuals ascribe meanings to those productions.

14. The primary purpose of the passage is to

(A) determine which of two hypotheses considered by a certain discipline is correct
(B) discredit the evidence offered for a claim made by a particular discipline
(C) argue that a certain discipline should adopt a particular methodology
(D) examine similar methodological weaknesses in two different disciplines
(E) compare the views of two different disciplines on an issue

15. Which one of the following most accurately describes the organization of the passage?

(A) The author takes issue with an assertion, suggests reasons why the assertion is supported by its proponents, introduces a new view that runs counter to the assertion, and presents examples to support the new view.
(B) The author takes issue with an assertion, presents examples that run counter to the assertion, suggests that a particular approach be taken by the proponents of the assertion, and discusses two questions that should be addressed in the new approach.
(C) The author takes issue with an assertion, introduces a new view that runs counter to the assertion, presents examples that support the new view, and gives reasons why proponents of the assertion should abandon it and adopt the new view.
(D) The author takes issue with an assertion, presents examples that run counter to the assertion, suggests a change in the approach taken by the proponents of the assertion, and discusses two ways in which the new approach will benefit the proponents.
(E) The author takes issue with an assertion, presents examples that run counter to the assertion, introduces a new view that runs counter to the assertion, and suggests ways in which a compromise may be found between the view and the assertion.

GO ON TO THE NEXT PAGE.

16. Which one of the following is the most logical continuation of the last paragraph of the passage?

   (A) Lacking such an emphasis, we cannot judge conclusively the degree to which cultural relationships can be described by an abstract model.
   (B) Without such an emphasis, we can be confident that the dominance view asserted by communications specialists will survive the criticisms leveled against it.
   (C) Unless they do so, we cannot know for certain whether the model developed describes accurately the impact of external cultural influences on the lives of people.
   (D) Until they agree to do so, we can remain secure in the knowledge that communications specialists will never fully gain the scientific credibility they so passionately crave.
   (E) But even with such an emphasis, it will be the extent to which the model accurately describes the economic relationship between cultures that determines its usefulness.

17. The author most likely discusses an anthropological study in the second paragraph primarily in order to

   (A) provide to international communications specialists a model of cultural relationships
   (B) describe to international communications specialists new ways of conducting their research
   (C) highlight the flaws in a similar study conducted by international communications specialists
   (D) cite evidence that contradicts claims made by international communications specialists
   (E) support the claim that international communications specialists need to take the diversity of individual viewing habits into account

18. Which one of the following can most reasonably be concluded about the television viewers who were the subject of the study discussed in the second paragraph?

   (A) They will gradually come to prefer imported television programs over domestic ones.
   (B) They are likely someday to give up oral poetry in favor of watching television exclusively.
   (C) They would likely watch more television if they did not have oral poetry.
   (D) They enjoy domestic television programs mainly because they have little access to imported ones.
   (E) They watch television for some of the same reasons that they enjoy oral poetry.

19. According to the author, an empirical study of the effect of external cultural influences on the lives of people in a society must begin by identifying

   (A) the viewing habits and tastes of the people in the society
   (B) an accurate model of how imported cultural productions influence domestic ones
   (C) the role of the external cultural influences in the daily life of the people in the society
   (D) shared aspects of domestic and imported productions popular with mass audiences
   (E) social factors that affect how external cultural productions are given meaning by viewers

20. Suppose a study is conducted that measures the amount of airtime allotted to imported television programming in the daily broadcasting schedules of several developing nations. Given the information in the passage, the results of that study would be most directly relevant to answering which one of the following questions?

   (A) How does the access to imported cultural productions differ among these nations?
   (B) What are the individual viewing habits of citizens in these nations?
   (C) How influential are the domestic television industries in these nations?
   (D) Do imported programs attract larger audiences than domestic ones in these nations?
   (E) What model best describes the relationship between imported cultural influences and domestic culture in these nations?

GO ON TO THE NEXT PAGE.

Computers have long been utilized in the sphere of law in the form of word processors, spreadsheets, legal research systems, and practice management systems. Most exciting, however, has been the
(5) prospect of using artificial intelligence techniques to create so-called legal reasoning systems—computer programs that can help to resolve legal disputes by reasoning from and applying the law. But the practical benefits of such automated reasoning
(10) systems have fallen short of optimistic early predictions and have not resulted in computer systems that can independently provide expert advice about substantive law. This is not surprising in light of the difficulty in resolving problems involving the
(15) meaning and applicability of rules set out in a legal text.

Early attempts at automated legal reasoning focused on the doctrinal nature of law. They viewed law as a set of rules, and the resulting computer
(20) systems were engineered to make legal decisions by determining the consequences that followed when its stored set of legal rules was applied to a collection of evidentiary data. Such systems underestimated the problems of interpretation that can arise at every
(25) stage of a legal argument. Examples abound of situations that are open to differing interpretations: whether a mobile home in a trailer park is a house or a motor vehicle, whether a couple can be regarded as married in the absence of a formal legal ceremony,
(30) and so on. Indeed, many notions invoked in the text of a statute may be deliberately left undefined so as to allow the law to be adapted to unforeseen circumstances. But in order to be able to apply legal rules to novel situations, systems have to be equipped
(35) with a kind of comprehensive knowledge of the world that is far beyond their capabilities at present or in the foreseeable future.

Proponents of legal reasoning systems now argue that accommodating reference to, and reasoning from,
(40) cases improves the chances of producing a successful system. By focusing on the practice of reasoning from precedents, researchers have designed systems called case-based reasoners, which store individual example cases in their knowledge bases. In contrast
(45) to a system that models legal knowledge based on a set of rules, a case-based reasoner, when given a concrete problem, manipulates the cases in its knowledge base to reach a conclusion based on a similar case. Unfortunately, in the case-based systems
(50) currently in development, the criteria for similarity among cases are system dependent and fixed by the designer, so that similarity is found only by testing for the presence or absence of predefined factors. This simply postpones the apparently intractable
(55) problem of developing a system that can discover for itself the factors that make cases similar in relevant ways.

21. Which one of the following most accurately expresses the main point of the passage?

(A) Attempts to model legal reasoning through computer programs have not been successful because of problems of interpreting legal discourse and identifying appropriate precedents.

(B) Despite signs of early promise, it is now apparent that computer programs have little value for legal professionals in their work.

(C) Case-based computer systems are vastly superior to those computer systems based upon the doctrinal nature of the law.

(D) Computers applying artificial intelligence techniques show promise for revolutionizing the process of legal interpretation in the relatively near future.

(E) Using computers can expedite legal research, facilitate the matching of a particular case to a specific legal principle, and even provide insights into possible flaws involving legal reasoning.

22. The logical relationship of lines 8–13 of the passage to lines 23–25 and 49–53 of the passage is most accurately described as

(A) a general assertion supported by two specific observations

(B) a general assertion followed by two arguments, one of which supports and one of which refutes the general assertion

(C) a general assertion that entails two more specific assertions

(D) a theoretical assumption refuted by two specific observations

(E) a specific observation that suggests two incompatible generalizations

23. In the passage as a whole, the author is primarily concerned with

(A) arguing that computers can fundamentally change how the processes of legal interpretation and reasoning are conducted in the future

(B) indicating that the law has subtle nuances that are not readily dealt with by computerized legal reasoning programs

(C) demonstrating that computers are approaching the point where they can apply legal precedents to current cases

(D) suggesting that, because the law is made by humans, computer programmers must also apply their human intuition when designing legal reasoning systems

(E) defending the use of computers as essential and indispensable components of the modern legal profession

GO ON TO THE NEXT PAGE.

24. The passage suggests that the author would be most likely to agree with which one of the following statements about computerized automated legal reasoning systems?

    (A) These systems have met the original expectations of computer specialists but have fallen short of the needs of legal practitioners.
    (B) Progress in research on these systems has been hindered, more because not enough legal documents are accessible by computer than because theoretical problems remain unsolved.
    (C) These systems will most likely be used as legal research tools rather than as aids in legal analysis.
    (D) Rule systems will likely replace case-based systems over time.
    (E) Developing adequate legal reasoning systems would require research breakthroughs by computer specialists.

25. It can be most reasonably inferred from the passage's discussion of requirements for developing effective automated legal reasoning systems that the author would agree with which one of the following statements?

    (A) Focusing on the doctrinal nature of law is the fundamental error made by developers of automated legal systems.
    (B) Contemporary computers do not have the required memory capability to store enough data to be effective legal reasoning systems.
    (C) Questions of interpretation in rule-based legal reasoning systems must be settled by programming more legal rules into the systems.
    (D) Legal statutes and reasoning may involve innovative applications that cannot be modeled by a fixed set of rules, cases, or criteria.
    (E) As professionals continue to use computers in the sphere of law they will develop the competence to use legal reasoning systems effectively.

26. Based on the passage, which one of the following can be most reasonably inferred concerning case-based reasoners?

    (A) The major problem in the development of these systems is how to store enough cases in their knowledge bases.
    (B) These systems are more useful than rule systems because case-based reasoners are based on a simpler view of legal reasoning.
    (C) Adding specific criteria for similarity among cases to existing systems would not overcome an important shortcoming of these systems.
    (D) These systems can independently provide expert advice about legal rights and duties in a wide range of cases.
    (E) These systems are being designed to attain a much more ambitious goal than had been set for rule systems.

27. Which one of the following is mentioned in the passage as an important characteristic of many statutes that frustrates the application of computerized legal reasoning systems?

    (A) complexity of syntax
    (B) unavailability of relevant precedents
    (C) intentional vagueness and adaptability
    (D) overly narrow intent
    (E) incompatibility with previous statutes

28. The examples of situations that are open to differing interpretations (lines 25–30) function in the passage to

    (A) substantiate the usefulness of computers in the sphere of law
    (B) illustrate a vulnerability of rule systems in computerized legal reasoning
    (C) isolate issues that computer systems are in principle incapable of handling
    (D) explain how legal rules have been adapted to novel situations
    (E) question the value of reasoning from precedents in interpreting legal rules

S T O P

IF YOU FINISH BEFORE TIME IS CALLED, YOU MAY CHECK YOUR WORK ON THIS SECTION ONLY.
DO NOT WORK ON ANY OTHER SECTION IN THE TEST.

SECTION III

Time—35 minutes

25 Questions

Directions: The questions in this section are based on the reasoning contained in brief statements or passages. For some questions, more than one of the choices could conceivably answer the question. However, you are to choose the best answer; that is, the response that most accurately and completely answers the question. You should not make assumptions that are by commonsense standards implausible, superfluous, or incompatible with the passage. After you have chosen the best answer, blacken the corresponding space on your answer sheet.

1. In 1974 the speed limit on highways in the United States was reduced to 55 miles per hour in order to save fuel. In the first 12 months after the change, the rate of highway fatalities dropped 15 percent, the sharpest one-year drop in history. Over the next 10 years, the fatality rate declined by another 25 percent. It follows that the 1974 reduction in the speed limit saved many lives.

   Which one of the following, if true, most strengthens the argument?

   (A) The 1974 fuel shortage cut driving sharply for more than a year.
   (B) There was no decline in the rate of highway fatalities during the twelfth year following the reduction in the speed limit.
   (C) Since 1974 automobile manufacturers have been required by law to install lifesaving equipment, such as seat belts, in all new cars.
   (D) The fatality rate in highway accidents involving motorists driving faster than 55 miles per hour is much higher than in highway accidents that do not involve motorists driving at such speeds.
   (E) Motorists are more likely to avoid accidents by matching their speed to that of the surrounding highway traffic than by driving at faster or slower speeds.

2. Some legislators refuse to commit public funds for new scientific research if they cannot be assured that the research will contribute to the public welfare. Such a position ignores the lessons of experience. Many important contributions to the public welfare that resulted from scientific research were never predicted as potential outcomes of that research. Suppose that a scientist in the early twentieth century had applied for public funds to study molds: who would have predicted that such research would lead to the discovery of antibiotics—one of the greatest contributions ever made to the public welfare?

   Which one of the following most accurately expresses the main point of the argument?

   (A) The committal of public funds for new scientific research will ensure that the public welfare will be enhanced.
   (B) If it were possible to predict the general outcome of a new scientific research effort, then legislators would not refuse to commit public funds for that effort.
   (C) Scientific discoveries that have contributed to the public welfare would have occurred sooner if public funds had been committed to the research that generated those discoveries.
   (D) In order to ensure that scientific research is directed toward contributing to the public welfare, legislators must commit public funds to new scientific research.
   (E) Lack of guarantees that new scientific research will contribute to the public welfare is not sufficient reason for legislators to refuse to commit public funds to new scientific research.

GO ON TO THE NEXT PAGE.

3. When workers do not find their assignments challenging, they become bored and so achieve less than their abilities would allow. On the other hand, when workers find their assignments too difficult, they give up and so again achieve less than what they are capable of achieving. It is, therefore, clear that no worker's full potential will ever be realized.

Which one of the following is an error of reasoning contained in the argument?

(A) mistakenly equating what is actual and what is merely possible

(B) assuming without warrant that a situation allows only two possibilities

(C) relying on subjective rather than objective evidence

(D) confusing the coincidence of two events with a causal relation between the two

(E) depending on the ambiguous use of a key term

4. Our tomato soup provides good nutrition: for instance, a warm bowl of it contains more units of vitamin C than does a serving of apricots or fresh carrots!

The advertisement is misleading if which one of the following is true?

(A) Few people depend exclusively on apricots and carrots to supply vitamin C to their diets.

(B) A liquid can lose vitamins if it stands in contact with the air for a protracted period of time.

(C) Tomato soup contains important nutrients other than vitamin C.

(D) The amount of vitamin C provided by a serving of the advertised soup is less than the amount furnished by a serving of fresh strawberries.

(E) Apricots and fresh carrots are widely known to be nutritious, but their contribution consists primarily in providing a large amount of vitamin A, not a large amount of vitamin C.

Questions 5–6

The government provides insurance for individuals' bank deposits, but requires the banks to pay the premiums for this insurance. Since it is depositors who primarily benefit from the security this insurance provides, the government should take steps to ensure that depositors who want this security bear the cost of it and thus should make depositors pay the premiums for insuring their own accounts.

5. Which one of the following principles, if established, would do most to justify drawing the conclusion of the argument on the basis of the reasons offered in its support?

(A) The people who stand to benefit from an economic service should always be made to bear the costs of that service.

(B) Any rational system of insurance must base the size of premiums on the degree of risk involved.

(C) Government-backed security for investors, such as bank depositors, should be provided only when it does not reduce incentives for investors to make responsible investments.

(D) The choice of not accepting an offered service should always be available, even if there is no charge for the service.

(E) The government should avoid any actions that might alter the behavior of corporations and individuals in the market.

6. Which one of the following is assumed by the argument?

(A) Banks are not insured by the government against default on the loans the banks make.

(B) Private insurance companies do not have the resources to provide banks or individuals with deposit insurance.

(C) Banks do not always cover the cost of the deposit-insurance premiums by paying depositors lower interest rates on insured deposits than the banks would on uninsured deposits.

(D) The government limits the insurance protection it provides by insuring accounts up to a certain legally defined amount only.

(E) The government does not allow banks to offer some kinds of accounts in which deposits are not insured.

GO ON TO THE NEXT PAGE.

7. When individual students are all treated equally in that they have identical exposure to curriculum material, the rate, quality, and quantity of learning will vary from student to student. If all students are to master a given curriculum, some of them need different types of help than others, as any experienced teacher knows.

If the statements above are both true, which one of the following conclusions can be drawn on the basis of them?

(A) Unequal treatment, in a sense, of individual students is required in order to ensure equality with respect to the educational tasks they master.

(B) The rate and quality of learning, with learning understood as the acquiring of the ability to solve problems within a given curriculum area, depend on the quantity of teaching an individual student receives in any given curriculum.

(C) The more experienced the teacher is, the more the students will learn.

(D) All students should have identical exposure to learn the material being taught in any given curriculum.

(E) Teachers should help each of their students to learn as much as possible.

8. George: Some scientists say that global warming will occur because people are releasing large amounts of carbon dioxide into the atmosphere by burning trees and fossil fuels. We can see, though, that the predicted warming is occurring already. In the middle of last winter, we had a month of springlike weather in our area, and this fall, because of unusually mild temperatures, the leaves on our town's trees were three weeks late in turning color.

Which one of the following would it be most relevant to investigate in evaluating the conclusion of George's argument?

(A) whether carbon dioxide is the only cause of global warming

(B) when leaves on the trees in the town usually change color

(C) what proportion of global emissions of carbon dioxide is due to the burning of trees by humans

(D) whether air pollution is causing some trees in the area to lose their leaves

(E) whether unusually warm weather is occurring elsewhere on the globe more frequently than before

9. Student representative: Our university, in expelling a student who verbally harassed his roommate, has erred by penalizing the student for doing what he surely has a right to do: speak his mind!

Dean of students: But what you're saying is that our university should endorse verbal harassment. Yet surely if we did that, we would threaten the free flow of ideas that is the essence of university life.

Which one of the following is a questionable technique that the dean of students uses in attempting to refute the student representative?

(A) challenging the student representative's knowledge of the process by which the student was expelled

(B) invoking a fallacious distinction between speech and other sorts of behavior

(C) misdescribing the student representative's position, thereby making it easier to challenge

(D) questioning the motives of the student representative rather than offering reasons for the conclusion defended

(E) relying on a position of power to silence the opposing viewpoint with a threat

10. Famous personalities found guilty of many types of crimes in well-publicized trials are increasingly sentenced to the performance of community service, though unknown defendants convicted of similar crimes almost always serve prison sentences. However, the principle of equality before the law rules out using fame and publicity as relevant considerations in the sentencing of convicted criminals.

The statements above, if true, most strongly support which one of the following conclusions?

(A) The principle of equality before the law is rigorously applied in only a few types of criminal trials.

(B) The number of convicted celebrities sentenced to community service should equal the number of convicted unknown defendants sentenced to community service.

(C) The principle of equality before the law can properly be overridden by other principles in some cases.

(D) The sentencing of celebrities to community service instead of prison constitutes a violation of the principle of equality before the law in many cases.

(E) The principle of equality before the law does not allow for leniency in sentencing.

GO ON TO THE NEXT PAGE.

11. Scientific research at a certain university was supported in part by an annual grant from a major foundation. When the university's physics department embarked on weapons-related research, the foundation, which has a purely humanitarian mission, threatened to cancel its grant. The university then promised that none of the foundation's money would be used for the weapons research, whereupon the foundation withdrew its threat, concluding that the weapons research would not benefit from the foundation's grant.

Which one of the following describes a flaw in the reasoning underlying the foundation's conclusion?

(A) It overlooks the possibility that the availability of the foundation's money for humanitarian uses will allow the university to redirect other funds from humanitarian uses to weapons research.

(B) It overlooks the possibility that the physics department's weapons research is not the only one of the university's research activities with other than purely humanitarian purposes.

(C) It overlooks the possibility that the university made its promise specifically in order to induce the foundation to withdraw its threat.

(D) It confuses the intention of not using a sum of money for a particular purpose with the intention of not using that sum of money at all.

(E) It assumes that if the means to achieve an objective are humanitarian in character, then the objective is also humanitarian in character.

12. To suit the needs of corporate clients, advertising agencies have successfully modified a strategy originally developed for political campaigns. This strategy aims to provide clients with free publicity and air time by designing an advertising campaign that is controversial, thus drawing prime-time media coverage and evoking public comment by officials.

The statements above, if true, most seriously undermine which one of the following assertions?

(A) The usefulness of an advertising campaign is based solely on the degree to which the campaign's advertisements persuade their audiences.

(B) Only a small percentage of eligible voters admit to being influenced by advertising campaigns in deciding how to vote.

(C) Campaign managers have transformed political campaigns by making increasing use of strategies borrowed from corporate advertising campaigns.

(D) Corporations are typically more concerned with maintaining public recognition of the corporate name than with enhancing goodwill toward the corporation.

(E) Advertising agencies that specialize in campaigns for corporate clients are not usually chosen for political campaigns.

13. The National Association of Fire Fighters says that 45 percent of homes now have smoke detectors, whereas only 30 percent of homes had them 10 years ago. This makes early detection of house fires no more likely, however, because over half of the domestic smoke detectors are either without batteries or else inoperative for some other reason.

In order for the conclusion above to be properly drawn, which one of the following assumptions would have to be made?

(A) Fifteen percent of domestic smoke detectors were installed less than 10 years ago.

(B) The number of fires per year in homes with smoke detectors has increased.

(C) Not all of the smoke detectors in homes are battery operated.

(D) The proportion of domestic smoke detectors that are inoperative has increased in the past ten years.

(E) Unlike automatic water sprinklers, a properly functioning smoke detector cannot by itself increase fire safety in a home.

GO ON TO THE NEXT PAGE.

14. Advertisement: HomeGlo Paints, Inc., has won the prestigious Golden Paintbrush Award given to the one paint manufacturer in the country that has increased the environmental safety of its product most over the past three years for HomeGlo Exterior Enamel. The Golden Paintbrush is awarded only on the basis of thorough tests by independent testing laboratories. So when you choose HomeGlo Exterior Enamel, you will know that you have chosen the most environmentally safe brand of paint manufactured in this country today.

The flawed reasoning in the advertisement most closely parallels that in which one of the following?

(A) The ZXC audio system received the overall top ranking for looks, performance, durability, and value in Listeners' Report magazine's ratings of currently produced systems. Therefore, the ZXC must have better sound quality than any other currently produced sound system.

(B) Morning Sunshine breakfast cereal contains, ounce for ounce, more of the nutrients needed for a healthy diet than any other breakfast cereal on the market today. Thus, when you eat Morning Sunshine, you will know you are eating the most nutritious food now on the market.

(C) The number of consumer visits increased more at Countryside Market last year than at any other market in the region. Therefore, Countryside's profits must also have increased more last year than those of any other market in the region.

(D) Jerrold's teachers recognize him as the student who has shown more academic improvement than any other student in the junior class this year. Therefore, if Jerrold and his classmates are ranked according to their current academic performance, Jerrold must hold the highest ranking.

(E) Margaret Durring's short story "The Power Lunch" won three separate awards for best short fiction of the year. Therefore, any of Margaret Durring's earlier stories certainly has enough literary merit to be included in an anthology of the best recent short fiction.

15. The consistency of ice cream is adversely affected by even slight temperature changes in the freezer. To counteract this problem, manufacturers add stabilizers to ice cream. Unfortunately, stabilizers, though inexpensive, adversely affect flavor.

Stabilizers are less needed if storage temperatures are very low. However, since energy costs are constantly going up, those costs constitute a strong incentive in favor of relatively high storage temperatures.

Which one of the following can be properly inferred from the passage?

(A) Even slight deviations from the proper consistency for ice cream sharply impair its flavor.

(B) Cost considerations favor sacrificing consistency over sacrificing flavor.

(C) It would not be cost-effective to develop a new device to maintain the constancy of freezer temperatures.

(D) Stabilizers function well only at very low freezer temperatures.

(E) Very low, stable freezer temperatures allow for the best possible consistency and flavor of ice cream.

16. Edwina: True appreciation of Mozart's music demands that you hear it exactly as he intended it to be heard; that is, exactly as he heard it. Since he heard it on eighteenth-century instruments, it follows that so should we.

Alberto: But what makes you think that Mozart ever heard his music played as he had intended it to be played? After all, Mozart was writing at a time when the performer was expected, as a matter of course, not just to interpret but to modify the written score.

Alberto adopts which one of the following strategies in criticizing Edwina's position?

(A) He appeals to an academic authority in order to challenge the factual basis of her conclusion.

(B) He attacks her judgment by suggesting that she does not recognize the importance of the performer's creativity to the audience's appreciation of a musical composition.

(C) He defends a competing view of musical authenticity.

(D) He attacks the logic of her argument by suggesting that the conclusion she draws does not follow from the premises she sets forth.

(E) He offers a reason to believe that one of the premises of her argument is false.

GO ON TO THE NEXT PAGE.

17. Since the introduction of the Impanian National Health scheme, Impanians (or their private insurance companies) have had to pay only for the more unusual and sophisticated medical procedures. When the scheme was introduced, it was hoped that private insurance to pay for these procedures would be available at modest cost, since the insurers would no longer be paying for the bulk of health care costs, as they had done previously. Paradoxically, however, the cost of private health insurance did not decrease but has instead increased dramatically in the years since the scheme's introduction.

Which one of the following, if true, does most to explain the apparently paradoxical outcome?

(A) The National Health scheme has greatly reduced the number of medical claims handled annually by Impania's private insurers, enabling these firms to reduce overhead costs substantially.

(B) Before the National Health scheme was introduced, more than 80 percent of all Impanian medical costs were associated with procedures that are now covered by the scheme.

(C) Impanians who previously were unable to afford regular medical treatment now use the National Health scheme, but the number of Impanians with private health insurance has not increased.

(D) Impanians now buy private medical insurance only at times when they expect that they will need care of kinds not available in the National Health scheme.

(E) The proportion of total expenditures within Impania that is spent on health care has declined since the introduction of the National Health scheme.

18. In clinical trials of new medicines, half of the subjects receive the drug being tested and half receive a physiologically inert substance—a placebo. Trials are designed with the intention that neither subjects nor experimenters will find out which subjects are actually being given the drug being tested. However, this intention is frequently frustrated because_____.

Which one of the following, if true, most appropriately completes the explanation?

(A) often the subjects who receive the drug being tested develop symptoms that the experimenters recognize as side effects of the physiologically active drug

(B) subjects who believe they are receiving the drug being tested often display improvements in their conditions regardless of whether what is administered to them is physiologically active or not

(C) in general, when the trial is intended to establish the experimental drug's safety rather than its effectiveness, all of the subjects are healthy volunteers

(D) when a trial runs a long time, few of the experimenters will work on it from inception to conclusion

(E) the people who are subjects for clinical trials must, by law, be volunteers and must be informed of the possibility that they will receive a placebo

19. It takes 365.25 days for the Earth to make one complete revolution around the Sun. Long-standing convention makes a year 365 days long, with an extra day added every fourth year, and the year is divided into 52 seven-day weeks. But since 52 times 7 is only 364, anniversaries do not fall on the same day of the week each year. Many scheduling problems could be avoided if the last day of each year and an additional day every fourth year belonged to no week, so that January 1 would be a Sunday every year.

The proposal above, once put into effect, would be most likely to result in continued scheduling conflicts for which one of the following groups?

(A) people who have birthdays or other anniversaries on December 30 or 31

(B) employed people whose strict religious observances require that they refrain from working every seventh day

(C) school systems that require students to attend classes a specific number of days each year

(D) employed people who have three-day breaks from work when holidays are celebrated on Mondays or Fridays

(E) people who have to plan events several years before those events occur

GO ON TO THE NEXT PAGE.

20. Graphologists claim that it is possible to detect permanent character traits by examining people's handwriting. For example, a strong cross on the "t" is supposed to denote enthusiasm. Obviously, however, with practice and perseverance people can alter their handwriting to include this feature. So it seems that graphologists must hold that permanent character traits can be changed.

The argument against graphology proceeds by

(A) citing apparently incontestable evidence that leads to absurd consequences when conjoined with the view in question

(B) demonstrating that an apparently controversial and interesting claim is really just a platitude

(C) arguing that a particular technique of analysis can never be effective when the people analyzed know that it is being used

(D) showing that proponents of the view have no theoretical justification for the view

(E) attacking a technique by arguing that what the technique is supposed to detect can be detected quite readily without it

Questions 21–22

Historian: There is no direct evidence that timber was traded between the ancient nations of Poran and Nayal, but the fact that a law setting tariffs on timber imports from Poran was enacted during the third Nayalese dynasty does suggest that during that period a timber trade was conducted.

Critic: Your reasoning is flawed. During its third dynasty, Nayal may well have imported timber from Poran, but certainly on today's statute books there remain many laws regulating activities that were once common but in which people no longer engage.

21. The critic's response to the historian's reasoning does which one of the following?

(A) It implies an analogy between the present and the past.

(B) It identifies a general principle that the historian's reasoning violates.

(C) It distinguishes between what has been established as a certainty and what has been established as a possibility.

(D) It establishes explicit criteria that must be used in evaluating indirect evidence.

(E) It points out the dissimilar roles that law plays in societies that are distinct from one another.

22. The critic's response to the historian is flawed because it

(A) produces evidence that is consistent with there not having been any timber trade between Poran and Nayal during the third Nayalese dynasty

(B) cites current laws without indicating whether the laws cited are relevant to the timber trade

(C) fails to recognize that the historian's conclusion was based on indirect evidence rather than direct evidence

(D) takes no account of the difference between a law's enactment at a particular time and a law's existence as part of a legal code at a particular time

(E) accepts without question the assumption about the purpose of laws that underlies the historian's argument

GO ON TO THE NEXT PAGE.

23. The workers at Bell Manufacturing will shortly go on strike unless the management increases their wages. As Bell's president is well aware, however, in order to increase the workers' wages, Bell would have to sell off some of its subsidiaries. So, some of Bell's subsidiaries will be sold.

The conclusion above is properly drawn if which one of the following is assumed?

(A) Bell Manufacturing will begin to suffer increased losses.
(B) Bell's management will refuse to increase its workers' wages.
(C) The workers at Bell Manufacturing will not be going on strike.
(D) Bell's president has the authority to offer the workers their desired wage increase.
(E) Bell's workers will not accept a package of improved benefits in place of their desired wage increase.

24. One sure way you can tell how quickly a new idea—for example, the idea of "privatization"—is taking hold among the population is to monitor how fast the word or words expressing that particular idea are passing into common usage. Professional opinions of whether or not words can indeed be said to have passed into common usage are available from dictionary editors, who are vitally concerned with this question.

The method described above for determining how quickly a new idea is taking hold relies on which one of the following assumptions?

(A) Dictionary editors are not professionally interested in words that are only rarely used.
(B) Dictionary editors have exact numerical criteria for telling when a word has passed into common usage.
(C) For a new idea to take hold, dictionary editors have to include the relevant word or words in their dictionaries.
(D) As a word passes into common usage, its meaning does not undergo any severe distortions in the process.
(E) Words denoting new ideas tend to be used before the ideas denoted are understood.

25. Because migrant workers are typically not hired by any one employer for longer than a single season, migrant workers can legally be paid less than the minimum hourly wage that the government requires employers to pay all their permanent employees. Yet most migrant workers work long hours each day for eleven or twelve months a year and thus are as much full-time workers as are people hired on a year-round basis. Therefore, the law should require that migrant workers be paid the same minimum hourly wage that other full-time workers must be paid.

The pattern of reasoning displayed above most closely parallels that displayed in which one of the following arguments?

(A) Because day-care facilities are now regulated at the local level, the quality of care available to children in two different cities can differ widely. Since such differences in treatment clearly are unfair, day care should be federally rather than locally regulated.
(B) Because many rural areas have few restrictions on development, housing estates in such areas have been built where no adequate supply of safe drinking water could be ensured. Thus, rural areas should adopt building codes more like those large cities have.
(C) Because some countries regulate gun sales more strictly than do other countries, some people can readily purchase a gun, whereas others cannot. Therefore, all countries should cooperate in developing a uniform international policy regarding gun sales.
(D) Because it is a democratic principle that laws should have the consent of those affected by them, liquor laws should be formulated not by politicians but by club and restaurant owners, since such laws directly affect the profitability of their businesses.
(E) Because food additives are not considered drugs, they have not had to meet the safety standards the government applies to drugs. But food additives can be as dangerous as drugs. Therefore, food additives should also be subject to safety regulations as stringent as those covering drugs.

S T O P

IF YOU FINISH BEFORE TIME IS CALLED, YOU MAY CHECK YOUR WORK ON THIS SECTION ONLY.
DO NOT WORK ON ANY OTHER SECTION IN THE TEST.

SECTION IV

Time—35 minutes

25 Questions

Directions: The questions in this section are based on the reasoning contained in brief statements or passages. For some questions, more than one of the choices could conceivably answer the question. However, you are to choose the best answer; that is, the response that most accurately and completely answers the question. You should not make assumptions that are by commonsense standards implausible, superfluous, or incompatible with the passage. After you have chosen the best answer, blacken the corresponding space on your answer sheet.

1. Studies have shown that treating certain illnesses with treatment X produces the same beneficial changes in patients' conditions as treating the same illnesses with treatment Y. Furthermore, treatment X is quicker and less expensive than treatment Y. Thus, in treating these illnesses, treatment X should be preferred to treatment Y.

Which one of the following, if true, would most weaken the argument above?

(A) Unlike treatment Y, treatment X has produced harmful side effects in laboratory animals.
(B) There are other illnesses for which treatment Y is more effective than treatment X.
(C) Until recently, treatment X was more expensive than treatment Y.
(D) Treatment Y is prescribed more often by physicians than treatment X.
(E) A third treatment, treatment Z, is even quicker and less expensive than treatment X.

2. Some political thinkers hope to devise a form of government in which every citizen's rights are respected. But such a form of government is impossible. For any government must be defined and controlled by laws that determine its powers and limits; and it is inevitable that some individuals will learn how to interpret these laws to gain a greater share of political power than others have.

Which one of the following is an assumption required by the argument?

(A) In any form of government that leads to unequal distribution of political power, the rights of the majority of people will be violated.
(B) A government can ensure that every citizen's rights are respected by keeping the citizens ignorant of the laws.
(C) Not all the laws that define a government's power and limits can be misinterpreted.
(D) In any form of government, if anybody gains a greater share of political power than others have, then somebody's rights will be violated.
(E) People who have more political power than others have tend to use it to acquire an even greater share of political power.

3. Safety considerations aside, nuclear power plants are not economically feasible. While the cost of fuel for nuclear plants is significantly lower than the cost of conventional fuels, such as coal and oil, nuclear plants are far more expensive to build than are conventional power plants.

Which one of the following, if true, most strengthens the argument?

(A) Safety regulations can increase the costs of running both conventional and nuclear power plants.
(B) Conventional power plants spend more time out of service than do nuclear power plants.
(C) The average life expectancy of a nuclear power plant is shorter than that of a conventional one.
(D) Nuclear power plants cost less to build today than they cost to build when their technology was newly developed.
(E) As conventional fuels become scarcer their cost will increase dramatically, which will increase the cost of running a conventional power plant.

4. Pundit: The average salary for teachers in our society is lower than the average salary for athletes. Obviously, our society values sports more than it values education.

The reasoning in the pundit's argument is questionable because the argument

(A) presumes, without providing justification, that sports have some educational value
(B) fails to consider that the total amount of money spent on education may be much greater than the total spent on sports
(C) fails to consider both that most teachers are not in the classroom during the summer and that most professional athletes do not play all year
(D) compares teachers' salaries only to those of professional athletes rather than also to the salaries of other professionals
(E) fails to compare salaries for teachers in the pundit's society to salaries for teachers in other societies

GO ON TO THE NEXT PAGE.

5. The area of mathematics called "gauge field theory," though investigated in the nineteenth century, has only relatively recently been applied to problems in contemporary quantum mechanics. Differential geometry, another area of mathematics, was investigated by Gauss in the early nineteenth century, long before Einstein determined that one of its offspring, tensor analysis, was the appropriate mathematics for exploring general relativity.

Which one of the following is best illustrated by the examples presented above?

(A) Applications of some new theories or techniques in mathematics are unrecognized until long after the discovery of those theories or techniques.

(B) Mathematicians are sometimes able to anticipate which branches of their subject will prove useful to future scientists.

(C) The discoveries of modern physics would not have been possible without major mathematical advances made in the nineteenth century.

(D) The nineteenth century stands out among other times as a period of great mathematical achievement.

(E) Mathematics tends to advance more quickly than any of the physical sciences.

6. Recently discovered bird fossils are about 20 million years older than the fossils of the birdlike dinosaurs from which the birds are generally claimed to have descended. So these newly discovered fossils show, contrary to the account espoused by most paleontologists, that no bird descended from any dinosaur.

The reasoning in the argument is flawed in that the argument

(A) draws a generalization that is broader than is warranted by the findings cited

(B) rejects the consensus view of experts in the field without providing any counterevidence

(C) attacks the adherents of the opposing view personally instead of addressing any reason for their view

(D) fails to consider the possibility that dinosaurs descended from birds

(E) ignores the possibility that dinosaurs and birds descended from a common ancestor

7. Whether one is buying men's or women's clothing, it pays to consider fashion trends. A classic suit may stay in style for as long as five years, so it is worthwhile to pay more to get a well-constructed one. A trendy hat that will go out of style in a year or two should be purchased as cheaply as possible.

Which one of the following most accurately expresses the principle underlying the reasoning above?

(A) Formal attire tends to be designed and constructed to last longer than casual attire.

(B) The amount of money one spends on a garment should be roughly proportionate to the length of time one plans to keep wearing it.

(C) One should not buy a cheaply made garment when a well-constructed garment is available.

(D) The amount of money one spends on clothing should be roughly the same whether one is purchasing men's or women's attire.

(E) It is more appropriate to spend money on office attire than on casual attire.

8. Engineers are investigating the suitability of Wantastiquet Pass as the site of a new bridge. Because one concern is whether erosion could eventually weaken the bridge's foundations, they contracted for two reports on erosion in the region. Although both reports are accurate, one claims that the region suffers relatively little erosion, while the other claims that regional erosion is heavy and a cause for concern.

Which one of the following, if true, most helps to explain how both reports could be accurate?

(A) Neither report presents an extensive chemical analysis of the soil in the region.

(B) Both reports include computer-enhanced satellite photographs.

(C) One report was prepared by scientists from a university, while the other report was prepared by scientists from a private consulting firm.

(D) One report focuses on regional topsoil erosion, while the other report focuses on riverbank erosion resulting from seasonal floods.

(E) One report cost nearly twice as much to prepare as did the other report.

GO ON TO THE NEXT PAGE.

9. Letter to the editor: I have never seen such flawed reasoning and distorted evidence as that which you tried to pass off as a balanced study in the article "Speed Limits, Fatalities, and Public Policy." The article states that areas with lower speed limits had lower vehicle-related fatality rates than other areas. However, that will not be true for long, since vehicle-related fatality rates are rising in the areas with lower speed limits. So the evidence actually supports the view that speed limits should be increased.

The reasoning in the letter writer's argument is flawed because the argument

(A) bases its conclusion on findings from the same article that it is criticizing

(B) fails to consider the possibility that automobile accidents that occur at high speeds often result in fatalities

(C) fails to consider the possibility that not everyone wants to drive faster

(D) fails to consider the possibility that the vehicle-related fatality rates in other areas are also rising

(E) does not present any claims as evidence against the opposing viewpoint

10. Human settlement of previously uninhabited areas tends to endanger species of wildlife. However, the Mississippi kite, a bird found on the prairies of North America, flourishes in areas that people have settled. In fact, during the five years since 1985 its population has risen far more rapidly in towns than in rural areas.

Which one of the following, if true, most helps to explain why the Mississippi kite population does not follow the usual pattern?

(A) Residents of prairie towns have been setting off loud firecrackers near kites' roosting spots because of the birds' habit of diving at people and frightening them.

(B) Towns on the prairies tend to be small, with a low density of human population and large numbers of wild birds and animals.

(C) Since the international migratory bird protection treaty of 1972, it has been illegal to shoot kites, and the treaty has been effectively enforced.

(D) Wildlife such as pigeons and raccoons had already adapted successfully to towns and cities long before there were towns on the North American prairies.

(E) Trees are denser in towns than elsewhere on the prairie, and these denser trees provide greater protection from hail and windstorms for kites' nests and eggs.

11. When a major record label signs a contract with a band, the label assumes considerable financial risk. It pays for videos, album art, management, and promotions. Hence, the band does not need to assume nearly as much risk as it would if it produced its own records independently. For this reason, it is only fair for a major label to take a large portion of the profits from the record sales of any band signed with it.

Which one of the following most accurately describes the role played in the argument by the claim that a band signed with a major label does not need to assume nearly as much risk as it would if it produced its own records independently?

(A) It is the only conclusion that the argument attempts to establish.

(B) It is one of two unrelated conclusions, each of which the same premises are used to support.

(C) It is a general principle from which the argument's conclusion follows as a specific instance.

(D) It describes a phenomenon for which the rest of the argument offers an explanation.

(E) Premises are used to support it, and it is used to support the main conclusion.

12. Commentator: Recently, articles criticizing the environmental movement have been appearing regularly in newspapers. According to Winslow, this is due not so much to an antienvironmental bias among the media as to a preference on the part of newspaper editors for articles that seem "daring" in that they seem to challenge prevailing political positions. It is true that editors like to run antienvironmental pieces mainly because they seem to challenge the political orthodoxy. But serious environmentalism is by no means politically orthodox, and antienvironmentalists can hardly claim to be dissidents, however much they may have succeeded in selling themselves as renegades.

The commentator's statements, if true, most strongly support which one of the following?

(A) Winslow is correct about the preference of newspaper editors for controversial articles.

(B) Critics of environmentalism have not successfully promoted themselves as renegades.

(C) Winslow's explanation is not consonant with the frequency with which critiques of environmentalism are published.

(D) The position attacked by critics of environmentalism is actually the prevailing political position.

(E) Serious environmentalism will eventually become a prevailing political position.

GO ON TO THE NEXT PAGE.

13. Philosopher: Some of the most ardent philosophical opponents of democracy have rightly noted that both the inherently best and the inherently worst possible forms of government are those that concentrate political power in the hands of a few. Thus, since democracy is a consistently mediocre form of government, it is a better choice than rule by the few.

Which one of the following principles, if valid, most helps to justify the philosopher's argument?

(A) A society should adopt a democratic form of government if and only if most members of the society prefer a democratic form of government.

(B) In choosing a form of government, it is better for a society to avoid the inherently worst than to seek to attain the best.

(C) The best form of government is the one that is most likely to produce an outcome that is on the whole good.

(D) Democratic governments are not truly equitable unless they are designed to prevent interest groups from exerting undue influence on the political process.

(E) It is better to choose a form of government on the basis of sound philosophical reasons than on the basis of popular preference.

14. Expert: What criteria distinguish addictive substances from nonaddictive ones? Some have suggested that any substance that at least some habitual users can cease to use is nonaddictive. However, if this is taken to be the sole criterion of nonaddictiveness, some substances that most medical experts classify as prime examples of addictive substances would be properly deemed nonaddictive. Any adequate set of criteria for determining a substance's addictiveness must embody the view, held by these medical experts, that a substance is addictive only if withdrawal from its habitual use causes most users extreme psychological and physiological difficulty.

Which one of the following can be properly inferred from the expert's statements?

(A) If a person experiences extreme psychological and physiological difficulty in ceasing to use a substance habitually, that substance is addictive.

(B) Fewer substances would be deemed addictive than are deemed so at present if an adequate definition of "addictive" were employed.

(C) A substance that some habitual users can cease to use with little or no psychological or physiological difficulty is addictive only if that is not true for most habitual users.

(D) A chemical substance habitually used by a person throughout life without significant psychological or physiological difficulty is nonaddictive.

(E) "Addiction" is a term that is impossible to define with precision.

GO ON TO THE NEXT PAGE.

15. Sociologist: A contention of many of my colleagues—
that the large difference between the wages of the
highest- and lowest-paid workers will inevitably
become a source of social friction—is unfounded.
Indeed, the high differential should have an
opposite effect, for it means that companies will
be able to hire freely in response to changing
conditions. Social friction arises not from large
wage differences, but from wage levels that are
static or slow changing.

Which one of the following is an assumption required
by the sociologist's argument?

(A) When companies can hire freely in response to
changing conditions, wage levels do not tend to
be static or slow changing.
(B) People who expect their wages to rise react
differently than do others to obvious disparities
in income.
(C) A lack of financial caution causes companies to
expand their operations.
(D) A company's ability to respond swiftly to
changing conditions always benefits its workers.
(E) Even relatively well-paid workers may become
dissatisfied with their jobs if their wages never
change.

16. Publisher: The new year is approaching, and with it
the seasonal demand for books on exercise and
fitness. We must do whatever it takes to ship books
in that category on time; our competitors have
demonstrated a high level of organization, and we
cannot afford to be outsold.

Which one of the following most accurately expresses
the main conclusion drawn in the publisher's argument?

(A) The company should make shipping books its
highest priority.
(B) By increasing its efficiency, the company can
maintain its competitive edge.
(C) The company will be outsold if it does not
maintain its competitors' high level of
organization.
(D) It is imperative that the company ship fitness and
exercise books on time.
(E) The company should do whatever is required
in order to adopt its competitors' shipping
practices.

17. Advertiser: There's nothing wrong with a tool that
has ten functions until you need a tool that can
perform an eleventh function! The VersaTool can
perform more functions than any other tool. If
you use the VersaTool, therefore, you will need
additional tools less often than you would using
any other multiple-function tool.

The reasoning in the advertiser's argument is most
vulnerable to criticism on the grounds that the VersaTool
might

(A) include some functions that are infrequently or
never needed
(B) include a number of functions that are difficult to
perform with any tool
(C) cost more than the combined cost of two other
multiple-function tools that together perform
more functions than the VersaTool
(D) be able to perform fewer often-needed functions
than some other multiple-function tool
(E) not be able to perform individual functions as
well as single-function tools

18. The flagellum, which bacteria use to swim, requires
many parts before it can propel a bacterium at all.
Therefore, an evolutionary ancestor of bacteria that
had only a few of these parts would gain no survival
advantage from them.

Which one of the following is an assumption on which
the argument depends?

(A) Any of bacteria's evolutionary ancestors that had
only a few of the parts of the flagellum would be
at a disadvantage relative to similar organisms
that had none of these parts.
(B) For parts now incorporated into the flagellum to
have aided an organism's survival, they would
have had to help it swim.
(C) All parts of the flagellum are vital to each of its
functions.
(D) No evolutionary ancestor of bacteria had only a
few of the parts of the flagellum.
(E) Any of bacteria's evolutionary ancestors that
lacked a flagellum also lacked the capacity to
swim.

GO ON TO THE NEXT PAGE.

19. Style manual: Archaic spellings and styles of punctuation in direct quotations from older works are to be preserved if they occur infrequently and do not interfere with a reader's comprehension. However, if they occur frequently, the editor may modernize them, inserting a note with an explanation to this effect in the text, or if similar modernizing has been done in more than one quotation, inserting a general statement in the preface. On the other hand, obvious typographical errors in quotations from modern works may be corrected without explanation.

Which one of the following follows logically from the statements above?

(A) If an editor corrects the spelling of a quoted word and the word occurs only once in the text, then an explanation should appear in a note or in the text.

(B) An editor may modernize an archaic spelling of a word found in a modern work without providing an explanation.

(C) An editor should modernize an archaic spelling of a word that is quoted from an older work if the spelling interferes with reader comprehension.

(D) An editor may modernize punctuation directly quoted from an older work if that punctuation occurs frequently and interferes with reader comprehension.

(E) If an editor modernizes only one of several similar instances of quoted archaic punctuation, an explanation should appear in the preface of the work.

20. Whoever murdered Jansen was undoubtedly in Jansen's office on the day of the murder, and both Samantha and Herbert were in Jansen's office on that day. If Herbert had committed the murder, the police would have found either his fingerprints or his footprints at the scene of the crime. But if Samantha was the murderer, she would have avoided leaving behind footprints or fingerprints. The police found fingerprints but no footprints at the scene of the crime. Since the fingerprints were not Herbert's, he is not the murderer. Thus Samantha must be the killer.

Which one of the following, if assumed, allows the conclusion that Samantha was the killer to be properly inferred?

(A) If there had been footprints at the scene of the crime, the police would have found them.

(B) Jansen's office was the scene of the crime.

(C) No one but Herbert and Samantha was in Jansen's office on the day of the murder.

(D) The fingerprints found at the scene of the crime were not Jansen's.

(E) The fingerprints found at the scene of the crime were not Samantha's.

21. Most opera singers who add demanding roles to their repertoires at a young age lose their voices early. It has been said that this is because their voices have not yet matured and hence lack the power for such roles. But young singers with great vocal power are the most likely to ruin their voices. The real problem is that most young singers lack the technical training necessary to avoid straining their vocal cords—especially when using their full vocal strength. Such misuse of the cords inevitably leads to a truncated singing career.

Which one of the following does the information above most strongly support?

(A) Young opera singers without great vocal power are unlikely to ruin their voices by singing demanding roles.

(B) Some young opera singers ruin their voices while singing demanding roles because their vocal cords have not yet matured.

(C) Only opera singers with many years of technical training should try to sing demanding roles.

(D) Only mature opera singers can sing demanding roles without undue strain on their vocal cords.

(E) Most young opera singers who sing demanding roles strain their vocal cords.

GO ON TO THE NEXT PAGE.

22. Food that is very high in fat tends to be unhealthy. These brownies are fat-free, while those cookies contain a high percentage of fat. Therefore, these fat-free brownies are healthier than those cookies are.

Which one of the following exhibits flawed reasoning most similar to the flawed reasoning exhibited by the argument above?

(A) Canned foods always contain more salt than frozen foods do. Therefore, these canned peas contain more salt than those frozen peas do.

(B) Vegetables that are overcooked generally have few vitamins. Therefore, these carrots, which are overcooked, contain fewer vitamins than those peas, which are uncooked.

(C) The human body needs certain amounts of many minerals to remain healthy. Therefore, this distilled water, which has no minerals, is unhealthy.

(D) Some types of nuts make Roy's throat itch. These cookies contain a greater percentage of nuts than that pie contains. Therefore, these cookies are more likely to make Roy's throat itch.

(E) Eating at a restaurant costs more than eating food prepared at home. Therefore, this home-cooked meal is less expensive than a restaurant meal of the same dishes would be.

23. Ethicist: It would be a mistake to say that just because someone is not inclined to do otherwise, she or he does not deserve to be praised for doing what is right, for although we do consider people especially virtuous if they successfully resist a desire to do what is wrong, they are certainly no less virtuous if they have succeeded in extinguishing all such desires.

The assertion that people are considered especially virtuous if they successfully resist a desire to do what is wrong plays which one of the following roles in the ethicist's argument?

(A) It is a claim for which the argument attempts to provide justification.

(B) It makes an observation that, according to the argument, is insufficient to justify the claim that the argument concludes is false.

(C) It is a claim, acceptance of which, the argument contends, is a primary obstacle to some people's having an adequate conception of virtue.

(D) It is, according to the argument, a commonly held opinion that is nevertheless false.

(E) It reports an observation that, according to the argument, serves as evidence for the truth of its conclusion.

GO ON TO THE NEXT PAGE.

24. Ecologists predict that the incidence of malaria will increase if global warming continues or if the use of pesticides is not expanded. But the use of pesticides is known to contribute to global warming, so it is inevitable that we will see an increase in malaria in the years to come.

The pattern of reasoning in which one of the following is most similar to that in the argument above?

(A) The crime rate will increase if the economy does not improve or if we do not increase the number of police officers. But we will be able to hire more police officers if the economy does improve. Therefore, the crime rate will not increase.

(B) If educational funds remain at their current level or if we fail to recruit qualified teachers, student performance will worsen. But we will fail to recruit qualified teachers. Therefore, student performance will worsen.

(C) If interest rates increase or demand for consumer goods does not decline, inflation will rise. But if there is a decline in the demand for consumer goods, that will lead to higher interest rates. Therefore, inflation will rise.

(D) If global warming continues or if the rate of ozone depletion is not reduced, there will be an increase in the incidence of skin cancer. But reduced use of aerosols ensures both that global warming will not continue and that ozone depletion will be reduced. Thus, the incidence of skin cancer will not increase.

(E) If deforestation continues at the current rate and the use of chemicals is not curtailed, wildlife species will continue to become extinct. But because of increasing population worldwide, it is inevitable that the current rate of deforestation will continue and that the use of chemicals will not be curtailed. Thus, wildlife species will continue to become extinct.

25. In ancient Greece, court witnesses were not cross-examined and the jury, selected from the citizenry, received no guidance on points of law; thus, it was extremely important for litigants to make a good impression on the jurors. For this reason, courtroom oratory by litigants is a good source of data on the common conceptions of morality held by the citizens of ancient Greece.

Which one of the following, if true, would most strengthen the argument?

(A) Litigants believed jurors were more likely to be impressed by litigants whose personality they preferred.

(B) Litigants believed jurors were more likely to subject the litigants' personal moral codes to close critical scrutiny than were people who did not sit on juries.

(C) Litigants believed jurors were likely to be impressed by litigants whose professed moral code most resembled their own.

(D) Litigants believed jurors to be more impressed by litigants who were of the same economic class as the jurors.

(E) Litigants believed jurors were likely to render their decisions based on a good understanding of the law.

S T O P

IF YOU FINISH BEFORE TIME IS CALLED, YOU MAY CHECK YOUR WORK ON THIS SECTION ONLY.
DO NOT WORK ON ANY OTHER SECTION IN THE TEST.

SECTION V

Time—35 minutes

22 Questions

Directions: Each group of questions in this section is based on a set of conditions. In answering some of the questions, it may be useful to draw a rough diagram. Choose the response that most accurately and completely answers each question and blacken the corresponding space on your answer sheet.

Questions 1–5

A clown will select a costume consisting of two pieces and no others: a jacket and overalls. One piece of the costume will be entirely one color, and the other piece will be plaid. Selection is subject to the following restrictions:

   If the jacket is plaid, then there must be exactly three colors in it.

   If the overalls are plaid, then there must be exactly two colors in them.

   The jacket and overalls must have exactly one color in common.

   Green, red, and violet are the only colors that can be in the jacket.

   Red, violet, and yellow are the only colors that can be in the overalls.

1. Which one of the following could be a complete and accurate list of the colors in the costume?

	Jacket	Overalls
(A)	red	red
(B)	red	violet, yellow
(C)	violet	green, violet
(D)	violet	red, violet
(E)	violet	red, violet, yellow

2. If there are exactly two colors in the costume, then which one of the following must be false?

(A) At least part of the jacket is green.
(B) At least part of the jacket is red.
(C) The overalls are red and violet.
(D) The overalls are red and yellow.
(E) The overalls are violet and yellow.

3. If at least part of the jacket is green, then which one of the following could be true?

(A) The overalls are plaid.
(B) No part of the jacket is red.
(C) No part of the jacket is violet.
(D) At least part of the overalls are yellow.
(E) At least part of the overalls are violet.

4. Which one of the following must be false?

(A) Both green and red are colors used in the costume.
(B) Both green and violet are colors used in the costume.
(C) Both green and yellow are colors used in the costume.
(D) Both red and violet are colors used in the costume.
(E) Both violet and yellow are colors used in the costume.

5. If there are exactly three colors in the costume, the overalls must be

(A) entirely red or else red and violet plaid
(B) entirely yellow or else violet and yellow plaid
(C) entirely violet or else red and violet plaid
(D) entirely red or else entirely yellow
(E) entirely red or else entirely violet

GO ON TO THE NEXT PAGE.

<u>Questions 6–10</u>

Six hotel suites—F, G, H, J, K, L—are ranked from most expensive (first) to least expensive (sixth). There are no ties. The ranking must be consistent with the following conditions:

   H is more expensive than L.
   If G is more expensive than H, then neither K nor L is more expensive than J.
   If H is more expensive than G, then neither J nor L is more expensive than K.
   F is more expensive than G, or else F is more expensive than H, but not both.

6. Which one of the following could be the ranking of the suites, from most expensive to least expensive?

   (A)   G, F, H, L, J, K
   (B)   H, K, F, J, G, L
   (C)   J, H, F, K, G, L
   (D)   J, K, G, H, L, F
   (E)   K, J, L, H, F, G

7. If G is the second most expensive suite, then which one of the following could be true?

   (A)   H is more expensive than F.
   (B)   H is more expensive than G.
   (C)   K is more expensive than F.
   (D)   K is more expensive than J.
   (E)   L is more expensive than F.

8. Which one of the following CANNOT be the most expensive suite?

   (A)   F
   (B)   G
   (C)   H
   (D)   J
   (E)   K

9. If L is more expensive than F, then which one of the following could be true?

   (A)   F is more expensive than H.
   (B)   F is more expensive than K.
   (C)   G is more expensive than H.
   (D)   G is more expensive than J.
   (E)   G is more expensive than L.

10. If H is more expensive than J and less expensive than K, then which one of the following could be true?

   (A)   F is more expensive than H.
   (B)   G is more expensive than F.
   (C)   G is more expensive than H.
   (D)   J is more expensive than L.
   (E)   L is more expensive than K.

GO ON TO THE NEXT PAGE.

Questions 11–15

A locally known guitarist's demo CD contains exactly seven different songs—S, T, V, W, X, Y, and Z. Each song occupies exactly one of the CD's seven tracks. Some of the songs are rock classics; the others are new compositions. The following conditions must hold:

    S occupies the fourth track of the CD.
    Both W and Y precede S on the CD.
    T precedes W on the CD.
    A rock classic occupies the sixth track of the CD.
    Each rock classic is immediately preceded on the CD by
       a new composition.
    Z is a rock classic.

11. Which one of the following could be the order of the songs on the CD, from the first track through the seventh?

    (A) T, W, V, S, Y, X, Z
    (B) V, Y, T, S, W, Z, X
    (C) X, Y, W, S, T, Z, S
    (D) Y, T, W, S, X, Z, V
    (E) Z, T, X, W, V, Y, S

12. Which one of the following is a pair of songs that must occupy consecutive tracks on the CD?

    (A) S and V
    (B) S and W
    (C) T and Z
    (D) T and Y
    (E) V and Z

13. Which one of the following songs must be a new composition?

    (A) S
    (B) T
    (C) W
    (D) X
    (E) Y

14. If W precedes Y on the CD, then which one of the following must be true?

    (A) S is a rock classic.
    (B) V is a rock classic.
    (C) Y is a rock classic.
    (D) T is a new composition.
    (E) W is a new composition.

15. If there are exactly two songs on the CD that both precede V and are preceded by Y, then which one of the following could be true?

    (A) V occupies the seventh track of the CD.
    (B) X occupies the fifth track of the CD.
    (C) Y occupies the third track of the CD.
    (D) T is a rock classic.
    (E) W is a rock classic.

GO ON TO THE NEXT PAGE.

<u>Questions 16–22</u>

A courier delivers exactly eight parcels—G, H, J, K, L, M, N, and O. No two parcels are delivered at the same time, nor is any parcel delivered more than once. The following conditions must apply:

L is delivered later than H.
K is delivered earlier than O.
H is delivered earlier than M.
O is delivered later than G.
M is delivered earlier than G.
Both N and J are delivered earlier than M.

16. Which one of the following could be the order of deliveries from first to last?

(A) N, H, K, M, J, G, O, L
(B) H, N, J, K, G, O, L, M
(C) J, H, N, M, K, O, G, L
(D) N, J, H, L, M, K, G, O
(E) K, N, J, M, G, H, O, L

17. Which one of the following must be true?

(A) At least one parcel is delivered earlier than K is delivered.
(B) At least two parcels are delivered later than G is delivered.
(C) At least four parcels are delivered later than H is delivered.
(D) At least four parcels are delivered later than J is delivered.
(E) At least four parcels are delivered earlier than M is delivered.

18. If M is the fourth parcel delivered, then which one of the following must be true?

(A) G is the fifth parcel delivered.
(B) O is the seventh parcel delivered.
(C) J is delivered later than H.
(D) K is delivered later than N.
(E) G is delivered later than L.

19. If H is the fourth parcel delivered, then each of the following could be true EXCEPT:

(A) K is the fifth parcel delivered.
(B) L is the sixth parcel delivered.
(C) M is the sixth parcel delivered.
(D) G is the seventh parcel delivered.
(E) O is the seventh parcel delivered.

20. Each of the following could be true EXCEPT:

(A) H is delivered later than K.
(B) J is delivered later than G.
(C) L is delivered later than O.
(D) M is delivered later than L.
(E) N is delivered later than H.

21. If K is the seventh parcel delivered, then each of the following could be true EXCEPT:

(A) G is the fifth parcel delivered.
(B) M is the fifth parcel delivered.
(C) H is the fourth parcel delivered.
(D) L is the fourth parcel delivered.
(E) J is the third parcel delivered.

22. If L is delivered earlier than K, then which one of the following must be false?

(A) N is the second parcel delivered.
(B) L is the third parcel delivered.
(C) H is the fourth parcel delivered.
(D) K is the fifth parcel delivered.
(E) M is the sixth parcel delivered.

S T O P

IF YOU FINISH BEFORE TIME IS CALLED, YOU MAY CHECK YOUR WORK ON THIS SECTION ONLY.
DO NOT WORK ON ANY OTHER SECTION IN THE TEST.

Acknowledgment is made to the following sources from which material has been adapted for use in this test booklet:

Clark R. Chapman, "Bombarding Mars Lately." ©1996 by Nature Publishing Group.

James P. Draper, ed., *Black Literature Criticism*. ©1992 by Gale Research Inc.

Garrett Hardin, *Living Within Limits: Ecology, Economics, and Population Taboos*. ©1993 by Oxford University Press.

Michael Tracey, "The Poisoned Chalice? International Television and the Idea of Dominance." ©1985 by the American Academy of Arts and Sciences.

Wait for the supervisor's instructions before you open the page to the topic.
Please print and sign your name and write the date in the designated spaces below.

Time: 35 Minutes

General Directions

You will have 35 minutes in which to plan and write an essay on the topic inside. Read the topic and the accompanying directions carefully. You will probably find it best to spend a few minutes considering the topic and organizing your thoughts before you begin writing. In your essay, be sure to develop your ideas fully, leaving time, if possible, to review what you have written. **Do not write on a topic other than the one specified. Writing on a topic of your own choice is not acceptable.**

No special knowledge is required or expected for this writing exercise. Law schools are interested in the reasoning, clarity, organization, language usage, and writing mechanics displayed in your essay. How well you write is more important than how much you write.

Confine your essay to the blocked, lined area on the front and back of the separate Writing Sample Response Sheet. Only that area will be reproduced for law schools. Be sure that your writing is legible.

Both this topic sheet and your response sheet must be turned over to the testing staff before you leave the room.

Topic Code	Print Your Full Name Here		
_____	Last	First	M.I.

Date	Sign Your Name Here
/ /	

Scratch Paper
Do not write your essay in this space.

LSAT Writing Sample Topic

The charitable grants manager of Highland Electricity has received funding requests for two worthy programs—*Market Your Art*, a business program for artists, and *Get Certified*, a technical skills program for adults seeking to change careers—but can grant only one. Write an essay in which you argue for one program over the other, keeping in mind the following two criteria:

- Highland wants to help as many people as possible through its charitable giving.
- Grants should enhance the company's corporate stature within its service area.

The first funding request is to provide a grant to an arts center that serves several communities in the utility's defined service territory. The grant money would be used to establish a year-long entrepreneurship program called *Market Your Art*, designed for artists who are new to the business of selling their art. Participants will learn about pricing their work, running a small business, working with art galleries, soliciting corporate work, and bidding for public contracts. Business professionals will work closely with individual artists, and enrollment is limited to around a dozen or so participants. Highland is well known for its financial support of local community projects, yet the utility has in the past turned down numerous funding requests from arts and cultural organizations because the proposed programs did not directly further its economic development objectives.

The second request is for a grant to a nonprofit jobs training program called *Get Certified*. Participants are generally those looking for a career change, and the focus is on needed technical skills. *Get Certified* is now in the final phase of a one-time multi-year grant and is in need of new funding. Although several hundred participants have successfully completed the program, it is not heavily represented inside the utility's service area. Nonetheless, *Get Certified* is well established, increasingly in demand, and may eventually expand to locations in Highland's service area. The utility's involvement at this early stage may provide opportunities for building additional relationships and good will.

Scratch Paper
Do not write your essay in this space.

Writing Sample Response Sheet

DO NOT WRITE
IN THIS SPACE

Begin your essay in the lined area below.
Continue on the back if you need more space.

Directions:

1. Use the Answer Key on the next page to check your answers.

2. Use the Scoring Worksheet below to compute your raw score.

3. Use the Score Conversion Chart to convert your raw score into the 120–180 scale.

Conversion Chart

For Converting Raw Score to the 120–180 LSAT Scaled Score

LSAT PrepTest 51

Reported Score	Raw Score Lowest	Raw Score Highest
180	98	100
179	97	97
178	96	96
177	95	95
176	94	94
175	—*	—*
174	93	93
173	92	92
172	91	91
171	90	90
170	89	89
169	87	88
168	86	86
167	85	85
166	83	84
165	82	82
164	80	81
163	79	79
162	77	78
161	75	76
160	74	74
159	72	73
158	70	71
157	68	69
156	67	67
155	65	66
154	63	64
153	61	62
152	60	60
151	58	59
150	56	57
149	54	55
148	53	53
147	51	52
146	49	50
145	47	48
144	46	46
143	44	45
142	42	43
141	41	41
140	39	40
139	38	38
138	36	37
137	35	35
136	33	34
135	32	32
134	30	31
133	29	29
132	28	28
131	26	27
130	25	25
129	24	24
128	22	23
127	21	21
126	20	20
125	19	19
124	18	18
123	16	17
122	15	15
121	14	14
120	0	13

Scoring Worksheet

1. Enter the number of questions you answered correctly in each section

    Number Correct

    SECTION I . . . . _____
    SECTION II . . . . _____
    SECTION III . . . . . . _EXP_
    SECTION IV . . . . . . _____
    SECTION V . . . . _____

2. Enter the sum here: _____

    This is your Raw Score.

*There is no raw score that will produce this scaled score for this form.

SECTION I

1.	D	8.	C	15.	C	22.	B
2.	A	9.	E	16.	B	23.	A
3.	B	10.	E	17.	C	24.	B
4.	B	11.	B	18.	E	25.	A
5.	D	12.	D	19.	B		
6.	C	13.	B	20.	B		
7.	C	14.	C	21.	D		

SECTION II

1.	B	8.	E	15.	B	22.	A
2.	B	9.	B	16.	C	23.	B
3.	E	10.	D	17.	D	24.	E
4.	A	11.	C	18.	E	25.	D
5.	C	12.	B	19.	B	26.	C
6.	A	13.	A	20.	A	27.	C
7.	D	14.	C	21.	A	28.	B

SECTION III (experimental)

1.	D	8.	E	15.	E	22.	D
2.	E	9.	C	16.	E	23.	C
3.	B	10.	D	17.	D	24.	D
4.	E	11.	A	18.	A	25.	E
5.	A	12.	A	19.	B		
6.	C	13.	D	20.	A		
7.	A	14.	D	21.	A		

SECTION IV

1.	A	8.	D	15.	A	22.	B
2.	D	9.	D	16.	D	23.	B
3.	C	10.	E	17.	D	24.	C
4.	B	11.	E	18.	B	25.	C
5.	A	12.	A	19.	D		
6.	A	13.	B	20.	C		
7.	B	14.	C	21.	E		

SECTION V

1.	D	8.	A	15.	E	22.	C
2.	A	9.	D	16.	D		
3.	E	10.	D	17.	C		
4.	C	11.	D	18.	D		
5.	E	12.	E	19.	A		
6.	B	13.	D	20.	B		
7.	C	14.	D	21.	C		

Endurance Practice Test 6

PrepTest 50 plus experimental
from PrepTest 1, Section III

SCAN CODE: LL9006

SECTION I
Time—35 minutes
28 Questions

Directions: Each passage in this section is followed by a group of questions to be answered on the basis of what is stated or implied in the passage. For some of the questions, more than one of the choices could conceivably answer the question. However, you are to choose the best answer; that is, the response that most accurately and completely answers the question, and blacken the corresponding space on your answer sheet.

One of the most prominent characteristics of the literature by United States citizens of Mexican descent is that it is frequently written in a combination of English and Spanish. By not limiting
(5) itself to one language, such writing resonates with its authors' bicultural experiences. Their work is largely Mexican in its sensibility, its traditions, and its myths, but its immediate geographical setting is the United States. And though Mexican American literature is
(10) solidly grounded in Mexican culture, it distinguishes itself from Mexican literature in its content and concerns.

Many Mexican Americans are only a generation away from the mostly agrarian culture of their
(15) ancestors, and the work of most Mexican American writers shows evidence of heavy influence from this culture. Their novels are often simple in structure, and some of the common themes in these novels include the struggle to overcome the agricultural
(20) adversity that caused their families to emigrate, and a feeling of being distanced from the traditions of rural Mexico and yet striving to hold on to them. These themes coexist with ever-present images of the land, which symbolizes the values of the characters'
(25) culture, such as the spiritual and religious benefits of working the land.

Much of Mexican writing, on the other hand, has been criticized for being dominated by the prominent literary establishment concentrated in Mexico City.
(30) Literary reputation and success in Mexico—including the attainment of publicly sponsored positions in the arts—are often bestowed or denied by this literary establishment. Moreover, the work of Mexican writers is often longer in form and marked by greater
(35) cosmopolitanism and interest in theoretical ideas and arguments than is Mexican American writing. Not surprisingly, the Mexican literary community views Mexican American literature as a variety of "regional" writing. But the apparent simplicity of
(40) what this community sees as parochial concerns belies the thematic richness of Mexican American writing.

The work of Mexican American writers can be richly textured in its complex mixture of concerns;
(45) among other things, their work is distinguished by an overarching concern with the complexities of cultural transition. Many Mexican American writers assert that rather than working to be absorbed into U.S. society, they are engaged in the process of creating a new
(50) identity. Physically distanced from Mexico and yet convinced of its importance, these writers depict a

new reality by creating "in-between" characters. These characters inhabit a social and cultural milieu which is neither that of Mexico nor that of the U.S.
(55) And while this new setting reflects the contemporary social realities of both Mexico and the U.S., it also derives a great deal of emotional power from an evocation of a romanticized memory of Mexico. What results is an intermediate cultural borderland in
(60) which nostalgia and reality are combined in the service of forging a new identity.

1. Which one of the following most accurately states the main point of the passage?

(A) Mexican American literature is characterized by a strong sense of transition, which is due to its writers' physical distance from Mexico and their clear vision of the future of Mexican culture.

(B) Unlike Mexican writing, which is largely tied to an urban literary establishment, Mexican American writing is a movement that attempts through its works to develop a literary voice for agrarian workers.

(C) The work of Mexican American writers reflects Mexican Americans' bicultural experiences, both in its close links with the culture of rural Mexico and in its striving to develop a new identity out of elements of Mexican culture and U.S. culture.

(D) Mexican American literature, although unique in its content and concerns as well as in its stylistic innovations, has not yet achieved the prominence and reputation of Mexican literature.

(E) Many Mexican Americans are only a generation away from the culture of their ancestors and because of this, Mexican American literature is distinguished by the presence of powerful spiritual images, which are an organic part of the Mexican American agrarian culture.

GO ON TO THE NEXT PAGE.

2. It can most reasonably be inferred from the passage that the author would agree with which one of the following statements?

    (A) While Mexican American writers are in the process of shaping their body of literature, one of their goals is to create a literary establishment in the U.S. essentially like the one concentrated in Mexico City.

    (B) The use of a mixture of both Spanish and English in current Mexican American literature is evidence of a brief transitional period.

    (C) The use of a romanticized Mexico in Mexican American literature is offensive to writers of the literary establishment of Mexico City, who find the images to be caricatures of their culture.

    (D) Mexican American literature is noteworthy more for its thematic content than for its narrative structure.

    (E) Mexican American writers are concerned that the importance of Mexico, currently central to their culture, will be diminished, and that Mexican American literature will be impoverished as a result.

3. It can most reasonably be inferred from the passage that many Mexican American writers tend to value which one of the following?

    (A) stylistic innovations that distinguish their work from that of Mexican writers

    (B) recognition from a U.S. literary establishment that is significantly different from that of Mexico

    (C) an identity that resists absorption by U.S. culture

    (D) critical acceptance of bilingual forms of literary expression

    (E) the ability to express in their literature a more complex fabric of concerns than is found in most U.S. literature

4. To which one of the following questions does the passage most clearly provide an answer?

    (A) What is an example of a specific literary work by a Mexican American writer?

    (B) For what reason are many Mexican American writings concerned with agrarian themes or topics?

    (C) What is the prevailing view of Mexican American literature among critics in the United States?

    (D) How has the literature of the United States influenced Mexican American writers?

    (E) Are the works of Mexican American writers written more in Spanish or in English?

5. It can most reasonably be inferred from the passage that the author holds which one of the following views?

    (A) Mexican American literature advocates an agrarian way of life as a remedy for the alienation of modern culture.

    (B) The Mexican American "in-between" character is an instance of a type found in the literature of immigrant groups in general.

    (C) A predominant strength of Mexican American writers is that they are not tied to a major literary establishment and so are free to experiment in a way many Mexican writers are not.

    (D) Writers of "regional" literature find it more difficult to attain reputation and success in Mexico than writers whose work is concerned with more urban themes.

    (E) History has an importance in Mexican American culture that it does not have in Mexican culture because Mexican Americans have attached greater importance to their ancestry.

GO ON TO THE NEXT PAGE.

In many Western societies, modern bankruptcy laws have undergone a shift away from a focus on punishment and toward a focus on bankruptcy as a remedy for individuals and corporations in financial
(5) trouble—and, perhaps unexpectedly, for their creditors. This shift has coincided with an ever-increasing reliance on declarations of bankruptcy by individuals and corporations with excessive debt, a trend that has drawn widespread criticism. However,
(10) any measure seeking to make bankruptcy protection less available would run the risk of preventing continued economic activity of financially troubled individuals and institutions. It is for this reason that the temptation to return to a focus on punishment of
(15) individuals or corporations that become insolvent must be resisted. Modern bankruptcy laws, in serving the needs of an interdependent society, serve the varied interests of the greatest number of citizens.

The harsh punishment for insolvency in centuries
(20) past included imprisonment of individuals and dissolution of enterprises, and reflected societies' beliefs that the accumulation of excessive debt resulted either from debtors' unwillingness to meet obligations or from their negligence. Insolvent debtors
(25) were thought to be breaking sacrosanct social contracts; placing debtors in prison was considered necessary in order to remove from society those who would violate such contracts and thereby defraud creditors. But creditors derive little benefit from
(30) imprisoned debtors unable to repay even a portion of their debt. And if the entity to be punished is a large enterprise, for example, an auto manufacturer, its dissolution would cause significant unemployment and the disruption of much-needed services.

(35) Modern bankruptcy law has attempted to address the shortcomings of the punitive approach. Two beliefs underlie this shift: that the public good ought to be paramount in considering the financial insolvency of individuals and corporations; and that
(40) the public good is better served by allowing debt-heavy corporations to continue to operate, and indebted individuals to continue to earn wages, than by disabling insolvent economic entities. The mechanism for executing these goals is usually a
(45) court-directed reorganization of debtors' obligations to creditors. Such reorganizations typically comprise debt relief and plans for court-directed transfers of certain assets from debtor to creditor. Certain strictures connected to bankruptcy—such as the fact
(50) that bankruptcies become matters of public record and are reported to credit bureaus for a number of years—may still serve a punitive function, but not by denying absolution of debts or financial reorganization. Through these mechanisms, today's
(55) bankruptcy laws are designed primarily to assure continued engagement in productive economic activity, with the ultimate goal of restoring businesses and individuals to a degree of economic health and providing creditors with the best hope of collecting.

6. Which one of the following most accurately expresses the main point of the passage?

(A) The modern trend in bankruptcy law away from punishment and toward the maintenance of economic activity serves the best interests of society and should not be abandoned.

(B) Bankruptcy laws have evolved in order to meet the needs of creditors, who depend on the continued productive activity of private citizens and profit-making enterprises.

(C) Modern bankruptcy laws are justified on humanitarian grounds, even though the earlier punitive approach was more economically efficient.

(D) Punishment for debt no longer holds deterrent value for debtors and is therefore a concept that has been largely abandoned as ineffective.

(E) Greater economic interdependence has triggered the formation of bankruptcy laws that reflect a convergence of the interests of debtors and creditors.

7. In stating that bankruptcy laws have evolved "perhaps unexpectedly" (line 5) as a remedy for creditors, the author implies that creditors

(A) are often surprised to receive compensation in bankruptcy courts

(B) have unintentionally become the chief beneficiaries of bankruptcy laws

(C) were a consideration, though not a primary one, in the formulation of bankruptcy laws

(D) are better served than is immediately apparent by laws designed in the first instance to provide a remedy for debtors

(E) were themselves active in the formulation of modern bankruptcy laws

8. The author's attitude toward the evolution of bankruptcy law can most accurately be described as

(A) approval of changes that have been made to inefficient laws

(B) confidence that further changes to today's laws will be unnecessary

(C) neutrality toward laws that, while helpful to many, remain open to abuse

(D) skepticism regarding the possibility of solutions to the problem of insolvency

(E) concern that inefficient laws may have been replaced by legislation too lenient to debtors

GO ON TO THE NEXT PAGE.

9. The primary purpose of the passage is to

(A) offer a critique of both past and present approaches to insolvency

(B) compare the practices of bankruptcy courts of the past with those of bankruptcy courts of the present

(C) criticize those who would change the bankruptcy laws of today

(D) reexamine today's bankruptcy laws in an effort to point to further improvements

(E) explain and defend contemporary bankruptcy laws

10. Which one of the following claims would a defender of the punitive theory of bankruptcy legislation be most likely to have made?

(A) Debt that has become so great that repayment is impossible is ultimately a moral failing and thus a matter for which the law should provide punitive sanctions.

(B) Because insolvency ultimately harms the entire economy, the law should provide a punitive deterrent to insolvency.

(C) The insolvency of companies or individuals is tolerable if the debt is the result of risk-taking, profit-seeking ventures that might create considerable economic growth in the long run.

(D) The dissolution of a large enterprise is costly to the economy as a whole and should not be allowed, even when that enterprise's insolvency is the result of its own fiscal irresponsibility.

(E) The employees of a large bankrupt enterprise should be considered just as negligent as the owner of a bankrupt sole proprietorship.

11. Which one of the following sentences could most logically be appended to the end of the last paragraph of the passage?

(A) Only when today's bankruptcy laws are ultimately seen as inadequate on a large scale will bankruptcy legislation return to its original intent.

(B) Punishment is no longer the primary goal of bankruptcy law, even if some of its side effects still function punitively.

(C) Since leniency serves the public interest in bankruptcy law, it is likely to do so in criminal law as well.

(D) Future bankruptcy legislation could include punitive measures, but only if such measures ultimately benefit creditors.

(E) Today's bankruptcy laws place the burden of insolvency squarely on the shoulders of creditors, in marked contrast to the antiquated laws that weighed heavily on debtors.

12. The information in the passage most strongly suggests which one of the following about changes in bankruptcy laws?

(A) Bankruptcy laws always result from gradual changes in philosophy followed by sudden shifts in policy.

(B) Changes in bankruptcy law were initiated by the courts and only grudgingly adopted by legislators.

(C) The adjustment of bankruptcy laws away from a punitive focus was at first bitterly opposed by creditors.

(D) Bankruptcy laws underwent change because the traditional approach proved inadequate and contrary to the needs of society.

(E) The shift away from a punitive approach to insolvency was part of a more general trend in society toward rehabilitation and away from retribution.

13. Which one of the following, if true, would most weaken the author's argument against harsh punishment for debtors?

(A) Extensive study of the economic and legal history of many countries has shown that most individuals who served prison time for bankruptcy subsequently exhibited greater economic responsibility.

(B) The bankruptcy of a certain large company has had a significant negative impact on the local economy even though virtually all of the affected employees were able to obtain similar jobs within the community.

(C) Once imprisonment was no longer a consequence of insolvency, bankruptcy filings increased dramatically, then leveled off before increasing again during the 1930s.

(D) The court-ordered liquidation of a large and insolvent company's assets threw hundreds of people out of work, but the local economy nevertheless demonstrated robust growth in the immediate aftermath.

(E) Countries that continue to imprison debtors enjoy greater economic health than do comparable countries that have ceased to do so.

GO ON TO THE NEXT PAGE.

As the twentieth century draws to a close, we are learning to see the extent to which accounts and definitions of cultures are influenced by human biases and purposes, benevolent in what they include,
(5) incorporate, and validate, less so in what they exclude and demote. A number of recent studies have argued that the anxieties and agendas of the present exert an extraordinary influence on the national identities we construct from the cultural past. For example, Greek
(10) civilization was known originally to have had roots in Egyptian and various other African and Eastern cultures, but some current scholars charge that its identity was revised during the course of the nineteenth century to support an image of European
(15) cultural dominance—its African and other cultural influences either actively purged or hidden from view by European scholars. Because ancient Greek writers themselves openly acknowledged their culture's hybrid past, nineteenth-century European
(20) commentators habitually passed over these acknowledgments without comment.

Another example is the use of "tradition" to determine national identity. Images of European authority over other cultures were shaped and
(25) reinforced during the nineteenth century, through the manufacture and reinterpretation of rituals, ceremonies, and traditions. At a time when many of the institutions that had helped maintain imperial societies were beginning to recede in influence, and
(30) when the pressures of administering numerous overseas territories and large new domestic constituencies mounted, the ruling elites of Europe felt the clear need to project their power backward in time, giving it a legitimacy that only longevity could
(35) impart. Thus in 1876, Queen Victoria of England was declared empress of India and was celebrated in numerous "traditional" jamborees, as if her rule were not mainly a matter of recent edict but of age-old custom.
(40) Similar constructions have also been made by native cultures about their precolonial past, as in the case of Algeria during its war of independence from France, when decolonization encouraged Algerians to create idealized images of what they believed their
(45) culture to have been prior to French occupation. This strategy is at work in what many revolutionary poets say and write during wars of independence elsewhere, giving their adherents something to revive and admire.
(50) Though for the most part colonized societies have won their independence, in many cultures the imperial attitudes of uniqueness and superiority underlying colonial conquest remain. There is in all nationally defined cultures an aspiration to
(55) sovereignty and dominance that expresses itself in definitions of cultural identity. At the same time, paradoxically, we have never been as aware as we are now of the fact that historical and cultural experiences partake of many social and cultural
(60) domains and even cross national boundaries,

despite the claims to the contrary made by purveyors of nationalist dogma. Far from being unitary, monolithic, or autonomous, cultures actually include more "foreign" elements than
(65) they consciously exclude.

14. Which one of the following statements most accurately expresses the main point of the passage?

(A) Either by ignoring a native culture's own self-understanding or by substituting fabricated traditions and rituals, imperial societies often obscure the heterogeneous cultures of the peoples they colonize.

(B) Attempts to reconstruct a native, precolonial culture by members of decolonized societies are essentially no different from European colonial creation of traditions and rituals to validate their authority.

(C) In attempting to impose a monolithic culture on the peoples they colonize, imperial societies adopt artifices very similar to the tactics employed by revisionist historians of ancient Greek culture.

(D) While most colonized societies have regained their independence, they retain trappings of imperial culture that will need to be discarded if they are to regain the traditions of their past.

(E) Despite nationalistic creation of images of cultures as unified and monolithic, we now more clearly understand the extent to which cultures are in fact made up of heterogeneous elements.

15. The passage provides information to answer all of the following questions EXCEPT:

(A) What kinds of influences affect the national identities people construct from their past?

(B) Why did nineteenth-century European commentators ignore some discussion of Greek culture by ancient Greek writers?

(C) In what ways did African cultural influence affect the culture of ancient Greece?

(D) Why was Queen Victoria of England declared empress of India in 1876?

(E) What is one reason why revolutionary poets speak and write as they do?

GO ON TO THE NEXT PAGE.

16. The author's attitude toward the studies mentioned in line 6 is most likely

(A) overall agreement with their conclusion about influences on cultural identity
(B) reservation over their preoccupation with colonialism
(C) skepticism toward the relevance of the examples they cite
(D) concern that they fail to explain ancient Greek culture
(E) unqualified disagreement with their insistence that cultures are monolithic

17. The author's use of the word "traditional" in line 37 is intended to indicate that the jamborees

(A) had been revived after centuries of neglect
(B) were legitimized by their historic use in the native culture
(C) exemplified the dominance of the imperial culture
(D) conferred spurious historical legitimacy upon colonial authority
(E) combined historic elements of imperial and native cultures

18. The "purveyors of nationalist dogma" mentioned in line 62 would be most likely to agree with which one of the following?

(A) Colonized nations should not attempt to regain their historical cultures.
(B) Imperial cultures should incorporate the traditions of their colonies.
(C) The cultural traditions of a nation should remain untainted by outside influences.
(D) A country's cultural identity partakes of many social and cultural domains.
(E) National histories are created to further aspirations to sovereignty and dominance.

19. Which one of the following would most likely be an example of one of the "rituals, ceremonies, and traditions" mentioned in lines 26–27?

(A) an annual ceremony held by an institution of the colonizing culture to honor the literary and theatrical achievements of members of the native culture
(B) a religious service of the colonizing culture that has been adapted to include elements of the native culture in order to gain converts
(C) a traditional play that is part of a colonized nation's original culture, but is highly popular among the leaders of the imperial culture
(D) a ritual dance, traditionally used to commemorate the union of two native deities, that is modified to depict the friendship between the colonial and native cultures
(E) a traditional village oratory competition in which members of the native culture endeavor to outdo one another in allegorical criticisms of the colonizing culture

20. In the context of the passage, the examples in the second and third paragraphs best exemplify which one of the following generalizations?

(A) Apparent traditions may be products of artifice.
(B) National identity generally requires cultural uniformity.
(C) Most colonial cultures are by nature artificial and contrived.
(D) Historical and cultural experiences may cross national boundaries.
(E) Revolutionary cultures are often more authentic than imperial cultures.

21. The primary purpose of the passage is to

(A) argue for the creation of a global culture made up of elements from many national cultures
(B) explain how the desire for cultural uniformity supports imperialist attitudes
(C) stress the importance of objectivity in studying the actual sources of cultural identity
(D) advance the claim that present concerns motivate the shaping of cultural identities
(E) reveal the imperialist motivations of some nineteenth-century scholarship

GO ON TO THE NEXT PAGE.

One of the foundations of scientific research is that an experimental result is credible only if it can be replicated—only if performing the experiment a second time leads to the same result. But physicists

(5) John Sommerer and Edward Ott have conceived of a physical system in which even the least change in the starting conditions—no matter how small, inadvertent, or undetectable—can alter results radically. The system is represented by a computer model of a

(10) mathematical equation describing the motion of a particle placed in a particular type of force field.

Sommerer and Ott based their system on an analogy with the phenomena known as riddled basins of attraction. If two bodies of water bound a large

(15) landmass and water is spilled somewhere on the land, the water will eventually make its way to one or the other body of water, its destination depending on such factors as where the water is spilled and the geographic features that shape the water's path and

(20) velocity. The basin of attraction for a body of water is the area of land that, whenever water is spilled on it, always directs the spilled water to that body.

In some geographical formations it is sometimes impossible to predict, not only the exact destination

(25) of the spilled water, but even which body of water it will end up in. This is because the boundary between one basin of attraction and another is riddled with fractal properties; in other words, the boundary is permeated by an extraordinarily high number of

(30) physical irregularities such as notches or zigzags. Along such a boundary, the only way to determine where spilled water will flow at any given point is actually to spill it and observe its motion; spilling the water at any immediately adjacent point could give

(35) the water an entirely different path, velocity, or destination.

In the system posited by the two physicists, this boundary expands to include the whole system: i.e., the entire force field is riddled with fractal properties,

(40) and it is impossible to predict even the general destination of the particle given its starting point. Sommerer and Ott make a distinction between this type of uncertainty and that known as "chaos"; under chaos, a particle's general destination would be

(45) predictable but its path and exact destination would not.

There are presumably other such systems because the equation the physicists used to construct the computer model was literally the first one they

(50) attempted, and the likelihood that they chose the only equation that would lead to an unstable system is small. If other such systems do exist, metaphorical examples of riddled basins of attraction may abound in the failed attempts of scientists to replicate

(55) previous experimental results—in which case, scientists would be forced to question one of the basic principles that guide their work.

22. Which one of the following most accurately expresses the main point of the passage?

(A)   Sommerer and Ott's model suggests that many of the fundamental experimental results of science are unreliable because they are contaminated by riddled basins of attraction.

(B)   Sommerer and Ott's model suggests that scientists who fail to replicate experimental results might be working within physical systems that make replication virtually impossible.

(C)   Sommerer and Ott's model suggests that experimental results can never be truly replicated because the starting conditions of an experiment can never be re-created exactly.

(D)   Sommerer and Ott's model suggests that most of the physical systems studied by scientists are in fact metaphorical examples of riddled basins of attraction.

(E)   Sommerer and Ott's model suggests that an experimental result should not be treated as credible unless that result can be replicated.

23. The discussion of the chaos of physical systems is intended to perform which one of the following functions in the passage?

(A)   emphasize the extraordinarily large number of physical irregularities in a riddled basin of attraction

(B)   emphasize the unusual types of physical irregularities found in Sommerer and Ott's model

(C)   emphasize the large percentage of a riddled basin of attraction that exhibits unpredictability

(D)   emphasize the degree of unpredictability in Sommerer and Ott's model

(E)   emphasize the number of fractal properties in a riddled basin of attraction

24. Given the information in the passage, Sommerer and Ott are most likely to agree with which one of the following?

(A)   It is sometimes impossible to determine whether a particular region exhibits fractal properties.

(B)   It is sometimes impossible to predict even the general destination of a particle placed in a chaotic system.

(C)   It is sometimes impossible to re-create exactly the starting conditions of an experiment.

(D)   It is usually possible to predict the exact path water will travel if it is spilled at a point not on the boundary between two basins of attraction.

(E)   It is usually possible to determine the path by which a particle traveled given information about where it was placed and its eventual destination.

GO ON TO THE NEXT PAGE.

25. Which one of the following most accurately describes the author's attitude toward the work of Sommerer and Ott?

(A) skeptical of the possibility that numerous unstable systems exist but confident that the existence of numerous unstable systems would call into question one of the foundations of science

(B) convinced of the existence of numerous unstable systems and unsure if the existence of numerous unstable systems calls into question one of the foundations of science

(C) convinced of the existence of numerous unstable systems and confident that the existence of numerous unstable systems calls into question one of the foundations of science

(D) persuaded of the possibility that numerous unstable systems exist and unsure if the existence of numerous unstable systems would call into question one of the foundations of science

(E) persuaded of the possibility that numerous unstable systems exist and confident that the existence of numerous unstable systems would call into question one of the foundations of science

26. According to the passage, Sommerer and Ott's model differs from a riddled basin of attraction in which one of the following ways?

(A) In the model, the behavior of a particle placed at any point in the system is chaotic; in a riddled basin of attraction, only water spilled at some of the points behaves chaotically.

(B) In a riddled basin of attraction, the behavior of water spilled at any point is chaotic; in the model, only particles placed at some of the points in the system behave chaotically.

(C) In the model, it is impossible to predict the destination of a particle placed at any point in the system; in a riddled basin of attraction, only some points are such that it is impossible to predict the destination of water spilled at each of those points.

(D) In a riddled basin of attraction, water spilled at two adjacent points always makes its way to the same destination; in the model, it is possible for particles placed at two adjacent points to travel to different destinations.

(E) In the model, two particles placed successively at a given point always travel to the same destination; in a riddled basin of attraction, water spilled at the same point on different occasions may make its way to different destinations.

27. Which one of the following best defines the term "basin of attraction," as that term is used in the passage?

(A) the set of all points on an area of land for which it is possible to predict the destination, but not the path, of water spilled at that point

(B) the set of all points on an area of land for which it is possible to predict both the destination and the path of water spilled at that point

(C) the set of all points on an area of land that are free from physical irregularities such as notches and zigzags

(D) the set of all points on an area of land for which water spilled at each point will travel to a particular body of water

(E) the set of all points on an area of land for which water spilled at each point will travel to the same exact destination

28. Which one of the following is most clearly one of the "metaphorical examples of riddled basins of attraction" mentioned in lines 52–53?

(A) A scientist is unable to determine if mixing certain chemicals will result in a particular chemical reaction because the reaction cannot be consistently reproduced since sometimes the reaction occurs and other times it does not despite starting conditions that are in fact exactly the same in each experiment.

(B) A scientist is unable to determine if mixing certain chemicals will result in a particular chemical reaction because the reaction cannot be consistently reproduced since it is impossible to bring about starting conditions that are in fact exactly the same in each experiment.

(C) A scientist is unable to determine if mixing certain chemicals will result in a particular chemical reaction because the reaction cannot be consistently reproduced since it is impossible to produce starting conditions that are even approximately the same from one experiment to the next.

(D) A scientist is able to determine that mixing certain chemicals results in a particular chemical reaction because it is possible to consistently reproduce the reaction even though the starting conditions vary significantly from one experiment to the next.

(E) A scientist is able to determine that mixing certain chemicals results in a particular chemical reaction because it is possible to consistently reproduce the reaction despite the fact that the amount of time it takes for the reaction to occur varies significantly depending on the starting conditions of the experiment.

S T O P

IF YOU FINISH BEFORE TIME IS CALLED, YOU MAY CHECK YOUR WORK ON THIS SECTION ONLY.
DO NOT WORK ON ANY OTHER SECTION IN THE TEST.

SECTION II

Time—35 minutes

25 Questions

<u>Directions:</u> The questions in this section are based on the reasoning contained in brief statements or passages. For some questions, more than one of the choices could conceivably answer the question. However, you are to choose the <u>best</u> answer; that is, the response that most accurately and completely answers the question. You should not make assumptions that are by commonsense standards implausible, superfluous, or incompatible with the passage. After you have chosen the best answer, blacken the corresponding space on your answer sheet.

1. Extract from lease: The tenant should record all preexisting damage on the preexisting damage list, because the tenant need not pay for preexisting damage recorded there. The tenant must pay for damage that was not recorded on the preexisting damage list, except for any damage caused by a circumstance beyond the tenant's control.

   In which one of the following instances does the extract from the lease most strongly support the view that the tenant is not required to pay for the damage?

   (A) a hole in the wall that was not recorded on the preexisting damage list and that was the result of an event within the tenant's control

   (B) a crack in a window caused by a factor beyond the tenant's control and not recorded on the preexisting damage list

   (C) a tear in the linoleum that was not preexisting but that was caused by one of the tenant's children

   (D) a missing light fixture that was present when the tenant moved in but was later removed by the tenant

   (E) paint splatters on the carpet that should have been recorded on the preexisting damage list but were not

2. Randy: After Mega Cable Television Company refused to carry the competing Azco News Service alongside its own news channels, the mayor used her influence to get Azco time on a community channel, demonstrating her concern for keeping a diversity of news programming in the city.

   Marion: The mayor's action is fully explained by cruder motives: she's rewarding Azco's owner, a political supporter of hers.

   Of the following, which one, if true, is the logically strongest counter Randy can make to Marion's objection?

   (A) The owner of Azco supported the mayor simply because he liked her political agenda, and not for any expected reward.

   (B) The mayor also used her influence to get time on a community channel for another news service, whose owner supported the mayor's opponent in the last election.

   (C) Azco's news coverage of the mayor has never been judged to be biased by an impartial, independent organization.

   (D) The many people whose jobs depend on Azco's continued presence on a community channel are a potential source of political support for the mayor.

   (E) The number of people who watch Mega Cable Television Company's programming has decreased during the mayor's term.

GO ON TO THE NEXT PAGE.

3. On the first day of trout season a team of biologists went with local trout anglers to the Macawber River. Each angler who caught at least 2 trout chose exactly 2 of these trout for the biologists to weigh. A total of 90 fish were weighed. The measurements show that at the beginning of this season the average trout in the Macawber River weighed approximately 1.6 kilograms.

The reasoning above is most vulnerable to criticism on the grounds that it

(A) makes a generalization from a sample that is unlikely to be representative

(B) relies on evidence that is anecdotal rather than scientific

(C) ignores the variations in weight that are likely to occur over the whole season

(D) fails to take into account measurements from the same time in previous seasons

(E) does not consider whether any fish other than trout were caught

4. A strong correlation exists between what people value and the way they act. For example, those who value wealth tend to choose higher-paying jobs in undesirable locations over lower-paying jobs in desirable locations. Thus, knowing what people value can help one predict their actions.

Which one of the following most accurately expresses the conclusion of the argument?

(A) Knowing how people behave allows one to infer what they value.

(B) People's claims concerning what they value are symptomatic of their actions.

(C) No two people who value different things act the same way in identical circumstances.

(D) People who value wealth tend to allow their desire for it to outweigh other concerns.

(E) What people value can be a reliable indicator of how they will act.

5. An analysis of the number and severity of health problems among the population of a certain community showed that elderly people who were born in the community and resided there all their lives had significantly worse health than elderly people who had moved there within the past five years.

Each of the following, if true, contributes to an explanation of the difference in health between these two groups EXCEPT:

(A) People who have the means to relocate tend to be in better-than-average health.

(B) Although most people who have moved into the community are young, most people who have lived in the community all their lives are elderly.

(C) The quality of health care available to the community is lower than that for the rest of the country.

(D) Changes in one's environment tend to have a beneficial effect on one's health.

(E) People in good health are more likely to move to new communities than are people in poor health.

6. Classical Roman architecture is beautiful, primarily because of its use of rounded arches and its symmetry. Postmodern architecture is dramatic, primarily because of its creative use both of materials and of the surrounding environment. An architectural style that combines elements of both classical Roman and postmodern architecture would therefore be both beautiful and dramatic.

The reasoning in the argument is flawed in that it

(A) presumes, without providing justification, that for an architectural style to have certain qualities, its components must have those qualities

(B) fails to justify its presumption that because postmodern architecture is dramatic, that is its most salient feature

(C) neglects to consider that an architectural style combining elements of two other architectural styles may lack certain qualities of one or both of those styles

(D) neglects to specify how the drama of an architectural style contributes to its beauty

(E) ignores the possibility that there are other architectural styles whose defining qualities include both drama and beauty

GO ON TO THE NEXT PAGE.

7. After being subjected to clinical tests like those used to evaluate the effectiveness of prescription drugs, a popular nonprescription herbal remedy was found to be as effective in treating painful joints as is a certain prescription drug that has been used successfully to treat this condition. The manufacturer of the herbal remedy cited the test results as proof that chemical agents are unnecessary for the successful treatment of painful joints.

The test results would provide the proof that the manufacturer claims they do if which one of the following is assumed?

(A) People are likely to switch from using prescription drugs to using herbal remedies if the herbal remedies are found to be as effective as the prescription drugs.

(B) The herbal remedy contains no chemical agents that are effective in treating painful joints.

(C) None of the people who participated in the test of the prescription drug had ever tried using an herbal remedy to treat painful joints.

(D) The researchers who analyzed the results of the clinical testing of the herbal remedy had also analyzed the results of the clinical testing of the prescription drug.

(E) The prescription drug treats the discomfort associated with painful joints without eliminating the cause of that condition.

8. When companies' profits would otherwise be reduced by an increase in the minimum wage (a wage rate set by the government as the lowest that companies are allowed to pay), the companies often reduce the number of workers they employ. Yet a recent increase in the minimum wage did not result in job cutbacks in the fast-food industry, where most workers are paid the minimum wage.

Which one of the following, if true, most helps to explain why the increase in the minimum wage did not affect the number of jobs in the fast-food industry?

(A) After the recent increase in the minimum wage, decreased job turnover in the fast-food industry allowed employers of fast-food workers to save enough on recruiting costs to cover the cost of the wage increase.

(B) If, in any industry, an increase in the minimum wage leads to the elimination of many jobs that pay the minimum wage, then higher-paying supervisory positions will also be eliminated in that industry.

(C) With respect to its response to increases in the minimum wage, the fast-food industry does not differ significantly from other industries that employ many workers at the minimum wage.

(D) A few employees in the fast-food industry were already earning more than the new, higher minimum wage before the new minimum wage was established.

(E) Sales of fast food to workers who are paid the minimum wage did not increase following the recent change in the minimum wage.

9. One should always capitalize the main words and the first and last words of a title. But one should never capitalize articles, or prepositions and conjunctions with fewer than five letters, when they occur in the middle of a title.

Which one of the following can be properly inferred from the statements above?

(A) If a word that is a preposition or conjunction should be capitalized, then it is the first or last word of the title.

(B) If a word in the middle of a title should be capitalized, then that word is neither an article nor a conjunction shorter than five letters.

(C) All prepositions and conjunctions with fewer than five letters should be uncapitalized in titles.

(D) If a word is neither a main word nor a first or last word of a title, then it should not be capitalized.

(E) Prepositions and conjunctions with five or more letters should be capitalized in any text.

10. Letter to the editor: Recently, the city council passed an ordinance that prohibits loitering at the local shopping mall. The council's declared goal was to eliminate overcrowding and alleviate pedestrian congestion, thereby improving the mall's business and restoring its family-oriented image. But despite these claims, reducing overcrowding and congestion cannot be the actual goals of this measure, because even when fully implemented, the ordinance would not accomplish them.

Which one of the following most accurately describes a flaw in the argument's reasoning?

(A) The argument ignores the possibility that an action may achieve its secondary goals even if it does not achieve its primary goals.

(B) The argument takes for granted that something cannot be the goal of an action performed unless the action will in fact achieve that goal.

(C) The argument dismisses a claim because of its source rather than because of its content.

(D) The argument takes for granted that an action that does not accomplish its stated goals will not have any beneficial effects.

(E) The argument treats a condition that is necessary for achieving an action's stated goals as if this condition were sufficient for achieving these goals.

GO ON TO THE NEXT PAGE.

11. Cynthia: Corporations amply fund research that generates marketable new technologies. But the fundamental goal of science is to achieve a comprehensive knowledge of the workings of the universe. The government should help fund those basic scientific research projects that seek to further our theoretical knowledge of nature.

　　Luis: The basic goal of government support of scientific research is to generate technological advances that will benefit society as a whole. So only research that is expected to yield practical applications in fields such as agriculture and medicine ought to be funded.

Cynthia's and Luis's statements provide the most support for the contention that they would disagree with each other about the truth of which one of the following statements?

(A) The government should help fund pure theoretical research because such research might have unforeseen practical applications in fields such as agriculture and medicine.
(B) A proposed study of the effects of chemical fertilizers on crops, for the purpose of developing more-resistant and higher-yielding breeds, should not receive government funding.
(C) Although some research projects in theoretical science yield practical benefits, most do not, and so no research projects in theoretical science should be funded by the government.
(D) Research for the sole purpose of developing new technologies ought to be financed exclusively by corporations.
(E) Knowledge gained through basic scientific research need not be expected to lead to new and useful technologies in order for the research to merit government funding.

12. One can never tell whether another person is acting from an ulterior motive; therefore, it is impossible to tell whether someone's action is moral, and so one should evaluate the consequences of an action rather than its morality.

Which one of the following principles, if valid, most helps to justify the reasoning above?

(A) The intention of an action is indispensable for an evaluation of its morality.
(B) The assigning of praise and blame is what is most important in the assessment of the value of human actions.
(C) One can sometimes know one's own motives for a particular action.
(D) There can be good actions that are not performed by a good person.
(E) One cannot know whether someone acted morally in a particular situation unless one knows what consequences that person's actions had.

13. Fossil-fuel producers say that it would be prohibitively expensive to reduce levels of carbon dioxide emitted by the use of fossil fuels enough to halt global warming. This claim is probably false. Several years ago, the chemical industry said that finding an economical alternative to the chlorofluorocarbons (CFCs) destroying the ozone layer would be impossible. Yet once the industry was forced, by international agreements, to find substitutes for CFCs, it managed to phase them out completely well before the mandated deadline, in many cases at a profit.

Which one of the following, if true, most strengthens the argument?

(A) In the time since the chemical industry phased out CFCs, the destruction of the ozone layer by CFCs has virtually halted, but the levels of carbon dioxide emitted by the use of fossil fuels have continued to increase.
(B) In some countries, the amount of carbon dioxide emitted by the use of fossil fuels has already been reduced without prohibitive expense, but at some cost in convenience to the users of such fuels.
(C) The use of CFCs never contributed as greatly to the destruction of the ozone layer as the carbon dioxide emitted by the use of fossil fuels currently contributes to global warming.
(D) There are ways of reducing carbon dioxide emissions that could halt global warming without hurting profits of fossil-fuel producers significantly more than phasing out CFCs hurt those of the chemical industry.
(E) If international agreements forced fossil-fuel producers to find ways to reduce carbon dioxide emissions enough to halt global warming, the fossil-fuel producers could find substitutes for fossil fuels.

GO ON TO THE NEXT PAGE.

14. If legislators are to enact laws that benefit constituents, they must be sure to consider what the consequences of enacting a proposed law will actually be. Contemporary legislatures fail to enact laws that benefit constituents. Concerned primarily with advancing their own political careers, legislators present legislation in polemical terms; this arouses in their colleagues either repugnance or enthusiasm for the legislation.

Which one of the following is an assumption on which the argument depends?

(A) Legislation will not benefit constituents unless legislators become less concerned with their own careers.
(B) Legislatures that enact laws that benefit constituents are successful legislatures.
(C) The passage of laws cannot benefit constituents unless constituents generally adhere to those laws.
(D) Legislators considering a proposed law for which they have repugnance or enthusiasm do not consider the consequences that it will actually have.
(E) The inability of legislators to consider the actual consequences of enacting a proposed law is due to their strong feelings about that law.

15. Anderson maintains that travel writing has diminished in quality over the last few decades. Although travel writing has changed in this time, Anderson is too harsh on contemporary travel writers. Today, when the general public is better traveled than in the past, travel writers face a challenge far greater than that of their predecessors: they must not only show their readers a place but also make them see it anew. That the genre has not only survived but also flourished shows the talent of today's practitioners.

Which one of the following most accurately describes the role played in the argument by the statement that the general public is better traveled today than in the past?

(A) It is claimed to be a result of good travel writing.
(B) It is cited as evidence that contemporary travel writing is intended for a wider readership.
(C) It is part of a purported explanation of why readers are disappointed with today's travel writers.
(D) It is cited as a reason that travel writing flourishes more today than it has in the past.
(E) It is cited as a condition that has transformed the task of the travel writer.

16. Among multiparty democracies, those with the fewest parties will have the most-productive legislatures. The fewer the number of parties in a democracy, the more issues each must take a stand on. A political party that must take stands on a wide variety of issues has to prioritize those issues; this promotes a tendency to compromise.

Which one of the following is an assumption required by the argument?

(A) The more political parties a nation has, the more likely it is that there will be disagreements within parties.
(B) The fewer the number of a nation's political parties, the more important it is that those parties can compromise with each other.
(C) The tendency to compromise makes the legislative process more productive.
(D) The legislatures of nondemocracies are less productive than are those of democracies.
(E) Legislators in a multiparty democracy never all agree on important issues.

GO ON TO THE NEXT PAGE.

17. Warm air tends to be humid, and as humidity of air increases, the amount of rainfall also increases. So, the fact that rainfall totals for most continents have been increasing over the past five years is strong evidence that the air temperature is increasing as well.

Which one of the following has a flawed pattern of reasoning most similar to the flawed pattern of reasoning in the argument above?

(A) Food that is fresh tends to be nutritious, and the more nutritious one's diet the healthier one is. People today are generally healthier than people were a century ago. So it is likely that people today eat food that is fresher than the food people ate a century ago.

(B) Your refusal to make public your personal finances indicates some sort of financial impropriety on your part, for people who do not reveal their personal finances generally are hiding some sort of financial impropriety.

(C) People tend not to want to travel on mass transit when they are carrying bags and packages, and the more bags and packages one carries, the more awkward travel on mass transit becomes. Therefore, people who carry bags and packages tend to use automobiles rather than mass transit.

(D) Statistics show that people are generally living longer and healthier lives than ever before. However, more people are overweight and fewer people exercise than ever before. Therefore, being lean and physically fit is essential neither to long life nor to good health.

(E) People tend to watch only those television programs that they enjoy and appreciate. Since there are more television viewers today than there were ten years ago, it must be the case that viewers today are satisfied with at least some of the programs shown on television.

18. Asked by researchers to sort objects by shape, most toddlers in a large study had no trouble doing so. When subsequently told to sort by color, the toddlers seemed to have difficulty following the new rule and almost invariably persisted with their first approach. The researchers suggest such failures to adapt to new rules often result from insufficient development of the prefrontal cortex in toddlers. The cortex is essential for functions like adapting to new rules, yet is slow to mature, continuing to develop right into adolescence.

Which one of the following is most supported by the information above?

(A) Toddlers unable to sort objects by color tend to have a less developed prefrontal cortex than other children of the same age.

(B) Only adolescents and adults can solve problems that require adapting to new rules.

(C) Certain kinds of behavior on the part of toddlers may not be willfully disobedient.

(D) The maturing of the prefrontal cortex is more important than upbringing in causing the development of adaptive behavior.

(E) Skill at adapting to new situations is roughly proportional to the level of development of the prefrontal cortex.

19. Dietitian: It is true that nutrients are most effective when provided by natural foods rather than artificial supplements. While it is also true that fat in one's diet is generally unhealthy, eating raw carrots (which are rich in beta carotene) by themselves is nonetheless not an effective means of obtaining vitamin A, since the body cannot transform beta carotene into vitamin A unless it is consumed with at least some fat.

The statement that fat in one's diet is generally unhealthy plays which one of the following roles in the dietitian's argument?

(A) It is mentioned as a reason for adopting a dietary practice that the dietitian provides a reason for not carrying to the extreme.

(B) It is mentioned as the reason that is least often cited by those who recommend a dietary practice the dietitian disfavors.

(C) It is mentioned as a generally accepted hypothesis that the dietitian attempts to undermine completely.

(D) It is attacked as inadequate evidence for the claim that nutrients are most effective when provided by natural foods rather than artificial supplements.

(E) It is cited as a bad reason for adopting a dietary habit that the dietitian recommends.

GO ON TO THE NEXT PAGE.

20. Industrial engineer: Some people have suggested that the problem of global warming should be addressed by pumping some of the carbon dioxide produced by the burning of fossil fuels into the deep ocean. Many environmentalists worry that this strategy would simply exchange one form of pollution for an equally destructive form. This worry is unfounded, however; much of the carbon dioxide now released into the atmosphere eventually ends up in the ocean anyway, where it does not cause environmental disturbances as destructive as global warming.

Which one of the following most accurately expresses the conclusion of the industrial engineer's argument as a whole?

(A) Global warming from the emission of carbon dioxide into the atmosphere could be reduced by pumping some of that carbon dioxide into the deep ocean.

(B) Environmentalists worry that the strategy of pumping carbon dioxide into the deep ocean to reduce global warming would simply exchange one form of pollution for another, equally destructive one.

(C) Worrying that pumping carbon dioxide into the deep ocean to reduce global warming would simply exchange one form of pollution for another, equally destructive, form is unfounded.

(D) Much of the carbon dioxide now released into the atmosphere ends up in the ocean where it does not cause environmental disturbances as destructive as global warming.

(E) To reduce global warming, the strategy of pumping into the deep ocean at least some of the carbon dioxide now released into the atmosphere should be considered.

21. Several people came down with an illness caused by a type of bacteria in seafood. Health officials traced the history of each person who became ill to the same restaurant and date. Careful testing showed that most people who ate seafood at the restaurant on that date had not come in contact with the bacteria in question. Despite this finding, health officials remained confident that contaminated seafood from this restaurant caused the cases of illness.

Which one of the following, if true, most helps to resolve the apparent discrepancy indicated above?

(A) Most people are immune to the effects of the bacteria in question.

(B) Those made ill by the bacteria had all been served by a waiter who subsequently became ill.

(C) All and only those who ate contaminated seafood at the restaurant on that date were allergic to the monosodium glutamate in a sauce that they used.

(D) The restaurant in question had recently been given a warning about violations of health regulations.

(E) All and only those who ate a particular seafood dish at the restaurant contracted the illness.

22. Economist: Real wages in this country will increase significantly only if productivity increases notably. Thus, it is unlikely that real wages will increase significantly in the near future, since this country's businesses are currently investing very little in new technology and this pattern is likely to continue for at least several more years.

Which one of the following, if assumed about the economist's country, allows the economist's conclusion to be properly drawn?

(A) Neither real wages nor productivity have increased in the last several years.

(B) Real wages will increase notably if a significant number of workers acquire the skills necessary to use new technology.

(C) Sooner or later real wages will increase significantly.

(D) Productivity will not increase if businesses do not make a substantial investment in new technology.

(E) The new technology in which businesses are currently investing is not contributing to an increase in productivity.

GO ON TO THE NEXT PAGE.

23. In scientific journals, authors and reviewers have praised companies in which they have substantial investments. These scientists, with their potential conflict of interest, call into question the integrity of scientific inquiry, so there should be full public disclosure of scientific authors' commercial holdings.

Which one of the following conforms most closely to the principle illustrated by the argument above?

(A) Managers within any corporation should not make investments in the companies for which they work.

(B) Claims about the effectiveness of pharmaceuticals should be based on scientific studies.

(C) People with access to otherwise private information regarding the value of stocks should not be allowed to sell or purchase those stocks.

(D) Magazine publishers should not be allowed to invest in the companies that advertise in their magazines.

(E) Financial advisers should inform their clients about any incentives the advisers receive for promoting investments in particular companies.

24. Columnist: The amount of acidic pollutants released into the air has decreased throughout the world over the last several decades. We can expect, then, an overall decrease in the negative environmental effects of acid rain, which is caused by these acidic pollutants.

Each of the following, if true, would weaken the columnist's argument EXCEPT:

(A) Some ecosystems have developed sophisticated mechanisms that reduce the negative effects of increased levels of acids in the environment.

(B) The amount of acid-neutralizing buffers released into the air has decreased in recent years.

(C) The current decrease in acidic pollutants is expected to end soon, as more countries turn to coal for the generation of electricity.

(D) The effects of acid rain are cumulative and largely independent of current acid rain levels.

(E) The soils of many ecosystems exposed to acid rain have been exhausted of minerals that help protect them from acid rain's harmful effects.

25. Columnist: It is sometimes claimed that the only factors relevant to determining moral guilt or innocence are the intentions of the person performing an action. However, external circumstances often play a crucial role in our moral judgment of an action. For example, a cook at a restaurant who absentmindedly put an ingredient in the stew that is not usually in the stew would ordinarily be regarded as forgetful, not immoral. If, however, someone eating at the restaurant happens to be severely allergic to that ingredient, eats the stew, and dies, many people would judge the cook to be guilty of serious moral negligence.

Which one of the following propositions is best illustrated by the columnist's statements?

(A) It is sometimes fair to judge the morality of others' actions even without considering all of the circumstances under which those actions were performed.

(B) We sometimes judge unfairly the morality of other people's actions.

(C) We should judge all negligent people to be equally morally blameworthy, regardless of the outcomes of their actions.

(D) People are sometimes held morally blameworthy as a result of circumstances some of which were outside their intentional control.

(E) The intentions of the person performing an action are rarely a decisive factor in making moral judgments about that action.

S T O P

IF YOU FINISH BEFORE TIME IS CALLED, YOU MAY CHECK YOUR WORK ON THIS SECTION ONLY.
DO NOT WORK ON ANY OTHER SECTION IN THE TEST.

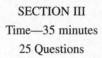
SECTION III
Time—35 minutes
25 Questions

Directions: The questions in this section are based on the reasoning contained in brief statements or passages. For some questions, more than one of the choices could conceivably answer the question. However, you are to choose the best answer; that is, the response that most accurately and completely answers the question. You should not make assumptions that are by commonsense standards implausible, superfluous, or incompatible with the passage. After you have chosen the best answer, blacken the corresponding space on your answer sheet.

1. It is difficult to keep deep wounds free of bacteria. Even strong antibiotics fail to kill the bacteria that live in such wounds. However, many physicians have succeeded in eliminating bacteria from deep wounds by packing the wound with a sweet substance like sugar.

    Which one of the following, if true, most helps to explain why treating deep wounds with sugar as described above is successful?

    (A) Bacteria that live in deep wounds thrive in a moist environment, and sugar has a dehydrating effect.
    (B) Sugar that is nearly pure is readily available for use in medical treatments.
    (C) Many kinds of bacteria can use sugar as a nutrient and will reproduce rapidly when sugar is available to them.
    (D) Some foods that contain sugar can weaken the effects of certain antibiotics.
    (E) Strong antibiotics were developed only recently, but the use of sugar as a treatment for wounds dates back to ancient times.

2. People who are red/green color-blind cannot distinguish between green and brown. Gerald cannot distinguish between green and brown. Therefore Gerald is red/green color-blind.

    Which one of the following most closely parallels the reasoning in the argument presented in the passage?

    (A) People who are fair-skinned suffer from sunburn. William is fair-skinned. Therefore William suffers from sunburn.
    (B) People who are suffering from sinusitis lose their sense of smell. Mary has lost her sense of smell. Therefore Mary is suffering from sinusitis.
    (C) People who have suffered from jaundice cannot become blood donors. Jean is a blood donor. Therefore Jean has not suffered from jaundice.
    (D) People who are color-blind cannot become airline pilots. Arthur is color-blind. Therefore Arthur cannot become an airline pilot.
    (E) People who are diabetic cannot eat large amounts of sugar. Freda is diabetic. Therefore Freda is on a special diet.

3. Early in this century Alfred Wegener developed the concept of continental drift. His ideas were rejected vehemently because he postulated no identifiable force strong enough to make the continents move. We have come to accept Wegener's theory, not because we have pinpointed such a force, but because new instruments have finally allowed continental movement to be confirmed by observation.

    The passage best illustrates which one of the following statements about science?

    (A) The aim of science is to define the manifold of nature within the terms of a single harmonious theory.
    (B) In accepting a mathematical description of nature, science has become far more accurate at identifying underlying forces.
    (C) The paradox of science is that every improvement in its measuring instruments seems to make adequate theories harder to work out.
    (D) Science, employing statistics and the laws of probability, is concerned not with the single event but with mass behavior.
    (E) When the events a theory postulates are detected, the theory is accepted even without an explanation of how those events are brought about.

GO ON TO THE NEXT PAGE.

4. The theory of military deterrence was based on a simple psychological truth, that fear of retaliation makes a would-be aggressor nation hesitate before attacking and is often sufficient to deter it altogether from attacking. Clearly, then, to maintain military deterrence, a nation would have to be believed to have retaliatory power so great that a potential aggressor nation would have reason to think that it could not defend itself against such retaliation.

If the statements above are true, which one of the following can be properly inferred?

(A) A would-be aggressor nation can be deterred from attacking only if it has certain knowledge that it would be destroyed in retaliation by the country it attacks.

(B) A nation will not attack another nation if it believes that its own retaliatory power surpasses that of the other nation.

(C) One nation's failing to attack another establishes that the nation that fails to attack believes that it could not withstand a retaliatory attack from the other nation.

(D) It is in the interests of a nation that seeks deterrence and has unsurpassed military power to let potential aggressors against it become aware of its power of retaliatory attack.

(E) Maintaining maximum deterrence from aggression by other nations requires that a nation maintain a retaliatory force greater than that of any other nation.

5. To the Editor:

In 1960, an astronomer proposed a mathematical model for determining whether extraterrestrial life exists. It was based on the assumptions that life as we know it could exist only on a planet and that many stars are, like our Sun, orbited by planets. On the basis that there are nine planets in our solar system and one of them has life as we know it, the astronomer predicted that there are as many as one million extraterrestrial civilizations across all solar systems. Yet astronomers to date have not detected even one planet outside our solar system. This indicates that the astronomer's model is wrong, and life as we know it exists only on the planet Earth.

Clay Moltz

Which one of the following, if accepted by Clay Moltz, would require him to reconsider his conclusion?

(A) Forms of life other than life as we know it exist on other planets.

(B) There are many stars that are not orbited by planets.

(C) Detecting planets outside our solar system requires more sophisticated instruments than are currently available.

(D) The soundness of the conclusion reached by applying a mathematical model depends on the soundness of the assumptions on which the model is based.

(E) Due to sheer distances and expanses of space involved, any extraterrestrial civilization would have great difficulty communicating with ours.

6. If Max were guilty, he would not ask the police to investigate. Therefore, his asking the police to investigate shows that he is not guilty.

The logical structure of the argument above is most similar to which one of the following?

(A) If Lucille were in the next room, I would not be able to see her. Therefore, the fact that I can see her shows that she is not in the next room.

(B) If Sam were rich, he would not spend his vacation in Alaska. Therefore, his spending his vacation in the Bahamas shows that he is rich.

(C) If Joe were over 40 he would not want to learn to ski. Therefore, the fact that he does not want to learn to ski shows that he is over 40.

(D) If Mark were a good cook, he would not put cinnamon in the chili. Therefore, the fact that he is not a good cook shows that he put cinnamon in the chili.

(E) If Sally were sociable, she would not avoid her friends. Therefore, the fact that she is sociable shows that she does not avoid her friends.

GO ON TO THE NEXT PAGE.

7. A population of game ducks at a western lake contains 55 males to every 45 females, while a population of game ducks at an eastern lake contains 65 males for every 35 females. Among those ducks that have not yet bred there are only slightly more males than females, but among older ducks the number of males greatly exceeds the number of females. Because there are appreciably more males among adult ducks than among young ducks, we can infer that the greater the disparity in overall sex ratios, the greater the percentage of older male ducks in the population.

Which one of the following can be inferred from the passage?

(A) The population of game ducks at the western lake contains a lower percentage of adult males than the population at the eastern lake contains.
(B) The population of game ducks at the eastern lake contains a higher percentage of nonadult game ducks than the population at the western lake contains.
(C) The total number of male game ducks is higher in the eastern lake's population than in the western lake's population.
(D) The number of nonadult ducks hatched in a breeding season is higher in the eastern lake's population than in the western lake's population.
(E) Adult female game ducks outnumber nonadult female game ducks in the eastern lake's population.

8. The common procedure for determining whether a food additive should be banned from use is to compare its health-related benefits with its potential risks. Yellow Dye No. 5, an additive used to color lemon soda, might cause allergic reactions in a few consumers. For most consumers of lemon soda, however, the coloring enhances their enjoyment of the beverage. This particular additive should not be banned, therefore, because its benefits greatly outweigh its risks.

A flaw in the argument is that the author

(A) implies that the dye entails no health-related risks
(B) treats enjoyment of a beverage as a health-related benefit
(C) ignores the possibility that some food additives are harmful to most people
(D) bases the argument on an unproven claim regarding a danger in using Yellow Dye No. 5
(E) presumes that most consumers heed the warning labels on beverage containers

9. Fines levied against those responsible for certain environmentally damaging accidents are now so high that it costs a company responsible for such an accident more to pay the fine than it would have cost to adopt measures that would have prevented the accident. Therefore, since businesses value their profits, those that might have such accidents will now install adequate environmental safeguards.

Which one of the following, if true, most seriously weakens the argument?

(A) Businesses generally greatly underestimate the risk of future accidents.
(B) Businesses are as concerned with long-term as they are with short-term strategies for maximizing profits.
(C) Businesses generally do the environmentally "right" thing only if doing so makes good business sense.
(D) Businesses treat fines that are levied against them as an ordinary business expense.
(E) Businesses are learning to exploit the public's environmental awareness in promoting themselves.

GO ON TO THE NEXT PAGE.

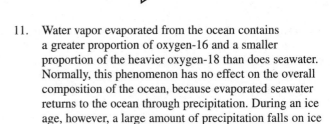

10. Even in a democracy, it is necessary to restrict the dissemination of advanced technological knowledge that is of commercial or national-security value. Dissemination to certain countries, those that are or will be competitors or enemies, should be selectively prohibited. There must, however, be free exchange of scientific information.

In order to act in accordance with the position above, it would be necessary to be able to rely on each of the following EXCEPT:

(A) It is possible to distinguish with confidence, despite any changes in the international environment, friendly or noncompetitive from hostile or competitive nations.

(B) In a democracy, it is not necessary that the public have detailed knowledge of the country's advanced technology in order, for example, to make informed decisions about the direction public policy should take.

(C) In most fields of science, basic scientific research is further advanced in countries that are democracies than in countries that are not democracies.

(D) In each field of science, it is possible to distinguish scientific information from advanced technological knowledge that is of commercial or national-security value.

(E) In cases where a company that uses advanced technology is a multinational organization, it is possible to keep information about the technology from being passed across designated national boundaries.

11. Water vapor evaporated from the ocean contains a greater proportion of oxygen-16 and a smaller proportion of the heavier oxygen-18 than does seawater. Normally, this phenomenon has no effect on the overall composition of the ocean, because evaporated seawater returns to the ocean through precipitation. During an ice age, however, a large amount of precipitation falls on ice caps, where it is trapped as ice.

Which one of the following conclusions about a typical ice age is most strongly supported by the statements above?

(A) The proportions of oxygen-16 and oxygen-18 are the same in vapor from seawater as in the seawater itself.

(B) The concentration of oxygen-18 in seawater is increased.

(C) Rain and snow contain relatively more oxygen-16 than they do in interglacial periods.

(D) During the ice age, more of the Earth's precipitation falls over land than falls over the ocean.

(E) The composition of seawater changes more slowly than it does in interglacial periods.

12. Some of the most prosperous nations in the world have experienced a pronounced drop in national savings rates—the percentage of after-tax income an average household saves. This trend will undoubtedly continue if the average age of these nations' populations continues to rise, since older people have fewer reasons to save than do younger people.

Which one of the following indicates an error in the reasoning leading to the prediction above?

(A) It fails to specify the many reasons younger people have for saving money, and it fails to identify which of those reasons is the strongest.

(B) It assumes that a negative savings rate—the result of the average household's spending all of its after-tax income as well as some of its existing savings—cannot ever come about in any nation.

(C) It fails to cite statistics showing that the average age of the population of certain nations is rising.

(D) It only takes into account the comparative number of reasons older and younger people, respectively, have for saving, and not the comparative strength of those reasons.

(E) It uses after-tax income as the base for computing the national savings rate without establishing by argument that after-tax income is a more appropriate base than before-tax income.

GO ON TO THE NEXT PAGE.

13. The term "pit bull" does not designate a breed of dog, as do the terms "German shepherd" and "poodle." It is like the terms "Seeing-Eye dog" and "police dog," which designate dogs according to what they do. If you take two German shepherds and place them side by side, you cannot tell by appearance alone which is the police dog and which is the Seeing-Eye dog.

Which one of the following is the main point of the passage?

(A) German shepherds can be pit bulls.
(B) Pit bulls can be distinguished from other kinds of dogs by appearance alone.
(C) A dog is a pit bull because of what it does, not because of its breed.
(D) German shepherds can function both as police dogs and as Seeing-Eye dogs.
(E) Some breeds of dogs cannot be distinguished from other breeds of dogs by appearance alone.

14. Historically, monetary systems have developed only in population centers with marketplaces. Through the fourth century B.C., Mesopotamian cities engaged in trade, but had never had marketplaces. By that period, however, Greek cities all had marketplaces, or agorae. The Greek cities' agorae were centrally located and goods were traded there either for money or for commodities.

If all of the statements in the passage are true, then which one of the following must also be true?

(A) In the fourth century B.C., Greek cities were the only population centers with monetary systems.
(B) The development of monetary systems has historically led to the development of marketplaces.
(C) In the fourth century B.C., the Greeks and the Mesopotamians traded with each other.
(D) After the fourth century B.C., Mesopotamian cities had marketplaces and monetary systems.
(E) The Mesopotamian cities of the fourth century B.C. did not have monetary systems.

Questions 15–16

Computer operating system software has become increasingly standardized. But when a large business with multiple, linked computer systems uses identical operating system software on all of its computers, a computer vandal who gains access to one computer automatically has access to the data on all the computers. Using a program known as a "virus," the vandal can then destroy much of the data on all the computers. If such a business introduced minor variations into its operating system software, unauthorized access to all the computers at the same time could be virtually eliminated. Furthermore, variations in operating system software can be created without any loss of computer compatibility to the business. Therefore, it is advisable for businesses to implement such variations.

15. Which one of the following, if true, supports the conclusion in the passage?

(A) Standardization of computer operating system software has increased computer compatibility among different businesses.
(B) Correcting any damage resulting from an invasion by a computer virus program is more expensive than preventing the damage.
(C) It is not costly for a business to maintain incompatible computer operating systems.
(D) There are other kinds of destructive computer programs that do not depend on intercomputer links.
(E) Not all businesses need to share data among their internal computer systems.

16. Which one of the following can be inferred from the passage?

(A) If a business does not introduce variety into its computer operating systems, it will lose data on its computers because of damage from virus programs.
(B) If a computer virus program is introduced into a business' computer, all of the data on that computer will be destroyed.
(C) If a business introduces variety into its linked computer operating systems, it will have increased overall protection for its systems, but will not have protected every computer from viral invasion.
(D) If a business does not have multiple, linked computer systems, its computers cannot be protected from computer viruses.
(E) If minor variations are created in computer operating system software, it will be easier to access the data on the computers that use that software.

GO ON TO THE NEXT PAGE.

17. It is the mark of a superior conductor that he or she has the authority to insist, even with a top orchestra, that rehearsal work must be intensified. This authority cannot simply be claimed; the conductor must earn it by winning the orchestra's respect for the artistic interpretations he or she is currently pursuing.

In taking the position outlined, the author presupposes which one of the following?

(A) Superior conductors devise different interpretations of a composition for each orchestra with which they perform it.
(B) Superior conductors are perfectionists who are never satisfied with any performance even by a top orchestra.
(C) Top orchestras are always ready to put in additional work on rehearsals if the conductor considers additional rehearsing necessary.
(D) Top orchestras can appreciate the merits of an interpretation even before they have brought it to full realization.
(E) Even top orchestras are not always led by superior conductors.

18. In the United States proven oil reserves—the amount of oil considered extractable from known fields—are at the same level as they were ten years ago. Yet over this same period no new oil fields of any consequence have been discovered, and the annual consumption of domestically produced oil has increased.

Which one of the following, if true, best reconciles the discrepancy described above?

(A) Over the past decade the annual consumption of imported oil has increased more rapidly than that of domestic oil in the United States.
(B) Conservation measures have lowered the rate of growth of domestic oil consumption from what it was a decade ago.
(C) Oil exploration in the United States has slowed due to increased concern over the environmental impact of such exploration.
(D) The price of domestically produced oil has fallen substantially over the past decade.
(E) Due to technological advances over the last decade, much oil previously considered unextractable is now considered extractable.

19. Train service suffers when a railroad combines commuter and freight service. By dividing its attention between its freight and commuter customers, a railroad serves neither particularly well. Therefore, if a railroad is going to be a successful business, then it must concentrate exclusively on one of these two markets.

For the argument to be logically correct, it must make which of the of the following assumptions?

(A) Commuter and freight service have little in common with each other.
(B) The first priority of a railroad is to be a successful business.
(C) Unless a railroad serves its customers well, it will not be a successful business.
(D) If a railroad concentrates on commuter service, it will be a successful business.
(E) Railroad commuters rarely want freight service as well.

20. Most people in the United States view neither big nor small business as particularly efficient or dynamic and regard both as providing consumers with fairly priced goods and services. However, most people consistently perceive small business as a force for good in society, whereas big business is perceived as socially responsible only in times of prosperity.

The statements above, if true, would provide the strongest support for which one of the following hypotheses?

(A) Most people in the United States give little thought to the value of business to society.
(B) If big business were more efficient, it would be perceived more favorably by the public generally.
(C) If small business were regarded as being more dynamic, it, too would receive strongly favorable ratings only in times of general prosperity.
(D) Even if people did not regard big business as providing consumers with value for their money, they would still regard it as socially responsible in times of general prosperity.
(E) Many people in the United States regard the social responsibility of big business as extending beyond providing consumers with fairly priced goods and services.

GO ON TO THE NEXT PAGE.

21. The energy an animal must expend to move uphill is proportional to its body weight, whereas the animal's energy output available to perform this task is proportional to its surface area. This is the reason that small animals, like squirrels, can run up a tree trunk almost as fast as they can move on level ground, whereas large animals tend to slow down when they are moving uphill.

Which one of the following is an assumption on which the explanation above depends?

(A) The amount of energy needed to move uphill is no greater for large animals than it is for small animals.
(B) Small animals can move more rapidly than large animals can.
(C) The ratio of surface area to body weight is smaller in large animals than it is in small animals.
(D) There is little variation in the ratio of energy output to body weight among animals.
(E) The amount of energy needed to run at a given speed is proportional to the surface area of the running animal.

22. The 1980s have been characterized as a period of selfish individualism that threatens the cohesion of society. But this characterization is true of any time. Throughout history all human actions have been motivated by selfishness. When the deeper implications are considered, even the simplest "unselfish" acts prove to be instances of selfish concern for the human species.

Which one of the following is a flaw in the argument?

(A) The claim that selfishness has been present throughout history is not actually relevant to the argument.
(B) No statistical evidence is provided to show that humans act selfishly more often than they act unselfishly.
(C) The argument assumes that selfishness is unique to the present age.
(D) The argument mentions only humans and does not consider the behavior of other species.
(E) The argument relies on two different uses of the term "selfish."

23. A medical journal used a questionnaire survey to determine whether a particular change in its format would increase its readership. Sixty-two percent of those who returned the questionnaire supported that change. On the basis of this outcome, the decision was made to introduce the new format.

Which one of the following, if it were determined to be true, would provide the best evidence that the journal's decision will have the desired effect?

(A) Of the readers who received questionnaires, 90 percent returned them.
(B) Other journals have based format changes on survey results.
(C) The percentage of surveyed readers who like the format change was almost the same as the percentage of the entire potential readership who would like the format change.
(D) It was determined that the new format would be less costly than the old format.
(E) Ninety percent of the readers who were dissatisfied with the old format and only 50 percent of the readers who liked the old format returned their questionnaires.

GO ON TO THE NEXT PAGE.

Questions 24–25

Shanna: Owners of any work of art, simply by virtue of ownership, ethically have the right to destroy that artwork if they find it morally or aesthetically distasteful, or if caring for it becomes inconvenient.

Jorge: Ownership of unique artworks, unlike ownership of other kinds of objects, carries the moral right to possess but not to destroy. A unique work of art with aesthetic or historical value belongs to posterity and so must be preserved, whatever the personal wishes of its legal owner.

24. Which one of the following principles, if accepted, would contribute most to Shanna's defense of her position against that of Jorge?

   (A)   Truly great works of art are never morally or aesthetically distasteful to any serious student of the history of art.

   (B)   The right of future generations to have their artistic heritage preserved is of greater importance than the rights of any presently living individual.

   (C)   It would be imprudent to allow the present stock of artworks to be destroyed without some guarantee that the artists of the future will produce works as great as those produced in the past.

   (D)   There are certain entities over which no one would be ethically justified in claiming absolute rights to ownership.

   (E)   The autonomy of individuals to do what they wish with what is theirs must not be compromised in the absence of a threat to anyone's health or safety.

25. On the basis of their statements, Shanna and Jorge are committed to disagreeing about the truth of which one of the following statements?

   (A)   Anyone who owns a portrait presenting his or her father in an unflattering light would for that reason alone be ethically justified in destroying it.

   (B)   People who own aesthetically valuable works of art have no moral obligation to make them available for public viewing.

   (C)   Valuable paintings by well-known artists are seldom intentionally damaged or destroyed by their owners.

   (D)   If a piece of sculpture is not unique, its owner has no ethical obligation to preserve it if doing so proves burdensome.

   (E)   It is legally permissible for a unique and historically valuable mural to be destroyed by its owner if he or she tires of it.

S T O P

IF YOU FINISH BEFORE TIME IS CALLED, YOU MAY CHECK YOUR WORK ON THIS SECTION ONLY. DO NOT WORK ON ANY OTHER SECTION IN THE TEST.

SECTION IV

Time—35 minutes

22 Questions

Directions: Each group of questions in this section is based on a set of conditions. In answering some of the questions, it may be useful to draw a rough diagram. Choose the response that most accurately and completely answers each question and blacken the corresponding space on your answer sheet.

Questions 1–5

At each of six consecutive stops—1, 2, 3, 4, 5, and 6—that a traveler must make in that order as part of a trip, she can choose one from among exactly four airlines—L, M, N, and O—on which to continue. Her choices must conform to the following constraints:

    Whichever airline she chooses at a stop, she chooses one of the other airlines at the next stop.

    She chooses the same airline at stop 1 as she does at stop 6.

    She chooses the same airline at stop 2 as she does at stop 4.

    Whenever she chooses either L or M at a stop, she does not choose N at the next stop.

    At stop 5, she chooses N or O.

1. Which one of the following could be an accurate list of the airlines the traveler chooses at each stop, in order from 1 through 6?

    (A)   L, M, M, L, O, L

    (B)   M, L, O, M, O, M

    (C)   M, N, O, N, O, M

    (D)   M, O, N, O, N, M

    (E)   O, M, L, M, O, N

2. If the traveler chooses N at stop 5, which one of the following could be an accurate list of the airlines she chooses at stops 1, 2, and 3, respectively?

    (A)   L, M, N

    (B)   L, O, N

    (C)   M, L, N

    (D)   M, L, O

    (E)   N, O, N

3. If the only airlines the traveler chooses for the trip are M, N, and O, and she chooses O at stop 5, then the airlines she chooses at stops 1, 2, and 3, must be, respectively,

    (A)   M, O, and N

    (B)   M, N, and O

    (C)   N, M, and O

    (D)   N, O, and M

    (E)   O, M, and N

4. Which one of the following CANNOT be an accurate list of the airlines the traveler chooses at stops 1 and 2, respectively?

    (A)   L, M

    (B)   L, O

    (C)   M, L

    (D)   M, O

    (E)   O, N

5. If the traveler chooses O at stop 2, which one of the following could be an accurate list of the airlines she chooses at stops 5 and 6, respectively?

    (A)   M, N

    (B)   N, L

    (C)   N, O

    (D)   O, L

    (E)   O, N

GO ON TO THE NEXT PAGE.

<u>Questions 6–11</u>

The members of a five-person committee will be selected from among three parents—F, G, and H—three students—K, L, and M—and four teachers—U, W, X, and Z. The selection of committee members will meet the following conditions:

The committee must include exactly one student.
F and H cannot both be selected.
M and Z cannot both be selected.
U and W cannot both be selected.
F cannot be selected unless Z is also selected.
W cannot be selected unless H is also selected.

6. Which one of the following is an acceptable selection of committee members?

(A) F, G, K, L, Z
(B) F, G, K, U, X
(C) G, K, W, X, Z
(D) H, K, U, W, X
(E) H, L, W, X, Z

7. If W and Z are selected, which one of the following is a pair of people who could also be selected?

(A) U and X
(B) K and L
(C) G and M
(D) G and K
(E) F and G

8. Which one of the following is a pair of people who CANNOT both be selected?

(A) F and G
(B) F and M
(C) G and K
(D) H and L
(E) M and U

9. If W is selected, then any one of the following could also be selected EXCEPT:

(A) F
(B) G
(C) L
(D) M
(E) Z

10. If the committee is to include exactly one parent, which one of the following is a person who must also be selected?

(A) K
(B) L
(C) M
(D) U
(E) X

11. If M is selected, then the committee must also include both

(A) F and G
(B) G and H
(C) H and K
(D) K and U
(E) U and X

GO ON TO THE NEXT PAGE.

<u>Questions 12–17</u>

Within a five-year period from 1991 to 1995, each of three friends—Ramon, Sue, and Taylor—graduated. In that period, each bought his or her first car. The graduations and car purchases must be consistent with the following:

Ramon graduated in some year before the year in which Taylor graduated.

Taylor graduated in some year before the year in which he bought his first car.

Sue bought her first car in some year before the year in which she graduated.

Ramon and Sue graduated in the same year as each other.

At least one of the friends graduated in 1993.

12. Which one of the following could be an accurate matching of each friend and the year in which she or he graduated?

(A) Ramon: 1991; Sue: 1991; Taylor: 1993
(B) Ramon: 1992; Sue: 1992; Taylor: 1993
(C) Ramon: 1992; Sue: 1993; Taylor: 1994
(D) Ramon: 1993; Sue: 1993; Taylor: 1992
(E) Ramon: 1993; Sue: 1993; Taylor: 1995

13. Which one of the following could have taken place in 1995?

(A) Ramon graduated.
(B) Ramon bought his first car.
(C) Sue graduated.
(D) Sue bought her first car.
(E) Taylor graduated.

14. Which one of the following must be false?

(A) Two of the friends each bought his or her first car in 1991.
(B) Two of the friends each bought his or her first car in 1992.
(C) Two of the friends each bought his or her first car in 1993.
(D) Two of the friends each bought his or her first car in 1994.
(E) Two of the friends each bought his or her first car in 1995.

15. Which one of the following must be true?

(A) None of the three friends graduated in 1991.
(B) None of the three friends graduated in 1992.
(C) None of the three friends bought his or her first car in 1993.
(D) None of the three friends graduated in 1994.
(E) None of the three friends bought his or her first car in 1995.

16. If Taylor graduated in the same year that Ramon bought his first car, then each of the following could be true EXCEPT:

(A) Sue bought her first car in 1991.
(B) Ramon graduated in 1992.
(C) Taylor graduated in 1993.
(D) Taylor bought his first car in 1994.
(E) Ramon bought his first car in 1995.

17. If Sue graduated in 1993, then which one of the following must be true?

(A) Sue bought her first car in 1991.
(B) Ramon bought his first car in 1992.
(C) Ramon bought his first car in 1993.
(D) Taylor bought his first car in 1994.
(E) Taylor bought his first car in 1995.

GO ON TO THE NEXT PAGE.

Questions 18–22

A child eating alphabet soup notices that the only letters left in her bowl are one each of these six letters: T, U, W, X, Y, and Z. She plays a game with the remaining letters, eating them in the next three spoonfuls in accord with certain rules. Each of the six letters must be in exactly one of the next three spoonfuls, and each of the spoonfuls must have at least one and at most three of the letters. In addition, she obeys the following restrictions:

The U is in a later spoonful than the T.
The U is not in a later spoonful than the X.
The Y is in a later spoonful than the W.
The U is in the same spoonful as either the Y or the Z, but not both.

18. Which one of the following could be an accurate list of the spoonfuls and the letters in each of them?

(A) first: Y
    second: T, W
    third: U, X, Z
(B) first: T, W
    second: U, X, Y
    third: Z
(C) first: T
    second: U, Z
    third: W, X, Y
(D) first: T, U, Z
    second: W
    third: X, Y
(E) first: W
    second: T, X, Z
    third: U, Y

19. If the Y is the only letter in one of the spoonfuls, then which one of the following could be true?

(A) The Y is in the first spoonful.
(B) The Z is in the first spoonful.
(C) The T is in the second spoonful.
(D) The X is in the second spoonful.
(E) The W is in the third spoonful.

20. If the Z is in the first spoonful, then which one of the following must be true?

(A) The T is in the second spoonful.
(B) The U is in the third spoonful.
(C) The W is in the first spoonful.
(D) The W is in the second spoonful.
(E) The X is in the third spoonful.

21. Which one of the following is a complete list of letters, any one of which could be the only letter in the first spoonful?

(A) T
(B) T, W
(C) T, X
(D) T, W, Z
(E) T, X, W, Z

22. If the T is in the second spoonful, then which one of the following could be true?

(A) Exactly two letters are in the first spoonful.
(B) Exactly three letters are in the first spoonful.
(C) Exactly three letters are in the second spoonful.
(D) Exactly one letter is in the third spoonful.
(E) Exactly two letters are in the third spoonful.

S T O P

IF YOU FINISH BEFORE TIME IS CALLED, YOU MAY CHECK YOUR WORK ON THIS SECTION ONLY.
DO NOT WORK ON ANY OTHER SECTION IN THE TEST.

SECTION V

Time—35 minutes

25 Questions

Directions: The questions in this section are based on the reasoning contained in brief statements or passages. For some questions, more than one of the choices could conceivably answer the question. However, you are to choose the best answer; that is, the response that most accurately and completely answers the question. You should not make assumptions that are by commonsense standards implausible, superfluous, or incompatible with the passage. After you have chosen the best answer, blacken the corresponding space on your answer sheet.

1. Students in a first-year undergraduate course were divided into two groups. All the students in both groups were given newspaper articles identical in every respect, except for the headline, which was different for each group. When the students were later asked questions about the contents of the article, the answers given by the two groups were markedly different, though within each group the answers were similar.

Which one of the following is most strongly supported by the information above?

(A) Readers base their impressions of what is in a newspaper on headlines alone.
(B) Newspaper headlines hamper a reader's ability to comprehend the corresponding articles.
(C) Careless reading is more common among first-year undergraduates than among more senior students.
(D) Newspaper headlines tend to be highly misleading.
(E) Newspaper headlines influence a reader's interpretation of the corresponding articles.

2. All works of art are beautiful and have something to teach us. Thus, since the natural world as a whole is both beautiful and instructive, it is a work of art.

The reasoning in the argument is flawed because the argument

(A) uses the inherently vague term "beautiful" without providing an explicit definition of that term
(B) attempts to establish an evaluative conclusion solely on the basis of claims about factual matters
(C) concludes, simply because an object possesses two qualities that are each common to all works of art, that the object is a work of art
(D) presumes, without providing justification, that only objects that are beautiful are instructive
(E) fails to consider the possibility that there are many things that are both beautiful and instructive but are not part of the natural world

3. When Copernicus changed the way we think about the solar system, he did so not by discovering new information, but by looking differently at information already available. Edward Jenner's discovery of a smallpox vaccine occurred when he shifted his focus to disease prevention from the then more common emphasis on cure. History is replete with breakthroughs of this sort.

The examples provided above illustrate which one of the following?

(A) Many valuable intellectual accomplishments occur by chance.
(B) Shifting from earlier modes of thought can result in important advances.
(C) The ability to look at information from a different point of view is rare.
(D) Understanding is advanced less often by better organization of available information than it is by the accumulation of new information.
(E) Dramatic intellectual breakthroughs are more easily accomplished in fields in which the amount of information available is relatively small.

4. Politician: Suppose censorship is wrong in itself, as modern liberals tend to believe. Then an actor's refusing a part in a film because the film glamorizes a point of view abhorrent to the actor would be morally wrong. But this conclusion is absurd. It follows that censorship is not, after all, wrong in itself.

The reasoning in the politician's argument is most vulnerable to criticism on the grounds that this argument

(A) presumes, without providing justification, that actors would subscribe to any tenet of modern liberalism
(B) uses the term "liberal" in order to discredit opponents' point of view
(C) takes for granted that there is a moral obligation to practice one's profession
(D) draws a conclusion that is inconsistent with a premise it accepts
(E) presumes, without providing justification, that declining a film role constitutes censorship in the relevant sense

GO ON TO THE NEXT PAGE.

Motor oil serves to lubricate engines and thus retard engine wear. A study was conducted to assess the effectiveness of various brands of motor oil by using them in taxicabs over a 6,000-mile test period. All the oils did equally well in retarding wear on pistons and cylinders, the relevant parts of the engine. Hence, cheaper brands of oil are the best buys.

Which one of the following, if true, most weakens the argument?

(A) Cheaper brands of motor oil are often used by knowledgeable automobile mechanics for their own cars.

(B) Tests other than of the ability to reduce engine wear also can reliably gauge the quality of motor oil.

(C) The lubricating properties of all motor oils deteriorate over time, and the rate of deterioration is accelerated by heat.

(D) The engines of some individual cars that have had their oil changed every 3,000 miles, using only a certain brand of oil, have lasted an extraordinarily long time.

(E) Ability to retard engine wear is not the only property of motor oil important to the running of an engine.

6. Elena: The best form of government is one that fosters the belief among its citizens that they have a say in how the government is run. Thus, democracy is the best form of government.

Marsha: But there are many forms of government under which citizens can be manipulated into believing they have a say when they don't.

Marsha's claim that it is possible for governments to manipulate people into thinking that they have a say when they do not is used to

(A) concur with Elena's claim that democracy is the best form of government

(B) support Marsha's unstated conclusion that the best form of government is one that appears to be democratic but really is not

(C) suggest that the premise Elena uses to support her conclusion could be used to support a conflicting conclusion

(D) support Marsha's unstated conclusion that most people seek only the appearance of democracy rather than democracy itself

(E) reject Elena's conclusion that the best form of government is democracy

7. Researcher: The use of the newest drug in treating this disease should be discontinued. The treatment usually wreaks havoc with the normal functioning of the human body, causing severe side effects such as total loss of hair, debilitating nausea, and intense pain in the joints.

The argument's reasoning is flawed because the argument

(A) fails to specify what is meant by "normal functioning of the human body"

(B) fails to consider the consequences of not administering the treatment

(C) presumes that every patient with the disease is treated with the drug

(D) does not consider the length of time needed for the treatment to begin taking effect

(E) does not acknowledge that the effects of the treatment may not be of the same severity in all cases

8. Otis: Aristotle's principle of justice says that we should treat relevantly similar cases similarly. Therefore, it is wrong for a dentist to schedule an after-hours appointment to suit a family friend but refuse to do it for anyone else.

Tyra: I accept Aristotle's principle of justice, but it's human nature to want to do special favors for friends. Indeed, that's what friends are—those for whom you would do special favors. It's not unjust for dentists to do that.

It can be inferred on the basis of their statements that Otis and Tyra disagree about whether

(A) Aristotle's principle of justice is widely applicable

(B) situations involving friends and situations involving others should be considered relevantly similar cases

(C) human nature makes it impossible to treat relevantly similar cases similarly

(D) dentists should be willing to schedule an after-hours appointment for anyone who asks

(E) Aristotle recognizes that friendship sometimes morally outweighs justice

GO ON TO THE NEXT PAGE.

9. Typically, people who have diets high in saturated fat have an increased risk of heart disease. Those who replace saturated fat in their diets with unsaturated fat decrease their risk of heart disease. Therefore, people who eat a lot of saturated fat can lower their risk of heart disease by increasing their intake of unsaturated fat.

Which one of the following, if assumed, most helps to justify the reasoning above?

(A) People who add unsaturated fat to their diets will eat less food that is high in saturated fat.

(B) Adding unsaturated fat to a diet brings health benefits other than a reduced risk of heart disease.

(C) Diet is the most important factor in a person's risk of heart disease.

(D) Taking steps to prevent heart disease is one of the most effective ways of increasing life expectancy.

(E) It is difficult to move from a diet that is high in saturated fat to a diet that includes very little fat.

10. Only people who are willing to compromise should undergo mediation to resolve their conflicts. Actual litigation should be pursued only when one is sure that one's position is correct. People whose conflicts are based on ideology are unwilling to compromise.

If the statements above are true, then which one of the following must be true?

(A) People who do not undergo mediation to resolve their conflicts should be sure that their positions are correct.

(B) People whose conflicts are not based on ideology should attempt to resolve their conflicts by means of litigation.

(C) People whose conflicts are based on ideology are not always sure that their positions are correct.

(D) People who are sure of the correctness of their positions are not people who should undergo mediation to resolve their conflicts.

(E) People whose conflicts are based on ideology are not people who should undergo mediation to resolve their conflicts.

11. Scientists have long thought that omega-3 fatty acids in fish oil tend to lower blood cholesterol and strongly suspected that a diet that includes a modest amount of fish would provide substantial health benefits. Now these views have acquired strong support from a recent study showing that middle-aged people who eat fish twice a week are nearly 30 percent less likely to develop heart disease than are those who do not eat fish.

Which one of the following is an assumption required by the argument?

(A) The test subjects in the recent study who did not eat fish were not vegetarians.

(B) The test subjects in the recent study who ate fish twice a week did not have a diet that was otherwise conducive to the development of heart disease.

(C) The test subjects in the recent study who did not eat fish were significantly more likely to eat red meat several times per week than were those who did eat fish.

(D) The test subjects in the recent study who ate fish twice a week were not significantly more likely than those who did not to engage regularly in activities known to augment cardiorespiratory health.

(E) The test subjects in the recent study who ate fish twice a week were no more likely than those who did not to have sedentary occupations.

GO ON TO THE NEXT PAGE.

12. Researcher: A number of studies have suggested that, on average, clients in short-term psychotherapy show similar levels of improvement regardless of the kind of psychotherapy they receive. So any client improvement in short-term psychotherapy must be the result of some aspect or aspects of therapy that are common to all psychotherapies—for example, the presence of someone who listens and gives attention to the client.

Which one of the following, if true, would most weaken the researcher's argument?

(A) The methods by which the studies measured whether clients improved primarily concerned immediate symptom relief and failed to address other important kinds of improvement.

(B) On average, clients improve more dramatically when they receive long-term psychotherapy, a year or longer in duration, than when clients receive short-term psychotherapy.

(C) The studies found that psychotherapy by a trained counselor does not result in any greater improvement, on average, among clients than does simple counseling by an untrained layperson.

(D) The specific techniques and interventions used by therapists practicing different kinds of psychotherapy differ dramatically.

(E) More-experienced therapists tend to use a wider range of techniques and interventions in psychotherapy than do inexperienced therapists.

13. Journalists sometimes use historical photographs to illustrate articles about current events. But this recycling of old photographs overstates the similarities between past and present, and thereby denies the individual significance of those current events. Hence, the use of historical photographs in this manner by journalists distorts public understanding of the present by presenting current events as mere repetitions of historical incidents.

Which one of the following, if assumed, enables the conclusion of the argument to be properly inferred?

(A) Any practice by which journalists present current events as mere repetitions of historical incidents overstates the similarities between past and present.

(B) If the work of a journalist overstates the similarities between past and present, then it distorts public understanding of the present by presenting current events as mere repetitions of historical incidents.

(C) If a journalistic practice distorts public understanding of the present by overstating the similarities between past and present, then it denies the individual significance of any articles about current events.

(D) No article about a current event treats that event as merely a repetition of historical incidents unless it uses historical photographs to illustrate that article.

(E) If journalists believe current events to be mere repetitions of historical incidents, then public understanding of the present will be distorted.

GO ON TO THE NEXT PAGE.

14. If Juan went to the party, it is highly unlikely that Maria would have enjoyed the party. But in fact it turned out that Maria did enjoy the party; therefore, it is highly unlikely that Juan was at the party.

The pattern of reasoning in the argument above is most similar to that in which one of the following?

(A) According to the newspaper, all eight teams in the soccer tournament have an equal chance of winning it. If so, then we will probably lose our goalie, since if we do lose our goalie we will probably not win the tournament.

(B) Kapinski, our new neighbor, is probably friendly, for Kapinski sells insurance and most people who sell insurance are friendly.

(C) If the lottery were fair, the person who won the lottery would not have been likely to win it. Thus, since this person would have been likely to win the lottery if it were unfair, the lottery was probably unfair.

(D) If Clarissa missed the bus today, it is quite unlikely that she would have gotten to work on time. So, it is quite unlikely that Clarissa missed the bus, since she actually was at work on time today.

(E) This year's election will probably be fair. But Popov probably will not win unless the election is unfair. So, Popov will not win the election.

15. Sonya: Anyone who lives without constant awareness of the fragility and precariousness of human life has a mind clouded by illusion. Yet those people who are perpetually cognizant of the fragility and precariousness of human life surely taint their emotional outlook on existence.

Sonya's statements, if true, most strongly support which one of the following?

(A) Anyone who places a higher priority on maintaining a positive emotional outlook than on dispelling illusion will be completely unaware of the fragility and precariousness of human life.

(B) Either no one has a tainted emotional outlook on existence, or no one has a mind clouded by illusion.

(C) It is impossible for anyone to live without some degree of self-deception.

(D) Everyone whose emotional outlook on existence is untainted has a mind clouded by illusion.

(E) It is better to be aware of the fragility and precariousness of human life than to have an untainted emotional outlook on existence.

16. In a study, shoppers who shopped in a grocery store without a shopping list and bought only items that were on sale for half price or less spent far more money on a comparable number of items than did shoppers in the same store who used a list and bought no sale items.

Which one of the following, if true, most helps to explain the apparent paradox in the study's results?

(A) Only the shoppers who used a list used a shopping cart.

(B) The shoppers who did not use lists bought many unnecessary items.

(C) Usually, only the most expensive items go on sale in grocery stores.

(D) The grocery store in the study carries many expensive items that few other grocery stores carry.

(E) The grocery store in the study places relatively few items on sale.

17. A group of mountain climbers was studied to determine how they were affected by diminished oxygen in the air at high altitudes. As they climbed past 6,100 meters above sea level, the climbers slurred words, took longer to understand simple sentences, and demonstrated poor judgment. This combination of worsened performances disproves the theory that the area of the brain controlling speech is distinct from that controlling other functions.

The argument is most vulnerable to criticism on the grounds that it overlooks the possibility that

(A) the climbers' performance in speech, comprehension, and reasoning was impaired because oxygen deprivation affected their entire brains

(B) the climbers' performance in speech, comprehension, and reasoning was better than average before they were studied

(C) the climbers showed different levels of impairment in their performance in speech, comprehension, and reasoning

(D) some of the effects described were apparent just before the climbers reached 6,100 meters

(E) many of the climbers had engaged in special training before the climb because they wanted to improve the efficiency with which their bodies use oxygen

GO ON TO THE NEXT PAGE.

18. It was once thought that pesticide TSX-400 was extremely harmful to the environment but that pesticides Envirochem and Zanar were environmentally harmless. TSX-400 was banned; Envirochem and Zanar were not. However, according to recent studies, Envirochem and Zanar each cause greater environmental harm than does TSX-400. If these studies are accurate, then either Envirochem and Zanar should be banned or TSX-400 should be legalized.

Which one of the following principles, if valid, most helps to justify the argumentation?

(A) Two pesticides should not both be legal if one is measurably more harmful to the environment than the other is.

(B) Two pesticides should both be legal only if neither is harmful to the environment.

(C) Two pesticides should both be illegal only if both are harmful to the environment.

(D) One pesticide should be legal and another illegal only if the former is less harmful to the environment than is the latter.

(E) One pesticide should be legal and another illegal if the former is harmless to the environment and the latter is harmful to it.

19. Recent studies have demonstrated that smokers are more likely than nonsmokers to develop heart disease. Other studies have established that smokers are more likely than others to drink caffeinated beverages. Therefore, even though drinking caffeinated beverages is not thought to be a cause of heart disease, there is a positive correlation between drinking caffeinated beverages and the development of heart disease.

The argument's reasoning is most vulnerable to criticism on the grounds that the argument fails to take into account the possibility that

(A) smokers who drink caffeinated beverages are less likely to develop heart disease than are smokers who do not drink caffeinated beverages

(B) something else, such as dietary fat intake, may be a more important factor in the development of heart disease than are the factors cited in the argument

(C) drinking caffeinated beverages is more strongly correlated with the development of heart disease than is smoking

(D) it is only among people who have a hereditary predisposition to heart disease that caffeine consumption is positively correlated with the development of heart disease

(E) there is a common cause of both the development of heart disease and behaviors such as drinking caffeinated beverages and smoking

20. The layouts of supermarkets are not accidental: they are part of a plan designed to make customers walk all the way to the back of the store just to pick up a loaf of bread, passing tempting displays the whole way. But supermarkets can alienate customers by placing popular items in the rear; surveys list inconvenience as shoppers' top reason for disliking supermarkets.

Which one of the following propositions does the passage most precisely illustrate?

(A) Supermarkets should focus on customers who want to purchase many items in a single trip.

(B) Alienation of customers is not good for business.

(C) Even well-thought-out plans can fail.

(D) Distracting customers is not good for business.

(E) Manipulation of people can have unwelcome consequences.

21. Doctor: Medication to reduce blood pressure often has unhealthy side effects. However, lifestyle changes such as exercising more and avoiding fatty foods reduce blood pressure just as effectively as taking medication does. Therefore, it is healthier to rely on these lifestyle changes than on medication to reduce blood pressure.

Which one of the following is an assumption that the doctor's argument requires?

(A) Other than medication, the only way to reduce blood pressure is by making lifestyle changes such as exercising more and avoiding fatty foods.

(B) If it is healthier to rely on a lifestyle change than on medication to reduce blood pressure, then that lifestyle change reduces blood pressure at least as effectively as medication does.

(C) The side effects, if any, of exercising more and avoiding fatty foods in order to reduce blood pressure are less unhealthy than those of taking medication to reduce blood pressure.

(D) If an alternative to medication relieves a medical condition just as effectively as medication does, then it is always healthier to rely on that alternative than on medication to relieve that medical condition.

(E) If two different methods of treating a medical condition have similar side effects, then it is healthier to rely on the more effective method.

GO ON TO THE NEXT PAGE.

22. Columnist: Several recent studies show, and insurance statistics confirm, that more pedestrians are killed every year in North American cities when crossing with the light than when crossing against it. Crossing against the light in North American cities is therefore less dangerous than crossing with the light.

The columnist's reasoning is most vulnerable to criticism on the grounds that it

(A) relies on sources that are likely to be biased in their reporting

(B) presumes, without providing justification, that because two things are correlated there must be a causal relationship between them

(C) does not adequately consider the possibility that a correlation between two events may be explained by a common cause

(D) ignores the possibility that the effects of the types of actions considered might be quite different in environments other than the ones studied

(E) ignores possible differences in the frequency of the two actions whose risk is being assessed

23. Many scientific studies have suggested that taking melatonin tablets can induce sleep. But this does not mean that melatonin is helpful in treating insomnia. Most of the studies examined only people without insomnia, and in many of the studies, only a few of the subjects given melatonin appeared to be significantly affected by it.

Which one of the following, if true, most strengthens the argument?

(A) A weaker correlation between taking melatonin and the inducement of sleep was found in the studies that included people with insomnia than in the studies that did not.

(B) None of the studies that suggested that taking melatonin tablets can induce sleep examined a fully representative sample of the human population.

(C) In the studies that included subjects with insomnia, only subjects without insomnia were significantly affected by doses of melatonin.

(D) Several people who were in control groups and only given placebos claimed that the tablets induced sleep.

(E) If melatonin were helpful in treating insomnia, then every person with insomnia who took doses of melatonin would appear to be significantly affected by it.

GO ON TO THE NEXT PAGE.

24. The asteroid that hit the Yucatán Peninsula 65 million years ago caused both long-term climatic change and a tremendous firestorm that swept across North America. We cannot show that it was this fire that caused the extinction of the triceratops, a North American dinosaur in existence at the time of the impact of the asteroid. Nor can we show that the triceratops became extinct due to the climatic changes resulting from the asteroid's impact. Hence, we cannot attribute the triceratops's extinction to the asteroid's impact.

Which one of the following has flawed reasoning most similar to the flawed reasoning in the argument above?

(A) I know that one cannot move this piano unless one can lift at least 150 kilograms. I doubt that either Leon or Pam can lift 150 kilograms alone. So I doubt that either Leon or Pam can move this piano alone. Thus, I doubt that Leon and Pam can move this piano together.

(B) Since we are quite sure that Cheng and Lin are the only candidates in the mayoral election, we can be quite sure that either Cheng or Lin will win the election. Therefore, either we know that Cheng will win or we know that Lin will win.

(C) It has not been conclusively proven that the accident was caused by John's driving at excessive speeds. Nor has it been conclusively proven that the accident was the result of John's weaving out of his lane. Hence, it has been conclusively proven that the cause of the accident was neither John's driving at excessive speeds nor John's weaving out of his lane.

(D) The flooding in the basement caused damage to the furnace and also caused a short in the electrical system. Fire investigators could not show that the damage to the furnace caused the fire that resulted shortly after the flooding, nor could they show that the fire was caused by the short in the electrical system. Therefore, we cannot claim that the flooding in the basement caused the fire.

(E) We have good reason to believe that the cause of the flooding along the coast was the unusually high tides. We also have good reason to believe that the cause of the unusually high tides was either the sun or the moon. So it is reasonable to maintain that the cause of the flooding was either the sun or the moon.

25. Economist: Although obviously cuts in personal income tax rates for the upper income brackets disproportionately benefit the wealthy, across-the-board cuts for all brackets tend to have a similar effect. Personal income tax rates are progressive (i.e., graduated), and if total revenue remains constant, then across-the-board cuts in these taxes require increasing the amount of revenue generated through nonprogressive taxes, thereby favoring the wealthy. Yet if nonprogressive taxes are not increased to compensate for the cuts, then the budget deficit will increase, requiring more government borrowing and driving up interest rates. This favors those who have money to lend, once again benefiting primarily the wealthy.

Which one of the following statements most accurately expresses the main conclusion of the economist's argument?

(A) Cuts in personal income tax rates for upper income brackets benefit the wealthy more than they benefit others.

(B) Across-the-board cuts in personal income tax rates do not generate enough additional economic activity to prevent a net loss of revenue.

(C) It is the wealthy who are favored by generating a high amount of revenue through nonprogressive taxes.

(D) It is primarily the wealthy who benefit from increases in the budget deficit, which drive up interest rates.

(E) Across-the-board personal income tax rate cuts generally benefit the wealthy more than they benefit others.

S T O P

IF YOU FINISH BEFORE TIME IS CALLED, YOU MAY CHECK YOUR WORK ON THIS SECTION ONLY.
DO NOT WORK ON ANY OTHER SECTION IN THE TEST.

Acknowledgment is made to the following sources from which material has been adapted for use in this test booklet:

Elise Hancock, "Unpredictable Outcomes Could Be 'Poison' to Science." ©1994 by The Johns Hopkins University.

"Motor Oil: What's Best for Your Car?" ©1996 by Consumer Reports.

Angela Pirist, "Why Tots Can't Play by the Rules." © 1996 by Sussex Publishers Inc.

Martha Robles, "An Historical Adventure: Notes on Chicano Literature." © 1992 by TriQuarterly.

Edward W. Said, *Culture and Imperialism.* © 1993 by Edward W. Said.

Wait for the supervisor's instructions before you open the page to the topic.
Please print and sign your name and write the date in the designated spaces below.

Time: 35 Minutes

General Directions

You will have 35 minutes in which to plan and write an essay on the topic inside. Read the topic and the accompanying directions carefully. You will probably find it best to spend a few minutes considering the topic and organizing your thoughts before you begin writing. In your essay, be sure to develop your ideas fully, leaving time, if possible, to review what you have written. **Do not write on a topic other than the one specified. Writing on a topic of your own choice is not acceptable.**

No special knowledge is required or expected for this writing exercise. Law schools are interested in the reasoning, clarity, organization, language usage, and writing mechanics displayed in your essay. How well you write is more important than how much you write.

Confine your essay to the blocked, lined area on the front and back of the separate Writing Sample Response Sheet. Only that area will be reproduced for law schools. Be sure that your writing is legible.

Both this topic sheet and your response sheet must be turned over to the testing staff before you leave the room.

Topic Code	Print Your Full Name Here		
_____	Last	First	M.I.

Date	Sign Your Name Here
/ /	

Scratch Paper
Do not write your essay in this space.

LSAT Writing Sample Topic

Directions: The scenario presented below describes two choices, either one of which can be supported on the basis of the information given. Your essay should consider both choices and argue for one and against the other, based on the two specified criteria and the facts provided. There is no "right" or "wrong" choice: a reasonable argument can be made for either.

Calvin, the hiring manager for Ocean Blue Cruise Line, is seeking a permanent chef for a cruise ship. In the meantime, he has found someone who can commit to a three-month contract and someone else who can commit to a six-month contact. Calvin has decided that Ocean Blue should enter into one of the limited-term contracts. Write an essay in which you argue for choosing one chef over the other, keeping in mind the following two criteria:

- Ocean Blue would like to hire a chef who can take over management of the large galley staff.
- Ocean Blue would like to hire a permanent chef as soon as possible.

Marie, who has served as executive chef in a large resort kitchen for the past three years, is available for a three-month contract, with no possibility of her staying on permanently. She has earned a strong reputation for competence in kitchen organization and management. Her objective, should she be offered the contract, is to reorganize and streamline the galley operations to sustain a degree of efficiency and productivity even after she leaves. Because Marie is also affiliated with a cooking school, Calvin would have the opportunity to establish contacts that might lead to the permanent hire he desires to make.

Jared is available to take on a six-month contract. Early in his career, he served as an assistant pastry chef on a cruise ship in a nonmanagement role. He has since had a very successful fourteen-year career managing a small cateering company, in which he was responsible for staffing, food planning, and quality control, but he has never managed a staff as large as the ship's galley staff and would have to learn on his feet. While the contract with Jared offers Ocean Blue a greater period of stability and security than the shorter three-month contract does, it takes the cruise line off the market for hiring a permanent employee for twice as long. However, Jared has indicated that he would probably be willing to accept the permanent position at the end of the contract.

Scratch Paper
Do not write your essay in this space.

Writing Sample Response Sheet

DO NOT WRITE
IN THIS SPACE

**Begin your essay in the lined area below.
Continue on the back if you need more space.**

Directions:

1. Use the Answer Key on the next page to check your answers.

2. Use the Scoring Worksheet below to compute your raw score.

3. Use the Score Conversion Chart to convert your raw score into the 120–180 scale.

Scoring Worksheet

1. Enter the number of questions you answered correctly in each section

Number Correct

SECTION I . . . . _____

SECTION II . . . . . . _____

SECTION III . . . . . . _EXP_

SECTION IV . . . . . . _____

SECTION V . . . . . . _____

2. Enter the sum here: _____
   This is your Raw Score.

Conversion Chart
For converting Raw Score to the 120–180 LSAT Scaled Score
LSAT Prep Test 50

Reported Score	Raw Score Lowest	Raw Score Highest
180	98	100
179	97	97
178	—*	—*
177	96	96
176	95	95
175	94	94
174	—*	—*
173	93	93
172	92	92
171	91	91
170	90	90
169	89	89
168	88	88
167	86	87
166	85	85
165	84	84
164	83	83
163	81	82
162	80	80
161	78	79
160	77	77
159	75	76
158	73	74
157	72	72
156	70	71
155	68	69
154	66	67
153	64	65
152	63	63
151	61	62
150	59	60
149	57	58
148	55	56
147	53	54
146	52	52
145	50	51
144	48	49
143	46	47
142	45	45
141	43	44
140	41	42
139	40	40
138	38	39
137	36	37
136	35	35
135	33	34
134	32	32
133	30	31
132	29	29
131	27	28
130	26	26
129	25	25
128	23	24
127	22	22
126	21	21
125	20	20
124	18	19
123	17	17
122	16	16
121	15	15
120	0	14

*There is no raw score that will produce this scaled score for this form.

SECTION I

1.	C	8.	A	15.	C	22.	B
2.	D	9.	E	16.	A	23.	D
3.	C	10.	A	17.	D	24.	C
4.	B	11.	B	18.	C	25.	E
5.	D	12.	D	19.	D	26.	C
6.	A	13.	E	20.	A	27.	D
7.	D	14.	E	21.	D	28.	B

SECTION II

1.	B	8.	A	15.	E	22.	D
2.	B	9.	B	16.	C	23.	E
3.	A	10.	B	17.	A	24.	A
4.	E	11.	E	18.	C	25.	D
5.	B	12.	A	19.	A		
6.	C	13.	D	20.	C		
7.	B	14.	D	21.	E		

SECTION III (experimental)

1.	A	8.	B	15.	B	22.	E
2.	B	9.	A	16.	C	23.	C
3.	E	10.	C	17.	D	24.	E
4.	D	11.	B	18.	E	25.	A
5.	C	12.	D	19.	C		
6.	A	13.	C	20.	E		
7.	A	14.	E	21.	C		

SECTION IV

1.	D	8.	B	15.	A	22.	A
2.	B	9.	A	16.	E		
3.	C	10.	E	17.	E		
4.	E	11.	B	18.	B		
5.	B	12.	B	19.	D		
6.	E	13.	B	20.	E		
7.	D	14.	C	21.	D		

SECTION V

1.	E	8.	B	15.	D	22.	E
2.	C	9.	A	16.	C	23.	C
3.	B	10.	E	17.	A	24.	D
4.	E	11.	D	18.	D	25.	E
5.	E	12.	A	19.	A		
6.	C	13.	B	20.	E		
7.	B	14.	D	21.	C		

Endurance Practice Test 7

**PrepTest 48 plus experimental
from PrepTest 5, Section IV**

SECTION I

Time—35 minutes

26 Questions

<u>Directions</u>: The questions in this section are based on the reasoning contained in brief statements or passages. For some questions, more than one of the choices could conceivably answer the question. However, you are to choose the <u>best</u> answer; that is, the response that most accurately and completely answers the question. You should not make assumptions that are by commonsense standards implausible, superfluous, or incompatible with the passage. After you have chosen the best answer, blacken the corresponding space on your answer sheet.

1. The effort involved in lying produces measurable physiological reactions such as a speedup of the heartbeat. Since lying is accompanied by physiological reactions, lie-detector tests that can detect these reactions are a sure way of determining when someone is lying.

Which one of the following statements, if true, most seriously weakens the argument?

(A) Lie-detector tests can measure only some of the physiological reactions that occur when someone is lying.

(B) People are often unaware that they are having physiological reactions of the sort measured by lie-detector tests.

(C) Lying about past criminal behavior does not necessarily produce stronger physiological reactions than does lying about other things.

(D) For people who are not lying, the tension of taking a lie-detector test can produce physiological reactions identical to the ones that accompany the act of lying.

(E) When employers use lie-detector tests as part of their preemployment screening, some candidates tested are highly motivated to lie.

2. Publishing executive: Our company must sell at least 100,000 books to make a profit this year. However, it is unlikely that we will sell that many, since of the twelve titles we will sell, the one with the best sales prospects, a novel, is unlikely to sell as many as 100,000 copies.

The publishing executive's argument is most vulnerable to criticism because it overlooks the possibility that

(A) the publishing company will sell considerably fewer than 100,000 copies of the novel

(B) the publishing company will not make a profit even if it sells more than 100,000 books

(C) what is true of the overall profitability of a publishing company is not true of its profitability in a particular year

(D) what is true of the sales prospects of the publishing company's individual titles is not true of the sales prospects of the group of titles as a whole

(E) the publishing company will sell even fewer books if it does not advertise its books efficiently

3. A recent study proves that at least some people possess an independent "sixth sense" that allows them to detect whether someone is watching them. In the study, subjects were seated one at a time in the center of a room facing away from a large window. On average, subjects decided correctly 60 percent of the time whether or not they were being watched through the window.

Which one of the following, if true, most supports the conclusion drawn from the study mentioned above?

(A) Most of the time, subjects said they were being watched.

(B) The person recording the experimental results was careful not to interact with the subjects after the experiment ended.

(C) A similar result was found when the subjects were watched from another room on a video monitor.

(D) The room in which the subjects were seated was not soundproof.

(E) The subjects were mostly graduate students in psychology from a nearby university.

GO ON TO THE NEXT PAGE.

4. Philosopher: We should not disapprove of the unearthing of truths that we would rather not acknowledge or that, by their dissemination, might influence society in pernicious ways.

Which one of the following conforms most closely to the principle stated by the philosopher?

(A) A law enforcement officer should not act upon illegally obtained information, even though such action might, in some cases, result in a benefit to society.

(B) Scientific research should not be restricted even if it could lead to harmful applications, such as the manufacture of sophisticated weapons.

(C) A physician should never withhold the truth from a patient, except in cases where depression induced by bad news might significantly affect the patient's recuperation.

(D) Investigative journalists who employ illegal means of obtaining information should not be subjected to moral disapproval, if the revelation of that information does more good for society than does its suppression.

(E) A poem need not adhere too strictly to the truth. Art is exempt from such requirements—it matters only that the poem provoke a response in the reader.

5. Compact discs (CDs) offer an improvement in artistic freedom over vinyl records. As the record needle moves in toward a vinyl record's center, it must fight centrifugal force. Wide, shallow, or jagged grooves will cause the needle to jump; consequently, the song nearest the center—the last song on the side—cannot have especially loud, high-pitched, or low-pitched passages. The CD suffers no such limitations, leaving artists free to end recordings with any song.

Which one of the following most accurately expresses the main conclusion of the argument?

(A) CDs provide greater artistic latitude than do vinyl records.

(B) On vinyl records, the song farthest from the center can have loud, high-pitched, or low-pitched passages.

(C) As the record needle moves in toward the vinyl record's center, the centrifugal force on the needle becomes stronger.

(D) CDs represent a considerable technological advance over vinyl records.

(E) CDs can have louder passages, as well as both higher- and lower-pitched passages, than can vinyl records.

6. The public interest comprises many interests and the broadcast media must serve all of them. Perhaps most television viewers would prefer an action show to an opera. But a constant stream of action shows on all channels is not in the public interest. Thus, _____.

Which one of the following most logically completes the argument?

(A) broadcasters' obligations are not satisfied if they look only to popularity to decide their programming schedules

(B) television networks should broadcast more artistic and cultural shows and fewer action shows

(C) the public interest should be considered whenever television producers develop a new program

(D) the popularity of a television program is a poor indicator of its artistic quality

(E) broadcast media could be rightly accused of neglecting the public interest only if all channels carried mostly action shows

7. Enthusiasm for the use of calculators in the learning of mathematics is misplaced. Teachers rightly observe that in some cases calculators enable students to focus on general principles rather than the tedious, largely rote calculations that constitute the application of these principles. But principles are more likely to be remembered when knowledge of them is grounded in habits ingrained by painstaking applications of those principles. The very fact that calculators make calculation easier, therefore, makes it reasonable to restrict their use.

Which one of the following, if true, most strengthens the argument?

(A) Some students who know how to use calculators also thoroughly understand the mathematical principles that calculators obey.

(B) Slide rules, which are less technologically sophisticated analogues of calculators, were widely used in the learning of mathematics several decades ago.

(C) It is much more important that students retain the knowledge of general principles than that this knowledge be easily acquired.

(D) Habits that are acquired by laborious and sometimes tedious practice are not as valuable as those that are painlessly mastered.

(E) Teachers' enthusiasm for new educational aids is often not proportional to the pedagogical effectiveness of those devices.

GO ON TO THE NEXT PAGE.

8. Commentator: Most journalists describe their individual political orientations as liberal, and it is often concluded that there is therefore a liberal bias in current journalism. This is not the case, however, because newspapers, magazines, radio, and television are all in the business of selling news and advertising, and therefore face market pressures that tend to keep them impartial, since in order to maximize profits they must target the broadest customer base possible.

Which one of the following most accurately expresses the main conclusion drawn by the commentator's argument?

(A) The individual political orientations of journalists do not constitute acceptable evidence regarding media bias.
(B) Major media face significant market pressures.
(C) Current journalism does not have a liberal political bias.
(D) Major media must target the broadest customer base possible in order to maximize profits.
(E) It is often maintained that current journalism has a liberal bias.

9. Theories generated by scientific research were used to develop several products that, although useful, damage the environment severely. The scientists who conducted the research, however, should not be held responsible for that damage, since they merely generated the theories and could neither foresee nor restrict the kinds of products that might be designed using those theories.

Which one of the following principles, if established, justifies the conclusion above?

(A) Individuals who develop something that has desirable characteristics should not be held responsible for any undesirable characteristics that the thing has if improperly used.
(B) Individuals are justified in performing an activity that has both desirable and undesirable foreseeable consequences only if they alone bear its undesirable consequences.
(C) Individuals should receive credit for the foreseeable desirable consequences of the activities they perform only if those individuals are to be held responsible for any unforeseeable undesirable consequences those activities might have.
(D) Individuals who perform an activity should not be held responsible for any unforeseen undesirable consequences that arise from the use to which others put the results of that activity.
(E) Individuals should be held responsible for the foreseeable undesirable consequences of the activities that they perform and receive credit for the foreseeable desirable consequences of those activities.

10. The administration at a certain university has explained this year's tuition increase by citing increased spending on faculty salaries and on need-based aid to students. However, this year's budget indicated that faculty salaries constitute a small part of the university's expenditure, and the only significant increases in scholarship aid have gone to academic scholarships awarded regardless of need. The administration's explanation is not believable.

Which one of the following, if true, most strengthens the argument that the administration's explanation is not believable?

(A) With this year's budget, the university has increased its total spending on scholarship aid by 5 percent.
(B) With this year's budget, the university increased the allotment for faculty salaries by 5 percent while tuition was increased by 6 percent.
(C) Faculty salaries at the university have increased in line with the national average, and substantial cuts in government student-loan programs have caused financial difficulties for many students at the university.
(D) Of the substantial items in the budget, the greatest increase was in administrative costs, facilities maintenance costs, and costs associated with the provision of athletic facilities.
(E) Because enrollment projections at the university are very unreliable, it is difficult to accurately estimate the amount of money the university will collect from tuition fees ahead of time.

11. Students asked by a psychologist to tell a lie before discussion groups vastly overestimated how many people in the discussion groups could tell they were lying. Other research has found that when volleyball players perform unusually poorly on the court, teammates notice this far less often than the players expect. Finally, in one research experiment a student wearing a funny T-shirt entered a room full of people. Questioning revealed that only a small fraction of the people in the room noticed the shirt, contrary to the student's expectations.

Which one of the following is best illustrated by the statements above?

(A) People tend to be far less aware of their own appearance and behavior than are other people.
(B) People tend not to notice the appearance or behavior of others.
(C) We are actually less observant of the appearance and behavior of others than we think ourselves to be.
(D) People will notice the appearance or behavior of others only if it is specifically highlighted in some way.
(E) People tend to believe their appearance and behavior are noticed by others more often than is actually the case.

GO ON TO THE NEXT PAGE.

12. Extinction is inevitable for all biological species. In fact, the vast majority of all species that have ever lived are now extinct. Since all species die out eventually, there is no justification for trying to protect species that are presently endangered, even those that can be saved from extinction now.

The reasoning in the argument above is most closely paralleled by the argument that there is no reason to

(A) look for a book in the library because it is sometimes checked out

(B) spend money on preventive maintenance of a car because no car can last indefinitely

(C) reinforce bridges against earthquakes in earthquake-prone areas because earthquakes occur only very infrequently

(D) take a route that will avoid the normal traffic jams because traffic jams can occur along any route

(E) plant a flower garden in soil that is not beneficial to plants because the plants are likely to die in such soil

13. Psychology professor: Applied statistics should be taught only by the various social science departments. These departments can best teach their respective students which statistical methodologies are most useful for their discipline, and how best to interpret collected data and the results of experiments.

Mathematics professor: I disagree. My applied statistics course covers much of the same material taught in the applied statistics courses in social science departments. In fact, my course uses exactly the same textbook as those courses!

Which one of the following most accurately describes a questionable aspect of the reasoning in the mathematics professor's response to the psychology professor?

(A) The response gives no evidence for its presumption that students willing to take a course in one department would choose a similar course in another.

(B) The response gives no evidence for its presumption that social science students should have the same competence in statistics as mathematics students.

(C) The response does not effectively address a key reason given in support of the psychology professor's position.

(D) The response depends for its plausibility on a personal attack made against the psychology professor.

(E) The response takes for granted that unless the course textbook is the same the course content will not be the same.

14. Among a sample of diverse coins from an unfamiliar country, each face of any coin portrays one of four things: a judge's head, an explorer's head, a building, or a tree. By examining the coins, a collector determines that none of them have heads on both sides and that all coins in the sample with a judge's head on one side have a tree on the other.

If the statements above are true, which one of the following must be true of the coins in the sample?

(A) All those with an explorer's head on one side have a building on the other.

(B) All those with a tree on one side have a judge's head on the other.

(C) None of those with a tree on one side have an explorer's head on the other.

(D) None of those with a building on one side have a judge's head on the other.

(E) None of those with an explorer's head on one side have a building on the other.

15. There are two supposedly conflicting hypotheses as to what makes for great national leaders: one is that such leaders successfully shape public opinion, and the other is that they are adept at reacting to it. However, treating these hypotheses as mutually exclusive is evidently a mistake. All leaders who have had success getting their programs passed by their country's legislature have been adroit both in shaping and reacting to public opinion.

Which one of the following is an assumption on which the argument depends?

(A) Having success getting programs passed by the legislature is indicative of being a great national leader.

(B) It is impossible to successfully shape public opinion without in some way reacting to it.

(C) To lead, one must either successfully shape public opinion or be adept at reacting to it, or both.

(D) Having a good rapport with the members of the legislature allows a leader to shape public opinion.

(E) To be a great leader one must not be swayed by public opinion.

GO ON TO THE NEXT PAGE.

16. Most business ethics courses and textbooks confine themselves to considering specific cases and principles. For example, students are often given lists of ethical rules for in-class discussion and role-playing. This approach fails to provide a framework for understanding specific principles and should thus be changed to include abstract ethical theory.

Which one of the following, if valid, most helps to justify the reasoning above?

(A) A moralizing approach that fails to recognize the diversity of the ethical rules in use is unacceptable.

(B) Courses that concentrate mainly on role-playing are undesirable because students must adopt alien personae.

(C) People have no obligation to always behave ethically unless they are acquainted with abstract ethical theory.

(D) Abstract ethical theory is the most appropriate of any context for understanding specific principles.

(E) An ethics course should acquaint students with a wide range of specific principles and appropriate applications.

17. Some classes of animal are so successful that they spread into virtually every ecosystem, whereas others gradually recede until they inhabit only small niches in geographically isolated areas and thereby become threatened. Insects are definitely of the former sort and ants are the most successful of these, ranging from the Arctic Circle to Tierra del Fuego. Hence, no species of ant is a threatened species.

The argument is flawed because it takes for granted that

(A) the Arctic Circle and Tierra del Fuego do not constitute geographically isolated areas

(B) because ants do not inhabit only a small niche in a geographically isolated area, they are unlike most other insects

(C) the only way a class of animal can avoid being threatened is to spread into virtually every ecosystem

(D) what is true of the constituent elements of a whole is also true of the whole

(E) what is true of a whole is also true of its constituent elements

18. Advocate: You claim that it is wrong to own gasoline-powered cars because they pollute too much; you have an electric car, which pollutes far less. But the company that made your car also makes millions of gasoline-powered vehicles, so your patronage benefits a producer of products to which you object. Thus, if you are right about gasoline-powered cars, you should not have your electric car either.

Which one of the following principles, if valid, would most help to justify the advocate's reasoning?

(A) An action can be wrong even if it has fewer negative consequences than another action.

(B) One should purchase a product only if it pollutes less than any competing product.

(C) One should purchase every product whose use has no negative consequences.

(D) One should not support an organization that does anything one believes to be wrong.

(E) One should not purchase products from companies that make no environmentally sound products.

19. Analyst: A recent survey showed that although professors of biology who teach but do not pursue research made up one twentieth of all science professors, they were appointed to fewer than one twentieth of all the scientific administrative positions in universities. We can conclude from this survey that failing to pursue research tends to bias university administrators against appointing these professors to scientific administrative positions.

Which one of the following, if true, most seriously weakens the support for the analyst's conclusion?

(A) In universities there are fewer scientific administrative positions than there are nonscientific administrative positions.

(B) Biologists who do research fill a disproportionately low number of scientific administrative positions in universities.

(C) Biology professors get more than one twentieth of all the science grant money available.

(D) Conducting biological research tends to take significantly more time than does teaching biology.

(E) Biologists who hold scientific administrative positions in the university tend to hold those positions for a shorter time than do other science professors.

GO ON TO THE NEXT PAGE.

20. Researcher: We have found that some cases of high blood pressure can be treated effectively with medicine. Since it is generally accepted that any illness caused by stress is treatable only by the reduction of stress, some cases of high blood pressure must not be caused by stress.

Which one of the following is an assumption required by the researcher's argument?

(A) The correlation between stress and all cases of high blood pressure is merely coincidental.

(B) The reduction of stress in a person's life can at times lower that person's blood pressure.

(C) Reduced stress does not reduce a person's responsiveness to medicine used to treat high blood pressure.

(D) Some conditions that are treated effectively by medicines are not also treatable through the reduction of stress.

(E) Medicine used to treat high blood pressure does not itself reduce stress.

21. Catmull: Although historians consider themselves to be social scientists, different historians never arrive at the same conclusions about specific events of the past. Thus historians never determine what actually happened; like novelists, they merely create interesting fictional stories about the many different problems that people have faced.

The reasoning in Catmull's argument is flawed because the argument

(A) draws a conclusion that simply restates a claim presented in support of that conclusion

(B) concludes, solely on the basis of the claim that different people have reached different conclusions about a topic, that none of these conclusions is true

(C) presumes, without providing justification, that unless historians' conclusions are objectively true, they have no value whatsoever

(D) bases its conclusion on premises that contradict each other

(E) mistakes a necessary condition for the objective truth of historians' conclusions for a sufficient condition for the objective truth of those conclusions

22. In a poll conducted by interviewing eligible voters in their homes just before the recent election, incumbent candidate Kenner was significantly ahead of candidate Muratori. Nonetheless, Muratori won the recent election.

Which one of the following, if true, most helps to resolve the apparent discrepancy described by the statements above?

(A) The positions taken by Muratori and Kenner on many election issues were not very similar to each other.

(B) Kenner had held elected office for many years before the recent election.

(C) In the year leading up to the election, Kenner was implicated in a series of political scandals.

(D) Six months before the recent election, the voting age was lowered by three years.

(E) In the poll, supporters of Muratori were more likely than others to describe the election as important.

GO ON TO THE NEXT PAGE.

23. Statistical analysis is a common tool for explanation in the physical sciences. It can only be used, however, to explain events that can be replicated to the last detail. Since human mental events never precisely recur, statistical analysis cannot be employed to explain these events. Therefore, they cannot be explained by the physical sciences.

Which one of the following arguments is most similar in its flawed reasoning to the argument above?

(A) Computer modeling is used to try to explain the way in which wind resistance affects the movement of bicycles. To use computer modeling, the phenomenon being modeled must be predictable. But wind resistance is not predictable. Therefore, the way in which wind resistance affects the movement of bicycles cannot be explained by computer modeling.

(B) The only way to explain how music affects the emotional state of a person is to appeal to the psychology of emotion. The psychology of emotion can be applied only to cases involving human beings. But not all music is created by human beings; some music is computer generated. Therefore, the way in which music affects the emotional state of a person cannot be explained.

(C) The best way to explain why an object has a particular color is in terms of the interaction of light and matter. It is sometimes impossible to find out what kind of matter constitutes an object. Therefore, the color of such objects has nothing to do with the interaction of light and matter.

(D) To determine which explanation of the origin of the universe is correct, we would need to know about the first moments of the existence of the universe. Due to the immense time that has passed since the universe began, it is impossible to get such information. Therefore, none of the explanations of the origin of the universe is likely to be correct.

(E) A good way to explain historical events is to construct a coherent narrative about those events. In order to construct such a narrative, a great many details about the events must be known. Virtually no details can be known of certain very ancient historical events. Therefore, no historical explanation can be given for these events.

24. Journalist: Although a recent poll found that more than half of all eligible voters support the idea of a political party whose primary concern is education, only 26 percent would like to join it, and only 16 percent would be prepared to donate money to it. Furthermore, there is overwhelming historical evidence that only a party that has at least 30 percent of eligible voters prepared to support it by either joining it or donating money to it is viable in the long run. Therefore, it is unlikely that an education party is viable in the long run.

The reasoning in the journalist's argument is most vulnerable to criticism on the grounds that the argument fails to consider that

(A) some of those who said they were willing to donate money to an education party might not actually do so if such a party were formed

(B) an education party could possibly be viable with a smaller base than is customarily needed

(C) the 16 percent of eligible voters prepared to donate money to an education party might donate almost as much money as a party would ordinarily expect to get if 30 percent of eligible voters contributed

(D) a party needs the appropriate support of at least 30 percent of eligible voters in order to be viable and more than half of all eligible voters support the idea of an education party

(E) some of the eligible voters who would donate money to an education party might not be prepared to join such a party

GO ON TO THE NEXT PAGE.

25. Almost all microbe species live together in dense, interdependent communities, supporting the environment for each other, and regulating the population balances for their different species through a complex system of chemical signals. For this reason, it is currently impossible to cultivate any one such species in isolation. Thus, microbiologists lack complete knowledge of most microbe species.

Which one of the following, if assumed, enables the argument's conclusion to be properly drawn?

(A) It is currently impossible for microbiologists to reproduce the complex systems of chemical signals with which microbe communities regulate the population balances for their different species.

(B) If it is currently impossible to reproduce the environmental supports and chemical signals in dense, interdependent communities of microbe species, then it is also impossible to cultivate any microbe species from such a community in isolation.

(C) No microbiologist can have complete knowledge of any species of organism unless that microbiologist can cultivate that species in isolation.

(D) At least some microbiologists lack complete knowledge of any microbe species that live together in dense, interdependent communities.

(E) No microbe species that normally lives together with other microbe species in dense, interdependent communities can survive outside such a community.

26. Reza: Language requires the use of verbal signs for objects as well as for feelings. Many animals can vocally express hunger, but only humans can ask for an egg or an apple by naming it. And using verbal signs for objects requires the ability to distinguish these objects from other objects, which in turn requires conceptual thought.

If all of Reza's statements are true, then which one of the following must also be true?

(A) Conceptual thought is required for language.

(B) Conceptual thought requires the use of verbal signs for objects.

(C) It is not possible to think conceptually about feelings.

(D) All humans are capable of conceptual thought.

(E) The vocal expressions of animals other than humans do not require conceptual thought.

S T O P

IF YOU FINISH BEFORE TIME IS CALLED, YOU MAY CHECK YOUR WORK ON THIS SECTION ONLY.
DO NOT WORK ON ANY OTHER SECTION IN THE TEST.

SECTION II

Time—35 minutes

27 Questions

<u>Directions</u>: Each passage in this section is followed by a group of questions to be answered on the basis of what is <u>stated</u> or <u>implied</u> in the passage. For some of the questions, more than one of the choices could conceivably answer the question. However, you are to choose the <u>best</u> answer; that is, the response that most accurately and completely answers the question, and blacken the corresponding space on your answer sheet.

Governments of developing countries occasionally enter into economic development agreements with foreign investors who provide capital and technological expertise that may not be
(5) readily available in such countries. Besides the normal economic risk that accompanies such enterprises, investors face the additional risk that the host government may attempt unilaterally to change in its favor the terms of the agreement or
(10) even to terminate the agreement altogether and appropriate the project for itself. In order to make economic development agreements more attractive to investors, some developing countries have attempted to strengthen the security of such
(15) agreements with clauses specifying that the agreements will be governed by "general principles of law recognized by civilized nations"—a set of legal principles or rules shared by the world's major legal systems. However, advocates of governments'
(20) freedom to modify or terminate such agreements argue that these agreements fall within a special class of contracts known as administrative contracts, a concept that originated in French law. They assert that under the theory of administrative contracts, a
(25) government retains inherent power to modify or terminate its own contract, and that this power indeed constitutes a general principle of law. However, their argument is flawed on at least two counts.
(30)   First, in French law not all government contracts are treated as administrative contracts. Some contracts are designated as administrative by specific statute, in which case the contractor is made aware of the applicable legal rules upon
(35) entering into agreement with the government. Alternatively, the contracting government agency can itself designate a contract as administrative by including certain terms not found in private civil contracts. Moreover, even in the case of
(40) administrative contracts, French law requires that in the event that the government unilaterally modifies the terms of the contract, it must compensate the contractor for any increased burden resulting from the government's action. In
(45) effect, the government is thus prevented from modifying those contractual terms that define the financial balance of the contract.
     Second, the French law of administrative contracts, although adopted by several countries, is
(50) not so universally accepted that it can be embraced

as a general principle of law. In both the United States and the United Kingdom, government contracts are governed by the ordinary law of contracts, with the result that the government can
(55) reserve the power to modify or terminate a contract unilaterally only by writing such power into the contract as a specific provision. Indeed, the very fact that termination and modification clauses are commonly found in government contracts suggests
(60) that a government's capacity to modify or terminate agreements unilaterally derives from specific contract provisions, not from inherent state power.

1. In the passage, the author is primarily concerned with doing which one of the following?

     (A)   pointing out flaws in an argument provided in support of a position
     (B)   analyzing the weaknesses inherent in the proposed solution to a problem
     (C)   marshaling evidence in support of a new explanation of a phenomenon
     (D)   analyzing the risks inherent in adopting a certain course of action
     (E)   advocating a new approach to a problem that has not been solved by traditional means

2. It can be inferred from the passage that the author would be most likely to agree with which one of the following assertions regarding the "general principles of law" mentioned in lines 16–17 of the passage?

     (A)   They fail to take into account the special needs and interests of developing countries that enter into agreements with foreign investors.
     (B)   They have only recently been invoked as criteria for adjudicating disputes between governments and foreign investors.
     (C)   They are more compatible with the laws of France and the United States than with those of the United Kingdom.
     (D)   They do not assert that governments have an inherent right to modify unilaterally the terms of agreements that they have entered into with foreign investors.
     (E)   They are not useful in adjudicating disputes between developing countries and foreign investors.

GO ON TO THE NEXT PAGE.

3. The author implies that which one of the following is true of economic development agreements?

    (A) They provide greater economic benefits to the governments that are parties to such agreements than to foreign investors.
    (B) They are interpreted differently by courts in the United Kingdom than they are by courts in the United States.
    (C) They have proliferated in recent years as a result of governments' attempts to make them more legally secure.
    (D) They entail greater risk to investors when the governments that enter into such agreements reserve the right to modify unilaterally the terms of the agreements.
    (E) They have become less attractive to foreign investors as an increasing number of governments that enter into such agreements consider them governed by the law of ordinary contracts.

4. According to the author, which one of the following is true of a contract that is designated by a French government agency as an administrative contract?

    (A) It requires the government agency to pay for unanticipated increases in the cost of delivering the goods and services specified in the contract.
    (B) It provides the contractor with certain guarantees that are not normally provided in private civil contracts.
    (C) It must be ratified by the passage of a statute.
    (D) It discourages foreign companies from bidding on the contract.
    (E) It contains terms that distinguish it from a private civil contract.

5. It can be inferred from the passage that under the "ordinary law of contracts" (lines 53–54), a government would have the right to modify unilaterally the terms of a contract that it had entered into with a foreign investor if which one of the following were true?

    (A) The government undertook a greater economic risk by entering into the contract than did the foreign investor.
    (B) The cost to the foreign investor of abiding by the terms of the contract exceeded the original estimates of such costs.
    (C) The modification of the contract did not result in any increased financial burden for the investor.
    (D) Both the government and the investor had agreed to abide by the general principles of law recognized by civilized nations.
    (E) The contract contains a specific provision allowing the government to modify the contract.

6. In the last paragraph, the author refers to government contracts in the United States and the United Kingdom primarily in order to

    (A) cite two governments that often reserve the right to modify unilaterally contracts that they enter into with foreign investors
    (B) support the assertion that there is no general principle of law governing contracts between private individuals and governments
    (C) cast doubt on the alleged universality of the concept of administrative contracts
    (D) provide examples of legal systems that might benefit from the concept of administrative contracts
    (E) provide examples of characteristics that typically distinguish government contracts from private civil contracts

7. Which one of the following best states the author's main conclusion in the passage?

    (A) Providing that an international agreement be governed by general principles of law is not a viable method of guaranteeing the legal security of such an agreement.
    (B) French law regarding contracts is significantly different from those in the United States and the United Kingdom.
    (C) Contracts between governments and private investors in most nations are governed by ordinary contract law.
    (D) An inherent power of a government to modify or terminate a contract cannot be considered a general principle of law.
    (E) Contracts between governments and private investors can be secured only by reliance on general principles of law.

8. The author's argument in lines 57–62 would be most weakened if which one of the following were true?

    (A) The specific provisions of government contracts often contain explicit statements of what all parties to the contracts already agree are inherent state powers.
    (B) Governments are more frequently put in the position of having to modify or terminate contracts than are private individuals.
    (C) Modification clauses in economic development agreements have frequently been challenged in international tribunals by foreign investors who were a party to such agreements.
    (D) The general principles of law provide that modification clauses cannot allow the terms of a contract to be modified in such a way that the financial balance of the contract is affected.
    (E) Termination and modification agreements are often interpreted differently by national courts than they are by international tribunals.

GO ON TO THE NEXT PAGE.

Nico Frijda writes that emotions are governed by a psychological principle called the "law of apparent reality": emotions are elicited only by events appraised as real, and the intensity of these
(5) emotions corresponds to the degree to which these events are appraised as real. This observation seems psychologically plausible, but emotional responses elicited by works of art raise counterexamples.

Frijda's law accounts for my panic if I am afraid
(10) of snakes and see an object I correctly appraise as a rattlesnake, and also for my identical response if I see a coiled garden hose I mistakenly perceive to be a snake. However, suppose I am watching a movie and see a snake gliding toward its victim. Surely I
(15) might experience the same emotions of panic and distress, though I know the snake is not real. These responses extend even to phenomena not conventionally accepted as real. A movie about ghosts, for example, may be terrifying to all viewers,
(20) even those who firmly reject the possibility of ghosts, but this is not because viewers are confusing cinematic depiction with reality. Moreover, I can feel strong emotions in response to objects of art that are interpretations, rather than
(25) representations, of reality: I am moved by Mozart's *Requiem*, but I know that I am not at a real funeral. However, if Frijda's law is to explain all emotional reactions, there should be no emotional response at all to aesthetic objects or events, because we know
(30) they are not real in the way a living rattlesnake is real.

Most psychologists, perplexed by the feelings they acknowledge are aroused by aesthetic experience, have claimed that these emotions are
(35) genuine, but different in kind from nonaesthetic emotions. This, however, is a descriptive distinction rather than an empirical observation and consequently lacks explanatory value. On the other hand, Gombrich argues that emotional responses to
(40) art are ersatz: art triggers remembrances of previously experienced emotions. These debates have prompted the psychologist Radford to argue that people do experience real melancholy or joy in responding to art, but that these are irrational
(45) responses precisely because people know they are reacting to illusory stimuli. Frijda's law does not help us to untangle these positions, since it simply implies that events we recognize as being represented rather than real cannot elicit emotion
(50) in the first place.

Frijda does suggest that a vivid imagination has "properties of reality"—implying, without explanation, that we make aesthetic objects or events "real" in the act of experiencing them.
(55) However, as Scruton argues, a necessary characteristic of the imaginative construction that can occur in an emotional response to art is that the person knows he or she is pretending. This is what distinguishes imagination from psychotic fantasy.

9. Which one of the following best states the central idea of the passage?

(A) The law of apparent reality fails to account satisfactorily for the emotional nature of belief.

(B) Theories of aesthetic response fail to account for how we distinguish unreasonable from reasonable responses to art.

(C) The law of apparent reality fails to account satisfactorily for emotional responses to art.

(D) Psychologists have been unable to determine what accounts for the changeable nature of emotional responses to art.

(E) Psychologists have been unable to determine what differentiates aesthetic from nonaesthetic emotional responses.

10. According to the passage, Frijda's law asserts that emotional responses to events are

(A) unpredictable because emotional responses depend on how aware the person is of the reality of an event

(B) weaker if the person cannot distinguish illusion from reality

(C) more or less intense depending on the degree to which the person perceives the event to be real

(D) more intense if the person perceives an event to be frightening

(E) weaker if the person judges an event to be real but unthreatening

11. The author suggests that Frijda's notion of the role of imagination in aesthetic response is problematic because it

(A) ignores the unselfconsciousness that is characteristic of emotional responses to art

(B) ignores the distinction between genuine emotion and ersatz emotion

(C) ignores the fact that a person who is imagining knows that he or she is imagining

(D) makes irrelevant distinctions between vivid and weak imaginative capacities

(E) suggests, in reference to the observation of art, that there is no distinction between real and illusory stimuli

GO ON TO THE NEXT PAGE.

12. The passage supports all of the following statements about the differences between Gombrich and Radford EXCEPT:

(A) Radford's argument relies on a notion of irrationality in a way that Gombrich's argument does not.

(B) Gombrich's position is closer to the position of the majority of psychologists than is Radford's.

(C) Gombrich, unlike Radford, argues that we do not have true emotions in response to art.

(D) Gombrich's argument rests on a notion of memory in a way that Radford's argument does not.

(E) Radford's argument, unlike Gombrich's, is not focused on the artificial quality of emotional responses to art.

13. Which one of the following best captures the progression of the author's argument in lines 9–31?

(A) The emotional responses to events ranging from the real to the depicted illustrate the irrationality of emotional response.

(B) A series of events that range from the real to the depicted conveys the contrast between real events and cinematic depiction.

(C) An intensification in emotional response to a series of events that range from the real to the depicted illustrates Frijda's law.

(D) A progression of events that range from the real to the depicted examines the precise nature of panic in relation to a feared object.

(E) The consistency of emotional responses to events that range from the real to the depicted challenges Frijda's law.

14. The author's assertions concerning movies about ghosts imply that all of the following statements are false EXCEPT:

(A) Movies about ghosts are terrifying in proportion to viewers' beliefs in the phenomenon of ghosts.

(B) Movies about imaginary phenomena like ghosts may be just as terrifying as movies about phenomena like snakes.

(C) Movies about ghosts and snakes are not terrifying because people know that what they are viewing is not real.

(D) Movies about ghosts are terrifying to viewers who previously rejected the possibility of ghosts because movies permanently alter the viewers' sense of reality.

(E) Movies about ghosts elicit a very different emotional response from viewers who do not believe in ghosts than movies about snakes elicit from viewers who are frightened by snakes.

15. Which one of the following statements best exemplifies the position of Radford concerning the nature of emotional response to art?

(A) A person watching a movie about guerrilla warfare irrationally believes that he or she is present at the battle.

(B) A person watching a play about a kidnapping feels nothing because he or she rationally realizes it is not a real event.

(C) A person gets particular enjoyment out of writing fictional narratives in which he or she figures as a main character.

(D) A person irrationally bursts into tears while reading a novel about a destructive fire, even while realizing that he or she is reading about a fictional event.

(E) A person who is afraid of snakes trips over a branch and irrationally panics.

GO ON TO THE NEXT PAGE.

Although bacteria are unicellular and among the simplest autonomous forms of life, they show a remarkable ability to sense their environment. They are attracted to materials they need and are
(5) repelled by harmful substances. Most types of bacteria swim very erratically; short smooth runs in relatively straight lines are followed by brief tumbles, after which the bacteria shoot off in random directions. This leaves researchers with the
(10) question of how such bacteria find their way to an attractant such as food or, in the case of photosynthetic bacteria, light, if their swimming pattern consists only of smooth runs and tumbles, the latter resulting in random changes in direction.

(15) One clue comes from the observation that when a chemical attractant is added to a suspension of such bacteria, the bacteria swim along a gradient of the attractant, from an area where the concentration of the attractant is weaker to an area
(20) where it is stronger. As they do so, their swimming is characterized by a decrease in tumbling and an increase in straight runs over relatively longer distances. As the bacteria encounter increasing concentrations of the attractant, their tendency to
(25) tumble is suppressed, whereas tumbling increases whenever they move away from the attractant. The net effect is that runs in the direction of higher concentrations of the attractant become longer and straighter as a result of the suppression of tumbling,
(30) whereas runs away from it are shortened by an increased tendency of the bacteria to tumble and change direction.

Biologists have proposed two mechanisms that bacteria might use in detecting changes in the
(35) concentration of a chemical attractant. First, a bacterium might compare the concentration of a chemical at the front and back of its cell body simultaneously. If the concentration is higher at the front of the cell, then it knows it is moving up the
(40) concentration gradient, from an area where the concentration is lower to an area where it is higher. Alternatively, it might measure the concentration at one instant and again after a brief interval, in which case the bacterium must retain a memory of the
(45) initial concentration. Researchers reasoned that if bacteria do compare concentrations at different times, then when suddenly exposed to a uniformly high concentration of an attractant, the cells would behave as if they were swimming up a concentration
(50) gradient, with long, smooth runs and relatively few tumbles. If, on the other hand, bacteria detect a chemical gradient by measuring it simultaneously at two distinct points, front and back, on the cell body, they would not respond to the jump in
(55) concentration because the concentration of the attractant in front and back of the cells, though high, would be uniform. Experimental evidence suggests that bacteria compare concentrations at different times.

16. It can be inferred from the passage that which one of the following experimental results would suggest that bacteria detect changes in the concentration of an attractant by measuring its concentration in front and back of the cell body simultaneously?

(A) When suddenly transferred from a medium in which the concentration of an attractant was uniformly low to one in which the concentration was uniformly high, the tendency of the bacteria to tumble and undergo random changes in direction increased.

(B) When suddenly transferred from a medium in which the concentration of an attractant was uniformly low to one in which the concentration was uniformly high, the bacteria exhibited no change in the pattern of their motion.

(C) When suddenly transferred from a medium in which the concentration of an attractant was uniformly low to one in which the concentration was uniformly high, the bacteria's movement was characterized by a complete absence of tumbling.

(D) When placed in a medium in which the concentration of an attractant was in some areas low and in others high, the bacteria exhibited an increased tendency to tumble in those areas where the concentration of the attractant was high.

(E) When suddenly transferred from a medium in which the concentration of an attractant was uniformly low to one that was completely free of attractants, the bacteria exhibited a tendency to suppress tumbling and move in longer, straighter lines.

GO ON TO THE NEXT PAGE.

17. It can be inferred from the passage that a bacterium would increase the likelihood of its moving away from an area where the concentration of a harmful substance is high if it did which one of the following?

(A) increased the speed at which it swam immediately after undergoing the random changes in direction that result from tumbling

(B) detected a concentration gradient of an attractant toward which it could begin to swim

(C) relied on the simultaneous measurement of the concentration of the substance in front and back of its body, rather than on the comparison of the concentration at different points in time

(D) exhibited a complete cessation of tumbling when it detected increases in the concentration of the substance

(E) exhibited an increased tendency to tumble as it encountered increasing concentrations of the substance, and suppressed tumbling as it detected decreases in the concentration of the substance

18. It can be inferred from the passage that when describing bacteria as "swimming up a concentration gradient" (lines 49–50), the author means that they were behaving as if they were swimming

(A) against a resistant medium that makes their swimming less efficient

(B) away from a substance to which they are normally attracted

(C) away from a substance that is normally harmful to them

(D) from an area where the concentration of a repellent is weaker to an area where it is completely absent

(E) from an area where the concentration of a substance is weaker to an area where it is stronger

19. The passage indicates that the pattern that characterizes a bacterium's motion changes in response to

(A) the kinds of chemical attractants present in different concentration gradients

(B) the mechanism that the bacterium adopts in determining the presence of an attractant

(C) the bacterium's detection of changes in the concentration of an attractant

(D) the extent to which neighboring bacteria are engaged in tumbling

(E) changes in the intervals of time that occur between the bacterium's measurement of the concentration of an attractant

20. Which one of the following best describes the organization of the third paragraph of the passage?

(A) Two approaches to a problem are discussed, a test that would determine which is more efficient is described, and a conclusion is made, based on experimental evidence.

(B) Two hypotheses are described, a way of determining which of them is more likely to be true is discussed, and one is said to be more accurate on the basis of experimental evidence.

(C) Two hypotheses are described, the flaws inherent in one of them are elaborated, and experimental evidence confirming the other is cited.

(D) An assertion that a species has adopted two different mechanisms to solve a particular problem is made, and evidence is then provided in support of that assertion.

(E) An assertion that one mechanism for solving a particular problem is more efficient than another is made, and evidence is then provided in support of that assertion.

21. The passage provides information in support of which one of the following assertions?

(A) The seemingly erratic motion exhibited by a microorganism can in fact reflect a mechanism by which it is able to control its movement.

(B) Biologists often overstate the complexity of simple organisms such as bacteria.

(C) A bacterium cannot normally retain a memory of a measurement of the concentration of an attractant.

(D) Bacteria now appear to have less control over their movement than biologists had previously hypothesized.

(E) Photosynthetic bacteria appear to have more control over their movement than do bacteria that are not photosynthetic.

GO ON TO THE NEXT PAGE.

Anthropologist David Mandelbaum makes a distinction between life-passage studies and life-history studies which emerged primarily out of research concerning Native Americans. Life-
(5) passage studies, he says, "emphasize the requirements of society, showing how groups socialize and enculturate their young in order to make them into viable members of society." Life histories, however, "emphasize the experiences and
(10) requirements of the individual, how the person copes with society rather than how society copes with the stream of individuals." Life-passage studies bring out the general cultural characteristics and commonalities that broadly define a culture, but are
(15) unconcerned with an individual's choices or how the individual perceives and responds to the demands and expectations imposed by the constraints of his or her culture. This distinction can clearly be seen in the autobiographies of Native American women.
(20) 　　For example, some early recorded autobiographies, such as *The Autobiography of a Fox Indian Woman,* a life passage recorded by anthropologist Truman Michelson, emphasizes prescribed roles. The narrator presents her story in
(25) a way that conforms with tribal expectations. Michelson's work is valuable as ethnography, as a reflection of the day-to-day responsibilities of Mesquakie women, yet as is often the case with life-passage studies, it presents little of the central
(30) character's psychological motivation. The Fox woman's life story focuses on her tribal education and integration into the ways of her people, and relates only what Michelson ultimately decided was worth preserving. The difference between the two
(35) types of studies is often the result of the amount of control the narrator maintains over the material; autobiographies in which there are no recorder-editors are far more reflective of the life-history category, for there are no outsiders shaping the
(40) story to reflect their preconceived notions of what the general cultural patterns are.
　　For example, in Maria Campbell's account of growing up as a Canadian Metis who was influenced strongly, and often negatively, by the non-Native
(45) American world around her, one learns a great deal about the life of Native American women, but Campbell's individual story, which is told to us directly, is always the center of her narrative. Clearly it is important to her to communicate to the
(50) audience what her experiences as a Native American have been. Through Campbell's story of her family the reader learns of the effect of poverty and prejudice on a people. The reader becomes an intimate of Campbell the writer, sharing her pain
(55) and celebrating her small victories. Although Campbell's book is written as a life history (the dramatic moments, the frustrations, and the fears are clearly hers), it reveals much about ethnic relations in Canada while reflecting the period in
(60) which it was written.

22. Which one of the following is the most accurate expression of the main point of the passage?

(A) The contributions of life-history studies to anthropology have made life-passage studies obsolete.

(B) Despite their dissimilar approaches to the study of culture, life-history and life-passage studies have similar goals.

(C) The autobiographies of Native American women illustrate the differences between life-history and life-passage studies.

(D) The roots of Maria Campbell's autobiography can be traced to earlier narratives such as *The Autobiography of a Fox Indian Woman.*

(E) Despite its shortcomings, the life-passage study is a more effective tool than the life-history study for identifying important cultural patterns.

23. The term "prescribed roles" in line 24 of the passage refers to the

(A) function of life-passage studies in helping ethnologists to understand cultural tradition

(B) function of life-history studies in helping ethnologists to gather information

(C) way in which a subject of a life passage views himself or herself

(D) roles clearly distinguishing the narrator of an autobiography from the recorder of an autobiography

(E) roles generally adopted by individuals in order to comply with cultural demands

24. The reference to the "psychological motivation" (line 30) of the subject of *The Autobiography of a Fox Indian Woman* serves primarily to

(A) dismiss as irrelevant the personal perspective in the life-history study

(B) identify an aspect of experience that is not commonly a major focus of life-passage studies

(C) clarify the narrator's self-acknowledged purpose in relating a life passage

(D) suggest a common conflict between the goals of the narrator and those of the recorder in most life-passage studies

(E) assert that developing an understanding of an individual's psychological motivation usually undermines objective ethnography

GO ON TO THE NEXT PAGE. •

25. Which one of the following statements about Maria Campbell can be inferred from material in the passage?

    (A) She was familiar with the very early history of her tribe but lacked insight into the motivations of non-Native Americans.
    (B) She was unfamiliar with Michelson's work but had probably read a number of life-passage studies about Native Americans.
    (C) She had training as a historian but was not qualified as an anthropologist.
    (D) Her family influenced her beliefs and opinions more than the events of her time did.
    (E) Her life history provides more than a record of her personal experience.

26. According to the passage, one way in which life-history studies differ from life-passage studies is that life-history studies are

    (A) usually told in the subject's native language
    (B) less reliable because they rely solely on the subject's recall
    (C) more likely to be told without the influence of an intermediary
    (D) more creative in the way they interpret the subject's cultural legacy
    (E) more representative of the historian's point of view than of the ethnographer's

27. Which one of the following pairings best illustrates the contrast between life passages and life histories?

    (A) a study of the attitudes of a society toward a mainstream religion and an analysis of techniques used to instruct members of that religious group
    (B) a study of how a preindustrial society maintains peace with neighboring societies and a study of how a postindustrial society does the same
    (C) a study of the way a military organization establishes and maintains discipline and a newly enlisted soldier's narrative describing his initial responses to the military environment
    (D) an analysis of a society's means of subsistence and a study of how its members celebrate religious holidays
    (E) a political history of a society focussing on leaders and parties and a study of how the electorate shaped the political landscape of the society

S T O P

IF YOU FINISH BEFORE TIME IS CALLED, YOU MAY CHECK YOUR WORK ON THIS SECTION ONLY.
DO NOT WORK ON ANY OTHER SECTION IN THE TEST.

SECTION III

Time—35 minutes

22 Questions

Directions: Each group of questions in this section is based on a set of conditions. In answering some of the questions, it may be useful to draw a rough diagram. Choose the response that most accurately and completely answers each question and blacken the corresponding space on your answer sheet.

Questions 1–6

Henri has exactly five electrical appliances in his dormitory room: a hairdryer, a microwave oven, a razor, a television, and a vacuum. As a consequence of fire department regulations, Henri can use these appliances only in accordance with the following conditions:

　Henri cannot use both the hairdryer and the razor simultaneously.

　Henri cannot use both the hairdryer and the television simultaneously.

　When Henri uses the vacuum, he cannot at the same time use any of the following: the hairdryer, the razor, and the television.

1. Which one of the following is a pair of appliances Henri could be using simultaneously?

    (A)　the hairdryer and the razor
    (B)　the hairdryer and the television
    (C)　the razor and the television
    (D)　the razor and the vacuum
    (E)　the television and the vacuum

2. Assume that Henri is using exactly two appliances and is not using the microwave oven. Which one of the following is a list of all the appliances, other than the microwave oven, that Henri CANNOT be using?

    (A)　hairdryer
    (B)　razor
    (C)　vacuum
    (D)　hairdryer, razor
    (E)　hairdryer, vacuum

3. Which one of the following CANNOT be true?

    (A)　Henri uses the hairdryer while using the microwave oven.
    (B)　Henri uses the microwave oven while using the razor.
    (C)　Henri uses the microwave oven while using two other appliances.
    (D)　Henri uses the television while using two other appliances.
    (E)　Henri uses the vacuum while using two other appliances.

4. If Henri were to use exactly three appliances, then what is the total number of different groups of three appliances any one of which could be the group of appliances he is using?

    (A)　one
    (B)　two
    (C)　three
    (D)　four
    (E)　five

5. Which one of the following statements, if true, guarantees that Henri is using no more than one of the following: the hairdryer, the razor, the television?

    (A)　Henri is using the hairdryer.
    (B)　Henri is using the television.
    (C)　Henri is not using the hairdryer.
    (D)　Henri is not using the microwave oven.
    (E)　Henri is not using the vacuum.

6. Which one of the following must be true?

    (A)　Henri uses at most three appliances simultaneously.
    (B)　Henri uses at most four appliances simultaneously.
    (C)　Henri uses at most one other appliance while using the microwave oven.
    (D)　Henri uses at most one other appliance while using the razor.
    (E)　Henri uses at least two other appliances while using the hairdryer.

GO ON TO THE NEXT PAGE.

Questions 7–12

A farmer harvests eight separate fields—G, H, J, K, L, M, P, and T. Each field is harvested exactly once, and no two fields are harvested simultaneously. Once the harvesting of a field begins, no other fields are harvested until the harvesting of that field is complete. The farmer harvests the fields in an order consistent with the following conditions:

Both P and G are harvested at some time before K.
Both H and L are harvested at some time before J.
K is harvested at some time before M but after L.
T is harvested at some time before M.

7. Which one of the following could be true?

(A) J is the first field harvested.
(B) K is the second field harvested.
(C) M is the sixth field harvested.
(D) G is the seventh field harvested.
(E) T is the eighth field harvested.

8. If M is the seventh field harvested, then any one of the following could be the fifth field harvested EXCEPT:

(A) H
(B) J
(C) K
(D) L
(E) P

9. Which one of the following CANNOT be the field that is harvested fifth?

(A) G
(B) J
(C) M
(D) P
(E) T

10. If J is the third field harvested, then which one of the following must be true?

(A) L is the first field harvested.
(B) H is the second field harvested.
(C) T is the fourth field harvested.
(D) K is the seventh field harvested.
(E) M is the eighth field harvested.

11. If H is the sixth field harvested, then which one of the following must be true?

(A) G is harvested at some time before T.
(B) H is harvested at some time before K.
(C) J is harvested at some time before M.
(D) K is harvested at some time before J.
(E) T is harvested at some time before K.

12. If L is the fifth field harvested, then which one of the following could be true?

(A) J is harvested at some time before G.
(B) J is harvested at some time before T.
(C) K is harvested at some time before T.
(D) M is harvested at some time before H.
(E) M is harvested at some time before J.

GO ON TO THE NEXT PAGE.

<u>Questions 13–17</u>

In a repair facility there are exactly six technicians: Stacy, Urma, Wim, Xena, Yolanda, and Zane. Each technician repairs machines of at least one of the following three types—radios, televisions, and VCRs—and no other types. The following conditions apply:

Xena and exactly three other technicians repair radios.
Yolanda repairs both televisions and VCRs.
Stacy does not repair any type of machine that Yolanda repairs.
Zane repairs more types of machines than Yolanda repairs.
Wim does not repair any type of machine that Stacy repairs.
Urma repairs exactly two types of machines.

13. For exactly how many of the six technicians is it possible to determine exactly which of the three types of machines each repairs?

(A) one
(B) two
(C) three
(D) four
(E) five

14. Which one of the following must be true?

(A) Of the types of machines repaired by Stacy there is exactly one type that Urma also repairs.
(B) Of the types of machines repaired by Yolanda there is exactly one type that Xena also repairs.
(C) Of the types of machines repaired by Wim there is exactly one type that Xena also repairs.
(D) There is more than one type of machine that both Wim and Yolanda repair.
(E) There is more than one type of machine that both Urma and Wim repair.

15. Which one of the following must be false?

(A) Exactly one of the six technicians repairs exactly one type of machine.
(B) Exactly two of the six technicians repair exactly one type of machine each.
(C) Exactly three of the six technicians repair exactly one type of machine each.
(D) Exactly one of the six technicians repairs exactly two types of machines.
(E) Exactly three of the six technicians repair exactly two types of machines each.

16. Which one of the following pairs of technicians could repair all and only the same types of machines as each other?

(A) Stacy and Urma
(B) Urma and Yolanda
(C) Urma and Xena
(D) Wim and Xena
(E) Xena and Yolanda

17. Which one of the following must be true?

(A) There is exactly one type of machine that both Urma and Wim repair.
(B) There is exactly one type of machine that both Urma and Xena repair.
(C) There is exactly one type of machine that both Urma and Yolanda repair.
(D) There is exactly one type of machine that both Wim and Yolanda repair.
(E) There is exactly one type of machine that both Xena and Yolanda repair.

GO ON TO THE NEXT PAGE.

Three folk groups—Glenside, Hilltopper, Levon—and three rock groups—Peasant, Query, Tinhead—each perform on one of two stages, north or south. Each stage has three two-hour performances: north at 6, 8, and 10; south at 8, 10, and 12. Each group performs individually and exactly once, consistent with the following conditions:

Peasant performs at 6 or 12.
Glenside performs at some time before Hilltopper.
If any rock group performs at 10, no folk group does.
Levon and Tinhead perform on different stages.
Query performs immediately after a folk group, though not necessarily on the same stage.

18. Which one of the following could be a complete and accurate ordering of performances on the north stage, from first to last?

(A) Glenside, Levon, Query
(B) Glenside, Query, Hilltopper
(C) Hilltopper, Query, Peasant
(D) Peasant, Levon, Tinhead
(E) Peasant, Query, Levon

19. Which one of the following groups must perform earlier than 10?

(A) Glenside
(B) Hilltopper
(C) Levon
(D) Peasant
(E) Tinhead

20. Which one of the following groups could perform at 6?

(A) Glenside
(B) Hilltopper
(C) Levon
(D) Query
(E) Tinhead

21. If Query performs at 12, then which one of the following could be an accurate ordering of the performances on the north stage, from first to last?

(A) Glenside, Levon, Query
(B) Peasant, Hilltopper, Tinhead
(C) Peasant, Tinhead, Glenside
(D) Peasant, Tinhead, Hilltopper
(E) Peasant, Tinhead, Levon

22. If a rock group performs at 10, then which one of the following must be true?

(A) A folk group performs at 6.
(B) A folk group performs at 8.
(C) A folk group performs at 12.
(D) A rock group performs at 8.
(E) A rock group performs at 12.

S T O P

IF YOU FINISH BEFORE TIME IS CALLED, YOU MAY CHECK YOUR WORK ON THIS SECTION ONLY.
DO NOT WORK ON ANY OTHER SECTION IN THE TEST.

SECTION IV
Time—35 minutes
27 Questions

Directions: Each passage in this section is followed by a group of questions to be answered on the basis of what is stated or implied in the passage. For some of the questions, more than one of the choices could conceivably answer the question. However, you are to choose the best answer; that is, the response that most accurately and completely answers the question, and blacken the corresponding space on your answer sheet.

One of the intriguing questions considered by anthropologists concerns the purpose our early ancestors had in first creating images of the world around them. Among these images are 25,000-year-
(5) old cave paintings made by the Aurignacians, a people who supplanted the Neanderthals in Europe and who produced the earliest known examples of representational art. Some anthropologists see these paintings as evidence that the Aurignacians had a
(10) more secure life than the Neanderthals. No one under constant threat of starvation, the reasoning goes, could afford time for luxuries such as art; moreover, the art is, in its latter stages at least, so astonishingly well-executed by almost any standard of excellence
(15) that it is highly unlikely it was produced by people who had not spent a great deal of time perfecting their skills. In other words, the high level of quality suggests that Aurignacian art was created by a distinct group of artists, who would likely have spent
(20) most of their time practicing and passing on their skills while being supported by other members of their community.

Curiously, however, the paintings were usually placed in areas accessible only with extreme effort
(25) and completely unilluminated by natural light. This makes it unlikely that these representational cave paintings arose simply out of a love of beauty or pride in artistry—had aesthetic enjoyment been the sole purpose of the paintings, they would presumably
(30) have been located where they could have been easily seen and appreciated.

Given that the Aurignacians were hunter-gatherers and had to cope with the practical problems of extracting a living from a difficult environment, many
(35) anthropologists hypothesize that the paintings were also intended to provide a means of ensuring a steady supply of food. Since it was common among pretechnological societies to believe that one can gain power over an animal by making an image of it,
(40) these anthropologists maintain that the Aurignacian paintings were meant to grant magical power over the Aurignacians' prey—typically large, dangerous animals such as mammoths and bison. The images were probably intended to make these animals
(45) vulnerable to the weapons of the hunters, an explanation supported by the fact that many of the pictures show animals with their hearts outlined in red, or with bright, arrow-shaped lines tracing paths to vital organs. Other paintings clearly show some
(50) animals as pregnant, perhaps in an effort to assure

plentiful hunting grounds. There is also evidence that ceremonies of some sort were performed before these images. Well-worn footprints of dancers can still be discerned in the clay floors of some caves, and
(55) pictures of what appear to be shamans, or religious leaders, garbed in fantastic costumes, are found among the painted animals.

1. Which one of the following most accurately describes the author's position regarding the claims attributed to anthropologists in the third paragraph?

    (A) implicit acceptance
    (B) hesitant agreement
    (C) noncommittal curiosity
    (D) detached skepticism
    (E) broad disagreement

2. The passage provides information that answers which one of the following questions?

    (A) For how long a period did the Neanderthals occupy Europe?
    (B) How long did it take for the Aurignacians to supplant the Neanderthals?
    (C) Did the Aurignacians make their homes in caves?
    (D) What are some of the animals represented in Aurignacian cave paintings?
    (E) What other prehistoric groups aside from the Aurignacians produced representational art?

GO ON TO THE NEXT PAGE.

3. The author would be most likely to agree with which one of the following statements?

    (A) The cave paintings indicate that the Aurignacians lived a relatively secure life compared to most other hunter-gatherer cultures.
    (B) Skill in art was essential to becoming an Aurignacian shaman.
    (C) Prehistoric hunter-gatherers did not create any art solely for aesthetic purposes.
    (D) All art created by the Aurignacians was intended to grant magical power over other beings.
    (E) The Aurignacians sought to gain magical power over their prey by means of ceremonial acts in addition to painted images.

4. The author mentions the relative inaccessibility of the Aurignacian cave paintings primarily to

    (A) stress the importance of the cave paintings to the lives of the artists who painted them by indicating the difficulties they had to overcome to do so
    (B) lay the groundwork for a fuller explanation of the paintings' function
    (C) suggest that only a select portion of the Aurignacian community was permitted to view the paintings
    (D) help explain why the paintings are still well preserved
    (E) support the argument that Aurignacian artists were a distinct and highly skilled group

5. The passage suggests that the author would be most likely to agree with which one of the following claims about the Aurignacians?

    (A) They were technologically no more advanced than the Neanderthals they supplanted.
    (B) They were the first humans known to have worn costumes for ceremonial purposes.
    (C) They had established some highly specialized social roles.
    (D) They occupied a less hostile environment than the Neanderthals did.
    (E) They carved images of their intended prey on their weapons to increase the weapons' efficacy.

GO ON TO THE NEXT PAGE.

The poet Louise Glück has said that she feels comfortable writing within a tradition often characterized as belonging only to male poets. About her own experience reading poetry, Glück notes that
(5) her gender did not keep her from appreciating the poems of Shakespeare, Blake, Keats, and other male poets. Rather she believed this was the tradition of her language and that it was for this reason her poetic inheritance. She thus views the canon of poets in
(10) English as a literary family to which she clearly belongs. Whereas many contemporary women poets have rejected this tradition as historically exclusionary and rhetorically inadequate for women, Glück embraces it with respect and admiration.

(15)   Glück's formative encounters with poetry also provided her with the theoretical underpinnings of her respect for this tradition; she notes that in her youth she could sense many of the great themes and subjects of poetry even before experiencing them in
(20) her own life. These subjects—loss, the passage of time, desire—are timeless, available to readers of any age, gender, or social background. Glück makes no distinction between these subjects as belonging to female or male poets alone, calling them "the great
(25) human subjects." If the aim of a poem is to explore the issue of human mortality, for example, then issues of gender distinction fade behind the presence of this universal reality.

Some of Glück's critics claim that this idea of the
(30) universal is suspect and that the idea that gender issues are transcended by addressing certain subjects may attribute to poetry an innocence that it does not have. They maintain that a female poet writing within a historically male-dominated tradition will on some
(35) level be unable to avoid accepting certain presuppositions, which, in the critics' view, are determined by a long-standing history of denigration and exclusion of female artists. Furthermore, they feel that this long-standing history cannot be confronted
(40) using tools—in Glück's case, poetic forms—forged by the traditions of this history. Instead critics insist that women poets should strive to create a uniquely female poetry by using new forms to develop a new voice.

(45)   Glück, however, observes that this ambition, with its insistence on an essentially female perspective, is as limiting as her critics believe the historically male-dominated tradition to be. She holds that to the extent that there are some gender differences that have been
(50) shaped by history, they will emerge in the differing ways that women and men write about the world—indeed, these differences will be revealed with more authority in the absence of conscious intention. She points out that the universal subjects of literature do
(55) not make literature itself timeless and unchanging. Literature, she maintains, is inescapably historical, and every work, both in what it includes and in what it omits, inevitably speaks of its social and historical context.

6. Which one of the following most accurately expresses the main point of the passage?

(A) In response to her critics, Glück argues that the attempt to develop a uniquely female voice is as restrictive as they believe the male tradition in poetry to be.

(B) Although critics have taken Glück to task for writing poetry that is generic in subject rather than specifically aimed at addressing women's concerns, she believes that poetry must instead concern itself with certain universal themes.

(C) In spite of critics who attempt to limit art to expressing the unique perspectives of the artist's gender, Glück believes that art in fact represents a perspective on its subject matter that is equally male and female.

(D) In opposition to some critics, Glück writes on universal themes rather than striving for a uniquely female voice, believing that whatever gender differences are present will emerge unconsciously in any case.

(E) Aside from the power and accomplishment of her writing, Glück has yet to offer a completely satisfying response to the critics' demand that her work reflect the conflict between male and female perspectives on poetic subject matter.

7. Based on the passage, with which one of the following statements regarding the poetic tradition in English would Glück be most likely to agree?

(A) This tradition is somewhat diminished for its lack of recognized female poets.

(B) This tradition transcends its social and historical context.

(C) The male-dominated aspect of this tradition can be overcome only by developing a uniquely female voice in poetry.

(D) The view of this tradition as an inheritance is necessary for a poet to be successful.

(E) This tradition, though male dominated, addresses universal subjects.

GO ON TO THE NEXT PAGE.

8. As it is used in the passage, "inheritance" (line 9) refers most specifically to

   (A) the burden that a historically male-dominated poetic canon places on a contemporary woman poet
   (B) the set of poetic forms and techniques considered acceptable within a linguistic culture
   (C) the poetry written in a particular language, whose achievement serves as a model for other poets writing in that language
   (D) the presumption that contemporary poets can write only on subjects already explored by the poets in that language who are considered to be the most celebrated
   (E) the imposition on a poet, based on the poetry of preceding generations in that language, of a particular writing style

9. Based on the description in the passage, a poem that reveals gender differences in the absence of any specific intention by the poet to do so is most like

   (A) a bird's flight that exposes unseen air currents
   (B) a ship's prow that indicates how strong a wave it is designed to withstand
   (C) a building's facade that superficially embellishes an ordinary structure
   (D) a railroad track, without which travel by train is impossible
   (E) a novel that deliberately conceals the motives of its main character

10. According to the passage, Glück believes that art reveals gender differences with more authority when which one of the following is true?

    (A) The artist refuses to accept certain presuppositions about gender.
    (B) The artist uses the tools of that art's tradition.
    (C) The artist does not consciously intend to reveal such differences.
    (D) The artist comments on gender issues through the use of other subject matter.
    (E) The artist embraces that art's tradition with respect.

11. Which one of the following statements about Glück is made in the passage?

    (A) She objects to the use of traditional poetic forms to confront the history of the poetic tradition.
    (B) She recognizes that the idea of the universal in poetry is questionable.
    (C) She claims to accept only male poets as her literary family.
    (D) She claims to write from a gender-neutral perspective.
    (E) She claims to have sensed the great themes and subjects of poetry while in her youth.

12. Based on the passage, which one of the following most accurately characterizes the author's attitude toward Glück's view of poetry?

    (A) respectful dismissal
    (B) grudging acceptance
    (C) detached indifference
    (D) tacit endorsement
    (E) enthusiastic acclaim

GO ON TO THE NEXT PAGE.

Although the rights of native peoples of Canada have yet to be comprehensively defined in Canadian law, most native Canadians assert that their rights include the right not only to govern themselves and (5) their land, but also to exercise ownership rights over movable cultural property—artifacts ranging from domestic implements to ceremonial costumes. Assignment of such rights to native communities has been difficult to achieve, but while traditional (10) Canadian statute and common law has placed ownership of movable property with current custodians such as museums, recent litigation by native Canadians has called such ownership into question.

(15) Canadian courts usually base decisions about ownership on a concept of private property, under which all forms of property are capable of being owned by individuals or by groups functioning legally as individuals. This system is based on a (20) philosophy that encourages the right of owners to use their property as they see fit without outside interference. But litigation by native Canadians challenges courts to recognize a concept of property ownership that clashes with the private property (25) concept. Although some tribes now recognize the notion of private property in their legal systems, they have traditionally employed a concept of collective ownership—and in all cases in which native Canadians have made legal claim to movable (30) property they have done so by invoking this latter concept, which is based on the philosophy that each member should have an equal say regarding the use of the community's resources. Under this collective ideology, access to and use of resources is determined (35) by the collective interests of the community. Furthermore, collective ownership casts an individual in the role of guardian or caretaker of property rather than as a titleholder; while every tribe member is an owner of the property, individual members cannot sell (40) this right, nor does it pass to their heirs when they die. Nevertheless, their children will enjoy the same rights, not as heirs but as communal owners.

Because the concept of collective property assigns ownership to individuals simply because they are (45) members of the community, native Canadians rarely possess the legal documents that the concept of private property requires to demonstrate ownership. Museums, which are likely to possess bills of sale or proof of prior possession to substantiate their claims (50) of ownership, are thus likely to be recognized as legally entitled to the property they hold, even when such property originated with native Canadian communities. But as their awareness of the inappropriateness of applying the private property (55) concept to all cultural groups grows, Canadian courts will gradually recognize that native Canadians, while they cannot demonstrate ownership as prescribed by the notion of private property, can clearly claim ownership as prescribed by the notion of collective (60) property, and that their claims to movable cultural property should be honored.

13. Which one of the following most accurately expresses the main idea of the passage?

(A) Litigation by native Canadians to regain control of their movable cultural property illustrates how the concept of private ownership has become increasingly obsolete and demonstrates that this concept should be replaced by the more modern concept of collective ownership.

(B) Litigation by native Canadians to regain control of their movable cultural property is likely to succeed more frequently as courts begin to acknowledge that the concept of collective ownership is more appropriate than the concept of private ownership in such cases.

(C) The conflict between the concepts of collective and private ownership that has led to litigation by native Canadians to regain control of their movable cultural property is in reality a debate over whether individuals should act as titleholders or merely as caretakers with respect to their property.

(D) The conflict between the concepts of collective and private ownership that has led to litigation by native Canadians to regain control of their movable cultural property cannot be resolved until the rights of native Canadians have been comprehensively defined in Canadian law.

(E) The conflict between the concepts of collective and private ownership that has led to litigation by native Canadians to regain control of their movable cultural property illustrates the need to expand the concept of private property to include cases of joint ownership by a collection of individuals.

14. According to the concept of private property as presented in the passage, which one of the following most completely describes the meaning of the term "property owner"?

(A) one who possesses a bill of sale to substantiate his or her claims to property ownership

(B) one who possesses proof of prior possession to substantiate his or her claims to property ownership

(C) one who is allowed to make use of his or her property in whatever manner he or she wishes

(D) one who is allowed to transfer ownership rights to his or her children as heirs

(E) one who is allowed to exercise property rights because of his or her membership in a community

GO ON TO THE NEXT PAGE.

15. The author's attitude toward the possibility of courts increasingly assigning ownership rights to native communities is best described as which one of the following?

(A) certain that it will never be realized and concerned that it should

(B) concerned that it will never be realized but hopeful that it will

(C) uncertain whether it will be realized but hopeful that it will

(D) uncertain whether it will be realized but confident that it should

(E) convinced that it will be realized and pleased that it will

16. The primary function of the first paragraph of the passage is to

(A) identify some of the specific types of property at issue in litigation by native Canadians to regain control of their movable cultural property from museums

(B) describe the role of the concept of property ownership in litigation by native Canadians to regain control of their movable cultural property from museums

(C) summarize the difficulties that have been experienced in attempting to develop a comprehensive definition of the rights of native Canadians under the law

(D) provide the context within which litigation by native Canadians to regain control of their movable cultural property is occurring

(E) discuss the difficulty of deciding legal cases that rest on a clash between two cultures' differing definitions of a legal concept

17. Given the information in the passage, Canadian courts hearing a dispute over movable cultural property between a museum and a group of native Canadians will be increasingly unlikely to treat which one of the following as a compelling reason for deciding the case in the museum's favor?

(A) The museum is able to produce evidence that the property did not originate in the native community.

(B) The museum cannot produce written documentation of its claims to ownership of the property.

(C) The group of native Canadians produces evidence that the property originated in their community.

(D) The group of native Canadians cannot produce written documentation of their claims to ownership of the property.

(E) The group of native Canadians do not belong to a tribe that employs a legal system that has adopted the concept of private property.

18. The passage suggests that the concepts of collective and private ownership differ in each of the following ways EXCEPT:

(A) The collective concept allows groups of individuals to own property; the private concept does not.

(B) The collective concept requires consideration of community interests; the private concept does not.

(C) The collective concept assigns ownership on the basis of membership in a community; the private concept does not.

(D) The private concept allows owners to function as titleholders to their property; the collective concept does not.

(E) The private concept permits individuals to sell property; the collective concept does not.

19. The passage most supports which one of the following statements about the tribal legal systems mentioned in the second paragraph of the passage?

(A) All tribes whose legal system employs the concept of collective property have engaged in litigation over control of movable cultural property.

(B) Only tribes that have engaged in litigation over control of movable property have a legal system that employs the concept of collective property.

(C) All tribes that have engaged in litigation over control of movable cultural property have a legal system that employs the concept of collective property.

(D) All tribes whose legal system recognizes the concept of private property can expect to succeed in litigation over control of movable cultural property.

(E) Only those tribes whose legal system recognizes the concept of private property can expect to succeed in litigation over control of movable cultural property.

GO ON TO THE NEXT PAGE.

The first thing any embryo must do before it can develop into an organism is establish early polarity—that is, it must set up a way to distinguish its top from its bottom and its back from its front. The
(5) mechanisms that establish the earliest spatial configurations in an embryo are far less similar across life forms than those relied on for later development, as in the formation of limbs or a nervous system: for example, the signals that the developing fruit fly uses
(10) to know its front end from its back end turn out to be radically different from those that the nematode, a type of worm, relies on, and both appear to be quite different from the polarity signals in the development of humans and other mammals.
(15)   In the fruit fly, polarity is established by signals inscribed in the yolklike cytoplasm of the egg before fertilization, so that when the sperm contributes its genetic material, everything is already set to go. Given all the positional information that must be
(20) distributed throughout the cell, it takes a fruit fly a week to make an egg, but once that well-appointed egg is fertilized, it is transformed from a single cell into a crawling larva in a day. By contrast, in the embryonic development of certain nematodes, the
(25) point where the sperm enters the egg appears to provide crucial positional information. Once that information is present, little bundles of proteins called p-granules, initially distributed uniformly throughout the cytoplasm, begin to congregate at one end of the
(30) yolk; when the fertilized egg divides, one of the resulting cells gets all the p-granules. The presence or absence of these granules in cells appears to help determine whether their subsequent divisions will lead to the formation of the worm's front or back
(35) half. A similar sperm-driven mechanism is also thought to establish body orientation in some comparatively simple vertebrates such as frogs, though apparently not in more complex vertebrates such as mammals. Research indicates that in human
(40) and other mammalian embryos, polarity develops much later, as many stages of cell division occur with no apparent asymmetries among cells. Yet how polarity is established in mammals is currently a tempting mystery to researchers.
(45)   Once an embryo establishes polarity, it relies on sets of essential genes that are remarkably similar among all life forms for elaboration of its parts. There is an astonishing conservation of mechanism in this process: the genes that help make eyes in flies
(50) are similar to the genes that make eyes in mice or humans. So a seeming paradox arises: when embryos of different species are at the one- or few-cell stage and still appear almost identical, the mechanisms of development they use are vastly different; yet when
(55) they start growing brains or extremities and become identifiable as distinct species, the developmental mechanisms they use are remarkably similar.

20. Which one of the following most accurately expresses the main point of the passage?

(A)   Species differ more in the mechanisms that determine the spatial orientation in an embryo than they do in their overall genetic makeup.

(B)   Embryos determine their front from their back and top from bottom by different methods, depending on whether the organism is simple or more complex.

(C)   While very similar genes help determine the later embryonic development of all organisms, the genetic mechanisms by which embryos establish early polarity vary dramatically from one organism to the next.

(D)   The mechanisms by which embryos establish early polarity differ depending on whether the signals by which polarity is achieved are inscribed in the cytoplasm of the egg or the p-granules of the sperm.

(E)   Despite their apparent dissimilarity from species to species, the means by which organisms establish polarity rely on essentially the same genetic mechanisms.

21. The passage suggests that the author would be most likely to agree with which one of the following statements?

(A)   The simpler the organism, the greater the speed at which it develops from fertilized egg to embryo.

(B)   Scientists have determined how polarity is established in most simple vertebrates.

(C)   Scientists will try to determine how polarity is established in humans.

(D)   Very few observations of embryonic development after polarity is established are generalizable to more than a single species.

(E)   Simpler organisms take longer to establish polarity than do more complex organisms.

GO ON TO THE NEXT PAGE.

22. The passage provides information to suggest that which one of the following relationships exists between the development of humans and the development of fruit flies?

(A) Since humans and fruit flies use similar genetic material in their development, analogies from fruit fly behavior can be useful in explaining human behavior.

(B) For the elaboration of parts, human development relies on genetic material quite different in nature, though not in quantity, from that of a fruit fly.

(C) Positional information for establishing polarity in a human embryo, as in that of the fruit fly, is distributed throughout the egg prior to fertilization.

(D) A study of the development of the fruit fly's visual system would more likely be applicable to questions of human development than would a study of the mechanisms that establish the fruit fly's polarity.

(E) While the fruit fly egg becomes a larva in a single day, a human embryo takes significantly longer to develop because humans cannot develop limbs until they have established a nervous system.

23. According to the passage, polarity is established in a human embryo

(A) after more stages of cell division than in frogs
(B) before the sperm enters the egg
(C) after positional information is provided by the massing of p-granules
(D) by the same sperm-driven mechanism as in the nematode
(E) in the same way as in simpler vertebrates

24. By "conservation of mechanism" (line 48) the author is probably referring to

(A) how the same mechanism can be used to form different parts of the same organism
(B) the fact that no genetic material is wasted in development
(C) how few genes a given organism requires in order to elaborate its parts
(D) a highly complex organism's requiring no more genetic material than a simpler one
(E) the fact that analogous structures in different species are brought about by similar genetic means

25. Which one of the following most accurately states the main purpose of the second paragraph?

(A) to illustrate the diversity of processes by which organisms establish early polarity
(B) to elaborate on the differences between embryonic formation in the fruit fly and in the nematode
(C) to suggest why the process of establishing early polarity in humans is not yet understood
(D) to demonstrate the significance and necessity for genetic development of establishing polarity
(E) to demonstrate that there are two main types of mechanism by which early polarity is established

26. According to the passage, which one of the following is a major difference between the establishment of polarity in the fruit fly and in the nematode?

(A) The fruit fly embryo takes longer to establish polarity than does the nematode embryo.
(B) The mechanisms that establish polarity are more easily identifiable in the nematode than in the fruit fly.
(C) Polarity signals for the fruit fly embryo are inscribed entirely in the egg and these signals for the nematode embryo are inscribed entirely in the sperm.
(D) Polarity in the fruit fly takes more stages of cell division to become established than in the nematode.
(E) Polarity is established for the fruit fly before fertilization and for the nematode through fertilization.

27. The author's primary purpose in the passage is to

(A) articulate a theory of how early polarity is established and support the theory by an analysis of data
(B) describe a phase in the development of organisms in which the genetic mechanisms used are disparate and discuss why this disparity is surprising
(C) provide a classification of the mechanisms by which different life forms establish early polarity
(D) argue that a certain genetic process must occur in all life forms, regardless of their apparent dissimilarity
(E) explain why an embryo must establish early polarity before it can develop into an organism

S T O P

IF YOU FINISH BEFORE TIME IS CALLED, YOU MAY CHECK YOUR WORK ON THIS SECTION ONLY.
DO NOT WORK ON ANY OTHER SECTION IN THE TEST.

SECTION V

Time—35 minutes

26 Questions

<u>Directions</u>: The questions in this section are based on the reasoning contained in brief statements or passages. For some questions, more than one of the choices could conceivably answer the question. However, you are to choose the <u>best</u> answer; that is, the response that most accurately and completely answers the question. You should not make assumptions that are by commonsense standards implausible, superfluous, or incompatible with the passage. After you have chosen the best answer, blacken the corresponding space on your answer sheet.

1. While 65 percent of the eligible voters who were recently polled favor Perkins over Samuels in the coming election, the results of that poll are dubious because it was not based on a representative sample. Given that Perkins predominantly advocates the interests of the upper-middle class and that the survey was conducted at high-priced shopping malls, it is quite probable that Perkins's supporters were overrepresented.

   Which one of the following statements most accurately expresses the main conclusion of the argument?

   (A) The poll was intentionally designed to favor Perkins over Samuels.
   (B) Samuels's supporters believe that they were probably not adequately represented in the poll.
   (C) The poll's results probably do not accurately represent the opinions of the voters in the coming election.
   (D) Samuels is quite likely to have a good chance of winning the coming election.
   (E) Those who designed the poll should have considered more carefully where to conduct the survey.

2. Sleep research has demonstrated that sleep is characterized by periods of different levels of brain activity. People experience dreams during only one of these periods, known as REM (rapid eye movement) sleep. Test subjects who are chronically deprived of REM sleep become irritable during waking life. This shows that REM sleep relieves the stresses of waking life.

   Which one of the following, if true, most strengthens the argument?

   (A) Test subjects who are chronically deprived of non-REM sleep also become irritable during waking life.
   (B) Chronically having bad dreams can cause stress, but so can chronically having pleasant but exciting dreams.
   (C) During times of increased stress, one's REM sleep is disturbed in a way that prevents one from dreaming.
   (D) Only some people awakened during REM sleep can report the dreams they were having just before being awakened.
   (E) Other factors being equal, people who normally have shorter periods of REM sleep tend to experience more stress.

GO ON TO THE NEXT PAGE.

3. Since 1989 the importation of ivory from African elephants into the United States and Canada has been illegal, but the importation of ivory from the excavated tusks of ancient mammoths remains legal in both countries. Following the ban, there was a sharp increase in the importation of ivory that importers identified as mammoth ivory. In 1989 customs officials lacked a technique for distinguishing elephant ivory from that of mammoths. Just after such a technique was invented and its use by customs officials became widely known, there was a dramatic decrease in the amount of ivory presented for importation into the U.S. and Canada that was identified by importers as mammoth ivory.

Which one of the following is most strongly supported by the information above?

(A) Customs officials still cannot reliably distinguish elephant ivory from mammoth ivory.

(B) Most of the ivory currently imported into the U.S. and Canada comes from neither African elephants nor mammoths.

(C) In the period since the technique for distinguishing elephant ivory from mammoth ivory was implemented, the population of African elephants has declined.

(D) Much of the ivory imported as mammoth ivory just after the ban on ivory from African elephants went into effect was actually elephant ivory.

(E) Shortly after the importation of ivory from African elephants was outlawed, there was a sharp increase in the total amount of all ivory presented for importation into the U.S. and Canada.

4. My suspicion that there is some truth to astrology has been confirmed. Most physicians I have talked to believe in it.

The flawed pattern of reasoning in the argument above is most similar to that in which one of the following?

(A) Professor Smith was convicted of tax evasion last year. So I certainly wouldn't give any credence to Smith's economic theories.

(B) I have come to the conclusion that several governmental social programs are wasteful. This is because most of the biology professors I have discussed this with think that this is true.

(C) Quantum mechanics seems to be emerging as the best physical theory we have today. Most prominent physicists subscribe to it.

(D) Most mechanical engineers I have talked to say that it is healthier to refrain from eating meat. So most mechanical engineers are vegetarians.

(E) For many years now, many people, some famous, have reported that they have seen or come in contact with unidentified flying objects. So there are probably extraterrestrial societies trying to contact us.

5. The best explanation for Mozart's death involves the recently detected fracture in his skull. The crack, most likely the result of an accident, could have easily torn veins in his brain, allowing blood to leak into his brain. When such bleeding occurs in the brain and the blood dries, many of the brain's faculties become damaged, commonly, though not immediately, leading to death. This explanation of Mozart's death is bolstered by the fact that the fracture shows signs of partial healing.

The claim that the fracture shows signs of partial healing figures in the argument in which one of the following ways?

(A) It shows that Mozart's death could have been avoided.

(B) It shows that the fracture did not occur after Mozart's death.

(C) It shows that the dried blood impaired Mozart's brain's faculties.

(D) It shows that Mozart's death occurred suddenly.

(E) It suggests that Mozart's death was accidental.

6. In the first phase of the Industrial Revolution, machines were invented whose main advantage was that they worked faster than human workers. This technology became widely used because it was economically attractive; many unskilled workers could be replaced by just a few skilled workers. Today managers are looking for technology that will allow them to replace highly paid skilled workers with a smaller number of less-skilled workers.

The examples presented above best illustrate which one of the following propositions?

(A) Employers utilize new technology because it allows them to reduce labor costs.

(B) Workers will need to acquire more education and skills to remain competitive in the labor market.

(C) In seeking employment, highly skilled workers no longer have an advantage over less-skilled workers.

(D) Technology eliminates many jobs but also creates just as many jobs.

(E) Whereas technological innovations were once concentrated in heavy industry, they now affect all industries.

GO ON TO THE NEXT PAGE.

7. For many types of crops, hybrid strains have been developed that have been found in test plantings to produce significantly higher yields than were produced by traditional nonhybrid strains of those crops planted alongside them. However, in many parts of the world where farmers have abandoned traditional nonhybrid strains in favor of the hybrid strains, crop yields have not increased.

Which one of the following, if true, most helps to resolve the apparent discrepancy?

(A) Most farmers who plant the hybrid strains of their crops have larger farms than do farmers who continue to plant traditional nonhybrid strains of the same crops.

(B) Hybrid strains of crops produced higher yields in some areas than did nonhybrid strains in those areas.

(C) The hybrid strains were tested under significantly better farming conditions than are found in most areas where farmers grow those strains.

(D) Many traditional nonhybrid strains of plants produce crops that taste better and thus sell better than the hybrid strains of those crops.

(E) Many governments subsidize farmers who plant only hybrid strains of staple crops.

8. This stamp is probably highly valuable, since it exhibits a printing error. The most important factors in determining a stamp's value, assuming it is in good condition, are its rarity and age. This is clearly a fine specimen, and it is quite old as well.

The conclusion is properly inferred if which one of the following is assumed?

(A) The older a stamp is, the more valuable it is.

(B) Printing errors are always confined to a few individual stamps.

(C) Most stamps with printing errors are already in the hands of collectors.

(D) Rarity and age are of equal importance to a stamp's value.

(E) Even old and rare stamps are usually not valuable if they are in poor condition.

9. A recent study of several hundred female physicians showed that their tendency to develop coronary disease was inversely proportional to their dietary intake of two vitamins, folate and B6. The researchers concluded that folate and B6 inhibit the development of heart disease in women.

Which one of the following would, if true, most weaken the researchers' conclusion?

(A) The foods that contain significant amounts of the vitamins folate and B6 also contain significant amounts of nonvitamin nutrients that inhibit heart disease.

(B) It is very unlikely that a chemical compound would inhibit coronary disease in women but not in men.

(C) Physicians are more likely than nonphysicians to know a great deal about the link between diet and health.

(D) The physicians in the study had not been screened in advance to ensure that none had preexisting heart conditions.

(E) The vitamins folate and B6 are present only in very small amounts in most foods.

10. The proposed coal-burning electric plant should be approved, since no good arguments have been offered against it. After all, all the arguments against it have been presented by competing electricity producers.

Which one of the following is an assumption on which the reasoning above depends?

(A) The competing electricity producers would stand to lose large amounts of revenue from the building of the coal-burning electric plant.

(B) If a person's arguments against a proposal are defective, then that person has a vested interest in seeing that the proposal is not implemented.

(C) Approval of the coal-burning electric plant would please coal suppliers more than disapproval would please suppliers of fuel to the competing electricity producers.

(D) If good arguments are presented for a proposal, then that proposal should be approved.

(E) Arguments made by those who have a vested interest in the outcome of a proposal are not good arguments.

GO ON TO THE NEXT PAGE.

11. Psychiatrist: While the first appearance of a phobia is usually preceded by a traumatizing event, not everyone who is traumatized by an event develops a phobia. Furthermore, many people with phobias have never been traumatized. These two considerations show that traumatizing events do not contribute to the occurrence of phobias.

The reasoning in the psychiatrist's argument is most vulnerable to criticism on the grounds that the argument

(A) treats the cause of the occurrence of a type of phenomenon as an effect of phenomena of that type

(B) presumes, without providing justification, that some psychological events have no causes that can be established by scientific investigation

(C) builds the conclusion drawn into the support cited for that conclusion

(D) takes for granted that a type of phenomenon contributes to the occurrence of another type of phenomenon only if phenomena of these two types are invariably associated

(E) derives a causal connection from mere association when there is no independent evidence of causal connection

12. Some species are called "indicator species" because the loss of a population of such a species serves as an early warning of problems arising from pollution. Environmentalists tracking the effects of pollution have increasingly paid heed to indicator species; yet environmentalists would be misguided if they attributed the loss of a population to pollution in all cases. Though declines in population often do signal environmental degradation, they are just as often a result of the natural evolution of an ecosystem. We must remember that, in nature, change is the status quo.

Which one of the following most accurately expresses the argument's conclusion?

(A) Environmentalists sometimes overreact to the loss of a specific population.

(B) The loss of a specific population should not always be interpreted as a sign of environmental degradation.

(C) Environmentalists' use of indicator species in tracking the effects of pollution is often problematic.

(D) The loss of a specific population is often the result of natural changes in an ecosystem and in such cases should not be resisted.

(E) The loss of a specific population as a result of pollution is simply part of nature's status quo.

13. Columnist: Tagowa's testimony in the Pemberton trial was not heard outside the courtroom, so we cannot be sure what she said. Afterward, however, she publicly affirmed her belief in Pemberton's guilt. Hence, since the jury found Pemberton not guilty, we can conclude that not all of the jury members believed Tagowa's testimony.

Which one of the following describes a flaw in the columnist's reasoning?

(A) It overlooks that a witness may think that a defendant is guilty even though that witness's testimony in no way implicates the defendant.

(B) It confuses facts about what certain people believe with facts about what ought to be the case.

(C) It presumes, without providing warrant, that juries find defendants guilty only if those defendants committed the crimes with which they are charged.

(D) It presumes, without providing warrant, that a jury's finding a defendant not guilty is evidence of dishonesty on the part of someone who testified against the defendant.

(E) It fails to consider that jury members sometimes disagree with each other about the significance of a particular person's testimony.

14. A new tax law aimed at encouraging the reforestation of cleared land in order to increase the amount of forested land in a particular region offers lumber companies tax incentives for each unit of cleared land they reforest. One lumber company has accordingly reduced its tax liability by purchasing a large tract of cleared land in the region and reforesting it. The company paid for the purchase by clearing a larger tract of land in the region, a tract that it had planned to hold in long-term reserve.

If the statements above are true, which one of the following must be true about the new tax law?

(A) It is a failure in encouraging the reforestation of cleared land in the region.

(B) It will have no immediate effect on the amount of forested land in the region.

(C) It will ultimately cause lumber companies to plant trees on approximately as much land as they harvest in the region.

(D) It can provide a motivation for companies to act in a manner contrary to the purpose of the law while taking advantage of the tax incentives.

(E) It will provide lumber companies with a tax incentive that will ultimately be responsible for a massive decrease in the number of mature forests in the region.

GO ON TO THE NEXT PAGE.

15. Trustee: The recent exhibit at the art museum was extensively covered by the local media, and this coverage seems to have contributed to the record-breaking attendance it drew. If the attendance at the exhibit had been low, the museum would have gone bankrupt and closed permanently, so the museum could not have remained open had it not been for the coverage from the local media.

The reasoning in the trustee's argument is most vulnerable to criticism on the grounds that the argument

(A) confuses a necessary condition for the museum's remaining open with a sufficient condition for the museum's remaining open

(B) takes for granted that no previous exhibit at the museum had received such extensive media coverage

(C) takes for granted that most people who read articles about the exhibit also attended the exhibit

(D) fails to address the possibility that the exhibit would have drawn enough visitors to prevent bankruptcy even without media coverage

(E) presupposes the very conclusion that it is trying to prove

16. Economist: A tax is effective if it raises revenue and burdens all and only those persons targeted by the tax. A tax is ineffective, however, if it does not raise revenue and it costs a significant amount of money to enforce.

Which one of the following inferences is most strongly supported by the principles stated by the economist?

(A) The tax on cigarettes burdens most, but not all, of the people targeted by it. Thus, if it raises revenue, the tax is effective.

(B) The tax on alcohol raises a modest amount of revenue, but it costs a significant amount of money to enforce. Thus, the tax is ineffective.

(C) The tax on gasoline costs a significant amount of money to enforce. Thus, if it does not raise revenue, the tax is ineffective.

(D) The tax on coal burdens all of the people targeted by it, and this tax does not burden anyone who is not targeted by it. Thus, the tax is effective.

(E) The tax on steel does not cost a significant amount of money to enforce, but it does not raise revenue either. Thus, the tax is ineffective.

17. A large amount of rainfall in April and May typically leads to an increase in the mosquito population and thus to an increased threat of encephalitis. People cannot change the weather. Thus people cannot decrease the threat of encephalitis.

The reasoning in the argument above is flawed in that the argument

(A) takes for granted that because one event precedes another the former must be the cause of the latter

(B) presumes, without providing justification, that a certain outcome would be desirable

(C) ignores the possibility that a certain type of outcome is dependent on more than one factor

(D) takes for granted that a threat that is aggravated by certain factors could not occur in the absence of those factors

(E) draws a conclusion about what is possible from a premise about what is actually the case

18. Leadership depends as much on making one's followers aware of their own importance as it does on conveying a vivid image of a collective goal. Only if they are convinced both that their efforts are necessary for the accomplishment of this goal, and that these efforts, if expended, will actually achieve it, will people follow a leader.

If all of the statements above are true, then which one of the following CANNOT be true?

(A) Some leaders who convince their followers of the necessity of their efforts in achieving a goal fail, nevertheless, to lead them to the attainment of that goal.

(B) One who succeeds in conveying to one's followers the relationship between their efforts and the attainment of a collective goal succeeds in leading these people to this goal.

(C) Only if one is a leader must one convince people of the necessity of their efforts for the attainment of a collective goal.

(D) Sometimes people succeed in achieving a collective goal without ever having been convinced that by trying to do so they would succeed.

(E) Sometimes people who remain unsure of whether their efforts are needed for the attainment of a collective goal nevertheless follow a leader.

GO ON TO THE NEXT PAGE.

19. Fifty chronic insomniacs participated in a one-month study conducted at an institute for sleep disorders. Half were given a dose of a new drug and the other half were given a placebo every night before going to bed at the institute. Approximately 80 percent of the participants in each group reported significant relief from insomnia during the first two weeks of the study. But in each group, approximately 90 percent of those who had reported relief claimed that their insomnia had returned during the third week of the study.

Which one of the following, if true, most helps to explain all the data from the study?

(A) Because it is easy to build up a tolerance to the new drug, most people will no longer experience its effects after taking it every night for two weeks.
(B) The psychological comfort afforded by the belief that one has taken a sleep-promoting drug is enough to prevent most episodes of insomnia.
(C) The new drug is very similar in chemical composition to another drug, large doses of which have turned out to be less effective than expected.
(D) Most insomniacs sleep better in a new environment, and the new drug has no effect on an insomniac's ability to sleep.
(E) Some insomniacs cannot reliably determine how much sleep they have had or how well they have slept.

20. Advertisement: The Country Classic is the only kind of car in its class that offers an antilock braking system that includes TrackAid. An antilock braking system keeps your wheels from locking up during hard braking, and TrackAid keeps your rear wheels from spinning on slippery surfaces. So if you are a safety-conscious person in the market for a car in this class, the Country Classic is the only car for you.

The advertisement is misleading if which one of the following is true?

(A) All of the cars that are in the same class as the Country Classic offer some kind of antilock braking system.
(B) Most kinds of cars that are in the same class as the Country Classic are manufactured by the same company that manufactures the Country Classic.
(C) Without an antilock braking system, the wheels of the Country Classic and other cars in its class are more likely to lock up during hard braking than they are to spin on slippery surfaces.
(D) Other cars in the same class as the Country Classic offer an antilock braking system that uses a method other than TrackAid to prevent rear wheels from spinning on slippery surfaces.
(E) The Country Classic is more expensive than any other car in its class.

21. Sociologist: Traditional norms in our society prevent sincerity by requiring one to ignore unpleasant realities and tell small lies. But a community whose members do not trust one another cannot succeed. So, if a community is to succeed, its members must be willing to face unpleasant realities and speak about them honestly.

The sociologist's conclusion follows logically if which one of the following is assumed?

(A) Sincerity is required if community members are to trust each other.
(B) The more sincere and open community members are, the more likely that community is to succeed.
(C) A community sometimes can succeed even if its members subscribe to traditional norms.
(D) Unless a community's members are willing to face unpleasant realities, they cannot be sincere.
(E) A community's failure is often caused by its members' unwillingness to face unpleasant realities and to discuss them honestly.

GO ON TO THE NEXT PAGE.

22. If there is an election, you can either vote or not. If you vote, you have the satisfaction of knowing you influenced the results of the election; if you do not vote, you have no right to complain about the results. So, following an election, either you will have the satisfaction of knowing you influenced its results or you will have no right to complain.

The reasoning in which one of the following most closely resembles that in the argument above?

(A) When you rent a car, you can either take out insurance or not. If you take out insurance you are covered, but if you are uninsured, you are personally liable for any costs incurred from an accident. So in case of an accident, you will be better off if you are insured.

(B) If you go for a walk, when you are finished either you will feel relaxed or you will not. If you feel relaxed, then your muscles will likely not be sore the next day, though your muscles will more likely become conditioned faster if they do feel sore. Therefore, either your muscles will feel sore, or they will become better conditioned.

(C) If you attend school, you will find the courses stimulating or you will not. If your teachers are motivated, you will find the courses stimulating. If your teachers are not motivated, you will not. So either your teachers are motivated, or their courses are not stimulating.

(D) If you use a computer, its messages are either easily readable or not. If the messages are easily readable, they are merely password protected. If they are not easily readable, they are electronically encrypted. So any message on the computer you use is either password protected or electronically encrypted.

(E) When manufacturers use a natural resource, they are either efficient or inefficient. If they are inefficient, the resource will be depleted quickly. If they are efficient, the resource will last much longer. So either manufacturers are efficient or they should be fined.

23. Company president: Our consultants report that, in general, the most efficient managers have excellent time management skills. Thus, to improve productivity I recommend that we make available to our middle-level managers a seminar to train them in techniques of time management.

Each of the following, if true, would weaken the support for the company president's recommendation EXCEPT:

(A) The consultants use the same criteria to evaluate managers' efficiency as they do to evaluate their time management skills.

(B) Successful time management is more dependent on motivation than on good technique.

(C) Most managers at other companies who have attended time management seminars are still unproductive.

(D) Most managers who are already efficient do not need to improve their productivity.

(E) Most managers who are efficient have never attended a time management seminar.

24. Many Seychelles warblers of breeding age forgo breeding, remaining instead with their parents and helping to raise their own siblings. This behavior, called cooperative breeding, results from the scarcity of nesting territory for the birds on the tiny island that, until recently, was home to the world's population of Seychelles warblers. Yet when healthy warblers were transplanted to a much larger neighboring island as part of an experiment, most of those warblers maintained a pattern of cooperative breeding.

Which one of the following, if true, most helps to explain the result of the experiment?

(A) Many of the Seychelles warblers that were transplanted to the neighboring island had not yet reached breeding age.

(B) The climate of the island to which Seychelles warblers were transplanted was the same as that of the warblers' native island.

(C) Most of the terrain on the neighboring island was not of the type in which Seychelles warblers generally build their nests.

(D) Cooperative breeding in species other than the Seychelles warbler often results when the environment cannot sustain a rise in the population.

(E) The Seychelles warblers had fewer competitors for nesting territory on the island to which they were transplanted than on their native island.

GO ON TO THE NEXT PAGE.

25. Therapist: In a recent study, researchers measured how quickly 60 different psychological problems waned as a large, diverse sample of people underwent weekly behavioral therapy sessions. About 75 percent of the 60 problems consistently cleared up within 50 weeks of therapy. This shows that 50 weekly behavioral therapy sessions are all that most people need.

The therapist's argument is logically most vulnerable to criticism on the grounds that it

(A) takes for granted that there are no psychological problems that usually take significantly longer to clear up than the 60 psychological problems studied

(B) fails to address the possibility that any given one of the 60 psychological problems studied might afflict most people

(C) takes for granted that no one suffers from more than one of the 60 psychological problems studied

(D) fails to address the possibility that some forms of therapy have never been proven to be effective as treatments for psychological problems

(E) takes for granted that the sample of people studied did not have significantly more psychological problems, on average, than the population as a whole

26. Researcher: It is commonly believed that species belonging to the same biological order, such as rodents, descended from a single common ancestor. However, I compared the genetic pattern in 3 rodent species—guinea pigs, rats, and mice—as well as in 13 nonrodent mammals, and found that while rats and mice are genetically quite similar, the genetic differences between guinea pigs and mice are as great as those between mice and some nonrodent species. Thus, despite their similar physical form, guinea pigs stem from a separate ancestor.

Which one of the following, if true, most seriously undermines the researcher's reasoning?

(A) The researcher examined the genetic material of only 3 of over 2,000 species of rodents.

(B) Some pairs of species not having a common ancestor are genetically more similar to each other than are some pairs that do have a common ancestor.

(C) The researcher selected nonrodent species that have the specific cell structures she wanted to analyze genetically, though many nonrodent mammals lack these cell structures.

(D) For some genuine biological orders, the most recent common ancestor dates from later epochs than does the most recent common ancestor of other biological orders.

(E) Peculiarities of body structure, such as distinctive teeth and olfactory structures, are shared by all rodents, including guinea pigs.

S T O P

IF YOU FINISH BEFORE TIME IS CALLED, YOU MAY CHECK YOUR WORK ON THIS SECTION ONLY.
DO NOT WORK ON ANY OTHER SECTION IN THE TEST.

Acknowledgment is made to the following sources from which material has been adapted for use in this test booklet:

Natalie Angier, "Heads or Tails? How Embryos Get It Right." ©1995 by The New York Times.

Catherine Bell, "Aboriginal Claims to Cultural Property in Canada: A Comparative Legal Analysis of the Repatriation Debate."
   © 1992 by the American Indian Law Review.

Louise Glück, *Proofs & Theories: Essays on Poetry*. ©1994 by Louise Glück.

"Why Bad Hair Days May Not Matter." ©1996 by Sussex Publishers Inc.

**Wait for the supervisor's instructions before you open the page to the topic.
Please print and sign your name and write the date in the designated spaces below.**

Time: 35 Minutes

General Directions

You will have 35 minutes in which to plan and write an essay on the topic inside. Read the topic and the accompanying directions carefully. You will probably find it best to spend a few minutes considering the topic and organizing your thoughts before you begin writing. In your essay, be sure to develop your ideas fully, leaving time, if possible, to review what you have written. **Do not write on a topic other than the one specified. Writing on a topic of your own choice is not acceptable.**

No special knowledge is required or expected for this writing exercise. Law schools are interested in the reasoning, clarity, organization, language usage, and writing mechanics displayed in your essay. How well you write is more important than how much you write.

Confine your essay to the blocked, lined area on the front and back of the separate Writing Sample Response Sheet. Only that area will be reproduced for law schools. Be sure that your writing is legible.

Both this topic sheet and your response sheet must be turned over to the testing staff before you leave the room.

Topic Code	Print Your Full Name Here		
_____	Last	First	M.I.

Date	Sign Your Name Here
/ /	

Scratch Paper
Do not write your essay in this space.

LSAT Writing Sample Topic

The owner of Avanti Pizza, which currently makes pizzas for pickup or delivery only, is considering expanding his business. He can either purchase a brick pizza oven or he can add a small dining room to his restaurant. Write an essay in which you argue for one option over the other, keeping in mind the following two criteria:

- Avanti's owner wants to increase profits by offering customers something of value that Avanti does not currently provide.
- Avanti's owner wants to distinguish his restaurant from local competitors.

Brick-oven pizza has become extremely popular, and Avanti's owner estimates that including it on the menu would substantially increase takeout and delivery business. The profit margin on such pizzas is higher than on conventional pizzas. In addition, Avanti's pizza chef could use the opportunity to introduce a selection of gourmet pizzas with creative toppings. Avanti's competitors consist of a well-established Italian restaurant, La Stella, and a franchisee of the large pizza delivery chain Pronto. Neither has a brick oven, although La Stella is rumored to be considering the option. The new oven could be up and running two weeks after the start of construction.

Avanti does not currently have space for a dining room, but the adjacent storefront property has recently become available on good lease terms. Obtaining permits and remodeling would take six months to a year, during which time the rest of the business could continue to operate. Avanti's chef would like to expand the menu to include dishes other than pizza, and with an eat-in option for customers she could easily do so. La Stella already offers sit-down dining, but in a relatively formal setting. Avanti could be more relaxed and family-friendly. In addition, Avanti could allow patrons to bring their own wine or beer, which would attract economy-minded customers. La Stella, which has a liquor license and a full bar, charges a substantial markup on all alcoholic beverages it serves.

Scratch Paper
Do not write your essay in this space.

LAST NAME (Print)

MI

FIRST NAME (Print)

SIGNATURE

Writing Sample Response Sheet

DO NOT WRITE
IN THIS SPACE

**Begin your essay in the lined area below.
Continue on the back if you need more space.**

Directions:

1. Use the Answer Key on the next page to check your answers.

2. Use the Scoring Worksheet below to compute your raw score.

3. Use the Score Conversion Chart to convert your raw score into the 120–180 scale.

Scoring Worksheet

1. Enter the number of questions you answered correctly in each section

	Number Correct
SECTION I	_____
SECTION II	__EXP__
SECTION III	_____
SECTION IV	_____
SECTION V	_____

2. Enter the sum here: _____
   This is your Raw Score.

Conversion Chart

For Converting Raw Score to the 120–180 LSAT Scaled Score
LSAT PrepTest 48

Reported Score	Raw Score Lowest	Raw Score Highest
180	100	101
179	—*	—*
178	99	99
177	98	98
176	—*	—*
175	97	97
174	96	96
173	—*	—*
172	95	95
171	94	94
170	93	93
169	92	92
168	90	91
167	89	89
166	88	88
165	86	87
164	85	85
163	83	84
162	81	82
161	80	80
160	78	79
159	76	77
158	74	75
157	72	73
156	70	71
155	68	69
154	66	67
153	64	65
152	62	63
151	60	61
150	58	59
149	56	57
148	54	55
147	52	53
146	50	51
145	49	49
144	47	48
143	45	46
142	43	44
141	41	42
140	39	40
139	38	38
138	36	37
137	34	35
136	33	33
135	31	32
134	30	30
133	29	29
132	27	28
131	26	26
130	25	25
129	23	24
128	22	22
127	21	21
126	20	20
125	19	19
124	18	18
123	17	17
122	16	16
121	15	15
120	0	14

*There is no raw score that will produce this scaled score for this test.

SECTION I

1.	D	8.	C	15.	A	22.	E
2.	D	9.	D	16.	D	23.	E
3.	C	10.	D	17.	E	24.	E
4.	B	11.	E	18.	D	25.	C
5.	A	12.	B	19.	B	26.	A
6.	A	13.	C	20.	E		
7.	C	14.	D	21.	B		

SECTION II (experimental)

1.	A	8.	A	15.	D	22.	C
2.	D	9.	C	16.	B	23.	E
3.	D	10.	C	17.	E	24.	B
4.	E	11.	C	18.	E	25.	E
5.	E	12.	B	19.	C	26.	C
6.	C	13.	E	20.	B	27.	C
7.	D	14.	B	21.	A		

SECTION III

1.	C	8.	B	15.	D	22.	B
2.	E	9.	C	16.	C		
3.	E	10.	E	17.	C		
4.	A	11.	D	18.	A		
5.	A	12.	E	19.	A		
6.	A	13.	C	20.	A		
7.	C	14.	A	21.	D		

SECTION IV

1.	A	8.	C	15.	E	22.	D
2.	D	9.	A	16.	D	23.	A
3.	E	10.	C	17.	D	24.	E
4.	B	11.	E	18.	A	25.	A
5.	C	12.	D	19.	C	26.	E
6.	D	13.	B	20.	C	27.	B
7.	E	14.	C	21.	C		

SECTION V

1.	C	8.	B	15.	D	22.	D
2.	E	9.	A	16.	C	23.	D
3.	D	10.	E	17.	C	24.	C
4.	B	11.	D	18.	E	25.	B
5.	B	12.	B	19.	D	26.	B
6.	A	13.	A	20.	D		
7.	C	14.	D	21.	A		

Endurance Practice Test 8

PrepTest 46 plus experimental
from PrepTest 4, Section I

SCAN CODE: LL9008

SECTION I

Time—35 minutes

27 Questions

<u>Directions:</u> Each passage in this section is followed by a group of questions to be answered on the basis of what is <u>stated</u> or <u>implied</u> in the passage. For some of the questions, more than one of the choices could conceivably answer the question. However, you are to choose the <u>best</u> answer; that is, the response that most accurately and completely answers the question, and blacken the corresponding space on your answer sheet.

Economists have long defined prosperity in terms of monetary value, gauging a given nation's prosperity solely on the basis of the total monetary value of the goods and services produced annually.
(5) However, critics point out that defining prosperity solely as a function of monetary value is questionable since it fails to recognize other kinds of values, such as quality of life or environmental health, that contribute directly to prosperity in a broader sense.
(10) For example, as the earth's ozone layer weakens and loses its ability to protect people from ultraviolet radiation, sales of hats, sunglasses, and sunscreens are likely to skyrocket, all adding to the nation's total expenditures. In this way, troubling reductions in
(15) environmental health and quality of life may in fact initiate economic activity that, by the economists' measure, bolsters prosperity.

It can also happen that communities seeking to increase their prosperity as measured strictly in
(20) monetary terms may damage their quality of life and their environment. The situation of one rural community illustrates this point: residents of the community value the local timber industry as a primary source of income, and they vocally protested
(25) proposed limitations on timber harvests as a threat to their prosperity. Implicitly adopting the economists' point of view, the residents argued that the harvest limitations would lower their wages or even cause the loss of jobs.
(30) But critics of the economists' view argue that this view of the situation overlooks a crucial consideration. Without the harvest limitations, they say, the land on which the community depends would be seriously damaged. Moreover, they point out that the residents
(35) themselves cite the abundance of natural beauty as one of the features that make their community a highly desirable place to live. But it is also extremely poor, and the critics point out that the residents could double their incomes by moving only 150 kilometers
(40) away. From their decision not to do so, the critics conclude that their location has substantial monetary value to them. The community will thus lose much more—even understood in monetary terms—if the proposed harvest limits are not implemented.
(45) Economists respond by arguing that to be a useful concept, prosperity must be defined in easily quantifiable terms, and that prosperity thus should not include difficult-to-measure values such as happiness or environmental health. But this position dodges the
(50) issue—emphasizing ease of calculation causes one to

disregard substantive issues that directly influence real prosperity. The economists' stance is rather like that of a literary critic who takes total sales to be the best measure of a book's value—true, the number of
(55) copies sold is a convenient and quantifiable measure, but it is a poor substitute for an accurate appraisal of literary merit.

1.   Which one of the following most accurately states the main point of the passage?

(A)   According to critics, communities that seek to increase their prosperity recognize the need to gauge the value and ensure the long-term health of their local environment.

(B)   Economists' definition of prosperity strictly in terms of monetary value is too narrow to truly capture our ordinary conception of this notion.

(C)   If economists were to alter and expand their definition of prosperity, it is likely that the economic and environmental health of most communities would appear worse under the new definition than under the old definition.

(D)   In contrast with the views of economists, some critics believe that prosperity can be neither scientifically measured nor accurately defined, and as a concept is therefore of little use for economists.

(E)   While they are generally an accurate and practical measure of current economic prosperity, figures for the total expenditures of a nation do not aid in providing an indication of that nation's future economic prospects.

GO ON TO THE NEXT PAGE.

2. The example in the passage of the timber industry and its effect on a poor rural community suggests that the critics would most likely agree with which one of the following statements?

    (A) Harvest limitations have little relationship to lower wages or fewer jobs in the community.

    (B) Harvest limitations should be imposed only when the limitations have wide public support in the community.

    (C) The advantages to the community that would be created by harvest limitations are likely to outweigh the disadvantages.

    (D) Communities protest harvest limitations primarily because they do not understand the long-term monetary impact of such regulation.

    (E) It is the arguments of economists that often cause residents of rural communities to view harvest limitations more negatively.

3. Based on the information in the passage, the author would be most likely to agree with which one of the following statements regarding the weakening of the earth's ozone layer?

    (A) Paradoxically, the weakening of the ozone layer actually contributes to environmental health and quality of life.

    (B) The environmental effects of this problem are likely to occur more gradually than the economic effects.

    (C) The appearance of prosperity that results from this problem has directed attention away from solving it.

    (D) This problem should be regarded primarily as threatening rather than contributing to true prosperity.

    (E) This problem has resulted in part from the failure of economists to recognize it in its formative stages.

4. According to the passage, economists defend their concept of prosperity in which one of the following ways?

    (A) by claiming that alternative definitions of the concept would not be easily quantifiable

    (B) by asserting that environmental preservation can cause the loss of jobs

    (C) by citing the relevance of nonmonetary values such as environmental health

    (D) by showing that the value of natural beauty can be understood in quantifiable terms

    (E) by detailing the historical development of their definition of the concept

5. The author compares the economists' position to that of a literary critic (lines 52–57) primarily to

    (A) introduce the idea that the assessment of worth is basically subjective

    (B) advocate an innovative method of measuring literary merit

    (C) suggest that quality of life is mainly an aesthetic issue

    (D) provide additional evidence that prosperity cannot be quantified

    (E) illustrate the limitations of the economists' position

6. In the passage, the author cites which one of the following claims?

    (A) that hats, sunglasses, and sunscreens provide an adequate substitute for the ozone layer

    (B) that environmental protection measures are unpopular and often rejected by communities

    (C) that the value of a locale's environment can be gauged by the incomes of its residents

    (D) that timber harvest limits are needed to save one area from environmental damage

    (E) that most nations measure their own prosperity in terms broader than monetary value

7. The primary purpose of the passage is to

    (A) argue that there is an inherent and potentially detrimental conflict between two schools of thought concerning a certain concept

    (B) summarize and illustrate the main points of the conflict between two schools of thought over the definition of a certain concept

    (C) question one school of thought's definition of a certain concept and suggest several possible alternative definitions

    (D) criticize one school of thought's definition of a certain concept by providing examples that illustrate the implications of adhering to this definition

    (E) bring one school of thought's perspective to bear on a concept traditionally considered to be the exclusive territory of another school of thought

GO ON TO THE NEXT PAGE.

Joy Kogawa's *Obasan* is an account of a
Japanese-Canadian family's experiences during World
War II. The events are seen froπm the viewpoint of a
young girl who watches her family disintegrate as it
(5) undergoes the relocation that occurred in both Canada
and the United States. Although the experience
depicted in *Obasan* is mainly one of dislocation,
Kogawa employs subtle techniques that serve to
emphasize her major character's heroism and to
(10) critique the majority culture. The former end is
achieved through the novel's form and the latter
through the symbols it employs.

The form of the novel parallels the three-stage
structure noted by anthropologists in their studies of
(15) rites of passage. According to these anthropologists, a
rite of passage begins with separation from a position
of security in a highly structured society; proceeds to
alienation in a deathlike state where one is stripped of
status, property, and rank; and concludes with
(20) reintegration into society accompanied by a
heightened status gained as a result of the second
stage. The process thus has the effect of transforming
a society's victim into a hero. The first eleven
chapters of *Obasan* situate the young protagonist
(25) Naomi Nakane in a close-knit, securely placed family
within Vancouver society. Chapters 12–32 chronicle
the fall into alienation, when Naomi's family is
dislodged from its structured social niche and
removed from the city into work camps or exile.
(30) Separated from her parents, Naomi follows her aunt
Aya Obasan to the ghost town of Slocan, where
Naomi joins the surrogate family of her uncle and
aunt. In chapters 33–39 this surrogate family nurtures
Naomi as she develops toward a final integration with
(35) the larger society and with herself: as an adult, when
she receives a bundle of family documents and letters
from her aunt, Naomi breaks through the personal
and cultural screens of silence and secretiveness that
have enshrouded her past, and reconciles herself with
(40) her history.

Kogawa's use of motifs drawn from Christian
rituals and symbols forms a subtle critique of the
professed ethics of the majority culture that has
shunned Naomi. In one example of such symbolism,
(45) Naomi's reacquaintance with her past is compared
with the biblical story of turning stone into bread.
The bundle of documents—which Kogawa refers to
as "stone-hard facts"—brings Naomi to the
recognition of her country's abuse of her people. But
(50) implicit in these hard facts, Kogawa suggests, is also
the "bread" of a spiritual sustenance that will allow
Naomi to affirm the durability of her people and
herself. Through the careful deployment of structure
and symbol, Kogawa thus manages to turn Naomi's
(55) experience—and by extension the wartime
experiences of many Japanese Canadians—into a
journey of heroic transformation and a critique of the
majority culture.

8. Which one of the following most accurately states the
main idea of the passage?

(A) While telling a story of familial disruption,
Obasan uses structure and symbolism to valorize
its protagonist and critique the majority culture.
(B) By means of its structure and symbolism, *Obasan*
mounts a harsh critique of a society that disrupts
its citizens' lives.
(C) Although intended primarily as social criticism,
given its structure *Obasan* can also be read as a
tale of heroic transformation.
(D) With its three-part structure that parallels rites
of passage, *Obasan* manages to valorize its
protagonist in spite of her traumatic experiences.
(E) Although intended primarily as a story of heroic
transformation, *Obasan* can also be read as a
work of social criticism.

9. Item removed from scoring.

GO ON TO THE NEXT PAGE.

10. Which one of the following most accurately describes the organization of the passage?

(A) Two points are made about a novel, the first supported with a brief example, the second reasserted without support.

(B) Two points are made about a novel, the first supported with an extended analogy, the second reasserted without support.

(C) Two points are made about a novel, the first reasserted without support, the second supported with an extended analogy.

(D) Two points are made about a novel, the first supported with a brief example, the second supported with an extended analogy.

(E) Two points are made about a novel, the first supported with an extended analogy, the second supported with a brief example.

11. It can be inferred that the heroism Naomi gains in the course of *Obasan* is manifested in her

(A) reconciliation with her past
(B) careful deployment of structure and symbol
(C) relationship with her surrogate family
(D) renewal of her religious beliefs
(E) denunciation of the majority culture

12. According to the anthropologists cited by the author, rites of passage are best described by which one of the following sequences of stages?

(A) alienation, dislocation, integration
(B) separation, alienation, reintegration
(C) integration, alienation, disintegration
(D) dislocation, reconciliation, reintegration
(E) disintegration, transformation, reintegration

13. According to the passage, the agent of Naomi's reconciliation with her past is

(A) her reunion with her parents
(B) the exile of her parents
(C) her critique of the majority society
(D) her separation from her aunt and uncle
(E) her receipt of documents and letters

14. The passage suggests that Joy Kogawa believes which one of the following about the society that shuns Naomi?

(A) It discouraged its citizens from seeking out their heritage.
(B) It endeavored to thwart its citizens' attempts at heroic transformation.
(C) It violated its own supposed religious ethics by doing so.
(D) It prohibited its citizens from participating in rites of passage.
(E) It demanded that loyalty to the government replace loyalty to the family.

15. Based on the passage, which one of the following aspects of Kogawa's work does the author of the passage appear to value most highly?

(A) her willingness to make political statements
(B) her imaginative development of characters
(C) her subtle use of literary techniques
(D) her knowledge of Christian rituals and symbols
(E) her objectivity in describing Naomi's tragic life

GO ON TO THE NEXT PAGE.

The pronghorn, an antelope-like mammal that lives on the western plains of North America, is the continent's fastest land animal, capable of running 90 kilometers per hour and of doing so for several
(5) kilometers. Because no North American predator is nearly fast enough to chase it down, biologists have had difficulty explaining why the pronghorn developed its running prowess. One biologist, however, has recently claimed that pronghorns run as
(10) fast as they do because of adaptation to predators known from fossil records to have been extinct for 10,000 years, such as American cheetahs and long-legged hyenas, either of which, it is believed, were fast enough to run down the pronghorn.
(15) Like all explanations that posit what is called a relict behavior—a behavior that persists though its only evolutionary impetus comes from long-extinct environmental conditions—this one is likely to meet with skepticism. Most biologists distrust explanations positing relict
(20) behaviors, in part because testing these hypotheses is so difficult due to the extinction of a principal component. They typically consider such historical explanations only when a lack of alternatives forces them to do so. But present-day observations sometimes yield
(25) evidence that supports relict behavior hypotheses.
In the case of the pronghorn, researchers have identified much supporting evidence, as several aspects of pronghorn behavior appear to have been shaped by enemies that no longer exist. For example,
(30) pronghorns—like many other grazing animals—roam in herds, which allows more eyes to watch for predators and diminishes the chances of any particular animal being attacked but can also result in overcrowding and increased competition for food. But, since
(35) pronghorns have nothing to fear from present-day carnivores and thus have nothing to gain from herding, their herding behavior appears to be another adaptation to extinct threats. Similarly, if speed and endurance were once essential to survival, researchers would
(40) expect pronghorns to choose mates based on these athletic abilities, which they do—with female pronghorns, for example, choosing the victor after male pronghorns challenge each other in sprints and chases.
Relict behaviors appear to occur in other animals
(45) as well, increasing the general plausibility of such a theory. For example, one study reports relict behavior in stickleback fish belonging to populations that have long been free of a dangerous predator, the sculpin. In the study, when presented with sculpin, these
(50) stickleback fish immediately engaged in stereotypical antisculpin behavior, avoiding its mouth and swimming behind to bite it. Another study found that ground squirrels from populations that have been free from snakes for 70,000 to 300,000 years still clearly recognize
(55) rattlesnakes, displaying stereotypical antirattlesnake behavior in the presence of the snake. Such fear, however, apparently does not persist interminably. Arctic ground squirrels, free of snakes for about 3 million years, appear to be unable to recognize the threat of a rattlesnake, exhibiting only disorganized caution even after being bitten repeatedly.

16. Which one of the following most accurately states the main point of the passage?

(A) Evidence from present-day animal behaviors, together with the fossil record, supports the hypothesis that the pronghorn's ability to far outrun any predator currently on the North American continent is an adaptation to predators long extinct.

(B) Although some biologists believe that certain animal characteristics, such as the speed of the pronghorn, are explained by environmental conditions that have not existed for many years, recent data concerning arctic ground squirrels make this hypothesis doubtful.

(C) Research into animal behavior, particularly into that of the pronghorn, provides strong evidence that most present-day characteristics of animals are explained by environmental conditions that have not existed for many years.

(D) Even in those cases in which an animal species displays characteristics clearly explained by long-vanished environmental conditions, evidence concerning arctic ground squirrels suggests that those characteristics will eventually disappear.

(E) Although biologists are suspicious of hypotheses that are difficult to test, there is now widespread agreement among biologists that many types of animal characteristics are best explained as adaptations to long-extinct predators.

17. Based on the passage, the term "principal component" (line 21) most clearly refers to which one of the following?

(A) behavior that persists even though the conditions that provided its evolutionary impetus are extinct

(B) the original organism whose descendants' behavior is being investigated as relict behavior

(C) the pronghorn's ability to run 90 kilometers per hour over long distances

(D) the environmental conditions in response to which relict behaviors are thought to have developed

(E) an original behavior of an animal of which certain present-day behaviors are thought to be modifications

GO ON TO THE NEXT PAGE.

18. The last paragraph most strongly supports which one of the following statements?

    (A) An absence of predators in an animal's environment can constitute just as much of a threat to the well-being of that animal as the presence of predators.
    (B) Relict behaviors are found in most wild animals living today.
    (C) If a behavior is an adaptation to environmental conditions, it may eventually disappear in the absence of those or similar conditions.
    (D) Behavior patterns that originated as a way of protecting an organism against predators will persist interminably if they are periodically reinforced.
    (E) Behavior patterns invariably take longer to develop than they do to disappear.

19. Which one of the following describes a benefit mentioned in the passage that grazing animals derive from roaming in herds?

    (A) The greater density of animals tends to intimidate potential predators.
    (B) The larger number of adults in a herd makes protection of the younger animals from predators much easier.
    (C) With many animals searching it is easier for the herd to find food and water.
    (D) The likelihood that any given individual will be attacked by a predator decreases.
    (E) The most defenseless animals can achieve greater safety by remaining in the center of the herd.

20. The passage mentions each of the following as support for the explanation of the pronghorn's speed proposed by the biologist referred to in line 8 EXCEPT:

    (A) fossils of extinct animals believed to have been able to run down a pronghorn
    (B) the absence of carnivores in the pronghorn's present-day environment
    (C) the present-day preference of pronghorns for athletic mates
    (D) the apparent need for a similar explanation to account for the herding behavior pronghorns now display
    (E) the occurrence of relict behavior in other species

21. The third paragraph of the passage provides the most support for which one of the following inferences?

    (A) Predators do not attack grazing animals that are assembled into herds.
    (B) Pronghorns tend to graze in herds only when they sense a threat from predators close by.
    (C) If animals do not graze for their food, they do not roam in herds.
    (D) Female pronghorns mate only with the fastest male pronghorn in the herd.
    (E) If pronghorns did not herd, they would not face significantly greater danger from present-day carnivores.

GO ON TO THE NEXT PAGE.

Many legal theorists have argued that the only morally legitimate goal in imposing criminal penalties against certain behaviors is to prevent people from harming others. Clearly, such theorists would oppose
(5) laws that force people to act purely for their own good or to refrain from certain harmless acts purely to ensure conformity to some social norm. But the goal of preventing harm to others would also justify legal sanctions against some forms of nonconforming
(10) behavior to which this goal might at first seem not to apply.

In many situations it is in the interest of each member of a group to agree to behave in a certain way on the condition that the others similarly agree.
(15) In the simplest cases, a mere coordination of activities is itself the good that results. For example, it is in no one's interest to lack a convention about which side of the road to drive on, and each person can agree to drive on one side assuming the others do
(20) too. Any fair rule, then, would be better than no rule at all. On the assumption that all people would voluntarily agree to be subject to a coordination rule backed by criminal sanctions, if people could be assured that others would also agree, it is argued to
(25) be legitimate for a legislature to impose such a rule. This is because prevention of harm underlies the rationale for the rule, though it applies to the problem of coordination less directly than to other problems, for the act that is forbidden (driving on the other side
(30) of the road) is not inherently harm-producing, as are burglary and assault; instead, it is the lack of a coordinating rule that would be harmful.

In some other situations involving a need for legally enforced coordination, the harm to be averted
(35) goes beyond the simple lack of coordination itself. This can be illustrated by an example of a coordination rule—instituted by a private athletic organization—which has analogies in criminal law. At issue is whether the use of anabolic steroids, which
(40) build muscular strength but have serious negative side effects, should be prohibited. Each athlete has at stake both an interest in having a fair opportunity to win and an interest in good health. If some competitors use steroids, others have the option of either
(45) endangering their health or losing their fair opportunity to win. Thus they would be harmed either way. A compulsory rule could prevent that harm and thus would be in the interest of all competitors. If they understand its function and trust the techniques
(50) for its enforcement, they will gladly consent to it. So while it might appear that such a rule merely forces people to act for their own good, the deeper rationale for coercion here—as in the above example—is a somewhat complex appeal to the legitimacy of
(55) enforcing a rule with the goal of preventing harm.

22. Which one of the following most accurately states the main point of the passage?

(A) In order to be morally justifiable, laws prohibiting activities that are not inherently harm-producing must apply equitably to everyone.
(B) It is justifiable to require social conformity where noncompliance would be harmful to either the nonconforming individual or the larger group.
(C) Achieving coordination can be argued to be a morally legitimate justification for rules that prevent directly harmful actions and others that prevent indirectly harmful actions.
(D) It is reasonable to hold that restricting individual liberty is always justified on the basis of mutually agreed-upon community standards.
(E) The principle of preventing harm to others can be used to justify laws that do not at first glance appear to be designed to prevent such harm.

23. It can be most reasonably inferred from the passage that the author considers which one of the following factors to be generally necessary for the justification of rules compelling coordination of people's activities?

(A) evidence that such rules do not force individuals to act for their own good
(B) enactment of such rules by a duly elected or appointed government lawmaking organization
(C) the assurance that criminal penalties are provided as a means of securing compliance with such rules
(D) some form of consent on the part of rational people who are subject to such rules
(E) a sense of community and cultural uniformity among those who are required to abide by such rules

GO ON TO THE NEXT PAGE.

24. It can be most reasonably inferred from the passage that the author would agree with which one of the following statements?

(A) In all situations in which compulsory rules are needed for the coordination of human activities, any uniformly enforced rule is as acceptable as any other.

(B) No private organizational rules designed to coordinate the activities of members have as complex a relation to the goal of preventing harm as have some criminal statutes.

(C) Every fair rule that could be effectively used to prescribe which side of the road to drive on is a rule whose implementation would likely cause less harm than it would prevent.

(D) There would be little need for formal regulation and enforcement of conventional driving patterns if all drivers understood and accepted the rationale behind such regulation and enforcement.

(E) Unlike rules forbidding such acts as burglary and assault, those that are designed primarily to prevent the inconvenience and chaos of uncoordinated activities should not involve criminal penalties.

25. The author distinguishes between two examples of coordinating rules on the basis of whether or not such rules

(A) prevent some harm beyond that which consists simply in a lack of coordination

(B) are intended to ensure conformity to a set of agreed-upon standards

(C) are voluntarily agreed upon by all those affected by such rules

(D) could be considered justifiable by the legal theorists discussed in the passage

(E) apply less directly to the problem of preventing harm than do rules against burglary and assault

26. Which one of the following is a rule that primarily addresses a problem of coordination most similar to that discussed in the second paragraph?

(A) a rule requiring that those who wish to dig for ancient artifacts secure the permission of relevant authorities and the owners of the proposed site before proceeding with their activities

(B) a rule requiring that pharmacists dispense certain kinds of medications only when directed to do so by physicians' prescriptions, rather than simply selling medicines at the customers' request

(C) a rule requiring that advertisers be able to substantiate the claims they make in advertisements, rather than simply saying whatever they think will help to attract customers

(D) a rule requiring that employees of a certain restaurant all wear identical uniforms during their hours of employment, rather than wearing whatever clothes they choose

(E) a rule requiring different aircraft to fly at different altitudes rather than flying at any altitude their pilots wish

27. In line 54, the author uses the expression "somewhat complex" primarily to describe reasoning that

(A) involves two layers of law, one governing the private sector and the other governing the public sector

(B) requires that those affected by the rule understand the motivation behind its imposition

(C) involves a case in which a harm to be prevented is indirectly related to the kind of act that is to be prohibited

(D) can convince athletes that their health is as important as their competitive success

(E) illustrates how appeals to the need for coordination can be used to justify many rules that do not involve coordination

S T O P

IF YOU FINISH BEFORE TIME IS CALLED, YOU MAY CHECK YOUR WORK ON THIS SECTION ONLY.
DO NOT WORK ON ANY OTHER SECTION IN THE TEST.

SECTION II

Time—35 minutes

25 Questions

Directions: The questions in this section are based on the reasoning contained in brief statements or passages. For some questions, more than one of the choices could conceivably answer the question. However, you are to choose the best answer; that is, the response that most accurately and completely answers the question. You should not make assumptions that are by commonsense standards implausible, superfluous, or incompatible with the passage. After you have chosen the best answer, blacken the corresponding space on your answer sheet.

1. Cox: The consumer council did not provide sufficient justification for its action when it required that Derma-35 be recalled from the market.

    Crockett: I disagree. Derma-35 in fact causes inflammation, but in citing only the side effect of blemishes as the justification for its decision, the council rightly acknowledged that blemishes are a legitimate health concern.

    Cox and Crockett disagree over whether

    (A)   Derma-35 should remain on the market
    (B)   blemishes are sometimes caused by inflammation
    (C)   the council based its decision on the threat of inflammation or on the threat of blemishes
    (D)   the council gave an adequate reason for its decision to recall Derma-35
    (E)   inflammation is a serious health threat

2. Literary historian: William Shakespeare, a humble actor, could have written the love poetry attributed to him. But the dramas attributed to him evince such insight into the minds of powerful rulers that they could only have been written by one who had spent much time among them; Francis Bacon associated with rulers, but Shakespeare did not.

    Which one of the following logically follows from the literary historian's claims?

    (A)   Bacon wrote the dramas attributed to Shakespeare, but could not have written the love poetry.
    (B)   Bacon wrote both the love poetry and the dramas attributed to Shakespeare.
    (C)   Shakespeare wrote neither the love poetry nor the dramas attributed to him.
    (D)   One person could not have written both the love poetry and the dramas attributed to Shakespeare.
    (E)   Shakespeare may have written the love poetry but did not write the dramas attributed to him.

3. Philosopher: Effective tests have recently been developed to predict fatal diseases having a largely genetic basis. Now, for the first time, a person can be warned well in advance of the possibility of such life-threatening conditions. However, medicine is not yet able to prevent most such conditions. Simply being informed that one will get a disease that is both fatal and incurable can itself be quite harmful to some people. This raises the question of whether such "early warning" tests should be made available at all.

    Which one of the following statements is best illustrated by the state of affairs described by the philosopher?

    (A)   The advance of medicine fails to provide solutions to every problem.
    (B)   The advance of medicine creates new contexts in which ethical dilemmas can arise.
    (C)   Medical technologies continue to advance, increasing our knowledge and understanding of disease.
    (D)   The more we come to learn, the more we realize how little we know.
    (E)   The advance of technology is of questionable value.

GO ON TO THE NEXT PAGE.

4. Chapin: Commentators have noted with concern the recent electoral success by extremist parties in several democratic countries. But these successes pose no threat to democracy in those countries. The extremists have won pluralities, not majorities. Furthermore, they have won only when the moderate parties were preoccupied with arguing among themselves.

Which one of the following, if assumed, enables Chapin's conclusion to be properly drawn?

(A) Parties that win pluralities but not majorities never directly or indirectly effect changes in their country's political arrangements.
(B) Multiparty political systems are always more democratic than two-party political systems are.
(C) Countries in which extremist parties win pluralities sometimes have democratic governments as strong as those in countries that lack extremist parties.
(D) Members of moderate parties who consider extremist parties to be a serious threat to democracy will sometimes put aside their differences with each other to oppose them.
(E) People are not always supporting a move toward an extremist government when they vote for extremist parties in democratic elections.

5. Futurist: Artists in the next century will be supported largely by private patrons. Because these patrons will almost invariably be supporters of the social order—whatever it happens to be at the time—art in the next century will rarely express social and political doctrines that are perceived to be subversive of that social order.

Which one of the following principles, if valid, provides the most support for the futurist's inference?

(A) Art patrons tend not to support artists whose art expresses social and political views that are in opposition to their own.
(B) Art patrons tend to be more interested in formal artistic problems than in the social and political issues of their time.
(C) Artists are as prone to attack the contemporary social and political order in their work as they are to defend it.
(D) Artists tend to become more critical of contemporary social and political arrangements after they are freed of their dependency on private patrons.
(E) Art patrons tend to oppose all social change except that initiated by artists.

6. University budget committee: Athletes experience fewer injuries on artificial-turf athletic fields than on natural-grass fields. Additionally, natural-grass fields are more expensive to maintain than fields made of artificial turf. Nevertheless, this committee recommends replacing the university's current artificial-turf field with a natural-grass field.

Which one of the following, if true, most helps to resolve the apparent discrepancy in the committee's position?

(A) The university's current artificial-turf athletic field has required extensive maintenance since its original installation.
(B) Most injuries sustained on artificial-turf fields take longer to heal and require more expensive physical therapy than do injuries sustained on natural-grass fields.
(C) It is difficult for spectators at athletic events to determine whether an athletic field is artificial turf or natural grass.
(D) Maintaining artificial-turf fields involves the occasional replacement of damaged sections of turf, whereas natural-grass fields require daily watering and periodic fertilization.
(E) Athletes who have spent most of their playing time on natural-grass fields generally prefer not to play on artificial-turf fields.

7. Although instinct enables organisms to make complex responses to stimuli, instinctual behavior involves no reasoning and requires far fewer nerve cells than does noninstinctual (also called flexible) behavior. A brain mechanism capable of flexible behavior must have a large number of neurons, and no insect brain has yet reached a size capable of providing a sufficiently large number of neurons.

Which one of the following can be properly inferred from the statements above?

(A) The behavior of organisms with elaborate brain mechanisms is usually not instinctual.
(B) Insect behavior is exclusively instinctual.
(C) All organisms with brains larger than insects' brains are capable of some measure of flexible behavior.
(D) All organisms with large brains are biologically equipped for flexible behavior.
(E) Only organisms with brains of insect size or smaller engage in purely instinctual behavior.

GO ON TO THE NEXT PAGE.

8. The laboratory experiment, the most effective method for teaching science, is disappearing from most secondary school curricula, and students are now simulating experiments with computers. This trend should be stopped. It results in many students' completing secondary school and going on to a university without knowing how to work with laboratory equipment.

Which one of the following, if true, most weakens the argument?

(A) Scientific knowledge is changing so rapidly it is difficult for secondary schools to keep up without using computers.

(B) In some secondary schools, teachers conduct laboratory experiments while students observe.

(C) Computers have proven to be a valuable tool for teaching secondary school students scientific terminology.

(D) Secondary schools and universities across the nation have put a great deal of money into purchasing computers.

(E) University students can learn science effectively without having had experience in working with laboratory equipment.

9. Alice: In democracies, politicians garner support by emphasizing the differences between their opponents and themselves. Because they must rule in accord with their rhetoric, policies in democracies fluctuate wildly as one party succeeds another.

Elwell: But despite election rhetoric, to put together majority coalitions in democracies, politicians usually end up softening their stands on individual issues once they are elected.

The statements above provide the most support for the claim that Alice and Elwell disagree about whether

(A) politicians heighten the differences between themselves and their opponents during elections

(B) basic policies change drastically when one party succeeds another in a democracy

(C) in a democracy the best way of ensuring continuity in policies is to form a coalition government

(D) most voters stay loyal to a particular political party even as it changes its stand on particular issues

(E) the desire of parties to build majority coalitions tends to support democratic systems

10. Air traffic controllers and nuclear power plant operators are not allowed to work exceptionally long hours, because to do so would jeopardize lives. Yet physicians in residency training are typically required to work 80-hour weeks. The aforementioned restrictions on working exceptionally long hours should also be applied to resident physicians, since they too are engaged in work of a life-or-death nature.

Which one of the following is an assumption the argument depends on?

(A) There is no indispensable aspect of residency training that requires resident physicians to work exceptionally long hours.

(B) Resident physicians have a more direct effect on the lives of others than do air traffic controllers and nuclear power plant operators.

(C) The more hours one works in a week, the less satisfactorily one performs one's work.

(D) Those who are not engaged in work that has life-or-death consequences should only sometimes be allowed to work exceptionally long hours.

(E) Some resident physicians would like to complete their residency training without working exceptionally long hours.

11. Career consultant: The most popular career advice suggests emphasizing one's strengths to employers and downplaying one's weaknesses. Research shows this advice to be incorrect. A study of 314 managers shows that those who use self-deprecating humor in front of their employees are more likely to be seen by them as even-handed, thoughtful, and concerned than are those who do not.

The career consultant's reasoning is most vulnerable to criticism on the grounds that it

(A) bases a conclusion about how one group will respond to self-deprecation on information about how a different group responds to it

(B) ignores the possibility that what was viewed positively in the managers' self-deprecating humor was the self-deprecation and not its humor

(C) ignores the possibility that non-self-deprecating humor might have been viewed even more positively than self-deprecating humor

(D) infers from the fact that self-deprecating humor was viewed positively that nonhumorous self-deprecation would not be viewed positively

(E) bases a conclusion about certain popular career advice on a critique of only one part of that advice

GO ON TO THE NEXT PAGE.

12. Researcher: We studied two groups of subjects over a period of six months. Over this period, one of the groups had a daily routine of afternoon exercise. The other group, the control group, engaged in little or no exercise during the study. It was found that those in the exercise group got 33 percent more deep-sleep at night than did the control group. Exercising in the afternoon tends to raise body temperature slightly until after bedtime, and this extra heat induces deeper sleep.

The researcher's statements, if true, most strongly support which one of the following?

(A) Regular afternoon exercise is one of the things required for adequate deep-sleep.
(B) Exercise in the morning is almost as likely to have as many beneficial effects on sleep as is exercise in the afternoon.
(C) The best way to get increased deep-sleep is to induce a slight increase in body temperature just before bedtime.
(D) No one in the control group experienced a rise in body temperature just before bedtime.
(E) Raising body temperature slightly by taking a warm bath just before bedtime will likely result in increased deep-sleep.

13. Companies wishing to boost sales of merchandise should use in-store displays to catch customers' attention. According to a marketing study, today's busy shoppers have less time for coupon-clipping and pay little attention to direct-mail advertising; instead, they make two-thirds of their buying decisions on the spot at the store.

Which one of the following is an assumption that the argument requires?

(A) Companies are increasingly using in-store displays to catch customers' attention.
(B) Coupons and direct-mail advertising were at one time more effective means of boosting sales of merchandise than they are now.
(C) In-store displays are more likely to influence buying decisions made on the spot at the store than to influence other buying decisions.
(D) In-store displays that catch customers' attention increase the likelihood that customers will decide on the spot to buy the company's merchandise.
(E) Many of today's shoppers are too busy to pay careful attention to in-store displays.

14. Roger Bacon, the thirteenth-century scientist, is said to have made important discoveries in optics. He was an early advocate of hands-on experimentation, and as a teacher warned his students against relying uncritically on the opinions of authorities. Nevertheless, this did not stop Bacon himself from appealing to authority when it was expedient for his own argumentation. Thus, Bacon's work on optics should be generally disregarded, in view of the contradiction between his statements and his own behavior.

The reasoning in the argument is flawed because the argument

(A) presumes, without providing justification, that authority opinion is often incorrect
(B) attacks Bacon's uncritical reliance on authority opinion
(C) uses Bacon's remarks to his students as evidence of his opinions
(D) ignores the fact that thirteenth-century science may not hold up well today
(E) criticizes Bacon's character in order to question his scientific findings

15. One's palate is to a great extent socially determined: that is, if we notice that a lot of people enjoy consuming a certain type of food, we will eventually come to like the food as well, once we have become accustomed to the food.

Which one of the following most closely conforms to the principle above?

(A) Maxine spoke to her neighbor about the many different ways he prepared pasta, and after trying some of his recipes found out that she loves to eat pasta.
(B) Mike dislikes lima beans, due to his having parents who dislike them and few family members who enjoy them.
(C) All of George's Ukrainian relatives love to eat pierogis, and by staying with them for several summers, George has become very fond of pierogis as well.
(D) Yolanda dislikes pickles because she has observed that many of her relatives wince when eating pickles.
(E) Sally found jalapeño peppers to be too hot when she first tried them, but now she can eat them without discomfort, because her family members use them frequently in their cooking.

GO ON TO THE NEXT PAGE.

16. The ability to access information via computer is a tremendous resource for visually impaired people. Only a limited amount of printed information is accessible in braille, large type, or audiotape. But a person with the right hardware and software can access a large quantity of information from libraries and museums around the world, and can have the computer read the information aloud, display it in large type, or produce a braille version. Thus, visually impaired people can now access information from computers more easily than they can from most traditional sources.

Which one of the following, if true, most strengthens the argument?

(A) A computerized speech synthesizer is often less expensive than a complete library of audiotapes.

(B) Relatively easy-to-use computer systems that can read information aloud, display it in large type, or produce a braille version of it are widely available.

(C) Many visually impaired people prefer traditional sources of information to computers that can read information aloud, display it in large type, or produce a braille version of it.

(D) Most visually impaired people who have access to information via computer also have access to this same information via more traditional sources.

(E) The rate at which printed information is converted into formats easily accessible to visually impaired people will increase.

17. Legislator: The recently released crime statistics clearly show that the new laws requiring stiffer punishments for violators have reduced the crime rate. In the areas covered by those laws, the incidence of crime has decreased by one-fourth over the four years since the legislation was enacted.

Analyst: The statistics are welcome news, but they do not provide strong evidence that the new laws caused the drop in crime. Many comparable areas that lack such legislation have reported a similar drop in the crime rate during the same period.

Which one of the following most accurately describes the strategy used by the analyst to call into question the legislator's argument?

(A) pointing out that the legislator has provided no evidence of the reliability of the statistics on which the legislator's conclusion is based

(B) arguing that the legislator has unreasonably concluded that one event has caused another without ruling out the possibility that both events are effects of a common cause

(C) objecting that the statistics on which the legislator is basing his conclusion are drawn from a time period that is too short to yield a meaningful data sample

(D) claiming that the legislator has attempted to establish a particular conclusion because doing so is in the legislator's self-interest rather than because of any genuine concern for the truth of the matter

(E) implying that the legislator has drawn a conclusion about cause and effect without considering how often the alleged effect has occurred in the absence of the alleged cause

GO ON TO THE NEXT PAGE.

18. Many physicists claim that quantum mechanics may ultimately be able to explain all fundamental phenomena, and that, therefore, physical theory will soon be complete. However, every theory in the history of physics that was thought to be final eventually had to be rejected for failure to explain some new observation. For this reason, we can expect that quantum mechanics will not be the final theory.

Which one of the following arguments is most similar in its reasoning to the argument above?

(A) Only a few species of plants now grow in very dry climates; therefore, few species of animals can live in those climates.

(B) Four companies have marketed a new food processing product; therefore, a fifth company will not be able to market a similar product.

(C) Your sister is a very good chess player but she has never won a chess tournament; therefore, she will not win this chess tournament.

(D) A rare virus infected a group of people a decade ago; therefore, it will not reinfect the same population now.

(E) Each team member has failed to live up to people's expectations; therefore, the team will not live up to people's expectations.

19. In an experiment, researchers played a series of musical intervals—two-note sequences—to a large, diverse group of six-month-old babies. They found that the babies paid significantly more attention when the intervals were perfect octaves, fifths, or fourths than otherwise. These intervals are prevalent in the musical systems of most cultures around the world. Thus, humans probably have a biological predisposition to pay more attention to those intervals than to others.

Which one of the following, if true, most strengthens the argument?

(A) Several similar experiments using older children and adults found that these subjects, too, had a general tendency to pay more attention to octaves, fifths, and fourths than to other musical intervals.

(B) None of the babies in the experiment had previous exposure to music from any culture.

(C) All of the babies in the experiment had been exposed to music drawn equally from a wide variety of cultures around the world.

(D) In a second experiment, these same babies showed no clear tendency to notice primary colors more than other colors.

(E) Octaves, fifths, and fourths were played more frequently during the experiment than other musical intervals were.

20. Professor Donnelly's exams are always more difficult than Professor Curtis's exams. The question about dinosaurs was on Professor Donnelly's last exam. Therefore, the question must be difficult.

Which one of the following exhibits both of the logical flaws exhibited in the argument above?

(A) Lewis is a better baker than Stockman. Lewis made this cake. Therefore, it must be better than most of Stockman's cakes.

(B) Porter's new book of poetry is better than any of her other books of poetry. This poem is from Porter's new book, so it must be good.

(C) Professor Whitburn is teaching English this year and always assigns a lot of reading. Therefore, this year's English class will have to do more reading than last year's class.

(D) Shield's first novel has a more complicated plot than any other that she has written. Hence, that plot must be very complex.

(E) Mathematics is more difficult than history. Therefore, my calculus test will be more difficult than my history test.

GO ON TO THE NEXT PAGE.

21. Ethicist: As a function of one's job and societal role, one has various duties. There are situations where acting in accord with one of these duties has disastrous consequences, and thus the duties are not absolute. However, it is a principle of morality that if one does not have overwhelming evidence that fulfilling such a duty will have disastrous consequences, one ought to fulfill it.

Which one of the following most closely conforms to the principle of morality cited by the ethicist?

(A) A teacher thinks that a certain student has received the course grade merited by the quality of his work. The teacher should fulfill her duty not to raise the student's grade, even though the lower grade might harm the student's chance of obtaining an internship.

(B) A person should not fulfill his duty to tell his friend the truth about the friend's new haircut, because lying will make the friend happier than the truth would.

(C) A police investigator discovers that a contractor has slightly overcharged wealthy customers in order to lower rates for a charity. The investigator should not fulfill his duty to report the contractor provided that the contractor stops the practice.

(D) A psychiatrist's patient tells her about his recurring nightmares of having committed a terrible crime. The psychiatrist should fulfill her duty to report this to the authorities because the patient may have broken the law, even though the psychiatrist also has a duty of confidentiality to her patients.

(E) A journalist thinks there is a slight chance that a story about a developing crisis will endanger innocent lives. Therefore, the journalist should await further developments before fulfilling his duty to file the story.

22. Detective: Laser-printer drums are easily damaged, and any nick in a drum will produce a blemish of similar dimensions on each page produced by that printer. So in matching a blemish on a page with a nick on a drum, we can reliably trace a suspicious laser-printed document to the precise printer on which it was produced.

Which one of the following, if true, most weakens the detective's argument?

(A) Criminals are unlikely to use their own laser printers to produce suspicious documents.

(B) Drum nicks are usually so small that it requires skill to accurately determine their size and shape.

(C) The manufacturing process often produces the same nick on several drums.

(D) Blemishes on documents are sometimes totally concealed by characters that are printed over them.

(E) Most suspicious documents are not produced on laser printers.

23. Whoever is kind is loved by somebody or other, and whoever loves anyone is happy. It follows that whoever is kind is happy.

The conclusion follows logically if which one of the following is assumed?

(A) Whoever loves someone loves everyone.
(B) Whoever loves everyone loves someone.
(C) Whoever is happy loves everyone.
(D) Whoever loves no one is loved by no one.
(E) Whoever loves everyone is kind.

GO ON TO THE NEXT PAGE.

24. It is now clear that the ancient Egyptians were the first society to produce alcoholic beverages. It had been thought that the ancient Babylonians were the first; they had mastered the process of fermentation for making wine as early as 1500 B.C. However, archaeologists have discovered an Egyptian cup dating from 2000 B.C. whose sides depict what appears to be an Egyptian brewery, and whose chemical residue reveals that it contained a form of alcoholic beer.

The reasoning above is most vulnerable to criticism on which one of the following grounds?

(A) It makes a generalization about Egyptian society based on a sample so small that it is likely to be unrepresentative.

(B) It uses the term "alcoholic beverage" in a different sense in the premises than in the conclusion.

(C) It presumes, without providing justification, that because one society developed a technology before another, the development in the latter was dependent on the development in the former.

(D) It ignores the possibility that the first known instance of a kind is not the first instance of that kind.

(E) It provides no evidence for the claim that the Babylonians produced wine as early as 1500 B.C.

25. Studies have shown that specialty sports foods contain exactly the same nutrients in the same quantities as do common foods from the grocery store. Moreover, sports foods cost from two to three times more than regular foods. So very few athletes would buy sports foods were it not for expensive advertising campaigns.

Which one of the following, if true, most weakens the argument?

(A) Sports foods are occasionally used by world-famous athletes.

(B) Many grocery stores carry sports foods alongside traditional inventories.

(C) Sports foods are easier than regular foods to carry and consume during training and competition.

(D) Regular foods contain vitamins and minerals that are essential to developing strength and endurance.

(E) Sports foods can nutritionally substitute for regular meals.

S T O P

**IF YOU FINISH BEFORE TIME IS CALLED, YOU MAY CHECK YOUR WORK ON THIS SECTION ONLY.
DO NOT WORK ON ANY OTHER SECTION IN THE TEST.**

SECTION III

Time—35 minutes

24 Questions

<u>Directions:</u> The questions in this section are based on the reasoning contained in brief statements or passages. For some questions, more than one of the choices could conceivably answer the question. However, you are to choose the <u>best</u> answer; that is, the response that most accurately and completely answers the question. You should not make assumptions that are by commonsense standards implausible, superfluous, or incompatible with the passage. After you have chosen the <u>best</u> answer, blacken the corresponding space on your answer sheet.

1. Rita: The original purpose of government farm-subsidy programs was to provide income stability for small family farmers, but most farm-subsidy money goes to a few farmers with large holdings. Payments to farmers whose income, before subsidies, is greater than $100,000 a year should be stopped.

    Thomas: It would be impossible to administer such a cutoff point. Subsidies are needed during the planting and growing season, but farmers do not know their income for a given calendar year until tax returns are calculated and submitted the following April.

    Which one of the following, if true, is the strongest counter Rita can make to Thomas' objection?

    (A) It has become difficult for small farmers to obtain bank loans to be repaid later by money from subsidies.
    (B) Having such a cutoff point would cause some farmers whose income would otherwise exceed $100,000 to reduce their plantings.
    (C) The income of a farmer varies because weather and market prices are not stable from year to year.
    (D) If subsidy payments to large farmers were eliminated, the financial condition of the government would improve.
    (E) Subsidy cutoffs can be determined on the basis of income for the preceding year.

2. Modern physicians often employ laboratory tests, in addition to physical examinations, in order to diagnose diseases accurately. Insurance company regulations that deny coverage for certain laboratory tests therefore decrease the quality of medical care provided to patients.

    Which one of the following is an assumption that would serve to justify the conclusion above?

    (A) Physical examinations and the uncovered laboratory tests together provide a more accurate diagnosis of many diseases than do physical examinations alone.
    (B) Many physicians generally oppose insurance company regulations that, in order to reduce costs, limit the use of laboratory tests.
    (C) Many patients who might benefit from the uncovered laboratory tests do not have any form of health insurance.
    (D) There are some illnesses that experienced physicians can diagnose accurately from physical examination alone.
    (E) Laboratory tests are more costly to perform than are physical examinations.

3. Oil analysts predict that if the price of oil falls by half, the consumer's purchase price for gasoline made from this oil will also fall by half.

    Which one of the following, if true, would cast the most serious doubt on the prediction made by the oil analysts?

    (A) Improved automobile technology and new kinds of fuel for cars have enabled some drivers to use less gasoline.
    (B) Gasoline manufacturers will not expand their profit margins.
    (C) There are many different gasoline companies that compete with each other to provide the most attractive price to consumers.
    (D) Studies in several countries show that the amount of gasoline purchased by consumers initially rises after the price of gasoline has fallen.
    (E) Refining costs, distribution costs, and taxes, none of which varies significantly with oil prices, constitute a large portion of the price of gasoline.

GO ON TO THE NEXT PAGE

4. A survey was recently conducted among ferry passengers on the North Sea. Among the results was this: more of those who had taken anti-seasickness medication before their trip reported symptoms of seasickness than those who had not taken such medication. It is clear, then, that despite claims by drug companies that clinical tests show the contrary, people would be better off not taking anti-seasickness medications.

Which one of the following, if true, would most weaken the conclusion above?

(A) Given rough enough weather, most ferry passengers will have some symptoms of seasickness.
(B) The clinical tests reported by the drug companies were conducted by the drug companies' staffs.
(C) People who do not take anti-seasickness medication are just as likely to respond to a survey on seasickness as people who do.
(D) The seasickness symptoms of the people who took anti-seasickness medication would have been more severe had they not taken the medication.
(E) People who have spent money on anti-seasickness medication are less likely to admit symptoms of seasickness than those who have not.

5. Economic considerations color every aspect of international dealings, and nations are just like individuals in that the lender sets the terms of its dealings with the borrower. That is why a nation that owes money to another nation cannot be a world leader.

The reasoning in the passage assumes which one of the following?

(A) A nation that does not lend to any other nation cannot be a world leader.
(B) A nation that can set the terms of its dealings with other nations is certain to be a world leader.
(C) A nation that has the terms of its dealings with another nation set by that nation cannot be a world leader.
(D) A nation that is a world leader can borrow from another nation as long as that other nation does not set the terms of the dealings between the two nations.
(E) A nation that has no dealings with any other nation cannot be a world leader.

Questions 6–7

Rotelle: You are too old to address effectively the difficult issues facing the country, such as nuclear power, poverty, and pollution.

Sims: I don't want to make age an issue in this campaign, so I will not comment on your youth and inexperience.

6. Sims does which one of the following?

(A) demonstrates that Rotelle's claim is incorrect
(B) avoids mentioning the issue of age
(C) proposes a way to decide which issues are important
(D) shows that Rotelle's statement is self-contradictory
(E) fails to respond directly to Rotelle's claim

7. Rotelle is committed to which one of the following?

(A) Many old people cannot effectively address the difficult issues facing the country.
(B) Those at least as old as Sims are the only people who cannot effectively address the difficult issues facing the country.
(C) Some young people can effectively address the difficult issues facing the country.
(D) If anyone can effectively address the difficult issues facing the country, that person must be younger than Sims.
(E) Addressing the difficult issues facing the country requires an understanding of young people's points of view.

GO ON TO THE NEXT PAGE.

8. Political theorist: The chief foundations of all governments are the legal system and the police force; and as there cannot be a good legal system where the police are not well paid, it follows that where the police are well paid there will be a good legal system.

The reasoning in the argument is not sound because it fails to establish that

(A) many governments with bad legal systems have poorly paid police forces

(B) bad governments with good legal systems must have poorly paid police forces

(C) a well-paid police force cannot be effective without a good legal system

(D) a well-paid police force is sufficient to guarantee a good legal system

(E) some bad governments have good legal systems

9. Court records from medieval France show that in the years 1300 to 1400 the number of people arrested in the French realm for "violent interpersonal crimes" (not committed in wars) increased by 30 percent over the number of people arrested for such crimes in the years 1200 to 1300. If the increase was not the result of false arrests, therefore, medieval France had a higher level of documented interpersonal violence in the years 1300 to 1400 than in the years 1200 to 1300.

Which one of the following statements, if true, most seriously weakens the argument?

(A) In the years 1300 to 1400 the French government's category of violent crimes included an increasing variety of interpersonal crimes that are actually nonviolent.

(B) Historical accounts by monastic chroniclers in the years 1300 to 1400 are filled with descriptions of violent attacks committed by people living in the French realm.

(C) The number of individual agreements between two people in which they swore oaths not to attack each other increased substantially after 1300.

(D) When English armies tried to conquer parts of France in the mid- to late 1300s, violence in the northern province of Normandy and the southwestern province of Gascony increased.

(E) The population of medieval France increased substantially during the first five decades of the 1300s, until the deadly bubonic plague decimated the population of France after 1348.

10. *Rhizobium* bacteria living in the roots of bean plants or other legumes produce fixed nitrogen, which is one of the essential plant nutrients and which for nonlegume crops, such as wheat, normally must be supplied by applications of nitrogen-based fertilizer. So if biotechnology succeeds in producing wheat strains whose roots will play host to *Rhizobium* bacteria, the need for artificial fertilizers will be reduced.

The argument above makes which one of the following assumptions?

(A) Biotechnology should be directed toward producing plants that do not require artificial fertilizer.

(B) Fixed nitrogen is currently the only soil nutrient that must be supplied by artificial fertilizer for growing wheat crops.

(C) There are no naturally occurring strains of wheat or other grasses that have *Rhizobium* bacteria living in their roots.

(D) Legumes are currently the only crops that produce their own supply of fixed nitrogen.

(E) *Rhizobium* bacteria living in the roots of wheat would produce fixed nitrogen.

11. Current legislation that requires designated sections for smokers and nonsmokers on the premises of privately owned businesses is an intrusion into the private sector that cannot be justified. The fact that studies indicate that nonsmokers might be harmed by inhaling the smoke from others' cigarettes is not the main issue. Rather, the main issue concerns the government's violation of the right of private businesses to determine their own policies and rules.

Which one of the following is a principle that, if accepted, could enable the conclusion to be properly drawn?

(A) Government intrusion into the policies and rules of private businesses is justified only when individuals might be harmed.

(B) The right of individuals to breathe safe air supersedes the right of businesses to be free from government intrusion.

(C) The right of businesses to self-determination overrides whatever right or duty the government may have to protect the individual.

(D) It is the duty of private businesses to protect employees from harm in the workplace.

(E) Where the rights of businesses and the duty of government conflict, the main issue is finding a successful compromise.

GO ON TO THE NEXT PAGE.

12. Leachate is a solution, frequently highly contaminated, that develops when water permeates a landfill site. If and only if the landfill's capacity to hold liquids is exceeded does the leachate escape into the environment, generally in unpredictable quantities. A method must be found for disposing of leachate. Most landfill leachate is sent directly to sewage treatment plants, but not all sewage plants are capable of handling the highly contaminated water.

Which one of the following can be inferred from the passage?

(A) The ability to predict the volume of escaping landfill leachate would help solve the disposal problem.
(B) If any water permeates a landfill, leachate will escape into the environment.
(C) No sewage treatment plants are capable of handling leachate.
(D) Some landfill leachate is sent to sewage treatment plants that are incapable of handling it.
(E) If leachate does not escape from a landfill into the environment, then the landfill's capacity to hold liquids has not been exceeded.

13. The soaring prices of scholarly and scientific journals have forced academic libraries used only by academic researchers to drastically reduce their list of subscriptions. Some have suggested that in each academic discipline subscription decisions should be determined solely by a journal's usefulness in that discipline, measured by the frequency with which it is cited in published writings by researchers in the discipline.

Which one of the following, if true, most seriously calls into question the suggestion described above?

(A) The nonacademic readership of a scholarly or scientific journal can be accurately gauged by the number of times articles appearing in it are cited in daily newspapers and popular magazines.
(B) The average length of a journal article in some sciences, such as physics, is less than half the average length of a journal article in some other academic disciplines, such as history.
(C) The increasingly expensive scholarly journals are less and less likely to be available to the general public from nonacademic public libraries.
(D) Researchers often will not cite a journal article that has influenced their work if they think that the journal in which it appears is not highly regarded by the leading researchers in the mainstream of the discipline.
(E) In some academic disciplines, controversies which begin in the pages of one journal spill over into articles in other journals that are widely read by researchers in the discipline.

14. The average level of fat in the blood of people suffering from acute cases of disease W is lower than the average level for the population as a whole. Nevertheless, most doctors believe that reducing blood-fat levels is an effective way of preventing acute W.

Which one of the following, if true, does most to justify this apparently paradoxical belief?

(A) The blood level of fat for patients who have been cured of W is on average the same as that for the population at large.
(B) Several of the symptoms characteristic of acute W have been produced in laboratory animals fed large doses of a synthetic fat substitute, though acute W itself has not been produced in this way.
(C) The progression from latent to acute W can occur only when the agent that causes acute W absorbs large quantities of fat from the patient's blood.
(D) The levels of fat in the blood of patients who have disease W respond abnormally slowly to changes in dietary intake of fat.
(E) High levels of fat in the blood are indicative of several diseases that are just as serious as W.

15. Baking for winter holidays is a tradition that may have a sound medical basis. In midwinter, when days are short, many people suffer from a specific type of seasonal depression caused by lack of sunlight. Carbohydrates, both sugars and starches, boost the brain's levels of serotonin, a neurotransmitter that improves the mood. In this respect, carbohydrates act on the brain in the same way as some antidepressants. Thus, eating holiday cookies may provide an effective form of self-prescribed medication.

Which one of the following can be properly inferred from the passage?

(A) Seasonal depression is one of the most easily treated forms of depression.
(B) Lack of sunlight lowers the level of serotonin in the brain.
(C) People are more likely to be depressed in midwinter than at other times of the year.
(D) Some antidepressants act by changing the brain's level of serotonin.
(E) Raising the level of neurotransmitters in the brain effectively relieves depression.

GO ON TO THE NEXT PAGE.

16. The current proposal to give college students a broader choice in planning their own courses of study should be abandoned. The students who are supporting the proposal will never be satisfied, no matter what requirements are established. Some of these students have reached their third year without declaring a major. One first-year student has failed to complete four required courses. Several others have indicated a serious indifference to grades and intellectual achievement.

A flaw in the argument is that it does which one of the following?

(A) avoids the issue by focusing on supporters of the proposal
(B) argues circularly by assuming the conclusion is true in stating the premises
(C) fails to define the critical term "satisfied"
(D) distorts the proposal advocated by opponents
(E) uses the term "student" equivocally

Questions 17–18

The question whether intelligent life exists elsewhere in the universe is certainly imprecise, because we are not sure how different from us something might be and still count as "intelligent life." Yet we cannot just decide to define "intelligent life" in some more precise way since it is likely that we will find and recognize intelligent life elsewhere in the universe only if we leave our definitions open to new, unimagined possibilities.

17. The argument can most reasonably be interpreted as an objection to which one of the following claims?

(A) The question whether intelligent life exists elsewhere in the universe is one that will never correctly be answered.
(B) Whether or not there is intelligent life elsewhere in the universe, our understanding of intelligent life is limited.
(C) The question about the existence of intelligent life elsewhere in the universe must be made more precise if we hope to answer it correctly.
(D) The question whether there is intelligent life elsewhere in the universe is so imprecise as to be meaningless.
(E) The question whether there is intelligent life elsewhere in the universe is one we should not spend our time trying to answer.

18. The passage, if seen as an objection to an antecedent claim, challenges that claim by

(A) showing the claim to be irrelevant to the issue at hand
(B) citing examples that fail to fit a proposed definition of "intelligent life"
(C) claiming that "intelligent life" cannot be adequately defined
(D) arguing that the claim, if acted on, would be counterproductive
(E) maintaining that the claim is not supported by the available evidence

GO ON TO THE NEXT PAGE.

19. The efficiency of microwave ovens in destroying the harmful bacteria frequently found in common foods is diminished by the presence of salt in the food being cooked. When heated in a microwave oven, the interior of unsalted food reaches temperatures high enough to kill bacteria that cause food poisoning, but the interior of salted food does not. Scientists theorize that salt effectively blocks the microwaves from heating the interior.

Which one of the following conclusions is most supported by the information above?

(A) The kinds of bacteria that cause food poisoning are more likely to be found on the exterior of food than in the interior of food.

(B) The incidence of serious food poisoning would be significantly reduced if microwave ovens were not used by consumers to cook or reheat food.

(C) The addition of salt to food that has been cooked or reheated in a microwave oven can increase the danger of food poisoning.

(D) The danger of food poisoning can be lessened if salt is not used to prepare foods that are to be cooked in a microwave oven.

(E) Salt is the primary cause of food poisoning resulting from food that is heated in microwave ovens.

20. Pamela: Business has an interest in enabling employees to care for children, because those children will be the customers, employees, and managers of the future. Therefore, businesses should adopt policies, such as day-care benefits, that facilitate parenting.

Lee: No individual company, though, will be patronized, staffed, and managed only by its own employees' children, so it would not be to a company's advantage to provide such benefits to employees when other companies do not.

In which one of the following pairs consisting of argument and objection does the objection function most similarly to the way Lee's objection functions in relation to Pamela's argument?

(A) New roads will not serve to relieve this area's traffic congestion, because new roads would encourage new construction and generate additional traffic.
Objection: Failure to build new roads would mean that traffic congestion would strangle the area even earlier.

(B) Humanity needs clean air to breathe, so each person should make an effort to avoid polluting the air.
Objection: The air one person breathes is affected mainly by pollution caused by others, so it makes no sense to act alone to curb air pollution.

(C) Advertised discounts on products draw customers' attention to the products, so advertised discounts benefit sales.
Objection: Customers already planning to purchase a product accelerate buying to take advantage of advertised discounts, and thus subsequent sales suffer.

(D) If people always told lies, then no one would know what the truth was, so people should always tell the truth.
Objection: If people always told lies, then everyone would know that the truth was the opposite of what was said.

(E) Human social institutions have always changed, so even if we do not know what those changes will be, we do know that the social institutions of the future will differ from those of the past.
Objection: The existence of change in the past does not ensure that there will always be change in the future.

GO ON TO THE NEXT PAGE.

21. Pedro: Unlike cloth diapers, disposable diapers are a threat to the environment. Sixteen billion disposable diapers are discarded annually, filling up landfills at an alarming rate. So people must stop buying disposable diapers and use cloth diapers.

Maria: But you forget that cloth diapers must be washed in hot water, which requires energy. Moreover, the resulting wastewater pollutes our rivers. When families use diaper services, diapers must be delivered by fuel-burning trucks that pollute the air and add to traffic congestion.

Maria objects to Pedro's argument by

(A) claiming that Pedro overstates the negative evidence about disposable diapers in the course of his argument in favor of cloth diapers

(B) indicating that Pedro draws a hasty conclusion, based on inadequate evidence about cloth diapers

(C) pointing out that there is an ambiguous use of the word "disposable" in Pedro's argument

(D) demonstrating that cloth diapers are a far more serious threat to the environment than disposable diapers are

(E) suggesting that the economic advantages of cloth diapers outweigh whatever environmental damage they may cause

22. In an experiment, two-year-old boys and their fathers made pie dough together using rolling pins and other utensils. Each father-son pair used a rolling pin that was distinctively different from those used by the other father-son pairs, and each father repeated the phrase "rolling pin" each time his son used it. But when the children were asked to identify all of the rolling pins among a group of kitchen utensils that included several rolling pins, each child picked only the one that he had used.

Which one of the following inferences is most supported by the information above?

(A) The children did not grasp the function of a rolling pin.

(B) No two children understood the name "rolling pin" to apply to the same object.

(C) The children understood that all rolling pins have the same general shape.

(D) Each child was able to identify correctly only the utensils that he had used.

(E) The children were not able to distinguish the rolling pins they used from other rolling pins.

GO ON TO THE NEXT PAGE.

23. When 100 people who have not used cocaine are tested for cocaine use, on average only 5 will test positive. By contrast, of every 100 people who have used cocaine 99 will test positive. Thus, when a randomly chosen group of people is tested for cocaine use, the vast majority of those who test positive will be people who have used cocaine.

A reasoning error in the argument is that the argument

(A) attempts to infer a value judgment from purely factual premises

(B) attributes to every member of the population the properties of the average member of the population

(C) fails to take into account what proportion of the population have used cocaine

(D) ignores the fact that some cocaine users do not test positive

(E) advocates testing people for cocaine use when there is no reason to suspect that they have used cocaine

24. If a society encourages freedom of thought and expression, then, during the time when it does so, creativity will flourish in that society. In the United States creativity flourished during the eighteenth century. It is clear, therefore, that freedom of thought was encouraged in the United States during eighteenth century.

An error of reasoning of the same kind as one contained in the passage is present in each of the following arguments EXCEPT:

(A) According to the airline industry, airfares have to rise if air travel is to be made safer; since airfares were just raised, we can rest assured that air travel will therefore become safer.

(B) We can conclude that the Hillside police department has improved its efficiency, because crime rates are down in Hillside, and it is an established fact that crime rates go down when police departments increase their efficiency.

(C) People who are really interested in the preservation of wildlife obviously do not go hunting for big game; since Gerda has never gone hunting for big game and intends never to do so, it is clear that she is really interested in the preservation of wildlife.

(D) If the contents of a bottle are safe to drink, the bottle will not be marked "poison," so, since the bottle is not marked "poison," its contents will be safe to drink.

(E) None of the so-called Western democracies is really democratic, because, for a country to be democratic, the opinion of each of its citizens must have a meaningful effect on government, and in none of these countries does each citizen's opinion have such an effect.

S T O P

IF YOU FINISH BEFORE TIME IS CALLED, YOU MAY CHECK YOUR WORK ON THIS SECTION ONLY. DO NOT WORK ON ANY OTHER SECTION IN THE TEST.

SECTION IV
Time—35 minutes
26 Questions

<u>Directions</u>: The questions in this section are based on the reasoning contained in brief statements or passages. For some questions, more than one of the choices could conceivably answer the question. However, you are to choose the <u>best</u> answer; that is, the response that most accurately and completely answers the question. You should not make assumptions that are by commonsense standards implausible, superfluous, or incompatible with the passage. After you have chosen the best answer, blacken the corresponding space on your answer sheet.

1. Sambar deer are physically incapable of digesting meat. Yet sambar deer have been reported feeding on box turtles after killing them.

   Which one of the following, if true, best resolves the discrepancy above?

   (A) Sambar deer eat only the bony shells of box turtles.
   (B) Sambar deer often kill box turtles by accident.
   (C) Sambar deer kill box turtles only occasionally.
   (D) Box turtles sometimes compete with sambar deer for food.
   (E) Box turtles are much slower and clumsier than are sambar deer.

2. Benson: In order to maintain the quality of life in our city, we need to restrict growth. That is why I support the new zoning regulations.

   Willett: I had heard such arguments ten years ago, and again five years ago. Each time the city council was justified in deciding not to restrict growth. Since there is nothing new in this idea of restricting growth, I oppose the regulations.

   Which one of the following most accurately describes a way in which Willett's reasoning is questionable?

   (A) It presumes that growth is necessarily good without offering support for that position.
   (B) It is based on attacking Benson personally rather than responding to Benson's reasoning.
   (C) It ignores the possibility that new reasons for restricting growth have arisen in the past five years.
   (D) It fails to take into account the variety of factors that contribute to the quality of life in a city.
   (E) It overlooks the possibility that the city council of ten years ago was poorly qualified to decide on zoning regulations.

3. A recent study involved feeding a high-salt diet to a rat colony. A few months after the experiment began, standard tests of the rats' blood pressure revealed that about 25 percent of the colony had normal, healthy blood pressure, about 70 percent of the colony had high blood pressure, and 5 percent of the colony had extremely high blood pressure. The conclusion from these results is that high-salt diets are linked to high blood pressure in rats.

   The answer to which one of the following questions is most relevant to evaluating the conclusion drawn above?

   (A) How much more salt than is contained in a rat's normal diet was there in the high-salt diet?
   (B) Did the high blood pressure have any adverse health effects on those rats that developed it?
   (C) What percentage of naturally occurring rat colonies feed on high-salt diets?
   (D) How many rats in the colony studied had abnormally high blood pressure before the study began?
   (E) Have other species of rodents been used in experiments of the same kind?

4. Detective: Bill has been accused of committing the burglary at the warehouse last night. But no one saw Bill in the vicinity of the warehouse. So we must conclude that Bill did not commit the burglary.

   The reasoning in the detective's argument is most vulnerable to criticism on the grounds that the argument

   (A) treats evidence that is irrelevant to the burglar's identity as if it were relevant
   (B) merely attacks the character of Bill's accusers
   (C) fails to provide independent evidence for the theory that Bill committed the burglary
   (D) treats a lack of evidence against Bill as if it exonerated Bill
   (E) fails to establish the true identity of the burglar

GO ON TO THE NEXT PAGE.

5. Psychologist: Because of a perceived social stigma against psychotherapy, and because of age discrimination on the part of some professionals, some elderly people feel discouraged about trying psychotherapy. They should not be, however, for many younger people have greatly benefited from it, and people in later life have certain advantages over the young—such as breadth of knowledge, emotional maturity, and interpersonal skills—that contribute to the likelihood of a positive outcome.

Which one of the following most accurately expresses the main conclusion of the psychologist's argument?

(A) Certain psychotherapists practice age discrimination.
(B) Elderly people are better able to benefit from psychotherapy than are younger people.
(C) Elderly people should not be reluctant to undergo psychotherapy.
(D) Characteristics associated with maturity are important factors in psychotherapy's success.
(E) Elderly people are less inclined to try psychotherapy than are younger people.

6. Heavy salting of Albritten's roads to melt winter ice and snow began about 20 years ago. The area's groundwater now contains approximately 100 milligrams of dissolved salt per liter. Groundwater in a nearby, less highly urbanized area, where little salt is used and where traffic patterns resemble those of Albritten 20 years ago, contains only about 10 milligrams of dissolved salt per liter. Since water that contains 250 or more milligrams of dissolved salt per liter tastes unacceptably salty, continuing the salting of Albritten's roads at its present rate will render Albritten's groundwater unpalatable within the next few decades.

Which one of the following, if true, most seriously weakens the argument?

(A) Even water that contains up to 5,000 milligrams of dissolved salt per liter is safe to drink.
(B) The concentration of dissolved salt in Albritten's groundwater is expected to reach 400 milligrams per liter within a few decades.
(C) Salting icy roads is the simplest way to prevent accidents on those roads.
(D) Albritten's groundwater contained roughly 90 milligrams of dissolved salt per liter 20 years ago.
(E) Salting of Albritten's roads is likely to decrease over the next few decades.

7. Numerous books describe the rules of etiquette. Usually the authors of such books merely codify standards of behavior by classifying various behaviors as polite or rude. However, this suggests that there is a single, objective standard of politeness. Clearly, standards of politeness vary from culture to culture, so it is absurd to label any one set of behaviors as correct and others as incorrect.

The reasoning in the argument is most vulnerable to criticism on the grounds that the argument

(A) reaches a conclusion about how people actually behave on the basis of assertions regarding how they ought to behave
(B) bases a generalization about all books of etiquette on the actions of a few authors
(C) fails to justify its presumption regarding the influence of rules of etiquette on individual behavior
(D) overlooks the possibility that authors of etiquette books are purporting to state what is correct behavior for one particular culture only
(E) attempts to lend itself credence by unfairly labeling the position of the authors of etiquette books "absurd"

8. In jazz history, there have been gifted pianists who, because they had no striking musical ideas, led no memorable recording sessions. But precisely because they lacked such ideas, they were able to respond quickly to the ideas of imaginative and difficult leaders. Thus, these pianists are often heard adding masterful touches to some of the greatest jazz recordings.

Which one of the following principles is best illustrated by the information above?

(A) The success of a group enterprise depends on the ability of the leader to recognize the weaknesses of others in the group.
(B) The production of any great work requires contributions from those who are unimaginative but technically skilled.
(C) People without forceful personalities cannot become great leaders in a field.
(D) A trait that is a weakness in some settings can contribute to greatness in other settings.
(E) No one can achieve great success without the help of others who are able to bring one's ideas to fruition.

GO ON TO THE NEXT PAGE.

9. Editorial: When legislators discover that some public service is not being adequately provided, their most common response is to boost the funding for that public service. Because of this, the least efficiently run government bureaucracies are the ones that most commonly receive an increase in funds.

The statements in the editorial, if true, most strongly support which one of the following?

(A) The least efficiently run government bureaucracies are the bureaucracies that legislators most commonly discover to be failing to provide some public service adequately.

(B) When legislators discover that a public service is not being adequately provided, they never respond to the problem by reducing the funding of the government bureaucracy providing that service.

(C) Throughout the time a government bureaucracy is run inefficiently, legislators repeatedly boost the funding for the public service that this bureaucracy provides.

(D) If legislators boost funding for a public service, the government bureaucracy providing that service will commonly become less efficient as a result.

(E) The most inefficiently run government bureaucracy receives the most funding of any government bureaucracy.

10. Fred argued that, since Kathleen is a successful film director, she has probably worked with famous actors. But, while Fred is right in supposing that most successful film directors work with famous actors, his conclusion is not warranted. For, as he knows, Kathleen works only on documentary films, and directors of documentaries rarely work with famous actors.

Which one of the following strategies is used above to criticize Fred's reasoning?

(A) maintaining that too little is known about Kathleen to justify any conclusion

(B) showing that Kathleen must not have worked with famous actors

(C) claiming that Fred has failed to take relevant information into account

(D) showing that Fred has mistakenly assumed that all successful film directors work with famous actors

(E) demonstrating that Fred has failed to show that most successful film directors work with famous actors

11. In early 1990, Queenston instituted a tax increase that gave its school system a larger operating budget. The school system used the larger budget to increase the total number of teachers in the system by 30 percent between 1990 and 1993. Nevertheless, there was no change in the average number of students per teacher between 1990 and 1993.

If the statements above are true, then on the basis of them which one of the following must also be true?

(A) No classes in Queenston's school system experienced an increase in enrollment between 1990 and 1993.

(B) The total number of students enrolled in Queenston's school system increased between 1990 and 1993.

(C) The operating budget of Queenston's school system increased by exactly 30 percent between 1990 and 1993.

(D) Most teachers who worked for Queenston's school system in 1990 were still working for the system in 1993.

(E) The quality of education in Queenston's school system improved between 1990 and 1993.

12. Our computer experts are asked from time to time to allocate funds for new hardware and software for our company. Unfortunately, these experts favor cutting-edge technologies, because that is what excites them, despite the fact that such experimental technologies are highly expensive, full of undiscovered "bugs," and thus are not the most profitable investments.

Of the following, which one conforms most closely to the principle illustrated by the situation described above?

(A) When senior executives choose to promote junior executives, they tend to favor those who share their professional interests, not those who have had the most education.

(B) When supermarkets choose foods, they choose the kinds that can be sold for the most profit, not the kinds of foods that are the most healthful for consumers.

(C) When librarians choose books for the library, they choose the kinds that they enjoy reading, not the kinds of books that serve the interests of the community.

(D) When students choose courses, they choose those that require the least amount of work, not those in which they might learn the most.

(E) When television executives choose programs to air, they choose the ones with the most sex and violence because that is what viewers want, not the shows with the highest artistic merit.

GO ON TO THE NEXT PAGE.

13. It is characteristic of great artists generally, and of great writers in particular, to have a discerning view of the basic social and political arrangements of the society in which they live. Therefore, the greater a writer one is, the more astute one will be in perceiving the basic social and political arrangements of one's society.

Which one of the following most accurately describes a flaw in the reasoning above?

(A) It assumes, without providing justification, that members of a group that is part of a larger group possess all of the characteristics possessed by members of the larger group.

(B) It assumes, without providing justification, that because something is sometimes the case it must always be the case.

(C) It assumes, without providing justification, that those artists with political insight do not have insight into matters outside of politics.

(D) It assumes, without providing justification, that only great individuals can make discerning criticisms of their societies.

(E) It assumes, without providing justification, that because people who have one quality tend to have a second quality, those who have more of the first quality will have more of the second.

14. Political scientist: The economies of a number of European countries are currently in severe difficulty. Germany is the only neighboring country that has the resources to resuscitate these economies. Therefore, Germany should begin aiding these economically troubled countries.

Which one of the following principles most helps to justify the political scientist's reasoning?

(A) Any nation that alone has an obligation to economically resuscitate neighboring countries ought to be the only nation to provide any economic aid.

(B) Any nation that alone has the capacity to economically resuscitate neighboring countries should exercise that capacity.

(C) Any nation that can afford to give economic aid to just a few other nations ought to aid just those few.

(D) Only nations that alone have the capacity to economically resuscitate neighboring countries should exercise that capacity.

(E) Only nations that can afford to give economic aid to just a few other nations ought to aid just those few.

15. Critic: Works of literature often present protagonists who scorn allegiance to their society and who advocate detachment rather than civic-mindedness. However, modern literature is distinguished from the literature of earlier eras in part because it more frequently treats such protagonists sympathetically. Sympathetic treatment of such characters suggests to readers that one should be unconcerned about contributing to societal good. Thus, modern literature can damage individuals who appropriate this attitude, as well as damage society at large.

Which one of the following is an assumption on which the critic's argument relies?

(A) Some individuals in earlier eras were more concerned about contributing to societal good than is any modern individual.

(B) It is to the advantage of some individuals that they be concerned with contributing to societal good.

(C) Some individuals must believe that their society is better than most before they can become concerned with benefiting it.

(D) The aesthetic merit of some literary works cannot be judged in complete independence of their moral effects.

(E) Modern literature is generally not as conducive to societal good as was the literature of earlier eras.

16. Psychologist: Some people contend that children should never be reprimanded. Any criticism, let alone punishment, they say, harms children's self-esteem. This view is laudable in its challenge to the belief that children should be punished whenever they misbehave, yet it gives a dangerous answer to the question of how often punishment should be inflicted. When parents never reprimand their children, they are in effect rewarding them for unacceptable behavior, and rewarded behavior tends to recur.

The view that children should never be reprimanded functions in the psychologist's argument as a statement of a position that the psychologist's argument

(A) is designed to discredit entirely

(B) is designed to establish as true

(C) is designed to establish as well intentioned

(D) claims has a serious flaw though is not without value

(E) claims is less reasonable than any other view mentioned

GO ON TO THE NEXT PAGE.

17. Traditionally, students at Kelly University have evaluated professors on the last day of class. But some professors at Kelly either do not distribute the paper evaluation forms or do so selectively, and many students cannot attend the last day of class. Soon, students will be able to use school computers to evaluate their professors at any time during the semester. Therefore, evaluations under the new system will accurately reflect the distribution of student opinion about teaching performance.

Which one of the following is an assumption required by the argument?

(A) Professors who distribute the paper evaluation forms selectively distribute them only to students they personally like.

(B) Students can wisely and insightfully assess a professor's performance before the end of the semester.

(C) The traditional system for evaluating teaching performance should not be used at any university.

(D) Nearly all professors who fail to distribute the paper evaluation forms do so because they believe the students will evaluate them unfavorably.

(E) Dissatisfied students are in general not more likely than satisfied students to submit a computerized evaluation.

18. A seriously maladaptive trait is unlikely to persist in a given animal population for long, since there is enough genetic variation in populations that some members will lack the trait. Those lacking the trait will compete more successfully for the available resources. Hence these members of the population survive and reproduce at a higher rate, crowding out those with the maladaptive trait.

The proposition that those lacking a maladaptive trait will compete more successfully for the available resources figures in the argument in which one of the following ways?

(A) It expresses a view that the argument as a whole is designed to discredit.

(B) It is the argument's main conclusion.

(C) It is a premise of the argument.

(D) It presents evidence that the argument attempts to undermine.

(E) It is an intermediate conclusion of the argument.

19. Tanya would refrain from littering if everyone else refrained from littering. None of her friends litter, and therefore she does not litter either.

Which one of the following uses flawed reasoning most similar to the flawed reasoning in the argument above?

(A) All residents of the same neighborhood have some goals in common. One group of neighborhood residents wants improvements made to a local park, so some other residents of that neighborhood must share this goal.

(B) If a talented artist is willing to starve for her career, then her friends should take her choice of profession seriously. Donna's friends take her choice of profession seriously, and she is willing to starve for her career, so she must be a talented artist.

(C) Herbert will stop selling office supplies in his store if none of his regular customers complains. Some of his regular customers never knew that Herbert sold office supplies, so those customers will not complain.

(D) If all whales need to surface for air, then whales must be easy to observe. Blue whales are easily observed, so they must surface for air.

(E) If all of a restaurant's customers like its food, it must be an exceptional restaurant. Everyone whom Sherryl consulted liked the food at Chez Louis, so it must be an exceptional restaurant.

GO ON TO THE NEXT PAGE.

20. Scientist: Genetic engineering has aided new developments in many different fields. But because these techniques require the manipulation of the genetic codes of organisms, they are said to be unethical. What the critics fail to realize is that this kind of manipulation has been going on for millennia; virtually every farm animal is the result of selective breeding for desired traits. Since selective breeding is genetic engineering of a crude sort, genetic engineering is not unethical.

Which one of the following is an assumption on which the scientist's argument depends?

(A) The manipulation of the genetic code of organisms is never unethical.

(B) Anything that is accomplished by nature is not unethical to accomplish with science.

(C) The manipulation of the genetic code through selective breeding for desired traits is not unethical.

(D) The manipulation of the genetic code through selective breeding for desired traits is important for human survival.

(E) Science can accomplish only what is already in some sense natural, and nothing natural is unethical.

21. Baumgartner's comparison of the environmental hazards of gasoline-powered cars with those of electric cars is misleading. He examines only production of the cars, whereas it is the product's total life cycle—production, use, and recycling—that matters in determining its environmental impact. A typical gasoline-powered car consumes 3 times more resources and produces 15 to 20 times more air pollution than a typical electric car.

Which one of the following most accurately expresses the conclusion of the argument?

(A) Baumgartner makes a deceptive comparison between the environmental hazards of gasoline-powered and electric cars.

(B) The use of a typical gasoline-powered car results in much greater resource depletion than does the use of a typical electric car.

(C) Baumgartner uses inaccurate data in his comparison of the environmental hazards of gasoline-powered and electric cars.

(D) The total life cycle of a product is what matters in assessing its environmental impact.

(E) The production of gasoline-powered cars creates more environmental hazards than does that of electric cars.

GO ON TO THE NEXT PAGE.

22. Over the last 10 years, there has been a dramatic increase in the number of people over the age of 65 living in this region. This is evident from the fact that during this time the average age of people living in this region has increased from approximately 52 to 57 years.

Which one of the following, if true, would most strengthen the argument?

(A) The number of people in the region under the age of 18 has increased over the last 10 years.

(B) The birth rate for the region decreased significantly over the last 10 years.

(C) The total number of people living in the region has decreased over the last 10 years.

(D) The number of people who moved into the region over the last 10 years is greater than the number of those who moved out.

(E) The average age for people in the region is higher than that for people in surrounding regions.

23. Editorial: A recently passed law limits freedom of speech in order to silence dissenters. It has been said that those who are ignorant of history will repeat its patterns. If this is true, then those responsible for passing the law must be ignorant of a great deal of history. Historically, silencing dissenters has tended to promote undemocratic policies and the establishment of authoritarian regimes.

The editorialist's reasoning is flawed in that it fails to take into account that

(A) the law may have other purposes in addition to silencing dissenters

(B) certain freedoms might sometimes need to be limited in order to ensure the protection of certain other freedoms

(C) some historical accounts report that legal restrictions on freedom of speech have occasionally undermined the establishment of authoritarian regimes

(D) many good laws have been passed by people who are largely ignorant of history

(E) even those who are not ignorant of history may repeat its patterns

24. Editorialist: Despite the importance it seems to have in our lives, money does not really exist. This is evident from the fact that all that would be needed to make money disappear would be a universal loss of belief in it. We witness this phenomenon on a small scale daily in the rises and falls of financial markets, whose fluctuations are often entirely independent of concrete causes and are the results of mere beliefs of investors.

The conclusion of the editorialist's argument can be properly drawn if which one of the following is assumed?

(A) Anything that exists would continue to exist even if everyone were to stop believing in it.

(B) Only if one can have mistaken beliefs about a thing does that thing exist, strictly speaking.

(C) In order to exist, an entity must have practical consequences for those who believe in it.

(D) If everyone believes in something, then that thing exists.

(E) Whatever is true of money is true of financial markets generally.

GO ON TO THE NEXT PAGE.

25. False chicory's taproot is always one half as long as the plant is tall. Furthermore, the more rain false chicory receives, the taller it tends to grow. In fact, false chicory plants that receive greater than twice the average rainfall of the species' usual habitat always reach above-average heights for false chicory.

If the statements above are true, then which one of the following must also be true?

(A) If two false chicory plants differ in height, then it is likely that the one with the shorter taproot has received less than twice the average rainfall of the species' usual habitat.

(B) If a false chicory plant has a longer-than-average taproot, then it is likely to have received more than twice the average rainfall of the species' usual habitat.

(C) It is not possible for a false chicory plant to receive only the average amount of rainfall of the species' usual habitat and be of above-average height.

(D) If the plants in one group of false chicory are not taller than those in another group of false chicory, then the two groups must have received the same amount of rainfall.

(E) If a false chicory plant receives greater than twice the average rainfall of the species' usual habitat, then it will have a longer taproot than that of an average-sized false chicory plant.

26. Fossilized teeth of an extinct species of herbivorous great ape have on them phytoliths, which are microscopic petrified remains of plants. Since only phytoliths from certain species of plants are found on the teeth, the apes' diet must have consisted only of those plants.

The argument assumes which one of the following?

(A) None of the plant species that left phytoliths on the apes' teeth has since become extinct.

(B) Plants of every type eaten by the apes left phytoliths on their teeth.

(C) Each of the teeth examined had phytoliths of the same plant species on it as all the other teeth.

(D) Phytoliths have also been found on the fossilized teeth of apes of other extinct species.

(E) Most species of great ape alive today have diets that consist of a fairly narrow range of plants.

S T O P

IF YOU FINISH BEFORE TIME IS CALLED, YOU MAY CHECK YOUR WORK ON THIS SECTION ONLY.
DO NOT WORK ON ANY OTHER SECTION IN THE TEST.

SECTION V

Time—35 minutes

22 Questions

<u>Directions:</u> Each group of questions in this section is based on a set of conditions. In answering some of the questions, it may be useful to draw a rough diagram. Choose the response that most accurately and completely answers each question and blacken the corresponding space on your answer sheet.

<u>Questions 1–6</u>

Exactly six guideposts, numbered 1 through 6, mark a mountain trail. Each guidepost pictures a different one of six animals—fox, grizzly, hare, lynx, moose, or porcupine. The following conditions must apply:

>The grizzly is pictured on either guidepost 3 or guidepost 4.
>The moose guidepost is numbered lower than the hare guidepost.
>The lynx guidepost is numbered lower than the moose guidepost but higher than the fox guidepost.

1. Which one of the following could be an accurate list of the animals pictured on the guideposts, listed in order from guidepost 1 through guidepost 6?

  (A)   fox, lynx, grizzly, porcupine, moose, hare
  (B)   fox, lynx, moose, hare, grizzly, porcupine
  (C)   fox, moose, grizzly, lynx, hare, porcupine
  (D)   lynx, fox, moose, grizzly, hare, porcupine
  (E)   porcupine, fox, hare, grizzly, lynx, moose

2. Which one of the following animals CANNOT be the one pictured on guidepost 3?

  (A)   fox
  (B)   grizzly
  (C)   lynx
  (D)   moose
  (E)   porcupine

3. If the moose is pictured on guidepost 3, then which one of the following is the lowest numbered guidepost that could picture the porcupine?

  (A)   guidepost 1
  (B)   guidepost 2
  (C)   guidepost 4
  (D)   guidepost 5
  (E)   guidepost 6

4. If guidepost 5 does not picture the moose, then which one of the following must be true?

  (A)   The lynx is pictured on guidepost 2.
  (B)   The moose is pictured on guidepost 3.
  (C)   The grizzly is pictured on guidepost 4.
  (D)   The porcupine is pictured on guidepost 5.
  (E)   The hare is pictured on guidepost 6.

5. Which one of the following animals could be pictured on any one of the six guideposts?

  (A)   fox
  (B)   hare
  (C)   lynx
  (D)   moose
  (E)   porcupine

6. If the moose guidepost is numbered exactly one higher than the lynx guidepost, then which one of the following could be true?

  (A)   Guidepost 5 pictures the hare.
  (B)   Guidepost 4 pictures the moose.
  (C)   Guidepost 4 pictures the porcupine.
  (D)   Guidepost 3 pictures the lynx.
  (E)   Guidepost 3 pictures the porcupine.

GO ON TO THE NEXT PAGE.

Questions 7–11

Each side of four cassette tapes—Tapes 1 through 4—contains exactly one of the following four genres: folk, hip-hop, jazz, and rock. The following conditions must apply:

Each genre is found on exactly two of the eight sides.
Tape 1 has jazz on at least one side, but neither hip-hop nor rock.
Tape 2 has no jazz.
Folk is not on any tape numbered exactly one higher than a tape that has any rock on it.

7. Which one of the following could be an accurate matching of tapes with the musical genres found on them?

(A) Tape 1: folk and jazz; Tape 2: folk and jazz; Tape 3: hip-hop and rock; Tape 4: hip-hop and rock

(B) Tape 1: folk and jazz; Tape 2: folk and rock; Tape 3: hip-hop and jazz; Tape 4: hip-hop and rock

(C) Tape 1: folk and jazz; Tape 2: folk and rock; Tape 3: two sides of jazz; Tape 4: two sides of hip-hop

(D) Tape 1: hip-hop and jazz; Tape 2: folk and hip-hop; Tape 3: folk and jazz; Tape 4: two sides of rock

(E) Tape 1: two sides of jazz; Tape 2: folk and rock; Tape 3: hip-hop and rock; Tape 4: folk and hip-hop

8. Which one of the following must be true?

(A) If Tape 1 has two sides of jazz, Tape 4 has at least one side of rock.

(B) If Tape 2 has two sides of folk, Tape 3 has at least one side of hip-hop.

(C) If Tape 2 has two sides of rock, Tape 4 has at least one side of folk.

(D) If Tape 3 has two sides of folk, Tape 2 has at least one side of jazz.

(E) If Tape 4 has two sides of hip-hop, Tape 3 has at least one side of folk.

9. Which one of the following could be true?

(A) Tape 1 has jazz on both sides while Tape 4 has folk and hip-hop.

(B) Tape 2 has hip-hop on one side while Tape 3 has hip-hop and jazz.

(C) Tape 3 has folk on both sides while Tape 4 has jazz and rock.

(D) Tape 3 has jazz on one side while Tape 4 has folk on both sides.

(E) Tapes 2 and 3 each have jazz on one side.

10. Which one of the following could be true?

(A) Tape 1 has two sides of folk.

(B) Tape 2 has both hip-hop and jazz.

(C) Tape 4 has both folk and rock.

(D) Tapes 1 and 4 each have a side of hip-hop.

(E) Tapes 3 and 4 each have a side of folk.

11. Which one of the following CANNOT be true?

(A) Tape 2 has rock on both sides while Tape 3 has hip-hop on both sides.

(B) Tape 3 has rock on both sides while Tape 2 has hip-hop on both sides.

(C) Tape 3 has rock on both sides while Tape 4 has hip-hop on both sides.

(D) Tape 4 has rock on both sides while Tape 2 has hip-hop on both sides.

(E) Tape 4 has rock on both sides while Tape 3 has hip-hop on both sides.

GO ON TO THE NEXT PAGE.

Questions 12–16

One afternoon, a single thunderstorm passes over exactly five towns—Jackson, Lofton, Nordique, Oceana, and Plattesville—dropping some form of precipitation on each. The storm is the only source of precipitation in the towns that afternoon. On some towns, it drops both hail and rain; on the remaining towns, it drops only rain. It passes over each town exactly once and does not pass over any two towns at the same time. The following must obtain:

  The third town the storm passes over is Plattesville.
  The storm drops hail and rain on the second town it passes over.
  The storm drops only rain on both Lofton and Oceana.
  The storm passes over Jackson at some time after it passes over Lofton and at some time after it passes over Nordique.

12. Which one of the following could be the order, from first to fifth, in which the storm passes over the towns?

(A) Lofton, Nordique, Plattesville, Oceana, Jackson
(B) Lofton, Oceana, Plattesville, Nordique, Jackson
(C) Nordique, Jackson, Plattesville, Oceana, Lofton
(D) Nordique, Lofton, Plattesville, Jackson, Oceana
(E) Nordique, Plattesville, Lofton, Oceana, Jackson

13. If the storm passes over Oceana at some time before it passes over Jackson, then each of the following could be true EXCEPT:

(A) The first town the storm passes over is Oceana.
(B) The fourth town the storm passes over is Lofton.
(C) The fourth town the storm passes over receives hail and rain.
(D) The fifth town the storm passes over is Jackson.
(E) The fifth town the storm passes over receives only rain.

14. If the storm drops only rain on each town it passes over after passing over Lofton, then which one of the following could be false?

(A) The first town the storm passes over is Oceana.
(B) The fourth town the storm passes over receives only rain.
(C) The fifth town the storm passes over is Jackson.
(D) Jackson receives only rain.
(E) Plattesville receives only rain.

15. If the storm passes over Jackson at some time before it passes over Oceana, then which one of the following could be false?

(A) The storm passes over Lofton at some time before it passes over Jackson.
(B) The storm passes over Lofton at some time before it passes over Oceana.
(C) The storm passes over Nordique at some time before it passes over Oceana.
(D) The fourth town the storm passes over receives only rain.
(E) The fifth town the storm passes over receives only rain.

16. If the storm passes over Oceana at some time before it passes over Lofton, then which one of the following must be true?

(A) The third town the storm passes over receives only rain.
(B) The fourth town the storm passes over receives only rain.
(C) The fourth town the storm passes over receives hail and rain.
(D) The fifth town the storm passes over receives only rain.
(E) The fifth town the storm passes over receives hail and rain.

GO ON TO THE NEXT PAGE.

Questions 17–22

A reporter is trying to uncover the workings of a secret committee. The committee has six members—French, Ghauri, Hsia, Irving, Magnus, and Pinsky—each of whom serves on at least one subcommittee. There are three subcommittees, each having three members, about which the following is known:

> One of the committee members serves on all three subcommittees.
> French does not serve on any subcommittee with Ghauri.
> Hsia does not serve on any subcommittee with Irving.

17. If French does not serve on any subcommittee with Magnus, which one of the following must be true?

(A) French serves on a subcommittee with Hsia.
(B) French serves on a subcommittee with Irving.
(C) Irving serves on a subcommittee with Pinsky.
(D) Magnus serves on a subcommittee with Ghauri.
(E) Magnus serves on a subcommittee with Irving.

18. If Pinsky serves on every subcommittee on which French serves and every subcommittee on which Ghauri serves, then which one of the following could be true?

(A) Magnus serves on every subcommittee on which French serves and every subcommittee on which Ghauri serves.
(B) Magnus serves on every subcommittee on which Hsia serves and every subcommittee on which Irving serves.
(C) Hsia serves on every subcommittee on which French serves and every subcommittee on which Ghauri serves.
(D) French serves on every subcommittee on which Pinsky serves.
(E) Hsia serves on every subcommittee on which Pinsky serves.

19. If Irving serves on every subcommittee on which Magnus serves, which one of the following could be true?

(A) Magnus serves on all of the subcommittees.
(B) Irving serves on more than one subcommittee.
(C) Irving serves on every subcommittee on which Pinsky serves.
(D) French serves on a subcommittee with Magnus.
(E) Ghauri serves on a subcommittee with Magnus.

20. Which one of the following could be true?

(A) French serves on all three subcommittees.
(B) Hsia serves on all three subcommittees.
(C) Ghauri serves on every subcommittee on which Magnus serves and every subcommittee on which Pinsky serves.
(D) Pinsky serves on every subcommittee on which Irving serves and every subcommittee on which Magnus serves.
(E) Magnus serves on every subcommittee on which Pinsky serves, and Pinsky serves on every subcommittee on which Magnus serves.

21. Which one of the following must be true?

(A) Ghauri serves on at least two subcommittees.
(B) Irving serves on only one subcommittee.
(C) French serves on a subcommittee with Hsia.
(D) Ghauri serves on a subcommittee with Irving.
(E) Magnus serves on a subcommittee with Pinsky.

22. Which one of the following must be true?

(A) Every subcommittee has either French or Ghauri as a member.
(B) Every subcommittee has either Hsia or Irving as a member.
(C) No subcommittee consists of French, Magnus, and Pinsky.
(D) Some committee member serves on exactly two subcommittees.
(E) Either Magnus or Pinsky serves on only one subcommittee.

S T O P

IF YOU FINISH BEFORE TIME IS CALLED, YOU MAY CHECK YOUR WORK ON THIS SECTION ONLY.
DO NOT WORK ON ANY OTHER SECTION IN THE TEST.

Acknowledgment is made to the following sources from which material has been adapted for use in this test booklet:

Cheng Lok Chua, "Witnessing the Japanese Canadian Experience in World War II: Processual Structure, Symbolism, and Irony in Joy Kogawa's *Obasan*." © 1992 by Temple University.

Joel Feinberg, *The Moral Limits of the Criminal Law*. ©1988 by Oxford University Press.

Myrna I. Lewis, "What's So Bad About Feeling Good? How Psychotherapy Can Help You Find Peace of Mind." ©1993 by the American Association of Retired Persons.

William Bryant Logan, "What Is Prosperity?" ©1995 by POINT.

James Shreeve, "Music of the Hemispheres" © October 1996 by Discover.

Carol Kaesuk Yoon, "Pronghorn's Speed May Be Legacy of Past Predators." © 1996 by The New York Times.

**Wait for the supervisor's instructions before you open the page to the topic.
Please print and sign your name and write the date in the designated spaces below.**

Time: 35 Minutes

General Directions

You will have 35 minutes in which to plan and write an essay on the topic inside. Read the topic and the accompanying directions carefully. You will probably find it best to spend a few minutes considering the topic and organizing your thoughts before you begin writing. In your essay, be sure to develop your ideas fully, leaving time, if possible, to review what you have written. **Do not write on a topic other than the one specified. Writing on a topic of your own choice is not acceptable.**

No special knowledge is required or expected for this writing exercise. Law schools are interested in the reasoning, clarity, organization, language usage, and writing mechanics displayed in your essay. How well you write is more important than how much you write.

Confine your essay to the blocked, lined area on the front and back of the separate Writing Sample Response Sheet. Only that area will be reproduced for law schools. Be sure that your writing is legible.

Both this topic sheet and your response sheet must be turned over to the testing staff before you leave the room.

Topic Code	Print Your Full Name Here		
_____	Last	First	M.I.

Date	Sign Your Name Here
/ /	

Scratch Paper
Do not write your essay in this space.

LSAT Writing Sample Topic

Directions: The scenario presented below describes two choices, either one of which can be supported on the basis of the information given. Your essay should consider both choices and argue <u>for</u> one and <u>against</u> the other, based on the two specified criteria and the facts provided. There is no "right" or "wrong" choice: a reasonable argument can be made for either.

The *Tribune*, a growing large-city newspaper with a civic-minded publisher, will be adding a new column to the Arts and Leisure section. The publisher must decide between a restaurant review and a theater review. Write an essay in which you argue for one proposal over the other, keeping in mind the following two criteria:

- The publisher wants to increase the paper's circulation, making it more attractive to advertisers.
- The publisher wants to contribute to the revitalization of the city's Lakewood district, which is a magnet for nightlife and is perceived as being crucial to the city's development.

The *Tribune's* chief competitor, the *Standard*, publishes a restaurant review that is one of the most popular lifestyle features. Surveys indicate that readers of the *Tribune* would be receptive to a restaurant review in its pages. An established reviewer from an alternative newspaper in a larger city would write the column. He lacks the prestige of the *Standard's* reviewer, but is less traditional and would probably appeal to a different audience. Several local restaurants have indicated that they would be more willing to advertise in the *Tribune* if it featured a restaurant review. Some of these are in the Lakewood district, whose already flourishing restaurant scene would likely improve with the interest another restaurant review column would generate.

It the *Tribune* were to publish a theater review, it would be the only one in the city, since the *Standard* does not publish one. The *Tribune* has the opportunity to hire a distinguished reviewer from a major metropolitan newspaper, who would like to return to her home city, where The *Tribune* is located. Her coming to the *Tribune* would be an event that would attract considerable publicity. The *Tribune's* current readers express little demand for a theater column, but interest in theater in the city is growing, and with a distinguished theater critic on a city newspaper, it would be spurred considerably. All of the city's major theaters are located in the Lakewood district, which would therefore benefit from such a development. Currently, advertising by theaters is a significantly smaller source of revenue to newspapers than advertising by restaurants.

Scratch Paper
Do not write your essay in this space.

SIGNATURE

Writing Sample Response Sheet

DO NOT WRITE
IN THIS SPACE

Begin your essay in the lined area below.
Continue on the back if you need more space.

KAPLAN

Directions:

1. Use the Answer Key on the next page to check your answers.

2. Use the Scoring Worksheet below to compute your raw score.

3. Use the Score Conversion Chart to convert your raw score into the 120–180 scale.

Scoring Worksheet

1. Enter the number of questions you answered correctly in each section

	Number Correct
SECTION I	_____
SECTION II	_____
SECTION III	__EXP__
SECTION IV	_____
SECTION V	_____

2. Enter the sum here: _____
   This is your Raw Score.

Conversion Chart
For converting Raw Score to the 120–180 LSAT Scaled Score
LSAT Prep Test 46

Reported Score	Raw Score Lowest	Raw Score Highest
180	98	99
179	97	97
178	96	96
177	—*	—*
176	95	95
175	94	94
174	—*	—*
173	93	93
172	92	92
171	91	91
170	90	90
169	89	89
168	88	88
167	87	87
166	85	86
165	84	84
164	83	83
163	81	82
162	80	80
161	78	79
160	77	77
159	75	76
158	74	74
157	72	73
156	71	71
155	69	70
154	67	68
153	66	66
152	64	65
151	62	63
150	61	61
149	59	60
148	57	58
147	56	56
146	54	55
145	52	53
144	51	51
143	49	50
142	47	48
141	46	46
140	44	45
139	42	43
138	41	41
137	39	40
136	37	38
135	36	36
134	34	35
133	32	33
132	31	31
131	29	30
130	28	28
129	26	27
128	24	25
127	23	23
126	21	22
125	20	20
124	18	19
123	17	17
122	15	16
121	14	14
120	0	13

*There is no raw score that will produce this scaled score for this form.

SECTION I

1.	B	8.	A	15.	C	22.	E
2.	C	9.	*	16.	A	23.	D
3.	D	10.	E	17.	D	24.	C
4.	A	11.	A	18.	C	25.	A
5.	E	12.	B	19.	D	26.	E
6.	D	13.	E	20.	B	27.	C
7.	D	14.	C	21.	E		

SECTION II

1.	D	8.	E	15.	C	22.	C
2.	E	9.	B	16.	B	23.	D
3.	B	10.	A	17.	E	24.	D
4.	A	11.	A	18.	C	25.	C
5.	A	12.	E	19.	B		
6.	B	13.	D	20.	B		
7.	B	14.	E	21.	A		

SECTION III (experimental)

1.	E	8.	D	15.	D	22.	B
2.	A	9.	A	16.	A	23.	C
3.	E	10.	E	17.	C	24.	E
4.	D	11.	C	18.	D		
5.	C	12.	E	19.	D		
6.	E	13.	D	20.	B		
7.	D	14.	C	21.	B		

SECTION IV

1.	A	8.	D	15.	B	22.	A
2.	C	9.	A	16.	D	23.	E
3.	D	10.	C	17.	E	24.	A
4.	D	11.	B	18.	C	25.	E
5.	C	12.	C	19.	E	26.	B
6.	D	13.	E	20.	C		
7.	D	14.	B	21.	A		

SECTION V

1.	A	8.	C	15.	D	22.	D
2.	A	9.	B	16.	B		
3.	D	10.	C	17.	C		
4.	A	11.	B	18.	C		
5.	E	12.	A	19.	B		
6.	A	13.	C	20.	D		
7.	B	14.	E	21.	E		

Endurance Practice Test 9

PrepTest 42 plus experimental from PrepTest 4, Section II

SCAN CODE: LL9009

SECTION I

Time—35 minutes

23 Questions

Directions: Each group of questions in this section is based on a set of conditions. In answering some of the questions, it may be useful to draw a rough diagram. Choose the response that most accurately and completely answers each question and blacken the corresponding space on your answer sheet.

Questions 1–5

A panel of five scientists will be formed. The panelists will be selected from among three botanists—F, G, and H—three chemists—K, L, and M—and three zoologists—P, Q, and R. Selection is governed by the following conditions:

  The panel must include at least one scientist of each of the three types.

  If more than one botanist is selected, then at most one zoologist is selected.

  F and K cannot both be selected.

  K and M cannot both be selected.

  If M is selected, both P and R must be selected.

1. Which one of the following is an acceptable selection of scientists for the panel?

    (A) F, G, K, P, Q
    (B) G, H, K, L, M
    (C) G, H, K, L, R
    (D) H, K, M, P, R
    (E) H, L, M, P, Q

2. If M is the only chemist selected for the panel, which one of the following must be true?

    (A) F and G are both selected.
    (B) G and H are both selected.
    (C) H and P are both selected.
    (D) F, G, and H are all selected.
    (E) P, Q, and R are all selected.

3. If four of the scientists selected are F, L, Q, and R, which one of the following must be the fifth scientist selected?

    (A) G
    (B) H
    (C) K
    (D) M
    (E) P

4. If P is the only zoologist selected, which one of the following must be true?

    (A) If K is selected, G cannot be selected.
    (B) If L is selected, F cannot be selected.
    (C) If exactly one chemist is selected, it must be K.
    (D) If exactly two chemists are selected, F cannot be selected.
    (E) If exactly two chemists are selected, G cannot be selected.

5. If both G and H are among the scientists selected, then the panel must include either

    (A) F or else K
    (B) F or else M
    (C) K or else M
    (D) M or else Q
    (E) P or else Q

GO ON TO THE NEXT PAGE.

Questions 6–12

A loading dock consists of exactly six bays numbered 1 through 6 consecutively from one side of the dock to the other. Each bay is holding a different one of exactly six types of cargo—fuel, grain, livestock, machinery, produce, or textiles. The following apply:

The bay holding grain has a higher number than the bay holding livestock.

The bay holding livestock has a higher number than the bay holding textiles.

The bay holding produce has a higher number than the bay holding fuel.

The bay holding textiles is next to the bay holding produce.

6. Which one of the following lists could accurately identify the cargo held in each of the loading dock's first three bays, listed in order from bay 1 to bay 3?

(A) fuel, machinery, textiles
(B) grain, machinery, fuel
(C) machinery, livestock, fuel
(D) machinery, textiles, fuel
(E) machinery, textiles, produce

7. Which one of the following CANNOT be the type of cargo held in bay 4?

(A) grain
(B) livestock
(C) machinery
(D) produce
(E) textiles

8. If there is exactly one bay between the bay holding machinery and the bay holding grain, then for exactly how many of the six bays is the type of cargo that bay is holding completely determined?

(A) two
(B) three
(C) four
(D) five
(E) six

9. Which one of the following could be the bay holding livestock?

(A) bay 1
(B) bay 2
(C) bay 3
(D) bay 5
(E) bay 6

10. Which one of the following must be false?

(A) The bay holding fuel is next to the bay holding machinery.
(B) The bay holding grain is next to the bay holding machinery.
(C) The bay holding livestock is next to the bay holding fuel.
(D) The bay holding produce is next to the bay holding livestock.
(E) The bay holding textiles is next to the bay holding fuel.

11. If the bay holding produce is next to the bay holding livestock, then each of the following could be true EXCEPT:

(A) Bay 2 is holding fuel.
(B) Bay 4 is holding produce.
(C) Bay 4 is holding textiles.
(D) Bay 5 is holding grain.
(E) Bay 5 is holding machinery.

12. If bay 4 is holding produce, then for exactly how many of the six bays is the type of cargo that bay is holding completely determined?

(A) two
(B) three
(C) four
(D) five
(E) six

GO ON TO THE NEXT PAGE.

Questions 13–18

A bakery makes exactly three kinds of cookie—oatmeal, peanut butter, and sugar. Exactly three batches of each kind of cookie are made each week (Monday through Friday) and each batch is made, from start to finish, on a single day. The following conditions apply:

No two batches of the same kind of cookie are made on the same day.
At least one batch of cookies is made on Monday.
The second batch of oatmeal cookies is made on the same day as the first batch of peanut butter cookies.
The second batch of sugar cookies is made on Thursday.

13. Which one of the following could be a complete and accurate list of the days on which the batches of each kind of cookie are made?

(A) oatmeal: Monday, Wednesday, Thursday
    peanut butter: Wednesday, Thursday, Friday
    sugar: Monday, Thursday, Friday
(B) oatmeal: Monday, Tuesday, Thursday
    peanut butter: Tuesday, Wednesday, Thursday
    sugar: Monday, Wednesday, Thursday
(C) oatmeal: Tuesday, Wednesday, Thursday
    peanut butter: Wednesday, Thursday, Friday
    sugar: Tuesday, Thursday, Friday
(D) oatmeal: Monday, Tuesday, Thursday
    peanut butter: Monday, Wednesday, Thursday
    sugar: Monday, Thursday, Friday
(E) oatmeal: Monday, Thursday, Friday
    peanut butter: Tuesday, Wednesday, Thursday
    sugar: Monday, Thursday, Friday

14. How many of the days, Monday through Friday, are such that at most two batches of cookies could be made on that day?

(A) one
(B) two
(C) three
(D) four
(E) five

15. If the first batch of peanut butter cookies is made on Tuesday, then each of the following could be true EXCEPT:

(A) Two different kinds of cookie have their first batch made on Monday.
(B) Two different kinds of cookie have their first batch made on Tuesday.
(C) Two different kinds of cookie have their second batch made on Wednesday.
(D) Two different kinds of cookie have their second batch made on Thursday.
(E) Two different kinds of cookie have their third batch made on Friday.

16. If no batch of cookies is made on Wednesday, then which one of the following must be true?

(A) Exactly three batches of cookies are made on Tuesday.
(B) Exactly three batches of cookies are made on Friday.
(C) At least two batches of cookies are made on Monday.
(D) At least two batches of cookies are made on Thursday.
(E) Fewer batches of cookies are made on Monday than on Tuesday.

17. If the number of batches made on Friday is exactly one, then which one of the following could be true?

(A) The first batch of sugar cookies is made on Monday.
(B) The first batch of oatmeal cookies is made on Tuesday.
(C) The third batch of oatmeal cookies is made on Friday.
(D) The first batch of peanut butter cookies is made on Wednesday.
(E) The second batch of peanut butter cookies is made on Tuesday.

18. If one kind of cookie's first batch is made on the same day as another kind of cookie's third batch, then which one of the following could be false?

(A) At least one batch of cookies is made on each of the five days.
(B) At least two batches of cookies are made on Wednesday.
(C) Exactly one batch of cookies is made on Monday.
(D) Exactly two batches of cookies are made on Tuesday.
(E) Exactly one batch of cookies is made on Friday.

GO ON TO THE NEXT PAGE.

Questions 19–23

For the school paper, five students—Jiang, Kramer, Lopez, Megregian, and O'Neill—each review one or more of exactly three plays: *Sunset*, *Tamerlane*, and *Undulation*, but do not review any other plays. The following conditions must apply:

Kramer and Lopez each review fewer of the plays than Megregian.

Neither Lopez nor Megregian reviews any play Jiang reviews.

Kramer and O'Neill both review *Tamerlane*.

Exactly two of the students review exactly the same play or plays as each other.

19. Which one of the following could be an accurate and complete list of the students who review only *Sunset*?

(A) Lopez
(B) O'Neill
(C) Jiang, Lopez
(D) Kramer, O'Neill
(E) Lopez, Megregian

20. Which one of the following must be true?

(A) Jiang reviews more of the plays than Lopez does.
(B) Megregian reviews more of the plays than Jiang does.
(C) Megregian reviews more of the plays than O'Neill does.
(D) O'Neill reviews more of the plays than Jiang does.
(E) O'Neill reviews more of the plays than Kramer does.

21. If exactly three of the students review *Undulation*, which one of the following could be true?

(A) Megregian does not review *Undulation*.
(B) O'Neill does not review *Undulation*.
(C) Jiang reviews *Undulation*.
(D) Lopez reviews *Tamerlane*.
(E) O'Neill reviews *Sunset*.

22. Which one of the following could be an accurate and complete list of the students who review *Tamerlane*?

(A) Jiang, Kramer
(B) Kramer, O'Neill
(C) Kramer, Lopez, O'Neill
(D) Kramer, Megregian, O'Neill
(E) Lopez, Megregian, O'Neill

23. If Jiang does not review *Tamerlane*, then which one of the following must be true?

(A) Jiang reviews *Sunset*.
(B) Lopez reviews *Undulation*.
(C) Megregian reviews *Sunset*.
(D) Megregian reviews *Tamerlane*.
(E) O'Neill reviews *Undulation*.

S T O P

IF YOU FINISH BEFORE TIME IS CALLED, YOU MAY CHECK YOUR WORK ON THIS SECTION ONLY.
DO NOT WORK ON ANY OTHER SECTION IN THE TEST.

SECTION II

Time—35 minutes

26 Questions

<u>Directions</u>: The questions in this section are based on the reasoning contained in brief statements or passages. For some questions, more than one of the choices could conceivably answer the question. However, you are to choose the <u>best</u> answer; that is, the response that most accurately and completely answers the question. You should not make assumptions that are by commonsense standards implausible, superfluous, or incompatible with the passage. After you have chosen the best answer, blacken the corresponding space on your answer sheet.

1. Carl is clearly an incompetent detective. He has solved a smaller percentage of the cases assigned to him in the last 3 years—only 1 out of 25—than any other detective on the police force.

   Which one of the following, if true, most seriously weakens the argument above?

   (A) Because the police chief regards Carl as the most capable detective, she assigns him only the most difficult cases, ones that others have failed to solve.

   (B) Before he became a detective, Carl was a neighborhood police officer and was highly respected by the residents of the neighborhood he patrolled.

   (C) Detectives on the police force on which Carl serves are provided with extensive resources, including the use of a large computer database, to help them solve crimes.

   (D) Carl was previously a detective in a police department in another city, and in the 4 years he spent there, he solved only 1 out of 30 crimes.

   (E) Many of the officers in the police department in which Carl serves were hired or promoted within the last 5 years.

2. It is well documented that people have positive responses to some words, such as "kind" and "wonderful," and negative responses to others, such as "evil" and "nausea." Recently, psychological experiments have revealed that people also have positive or negative responses to many nonsense words. This shows that people's responses to words are conditioned not only by what the words mean, but also by how they sound.

   The claim that people have positive or negative responses to many nonsense words plays which one of the following roles in the argument?

   (A) It is a premise offered in support of the conclusion that people have either a positive or a negative response to any word.

   (B) It is a conclusion for which the only support provided is the claim that people's responses to words are conditioned both by what the words mean and by how they sound.

   (C) It is a generalization partially supported by the claim that meaningful words can trigger positive or negative responses in people.

   (D) It is a premise offered in support of the conclusion that people's responses to words are engendered not only by what the words mean, but also by how they sound.

   (E) It is a conclusion supported by the claim that people's responses under experimental conditions are essentially different from their responses in ordinary situations.

GO ON TO THE NEXT PAGE.

3. People with high blood pressure are generally more nervous and anxious than are people who do not have high blood pressure. This fact shows that this particular combination of personality traits—the so-called hypertensive personality—is likely to cause a person with these traits to develop high blood pressure.

The reasoning in the argument is most vulnerable to criticism on the ground that the argument

(A) fails to define the term "hypertensive personality"
(B) presupposes that people have permanent personality traits
(C) simply restates the claim that there is a "hypertensive personality" without providing evidence to support that claim
(D) takes a correlation between personality traits and high blood pressure as proof that the traits cause high blood pressure
(E) focuses on nervousness and anxiety only, ignoring other personality traits that people with high blood pressure might have

4. In his book, published in 1892, Grey used the same metaphor that Jordan used in her book, which was published in 1885. The metaphor is so unusual that there is little chance that two different people independently created it. Therefore, it is highly likely that Grey read Jordan's book.

Which one of the following, if true, most weakens the argument?

(A) A text that was probably known to both Jordan and Grey was published in 1860 and also contained the same unusual metaphor.
(B) The passage in Grey's book that employs the unusual metaphor expresses an idea that bears little relation to any ideas expressed in Jordan's book.
(C) Both Grey's book and Jordan's book were written for the same audience.
(D) Jordan used the same metaphor in a work that she wrote in 1894 and published in 1895.
(E) According to most scholars, Grey was generally a more inventive writer than Jordan and developed many original metaphors.

5. Medical specialists report that patients with back muscle injuries who receive a combination of drugs and physical therapy do only as well as those who receive physical therapy alone. Yet the specialists state that drugs are a necessary part of the treatment of all patients who receive them for back muscle injuries.

Which one of the following, if true, most helps to reconcile the medical specialists' two claims?

(A) Medical specialists treat all patients who have serious back muscle injuries with either physical therapy alone or a combination of drugs and physical therapy.
(B) Medical specialists who prescribe these treatments make accurate judgments about who needs both drugs and physical therapy and who needs physical therapy alone.
(C) Some back muscle injuries have been completely healed by a combination of drugs and physical therapy.
(D) Some back muscle injuries that have been aggravated by improper attempts at physical therapy, such as home massage, have been successfully treated with drugs.
(E) Patients with injuries to other muscles show more improvement when treated with both drugs and physical therapy than when treated with physical therapy alone.

6. Commentator: In many countries the influence of fringe movements is increasing. The great centrifugal engine of modern culture turns faster and faster, spinning off fashions, ideologies, religions, artistic movements, economic theories, cults, and dogmas in fabulous profusion. Hence, modern culture threatens the national identities that now exist in the world.

Which one of the following statements, if true, most seriously weakens the commentator's argument?

(A) New national identities are often forged out of conflicts among diverse groups.
(B) A stable national identity is typically a composite of a staggering number of subcultures.
(C) The rate of cultural change in most countries will soon change drastically.
(D) It is preferable to have a pluralistic rather than a monolithic national culture.
(E) A culture with a solidified national identity tends to have more social problems than one without such an identity.

GO ON TO THE NEXT PAGE.

7. Packaging is vital to a product's commercial success. For example, the maker of a popular drink introduced a "new, improved" version which succeeded in blind taste tests. However, customers did not buy the product when marketed, mainly because the can, almost identical to that used for the earlier version of the beverage, made consumers expect that the new product would share certain features of the old, an expectation not satisfied by the new product.

Which one of the following is most strongly supported by the information above?

(A) Proper product packaging is more important than the quality of the product.

(B) Products generally succeed in the market if they are packaged in a manner that accurately reflects their nature.

(C) Changing the packaging of a product will not improve the product's sales unless the product is also changed.

(D) To succeed in the market, a new product should not be packaged in a way that creates expectations that it does not meet.

(E) An improved version of an existing product will sell better than the earlier version unless the improved version is packaged like the earlier one.

8. Larew: People in the lowest income quintile had a much higher percentage increase in average income over the last ten years than did those in the highest quintile. So their economic prosperity increased relative to the highest quintile's.

Mendota: I disagree. The average income for the lowest quintile may have increased by a greater percentage, but the absolute amount of the increase in average income was surely greater for the highest quintile.

Larew and Mendota disagree about whether

(A) change in the economic prosperity of the lowest income quintile relative to the highest is accurately measured by comparing their percentage changes in average income

(B) change in the economic prosperity of the lowest income quintile is more accurately measured in terms relative to the highest income quintile than in terms relative only to the lowest income quintile

(C) changes in the average income of people in the lowest quintile should ever be compared to changes in the average income of people in the highest quintile

(D) there were any improvements at all in the economic situation of those in the lowest income quintile during the ten years being considered

(E) the average income of people in the lowest quintile increased by a greater percentage over the last decade than did that of people in the highest quintile

9. Challenge can be an important source of self-knowledge, since those who pay attention to how they react, both emotionally and physically, to challenge can gain useful insights into their own weaknesses.

Which one of the following most closely conforms to the principle above?

(A) A concert pianist should not have an entirely negative view of a memory lapse during a difficult performance. By understanding why the memory lapse occurred, the pianist can better prepare for future performances.

(B) A salesperson should understand that the commission earned is not the only reward of making a sale. Salespeople should also take satisfaction from the fact that successful sales reflect well on their personalities.

(C) Compassion is valuable not only for the wonderful feelings it brings, but also for the opportunities it affords to enrich the lives of other people.

(D) While some of the value of competition comes from the pleasure of winning, the primary reward of competition is competition itself.

(E) Even people who dread public speaking should accept invitations to speak before large groups. People will admire their courage and they will experience the fulfillment of having attempted something that is difficult for them.

10. In some countries, national planners have attempted to address the problems resulting from increasing urbanization by reducing migration from rural areas. But some economists have suggested an alternative approach. These economists assert that planners could solve these problems effectively by trading goods or services produced by a predominantly urban population in order to obtain the agricultural products that were previously produced domestically.

Which one of the following, if true, would provide the most support for the economists' assertion?

(A) Government subsidies to urban manufacturers can ease the problems caused by the migration of people from rural to urban areas.

(B) All problems that have economic causes must have economic solutions.

(C) A scarcity of agricultural products is a central element of many problems created by urbanization.

(D) Problems associated with migration to cities from rural areas are primarily due to trade imbalances between countries.

(E) Free trade policies can exacerbate the problems caused by increasing urbanization.

GO ON TO THE NEXT PAGE.

11. Inez: The book we are reading, *The Nature of Matter*, is mistitled. A title should summarize the content of the whole book, but nearly half of this book is devoted to discussing a different, albeit closely related subject: energy.

Antonio: I do not think that the author erred; according to modern physics, matter and energy are two facets of the same phenomenon.

Which one of the following is most strongly supported by the conversation above?

(A) Inez believes that the book should be called *The Nature of Energy*.
(B) Antonio believes that there are no differences between matter and energy.
(C) Inez and Antonio disagree on whether matter and energy are related.
(D) Inez and Antonio disagree about the overall value of the book.
(E) Inez believes that the book's title should not mention matter without mentioning energy.

12. Politician: Those economists who claim that consumer price increases have averaged less than 3 percent over the last year are mistaken. They clearly have not shopped anywhere recently. Gasoline is up 10 percent over the last year; my auto insurance, 12 percent; newspapers, 15 percent; propane, 13 percent; bread, 50 percent.

The reasoning in the politician's argument is most vulnerable to criticism on the grounds that the argument

(A) impugns the character of the economists rather than addressing their arguments
(B) fails to show that the economists mentioned are not experts in the area of consumer prices
(C) mistakenly infers that something is not true from the claim that it has not been shown to be so
(D) uses evidence drawn from a small sample that may well be unrepresentative
(E) attempts to persuade by making an emotional appeal

13. Sherrie: Scientists now agree that nicotine in tobacco is addictive inasmuch as smokers who try to stop smoking suffer withdrawal symptoms. For this reason alone, tobacco should be treated the same way as other dangerous drugs. Governments worldwide have a duty to restrict the manufacture and sale of tobacco.

Fran: By your own admission, "addictive" is broad enough to include other commonly consumed products, such as coffee and soft drinks containing caffeine. But of course the manufacture and sale of these products should not be restricted.

The dialogue above lends the most support to the claim that Sherrie and Fran disagree with each other about which one of the following statements?

(A) The manufacture and sale of all drugs should be regulated by governments.
(B) Coffee and soft drinks that contain caffeine should not be regulated by governments.
(C) Agreement by scientists that a substance is addictive justifies government restrictions on products containing that substance.
(D) Scientists are not proper authorities with respect to the question of whether a given substance is addictive.
(E) Scientists and governments have a duty to cooperate in regulating drugs to protect the public health.

14. In 1963, a young macaque monkey was observed venturing into a hot spring to retrieve food which had fallen in. Soon, other macaques began to enter the spring, and over a few years this behavior was adopted by the entire troop. Prior to 1963, no macaques had ever been observed in the hot spring; by 1990, the troop was regularly spending time there during the winters. Thus, these macaques are able to adopt and pass on new patterns of social behavior, and are not complete captives of their genetic heritage.

Which one of the following is an assumption required by the argument above?

(A) Mutations in the genetic heritage of a certain variety of macaques can occur over a time span as short as a few years or decades.
(B) New patterns of behavior that emerge in macaque populations over the course of a few years or decades are not necessarily genetically predetermined.
(C) Only when behaviors become typical among an animal population can we conclude that a genetic alteration has occurred in that variety or species.
(D) The social behaviors of macaques are completely independent of their genetic heritage.
(E) The macaques' new pattern of behavior will persist over several generations.

GO ON TO THE NEXT PAGE.

15. Technological innovation rarely serves the interests of society as a whole. This can be seen from the fact that those responsible for technological advances are almost without exception motivated by considerations of personal gain rather than societal benefit in that they strive to develop commercially viable technology.

The argument is most vulnerable to criticism on the grounds that it

(A) contains a premise that cannot possibly be true
(B) takes for granted that technology beneficial to society as a whole cannot be commercially viable
(C) fails to consider the possibility that actions motivated by a desire for personal gain often do not result in personal gain
(D) takes for granted that an action is unlikely to produce a certain outcome unless it is motivated by a desire to produce that outcome
(E) draws a conclusion about the practical consequences of people's actions on the basis of theoretical views about what people should or should not do

16. There are two kinds of horror stories: those that describe a mad scientist's experiments and those that describe a monstrous beast. In some horror stories about monstrous beasts, the monster symbolizes a psychological disturbance in the protagonist. Horror stories about mad scientists, on the other hand, typically express the author's feeling that scientific knowledge alone is not enough to guide human endeavor. However, despite these differences, both kinds of horror stories share two features: they describe violations of the laws of nature and they are intended to produce dread in the reader.

If the statements above are true, which one of the following would also have to be true?

(A) All descriptions of monstrous beasts describe violations of the laws of nature.
(B) Any story that describes a violation of a law of nature is intended to invoke dread in the reader.
(C) Horror stories of any kind usually describe characters who are psychologically disturbed.
(D) Most stories about mad scientists express the author's antiscientific views.
(E) Some stories that employ symbolism describe violations of the laws of nature.

17. Politician: Some of my opponents have argued on theoretical grounds in favor of reducing social spending. Instead of arguing that there is excessive public expenditure on social programs, my opponents should focus on the main cause of deficit spending: the fact that government is bloated with bureaucrats and self-aggrandizing politicians. It is unwarranted, therefore, to reduce social expenditure.

A reasoning flaw in the politician's argument is that the argument

(A) does not address the arguments advanced by the politician's opponents
(B) makes an attack on the character of opponents
(C) takes for granted that deficit spending has just one cause
(D) portrays opponents' views as more extreme than they really are
(E) fails to make clear what counts as excessive spending

18. While it is true that bees' vision is well suited to the task of identifying flowers by their colors, it is probable that flowers developed in response to the type of vision that bees have, rather than bees' vision developing in response to flower color.

Which one of the following, if true, most strongly supports the statement above?

(A) Many insects that have vision very similar to that of bees do not depend on perceiving an object's color.
(B) Some flowers rely on insects other than bees.
(C) The number of different species of flowers is greater than the number of different species of bees.
(D) Many nonflowering plants rely on bees.
(E) Present-day bees rely exclusively on flowers for their food.

GO ON TO THE NEXT PAGE.

19. Professor: It has been argued that freedom of thought is a precondition for intellectual progress, because freedom of thought allows thinkers to pursue their ideas, regardless of whom these ideas offend, in whatever direction they lead. However, it is clear that one must mine the full implications of interrelated ideas to make intellectual progress, and for this, thinkers need intellectual discipline. Therefore, this argument for freedom of thought fails.

The conclusion drawn by the professor follows logically if which one of the following is assumed?

(A) Thinkers who limit their line of thought to a particular orthodoxy are hindered in their intellectual progress.

(B) Thinkers can mine the full implications of interrelated ideas only in the context of a society that values intellectual progress.

(C) In societies that protect freedom of thought, thinkers invariably lack intellectual discipline.

(D) Freedom of thought engenders creativity, which aids the discovery of truth.

(E) Without intellectual discipline, thinkers can have no freedom of thought.

20. People who have specialized knowledge about a scientific or technical issue are systematically excluded from juries for trials where that issue is relevant. Thus, trial by jury is not a fair means of settling disputes involving such issues.

Which one of the following, if true, most seriously weakens the argument?

(A) The more complicated the issue being litigated, the less likely it is that a juror without specialized knowledge of the field involved will be able to comprehend the testimony being given.

(B) The more a juror knows about a particular scientific or technical issue involved in a trial, the more likely it is that the juror will be prejudiced in favor of one of the litigating parties before the trial begins.

(C) Appointing an impartial arbitrator is not a fair means of settling disputes involving scientific or technical issues, because arbitrators tend to favor settlements in which both parties compromise on the issues.

(D) Experts who give testimony on scientific or technical issues tend to hedge their conclusions by discussing the possibility of error.

(E) Expert witnesses in specialized fields often command fees that are so high that many people involved in litigation cannot afford their services.

21. If one has evidence that an act will benefit other people and performs that act to benefit them, then one will generally succeed in benefiting them.

Which one of the following best illustrates the proposition above?

(A) A country's leaders realized that fostering diplomatic ties with antagonistic nations reduces the chances of war with those nations. Because those leaders worried that war would harm their chances of being reelected, they engaged in diplomatic discussions with a hostile country, and the two countries avoided a confrontation.

(B) A government study concluded that a proposed bureaucratic procedure would allow people to register their cars without waiting in line. The government adopted the procedure for this reason, and, as with most bureaucratic procedures, it was not successful.

(C) Betsy overheard a heating contractor say that regularly changing the filter in a furnace helps to keep the furnace efficient. So Betsy has regularly changed the furnace filter in her daughter's house. As a result, the furnace has never required maintenance due to becoming clogged with dust or dirt.

(D) Sejal learned in a psychology class that the best way to help someone overcome an addiction is to confront that person. So she confronted her friend Bob, who was struggling with a chemical dependency.

(E) Zachary hoped that psychotherapy could help his parents overcome their marital difficulties. He persuaded his parents to call a psychotherapist, and eventually their problems were resolved.

GO ON TO THE NEXT PAGE.

22. Radio airplay restrictions are nationally imposed regulations. The City Club has compiled a guide to all nationally imposed regulations except those related to taxation or to labor law. Radio airplay restrictions are related neither to taxation nor to labor law, so the City Club's guide covers radio airplay restrictions.

Which one of the following exhibits a pattern of reasoning most similar to that exhibited by the argument above?

(A) All prepackaged desserts pose a risk of tooth decay. The Nutrition Foundation recommends avoiding all prepackaged desserts that are not high in vitamins or protein. Many prepackaged snack foods are low in vitamins or protein, so the Nutrition Foundation recommends avoiding prepackaged snack foods as well.

(B) Coreopsis is a perennial. The Garden Club awards a prize each year for each perennial except those that are shrubs or not native to North America. Coreopsis is native to North America and is not a shrub. So the Garden Club awards a prize each year for coreopsis.

(C) The Windsor Coalition is an example of a community organizing to discourage overdevelopment. The Neighborhood Association is in favor of this sort of community organizing, except when it poses a threat to regional economic growth. Therefore, the Neighborhood Association is in favor of the Windsor Coalition.

(D) Compact discs are a kind of data storage device. Leotol Corporation does not produce data storage devices that use analog storage methods. Compact discs do not use analog storage methods, so it follows that Leotol Corporation produces compact discs.

(E) Traffic laws are a type of government regulation. The association supports traffic laws that are in the public interest, even if they have not been shown to reduce the accident rate. Thus, the association should support all government regulations that are in the public interest.

23. Physics professor: Some scientists claim that superheated plasma in which electrical resistance fails is a factor in causing so-called "ball lightning." If this were so, then such lightning would emit intense light and, since plasma has gaslike properties, would rise in the air. However, the instances of ball lightning that I observed were of low intensity and floated horizontally before vanishing. Thus, superheated plasma with failed electrical resistance is never a factor in causing ball lightning.

The physics professor's conclusion follows logically if which one of the following is assumed?

(A) Superheated plasma in which electrical resistance fails does not cause types of lightning other than ball lightning.

(B) The phenomena observed by the physics professor were each observed by at least one other person.

(C) Ball lightning can occur as the result of several different factors.

(D) Superheating of gaslike substances causes bright light to be emitted.

(E) All types of ball lightning have the same cause.

GO ON TO THE NEXT PAGE.

24. Advertisement: Our oat bran cereal is the only one that has printed right on its package all of its claimed health benefits. And really health-conscious consumers have demonstrated that these health claims are true by buying our cereal since they would not have bought our cereal unless the claims were true. How do we know these consumers are really health-conscious? No really health-conscious consumer would buy food in a package that did not have accurate information about the food's health benefits printed on it.

Which one of the following employs a flawed argumentative strategy that is most closely parallel to the flawed argumentative strategy in the advertisement above?

(A) Greeting one's coworkers must be a polite thing to do, because people who are considered polite always greet their coworkers. The proof that these people really are polite is that they are consistently polite in their daily lives.

(B) This card game must be intellectually challenging, because it is played by highly intelligent people, who play only intellectually challenging card games. In fact, these players' intelligence is demonstrated by the fact that they play this game.

(C) When coffee is being chosen, Brand Z is the coffee chosen by people with highly developed taste in coffee. These people showed their highly developed taste in coffee by correctly distinguishing eight brands of coffee from each other in a taste test.

(D) That jacket must have been made for a very short person, because only very short people were able to fit into it. We know that they were very short because we saw them before they tried on the jacket.

(E) This painting is a poor imitation, because only people with poor eyesight mistook it for the original. That these people have poor eyesight is demonstrated by the fact that they also mistook a vase of flowers in the painting for a peacock.

25. A study of 86 patients, all of whom suffered from disease T and received the same standard medical treatment, divided the patients into 2 equal groups. One group's members all attended weekly support group meetings, but no one from the other group attended support group meetings. After 10 years, 41 patients from each group had died. Clearly, support group meetings do not help patients with disease T live longer.

Which one of the following statements, if true, most seriously weakens the argument?

(A) Of the 4 patients who survived more than 10 years, the 2 who had attended weekly support group meetings lived longer than the 2 who had not.

(B) For many diseases, attending weekly support group meetings is part of the standard medical treatment.

(C) The members of the group that attended weekly support group meetings lived 2 years longer, on average, than the members of the other group.

(D) Some physicians have argued that attending weekly support group meetings gives patients less faith in the standard treatment for disease T.

(E) Everyone in the group whose members attended weekly support group meetings reported after 1 year that those meetings had helped them to cope with the disease.

26. Astronomer: I have asserted that our solar system does not contain enough meteoroids and other cosmic debris to have caused the extensive cratering on the far side of the moon. My opponents have repeatedly failed to demonstrate the falsity of this thesis. Their evidence is simply inconclusive; thus they should admit that my thesis is correct.

The reasoning in the astronomer's argument is flawed because this argument

(A) criticizes the astronomer's opponents rather than their arguments

(B) infers the truth of the astronomer's thesis from the mere claim that it has not been proven false

(C) ignores the possibility that alternative explanations may exist for the cratering

(D) presumes that the astronomer's thesis should not be subject to rational discussion and criticism

(E) fails to precisely define the key word "meteoroids"

S T O P

IF YOU FINISH BEFORE TIME IS CALLED, YOU MAY CHECK YOUR WORK ON THIS SECTION ONLY.
DO NOT WORK ON ANY OTHER SECTION IN THE TEST.

SECTION III

Time—35 minutes

27 Questions

<u>Directions</u>: Each passage in this section is followed by a group of questions to be answered on the basis of what is <u>stated</u> or <u>implied</u> in the passage. For some of the questions, more than one of the choices could conceivably answer the question. However, you are to choose the <u>best</u> answer; that is, the response that most accurately and completely answers the question, and blacken the corresponding space on your answer sheet.

The extent of a nation's power over its coastal ecosystems and the natural resources in its coastal waters has been defined by two international law doctrines: freedom of the seas and adjacent state
(5) sovereignty. Until the mid-twentieth century, most nations favored application of broad open-seas freedoms and limited sovereign rights over coastal waters. A nation had the right to include within its territorial dominion only a very narrow band of
(10) coastal waters (generally extending three miles from the shoreline), within which it had the authority, but not the responsibility, to regulate all activities. But, because this area of territorial dominion was so limited, most nations did not establish rules for
(15) management or protection of their territorial waters.

Regardless of whether or not nations enforced regulations in their territorial waters, large ocean areas remained free of controls or restrictions. The citizens of all nations had the right to use these
(20) unrestricted ocean areas for any innocent purpose, including navigation and fishing. Except for controls over its own citizens, no nation had the responsibility, let alone the unilateral authority, to control such activities in international waters. And, since there
(25) were few standards of conduct that applied on the "open seas," there were few jurisdictional conflicts between nations.

The lack of standards is traceable to popular perceptions held before the middle of this century.
(30) By and large, marine pollution was not perceived as a significant problem, in part because the adverse effect of coastal activities on ocean ecosystems was not widely recognized, and pollution caused by human activities was generally believed to be limited
(35) to that caused by navigation. Moreover, the freedom to fish, or overfish, was an essential element of the traditional legal doctrine of freedom of the seas that no maritime country wished to see limited. And finally, the technology that later allowed exploitation
(40) of other ocean resources, such as oil, did not yet exist.

To date, controlling pollution and regulating ocean resources have still not been comprehensively addressed by law, but international law—established through the customs and practices of nations—does
(45) not preclude such efforts. And two recent developments may actually lead to future international rules providing for ecosystem management. First, the establishment of extensive fishery zones, extending territorial authority as far as
(50) 200 miles out from a country's coast, has provided

the opportunity for nations individually to manage larger ecosystems. This opportunity, combined with national self-interest in maintaining fish populations, could lead nations to reevaluate policies for
(55) management of their fisheries and to address the problem of pollution in territorial waters. Second, the international community is beginning to understand the importance of preserving the resources and ecology of international waters and to show signs of
(60) accepting responsibility for doing so. As an international consensus regarding the need for comprehensive management of ocean resources develops, it will become more likely that international standards and policies for broader
(65) regulation of human activities that affect ocean ecosystems will be adopted and implemented.

1. According to the passage, until the mid-twentieth century there were few jurisdictional disputes over international waters because

    (A) the nearest coastal nation regulated activities
    (B) few controls or restrictions applied to ocean areas
    (C) the ocean areas were used for only innocent purposes
    (D) the freedom of the seas doctrine settled all claims concerning navigation and fishing
    (E) broad authority over international waters was shared equally among all nations

GO ON TO THE NEXT PAGE.

2. According to the international law doctrines applicable before the mid-twentieth century, if commercial activity within a particular nation's territorial waters threatened all marine life in those waters, the nation would have been

   (A) formally censured by an international organization for not properly regulating marine activities
   (B) called upon by other nations to establish rules to protect its territorial waters
   (C) able but not required to place legal limits on such commercial activities
   (D) allowed to resolve the problem at its own discretion providing it could contain the threat to its own territorial waters
   (E) permitted to hold the commercial offenders liable only if they were citizens of that particular nation

3. The author suggests that, before the mid-twentieth century, most nations' actions with respect to territorial and international waters indicated that

   (A) managing ecosystems in either territorial or international waters was given low priority
   (B) unlimited resources in international waters resulted in little interest in territorial waters
   (C) nations considered it their responsibility to protect territorial but not international waters
   (D) a nation's authority over its citizenry ended at territorial lines
   (E) although nations could extend their territorial dominion beyond three miles from their shoreline, most chose not to do so

4. The author cites which one of the following as an effect of the extension of territorial waters beyond the three-mile limit?

   (A) increased political pressure on individual nations to establish comprehensive laws regulating ocean resources
   (B) a greater number of jurisdictional disputes among nations over the regulation of fishing on the open seas
   (C) the opportunity for some nations to manage large ocean ecosystems
   (D) a new awareness of the need to minimize pollution caused by navigation
   (E) a political incentive for smaller nations to solve the problems of pollution in their coastal waters

5. According to the passage, before the middle of the twentieth century, nations failed to establish rules protecting their territorial waters because

   (A) the waters appeared to be unpolluted and to contain unlimited resources
   (B) the fishing industry would be adversely affected by such rules
   (C) the size of the area that would be subject to such rules was insignificant
   (D) the technology needed for pollution control and resource management did not exist
   (E) there were few jurisdictional conflicts over nations' territorial waters

6. The passage as a whole can best be described as

   (A) a chronology of the events that have led up to a present-day crisis
   (B) a legal inquiry into the abuse of existing laws and the likelihood of reform
   (C) a political analysis of the problems inherent in directing national attention to an international issue
   (D) a historical analysis of a problem that requires international attention
   (E) a proposal for adopting and implementing international standards to solve an ecological problem

GO ON TO THE NEXT PAGE.

The human species came into being at the time of the greatest biological diversity in the history of the Earth. Today, as human populations expand and alter the natural environment, they are reducing
(5) biological diversity to its lowest level since the end of the Mesozoic era, 65 million years ago. The ultimate consequences of this biological collision are beyond calculation, but they are certain to be harmful. That, in essence, is the biodiversity crisis.

(10) The history of global diversity can be summarized as follows: after the initial flowering of multicellular animals, there was a swift rise in the number of species in early Paleozoic times (between 600 and 430 million years ago), then plateaulike stagnation
(15) for the remaining 200 million years of the Paleozoic era, and finally a slow but steady climb through the Mesozoic and Cenozoic eras to diversity's all-time high. This history suggests that biological diversity was hard won and a long time in coming.
(20) Furthermore, this pattern of increase was set back by five massive extinction episodes. The most recent of these, during the Cretaceous period, is by far the most famous, because it ended the age of the dinosaurs, conferred hegemony on the mammals, and
(25) ultimately made possible the ascendancy of the human species. But the Cretaceous crisis was minor compared with the Permian extinctions 240 million years ago, during which between 77 and 96 percent of marine animal species perished. It took 5 million
(30) years, well into Mesozoic times, for species diversity to begin a significant recovery.

Within the past 10,000 years biological diversity has entered a wholly new era. Human activity has had a devastating effect on species diversity, and the
(35) rate of human-induced extinctions is accelerating. Half of the bird species of Polynesia have been eliminated through hunting and the destruction of native forests. Hundreds of fish species endemic to Lake Victoria are now threatened with extinction
(40) following the careless introduction of one species of fish, the Nile perch. The list of such biogeographic disasters is extensive.

Because every species is unique and irreplaceable, the loss of biodiversity is the most profound process
(45) of environmental change. Its consequences are also the least predictable because the value of the Earth's biota (the fauna and flora collectively) remains largely unstudied and unappreciated; unlike material and cultural wealth, which we understand because
(50) they are the substance of our everyday lives, biological wealth is usually taken for granted. This is a serious strategic error, one that will be increasingly regretted as time passes. The biota is not only part of a country's heritage, the product of millions of years
(55) of evolution centered on that place; it is also a potential source for immense untapped material wealth in the form of food, medicine, and other commercially important substances.

7. Which one of the following best expresses the main idea of the passage?

(A) The reduction in biodiversity is an irreversible process that represents a setback both for science and for society as a whole.

(B) The material and cultural wealth of a nation are insignificant when compared with the country's biological wealth.

(C) The enormous diversity of life on Earth could not have come about without periodic extinctions that have conferred preeminence on one species at the expense of another.

(D) The human species is in the process of initiating a massive extinction episode that may make past episodes look minor by comparison.

(E) The current decline in species diversity is a human-induced tragedy of incalculable proportions that has potentially grave consequences for the human species.

8. Which one of the following situations is most analogous to the history of global diversity summarized in lines 10–18 of the passage?

(A) The number of fish in a lake declines abruptly as a result of water pollution, then makes a slow comeback after cleanup efforts and the passage of ordinances against dumping.

(B) The concentration of chlorine in the water supply of a large city fluctuates widely before stabilizing at a constant and safe level.

(C) An old-fashioned article of clothing goes in and out of style periodically as a result of features in fashion magazines and the popularity of certain period films.

(D) After valuable mineral deposits are discovered, the population of a geographic region booms, then levels off and begins to decrease at a slow and steady rate.

(E) The variety of styles stocked by a shoe store increases rapidly after the store opens, holds constant for many months, and then gradually creeps upward.

GO ON TO THE NEXT PAGE.

9. The author suggests which one of the following about the Cretaceous crisis?

(A) It was the second most devastating extinction episode in history.
(B) It was the most devastating extinction episode up until that time.
(C) It was less devastating to species diversity than is the current biodiversity crisis.
(D) The rate of extinction among marine animal species as a result of the crisis did not approach 77 percent.
(E) The dinosaurs comprised the great majority of species that perished during the crisis.

10. The author mentions the Nile perch in order to provide an example of

(A) a species that has become extinct through human activity
(B) the typical lack of foresight that has led to biogeographic disaster
(C) a marine animal species that survived the Permian extinctions
(D) a species that is a potential source of material wealth
(E) the kind of action that is necessary to reverse the decline in species diversity

11. All of the following are explicitly mentioned in the passage as contributing to the extinction of species EXCEPT

(A) hunting
(B) pollution
(C) deforestation
(D) the growth of human populations
(E) human-engineered changes in the environment

12. The passage suggests which one of the following about material and cultural wealth?

(A) Because we can readily assess the value of material and cultural wealth, we tend not to take them for granted.
(B) Just as the biota is a source of potential material wealth, it is an untapped source of cultural wealth as well.
(C) Some degree of material and cultural wealth may have to be sacrificed if we are to protect our biological heritage.
(D) Material and cultural wealth are of less value than biological wealth because they have evolved over a shorter period of time.
(E) Material wealth and biological wealth are interdependent in a way that material wealth and cultural wealth are not.

13. The author would be most likely to agree with which one of the following statements about the consequences of the biodiversity crisis?

(A) The loss of species diversity will have as immediate an impact on the material wealth of nations as on their biological wealth.
(B) The crisis will likely end the hegemony of the human race and bring about the ascendancy of another species.
(C) The effects of the loss of species diversity will be dire, but we cannot yet tell how dire.
(D) It is more fruitful to discuss the consequences of the crisis in terms of the potential loss to humanity than in strictly biological terms.
(E) The consequences of the crisis can be minimized, but the pace of extinctions cannot be reversed.

GO ON TO THE NEXT PAGE.

Women's participation in the revolutionary events in France between 1789 and 1795 has only recently been given nuanced treatment. Early twentieth-century historians of the French Revolution are
(5) typified by Jaures, who, though sympathetic to the women's movement of his own time, never even mentions its antecedents in revolutionary France. Even today most general histories treat only cursorily a few individual women, like Marie Antoinette. The
(10) recent studies by Landes, Badinter, Godineau, and Roudinesco, however, should signal a much-needed reassessment of women's participation.

Godineau and Roudinesco point to three significant phases in that participation. The first, up
(15) to mid-1792, involved those women who wrote political tracts. Typical of their orientation to theoretical issues—in Godineau's view, without practical effect—is Marie Gouze's *Declaration of the Rights of Women.* The emergence of vocal middle-
(20) class women's political clubs marks the second phase. Formed in 1791 as adjuncts of middle-class male political clubs, and originally philanthropic in function, by late 1792 independent clubs of women began to advocate military participation for women.
(25) In the final phase, the famine of 1795 occasioned a mass women's movement: women seized food supplies, held officials hostage, and argued for the implementation of democratic politics. This phase ended in May of 1795 with the military suppression
(30) of this multiclass movement. In all three phases women's participation in politics contrasted markedly with their participation before 1789. Before that date some noblewomen participated indirectly in elections, but such participation by more
(35) than a narrow range of the population—women or men—came only with the Revolution.

What makes the recent studies particularly compelling, however, is not so much their organization of chronology as their unflinching
(40) willingness to confront the reasons for the collapse of the women's movement. For Landes and Badinter, the necessity of women's having to speak in the established vocabularies of certain intellectual and political traditions diminished the ability of the
(45) women's movement to resist suppression. Many women, and many men, they argue, located their vision within the confining tradition of Jean-Jacques Rousseau, who linked male and female roles with public and private spheres respectively. But, when
(50) women went on to make political alliances with radical Jacobin men, Badinter asserts, they adopted a vocabulary and a violently extremist viewpoint that unfortunately was even more damaging to their political interests.
(55) Each of these scholars has a different political agenda and takes a different approach—Godineau, for example, works with police archives while Roudinesco uses explanatory schema from modern psychology. Yet, admirably, each gives center stage
(60) to a group that previously has been marginalized, or

at best undifferentiated, by historians. And in the case of Landes and Badinter, the reader is left with a sobering awareness of the cost to the women of the Revolution of speaking in borrowed voices.

14. Which one of the following best states the main point of the passage?

(A) According to recent historical studies, the participation of women in the revolutionary events of 1789–1795 can most profitably be viewed in three successive stages.

(B) The findings of certain recent historical studies have resulted from an earlier general reassessment, by historians, of women's participation in the revolutionary events of 1789–1795.

(C) Adopting the vocabulary and viewpoint of certain intellectual and political traditions resulted in no political advantage for women in France in the years 1789–1795.

(D) Certain recent historical studies have provided a much-needed description and evaluation of the evolving roles of women in the revolutionary events of 1789–1795.

(E) Historical studies that seek to explain the limitations of the women's movement in France during the years 1789–1795 are much more convincing than are those that seek only to describe the general features of that movement.

GO ON TO THE NEXT PAGE.

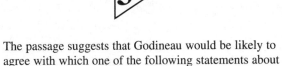
15. The passage suggests that Godineau would be likely to agree with which one of the following statements about Marie Gouze's Declaration of the Rights of Women?

    (A) This work was not understood by many of Gouze's contemporaries.
    (B) This work indirectly inspired the formation of independent women's political clubs.
    (C) This work had little impact on the world of political action.
    (D) This work was the most compelling produced by a French woman between 1789 and 1792.
    (E) This work is typical of the kind of writing French women produced between 1793 and 1795.

16. According to the passage, which one of the following is a true statement about the purpose of the women's political clubs mentioned in line 20?

    (A) These clubs fostered a mass women's movement.
    (B) These clubs eventually developed a purpose different from their original purpose.
    (C) These clubs were founded to advocate military participation for women.
    (D) These clubs counteracted the original purpose of male political clubs.
    (E) These clubs lost their direction by the time of the famine of 1795.

17. The primary function of the first paragraph of the passage is to

    (A) outline the author's argument about women's roles in France between 1789 and 1795
    (B) anticipate possible challenges to the findings of the recent studies of women in France between 1789 and 1795
    (C) summarize some long-standing explanations of the role of individual women in France between 1789 and 1795
    (D) present a context for the discussion of recent studies of women in France between 1789 and 1795
    (E) characterize various eighteenth-century studies of women in France

18. The passage suggests that Landes and Badinter would be likely to agree with which one of the following statements about the women's movement in France in the 1790s?

    (A) The movement might have been more successful if women had developed their own political vocabularies.
    (B) The downfall of the movement was probably unrelated to its alliance with Jacobin men.
    (C) The movement had a great deal of choice about whether to adopt a Rousseauist political vocabulary.
    (D) The movement would have triumphed if it had not been suppressed by military means.
    (E) The movement viewed a Rousseauist political tradition, rather than a Jacobin political ideology, as detrimental to its interests.

19. In the context of the passage, the word "cost" in line 63 refers to the

    (A) dichotomy of private roles for women and public roles for men
    (B) almost nonexistent political participation of women before 1789
    (C) historians' lack of differentiation among various groups of women
    (D) political alliances women made with radical Jacobin men
    (E) collapse of the women's movement in the 1790s

20. The author of the passage is primarily concerned with

    (A) criticizing certain political and intellectual traditions
    (B) summarizing the main points of several recent historical studies and assessing their value
    (C) establishing a chronological sequence and arguing for its importance
    (D) comparing and contrasting women's political activities before and after the French Revolution
    (E) reexamining a long-held point of view and isolating its strengths and weaknesses

GO ON TO THE NEXT PAGE.

Art historians' approach to French Impressionism has changed significantly in recent years. While a decade ago Rewald's *History of Impressionism,* which emphasizes Impressionist painters' stylistic
(5) innovations, was unchallenged, the literature on Impressionism has now become a kind of ideological battlefield, in which more attention is paid to the subject matter of the paintings, and to the social and moral issues raised by it, than to their style.
(10) Recently, politically charged discussions that address the Impressionists' unequal treatment of men and women and the exclusion of modern industry and labor from their pictures have tended to crowd out the stylistic analysis favored by Rewald and his
(15) followers. In a new work illustrating this trend, Robert L. Herbert dissociates himself from formalists whose preoccupation with the stylistic features of Impressionist painting has, in Herbert's view, left the history out of art history; his aim is to
(20) restore Impressionist paintings "to their sociocultural context." However, his arguments are not, finally, persuasive.

In attempting to place Impressionist painting in its proper historical context, Herbert has redrawn the
(25) traditional boundaries of Impressionism. Limiting himself to the two decades between 1860 and 1880, he assembles under the Impressionist banner what can only be described as a somewhat eccentric grouping of painters. Cezanne, Pisarro, and Sisley
(30) are almost entirely ignored, largely because their paintings do not suit Herbert's emphasis on themes of urban life and suburban leisure, while Manet, Degas, and Caillebotte—who paint scenes of urban life but whom many would hardly characterize as
(35) Impressionists—dominate the first half of the book. Although this new description of Impressionist painting provides a more unified conception of nineteenth-century French painting by grouping quite disparate modernist painters together and
(40) emphasizing their common concerns rather than their stylistic differences, it also forces Herbert to overlook some of the most important genres of Impressionist painting—portraiture, pure landscape, and still-life painting.
(45) Moreover, the rationale for Herbert's emphasis on the social and political realities that Impressionist paintings can be said to communicate rather than on their style is finally undermined by what even Herbert concedes was the failure of Impressionist
(50) painters to serve as particularly conscientious illustrators of their social milieu. They left much ordinary experience—work and poverty, for example—out of their paintings, and what they did put in was transformed by a style that had only an
(55) indirect relationship to the social realities of the world they depicted. Not only were their pictures inventions rather than photographs, they were inventions in which style to some degree disrupted description. Their paintings in effect have two levels
(60) of "subject": what is represented and how it is

represented, and no art historian can afford to emphasize one at the expense of the other.

21. Which one of the following best expresses the main point of the passage?

(A) The style of Impressionist paintings has only an indirect relation to their subject matter.
(B) The approach to Impressionism that is illustrated by Herbert's recent book is inadequate.
(C) The historical context of Impressionist paintings is not relevant to their interpretation.
(D) Impressionism emerged from a historical context of ideological conflict and change.
(E) Any adequate future interpretation of Impressionism will have to come to terms with Herbert's view of this art movement.

22. According to the passage, Rewald's book on Impressionism was characterized by which one of the following?

(A) evenhanded objectivity about the achievements of Impressionism
(B) bias in favor of certain Impressionist painters
(C) an emphasis on the stylistic features of Impressionist painting
(D) an idiosyncratic view of which painters were to be classified as Impressionists
(E) a refusal to enter into the ideological debates that had characterized earlier discussions of Impressionism

23. The author implies that Herbert's redefinition of the boundaries of Impressionism resulted from which one of the following?

(A) an exclusive emphasis on form and style
(B) a bias in favor of the representation of modern industry
(C) an attempt to place Impressionism within a specific sociocultural context
(D) a broadening of the term "Impressionism" to include all of nineteenth-century French painting
(E) an insufficient familiarity with earlier interpretations of Impressionism

GO ON TO THE NEXT PAGE.

24. The author states which one of the following about modern industry and labor as subjects for painting?

   (A)   The Impressionists neglected these subjects in their paintings.
   (B)   Herbert's book on Impressionism fails to give adequate treatment of these subjects.
   (C)   The Impressionists' treatment of these subjects was idealized.
   (D)   Rewald's treatment of Impressionist painters focused inordinately on their representations of these subjects.
   (E)   Modernist painters presented a distorted picture of these subjects.

25. Which one of the following most accurately describes the structure of the author's argument in the passage?

   (A)   The first two paragraphs each present independent arguments for a conclusion that is drawn in the third paragraph.
   (B)   A thesis is stated in the first paragraph and revised in the second paragraph, and the revised thesis is supported with an argument in the third paragraph.
   (C)   The first two paragraphs discuss and criticize a thesis, and the third paragraph presents an alternative thesis.
   (D)   A claim is made in the first paragraph, and the next two paragraphs each present reasons for accepting that claim.
   (E)   An argument is presented in the first paragraph, a counterargument is presented in the second paragraph, and the third paragraph suggests a way to resolve the dispute.

26. The author's statement that Impressionist paintings "were inventions in which style to some degree disrupted description" (lines 57–59) serves to

   (A)   strengthen the claim that Impressionists sought to emphasize the differences between painting and photography
   (B)   weaken the argument that style is the only important feature of Impressionist paintings
   (C)   indicate that Impressionists recognized that they had been strongly influenced by photography
   (D)   support the argument that an exclusive emphasis on the Impressionists' subject matter is mistaken
   (E)   undermine the claim that Impressionists neglected certain kinds of subject matter

27. The author would most likely regard a book on the Impressionists that focused entirely on their style as

   (A)   a product of the recent confusion caused by Herbert's book on Impressionism
   (B)   emphasizing what Impressionists themselves took to be their primary artistic concern
   (C)   an overreaction against the traditional interpretation of Impressionism
   (D)   neglecting the most innovative aspects of Impressionism
   (E)   addressing only part of what an adequate treatment should cover

S T O P

IF YOU FINISH BEFORE TIME IS CALLED, YOU MAY CHECK YOUR WORK ON THIS SECTION ONLY.
DO NOT WORK ON ANY OTHER SECTION IN THE TEST.

SECTION IV

Time—35 minutes

26 Questions

Directions: Each passage in this section is followed by a group of questions to be answered on the basis of what is <u>stated</u> or <u>implied</u> in the passage. For some of the questions, more than one of the choices could conceivably answer the question. However, you are to choose the <u>best</u> answer; that is, the response that most accurately and completely answers the question, and blacken the corresponding space on your answer sheet.

Most of what has been written about Thurgood Marshall, a former United States Supreme Court justice who served from 1967 to 1991, has just focused on his judicial record and on the ideological content of his
(5) earlier achievements as a lawyer pursuing civil rights issues in the courts. But when Marshall's career is viewed from a technical perspective, his work with the NAACP (National Association for the Advancement of Colored People) reveals a strategic and methodological
(10) legacy to the field of public interest law. Though the NAACP, under Marshall's direction, was not the first legal organization in the U.S. to be driven by a political and social agenda, he and the NAACP developed innovations that forever changed the landscape of
(15) public interest law: during the 1940s and 1950s, in their campaign against state-sanctioned racial segregation, Marshall and the NAACP, instead of simply pursuing cases as the opportunity arose, set up a predetermined legal campaign that was meticulously
(20) crafted and carefully coordinated.

One aspect of this campaign, the test case strategy, involved sponsoring litigation of tactically chosen cases at the trial court level with careful evaluation of the precedential nuances and potential impact of each
(25) decision. This allowed Marshall to try out different approaches and discover which was the best to be used. An essential element in the success of this tactic was the explicit recognition that in a public interest legal campaign, choosing the right plaintiff can mean the
(30) difference between success and failure. Marshall carefully selected cases with sympathetic litigants, whose public appeal, credibility, and commitment to the NAACP's goals were unsurpassed.

In addition, Marshall used sociological and
(35) psychological statistics—presented in expert testimony, for example, about the psychological impact of enforced segregation—as a means of transforming constitutional law by persuading the courts that certain discriminatory laws produced public harms in violation
(40) of constitutional principles. This tactic, while often effective, has been criticized by some legal scholars as a pragmatic attempt to give judges nonlegal material with which to fill gaps in their justifications for decisions where the purely legal principles appear
(45) inconclusive.

Since the time of Marshall's work with the NAACP, the number of public interest law firms in the U.S. has grown substantially, and they have widely adopted his combination of strategies for litigation,

(50) devoting them to various public purposes. These strategies have been used, for example, in consumer advocacy campaigns and, more recently, by politically conservative public interest lawyers seeking to achieve, through litigation, changes in the law that they have not
(55) been able to accomplish in the legislature. If we focus on the particular content of Marshall's goals and successes, it might seem surprising that his work has influenced the quest for such divergent political objectives, but the techniques that he honed—
(60) originally considered to be a radical departure from accepted conventions—have become the norm for U.S. public interest litigation today.

1. Which one of the following most accurately expresses the main point of the passage?

(A) In his role as a lawyer for the NAACP, Marshall developed a number of strategies for litigation which, while often controversial, proved to be highly successful in arguing against certain discriminatory laws.

(B) The litigation strategies that Marshall devised in pursuit of the NAACP's civil rights goals during the 1940s and 1950s constituted significant innovations that have since been adopted as standard tactics for public interest lawyers.

(C) Although commentary on Marshall has often focused only on a single ideological aspect of his accomplishments, a reinvestigation of his record as a judge reveals its influence on current divergent political objectives.

(D) In his work with the NAACP during the 1940s and 1950s, Marshall adopted a set of tactics that were previously considered a radical departure from accepted practice, but which he adapted in such a way that they eventually became accepted conventions in the field of law.

(E) Contrary to the impression commonly given by commentary on Marshall, his contributions to the work of the NAACP have had more of a lasting impact than his achievements as a U.S. Supreme Court justice.

GO ON TO THE NEXT PAGE.

2. Which one of the following most accurately describes two main functions of the first sentence of the passage?

    (A) It disputes a claim that has often been accepted and summarizes Marshall's achievements.
    (B) It establishes the passage's main topic and indicates the controversial nature of Marshall's ideologies.
    (C) It introduces two aspects of Marshall's career and outlines the historical significance of both.
    (D) It identifies Marshall's better-known achievements and suggests that commentary has neglected certain other achievements.
    (E) It provides a new perspective on Marshall's achievements and corrects a historical inaccuracy.

3. Which one of the following pairs of tactics used by an environmental-advocacy public interest law firm is most closely analogous to the strategies that Marshall utilized during his work with the NAACP?

    (A) a decision to pursue a pollution case based on its potential legal implications for a large class of related cases; and testimony by a noted medical authority whose data support the claim that the pollution in question causes widespread medical problems
    (B) acceptance of a pollution case based on the practical urgency of its expected impact on the environment if a ruling in favor of the plaintiff is rendered; and assignment of the case to the most widely known members of the firm
    (C) preference for pursuing a series of cases that are to be tried in courts having a record of decisions that are favorable to environmental interests; and taking these cases to judges who strictly uphold constitutional principles
    (D) acceptance of a pollution damage case based primarily on the potential plaintiff's needs; and careful orchestration of pretrial publicity designed to acquaint the public with the relevant issues
    (E) thorough and painstaking research of precedents relating to a current pollution case; and consultations with lawyers for the defense regarding a pretrial settlement

4. It can be most reasonably inferred from the passage that the author views the test case strategy developed by Marshall as

    (A) arbitrary
    (B) inflexible
    (C) unprecedented
    (D) necessary
    (E) subjective

5. The passage provides the most support for which one of the following statements?

    (A) The ideological motivations for Marshall's work with the NAACP changed during his tenure on the U.S. Supreme Court.
    (B) Marshall declined to pursue some cases that were in keeping with the NAACP's goals but whose plaintiffs' likely impression on the public he deemed to be unfavorable.
    (C) Marshall's tactics were initially opposed by some other members of the NAACP who favored a more traditional approach.
    (D) Marshall relied more on expert testimony in lower courts, whose judges were more likely than higher court judges to give weight to statistical evidence.
    (E) Marshall's colleagues at the NAACP subsequently revised his methods and extended their applications to areas of law and politics beyond those for which they were designed.

6. Based on the passage, it can be most reasonably inferred that the author would agree with which one of the following statements?

    (A) In light of a reconsideration of Marshall's career, it seems that commentary has undervalued both his innovations in litigation strategy and his accomplishments on the U.S. Supreme Court.
    (B) The most controversial of Marshall's methods was, somewhat paradoxically, the most unequivocally successful part of his overall campaign with the NAACP.
    (C) Lawyers representing private interests had previously used sociological evidence in court cases.
    (D) In response to Marshall's successes in NAACP litigations, the first public interest law firms were established, and they represented a radical change from previous types of U.S. law firms.
    (E) Marshall's techniques lend themselves to being used even for purposes that Marshall might not have intended.

7. According to the passage, some legal scholars have criticized which one of the following?

    (A) the ideology Marshall used to support his goals
    (B) recent public interest campaigns
    (C) the use of Marshall's techniques by politically conservative lawyers
    (D) the use of psychological statistics in court cases
    (E) the set of criteria for selecting public interest litigants

GO ON TO THE NEXT PAGE.

The painter Roy Lichtenstein helped to define pop art—the movement that incorporated commonplace objects and commercial-art techniques into paintings—by paraphrasing the style of comic books in his work.

(5) His merger of a popular genre with the forms and intentions of fine art generated a complex result: while poking fun at the pretensions of the art world, Lichtenstein's work also managed to convey a seriousness of theme that enabled it to transcend mere

(10) parody.

That Lichtenstein's images were fine art was at first difficult to see, because, with their word balloons and highly stylized figures, they looked like nothing more than the comic book panels from which they were

(15) copied. Standard art history holds that pop art emerged as an impersonal alternative to the histrionics of abstract expressionism, a movement in which painters conveyed their private attitudes and emotions using nonrepresentational techniques. The truth is that by the

(20) time pop art first appeared in the early 1960s, abstract expressionism had already lost much of its force. Pop art painters weren't quarreling with the powerful early abstract expressionist work of the late 1940s but with a second generation of abstract expressionists whose

(25) work seemed airy, high-minded, and overly lyrical. Pop art paintings were full of simple black lines and large areas of primary color. Lichtenstein's work was part of a general rebellion against the fading emotional power of abstract expressionism, rather than an aloof

(30) attempt to ignore it.

But if rebellion against previous art by means of the careful imitation of a popular genre were all that characterized Lichtenstein's work, it would possess only the reflective power that parodies have in relation

(35) to their subjects. Beneath its cartoonish methods, his work displayed an impulse toward realism, an urge to say that what was missing from contemporary painting was the depiction of contemporary life. The stilted romances and war stories portrayed in the comic books

(40) on which he based his canvases, the stylized automobiles, hot dogs, and table lamps that appeared in his pictures, were reflections of the culture Lichtenstein inhabited. But, in contrast to some pop art, Lichtenstein's work exuded not a jaded cynicism about

(45) consumer culture, but a kind of deliberate naivete, intended as a response to the excess of sophistication he observed not only in the later abstract expressionists but in some other pop artists. With the comics— typically the domain of youth and innocence—as his

(50) reference point, a nostalgia fills his paintings that gives them, for all their surface bravado, an inner sweetness. His persistent use of comic-art conventions demonstrates a faith in reconciliation, not only between cartoons and fine art, but between parody and true

(55) feeling.

8. Which one of the following most accurately states the main point of the passage?

(A) Lichtenstein's use of comic book elements in his paintings, considered simply a parodic reaction to the high-mindedness of later abstract expressionism, is also an attempt to re-create the emotionally powerful work of earlier abstract expressionists.

(B) Lichtenstein's use of comic book elements is not solely a parodic reaction to the high-mindedness of later abstract expressionism but also demonstrates an attempt to achieve realistic and nostalgic effects simultaneously in his paintings.

(C) Lichtenstein's use of comic book elements obscures the emotional complexity contained in his paintings, a situation that has prevented his work from being recognized as fine art in the expressionist tradition.

(D) Lichtenstein's use of comic book elements appears to mark his paintings as parodic reactions to the whole of abstract expressionism when they are instead a rebellion against the high-mindedness of the later abstract expressionists.

(E) Lichtenstein's use of comic book elements in his paintings, though a response to the excessive sophistication of the art world, is itself highly sophisticated in that it manages to reconcile pop art and fine art.

9. Which one of the following best captures the author's attitude toward Lichtenstein's work?

(A) enthusiasm for its more rebellious aspects

(B) respect for its successful parody of youth and innocence

(C) pleasure in its blatant rejection of abstract expressionism

(D) admiration for its subtle critique of contemporary culture

(E) appreciation for its ability to incorporate both realism and naivete

GO ON TO THE NEXT PAGE.

10. The author most likely lists some of the themes and objects influencing and appearing in Lichtenstein's paintings (lines 38–43) primarily to

   (A) show that the paintings depict aspects of contemporary life
   (B) support the claim that Lichtenstein's work was parodic in intent
   (C) contrast Lichtenstein's approach to art with that of abstract expressionism
   (D) suggest the emotions that lie at the heart of Lichtenstein's work
   (E) endorse Lichtenstein's attitude toward consumer culture

11. Based on the passage, which one of the following would be an example of pop art that is most in keeping with the spirit of Lichtenstein's work?

   (A) a painting that uses realistic techniques to represent several simple objects arranged on a table
   (B) a painting that parodies human figures by depicting them as stick figures
   (C) a painting that conveys its creator's inner turmoil through the use of bold lines and primary colors
   (D) a painting that employs vague shapes and images to make a statement about consumer culture
   (E) a painting that depicts products as they appear in magazine advertisements to comment on society's values

12. Which one of the following, if true, would most challenge the author's characterization of Lichtenstein?

   (A) Lichtenstein frequently attended exhibitions by abstract expressionist painters in the 1960s.
   (B) Lichtenstein praised a contemporary abstract expressionist in the 1960s for producing an atypically emotional painting.
   (C) Lichtenstein praised an early abstract expressionist for producing emotional paintings.
   (D) Lichtenstein criticized a pop artist in the 1960s for producing emotional paintings.
   (E) Lichtenstein criticized a pop artist in the 1960s for producing paintings void of emotion.

13. The primary purpose of the passage is most likely to

   (A) express curiosity about an artist's work
   (B) clarify the motivation behind an artist's work
   (C) contrast two opposing theories about an artist's work
   (D) describe the evolution of an artist's work
   (E) refute a previous overestimation of an artist's work

14. Based on the passage, which one of the following does the author appear to believe about the rebellious aspect of Lichtenstein's work?

   (A) It was directed less against abstract expressionism exclusively than against overly sophisticated art.
   (B) It was directed less against later abstract expressionism than against commercial art.
   (C) It was directed less against later abstract expressionism exclusively than against abstract expressionism in general.
   (D) It was an objection to the consumerism of the culture.
   (E) It was an objection to the simplicity of line and color used by pop artists.

15. Based on the passage, which one of the following can most reasonably be inferred about abstract expressionism?

   (A) Over time, it moved from abstraction to realism.
   (B) Over time, it moved from intensity to lyricism.
   (C) Over time, it moved from intellectualism to emotionalism.
   (D) Over time, it moved from obscurity to clarity.
   (E) Over time, it moved from density to sparseness.

GO ON TO THE NEXT PAGE.

Because the market system enables entrepreneurs and investors who develop new technology to reap financial rewards from their risk of capital, it may seem that the primary result of this activity is that some
(5) people who have spare capital accumulate more. But in spite of the fact that the profits derived from various technological developments have accrued to relatively few people, the developments themselves have served overall as a remarkable democratizing force. In fact,
(10) under the regime of the market, the gap in benefits accruing to different groups of people has been narrowed in the long term.

This tendency can be seen in various well-known technological developments. For example, before the
(15) printing press was introduced centuries ago, few people had access to written materials, much less to scribes and private secretaries to produce and transcribe documents. Since printed materials have become widely available, however, people without special
(20) position or resources—and in numbers once thought impossible—can take literacy and the use of printed texts for granted. With the distribution of books and periodicals in public libraries, this process has been extended to the point where people in general can have
(25) essentially equal access to a vast range of texts that would once have been available only to a very few. A more recent technological development extends this process beyond printed documents. A child in school with access to a personal computer and modem—
(30) which is becoming fairly common in technologically advanced societies—has computing power and database access equal to that of the best-connected scientists and engineers at top-level labs of just fifteen years ago, a time when relatively few people had
(35) personal access to any computing power. Or consider the uses of technology for leisure. In previous centuries only a few people with abundant resources had the ability and time to hire professional entertainment, and to have contact through travel and written
(40) communication—both of which were prohibitively expensive—with distant people. But now broadcast technology is widely available, and so almost anyone can have an entertainment cornucopia unimagined in earlier times. Similarly, the development of
(45) inexpensive mail distribution and telephone connections and, more recently, the establishment of the even more efficient medium of electronic mail have greatly extended the power of distant communication.

This kind of gradual diffusion of benefits across
(50) society is not an accident of these particular technological developments, but rather the result of a general tendency of the market system. Entrepreneurs and investors often are unable to maximize financial success without expanding their market, and this
(55) involves structuring their prices to the consumers so as to make their technologies genuinely accessible to an ever-larger share of the population. In other words, because market competition drives prices down, it tends to diffuse access to new technology across
(60) society as a result.

16. Which one of the following does the passage identify as being a result of a technological development?

(A) burgeoning scientific research
(B) educational uses of broadcasting
(C) widespread exchange of political ideas
(D) faster means of travel
(E) increased access to databases

17. As used in the passage, the word "democratizing" (line 9) most nearly means equalizing which one of the following?

(A) distribution of tangible and intangible goods
(B) opportunity to create new technology
(C) accumulation of financial assets in investments
(D) participation in the regulation of society through either public or private institutions
(E) generally acknowledged social status in a community

18. Which one of the following most accurately represents the primary function of the reference to maximization of financial success (lines 52–54)?

(A) It forms part of the author's summary of the benefits that have resulted from the technological developments described in the preceding paragraph.
(B) It serves as the author's logical conclusion from data presented in the preceding paragraph regarding the social consequences of technological development.
(C) It forms part of a speculative hypothesis that the author presents for its interest in relation to the main topic rather than as part of an argument.
(D) It serves as part of a causal explanation that reinforces the thesis in the first paragraph regarding the benefits of technological development.
(E) It forms part of the author's concession that certain factors complicate the argument presented in the first two paragraphs.

GO ON TO THE NEXT PAGE.

19. It can be most reasonably inferred from the passage that the author would agree with which one of the following statements?

    (A) The profits derived from computer technology have accrued to fewer people than have the profits derived from any other technological development.

    (B) Often the desire of some people for profits motivates changes that are beneficial for large numbers of other people.

    (C) National boundaries are rarely barriers to the democratizing spread of technology.

    (D) Typically, investment in technology is riskier than many other sorts of investment.

    (E) Greater geographical mobility of populations has contributed to the profits of entrepreneurs and investors in technology.

20. From the passage it can be most reasonably inferred that the author would agree with which one of the following statements?

    (A) The democratizing influence of technology generally contributes to technological obsolescence.

    (B) Wholly unregulated economies are probably the fastest in producing an equalization of social status.

    (C) Expanded access to printed texts across a population has historically led to an increase in literacy in that population.

    (D) The invention of the telephone has had a greater democratizing influence on society than has the invention of the printing press.

    (E) Near equality of financial assets among people is a realistic goal for market economies.

GO ON TO THE NEXT PAGE.

Neurobiologists once believed that the workings of the brain were guided exclusively by electrical signals; according to this theory, communication between neurons (brain cells) is possible because electrical
(5) impulses travel from one neuron to the next by literally leaping across the synapses (gaps between neurons). But many neurobiologists puzzled over how this leaping across synapses might be achieved, and as early as 1904 some speculated that electrical impulses
(10) are transmitted between neurons chemically rather than electrically. According to this alternative theory, the excited neuron secretes a chemical called a neurotransmitter that binds with its corresponding receptor molecule in the receiving neuron. This binding
(15) of the neurotransmitter renders the neuron permeable to ions, and as the ions move into the receiving neuron they generate an electrical impulse that runs through the cell; the electrical impulse is thereby transmitted to the receiving neuron.
(20)   This theory has gradually won acceptance in the scientific community, but for a long time little was known about the mechanism by which neurotransmitters manage to render the receiving neuron permeable to ions. In fact, some scientists
(25) remained skeptical of the theory because they had trouble imagining how the binding of a chemical to a receptor at the cell surface could influence the flow of ions through the cell membrane. Recently, however, researchers have gathered enough evidence for a
(30) convincing explanation: that the structure of receptors plays the pivotal role in mediating the conversion of chemical signals into electrical activity.
     The new evidence shows that receptors for neurotransmitters contain both a neurotransmitter
(35) binding site and a separate region that functions as a channel for ions; attachment of the neurotransmitter to the binding site causes the receptor to change shape and so results in the opening of its channel component. Several types of receptors have been isolated that
(40) conform to this structure, among them the receptors for acetylcholine, gamma-aminobutyric acid (GABA), glycine, and serotonin. These receptors display enough similarities to constitute a family, known collectively as neurotransmitter-gated ion channels.
(45)   It has also been discovered that each of the receptors in this family comes in several varieties so that, for example, a GABA receptor in one part of the brain has slightly different properties than a GABA receptor in another part of the brain. This discovery is
(50) medically significant because it raises the possibility of the highly selective treatment of certain brain disorders. As the precise effect on behavior of every variety of each neurotransmitter-gated ion channel is deciphered, pharmacologists may be able to design
(55) drugs targeted to specific receptors on defined categories of neurons that will selectively impede or enhance these effects. Such drugs could potentially help ameliorate any number of debilitating conditions, including mood disorders, tissue damage associated
(60) with stroke, or Alzheimer's disease.

21. Which one of the following most completely and accurately states the main point of the passage?

(A) Evidence shows that the workings of the brain are guided, not by electrical signals, but by chemicals, and that subtle differences among the receptors for these chemicals may permit the selective treatment of certain brain disorders.

(B) Evidence shows that the workings of the brain are guided, not by electrical signals, but by chemicals, and that enough similarities exist among these chemicals to allow scientists to classify them as a family.

(C) Evidence shows that electrical impulses are transmitted between neurons chemically rather than electrically, and that enough similarities exist among these chemicals to allow scientists to classify them as a family.

(D) Evidence shows that electrical impulses are transmitted between neurons chemically rather than electrically, and that subtle differences among the receptors for these chemicals may permit the selective treatment of certain brain disorders.

(E) Evidence shows that receptor molecules in the brain differ subtly from one another, and that these differences can be exploited to treat certain brain disorders through the use of drugs that selectively affect particular parts of the brain.

22. Based on the passage, the author's attitude toward the discovery presented in the last paragraph is most accurately described as

(A) certainty that its possible benefits will be realized
(B) optimism about its potential applications
(C) apprehension about the possibility of its misuse
(D) concern that its benefits are easily exaggerated
(E) skepticism toward its assumptions about the brain

23. Each of the following statements is affirmed by the passage EXCEPT:

(A) The secretion of certain chemicals plays a role in neuron communication.
(B) The flow of ions through neurons plays a role in neuron communication.
(C) The binding of neurotransmitters to receptors plays a role in neuron communication.
(D) The structure of receptors on neuron surfaces plays a role in neuron communication.
(E) The size of neurotransmitter binding sites on receptors plays a role in neuron communication.

GO ON TO THE NEXT PAGE.

24. The author most likely uses the phrase "defined categories of neurons" in lines 55–56 in order to refer to neurons that

(A) possess channels for ions
(B) respond to drug treatment
(C) contain receptor molecules
(D) influence particular brain functions
(E) react to binding by neurotransmitters

25. Which one of the following most accurately describes the organization of the passage?

(A) explanation of a theory; presentation of evidence in support of the theory; presentation of evidence in opposition to the theory; argument in favor of rejecting the theory; discussion of the implications of rejecting the theory
(B) explanation of a theory; presentation of evidence in support of the theory; explanation of an alternative theory; presentation of information to support the alternative theory; discussion of an experiment that can help determine which theory is correct
(C) explanation of a theory; description of an obstacle to the theory's general acceptance; presentation of an explanation that helps the theory overcome the obstacle; discussion of a further implication of the theory
(D) explanation of a theory; description of an obstacle to the theory's general acceptance; argument that the obstacle is insurmountable and that the theory should be rejected; discussion of the implications of rejecting the theory
(E) explanation of a theory; description of how the theory came to win scientific acceptance; presentation of new information that challenges the theory; modification of the theory to accommodate the new information; discussion of an implication of the modification

26. The primary purpose of the passage is most likely to

(A) propose a new theory about the workings of the brain
(B) introduce evidence that challenges a widely accepted theory about the workings of the brain
(C) describe the approach scientists use when studying the workings of the brain
(D) discuss new support for a widely accepted theory about the workings of the brain
(E) illustrate the practical utility of scientific research into the workings of the brain

S T O P

IF YOU FINISH BEFORE TIME IS CALLED, YOU MAY CHECK YOUR WORK ON THIS SECTION ONLY.
DO NOT WORK ON ANY OTHER SECTION IN THE TEST.

SECTION V

Time—35 minutes

26 Questions

Directions: The questions in this section are based on the reasoning contained in brief statements or passages. For some questions, more than one of the choices could conceivably answer the question. However, you are to choose the best answer; that is, the response that most accurately and completely answers the question. You should not make assumptions that are by commonsense standards implausible, superfluous, or incompatible with the passage. After you have chosen the best answer, blacken the corresponding space on your answer sheet.

1. Many newborn babies have a yellowish tinge to their skin because their blood contains a high level of the pigment bilirubin. One group of doctors treats newborns to reduce high levels of bilirubin, since bilirubin, if it enters the brain, might cause the tetanus that sometimes occurs in newborns. However, a second group of doctors argues for allowing bilirubin levels in newborn babies to remain high, since the brain's own natural defenses normally prevent bilirubin from entering.

Which one of the following, if true, most helps to support the position of the second group of doctors?

(A) The treatment that most effectively reduces high levels of bilirubin in newborns has no known negative side effects.

(B) Some diseases that occur in newborns can weaken the brain's natural defenses and allow bilirubin to enter.

(C) In newborns the pigment bilirubin, like other pigments, occurs not only in the blood but also in fluids involved in digestion.

(D) Bilirubin neutralizes certain potentially damaging substances to which newborns are exposed at birth.

(E) Among doctors who recommend treating newborns to reduce high levels of bilirubin, there is general agreement about what levels should be considered excessively high.

2. Economist: Some sociologists argue that because capitalism intrinsically involves competition, it weakens the ties between the people of a community. Although this may formerly have been true, modern capitalism requires that there be large corporations. Thus, modern capitalism promotes, rather than weakens, communal ties.

Which one of the following is an assumption on which the economist's argument depends?

(A) Few economic systems are more successful than modern capitalism in fostering communal ties between citizens.

(B) Modern capitalism is designed primarily to distribute goods and services, not to create communal ties between people.

(C) Corporations that compete with each other must develop some ties to each other in order to reach agreement on the rules of the competition.

(D) Having large corporations in a modern capitalist system promotes the strength of communal ties.

(E) An economic system that does not encourage large corporations will be less successful economically than one that does.

GO ON TO THE NEXT PAGE.

3. Teacher: Participating in organized competitive athletics may increase a child's strength and coordination. As critics point out, however, it also instills in those children who are not already well developed in these respects a feeling of inferiority that never really disappears. Yet, since research has shown that adults with feelings of inferiority become more successful than those free of such anxieties, funding for children's athletic programs should not be eliminated.

    Which one of the following most accurately describes the role played in the teacher's argument by the assertion that participating in organized competitive athletics may increase a child's strength and coordination?

    (A) It is mentioned as one possible reason for adopting a policy for which the teacher suggests an additional reason.
    (B) It is a claim that the teacher attempts to refute with counterarguments.
    (C) It is a hypothesis for which the teacher offers additional evidence.
    (D) It is cited as an insufficient reason for eliminating funding for children's athletic programs.
    (E) It is cited as an objection that has been raised to the position that the teacher is supporting.

4. Columnist: Donating items to charity may be a sign of generosity, but any generosity it may demonstrate is rarely a permanent virtue, since most donors make donations only intermittently.

    Which one of the following most accurately describes a flaw in the columnist's argument?

    (A) The argument takes for granted that truly generous people are the most virtuous.
    (B) The argument attacks the character of those whose values are different from those of the columnist.
    (C) The argument takes for granted that a character trait is present only when manifested.
    (D) The argument generalizes from too small a sample of cases.
    (E) The argument takes for granted that most people donate out of generosity.

5. Researchers have found that, hours after birth, infants are able to distinguish faces from other images. Infants stare at drawings of faces for longer periods of time than they do at blank ovals or drawings in which facial features are scrambled.

    Which one of the following, if true, most helps to explain the ability of newborn infants described above?

    (A) Certain abilities of facial pattern recognition are innate in humans, rather than learned.
    (B) The longer an infant stares at an object, the more interesting the infant finds that object.
    (C) Infants learn to associate human faces with the necessities of comfort and nourishment.
    (D) The less an infant stares at an object, the weaker the preference the infant has for that object.
    (E) Infants learn to associate the sound of human voices with the images of human faces.

6. Violent crime in this town is becoming a serious problem. Compared to last year, local law enforcement agencies have responded to 17 percent more calls involving violent crimes, showing that the average citizen of this town is more likely than ever to become a victim of a violent crime.

    Which one of the following, if true, most seriously weakens the argument?

    (A) The town's overall crime rate appears to have risen slightly this year compared to the same period last year.
    (B) In general, persons under the age of 65 are less likely to be victims of violent crimes than persons over the age of 65.
    (C) As a result of the town's community outreach programs, more people than ever are willing to report violent crimes to the proper authorities.
    (D) In response to worries about violent crime, the town has recently opened a community center providing supervised activities for teenagers.
    (E) Community officials have shown that a relatively small number of repeat offenders commit the majority of violent crimes in the town.

GO ON TO THE NEXT PAGE.

7. Two different dates have been offered as the approximate end point of the last ice age in North America. The first date was established by testing insect fragments found in samples of sediments to determine when warmth-adapted open-ground beetles replaced cold-adapted arctic beetles. The second date was established by testing pollen grains in those same samples to determine when ice masses yielded to spruce forests. The first date is more than 500 years earlier than the second.

The statements above, if true, most strongly support which one of the following conclusions about the last ice age and its aftermath in North America?

(A) Toward the end of the ice age, warmth-adapted open-ground beetles ceased to inhabit areas where the predominant tree cover consisted of spruce forests.

(B) Among those sediments deposited toward the end of the ice age, those found to contain cold-adapted arctic beetle fragments can also be expected to contain spruce-pollen grains.

(C) Ice masses continued to advance through North America for several hundred years after the end of the ice age.

(D) The species of cold-adapted arctic beetle that inhabited areas covered by ice masses died out toward the end of the last ice age.

(E) Toward the end of the ice age, warmth-adapted open-ground beetles colonized the new terrain opened to them faster than soil changes and seed dispersion established new spruce forests.

8. When presented with the evidence against him, Ellison freely admitted to engaging in illegal transactions using company facilities. However, the company obtained the evidence by illegally recording Ellison's conversations. Therefore, although the company may demand that he immediately cease, it cannot justifiably take any punitive measures against him.

Which one of the following judgments best illustrates the principle illustrated by the argument above?

(A) After Price confessed to having stolen money from Long over a period of several years, Long began stealing from Price. Despite Price's guilt, Long was not justified in taking illegal action against him.

(B) Shakila's secretary has admitted that he is illegally receiving cable television without paying for it. Shakila would not be justified in reporting him, though, since she once did the same thing.

(C) After Takashi told Sarah's parents that he had seen her at the movies on Tuesday, Sarah confessed to sneaking out that day. On Monday, however, Takashi had violated the local curfew for minors. Hence Sarah's parents cannot justifiably punish her in this case.

(D) After a conservation officer discovered them, Kuttner admitted that he had set the illegal animal traps on his land. But, because she was trespassing at the time, the conservation officer cannot justifiably punish Kuttner in this case.

(E) Ramirez was forced by the discovery of new evidence to admit that she lied about her role in managing the chief of staff's financial affairs. Nevertheless, the board of directors cannot justifiably take action against Ramirez, because in past instances it has pardoned others guilty of similar improprieties.

GO ON TO THE NEXT PAGE.

9. In a recent study, each member of two groups of people, Group A (composed of persons sixty-five to seventy-five years old) and Group B (composed of college students), was required to make a telephone call to a certain number at a specified time. The time when each call was initiated was recorded electronically. Group A proved far better at remembering to make a telephone call precisely at a specified time than did Group B. There were fourteen lapses in Group B but only one lapse in Group A. Clearly, at least one type of memory does not suffer as a person ages.

Which one of the following, if all of them are true, is LEAST helpful in establishing that the conclusion above is properly drawn?

(A) There was the same number of people in each group.

(B) The same group of researchers answered the calls made by the callers in both study groups.

(C) Among the college students there were no persons more than forty years old.

(D) Both groups had unrestricted access to telephones for making the required calls.

(E) The members of the two groups received their instructions approximately the same amount of time before they were to make their telephone calls.

10. Prediction, the hallmark of the natural sciences, appears to have been made possible by reducing phenomena to mathematical expressions. Some social scientists also want the power to predict accurately and assume they ought to perform the same reduction. But this would be a mistake; it would neglect data that are not easily mathematized and thereby would only distort the social phenomena.

Which one of the following most accurately expresses the main conclusion of the argument?

(A) The social sciences do not have as much predictive power as the natural sciences.

(B) Mathematics plays a more important role in the natural sciences than it does in the social sciences.

(C) There is a need in the social sciences to improve the ability to predict.

(D) Phenomena in the social sciences should not be reduced to mathematical formulas.

(E) Prediction is responsible for the success of the natural sciences.

11. Studies have shown that the more high-stress points a bridge has, the more likely it is to fracture eventually. This might lead one to expect fractures to develop at high-stress points. Surprisingly, however, fractures develop not at high-stress points but elsewhere on the bridge.

Which one of the following, if true, contributes most to an explanation of why bridges fracture elsewhere than at high-stress points?

(A) In many structures other than bridges, such as ship hulls and airplane bodies, fractures do not develop at high-stress points.

(B) Fractures do not develop at high-stress points, because bridges are reinforced at those points; however, stress is transferred to other points on the bridge where it causes fractures.

(C) In many structures, the process of fracturing often causes high-stress points to develop.

(D) Structures with no high-stress points can nonetheless have a high probability of fracturing.

(E) Improper bridge construction, e.g., low-quality welding or the use of inferior steel, often leads both to the development of high-stress points and to an increased probability of fracturing.

12. Many people say that the press should not pry into the personal lives of private individuals. But the press has the right to publish any story of interest to the public unless that story is libelous. So, if a story about a private individual is not libelous, the press has an obligation to publish it, for such information is clearly of interest to the public.

The argument's reasoning is vulnerable to criticism on the grounds that the argument presumes, without giving warrant, that

(A) the press can publish nonlibelous stories about private individuals without prying into their personal lives

(B) one's having a right to do something entails one's having an obligation to do it

(C) the publishing of information about the personal lives of private individuals cannot be libelous

(D) if one has an obligation to do something then one has a right to do it

(E) the press's right to publish always outweighs the individual's right not to be libeled

GO ON TO THE NEXT PAGE.

13. Consumer advocate: A recent study concluded that top-loading washing machines are superior overall to front-loaders. But front-loaders have the controls and access in front. This is more convenient for wheelchair users, some of whom find it highly inconvenient to remove laundry from top-loaders. So for some consumers front-loaders are superior.

Which one of the following is an assumption upon which the consumer advocate's argument depends?

(A) For some consumers the convenience of front-loaders outweighs the advantages of top-loaders in assessing which is superior.

(B) Washing machines of a given type should be compared only with washing machines of that type.

(C) Convenience is the only important factor in determining which type of washing machine is superior.

(D) Retrieving clothes from a top-loader is convenient for people who do not use wheelchairs.

(E) Retrieving clothes from front-loaders is inconvenient for people who are not wheelchair users.

14. Over 90 percent of the human brain currently serves no purpose, as is evident from the fact that many people with significant brain damage show no discernible adverse effects. So once humans begin to tap into this tremendous source of creativity and innovation, many problems that today seem insurmountable will be within our ability to solve.

Which one of the following most accurately describes a flaw in the argument?

(A) The argument presumes, without providing justification, that the effects of brain damage are always easily detectable.

(B) The argument presumes, without providing justification, that the only reason that any problem remains unsolved is a lack of creativity and innovation.

(C) The argument infers that certain parts of the brain do nothing merely on the basis of the assertion that we do not know what they do.

(D) The argument infers that problems will be solved merely on the basis of the claim that they will be within our ability to solve.

(E) The argument presumes, without providing justification, that the currently unused parts of the brain are a potential source of tremendous creativity and innovation.

15. Some scientists have expressed reservations about quantum theory because of its counterintuitive consequences. But despite rigorous attempts to show that quantum theory's predictions were inaccurate, they were shown to be accurate within the generally accepted statistical margin of error. These results, which have not been equaled by quantum theory's competitors, warrant acceptance of quantum theory.

Which one of the following principles most helps to justify the reasoning above?

(A) A scientific theory should be accepted if it has fewer counterintuitive consequences than do its competitors.

B) A scientific theory should be accepted if it has been subjected to serious attempts to disprove it and has withstood all of them.

(C) The consequences of a scientific theory should not be considered counterintuitive if the theory's predictions have been found to be accurate.

(D) A theory should not be rejected until it has been subjected to serious attempts to disprove it.

(E) A theory should be accepted only if its predictions have not been disproved by experiment.

16. Psychologist: The obligation to express gratitude cannot be fulfilled anonymously. However much society may have changed over the centuries, human psychology is still driven primarily by personal interaction. Thus, the important social function of positively reinforcing those behaviors that have beneficial consequences for others can be served only if the benefactor knows the source of the gratitude.

Which one of the following most accurately describes the role played in the psychologist's argument by the claim that the obligation to express gratitude cannot be fulfilled anonymously?

(A) It is an illustration of a premise that is used to support the argument's conclusion.

(B) It is used to counter a consideration that might be taken to undermine the argument's conclusion.

(C) It is used to support indirectly a claim that the argument in turn uses to support directly the conclusion.

(D) It is used to identify the social benefit with which the argument is concerned.

(E) It is the conclusion that the argument is intended to support.

GO ON TO THE NEXT PAGE.

17. Curator: Our museum displays only twentieth-century works, which are either on loan from private collectors or in the museum's permanent collection. Prints of all of the latter works are available in the museum store. The museum store also sells prints of some works that are not part of the museum's permanent collection, such as Hopper's *Nighthawks*.

    If the curator's statements are true, which one of the following must be true?

    (A) Every print in the museum store is of a work that is either on loan to the museum from a private collector or part of the museum's permanent collection.
    (B) Every print that is sold in the museum store is a copy of a twentieth-century work.
    (C) There are prints in the museum store of every work that is displayed in the museum and not on loan from a private collector.
    (D) Hopper's *Nighthawks* is both a twentieth-century work and a work on loan to the museum from a private collector.
    (E) Hopper's *Nighthawks* is not displayed in the museum.

18. Nutritionist: Because humans have evolved very little since the development of agriculture, it is clear that humans are still biologically adapted to a diet of wild foods, consisting mainly of raw fruits and vegetables, nuts and seeds, lean meat, and seafood. Straying from this diet has often resulted in chronic illness and other physical problems. Thus, the more our diet consists of wild foods, the healthier we will be.

    The claim that humans are still biologically adapted to a diet of wild foods plays which one of the following roles in the nutritionist's argument?

    (A) It is a conclusion for which the only support offered is the claim that straying from a diet of wild foods has often resulted in chronic illness and other physical problems.
    (B) It is a premise for which no justification is provided, but which is used to support the argument's main conclusion.
    (C) It is a phenomenon for which the main conclusion of the nutritionist's argument is cited as an explanation.
    (D) It is an intermediate conclusion for which one claim is offered as support, and which is used in turn to support the argument's main conclusion.
    (E) It is a premise offered in support of the claim that humans have evolved very little since the development of agriculture.

19. Editorialist: Some people argue that we have an obligation not to cut down trees. However, there can be no obligation to an entity unless that entity has a corresponding right. So if we have an obligation toward trees, then trees have rights. But trees are not the sort of things that can have rights. Therefore, we have no obligation not to cut down trees.

    The editorialist's argument depends on assuming which one of the following?

    (A) If an entity has a right to certain treatment, we have an obligation to treat it that way.
    (B) Any entity that has rights also has obligations.
    (C) Only conscious entities are the sort of things that can have rights.
    (D) Avoiding cutting down trees is not an obligation owed to some entity other than trees.
    (E) One does not always have the right to cut down the trees on one's own property.

20. A recent study suggests that consuming three glasses of wine daily substantially decreases the risk of stroke. Critics of the study, defending earlier research recommending one glass of wine daily, claim that binge drinkers (who drink once a week or less, but drink three or more drinks when they do drink) are the people most likely to drink three glasses of wine in one day and are more likely to die from sudden heart attacks than are other drinkers. According to these critics, drinking three glasses of wine daily would not benefit health overall, since the decrease in the risk of stroke associated with that level of consumption is negated by its associated increased risk of sudden heart attack.

    The critics' argument is most vulnerable to criticism on the grounds that it

    (A) inappropriately attributes the consequences of binge drinking to persons whose regular consumption of wine is three glasses a day
    (B) confuses the risk of sudden alcohol-induced heart attacks with other health risks
    (C) presumes, without providing justification, that there is no significant difference between wine and other alcoholic beverages in terms of health benefits and risks
    (D) fails to address specifically the reduction in risk of stroke conferred by the level of consumption in the recent study
    (E) overlooks the difference between strokes that result in death and less severe strokes

GO ON TO THE NEXT PAGE.

21. Scientist: Isaac Newton's *Principia*, the seventeenth-century work that served as the cornerstone of physics for over two centuries, could at first be understood by only a handful of people, but a basic understanding of Newton's ideas eventually spread throughout the world. This shows that the barriers to communication between scientists and the public are not impermeable. Thus recent scientific research, most of which also can be described only in language that seems esoteric to most contemporary readers, may also become part of everyone's intellectual heritage.

Which one of the following most accurately describes the role played in the scientist's argument by the claim that recent scientific research can often be described only in language that seems esoteric to most contemporary readers?

(A) It is raised as a potential objection to the argument's main conclusion, but its truth is called into doubt by the preceding statements.

(B) It is a premise that supports the argument's main conclusion by suggesting that the results of recent scientific research are only superficially different from claims made in Newton's *Principia*.

(C) It is cited as further evidence for the conclusion that the barriers to communication between scientists and the public are not impermeable.

(D) It is a claim that serves mainly to help establish the relevance of the preceding statements to the argument's final conclusion.

(E) It serves to cast doubt on an alleged similarity between Newton's *Principia* and recent scientific research.

22. Only a minority of those who engage in political action do so out of a sense of social justice. Therefore, some people who have a sense of social justice do not engage in political action.

Which one of the following uses flawed reasoning most similar to that used in the argument above?

(A) Most scholars are not motivated by a desire to win prestigious academic prizes. Thus, some of those who want to win prestigious academic prizes are not scholars.

(B) Only foolish politicians disregard the wishes of most voters. Thus, most voters deserve to be represented by foolish politicians.

(C) Some corporations only feign a concern for the environment when they advertise a product as environmentally friendly. Thus, no corporation has a genuine concern for the environment.

(D) Some parents show no interest in the curricula used in the schools that their children attend. Thus, some of the decisions regarding school curricula should be made without regard for the wishes of the children's parents.

(E) Only a small percentage of the profits that companies make are directly attributable to good management decisions. Thus, even companies that are managed badly will usually turn a profit.

23. Columnist: Even if the primary purpose of university education is to make students employable, such education should emphasize the liberal arts rather than the more narrow kind of technical training that prepares one for a particular sort of job. This is because the reasoning skills one acquires from a liberal arts education allow one to adapt to new intellectual challenges and thus to perform jobs for which one has received no specialized training.

Which one of the following, if true, most strengthens the columnist's argument?

(A) It is better for people to have good educations than good jobs.

(B) Many people with narrow technical training manage to find jobs.

(C) Having a series of different jobs is more interesting than having only one job.

(D) Having a general understanding of life is more important than possessing practical skills.

(E) Technical training does not help students acquire reasoning skills.

GO ON TO THE NEXT PAGE.

24. Provinces and states with stringent car safety requirements, including required use of seat belts and annual safety inspections, have on average higher rates of accidents per kilometer driven than do provinces and states with less stringent requirements. Nevertheless, most highway safety experts agree that more stringent requirements do reduce accident rates.

    Which one of the following, if true, most helps to reconcile the safety experts' belief with the apparently contrary evidence described above?

    (A)   Annual safety inspections ensure that car tires are replaced before they grow old.
    (B)   Drivers often become overconfident after their cars have passed a thorough safety inspection.
    (C)   The roads in provinces and states with stringent car safety requirements are far more congested and therefore dangerous than in other provinces and states.
    (D)   Psychological studies show that drivers who regularly wear seat belts often come to think of themselves as serious drivers, which for a few people discourages reckless driving.
    (E)   Provinces and states with stringent car safety requirements have, on average, many more kilometers of roads than do other provinces and states.

25. It is difficult to grow cacti in a humid climate. It is difficult to raise orange trees in a cold climate. In most parts of a certain country, it is either easy to grow cacti or easy to raise orange trees.

    If the statements above are true, which one of the following must be false?

    (A)   Half of the country is both humid and cold.
    (B)   Most of the country is hot.
    (C)   Some parts of the country are neither cold nor humid.
    (D)   It is not possible to raise cacti in the country.
    (E)   Most parts of the country are humid.

26. Essayist: Common sense, which is always progressing, is nothing but a collection of theories that have been tested over time and found useful. When alternative theories that prove even more useful are developed, they gradually take the place of theories already embodied in common sense. This causes common sense to progress, but, because it absorbs new theories slowly, it always contains some obsolete theories.

    If all of the essayist's statements are true, then which one of the following must be true?

    (A)   At least some new theories that have not yet been found to be more useful than any theory currently part of common sense will never be absorbed into the body of common sense.
    (B)   Of the useful theories within the body of common sense, the older ones are generally less useful than the newer ones.
    (C)   The frequency with which new theories are generated prevents their rapid absorption into the body of common sense.
    (D)   Each theory within the body of common sense is eventually replaced with a new theory that is more useful.
    (E)   At least some theories that have been tested over time and found useful are less useful than some other theories that have not been fully absorbed into the body of common sense.

S T O P

IF YOU FINISH BEFORE TIME IS CALLED, YOU MAY CHECK YOUR WORK ON THIS SECTION ONLY.
DO NOT WORK ON ANY OTHER SECTION IN THE TEST.

Acknowledgment is made to the following sources from which material has been adapted for use in this test booklet:

Acknowledgments for PrepTest 42:

Jean-Pierre Changeux, "Chemical Signaling in the Brain." ©November 1993 by Scientific American, Inc.

Adam Gopnik, "The Wise Innocent." ©1993 by The New Yorker Magazine, Inc.

Stephen Weinbert, "Life in the Universe." ©October 1994 by Scientific American, Inc.

Acknowledgments for PrepTest 4:

From "Management of Large Marine Ecosystems: Developing a New Rule of Customary International Law" by Martin H. Belsky, *San Diego Law Review*, Volume 22, 1985. ©1985 by the University of San Diego. Used by permission.

**Wait for the supervisor's instructions before you open the page to the topic.
Please print and sign your name and write the date in the designated spaces below.**

Time: 35 Minutes

General Directions

You will have 35 minutes in which to plan and write an essay on the topic inside. Read the topic and the accompanying directions carefully. You will probably find it best to spend a few minutes considering the topic and organizing your thoughts before you begin writing. In your essay, be sure to develop your ideas fully, leaving time, if possible, to review what you have written. **Do not write on a topic other than the one specified. Writing on a topic of your own choice is not acceptable.**

No special knowledge is required or expected for this writing exercise. Law schools are interested in the reasoning, clarity, organization, language usage, and writing mechanics displayed in your essay. How well you write is more important than how much you write.

Confine your essay to the blocked, lined area on the front and back of the separate Writing Sample Response Sheet. Only that area will be reproduced for law schools. Be sure that your writing is legible.

Both this topic sheet and your response sheet must be turned over to the testing staff before you leave the room.

Topic Code	Print Your Full Name Here		
_____	Last	First	M.I.
Date	**Sign Your Name Here**		
/ /			

Scratch Paper
Do not write your essay in this space.

LSAT Writing Sample Topic

The executors of the estate of a late, famous author recently found the manuscript of an unfinished novel among the author's papers. They must decide whether to publish the manuscript or donate it to a university library. In order to avoid unfortunate comparisons between a heavily edited published version and the original manuscript, they will not do both. Write an argument for choosing one option over the other based on the following considerations:

- The executors want to preserve the author's reputation as a literary genius.
- The executors want to maximize interest in the author's work among both scholars and the public.

Critics who have read the manuscript agree that the work is intriguingly experimental but that it is not among the author's best. If the novel is to be published, it will require heavy editing to make it seem complete. Its style differs greatly from that of the author's most popular novels, so it is unclear how well the novel will sell. Most of the author's other novels stayed on the bestsellers list for months after publication, but it has been more than a decade since her last work was published. The publisher promises a large printing, wide distribution, and an aggressive marketing campaign. If the work is published, the executors will sell the original manuscript to a private collector who would not allow it to be copied or viewed by scholars.

Scholars have voiced a strong preference for access to the unedited manuscript. One prominent scholar has expressed dismay at the publisher's intention to alter the original manuscript in order to make the novel marketable. If donated, the manuscript will become part of a permanent display in the university's library, which is open to the public. Individual copies will be made available for a nominal fee to scholars and any others upon request. The donation of the manuscript to the university would likely revive warning scholarly interest in the author and lead to a new wave of commentaries by literary critics and biographers. Past commentaries on the author's life and work have sold well even beyond academic critics.

Scratch Paper
Do not write your essay in this space.

Writing Sample Response Sheet

DO NOT WRITE
IN THIS SPACE

Begin your essay in the lined area below.
Continue on the back if you need more space.

KAPLAN

Directions:

1. Use the Answer Key on the next page to check your answers.

2. Use the Scoring Worksheet below to compute your raw score.

3. Use the Score Conversion Chart to convert your raw score into the 120–180 scale.

Scoring Worksheet

1. Enter the number of questions you answered correctly in each section

	Number Correct
SECTION I	_____
SECTION II	_____
SECTION III	EXP
SECTION IV	_____
SECTION V	_____

2. Enter the sum here: _____

   This is your Raw Score.

Conversion Chart

For Converting Raw Score to the 120–180 LSAT Scaled Score

LSAT PrepTest 42

Reported Score	Raw Score Lowest	Raw Score Highest
180	99	101
179	—*	—*
178	98	98
177	97	97
176	96	96
175	95	95
174	94	94
173	—*	—*
172	92	93
171	91	91
170	90	90
169	89	89
168	87	88
167	86	86
166	85	85
165	83	84
164	81	82
163	80	80
162	78	79
161	76	77
160	75	75
159	73	74
158	71	72
157	69	70
156	67	68
155	66	66
154	64	65
153	62	63
152	60	61
151	58	59
150	56	57
149	55	55
148	53	54
147	51	52
146	49	50
145	48	48
144	46	47
143	44	45
142	43	43
141	41	42
140	39	40
139	38	38
138	36	37
137	35	35
136	33	34
135	32	32
134	30	31
133	29	29
132	28	28
131	26	27
130	25	25
129	24	24
128	23	23
127	22	22
126	21	21
125	20	20
124	19	19
123	18	18
122	17	17
121	16	16
120	0	15

*There is no raw score that will produce this scaled score for this test.

SECTION I

1.	C	8.	C	15.	C	22.	D
2.	E	9.	D	16.	D	23.	D
3.	E	10.	C	17.	A		
4.	D	11.	C	18.	E		
5.	A	12.	C	19.	A		
6.	A	13.	A	20.	B		
7.	A	14.	A	21.	E		

SECTION II

1.	A	8.	A	15.	D	22.	B
2.	D	9.	A	16.	E	23.	E
3.	D	10.	C	17.	A	24.	B
4.	A	11.	E	18.	A	25.	C
5.	B	12.	D	19.	C	26.	B
6.	B	13.	C	20.	B		
7.	D	14.	B	21.	C		

SECTION III (experimental)

1.	B	8.	E	15.	C	22.	C
2.	C	9.	D	16.	B	23.	C
3.	A	10.	B	17.	D	24.	A
4.	C	11.	B	18.	A	25.	D
5.	C	12.	A	19.	E	26.	D
6.	D	13.	C	20.	B	27.	E
7.	E	14.	D	21.	B		

SECTION IV

1.	B	8.	B	15.	B	22.	B
2.	D	9.	E	16.	E	23.	E
3.	A	10.	A	17.	A	24.	D
4.	C	11.	E	18.	D	25.	C
5.	B	12.	D	19.	B	26.	D
6.	E	13.	B	20.	C		
7.	D	14.	A	21.	D		

SECTION V

1.	D	8.	D	15.	B	22.	A
2.	D	9.	B	16.	E	23.	E
3.	A	10.	D	17.	C	24.	C
4.	C	11.	B	18.	D	25.	A
5.	A	12.	B	19.	D	26.	E
6.	C	13.	A	20.	A		
7.	E	14.	E	21.	D		

Endurance Practice Test 10

PrepTest 40 plus experimental
from PrepTest 3, Section IV

SCAN CODE: LL9010

SECTION I

Time—35 minutes

24 Questions

Directions: The questions in this section are based on the reasoning contained in brief statements or passages. For some questions, more than one of the choices could conceivably answer the question. However, you are to choose the best answer; that is, the response that most accurately and completely answers the question. You should not make assumptions that are by commonsense standards implausible, superfluous, or incompatible with the passage. After you have chosen the best answer, blacken the corresponding space on your answer sheet.

1. The translator of poetry must realize that word-for-word equivalents do not exist across languages, any more than piano sounds exist in the violin. The violin can, however, play recognizably the same music as the piano, but only if the violinist is guided by the nature and possibilities of the violin as well as by the original composition.

As applied to the act of translating poetry from one language into another, the analogy above can best be understood as saying that

(A) poetry cannot be effectively translated because, unlike music, it is composed of words with specific meanings

(B) some languages are inherently more musical and more suitable to poetic composition than others

(C) the translator should be primarily concerned with reproducing the rhythms and sound patterns of the original, not with transcribing its meaning exactly

(D) the translator must observe the spirit of the original and also the qualities of expression that characterize the language into which the original is translated

(E) poetry is easier to translate if it focuses on philosophical insights or natural descriptions rather than on subjective impressions

2. Behind the hope that computers can replace teachers is the idea that the student's understanding of the subject being taught consists in knowing facts and rules, the job of a teacher being to make the facts and rules explicit and convey them to the student, either by practice drills or by coaching. If that were indeed the way the mind works, the teacher could transfer facts and rules to the computer, which would replace the teacher as drillmaster and coach. But since understanding does not consist merely of knowing facts and rules, but of the grasp of the general concepts underlying them, the hope that the computer will eventually replace the teacher is fundamentally misguided.

Which one of the following, if true, would most seriously undermine the author's conclusion that computers will not eventually be able to replace teachers?

(A) Computers are as good as teachers at drilling students on facts and rules.

(B) The job of a teacher is to make students understand the general concepts underlying specific facts and rules.

(C) It is possible to program computers so that they can teach the understanding of general concepts that underlie specific facts and rules.

(D) Because they are not subject to human error, computers are better than teachers at conveying facts and rules.

(E) It is not possible for students to develop an understanding of the concepts underlying facts and rules through practice drills and coaching.

GO ON TO THE NEXT PAGE.

3. If the city council maintains spending at the same level as this year's, it can be expected to levy a sales tax of 2 percent next year. Thus, if the council levies a higher tax, it will be because the council is increasing its expenditures.

Which one of the following exhibits a pattern of reasoning most closely similar to that of the argument above?

(A) If house-building costs are not now rising, builders cannot be expected to increase the prices of houses. Thus, if they decrease the prices of houses, it will be because that action will enable them to sell a greater number of houses.

(B) If shops wish to reduce shoplifting, they should employ more store detectives. Thus, if shops do not, they will suffer reduced profits because of their losses from stolen goods.

(C) If the companies in the state do not increase their workers' wages this year, the prices they charge for their goods can be expected to be much the same as they were last year. Thus, if the companies do increase prices, it will be because they have increased wages.

(D) If airlines wish to make profits this year that are similar to last year's, they should not increase their prices this year. Thus, if they charge more, they should be expected to improve their services.

(E) If newspaper publishers wish to publish good papers, they should employ good journalists. Thus, if they employ poor journalists, it will not be surprising if their circulation falls as a result.

4. The mind and the immune system have been shown to be intimately linked, and scientists are consistently finding that doing good deeds benefits one's immune system. The bone marrow and spleen, which produce the white blood cells needed to fight infection, are both connected by neural pathways to the brain. Recent research has shown that the activity of these white blood cells is stimulated by beneficial chemicals produced by the brain as a result of magnanimous behavior.

The statements above, if true, support the view that

(A) good deeds must be based on unselfish motives

(B) lack of magnanimity is the cause of most serious illnesses

(C) magnanimous behavior can be regulated by the presence or absence of certain chemicals in the brain

(D) magnanimity is beneficial to one's own interests

(E) the number of white blood cells will increase radically if behavior is consistently magnanimous

5. The high cost of production is severely limiting which operas are available to the public. These costs necessitate reliance on large corporate sponsors, who in return demand that only the most famous operas be produced. Determining which operas will be produced should rest only with ticket purchasers at the box office, not with large corporate sponsors. If we reduce production budgets so that operas can be supported exclusively by box-office receipts and donations from individuals, then the public will be able to see less famous operas.

Which one of the following, if true, would weaken the argument?

(A) A few opera ticket purchasers go to the opera for the sake of going to the opera, not to see specific operatic productions.

(B) The reduction of opera production budgets would not reduce the desire of large corporate sponsors to support operas.

(C) Without the support of large corporate sponsors, opera companies could not afford to produce any but the most famous of operas.

(D) Large corporate sponsors will stop supporting opera productions if they are denied control over which operas will be produced.

(E) The combination of individual donations and box-office receipts cannot match the amounts of money obtained through sponsorship by large corporations.

6. When machines are invented and technologies are developed, they alter the range of choices open to us. The clock, for example, made possible the synchronization of human affairs, which resulted in an increase in productivity. At the same time that the clock opened up some avenues, it closed others. It has become harder and harder to live except by the clock, so that now people have no choice in the matter at all.

Which one of the following propositions is best illustrated by the example presented in the passage?

(A) New machines and technologies can enslave as well as liberate us.

(B) People should make a concerted effort to free themselves from the clock.

(C) Some new machines and technologies bring no improvement to our lives.

(D) The increase in productivity was not worth our dependence on the clock.

(E) Most new machines and technologies make our lives more synchronized and productive.

GO ON TO THE NEXT PAGE.

7. To become an expert on a musical instrument, a person must practice. If people practice a musical instrument for three hours each day, they will eventually become experts on that instrument. Therefore, if a person is an expert on a musical instrument, that person must have practiced for at least three hours each day.

Which one of the following most accurately describes a flaw in the reasoning above?

(A) The conclusion fails to take into account that people who practice for three hours every day might not yet have reached a degree of proficiency that everyone would consider expert.

(B) The conclusion fails to take into account that practicing for less than three hours each day may be enough for some people to become experts.

(C) The conclusion fails to take into account that if a person has not practiced for at least three hours a day, the person has not become an expert.

(D) The conclusion fails to take into account that three consecutive hours of daily practice is not recommended by all music teachers.

(E) The conclusion fails to take into account that few people have the spare time necessary to devote three hours daily to practice.

8. On the basis of incontestable proof that car safety seats will greatly reduce the number of serious injuries sustained by children in car accidents, laws have been passed mandating the use of these seats. Unexpectedly, it has since been found that a large number of children who are riding in safety seats continue to receive serious injuries that safety seats were specifically designed to avoid, and in the prevention of which they in fact have proven to be effective.

Which one of the following, if true, could by itself adequately explain the unexpected finding reported in the passage?

(A) Many parents are defying the law by not using safety seats for their children.

(B) Children are more likely to make automobile trips now than they were before the introduction of the safety seat.

(C) The high cost of child safety seats has caused many parents to delay purchasing them.

(D) The car safety seat was not designed to prevent all types of injuries, so it is not surprising that some injuries are sustained.

(E) The protection afforded by child safety seats depends on their being used properly, which many parents fail to do.

9. An easy willingness to tell funny stories or jokes about oneself is the surest mark of supreme self-confidence. This willingness, often not acquired until late in life, is even more revealing than is good-natured acquiescence in having others poke fun at one.

Which one of the following inferences is most supported by the statements above?

(A) A person who lacks self-confidence will enjoy neither telling nor hearing funny stories about himself or herself.

(B) People with high self-confidence do not tell funny stories or jokes about others.

(C) Highly self-confident people tell funny stories and jokes in order to let their audience know that they are self-confident.

(D) Most people would rather tell a funny story or a joke than listen to one being told.

(E) Telling funny stories or jokes about people in their presence is a way of expressing one's respect for them.

GO ON TO THE NEXT PAGE.

Questions 10–11

Nature constantly adjusts the atmospheric carbon level. An increase in the level causes the atmosphere to hold more heat, which causes more water to evaporate from the oceans, which causes increased rain. Rain washes some carbon from the air into the oceans, where it eventually becomes part of the seabed. A decrease in atmospheric carbon causes the atmosphere to hold less heat, which causes decreased evaporation from the oceans, which causes less rain, and thus less carbon is washed into the oceans. Yet some environmentalists worry that burning fossil fuels may raise atmospheric carbon to a dangerous level. It is true that a sustained increase would threaten human life. But the environmentalists should relax—nature will continually adjust the carbon level.

10. Each of the following can be inferred from the information in the passage EXCEPT:

(A) A decrease in the level of atmospheric heat causes a decrease in the amount of carbon that rain washes into the oceans from the air.
(B) An increase in the level of carbon in the atmosphere causes increased evaporation of ocean water.
(C) An increase in the level of atmospheric heat causes increased rainfall.
(D) A decrease in the level of carbon in the atmosphere causes decreased evaporation of ocean water.
(E) A decrease in the level of atmospheric heat causes a decrease in the level of carbon in the atmosphere.

11. Which one of the following, if true, would most weaken the argument in the passage?

(A) Plant life cannot survive without atmospheric carbon.
(B) It is not clear that breathing excess carbon in the atmosphere will have a negative effect on human life.
(C) Carbon is part of the chemical "blanket" that keeps the Earth warm enough to sustain human life.
(D) Breathing by animals releases almost 30 times as much carbon as does the burning of fossil fuels.
(E) The natural adjustment process, which occurs over millions of years, allows wide fluctuations in the carbon level in the short term.

12. The more television children watch, the less competent they are in mathematical knowledge. More than a third of children in the United States watch television for more than five hours a day; in South Korea the figure is only 7 percent. But whereas less than 15 percent of children in the United States understand advanced measurement and geometric concepts, 40 percent of South Korean children are competent in these areas. Therefore, if United States children are to do well in mathematics, they must watch less television.

Which one of the following is an assumption upon which the argument depends?

(A) Children in the United States are less interested in advanced measurement and geometric concepts than are South Korean children.
(B) South Korean children are more disciplined about doing schoolwork than are children in the United States.
(C) Children who want to do well in advanced measurement and geometry will watch less television.
(D) A child's ability in advanced measurement and geometry increases if he or she watches less than one hour of television a day.
(E) The instruction in advanced measurement and geometric concepts available to children in the United States is not substantially worse than that available to South Korean children.

GO ON TO THE NEXT PAGE.

Questions 13–14

The only way that bookstores can profitably sell books at below-market prices is to get the books at a discount from publishers. Unless bookstores generate a high sales volume, however, they cannot get discounts from publishers. To generate such volume, bookstores must either cater to mass tastes or have exclusive access to a large specialized market, such as medical textbooks, or both.

13. Which one of the following can be properly inferred from the passage?

(A) If a bookstore receives discounts from publishers, it will profitably sell books at below-market prices.

(B) A bookstore that caters to mass tastes or has exclusive access to a large specialized market will have a high sales volume.

(C) A bookstore that profitably sells books at below-market prices gets discounts from publishers.

(D) A bookstore that does not sell books at below-market prices does not get discounts from publishers.

(E) A bookstore that not only caters to mass tastes but also has exclusive access to a large specialized market cannot profitably sell books at below-market prices.

14. If all the statements in the passage are true and if it is also true that a bookstore does not cater to mass tastes, which one of the following CANNOT be true?

(A) The bookstore profitably sells some of its books at below-market prices.

(B) The bookstore does not profitably sell any of its books at below-market prices.

(C) Either the bookstore has exclusive access to a large specialized market or else it does not get a discount from any publishers.

(D) The bookstore does not have exclusive access to a large specialized market but profitably sells some of its books at below-market prices.

(E) The bookstore does not have exclusive access to a large specialized market, nor does it get a discount from any publishers.

15. Extinction is the way of nature. Scientists estimate that over half of the species that have ever come into existence on this planet were already extinct before humans developed even the most primitive of tools. This constant natural process of species emergence and extinction, however, is ignored by those who wish to trace the blame for more recent extinctions to humanity's use of technology, with its consequent effects on the environment. These people must be made to understand that the species that have become extinct in modern times would have become extinct by now even if humans had never acquired technology.

Which one of the following identifies a reasoning error in the passage?

(A) The author mistakenly assumes that technology has not caused any harm to the environment.

(B) The author ignores the fact that some species that are not yet extinct are in danger of extinction.

(C) The author fails to consider that there are probably species in existence that have not yet been identified and studied by scientists.

(D) The author cites scientists who support the theory that over half of all species that ever existed have become extinct, but fails to mention any scientists who do not support that theory.

(E) The author provides no specific evidence that the species that have become extinct in modern times are the same species that would have become extinct in the absence of human technology.

GO ON TO THE NEXT PAGE.

16. The public is aware of the possibility of biases in the mass media and distrusts the media as too powerful. The body of information against which the public evaluates the plausibility of each new media report comes, however, from what the public has heard of through the mass media.

If the view above is correct, it provides a reason for accepting which one of the following conclusions?

(A) If there is a pervasive bias in the presentation of news by the mass media, it would be hard for the public to discern that bias.
(B) The mass media tailor their reports to conform to a specific political agenda.
(C) The biases that news media impose on reporting tend not to be conscious distortions but rather part of a sense they share about what is interesting and believable.
(D) News reporters and their public hold largely the same views about what is most important in society, because news reporters come out of that society.
(E) When a news event occurs that contradicts a stereotype formerly incorporated into reporting by the mass media, the public is predisposed to believe reports of the event.

17. In a bureaucracy, all decisions are arrived at by a process that involves many people. There is no one person who has the authority to decide whether a project will proceed or not. As a consequence, in bureaucracies, risky projects are never undertaken.

The conclusion follows logically from the premises if which one of the following is assumed?

(A) All projects in a bureaucracy require risk.
(B) Decisive individuals choose not to work in a bureaucracy.
(C) An individual who has decision-making power will take risks.
(D) The only risky projects undertaken are those for which a single individual has decision-making power.
(E) People sometimes take risks as individuals that they would not take as part of a group.

18. "Physicalists" expect that ultimately all mental functions will be explainable in neurobiological terms. Achieving this goal requires knowledge of neurons and their basic functions, a knowledge of how neurons interact, and a delineation of the psychological faculties to be explained. At present, there is a substantial amount of fundamental knowledge about the basic functions of neurons, and the scope and character of such psychological capacities as visual perception and memory are well understood. Thus, as the physicalists claim, mental functions are bound to receive explanations in neurobiological terms in the near future.

Which one of the following indicates an error in the reasoning in the passage?

(A) The conclusion contradicts the claim of the physicalists.
(B) The passage fails to describe exactly what is currently known about the basic functions of neurons.
(C) The word "neurobiological" is used as though it had the same meaning as the word "mental."
(D) The argument does not indicate whether it would be useful to explain mental functions in neurobiological terms.
(E) The passage does not indicate that any knowledge has been achieved about how neurons interact.

19. Because a large disparity in pay between the public and private sectors has developed in recent years, many experienced and extremely capable government administrators have quit their posts and taken positions in private-sector management. Government will be able to recapture these capable administrators by raising salaries to a level comparable to those of the private sector. In that way, the functioning of public agencies will be improved.

The position taken above presupposes which one of the following?

(A) Experience gained from private-sector management will be very valuable in government administration.
(B) The most important factor determining how well government agencies function is the amount of experience the administrators have.
(C) Unless government action is taken, the disparity in pay between government administration and private-sector management will continue to increase.
(D) People who moved from jobs in government administration to private-sector management would choose to change careers again.
(E) If the disparity in pay between government administration and private-sector management increases, administrators will move to the public sector in large numbers.

GO ON TO THE NEXT PAGE.

20. Politician: Homelessness is a serious social problem, but further government spending to provide low-income housing is not the cure for homelessness. The most cursory glance at the real-estate section of any major newspaper is enough to show that there is no lack of housing units available to rent. So the frequent claim that people are homeless because of a lack of available housing is wrong.

That homelessness is a serious social problem figures in the argument in which one of the following ways?

(A) It suggests an alternative perspective to the one adopted in the argument.

(B) It sets out a problem the argument is designed to resolve.

(C) It is compatible either with accepting the conclusion or with denying it.

(D) It summarizes a position the argument as a whole is directed toward discrediting.

(E) It is required in order to establish the conclusion.

21. Leona: If the average consumption of eggs in the United States were cut in half, an estimated 5,000 lives might be saved each year.

Thomas: How can that be? That would mean that if people adopt this single change in diet for ten years, the population ten years from now will be greater by 50,000 people than it otherwise would have been.

Which one of the following is a statement that Leona could offer Thomas to clarify her own claim and to address the point he has made?

(A) It is possible for the population to grow by 5,000 people for every year if the base year chosen for purposes of comparison is one with unusually low population growth.

(B) It is accurate to say that 5,000 lives have been saved as long as 5,000 people who would have died in a given year as a result of not changing their diet, did not do so—even if they died for some other reason.

(C) If egg consumption were reduced by more than half, the estimated number of lives saved each year could be even more than 5,000.

(D) The actual rate of population growth depends not only on the birth rate, but also on changes in life expectancy.

(E) For the average consumption of eggs to be cut by half, many individual consumers would have to cut their own consumption by much more than half.

22. The United States Food and Drug Administration (FDA) regulates the introduction of new therapeutic agents into the marketplace. Consequently, it plays a critical role in improving health care in the United States. While it is those in the academic and government research communities who engage in the long process of initial discovery and clinical testing of new therapeutic agents, it is the FDA's role and responsibility to facilitate the transfer of new discoveries from the laboratory to the marketplace. Only after the transfer can important new therapies help patients.

Which one of the following statements can be inferred from the passage?

(A) The FDA is responsible for ensuring that any therapeutic agent that is marketed is then regulated.

(B) Before new therapeutic agents reach the marketplace they do not help patients.

(C) The research community is responsible for the excessively long testing period for new drugs, not the FDA.

(D) The FDA should work more closely with researchers to ensure that the quality of therapeutic agents is maintained.

(E) If a new medical discovery has been transferred from the laboratory to the marketplace, it will help patients.

GO ON TO THE NEXT PAGE.

23. In a new police program, automobile owners in some neighborhoods whose cars are not normally driven between 1 A.M. and 5 A.M. can display a special decal in the cars' windows and authorize police to stop the cars during those hours to check the drivers' licenses. The theft rate for cars bearing such decals is much lower than had been usual for cars in those neighborhoods.

If it is concluded from the statements above that automobile theft has been reduced by the program, which one of the following would it be most important to answer in evaluating that conclusion?

(A) Are owners who are cautious enough to join the program taking other special measures to protect their cars against theft?

(B) In how many neighborhoods is the police program operating?

(C) Are cars in neighborhoods that are actively participating in the program sometimes stolen during daylight hours?

(D) Will owners who have placed decals on their cars' windows but who find it necessary to drive between 1 A.M. and 5 A.M. be harassed by police?

(E) Are the neighborhoods in which the program has been put into effect a representative cross section of neighborhoods with respect to the types of automobiles owned by residents?

24. It has been claimed that an action is morally good only if it benefits another person and was performed with that intention; whereas an action that harms another person is morally bad either if such harm was intended or if reasonable forethought would have shown that the action was likely to cause harm.

Which one of the following judgments most closely conforms to the principle cited above?

(A) Pamela wrote a letter attempting to cause trouble between Edward and his friend; this action of Pamela's was morally bad, even though the letter, in fact, had an effect directly opposite from the one intended.

(B) In order to secure a promotion, Jeffrey devoted his own time to resolving a backlog of medical benefits claims; Jeffrey's action was morally good since it alone enabled Sara's claim to be processed in time for her to receive much-needed treatment.

(C) Intending to help her elderly neighbor by clearing his walkway after a snowstorm, Teresa inadvertently left ice on his steps; because of this exposed ice, her neighbor had a bad fall, thus showing that morally good actions can have bad consequences.

(D) Marilees, asked by a homeless man for food, gave the man her own sandwich; however, because the man tried to talk while he was eating the sandwich, it caused him to choke, and thus Marilees unintentionally performed a morally bad action.

(E) Jonathan agreed to watch his three-year-old niece while she played but, becoming engrossed in conversation, did not see her run into the street where she was hit by a bicycle; even though he intended no harm, Jonathan's action was morally bad.

S T O P

IF YOU FINISH BEFORE TIME IS CALLED, YOU MAY CHECK YOUR WORK ON THIS SECTION ONLY.
DO NOT WORK ON ANY OTHER SECTION IN THE TEST.

SECTION II

Time—35 minutes

25 Questions

<u>Directions</u>: The questions in this section are based on the reasoning contained in brief statements or passages. For some questions, more than one of the choices could conceivably answer the question. However, you are to choose the <u>best</u> answer; that is, the response that most accurately and completely answers the question. You should not make assumptions that are by commonsense standards implausible, superfluous, or incompatible with the passage. After you have chosen the best answer, blacken the corresponding space on your answer sheet.

1. Considering that Mark Twain is Samuel Clemens, I have always found it amazing that very few people know that Samuel Clemens was a writer, since almost everybody knows that Mark Twain was one.

   Which one of the following, if true, would most effectively resolve the apparent paradox above?

   (A) Most people probably have not read anything by Samuel Clemens.
   (B) Everyone who knows that Samuel Clemens was a writer also knows that Mark Twain was one.
   (C) Most people do not know that Mark Twain is Samuel Clemens.
   (D) Many people believe apparently conflicting things about authors.
   (E) Some people know that "Mark Twain" is a pseudonym for Samuel Clemens.

2. Advertisement: The pride the people at Austin Stables take in their work accounts for their success in producing more winning racehorses than any other stable. Such a tradition of pride is not only found in the business of horse racing. For generations we at Barr Motor Company have demonstrated similar pride. You can rely on Barr Motor Company to produce more winning automobiles than our competitors.

   The advertisement proceeds by

   (A) demonstrating that Barr Motor Company has more repeat customers than its competitors
   (B) using an analogy to reach the conclusion that Barr Motor Company is superior to its competitors
   (C) proving that Barr Motor Company has a long-standing tradition of pride
   (D) understating the role that pride plays in accounting for the success of Austin Stables
   (E) asserting that Barr Motor Company has an older tradition of pride than does Austin Stables

3. Having lived through extraordinary childhood circumstances, Robin has no conception of the moral difference between right and wrong, only between what is legally permitted and what is not. When Robin committed an offense, Robin did not recognize the fact that it was a morally wrong act, despite knowing that it was illegal.

   From the statements above, which one of the following can be properly inferred?

   (A) Robin committed no offense that was not legally permissible.
   (B) Robin did something that was morally wrong.
   (C) Moral ignorance is never excusable in the eyes of the law.
   (D) Robin's childhood could have provided more adequate moral training even in the circumstances.
   (E) Robin could now be brought to see the moral difference between right and wrong.

GO ON TO THE NEXT PAGE.

4. Anne: Halley's Comet, now in a part of its orbit relatively far from the Sun, recently flared brightly enough to be seen by telescope. No comet has ever been observed to flare so far from the Sun before, so such a flare must be highly unusual.

    Sue: Nonsense. Usually no one bothers to try to observe comets when they are so far from the Sun. This flare was observed only because an observatory was tracking Halley's Comet very carefully.

    Sue challenges Anne's reasoning by

    (A) pointing out that Anne's use of the term "observed" is excessively vague
    (B) drawing attention to an inconsistency between two of Anne's claims
    (C) presenting evidence that directly contradicts Anne's evidence
    (D) offering an alternative explanation for the evidence Anne cites
    (E) undermining some of Anne's evidence while agreeing with her conclusion

5. Psychologist: There are theories that posit completely different causal mechanisms from those posited by Freudian psychological theory and that are more successful at predicting human behavior. Therefore, Freudian theories of behavior, no matter how suggestive or complex they are, ought to be abandoned in favor of these other theories.

    Which one of the following is an assumption on which the psychologist's argument depends?

    (A) Freudian theories have offered interesting suggestions, which have been shown to be false, about the causes of human behavior.
    (B) A psychological theory with greater predictive success than another is scientifically preferable to it.
    (C) Freudian theory has had little success in predicting how people will behave in various situations.
    (D) Measuring the predictive success of a psychological theory involves considering other theories that attempt to explain the same phenomena.
    (E) Scientific theories become impractical if they posit causal mechanisms beyond a certain level of complexity.

6. Skeletal remains of early humans indicate clearly that our ancestors had fewer dental problems than we have. So, most likely, the diet of early humans was very different from ours.

    Which one of the following, if true, most strengthens the argument?

    (A) A healthy diet leads to healthy teeth.
    (B) Skeletal remains indicate that some early humans had a significant number of cavities.
    (C) The diet of early humans was at least as varied as is our diet.
    (D) Early humans had a shorter average life span than we do, and the most serious dental problems now tend to develop late in life.
    (E) Diet is by far the most significant factor contributing to dental health.

GO ON TO THE NEXT PAGE.

7. In preagricultural societies, social roles were few and were easily predicted for each phase of a person's life. Accordingly, interpersonal relations, although not always pleasant or fair, were stable and predictable. Modern society, on the other hand, has thousands of different social roles. Technology and consumerism require that each of us fill highly particularized niches, and these niches are differentiating at an astonishing pace. Therefore, _____.

Which one of the following most logically completes the argument?

(A) modern society is characterized by greater injustice and unpleasantness than were preagricultural societies

(B) interpersonal relations in modern societies are less stable and less predictable than they were in preagricultural societies

(C) the most important difference between modern and preagricultural societies is the variety and type of social roles permitted in each

(D) in modern societies, people must rely on technology to effectively predict and interpret other people's actions

(E) preagricultural societies lacked the complex social system that is needed to provide each person with an appropriate and stable social role or niche

8. Some students attending a small university with a well-known choir live off campus. From the fact that all music majors are members of the choir, a professor in the music department concluded that none of the students who live off campus is a music major.

The professor's conclusion is properly drawn if which one of the following is assumed?

(A) None of the students who live off campus is a member of the choir.

(B) None of the students who are music majors has failed to join the choir.

(C) Some of the students who do not live off campus are not music majors.

(D) All students who live on campus are music majors.

(E) All students who are members of the choir are music majors.

9. Journalist: A free marketplace of ideas ensures that all ideas get a fair hearing. Even ideas tainted with prejudice and malice can prompt beneficial outcomes. In most countries, however, the government is responsible for over half the information released to the public through all media. For this reason, the power of governments over information needs to be curtailed. Everyone grants that governments should not suppress free expression, yet governments continue to construct near monopolies on the publication and dissemination of enormous amounts of information.

Which one of the following most accurately expresses the conclusion of the journalist's argument?

(A) The freedom of the marketplace of ideas is in jeopardy.

(B) Preserving a free marketplace of ideas is important.

(C) The control that governments have over information needs to be reduced.

(D) Ideas that have malicious content or stem from questionable sources can be valuable.

(E) Governments have near monopolies on the dissemination of many kinds of information.

GO ON TO THE NEXT PAGE.

10. Charlene: Environmental cleanup increasingly relies on microorganisms to metabolize pollutants. This has its limitations, though, since microbes become less active when a region's temperature drops below normal.

Olaf: I don't think that's right. Researchers studying oil spills in the Arctic and subtropical regions measured the carbon dioxide output of organisms that digest petroleum pollutants and found that Arctic and subtropical microbes ate oil at nearly the same rate.

Olaf's reply suggests that he misinterprets Charlene's use of the term

(A) relies
(B) normal
(C) cleanup
(D) limitations
(E) active

11. According to the theory of continental drift, in prehistoric times, many of today's separate continents were part of a single huge landmass. As the plates on which this landmass rested began to move, the mass broke apart, and ocean water filled the newly created chasms. It is hypothesized, for example, that South America was once joined on its east coast with what is now the west coast of Africa.

Which one of the following discoveries, if it were made, would most support the above hypothesis about South America and Africa?

(A) A large band of ancient rock of a rare type along the east coast of South America is of the same type as a band on the west coast of Africa.
(B) Many people today living in Brazil are genetically quite similar to many western Africans.
(C) The climates of western Africa and of the east coast of South America resemble each other.
(D) Some of the oldest tribes of people living in eastern South America speak languages linguistically similar to various languages spoken by certain western African peoples.
(E) Several species of plants found in western Africa closely resemble plants growing in South America.

12. Several legislators claim that the public finds many current movies so violent as to be morally offensive. However, these legislators have misrepresented public opinion. In a survey conducted by a movie industry guild, only 17 percent of respondents thought that movies are overly violent, and only 3 percent found any recent movie morally offensive. These low percentages are telling, because the respondents see far more current movies than does the average moviegoer.

The reasoning in the argument is flawed in that the argument

(A) attempts to undermine the legislators' credibility instead of addressing their argument
(B) bases its conclusion on subjective judgments rather than on an objective criterion of moral offensiveness
(C) fails to consider the possibility that violent movies increase the prevalence of antisocial behavior
(D) generalizes from a sample that is unlikely to be representative of public sentiment
(E) presumes, without providing justification, that the people surveyed based their responses on a random sampling of movies

GO ON TO THE NEXT PAGE.

13. James: Many people claim that the voting public is unable to evaluate complex campaign issues. The television commercials for Reade in the national campaign, however, discuss complex campaign issues, and Reade is, at present, more popular than any other candidate.

Maria: Yes, Reade is the most popular. However, you are incorrect in claiming that this is because of Reade's discussion of complex campaign issues. Reade simply strikes the voters as the most competent and trustworthy candidate.

Which one of the following, if true, most supports Maria's counter to James?

(A) Reade's opponents are discussing some of the same issues as Reade.

(B) Reade's opponents charge that Reade oversimplifies complex campaign issues.

(C) Polling data show that Reade's present popularity will probably diminish over time.

(D) Polling data show that most voters cannot identify Reade's positions on campaign issues.

(E) Polling data show that some voters consider Reade competent and trustworthy.

14. Some critics claim that the power of the media to impose opinions upon people concerning the important issues of the day is too great. But this is not true. It would be true if on major issues the media purveyed a range of opinion narrower than that found among consumers of media. The fact that this assumption is untrue shows the critics' claim to be false.

Which one of the following most accurately describes a reasoning flaw in the argument?

(A) The argument launches a personal attack against the critics rather than addressing the reasons they present in support of their claim.

(B) The argument takes for granted that the media give at least as much exposure as they should to a wide range of opinion on the important issues of the day.

(C) The argument takes for granted that if the truth of one claim implies the truth of a second claim, then the falsity of the first claim proves the falsity of the second claim.

(D) The argument, instead of providing adequate reasons in support of its conclusion, makes an appeal to popular opinion.

(E) The argument takes for granted that it is desirable for a wide range of opinion on the important issues of the day to receive media exposure.

15. Marta: There have been complaints about the lack of recreational areas in our city. Some people favor turning the old railway land into walking trails, but there may be more productive ways of using that land.

Arthur: But the old railway land is ideal for walking trails. Our citizens have gone too long with inadequate recreational areas; we should not dismiss this proposal for walking trails without further consideration.

Arthur's criticism suggests that he interpreted Marta to be

(A) maintaining that converting the old railway land into walking trails would be an entirely unproductive use of that land

(B) favoring the development of recreational areas other than walking trails

(C) assuming that the complaints concerning a shortage of recreational areas are ill founded

(D) recommending that the proposal for converting the old railway land into walking trails should be promptly dismissed

(E) asserting that it may not be possible to convert the old railway land into adequate walking trails

GO ON TO THE NEXT PAGE.

16. In countries where government officials are neither selected by free elections nor open to criticism by a free press, the lives of citizens are controlled by policies they have had no role in creating. This is why such countries are prone to civil disorder, in spite of the veneer of calm such countries often present to a visitor. When people do not understand the purpose of the restrictions placed on their behavior they have a greater tendency to engage in civil disorder as an expression of their frustration.

Which one of the following is an assumption on which the argument depends?

(A) People who have had a role in making the laws that govern their own behavior act more rationally than those who have not.

(B) A free press is better able to convey to citizens the purpose of government policy than is a press controlled by the government.

(C) Civil disorder cannot be prevented by security forces alone, however great the powers granted them by the government.

(D) People tend not to understand the purpose of restrictions unless they participate in their formulation.

(E) Civil disorder does not generally occur in countries that have either free elections or a free press.

17. Researcher: Hard water contains more calcium and magnesium than soft water contains. Thus, those who drink mostly soft water incur an increased risk of heart disease, stroke, and hypertension, for people being treated for these conditions tend to have lower levels of magnesium in their blood.

Which one of the following, if true, most undermines the researcher's argument?

(A) Magnesium deficiency is not uncommon, even in relatively prosperous countries with an otherwise generally adequate diet.

(B) Magnesium is needed to prevent sodium from increasing blood pressure.

(C) As people age, their ability to metabolize magnesium deteriorates.

(D) The ingestion of magnesium supplements inhibits the effectiveness of many medicines used to treat high blood pressure and heart disease.

(E) Compounds commonly used to treat hypertension and heart disease diminish the body's capacity to absorb and retain magnesium.

18. Bookstore owner: Consumers should buy books only from an independent bookstore, not from a bookstore that belongs to a bookstore chain. An independent bookstore tends to carry a much wider variety of books than does a chain bookstore, so because chains often threaten the existence of independent bookstores, they tend to reduce the variety of books available to consumers.

Which one of the following principles, if valid, most helps to justify the bookstore owner's argumentation?

(A) Chain bookstores should not force independent bookstores out of business when doing so would reduce the variety of books available to consumers.

(B) Consumers should buy books from only those bookstores whose existence does not tend to reduce the variety of books available to consumers.

(C) The best interest of the bookselling business is not served when consumers purchase books from businesses whose existence tends to reduce the variety of books available to consumers.

(D) Consumers should not make purchases from any bookstore that deliberately forces competing bookstores out of business.

(E) If consumers have no access to any independent bookstore, they should buy books from the chain bookstore with the greatest diversity of books.

GO ON TO THE NEXT PAGE.

19. Anger in response to insults is unreasonable, for insults are merely assertions that someone has undesirable characteristics. If such an assertion is false, the insulted party ought to pity the ignorance prompting the insult. If it is true, the insulted party should be grateful for such useful information.

Which one of the following, if assumed, enables the argument's conclusion to be properly drawn?

(A) Actions prompted by ignorance do not warrant hostile reactions.
(B) Anger is an unreasonable response to useful information.
(C) Anger is an unreasonable response to any action that should prompt pity or gratitude.
(D) Gratitude and pity are reasonable responses to some forms of hostile or insensitive behavior.
(E) Pity is the only reasonable reaction to people with undesirable characteristics.

20. Evidence suggests that we can manufacture a car with twice the fuel efficiency of a normal car, and it has been shown that we can produce a car that meets safety standards for side-impact crashes. So we can make a car that does both.

The flawed reasoning in the argument above is most similar to that in which one of the following?

(A) Since there is no dishwasher currently available that uses energy efficiently and there is no dishwasher currently available that effectively cleans pans, no dishwasher currently available is well engineered. For, to be well engineered, a dishwasher must use energy efficiently and clean pans effectively.
(B) Kameko might catch a cold this winter and she might go outside without a hat this winter. Therefore, it is possible that Kameko will catch a cold because she goes outside without a hat this winter.
(C) Susan says that it is cold outside, and Nathan says that it is snowing; therefore, it is both cold and snowing outside.
(D) It is possible to write a best-selling novel and it is possible to write one that appeals to the critics. Therefore, an author could write a critically acclaimed novel that gains a large readership.
(E) There are machines that brew coffee and there are machines that toast bread. And it is possible to make a machine that does both. So there will someday be a machine that does both.

21. Pizzerias are the only restaurants that routinely record the names, addresses, and menu selections of their customers. Simply by organizing these data, they can easily identify regular, average, and infrequent customers. Therefore, pizzerias utilize direct-mail marketing more effectively than do other restaurants.

Which one of the following, if assumed, enables the argument's conclusion to be properly inferred?

(A) Restaurants other than pizzerias cannot easily identify regular, average, and infrequent customers.
(B) For restaurants, utilizing direct-mail marketing requires the names, addresses, and menu selections of at least some customers.
(C) For restaurants, the identification of regular, average, and infrequent customers generally involves recording the names, addresses, and menu selections of at least some customers.
(D) Utilizing direct-mail marketing is rarely beneficial for restaurants that cannot identify regular, average, and infrequent customers.
(E) Restaurants that routinely record names, addresses, and menu selections of their customers always utilize direct-mail marketing more effectively than do any other restaurants.

22. All highly successful salespersons are both well organized and self-motivated, characteristics absent from many salespersons who are not highly successful. Further, although only those who are highly successful are well known among their peers, no salespersons who are self-motivated regret their career choices.

If all of the statements above are true, which one of the following must be true?

(A) No self-motivated salespersons who are not highly successful are well organized.
(B) All salespersons who are well organized but not highly successful are self-motivated.
(C) No salespersons who are well known among their peers regret their career choices.
(D) All salespersons who are not well organized regret their career choices.
(E) All salespersons who do not regret their career choices are highly successful.

GO ON TO THE NEXT PAGE.

23. The fact that people who exercise vigorously are sick less often than average does not prove that vigorous exercise prevents illness, for whether one exercises vigorously or not depends in part on one's preexisting state of health.

The reasoning in which one of the following arguments is most similar to that in the argument above?

(A) Having strong verbal skills encourages people to read more, so the fact that habitual readers tend to be verbally skilled does not prove that reading produces verbal skill.

(B) Musical and mathematical skills are often produced by the same talent for perceiving abstract patterns, so the fact that some mathematicians are not skilled musicians does not prove that they lack the talent that can produce musical skill.

(C) Since how people choose to dress often depends on how their friends dress, the fact that a person chooses a style of dress does not prove that he or she truly prefers that style to any other.

(D) The fact that taller children often outperform other children at basketball does not show that height is a decisive advantage in basketball, for taller children tend to play basketball more frequently than do other children.

(E) The fact that two diseases have similar symptoms does not establish that they have the same underlying cause, for dissimilar causes can have similar effects.

24. Biologist: We know the following things about plant X. Specimens with fuzzy seeds always have long stems but never have white flowers. Specimens with curled leaves always have white flowers, and specimens with thorny seedpods always have curled leaves. A specimen of plant X in my garden has a long stem and curled leaves.

From the biologist's statements, which one of the following can be properly inferred about the specimen of plant X in the biologist's garden?

(A) It has white flowers and thorny seedpods.
(B) It has white flowers but lacks thorny seedpods.
(C) It has white flowers but lacks fuzzy seeds.
(D) It has fuzzy seeds and thorny seedpods.
(E) It lacks both white flowers and fuzzy seeds.

25. Unquestionably, inventors of useful devices deserve credit for their ingenuity, but the engineers who help develop an invention get too little recognition. Although inventors sometimes serve as their own engineers, more often, engineers must translate an inventor's insight into something workable and useful. Therefore, engineers also deserve credit for their contribution.

The claim that inventors sometimes serve as their own engineers plays which one of the following roles in the argument?

(A) It separates the practical and theoretical aspects of the argument.

(B) It indicates that the problem identified in the argument does not arise in every instance.

(C) It supports an earlier statement regarding what is at issue in the argument.

(D) It concedes that a distinction on which the argument relies is unclear.

(E) It introduces an alternative solution to the problem the argument is addressing.

S T O P

IF YOU FINISH BEFORE TIME IS CALLED, YOU MAY CHECK YOUR WORK ON THIS SECTION ONLY.
DO NOT WORK ON ANY OTHER SECTION IN THE TEST.

SECTION III

Time—35 minutes

23 Questions

Directions: Each group of questions in this section is based on a set of conditions. In answering some of the questions, it may be useful to draw a rough diagram. Choose the response that most accurately and completely answers each question and blacken the corresponding space on your answer sheet.

Questions 1–5

Charlie makes a soup by adding exactly six kinds of foods— kale, lentils, mushrooms, onions, tomatoes, and zucchini—to a broth, one food at a time. No food is added more than once. The order in which Charlie adds the foods to the broth must be consistent with the following:

    If the mushrooms are added third, then the lentils are added last.

    If the zucchini is added first, then the lentils are added at some time before the onions.

    Neither the tomatoes nor the kale is added fifth.

    The mushrooms are added at some time before the tomatoes or the kale, but not before both.

1. Which one of the following could be the order in which the foods are added to the broth?

    (A)   kale, mushrooms, onions, lentils, tomatoes, zucchini
    (B)   kale, zucchini, mushrooms, tomatoes, lentils, onions
    (C)   lentils, mushrooms, zucchini, kale, onions, tomatoes
    (D)   zucchini, lentils, kale, mushrooms, onions, tomatoes
    (E)   zucchini, tomatoes, onions, mushrooms, lentils, kale

2. Which one of the following foods CANNOT be added first?

    (A)   kale
    (B)   lentils
    (C)   mushrooms
    (D)   onions
    (E)   tomatoes

3. If the lentils are added last, then which one of the following must be true?

    (A)   At least one of the foods is added at some time before the zucchini.
    (B)   At least two of the foods are added at some time before the kale.
    (C)   The mushrooms are added third.
    (D)   The zucchini is added third.
    (E)   The tomatoes are added fourth.

4. Which one of the following could be an accurate partial ordering of the foods added to the broth?

    (A)   lentils: second; mushrooms: third
    (B)   mushrooms: fourth; lentils: last
    (C)   onions: second; mushrooms: fifth
    (D)   zucchini: first; lentils: last
    (E)   zucchini: first; mushrooms: second

5. If the zucchini is added first, then which one of the following CANNOT be true?

    (A)   The kale is added second.
    (B)   The tomatoes are added second.
    (C)   The lentils are added third.
    (D)   The lentils are added fourth.
    (E)   The onions are added fourth.

GO ON TO THE NEXT PAGE.

<u>Questions 6–10</u>

A study sponsored by a consumer group tests exactly five of seven cold medications—F, G, H, I, K, L, and M—and ranks the medications tested from first (best) to fifth (worst). There are no ties. The following conditions must apply:

L ranks second.
Either F or G ranks first.
I is tested.
H ranks better than G if both are tested.
K ranks better than F if both are tested.
If M is tested, both F and H are also tested.

6. Which one of the following could be the five cold medications that the study ranks, listed from first to fifth?

(A) F, I, L, H, G
(B) F, L, G, H, M
(C) F, L, I, G, M
(D) F, L, I, H, M
(E) F, L, K, I, G

7. Which one of the following could be true of the study?

(A) G ranks better than M.
(B) H ranks better than F.
(C) I ranks better than F.
(D) K ranks better than G.
(E) M ranks better than G.

8. Which one of the following cold medications must be among those tested in the study?

(A) F
(B) G
(C) H
(D) K
(E) M

9. Which one of the following is a complete and accurate list of the cold medications any one of which could be the cold medication ranked fifth?

(A) F, G, H, M
(B) G, H, I, M
(C) G, H, L, M
(D) F, G, H, I, K
(E) F, G, H, I, M

10. If I ranks third, each of the following could also be true of the study EXCEPT:

(A) M ranks better than H.
(B) K ranks better than G.
(C) I ranks better than F.
(D) H ranks better than M.
(E) G ranks better than K.

GO ON TO THE NEXT PAGE.

Questions 11–17

Each nonstop flight offered by Zephyr Airlines departs from one and arrives at another of five cities: Honolulu, Montreal, Philadelphia, Toronto, and Vancouver. Any two cities are said to be connected with each other if Zephyr offers nonstop flights between them. Each city is connected with at least one other city. The following conditions govern Zephyr's nonstop flights:

Montreal is connected with exactly one other city.
Honolulu is not connected with Toronto.
Any city that is connected with Honolulu is also connected with Toronto.
If Philadelphia is connected with Toronto, then Philadelphia is not connected with Vancouver.

11. Which one of the following could be a complete and accurate list of Zephyr Airlines' connected cities?

(A) Honolulu and Vancouver; Montreal and Toronto; Philadelphia and Vancouver; Toronto and Vancouver

(B) Honolulu and Vancouver; Montreal and Philadelphia; Montreal and Toronto; Philadelphia and Toronto; Toronto and Vancouver

(C) Honolulu and Philadelphia; Honolulu and Montreal; Philadelphia and Toronto; Toronto and Vancouver

(D) Honolulu and Philadelphia; Montreal and Toronto; Philadelphia and Toronto; Philadelphia and Vancouver; Toronto and Vancouver

(E) Honolulu and Philadelphia; Honolulu and Toronto; Montreal and Philadelphia; Philadelphia and Vancouver

12. If exactly three cities are each connected with Philadelphia, then which one of the following could be a pair of connected cities?

(A) Honolulu and Montreal
(B) Honolulu and Vancouver
(C) Montreal and Toronto
(D) Montreal and Vancouver
(E) Philadelphia and Vancouver

13. Which one of the following is a pair of cities that CANNOT be connected?

(A) Honolulu and Montreal
(B) Honolulu and Philadelphia
(C) Montreal and Philadelphia
(D) Montreal and Vancouver
(E) Philadelphia and Toronto

14. Which one of the following could be true?

(A) Montreal and Philadelphia are connected with each other, but neither is connected with any other city.

(B) Montreal and Toronto are connected with each other, but neither is connected with any other city.

(C) Philadelphia and Toronto are connected with each other, but neither is connected with any other city.

(D) Philadelphia and Vancouver are connected with each other, but neither is connected with any other city.

(E) Toronto and Vancouver are connected with each other, but neither is connected with any other city.

15. If Toronto is the only city that is connected with Philadelphia, then which one of the following could be true?

(A) Exactly one city is connected with Toronto.
(B) Exactly one city is connected with Vancouver.
(C) Exactly two cities are each connected with Honolulu.
(D) Exactly two cities are each connected with Toronto.
(E) Exactly four cities are each connected with Toronto.

16. At most how many pairs of cities could be connected?

(A) four
(B) five
(C) six
(D) seven
(E) eight

17. If four of the cities are each connected with the remaining city, then the cities in which one of the following pairs must be connected with each other?

(A) Honolulu and Montreal
(B) Honolulu and Philadelphia
(C) Honolulu and Vancouver
(D) Montreal and Philadelphia
(E) Montreal and Toronto

GO ON TO THE NEXT PAGE.

Questions 18–23

For a behavioral study, a researcher will select exactly six individual animals from among three monkeys—F, G, and H—three pandas—K, L, and N—and three raccoons—T, V, and Z. The selection of animals for the study must meet the following conditions:

F and H are not both selected.
N and T are not both selected.
If H is selected, K is also selected.
If K is selected, N is also selected.

18. Which one of the following is an acceptable selection of animals for the study?

(A) F, G, K, N, T, V
(B) F, H, K, N, V, Z
(C) G, H, K, L, V, Z
(D) G, H, K, N, V, Z
(E) G, H, L, N, V, Z

19. If H and L are among the animals selected, which one of the following could be true?

(A) F is selected.
(B) T is selected.
(C) Z is selected.
(D) Exactly one panda is selected.
(E) Exactly two pandas are selected.

20. Each of the following is a pair of animals that could be selected together EXCEPT

(A) F and G
(B) H and K
(C) K and T
(D) L and N
(E) T and V

21. If all three of the raccoons are selected, which one of the following must be true?

(A) K is selected.
(B) L is selected.
(C) Exactly one monkey is selected.
(D) Exactly two pandas are selected.
(E) All three of the monkeys are selected.

22. If T is selected, which one of the following is a pair of animals that must be among the animals selected?

(A) F and G
(B) G and H
(C) K and L
(D) K and Z
(E) L and N

23. The selection of animals must include

(A) at most two of each kind of animal
(B) at least one of each kind of animal
(C) at least two pandas
(D) exactly two monkeys
(E) exactly two raccoons

S T O P

IF YOU FINISH BEFORE TIME IS CALLED, YOU MAY CHECK YOUR WORK ON THIS SECTION ONLY.
DO NOT WORK ON ANY OTHER SECTION IN THE TEST.

SECTION IV

Time—35 minutes

26 Questions

Directions: The questions in this section are based on the reasoning contained in brief statements or passages. For some questions, more than one of the choices could conceivably answer the question. However, you are to choose the best answer; that is, the response that most accurately and completely answers the question. You should not make assumptions that are by commonsense standards implausible, superfluous, or incompatible with the passage. After you have chosen the best answer, blacken the corresponding space on your answer sheet.

1. Big-budget movies often gross two or three times the cost of their production and marketing. However, most of the movie industry's total revenue comes from low-budget movies.

Which one of the following, if true, most helps to resolve the apparent discrepancy above?

(A) Big-budget movies need to sell many more tickets than do low-budget movies, just to recoup their production costs.

(B) There are many more low-budget movies produced than there are big- and medium-budget movies.

(C) The movie industry's revenues, when adjusted for inflation, have declined sharply in the last 30 years.

(D) Big-budget movies, because of their elaborate special effects, cost more in insurance premiums than low-budget movies do.

(E) The more time a company spends on making a movie the more expensive the movie is.

2. Dr. Theresa Pagano, a biologist, has found that the checkerspot butterfly is becoming more prevalent in regions farther north than before and less prevalent in regions farther south. The northward shift of the butterflies is almost perfectly correlated with the northward shift of the warm zones in the global climate, and Dr. Pagano has therefore concluded that the changing climate is responsible for the northward movement of the butterflies.

Each of the following, if true, supports Dr. Pagano's reasoning EXCEPT:

(A) Checkerspot butterfly colonies observed under laboratory conditions are critically affected by small temperature changes.

(B) Climate does not affect checkerspot butterflies themselves directly, but the plants they depend on thrive best in warm climates.

(C) Experimental evidence suggests that the checkerspot butterfly can adapt easily to a wide range of temperatures and geographic conditions.

(D) In recent years, abnormally low average temperatures have been correlated with a reduced checkerspot butterfly population.

(E) Several studies have shown that several other species of butterfly closely related to the checkerspot butterfly survive only in warm climates.

GO ON TO THE NEXT PAGE.

3. Professor: The best users of a language are its
    great authors. However, these authors often
    use language in ways that are innovative and
    idiosyncratic, and are therefore less respectful of
    the strictures of proper usage than most of us are.

    The Professor's statements, if true, most support which
    one of the following?

    (A) People who want to become great writers should
         not imitate great authors' use of language.
    (B) Writers who do not observe proper language
         usage risk developing a peculiar or idiosyncratic
         style.
    (C) Those most talented at using a language are not
         as likely as most other people to observe proper
         language usage.
    (D) People who use an innovative or idiosyncratic
         writing style often incur criticism of their
         language usage.
    (E) The standard for what constitutes proper language
         usage should be set by the best users of a
         language.

4. The purpose of the physical sciences is to predict the
    order in which events will succeed one another. Human
    behavior, also, can sometimes be successfully predicted.
    However, even successful predictions of human behavior
    do not provide an understanding of it, for understanding
    a human action requires knowing its goal, even though
    such knowledge of goals either cannot or need not be
    obtained in the case of nonhuman behavior.

    Which one of the following most accurately expresses
    the argument's conclusion?

    (A) Successful predictions of human behavior do not
         constitute an understanding of that behavior.
    (B) One cannot predict an instance of human
         behavior without an understanding of the agent's
         purpose in engaging in that behavior.
    (C) In some cases, but not in others, understanding
         an event consists in the ability to predict the
         occurrence of that event.
    (D) The goal of the physical sciences is to predict the
         order in which events will occur.
    (E) The methods used to predict human behavior
         must involve reference to the psychological
         states of human agents.

5. Sickles found at one archaeological site had scratched
    blades, but those found at a second site did not. Since
    sickle blades always become scratched whenever they
    are used to harvest grain, this evidence shows that the
    sickles found at the first site were used to harvest grain,
    but the sickles found at the second site were not.

    Which one of the following, if shown to be a realistic
    possibility, would undermine the argument?

    (A) Some sickles that have not yet been found at the
         first site do not have scratched blades.
    (B) The scratches on the blades of the sickles found
         at the first site resulted from something other
         than harvesting grain.
    (C) Sickles at both sites had ritual uses whether or
         not those sickles were used to harvest grain.
    (D) At the second site tools other than sickles were
         used to harvest grain.
    (E) The sickles found at the first site were made by
         the same people who made the sickles found at
         the second site.

6. Pain perception depends only partly on physiology.
    During World War II a significantly lower percentage of
    injured soldiers requested morphine than did civilians
    recuperating from surgery. The soldier's response to
    injury was relief, joy at being alive, even euphoria;
    to the civilians, surgery was a depressing, calamitous
    event. So it would seem that the meaning one attaches to
    a wound can affect the amount of pain one perceives.

    The claim that pain perception depends only partly on
    physiology figures in the argument in which one of the
    following ways?

    (A) It is an assumption on which the argument
         depends.
    (B) It undermines the argument's main conclusion.
    (C) It summarizes a position that the argument is
         meant to discredit.
    (D) It is information that the argument takes for
         granted.
    (E) It is the main conclusion of the argument.

GO ON TO THE NEXT PAGE.

7. If cold fusion worked, it would provide almost limitless power from very inexpensive raw materials, materials far cheaper than coal or oil. But replacing all the traditional electric generators that use these fuels with cold-fusion power plants would result in a reduction of no more than 25 percent in the average residential electric bill.

Each of the following, if true, would help to resolve the apparent discrepancy between the predictions above EXCEPT:

(A) Cold-fusion power plants would be more expensive to build and maintain than traditional electric generators are.
(B) Environmental regulations now placed on burning coal or fuel oil are less costly than the regulations that would be placed on cold fusion.
(C) Most electric companies would be willing to incorporate cold-fusion technology into their power plants.
(D) Only a relatively small portion of any residential electric bill is determined by the electric company's expenses for fuel.
(E) Personnel costs for the distribution of power to consumers are unrelated to the type of raw materials an electric company uses.

8. Everyone likes repertory theater. Actors like it because playing different roles each night decreases their level of boredom. Stagehands like it because changing sets every night means more overtime and, thus, higher pay. Theater managers like it because, if plays that reflect audience demand are chosen for production, most performances generate large revenues. It is evident, therefore, that more theaters should change to repertory.

The argument above would be strengthened if which one of the following were true?

(A) In a repertory theater, a large capital outlay is required at the beginning of each season.
(B) In a repertory theater, patrons need to pay overly close attention to the schedule in order to make their theater plans.
(C) In a repertory theater, storage space for sets for more than one production must be available.
(D) In a repertory theater, plays can be rescheduled to meet audience demand.
(E) In a repertory theater, some actors who change roles from night to night find it difficult to master all of the roles they play.

9. Writer: I collaborated with another writer on my last book, instead of writing alone as I usually do. Because the book sold so well as a result of this joint effort, I should collaborate with a writer on my next book so that book will sell well too.

Which one of the following principles, if valid, most helps to justify the reasoning above?

(A) If a person's book sells well because of a collaboration, that person's next book will sell well, if he or she collaborates with the same writer.
(B) A book sells well only if its author collaborated on the book with another writer.
(C) If a person's book sells well because of a collaboration, future collaborations on the part of that person will produce other books that sell well.
(D) Writers who do not collaborate on books have a smaller chance of writing a book that will sell well.
(E) Writers who collaborate on books, if they are good writers, usually produce books that sell well.

10. Researcher: All defects in short-term memory are caused by a malfunction of a part of the brain called the hippocampus. In short-term memory, the mind holds a piece of information for only a few moments, after which it is either stored in long-term memory or forgotten. Learning is the accumulation of new information in long-term memory. Thus, whenever a child exhibits a learning deficit, the hippocampus is malfunctioning.

The reasoning in the researcher's argument is most vulnerable to criticism on the grounds that this argument

(A) draws a general conclusion based on too small a sample of learning deficits
(B) presumes, without giving justification, that all learning deficits in children involve short-term memory
(C) presumes, without giving justification, that short-term memory is disabled whenever the hippocampus is disabled
(D) fails to quantify precisely the length of time during which the mind holds a piece of information in short-term memory
(E) takes for granted that learning deficits in adults have a cause unrelated to the cause of learning deficits in children

GO ON TO THE NEXT PAGE.

11. Historian: One traditional childrearing practice in the nineteenth century was to make a child who misbehaved sit alone outside. Anyone passing by would conclude that the child had misbehaved. Nowadays, many child psychologists would disapprove of this practice because they believe that such practices damage the child's self-esteem and that damage to children's self-esteem makes them less confident as adults. However, no one disagrees that adults raised under that traditional practice were, on average, as confident as adults not so raised.

Which one of the following can be properly inferred from the historian's statements?

(A) The beliefs of many present-day child psychologists about the consequences of loss of self-esteem are incorrect.

(B) Some of the most confident adults, as well as some of the least confident adults, were raised under the traditional practice in question.

(C) With the traditional childrearing practice, passersby did not always make correct inferences about children's behavior by observing them outdoors.

(D) The most confident adults are those who developed the highest level of self-esteem in childhood.

(E) If children's loss of self-esteem makes them less confident as adults, then the traditional childrearing practice in question did not tend to cause significant loss of self-esteem.

12. Novelist: Any author who thinks a sentence is ungrammatical will not write it down in the first place, and thus will have no need to use a grammar book. On the other hand, any author who is sure a sentence she or he has written is grammatical will not feel a need to consult a grammar book. Thus, grammar books are useless as reference sources for authors.

The reasoning in the novelist's argument is flawed because the argument

(A) infers, from the claim that authors should not consult grammar books, that they will not in fact do so

(B) infers, from the claim that an author does not mistakenly think that a sentence is ungrammatical, that the author will feel sure that it is grammatical

(C) overlooks the possibility that grammar books are useful as reference sources for people who are not authors

(D) presumes, without providing justification, that grammar books cannot have any use except as reference sources

(E) ignores the possibility that there is a middle ground between being sure that a sentence is grammatical and thinking that it is ungrammatical

13. Britain is now rabies free. Nevertheless, Britain's strict quarantine of imported domesticated animals, designed to prevent widespread outbreaks of rabies there, cannot succeed indefinitely in preventing such outbreaks. Bats, which are very susceptible to rabies, fly into Britain from continental Europe. Since wild bats cannot be quarantined, this policy cannot control rabies spread by wild bats.

Which one of the following is an argumentative strategy employed in the argument?

(A) trying to undermine support for a certain policy by pointing out that factors other than the policy itself could account for the results attributed to that policy

(B) raising a possible objection to a certain policy in order to show that the objection is in fact irrelevant to the particular situation the policy was designed to address

(C) providing evidence that because the officials charged with enforcing a certain policy often fail to perform their duty that policy is sure to have little effect

(D) showing that because a certain policy is not universally adopted that policy cannot accomplish what it was designed to do

(E) arguing that a certain policy is bound to fail because an event that is likely to defeat the aim of the policy falls outside the policy's influence

14. Franklin: The only clue I have as to the identity of the practical joker is the handwriting on the note. Ordinarily I would suspect Miller, who has always been jealous of me, but the handwriting is not hers. So the joker is apparently someone else.

Which one of the following provides the strongest grounds for criticizing Franklin's reasoning?

(A) It fails to consider the possibility that there was more than one practical joker.

(B) It fails to indicate the degree to which handwriting samples should look alike in order to be considered of the same source.

(C) It provides no explanation for why Miller should be the prime suspect.

(D) It provides no explanation for why only one piece of evidence was obtained.

(E) It takes for granted that if the handwriting on the note had been Miller's, then the identity of the joker would have been ascertained to be Miller.

GO ON TO THE NEXT PAGE.

15. People who have doctorates in the liberal arts are interested in improving their intellects. Companies, however, rarely hire people who are not concerned with the financial gain that can be obtained by hard work in the business world. As a result, companies rarely hire people who have doctorates in the liberal arts.

The conclusion of the argument follows logically if which one of the following is assumed?

(A) Companies would hire people with doctorates in the liberal arts if such people were interested in the money available in the business world.
(B) Some people who are interested in the liberal arts do not care about money.
(C) The only people not interested in making money in the business world are people who are interested in improving their intellects.
(D) People with doctorates in the liberal arts are interested in employment in the business world.
(E) Only people not concerned with making money in the business world are interested in improving their intellects.

16. Logan: Newspapers have always focused on ephemeral matters while ignoring important societal changes. For this and other reasons, old newspapers are useless to both amateur and professional historians.

Mendez: But news stories, along with popular art, provide a wealth of information about what the people of an era thought and felt.

On the basis of their statements, Logan and Mendez are committed to disagreeing over whether

(A) newspapers accurately report the most important changes taking place in a society
(B) the study of previous eras should include investigations of the conventions of newspaper reporting
(C) popular art is an important source of information about what the people of previous eras thought and felt
(D) newspapers ought to focus more on the types of stories they have glossed over in the past
(E) newspaper reports from former eras are useful sources of material for understanding the past

17. People who have never been asked to do more than they can easily do are people who never do all they can. Alex is someone who has clearly not done all that he is capable of doing, so obviously no one has ever pushed him to do more than what comes to him easily.

The flawed reasoning in which one of the following is most similar to the flawed reasoning in the argument above?

(A) Anybody who has a dog knows the true value of companionship, and Alicia has demonstrated that she knows the true value of companionship; thus we can safely conclude that Alicia has a dog.
(B) Anyone who discovers something new is someone who has examined all the possible solutions to a problem. Fran has surely never discovered something new. Therefore, Fran has never explored all the possible solutions to a problem.
(C) Any person who does not face sufficient challenges is a person who does not accomplish everything he or she can. Jill is a person who accomplishes everything she can, so Jill is a person who faces sufficient challenges.
(D) By definition, a polygon is any closed plane figure bounded by straight lines. That object pictured on the chalkboard is certainly a closed plane figure bounded by a large number of straight lines, so that object pictured on the chalkboard must be a polygon.
(E) People who have never lost something that they cannot afford to lose will be lax about keeping their property secure. Jon is lax about keeping property secure when it is something he can afford to lose, so Jon must never have lost anything.

GO ON TO THE NEXT PAGE.

18. It has been a staple of drama to feature an innocent young protagonist, eager to make a mark on the world, who is stymied by an indifferent or hostile society. Since the playwrights of such works wished the audience to empathize with the protagonist, historians do not regard these plays as serious revelations of what the societies presented in the plays were really like.

Which one of the following, if true, most helps to explain the viewpoint of the historians described above?

(A) The historians believe that playwrights tend to be more critical of their own societies than of other societies.

(B) The historians believe that playwrights tend to exaggerate the weaknesses of a society for the sake of dramatic effect.

(C) The historians believe that plays tend to provide useful information about the time and society in which they were written.

(D) The historians believe that plays often contain serious revelations of what the societies presented in those plays were like.

(E) The historians believe that only the most popular plays within a society accurately portray that society.

19. Fishing columnist: When an independent research firm compared the five best-selling baits, it found that Benton baits work best for catching trout. It asked a dozen top anglers to try out the five best-selling baits as they fished for speckled trout in a pristine northern stream, and every angler had the most success with a Benton bait. These results show that Benton is the best bait for anyone who is fishing for trout.

Each of the following describes a flaw in the reasoning in the fishing columnist's argument EXCEPT:

(A) The argument overlooks the possibility that some other bait is more successful than any of the five best-selling baits.

(B) The argument overlooks the possibility that what works best for expert anglers will not work best for ordinary anglers.

(C) The argument overlooks the possibility that the relative effectiveness of different baits changes when used in different locations.

(D) The argument overlooks the possibility that two best-selling brands of bait may be equally effective.

(E) The argument overlooks the possibility that baits that work well with a particular variety of fish may not work well with other varieties of that fish.

20. Investment banker: Democracies require free-market capitalist economies, because a more controlled economy is incompatible with complete democracy. But history shows that repressive measures against certain capitalistic developments are required during the transition from a totalitarian regime to a democracy. Thus, people who bemoan the seemingly anticapitalistic measures certain governments are currently taking are being hasty.

Which one of the following is an assumption required by the investment banker's argument?

(A) No current government has reached as complete a state of democracy as it is possible for a government to reach.

(B) The more democratic a country is, the less regulated its economy must be.

(C) The need for economic stability makes the existence of partially democratic governments more probable than the existence of fully democratic governments.

(D) A free-market economy is incompatible with a nondemocratic regime.

(E) The nations whose anticapitalistic measures the people in question bemoan had totalitarian regimes in the recent past.

21. Administrator: Because revenue fell by 15 percent this year, the university needs to reduce next year's budget. This could be accomplished by eliminating faculty positions. It could also be accomplished by reducing faculty salaries. Since we will not eliminate any faculty positions, we must reduce faculty salaries.

The administrator's reasoning is flawed because the administrator

(A) presumes, without providing justification, that more money would be saved by reducing faculty salaries than would be saved by eliminating faculty positions

(B) presumes, without providing justification, that the budget cannot be reduced unless faculty positions are eliminated or faculty salaries are reduced

(C) ignores the possibility that, though budget cuts will be needed, they will not need to be as high as 15 percent

(D) presumes, without providing justification, that some faculty members will leave their jobs rather than accept a reduced salary

(E) ignores the possibility that the budget could be reduced by eliminating some faculty positions and reducing the remaining faculty members' salaries

GO ON TO THE NEXT PAGE.

22. Repressors—people who unconsciously inhibit their display of emotion—exhibit significant increases in heart rate when they encounter emotion-provoking situations. Nonrepressors have similar physiological responses when they encounter such situations and consciously inhibit their display of emotion. Thus the very act of inhibiting displays of emotion, whether done consciously or unconsciously, causes a sharp rise in heart rate.

Which one of the following is an assumption required by the argument?

(A) Encountering an emotion-provoking situation is not sufficient to cause nonrepressors' heart rates to rise sharply.

(B) Nonrepressors can inhibit facial and bodily displays of emotion as well as repressors do.

(C) Despite their outward calm, repressors normally feel even more excited than do nonrepressors in an emotion-provoking situation.

(D) People who are ordinarily very emotional can refrain from feeling strong emotions when experimenters ask them to do so.

(E) In situations that do not tend to provoke emotions, the average heart rate of repressors is the same as that of nonrepressors.

23. A television manufacturing plant has a total of 1,000 workers, though an average of 10 are absent on any given day for various reasons. On days when exactly 10 workers are absent, the plant produces televisions at its normal rate. Thus, it is reasonable to assume that the plant could fire 10 workers without any loss in production.

The argument is most vulnerable to criticism on the grounds that it

(A) ignores the possibility that if 10 workers were fired, each of the remaining workers would produce more televisions than previously

(B) fails to show that the absentee rate would drop if 10 workers were fired

(C) takes for granted that the normal rate of production can be attained only when no more than the average number of workers are absent

(D) overlooks the possibility that certain workers are crucial to the production of televisions

(E) takes for granted that the rate of production is not affected by the number of workers employed at the plant

24. New evidence suggests that the collapse of Egypt's old kingdom some 4,000 years ago was caused by environmental catastrophe rather than internal social upheaval. Ocean sediments reveal a period of global cooling at the time, a condition generally associated with extended droughts. There were, no doubt, serious social problems in Egypt at the time, but they resulted from a severe dry spell.

Which one of the following, if true, would most strengthen the argument?

(A) Historically, most civilizations have succumbed to internal strife rather than external factors.

(B) The social problems in Egypt's old kingdom at the time of its collapse were serious enough to have caused the collapse.

(C) At the time of the collapse of the old kingdom, several isolated but well-established civilizations near Egypt underwent sudden declines.

(D) Egyptian records recovered from the time of the collapse explicitly refer to the deteriorating conditions of the society.

(E) Shortly after the collapse of the old kingdom, Egypt was thrust into a civil war that lasted most of the next two centuries.

GO ON TO THE NEXT PAGE.

25. Inflation rates will not stabilize unless the rate of economic growth decreases. Yet in order to slow the economy, the full cooperation of world leaders will be required. Thus, it would be overly optimistic to expect stable inflation rates in the near future.

    Which one of the following is most closely parallel in its reasoning to the reasoning in the argument above?

    (A) If factory safety is a serious concern, each employee must report potentially hazardous situations. Only with full employee participation in the safety program will these hazards be corrected and accidents be prevented. Thus, without everyone's cooperation we cannot expect improved factory safety.

    (B) If the board is serious about improving management efficiency, it must eliminate organizational redundancy. Unfortunately, it will not be possible to eliminate wasteful redundancy without dismissing a number of senior employees. Thus, no option is available but to dismiss some senior employees.

    (C) Only if we thoroughly examine all options will we be able to arrive at the optimal decision. Such a thorough examination, however, will necessitate a delay in the presentation of our proposal. Therefore, we will be able to arrive at an optimal decision only if we delay the presentation of our proposal.

    (D) If we are to produce the safest vehicles possible, we must conduct objective structural tests. However, the performance of such objective tests will inevitably result in huge cost overruns. It is therefore unavoidable that the level of vehicle safety will not be optimal.

    (E) If honesty is the best policy, we should report our company's poor performance in the last year. But if we do so, we will put our jobs at risk and our stockholders will complain. Therefore, we must not report our poor performance.

26. The number of applications for admission reported by North American Ph.D. programs in art history has declined in each of the last four years. We can conclude from this that interest among recent North American college and university graduates in choosing art history as a career has declined in the last four years.

    Each of the following, if true, weakens the argument EXCEPT:

    (A) The number of North American Ph.D. programs in art history that opted to report data about applications for admission has declined in each of the last four years.

    (B) The average age of applicants for admission to North American Ph.D. programs in art history has increased in each of the last four years.

    (C) The number of errors in data about applications for admission to North American Ph.D. programs in art history has increased substantially during the last four years.

    (D) The number of North American employers willing to hire individuals without a Ph.D. for jobs in art history has increased in each of the last four years.

    (E) The percentage of applications for admission received from outside North America by North American Ph.D. programs in art history has declined substantially in the last four years.

S T O P

IF YOU FINISH BEFORE TIME IS CALLED, YOU MAY CHECK YOUR WORK ON THIS SECTION ONLY. DO NOT WORK ON ANY OTHER SECTION IN THE TEST.

SECTION V

Time—35 minutes

27 Questions

<u>Directions</u>: Each passage in this section is followed by a group of questions to be answered on the basis of what is <u>stated</u> or <u>implied</u> in the passage. For some of the questions, more than one of the choices could conceivably answer the question. However, you are to choose the <u>best</u> answer; that is, the response that most accurately and completely answers the question, and blacken the corresponding space on your answer sheet.

Social scientists have traditionally defined multipolar international systems as consisting of three or more nations, each of roughly equal military and economic strength. Theoretically, the members of such
(5) systems create shifting, temporary alliances in response to changing circumstances in the international environment. Such systems are, thus, fluid and flexible. Frequent, small confrontations are one attribute of multipolar systems and are usually the result of less
(10) powerful members grouping together to counter threats from larger, more aggressive members seeking hegemony. Yet the constant and inevitable counterbalancing typical of such systems usually results in stability. The best-known example of a
(15) multipolar system is the Concert of Europe, which coincided with general peace on that continent lasting roughly 100 years beginning around 1815.

Bipolar systems, on the other hand, involve two major members of roughly equal military and
(20) economic strength vying for power and advantage. Other members of lesser strength tend to coalesce around one or the other pole. Such systems tend to be rigid and fixed, in part due to the existence of only one axis of power. Zero-sum political and military
(25) maneuverings, in which a gain for one side results in an equivalent loss for the other, are a salient feature of bipolar systems. Overall superiority is sought by both major members, which can lead to frequent confrontations, debilitating armed conflict, and,
(30) eventually, to the capitulation of one or the other side. Athens and Sparta of ancient Greece had a bipolar relationship, as did the United States and the USSR during the Cold War.

However, the shift in the geopolitical landscape
(35) following the end of the Cold War calls for a reassessment of the assumptions underlying these two theoretical concepts. The emerging but still vague multipolar system in Europe today brings with it the unsettling prospect of new conflicts and shifting
(40) alliances that may lead to a diminution, rather than an enhancement, of security. The frequent, small confrontations that are thought to have kept the Concert of Europe in a state of equilibrium would today, as nations arm themselves with modern
(45) weapons, create instability that could destroy the system. And the larger number of members and shifting alliance patterns peculiar to multipolar systems would create a bewildering tangle of conflicts.

This reassessment may also lead us to look at the
(50) Cold War in a new light. In 1914 smaller members of

the multipolar system in Europe brought the larger members into a war that engulfed the continent. The aftermath—a crippled system in which certain members were dismantled, punished, or voluntarily
(55) withdrew—created the conditions that led to World War II. In contrast, the principal attributes of bipolar systems—two major members with only one possible axis of conflict locked in a rigid yet usually stable struggle for power—may have created the necessary
(60) parameters for general peace in the second half of the twentieth century.

1. Which one of the following most accurately expresses the main point of the passage?

(A) Peace can be maintained in Europe only if a new bipolar system emerges to replace Cold War alliances.

(B) All kinds of international systems discussed by social scientists carry within themselves the seeds of their own collapse and ultimately endanger international order.

(C) The current European geopolitical landscape is a multipolar system that strongly resembles the Concert of Europe which existed through most of the nineteenth century.

(D) Multipolarity fostered the conditions that led to World War II and is incompatible with a stable, modern Europe.

(E) The characterization of multipolar systems as stable and bipolar systems as open to debilitating conflict needs to be reconsidered in light of the realities of post-Cold War Europe.

GO ON TO THE NEXT PAGE.

2. Which one of the following statements most accurately describes the function of the final paragraph?

(A) The weaknesses of both types of systems are discussed in the context of twentieth-century European history.

(B) A prediction is made regarding European security based on the attributes of both types of systems.

(C) A new argument is introduced in favor of European countries embracing a new bipolar system.

(D) Twentieth-century European history is used to expand on the argument in the previous paragraph.

(E) The typical characteristics of the major members of a bipolar system are reviewed.

3. The author's reference to the possibility that confrontations may lead to capitulation (lines 27–30) serves primarily to

(A) indicate that bipolar systems can have certain unstable characteristics

(B) illustrate how multipolar systems can transform themselves into bipolar systems

(C) contrast the aggressive nature of bipolar members with the more rational behavior of their multipolar counterparts

(D) indicate the anarchic nature of international relations

(E) suggest that military and economic strength shifts in bipolar as frequently as in multipolar systems

4. With respect to the Cold War, the author's attitude can most accurately be described as

(A) fearful that European geopolitics may bring about a similar bipolar system

(B) surprised that it did not end with a major war

(C) convinced that it provides an important example of bipolarity maintaining peace

(D) regretful that the major European countries were so ambivalent about it

(E) confident it will mark only a brief hiatus between long periods of European multipolarity

5. Which one of the following statements concerning the Concert of Europe (lines 14–17) can most reasonably be inferred from the passage?

(A) Each of the many small confrontations that occurred under the Concert of Europe threatened the integrity of the system.

(B) It provided the highest level of security possible for Europe in the late nineteenth century.

(C) All the factors contributing to stability during the late nineteenth century continue to contribute to European security.

(D) Equilibrium in the system was maintained as members grouped together to counterbalance mutual threats.

(E) It was more stable than most multipolar systems because its smaller members reacted promptly to aggression by its larger members.

GO ON TO THE NEXT PAGE.

In spite of a shared language, Latin American poetry written in Spanish differs from Spanish poetry in many respects. The Spanish of Latin American poets is more open than that of Spanish poets, more exposed
(5) to outside influences—indigenous, English, French, and other languages. While some literary critics maintain that there is as much linguistic unity in Latin American poetry as there is in Spanish poetry, they base this claim on the fact that Castilian Spanish, the
(10) official and literary version of the Spanish language based largely on the dialect originally spoken in the Castile region of Spain, was transplanted to the Americas when it was already a relatively standardized idiom. Although such unity may have characterized the
(15) earliest Latin American poetry, after centuries in the Americas the language of Latin American poetry cannot help but reveal the influences of its unique cultural history.

Latin American poetry is critical or irreverent in its
(20) attitude toward language, where that of Spanish poets is more accepting. For example, the Spanish-language incarnations of modernism and the avant-garde, two literary movements that used language in innovative and challenging ways, originated with Latin American
(25) poets. By contrast, when these movements later reached Spain, Spanish poets greeted them with reluctance. Spanish poets, even those of the modern era, seem to take their language for granted, rarely using it in radical or experimental ways.

(30) The most distinctive note in Latin American poetry is its enthusiastic response to the modern world, while Spanish poetry displays a kind of cultural conservatism—the desire to return to an ideal culture of the distant past. Because no Spanish-language
(35) culture lies in the equally distant (i.e., pre-Columbian) past of the Americas, but has instead been invented by Latin Americans day by day, Latin American poetry has no such long-standing past to romanticize. Instead, Latin American poetry often displays a curiosity about
(40) the literature of other cultures, an interest in exploring poetic structures beyond those typical of Spanish poetry. For example, the first Spanish-language haiku—a Japanese poetic form—were written by José Juan Tablada, a Mexican. Another of the Latin
(45) American poets' responses to this absence is the search for a world before recorded history—not only that of Spain or the Americas, but in some cases of the planet; the Chilean poet Pablo Neruda's work, for example, is noteworthy for its development of an ahistorical
(50) mythology for the creation of the earth. For Latin American poets there is no such thing as the pristine cultural past affirmed in the poetry of Spain: there is only the fluid interaction of all world cultures, or else the extensive time before cultures began.

6. The discussion in the second paragraph is intended primarily to

(A) argue that Latin American poets originated modernism and the avant-garde
(B) explain how Spanish poetry and Latin American poetry differ in their attitudes toward the Spanish language
(C) demonstrate why Latin American poetry is not well received in Spain
(D) show that the Castilian Spanish employed in Spanish poetry has remained relatively unchanged by the advent of modernism and the avant-garde
(E) illustrate the extent to which Spanish poetry romanticizes Spanish-language culture

7. Given the information in the passage, which one of the following is most analogous to the evolution of Latin American poetry?

(A) A family moves its restaurant to a new town and incorporates local ingredients into its traditional recipes.
(B) A family moves its business to a new town after the business fails in its original location.
(C) A family with a two-hundred-year-old house labors industriously in order to restore the house to its original appearance.
(D) A family does research into its ancestry in order to construct its family tree.
(E) A family eagerly anticipates its annual vacation but never takes photographs or purchases souvenirs to preserve its memories.

8. The passage's claims about Spanish poetry would be most weakened if new evidence indicating which one of the following were discovered?

(A) Spanish linguistic constructs had greater influence on Latin American poets than had previously been thought.
(B) Castilian Spanish was still evolving linguistically at the time of the inception of Latin American poetry.
(C) Spanish poets originated an influential literary movement that used language in radical ways.
(D) Castilian Spanish was influenced during its evolution by other Spanish dialects.
(E) Spanish poets rejected the English and French incarnations of modernism.

GO ON TO THE NEXT PAGE.

9. The passage affirms each of the following EXCEPT:

   (A) The first haiku in the Spanish language were written by a Latin American poet.
   (B) Spanish poetry is rarely innovative or experimental in its use of language.
   (C) Spanish poetry rarely incorporates poetic traditions from other cultures.
   (D) Latin American poetry tends to take the Spanish language for granted.
   (E) Latin American poetry incorporates aspects of various other languages.

10. Which one of the following can most reasonably be inferred from the passage about Latin American poetry's use of poetic structures from other world cultures?

    (A) The use of poetic structures from other world cultures is an attempt by Latin American poets to create a cultural past.
    (B) The use of poetic structures from other world cultures by Latin American poets is a response to their lack of a long-standing Spanish-language cultural past in the Americas.
    (C) The use of poetic structures from other world cultures has led Latin American poets to reconsider their lack of a long-standing Spanish-language cultural past in the Americas.
    (D) Latin American poets who write about a world before recorded history do not use poetic structures from other world cultures.
    (E) Latin American poetry does not borrow poetic structures from other world cultures whose literature exhibits cultural conservatism.

11. Based on the passage, the author most likely holds which one of the following views toward Spanish poetry's relationship to the Spanish cultural past?

    (A) This relationship has inspired Spanish poets to examine their cultural past with a critical eye.
    (B) This relationship forces Spanish poets to write about subjects with which they feel little natural affinity.
    (C) This relationship is itself the central theme of much Spanish poetry.
    (D) This relationship infuses Spanish poetry with a romanticism that is reluctant to embrace the modern era.
    (E) This relationship results in poems that are of little interest to contemporary Spanish readers.

12. Which one of the following inferences is most supported by the passage?

    (A) A tradition of cultural conservatism has allowed the Spanish language to evolve into a stable, reliable form of expression.
    (B) It was only recently that Latin American poetry began to incorporate elements of other languages.
    (C) The cultural conservatism of Spanish poetry is exemplified by the uncritical attitude of Spanish poets toward the Spanish language.
    (D) Latin American poets' interest in other world cultures is illustrated by their use of Japanese words and phrases.
    (E) Spanish poetry is receptive to the influence of some Spanish-language poets outside of Spain.

GO ON TO THE NEXT PAGE.

According to the theory of gravitation, every particle of matter in the universe attracts every other particle with a force that increases as either the mass of the particles increases, or their proximity to one
(5) another increases, or both. Gravitation is believed to shape the structures of stars, galaxies, and the entire universe. But for decades cosmologists (scientists who study the universe) have attempted to account for the finding that at least 90 percent of the universe seems to
(10) be missing: that the total amount of observable matter—stars, dust, and miscellaneous debris—does not contain enough mass to explain why the universe is organized in the shape of galaxies and clusters of galaxies. To account for this discrepancy, cosmologists
(15) hypothesize that something else, which they call "dark matter," provides the gravitational force necessary to make the huge structures cohere.

What is dark matter? Numerous exotic entities have been postulated, but among the more attractive
(20) candidates—because they are known actually to exist—are neutrinos, elementary particles created as a by-product of nuclear fusion, radioactive decay, or catastrophic collisions between other particles. Neutrinos, which come in three types, are by far the
(25) most numerous kind of particle in the universe; however, they have long been assumed to have no mass. If so, that would disqualify them as dark matter. Without mass, matter cannot exert gravitational force; without such force, it cannot induce other matter to
(30) cohere.

But new evidence suggests that a neutrino does have mass. This evidence came by way of research findings supporting the existence of a long-theorized but never observed phenomenon called oscillation,
(35) whereby each of the three neutrino types can change into one of the others as it travels through space. Researchers held that the transformation is possible only if neutrinos also have mass. They obtained experimental confirmation of the theory by generating
(40) one neutrino type and then finding evidence that it had oscillated into the predicted neutrino type. In the process, they were able to estimate the mass of a neutrino at from 0.5 to 5 electron volts.

While slight, even the lowest estimate would yield
(45) a lot of mass given that neutrinos are so numerous, especially considering that neutrinos were previously assumed to have no mass. Still, even at the highest estimate, neutrinos could only account for about 20 percent of the universe's "missing" mass.
(50) Nevertheless, that is enough to alter our picture of the universe even if it does not account for all of dark matter. In fact, some cosmologists claim that this new evidence offers the best theoretical solution yet to the dark matter problem. If the evidence holds up, these
(55) cosmologists believe, it may add to our understanding of the role elementary particles play in holding the universe together.

13. Which one of the following most accurately expresses the main idea of the passage?

(A) Although cosmologists believe that the universe is shaped by gravitation, the total amount of observable matter in the universe is greatly insufficient to account for the gravitation that would be required to cause the universe to be organized into galaxies.

(B) Given their inability to account for more than 20 percent of the universe's "missing" mass, scientists are beginning to speculate that our current understanding of gravity is significantly mistaken.

(C) Indirect evidence suggesting that neutrinos have mass may allow neutrinos to account for up to 20 percent of dark matter, a finding that could someday be extended to a complete solution of the dark matter problem.

(D) After much speculation, researchers have discovered that neutrinos oscillate from one type into another as they travel through space, a phenomenon that proves that neutrinos have mass.

(E) Although it has been established that neutrinos have mass, such mass does not support the speculation of cosmologists that neutrinos constitute a portion of the universe's "missing" mass.

14. Which one of the following titles most completely and accurately expresses the contents of the passage?

(A) "The Existence of Dark Matter: Arguments For and Against"

(B) "Neutrinos and the Dark Matter Problem: A Partial Solution?"

(C) "Too Little, Too Late: Why Neutrinos Do Not Constitute Dark Matter"

(D) "The Role of Gravity: How Dark Matter Shapes Stars"

(E) "The Implications of Oscillation: Do Neutrinos Really Have Mass?"

GO ON TO THE NEXT PAGE.

15. Based on the passage, the author most likely holds which one of the following views?

(A) Observable matter constitutes at least 90 percent of the mass of the universe.

(B) Current theories are incapable of identifying the force that causes all particles in the universe to attract one another.

(C) The key to the problem of dark matter is determining the exact mass of a neutrino.

(D) It is unlikely that any force other than gravitation will be required to account for the organization of the universe into galaxies.

(E) Neutrinos probably account for most of the universe's "missing" mass.

16. As described in the last paragraph of the passage, the cosmologists' approach to solving the dark matter problem is most analogous to which one of the following?

(A) A child seeking information about how to play chess consults a family member and so learns of a book that will instruct her in the game.

(B) A child seeking to earn money by delivering papers is unable to earn enough money for a bicycle and so decides to buy a skateboard instead.

(C) A child hoping to get a dog for his birthday is initially disappointed when his parents bring home a cat but eventually learns to love the animal.

(D) A child seeking money to attend a movie is given some of the money by one of his siblings and so decides to go to each of his other siblings to ask for additional money.

(E) A child enjoys playing sports with the neighborhood children but her parents insist that she cannot participate until she has completed her household chores.

17. The author's attitude toward oscillation can most accurately be characterized as being

(A) satisfied that it occurs and that it suggests that neutrinos have mass

(B) hopeful that it will be useful in discovering other forms of dark matter

(C) concerned that it is often misinterpreted to mean that neutrinos account for all of dark matter

(D) skeptical that it occurs until further research can be done

(E) convinced that it cannot occur outside an experimental setting

18. Which one of the following phrases could replace the word "cohere" at line 30 without substantively altering the author's meaning?

(A) exert gravitational force

(B) form galactic structures

(C) oscillate into another type of matter

(D) become significantly more massive

(E) fuse to produce new particles

19. The passage states each of the following EXCEPT:

(A) There are more neutrinos in the universe than there are non-neutrinos.

(B) Observable matter cannot exert enough gravitational force to account for the present structure of the universe.

(C) Scientific experiments support the theory of neutrino oscillation.

(D) Neutrinos likely cannot account for all of the universe's "missing" mass.

(E) Dark matter may account for a large portion of the universe's gravitational force.

GO ON TO THE NEXT PAGE.

Leading questions—questions worded in such a way as to suggest a particular answer—can yield unreliable testimony either by design, as when a lawyer tries to trick a witness into affirming a particular
(5) version of the evidence of a case, or by accident, when a questioner unintentionally prejudices the witness's response. For this reason, a judge can disallow such questions in the courtroom interrogation of witnesses. But their exclusion from the courtroom by no means
(10) eliminates the remote effects of earlier leading questions on eyewitness testimony. Alarmingly, the beliefs about an event that a witness brings to the courtroom may often be adulterated by the effects of leading questions that were introduced intentionally or
(15) unintentionally by lawyers, police investigators, reporters, or others with whom the witness has already interacted.

Recent studies have confirmed the ability of leading questions to alter the details of our memories
(20) and have led to a better understanding of how this process occurs and, perhaps, of the conditions that make for greater risks that an eyewitness's memories have been tainted by leading questions. These studies suggest that not all details of our experiences become
(25) clearly or stably stored in memory—only those to which we give adequate attention. Moreover, experimental evidence indicates that if subtly introduced new data involving remembered events do not actively conflict with our stored memory data, we
(30) tend to process such new data similarly whether they correspond to details as we remember them, or to gaps in those details. In the former case, we often retain the new data as a reinforcement of the corresponding aspect of the memory, and in the latter case, we often
(35) retain them as a construction to fill the corresponding gap. An eyewitness who is asked, prior to courtroom testimony, "How fast was the car going when it passed the stop sign?" may respond to the query about speed without addressing the question of the stop sign. But
(40) the "stop sign" datum has now been introduced, and when later recalled, perhaps during courtroom testimony, it may be processed as belonging to the original memory even if the witness actually saw no stop sign.
(45) The farther removed from the event, the greater the chance of a vague or incomplete recollection and the greater the likelihood of newly suggested information blending with original memories. Since we can be more easily misled with respect to fainter and more
(50) uncertain memories, tangential details are more apt to become constructed out of subsequently introduced information than are more central details. But what is tangential to a witness's original experience of an event may nevertheless be crucial to the courtroom issues
(55) that the witness's memories are supposed to resolve. For example, a perpetrator's shirt color or hairstyle might be tangential to one's shocked observance of an armed robbery, but later those factors might be crucial to establishing the identity of the perpetrator.

20. Which one of the following most accurately expresses the main point of the passage?

(A) The unreliability of memories about incidental aspects of observed events makes eyewitness testimony especially questionable in cases in which the witness was not directly involved.

(B) Because of the nature of human memory storage and retrieval, the courtroom testimony of eyewitnesses may contain crucial inaccuracies due to leading questions asked prior to the courtroom appearance.

(C) Researchers are surprised to find that courtroom testimony is often dependent on suggestion to fill gaps left by insufficient attention to detail at the time that the incident in question occurred.

(D) Although judges can disallow leading questions from the courtroom, it is virtually impossible to prevent them from being used elsewhere, to the detriment of many cases.

(E) Stricter regulation should be placed on lawyers whose leading questions can corrupt witnesses' testimony by introducing inaccurate data prior to the witnesses' appearance in the courtroom.

21. It can be reasonably inferred from the passage that which one of the following, if it were effectively implemented, would most increase the justice system's ability to prevent leading questions from causing mistaken court decisions?

(A) a policy ensuring that witnesses have extra time to answer questions concerning details that are tangential to their original experiences of events

(B) thorough revision of the criteria for determining which kinds of interrogation may be disallowed in courtroom testimony under the category of "leading questions"

(C) increased attention to the nuances of all witnesses' responses to courtroom questions, even those that are not leading questions

(D) extensive interviewing of witnesses by all lawyers for both sides of a case prior to those witnesses' courtroom appearance

(E) availability of accurate transcripts of all interrogations of witnesses that occurred prior to those witnesses' appearance in court

22. Which one of the following is mentioned in the passage as a way in which new data suggested to a witness by a leading question are sometimes processed?

(A) They are integrated with current memories as support for those memories.

(B) They are stored tentatively as conjectural data that fade with time.

(C) They stay more vivid in memory than do previously stored memory data.

(D) They are reinterpreted so as to be compatible with the details already stored in memory.

(E) They are retained in memory even when they conflict with previously stored memory data.

GO ON TO THE NEXT PAGE.

23. In discussing the tangential details of events, the passage contrasts their original significance to witnesses with their possible significance in the courtroom (lines 52–59). That contrast is most closely analogous to which one of the following?

    (A) For purposes of flavor and preservation, salt and vinegar are important additions to cucumbers during the process of pickling, but these purposes could be attained by adding other ingredients instead.

    (B) For the purpose of adding a mild stimulant effect, caffeine is included in some types of carbonated drinks, but for the purposes of appealing to health-conscious consumers, some types of carbonated drinks are advertised as being caffeine-free.

    (C) For purposes of flavor and tenderness, the skins of apples and some other fruits are removed during preparation for drying, but grape skins are an essential part of raisins, and thus grape skins are not removed.

    (D) For purposes of flavor and appearance, wheat germ is not needed in flour and is usually removed during milling, but for purposes of nutrition, the germ is an important part of the grain.

    (E) For purposes of texture and appearance, some fat may be removed from meat when it is ground into sausage, but the removal of fat is also important for purposes of health.

24. Which one of the following questions is most directly answered by information in the passage?

    (A) In witnessing what types of crimes are people especially likely to pay close attention to circumstantial details?

    (B) Which aspects of courtroom interrogation cause witnesses to be especially reluctant to testify in extensive detail?

    (C) Can the stress of having to testify in a courtroom situation affect the accuracy of memory storage and retrieval?

    (D) Do different people tend to possess different capacities for remembering details accurately?

    (E) When is it more likely that a detail of an observed event will be accurately remembered?

25. The second paragraph consists primarily of material that

    (A) corroborates and adds detail to a claim made in the first paragraph

    (B) provides examples illustrating the applications of a theory discussed in the first paragraph

    (C) forms an argument in support of a proposal that is made in the final paragraph

    (D) anticipates and provides grounds for the rejection of a theory alluded to by the author in the final paragraph

    (E) explains how newly obtained data favor one of two traditional theories mentioned elsewhere in the second paragraph

26. It can be most reasonably inferred from the passage that the author holds that the recent studies discussed in the passage

    (A) have produced some unexpected findings regarding the extent of human reliance on external verification of memory details

    (B) shed new light on a longstanding procedural controversy in the law

    (C) may be of theoretical interest despite their tentative nature and inconclusive findings

    (D) provide insights into the origins of several disparate types of logically fallacious reasoning

    (E) should be of more than abstract academic interest to the legal profession

27. Which one of the following can be most reasonably inferred from the information in the passage?

    (A) The tendency of leading questions to cause unreliable courtroom testimony has no correlation with the extent to which witnesses are emotionally affected by the events that they have observed.

    (B) Leading questions asked in the process of a courtroom examination of a witness are more likely to cause inaccurate testimony than are leading questions asked outside the courtroom.

    (C) The memory processes by which newly introduced data tend to reinforce accurately remembered details of events are not relevant to explaining the effects of leading questions.

    (D) The risk of testimony being inaccurate due to certain other factors tends to increase as an eyewitness's susceptibility to giving inaccurate testimony due to the effects of leading questions increases.

    (E) The traditional grounds on which leading questions can be excluded from courtroom interrogation of witnesses have been called into question by the findings of recent studies.

S T O P

IF YOU FINISH BEFORE TIME IS CALLED, YOU MAY CHECK YOUR WORK ON THIS SECTION ONLY.
DO NOT WORK ON ANY OTHER SECTION IN THE TEST.

Wait for the supervisor's instructions before you open the page to the topic. Please print and sign your name and write the date in the designated spaces below.

Time: 35 Minutes

General Directions

You will have 35 minutes in which to plan and write an essay on the topic inside. Read the topic and the accompanying directions carefully. You will probably find it best to spend a few minutes considering the topic and organizing your thoughts before you begin writing. In your essay, be sure to develop your ideas fully, leaving time, if possible, to review what you have written. **Do not write on a topic other than the one specified. Writing on a topic of your own choice is not acceptable.**

No special knowledge is required or expected for this writing exercise. Law schools are interested in the reasoning, clarity, organization, language usage, and writing mechanics displayed in your essay. How well you write is more important than how much you write.

Confine your essay to the blocked, lined area on the front and back of the separate Writing Sample Response Sheet. Only that area will be reproduced for law schools. Be sure that your writing is legible.

Both this topic sheet and your response sheet must be turned over to the testing staff before you leave the room.

Topic Code	Print Your Full Name Here		
_____	Last	First	M.I.

Date	Sign Your Name Here
/ /	

Scratch Paper
Do not write your essay in this space.

LSAT Writing Sample Topic

<u>Directions</u>: The scenario presented below describes two choices, either one of which can be supported on the basis of the information given. Your essay should consider both choices and argue <u>for</u> one and <u>against</u> the other, based on the two specified criteria and the facts provided. There is no "right" or "wrong" choice: a reasonable argument can be made for either.

The Brighton Land Conservancy, an organization dedicated to protecting wilderness areas, is contemplating its next land acquision. It has been offered two tracts of environmentally sensitive land, but it has sufficient funds in its budget to acquire only one. Write an essay in which you argue for the purchase of one tract over the other based on the following considerations.

• The Land Conservancy wants to preserve as much of the most environmentally sensitive land in the area as it can.
• The Land Conservancy wants to increase public appreciation of and contact with natural places.

The first tract, Elkton Marsh, consists of 3 square miles (5 square kilometers) of freshwater tidal marsh land. The parcel is relatively small and is surrounded by commercial development, but it is home to six officialy endangered native plant species. The marsh ecosystem functions as a nursery, pollution filter, and water purifier for a nearby river. It also serves as a rare haven for migratory waterfowl passing through the area. Elkton Marsh is close to major population centers and will be open to the public for nature study if it is acquired by the Conservancy; however, because of its small size and delicate ecology, it can sustain only a small number of visitors.

The second tract, Cobbett Woods, is a 7 square mile (11 square kilometer) parcel of wooded wetland comprising the area's best example of a coastal-plain forest. The woods contain eight rare plant species, two of which have been officially classified as endangered. They are also home to a native species of owl whose numbers are declining precipitously. The parcel features the area's oldest willow oak tree, a massive 300 year-old specimen. Cobbett Woods is contiguous to a 5 square mile (8 square kilometer) tract that is already protected from development by conservation easements. The combined tracts will be open for camping and nature study if the Conservancy acquires Cobbett Woods, which is located in a sparsely populated area approximately an hour's drive from the nearest large city.

Scratch Paper
Do not write your essay in this space.

LAST NAME (Print)   MI   FIRST NAME (Print)

SIGNATURE

Writing Sample Response Sheet

DO NOT WRITE
IN THIS SPACE

Begin your essay in the lined area below.
Continue on the back if you need more space.

Directions:

1. Use the Answer Key on the next page to check your answers.

2. Use the Scoring Worksheet below to compute your raw score.

3. Use the Score Conversion Chart to convert your raw score into the 120–180 scale.

Scoring Worksheet

1. Enter the number of questions you answered correctly in each section

	Number Correct
SECTION I	_EXP_
SECTION II	_____
SECTION III	_____
SECTION IV	_____
SECTION V	_____

2. Enter the sum here: _____

   This is your Raw Score.

Conversion Chart

For Converting Raw Score to the 120–180 LSAT Scaled Score

LSAT PrepTest XL

Reported Score	Raw Score	
	Lowest	Highest
180	99	101
179	—*	—*
178	98	98
177	97	97
176	96	96
175	—*	—*
174	95	95
173	94	94
172	93	93
171	92	92
170	91	91
169	89	90
168	88	88
167	87	87
166	85	86
165	84	84
164	83	83
163	81	82
162	79	80
161	78	78
160	76	77
159	74	75
158	73	73
157	71	72
156	69	70
155	67	68
154	66	66
153	64	65
152	62	63
151	60	61
150	58	59
149	57	57
148	55	56
147	53	54
146	51	52
145	50	50
144	48	49
143	46	47
142	44	45
141	42	43
140	41	41
139	39	40
138	37	38
137	36	36
136	34	35
135	33	33
134	31	32
133	29	30
132	28	28
131	27	27
130	25	26
129	24	24
128	22	23
127	21	21
126	20	20
125	19	19
124	18	18
123	16	17
122	15	15
121	—*	—*
120	0	14

*There is no raw score that will produce this scaled score for this test.

SECTION I (experimental)

1.	D	8.	E	15.	E	22.	B
2.	C	9.	A	16.	A	23.	A
3.	C	10.	E	17.	D	24.	E
4.	D	11.	E	18.	E		
5.	C	12.	E	19.	D		
6.	A	13.	C	20.	C		
7.	B	14.	D	21.	B		

SECTION II

1.	C	8.	A	15.	D	22.	C
2.	B	9.	C	16.	D	23.	A
3.	B	10.	B	17.	E	24.	C
4.	D	11.	A	18.	B	25.	B
5.	B	12.	D	19.	C		
6.	E	13.	D	20.	D		
7.	B	14.	C	21.	E		

SECTION III

1.	D	8.	A	15.	D	22.	A
2.	C	9.	E	16.	B	23.	B
3.	A	10.	B	17.	C		
4.	C	11.	A	18.	D		
5.	D	12.	B	19.	C		
6.	D	13.	A	20.	C		
7.	C	14.	A	21.	B		

SECTION IV

1.	B	8.	D	15.	E	22.	A
2.	C	9.	C	16.	E	23.	B
3.	C	10.	B	17.	A	24.	C
4.	A	11.	E	18.	B	25.	D
5.	B	12.	E	19.	D	26.	B
6.	E	13.	E	20.	E		
7.	C	14.	A	21.	B		

SECTION V

1.	E	8.	C	15.	D	22.	A
2.	D	9.	D	16.	D	23.	D
3.	A	10.	B	17.	A	24.	E
4.	C	11.	D	18.	B	25.	A
5.	D	12.	C	19.	A	26.	E
6.	B	13.	C	20.	B	27.	D
7.	A	14.	B	21.	E		

Answer
Grids

USE ONLY A NO 2. OR HB PENCIL TO COMPLETE THIS ANSWER SHEET. DO NOT USE INK.

● Right Mark   ⊘ ⊗ ⊙ Wrong Marks

1 LAST NAME | FIRST NAME | MI

(Grid of bubbles A through Z for each letter position)

2 SOCIAL SECURITY/ SOCIAL INSURANCE NO.

3 KAPLAN ENROLLMENT ID

(Bubbles 0–9)

4 TODAY'S DATE

MONTH	DAY	YEAR
○ Jan		
○ Feb		
○ Mar	⓪ ⓪	⓪ ⓪
○ Apr	① ①	① ①
○ May	② ②	② ②
○ June	③ ③	③ ③
○ July	④	④ ④
○ Aug	⑤	⑤ ⑤
○ Sept	⑥	⑥ ⑥
○ Oct	⑦	⑦ ⑦
○ Nov	⑧	⑧ ⑧
○ Dec	⑨	⑨ ⑨

5 RACIAL/ETHNIC DESCRIPTION

6 GENDER

7 DOMINANT LANGUAGE

8 ENGLISH FLUENCY

9 TEST BOOK SERIAL NO.

10 TEST FORM

11 TEST DATE

12 CENTER NUMBER

13 TEST FORM CODE

(Bubbles 0–9)

=== **Law School Admission Test*** ===

Mark one and only one answer to each question. Be sure to fill in completely the space for your intended answer choice. If you erase, do so completely. Make no stray marks.

SECTION 1	SECTION 2	SECTION 3	SECTION 4	SECTION 5
1 Ⓐ Ⓑ Ⓒ Ⓓ Ⓔ	1 Ⓐ Ⓑ Ⓒ Ⓓ Ⓔ	1 Ⓐ Ⓑ Ⓒ Ⓓ Ⓔ	1 Ⓐ Ⓑ Ⓒ Ⓓ Ⓔ	1 Ⓐ Ⓑ Ⓒ Ⓓ Ⓔ
2 Ⓐ Ⓑ Ⓒ Ⓓ Ⓔ	2 Ⓐ Ⓑ Ⓒ Ⓓ Ⓔ	2 Ⓐ Ⓑ Ⓒ Ⓓ Ⓔ	2 Ⓐ Ⓑ Ⓒ Ⓓ Ⓔ	2 Ⓐ Ⓑ Ⓒ Ⓓ Ⓔ
3 Ⓐ Ⓑ Ⓒ Ⓓ Ⓔ	3 Ⓐ Ⓑ Ⓒ Ⓓ Ⓔ	3 Ⓐ Ⓑ Ⓒ Ⓓ Ⓔ	3 Ⓐ Ⓑ Ⓒ Ⓓ Ⓔ	3 Ⓐ Ⓑ Ⓒ Ⓓ Ⓔ
4 Ⓐ Ⓑ Ⓒ Ⓓ Ⓔ	4 Ⓐ Ⓑ Ⓒ Ⓓ Ⓔ	4 Ⓐ Ⓑ Ⓒ Ⓓ Ⓔ	4 Ⓐ Ⓑ Ⓒ Ⓓ Ⓔ	4 Ⓐ Ⓑ Ⓒ Ⓓ Ⓔ
5 Ⓐ Ⓑ Ⓒ Ⓓ Ⓔ	5 Ⓐ Ⓑ Ⓒ Ⓓ Ⓔ	5 Ⓐ Ⓑ Ⓒ Ⓓ Ⓔ	5 Ⓐ Ⓑ Ⓒ Ⓓ Ⓔ	5 Ⓐ Ⓑ Ⓒ Ⓓ Ⓔ
6 Ⓐ Ⓑ Ⓒ Ⓓ Ⓔ	6 Ⓐ Ⓑ Ⓒ Ⓓ Ⓔ	6 Ⓐ Ⓑ Ⓒ Ⓓ Ⓔ	6 Ⓐ Ⓑ Ⓒ Ⓓ Ⓔ	6 Ⓐ Ⓑ Ⓒ Ⓓ Ⓔ
7 Ⓐ Ⓑ Ⓒ Ⓓ Ⓔ	7 Ⓐ Ⓑ Ⓒ Ⓓ Ⓔ	7 Ⓐ Ⓑ Ⓒ Ⓓ Ⓔ	7 Ⓐ Ⓑ Ⓒ Ⓓ Ⓔ	7 Ⓐ Ⓑ Ⓒ Ⓓ Ⓔ
8 Ⓐ Ⓑ Ⓒ Ⓓ Ⓔ	8 Ⓐ Ⓑ Ⓒ Ⓓ Ⓔ	8 Ⓐ Ⓑ Ⓒ Ⓓ Ⓔ	8 Ⓐ Ⓑ Ⓒ Ⓓ Ⓔ	8 Ⓐ Ⓑ Ⓒ Ⓓ Ⓔ
9 Ⓐ Ⓑ Ⓒ Ⓓ Ⓔ	9 Ⓐ Ⓑ Ⓒ Ⓓ Ⓔ	9 Ⓐ Ⓑ Ⓒ Ⓓ Ⓔ	9 Ⓐ Ⓑ Ⓒ Ⓓ Ⓔ	9 Ⓐ Ⓑ Ⓒ Ⓓ Ⓔ
10 Ⓐ Ⓑ Ⓒ Ⓓ Ⓔ	10 Ⓐ Ⓑ Ⓒ Ⓓ Ⓔ	10 Ⓐ Ⓑ Ⓒ Ⓓ Ⓔ	10 Ⓐ Ⓑ Ⓒ Ⓓ Ⓔ	10 Ⓐ Ⓑ Ⓒ Ⓓ Ⓔ
11 Ⓐ Ⓑ Ⓒ Ⓓ Ⓔ	11 Ⓐ Ⓑ Ⓒ Ⓓ Ⓔ	11 Ⓐ Ⓑ Ⓒ Ⓓ Ⓔ	11 Ⓐ Ⓑ Ⓒ Ⓓ Ⓔ	11 Ⓐ Ⓑ Ⓒ Ⓓ Ⓔ
12 Ⓐ Ⓑ Ⓒ Ⓓ Ⓔ	12 Ⓐ Ⓑ Ⓒ Ⓓ Ⓔ	12 Ⓐ Ⓑ Ⓒ Ⓓ Ⓔ	12 Ⓐ Ⓑ Ⓒ Ⓓ Ⓔ	12 Ⓐ Ⓑ Ⓒ Ⓓ Ⓔ
13 Ⓐ Ⓑ Ⓒ Ⓓ Ⓔ	13 Ⓐ Ⓑ Ⓒ Ⓓ Ⓔ	13 Ⓐ Ⓑ Ⓒ Ⓓ Ⓔ	13 Ⓐ Ⓑ Ⓒ Ⓓ Ⓔ	13 Ⓐ Ⓑ Ⓒ Ⓓ Ⓔ
14 Ⓐ Ⓑ Ⓒ Ⓓ Ⓔ	14 Ⓐ Ⓑ Ⓒ Ⓓ Ⓔ	14 Ⓐ Ⓑ Ⓒ Ⓓ Ⓔ	14 Ⓐ Ⓑ Ⓒ Ⓓ Ⓔ	14 Ⓐ Ⓑ Ⓒ Ⓓ Ⓔ
15 Ⓐ Ⓑ Ⓒ Ⓓ Ⓔ	15 Ⓐ Ⓑ Ⓒ Ⓓ Ⓔ	15 Ⓐ Ⓑ Ⓒ Ⓓ Ⓔ	15 Ⓐ Ⓑ Ⓒ Ⓓ Ⓔ	15 Ⓐ Ⓑ Ⓒ Ⓓ Ⓔ
16 Ⓐ Ⓑ Ⓒ Ⓓ Ⓔ	16 Ⓐ Ⓑ Ⓒ Ⓓ Ⓔ	16 Ⓐ Ⓑ Ⓒ Ⓓ Ⓔ	16 Ⓐ Ⓑ Ⓒ Ⓓ Ⓔ	16 Ⓐ Ⓑ Ⓒ Ⓓ Ⓔ
17 Ⓐ Ⓑ Ⓒ Ⓓ Ⓔ	17 Ⓐ Ⓑ Ⓒ Ⓓ Ⓔ	17 Ⓐ Ⓑ Ⓒ Ⓓ Ⓔ	17 Ⓐ Ⓑ Ⓒ Ⓓ Ⓔ	17 Ⓐ Ⓑ Ⓒ Ⓓ Ⓔ
18 Ⓐ Ⓑ Ⓒ Ⓓ Ⓔ	18 Ⓐ Ⓑ Ⓒ Ⓓ Ⓔ	18 Ⓐ Ⓑ Ⓒ Ⓓ Ⓔ	18 Ⓐ Ⓑ Ⓒ Ⓓ Ⓔ	18 Ⓐ Ⓑ Ⓒ Ⓓ Ⓔ
19 Ⓐ Ⓑ Ⓒ Ⓓ Ⓔ	19 Ⓐ Ⓑ Ⓒ Ⓓ Ⓔ	19 Ⓐ Ⓑ Ⓒ Ⓓ Ⓔ	19 Ⓐ Ⓑ Ⓒ Ⓓ Ⓔ	19 Ⓐ Ⓑ Ⓒ Ⓓ Ⓔ
20 Ⓐ Ⓑ Ⓒ Ⓓ Ⓔ	20 Ⓐ Ⓑ Ⓒ Ⓓ Ⓔ	20 Ⓐ Ⓑ Ⓒ Ⓓ Ⓔ	20 Ⓐ Ⓑ Ⓒ Ⓓ Ⓔ	20 Ⓐ Ⓑ Ⓒ Ⓓ Ⓔ
21 Ⓐ Ⓑ Ⓒ Ⓓ Ⓔ	21 Ⓐ Ⓑ Ⓒ Ⓓ Ⓔ	21 Ⓐ Ⓑ Ⓒ Ⓓ Ⓔ	21 Ⓐ Ⓑ Ⓒ Ⓓ Ⓔ	21 Ⓐ Ⓑ Ⓒ Ⓓ Ⓔ
22 Ⓐ Ⓑ Ⓒ Ⓓ Ⓔ	22 Ⓐ Ⓑ Ⓒ Ⓓ Ⓔ	22 Ⓐ Ⓑ Ⓒ Ⓓ Ⓔ	22 Ⓐ Ⓑ Ⓒ Ⓓ Ⓔ	22 Ⓐ Ⓑ Ⓒ Ⓓ Ⓔ
23 Ⓐ Ⓑ Ⓒ Ⓓ Ⓔ	23 Ⓐ Ⓑ Ⓒ Ⓓ Ⓔ	23 Ⓐ Ⓑ Ⓒ Ⓓ Ⓔ	23 Ⓐ Ⓑ Ⓒ Ⓓ Ⓔ	23 Ⓐ Ⓑ Ⓒ Ⓓ Ⓔ
24 Ⓐ Ⓑ Ⓒ Ⓓ Ⓔ	24 Ⓐ Ⓑ Ⓒ Ⓓ Ⓔ	24 Ⓐ Ⓑ Ⓒ Ⓓ Ⓔ	24 Ⓐ Ⓑ Ⓒ Ⓓ Ⓔ	24 Ⓐ Ⓑ Ⓒ Ⓓ Ⓔ
25 Ⓐ Ⓑ Ⓒ Ⓓ Ⓔ	25 Ⓐ Ⓑ Ⓒ Ⓓ Ⓔ	25 Ⓐ Ⓑ Ⓒ Ⓓ Ⓔ	25 Ⓐ Ⓑ Ⓒ Ⓓ Ⓔ	25 Ⓐ Ⓑ Ⓒ Ⓓ Ⓔ
26 Ⓐ Ⓑ Ⓒ Ⓓ Ⓔ	26 Ⓐ Ⓑ Ⓒ Ⓓ Ⓔ	26 Ⓐ Ⓑ Ⓒ Ⓓ Ⓔ	26 Ⓐ Ⓑ Ⓒ Ⓓ Ⓔ	26 Ⓐ Ⓑ Ⓒ Ⓓ Ⓔ
27 Ⓐ Ⓑ Ⓒ Ⓓ Ⓔ	27 Ⓐ Ⓑ Ⓒ Ⓓ Ⓔ	27 Ⓐ Ⓑ Ⓒ Ⓓ Ⓔ	27 Ⓐ Ⓑ Ⓒ Ⓓ Ⓔ	27 Ⓐ Ⓑ Ⓒ Ⓓ Ⓔ
28 Ⓐ Ⓑ Ⓒ Ⓓ Ⓔ	28 Ⓐ Ⓑ Ⓒ Ⓓ Ⓔ	28 Ⓐ Ⓑ Ⓒ Ⓓ Ⓔ	28 Ⓐ Ⓑ Ⓒ Ⓓ Ⓔ	28 Ⓐ Ⓑ Ⓒ Ⓓ Ⓔ
29 Ⓐ Ⓑ Ⓒ Ⓓ Ⓔ	29 Ⓐ Ⓑ Ⓒ Ⓓ Ⓔ	29 Ⓐ Ⓑ Ⓒ Ⓓ Ⓔ	29 Ⓐ Ⓑ Ⓒ Ⓓ Ⓔ	29 Ⓐ Ⓑ Ⓒ Ⓓ Ⓔ
30 Ⓐ Ⓑ Ⓒ Ⓓ Ⓔ	30 Ⓐ Ⓑ Ⓒ Ⓓ Ⓔ	30 Ⓐ Ⓑ Ⓒ Ⓓ Ⓔ	30 Ⓐ Ⓑ Ⓒ Ⓓ Ⓔ	30 Ⓐ Ⓑ Ⓒ Ⓓ Ⓔ

14 PLEASE PRINT ALL INFORMATION

LAST NAME   FIRST

EMAIL

PHONE NUMBER

MAILING ADDRESS

CLASS CODE

KAPLAN

TEST PREP
www.kaptest.com/lsat
1-800-KAP-TEST

SCANTRON Mark Reflex® EM-284925-1:654321   LL3225A

General Directions for the LSAT* Answer Sheet

The actual testing time for this portion of the test will be 2 hours 55 minutes. There are five sections, each with a time limit of 35 minutes. The supervisor will tell you when to begin and end each section. If you finish a section before time is called, you may check your work on that section only; do not turn to any other section of the test book and do not work on any other section either in the test book or on the answer sheet.

There are several different types of questions on the test, and each question type has its own directions. Be sure you understand the directions for each question type before attempting to answer any questions in that section.

Not everyone will finish all the questions in the time allowed. Do not hurry, but work steadily and as quickly as you can without sacrificing accuracy. You are advised to use your time effectively. If a question seems too difficult, go on to the next one and return to the difficult question after completing the section. MARK THE BEST ANSWER YOU CAN FOR EVERY QUESTION. NO DEDUCTIONS WILL BE MADE FOR WRONG ANSWERS. YOUR SCORE WILL BE BASED ONLY ON THE NUMBER OF QUESTIONS YOU ANSWER CORRECTLY.

ALL YOUR ANSWERS MUST BE MARKED ON THE ANSWER SHEET. Answer spaces for each question are lettered to correspond with the letters of the potential answers to each question in the test book. After you have decided which of the answers is correct, blacken the corresponding space on the answer sheet. BE SURE THAT EACH MARK IS BLACK AND COMPLETELY FILLS THE ANSWER SPACE. Give only one answer to each question. If you change an answer, be sure that all previous marks are erased completely. Since the answer sheet is machine scored, incomplete erasures may be interpreted as intended answers. ANSWERS RECORDED IN THE TEST BOOK WILL NOT BE SCORED.

There may be more questions noted on this answer sheet than there are questions in a section. Do not be concerned but be certain that the section and number of the question you are answering matches the answer sheet section and question number. Additional answer spaces in any answer sheet section should be left blank. Begin your next section in the number one answer space for that section.

Kaplan takes various steps to ensure that answer sheets are returned from test centers in a timely manner for processing. In the unlikely event that an answer sheet(s) is not received, Kaplan will permit the examinee to either retest at no additional fee or to receive a refund of his or her test fee. THESE REMEDIES ARE THE EXCLUSIVE REMEDIES AVAILABLE IN THE UNLIKELY EVENT THAT AN ANSWER SHEET IS NOT RECEIVED BY KAPLAN.

Score Cancellation

Complete this section only if you are absolutely certain you want to cancel your score. A CANCELLATION REQUEST CANNOT BE RESCINDED. IF YOU ARE AT ALL UNCERTAIN, YOU SHOULD NOT COMPLETE THIS SECTION.

To cancel your score from this administration, you must:

A. fill in both ovals here..... ○ ○

B. read the following statement. Then sign your name and enter the date. YOUR SIGNATURE ALONE IS NOT SUFFICIENT FOR SCORE CANCELLATION. BOTH OVALS MUST BE FILLED IN FOR SCANNING EQUIPMENT TO RECOGNIZE YOUR REQUEST FOR SCORE CANCELLATION.

I certify that I wish to cancel my test score from this administration. I understand that my request is irreversible and that my score will not be sent to me or to the law schools to which I apply.

Sign your name in full

_____

Date

_____

HOW DID YOU PREPARE FOR THE LSAT*?
(Select all that apply.)

Responses to this item are voluntary and will be used for statistical research purposes only.

○ By attending a Kaplan LSAT* prep course or tutoring program
○ By attending a non-Kaplan prep course or tutoring program (Please specify:_____)
○ By using a Kaplan LSAT* prep book
○ By using a non-Kaplan prep book (Please specify: _____)
○ By working through the sample questions and free sample tests provided by the LSAC
○ By working through official LSAT* PrepTests and/or other LSAC test prep products
○ Other preparation (Please specify: _____)
○ No preparation

CERTIFYING STATEMENT

Please write (DO NOT PRINT) the following statement. Sign and date.

I certify that I am the examinee whose name appears on this answer sheet and that I am here to take the LSAT for the sole purpose of being considered for application to law school. I further certify that I will neither assist nor receive assistance from any other candidate, and I agree not to copy or retain examination questions or to transmit them to or discuss them with any other person in any form.

_____
_____
_____
_____
_____
_____
_____
_____
_____
_____

SIGNATURE: _____ TODAY'S DATE: ____/____/____
                                                        MONTH DAY YEAR

*LSAT is a registered trademark of the Law School Admissions Council, Inc.

USE ONLY A NO 2. OR HB PENCIL TO COMPLETE THIS ANSWER SHEET. DO NOT USE INK.

● Right Mark ⊘ ⊗ ⊙ Wrong Marks

1 LAST NAME | FIRST NAME | MI

2 SOCIAL SECURITY/ SOCIAL INSURANCE NO.

3 KAPLAN ENROLLMENT ID

4 TODAY'S DATE

MONTH	DAY	YEAR
Jan		
Feb		
Mar		
Apr		
May		
June		
July		
Aug		
Sept		
Oct		
Nov		
Dec		

5 RACIAL/ETHNIC DESCRIPTION

6 GENDER

7 DOMINANT LANGUAGE

8 ENGLISH FLUENCY

9 TEST BOOK SERIAL NO.

10 TEST FORM

11 TEST DATE

12 CENTER NUMBER

13 TEST FORM CODE

=== Law School Admission Test* ===

Mark one and only one answer to each question. Be sure to fill in completely the space for your intended answer choice. If you erase, do so completely. Make no stray marks.

SECTION 1 | **SECTION 2** | **SECTION 3** | **SECTION 4** | **SECTION 5**

(Questions 1–30, each with answer bubbles A B C D E for each of the five sections)

14 PLEASE PRINT ALL INFORMATION

LAST NAME FIRST

EMAIL

PHONE NUMBER

MAILING ADDRESS

CLASS CODE

KAPLAN

TEST PREP

www.kaptest.com/lsat
1-800-KAP-TEST

LSAT is a registered trademark of the Law School Admissions Council, Inc.

SCANTRON Mark Reflex® EM-284925-1:654321 LL3225A

General Directions for the LSAT* Answer Sheet

The actual testing time for this portion of the test will be 2 hours 55 minutes. There are five sections, each with a time limit of 35 minutes. The supervisor will tell you when to begin and end each section. If you finish a section before time is called, you may check your work on that section <u>only</u>; do not turn to any other section of the test book and do not work on any other section either in the test book or on the answer sheet.

There are several different types of questions on the test, and each question type has its own directions. <u>Be sure you understand the directions for each question type before attempting to answer any questions in that section.</u>

Not everyone will finish all the questions in the time allowed. Do not hurry, but work steadily and as quickly as you can without sacrificing accuracy. You are advised to use your time effectively. If a question seems too difficult, go on to the next one and return to the difficult question after completing the section. MARK THE BEST ANSWER YOU CAN FOR EVERY QUESTION. NO DEDUCTIONS WILL BE MADE FOR WRONG ANSWERS. YOUR SCORE WILL BE BASED ONLY ON THE NUMBER OF QUESTIONS YOU ANSWER CORRECTLY.

ALL YOUR ANSWERS MUST BE MARKED ON THE ANSWER SHEET. Answer spaces for each question are lettered to correspond with the letters of the potential answers to each question in the test book. After you have decided which of the answers is correct, blacken the corresponding space on the answer sheet. BE SURE THAT EACH MARK IS BLACK AND COMPLETELY FILLS THE ANSWER SPACE. Give only one answer to each question. If you change an answer, be sure that all previous marks are <u>erased completely</u>. Since the answer sheet is machine scored, incomplete erasures may be interpreted as intended answers. ANSWERS RECORDED IN THE TEST BOOK WILL NOT BE SCORED.

There may be more questions noted on this answer sheet than there are questions in a section. Do not be concerned but be certain that the section and number of the question you are answering matches the answer sheet section and question number. Additional answer spaces in any answer sheet section should be left blank. Begin your next section in the number one answer space for that section.

Kaplan takes various steps to ensure that answer sheets are returned from test centers in a timely manner for processing. In the unlikely event that an answer sheet(s) is not received, Kaplan will permit the examinee to either retest at no additional fee or to receive a refund of his or her test fee. THESE REMEDIES ARE THE EXCLUSIVE REMEDIES AVAILABLE IN THE UNLIKELY EVENT THAT AN ANSWER SHEET IS NOT RECEIVED BY KAPLAN.

Score Cancellation

Complete this section only if you are absolutely certain you want to cancel your score. A CANCELLATION REQUEST CANNOT BE RESCINDED. IF YOU ARE AT ALL UNCERTAIN, YOU SHOULD <u>NOT</u> COMPLETE THIS SECTION.

To cancel your score from this administration, you <u>must</u>:

A. fill in both ovals here..... ◯ ◯

B. read the following statement. Then sign your name and enter the date.
YOUR SIGNATURE ALONE IS NOT SUFFICIENT FOR SCORE CANCELLATION. BOTH OVALS MUST BE FILLED IN FOR SCANNING EQUIPMENT TO RECOGNIZE YOUR REQUEST FOR SCORE CANCELLATION.

I certify that I wish to cancel my test score from this administration. I understand that my request is irreversible and that my score will not be sent to me or to the law schools to which I apply.

_____
Sign your name in full

_____
Date

HOW DID YOU PREPARE FOR THE LSAT*?
(Select all that apply.)

Responses to this item are voluntary and will be used for statistical research purposes only.

- ◯ By attending a Kaplan LSAT* prep course or tutoring program
- ◯ By attending a non-Kaplan prep course or tutoring program (Please specify:_____)
- ◯ By using a Kaplan LSAT* prep book
- ◯ By using a non-Kaplan prep book (Please specify: _____)
- ◯ By working through the sample questions and free sample tests provided by the LSAC
- ◯ By working through official LSAT* PrepTests and/or other LSAC test prep products
- ◯ Other preparation (Please specify: _____)
- ◯ No preparation

CERTIFYING STATEMENT

Please write (DO NOT PRINT) the following statement. Sign and date.

I certify that I am the examinee whose name appears on this answer sheet and that I am here to take the LSAT for the sole purpose of being considered for application to law school. I further certify that I will neither assist nor receive assistance from any other candidate, and I agree not to copy or retain examination questions or to transmit them to or discuss them with any other person in any form.

_____
_____
_____
_____
_____
_____
_____
_____

SIGNATURE: _____ TODAY'S DATE: ____ / ____ / ____
                                                              MONTH   DAY   YEAR

*LSAT is a registered trademark of the Law School Admissions Council, Inc.

USE ONLY A NO 2. OR HB PENCIL TO COMPLETE THIS ANSWER SHEET. DO NOT USE INK.

● Right Mark   ⊘ ⊗ ⊙ Wrong Marks

1 LAST NAME   FIRST NAME   MI

(A) through (Z) bubble grid

2 SOCIAL SECURITY/ SOCIAL INSURANCE NO.

3 KAPLAN ENROLLMENT ID

0 1 2 3 4 5 6 7 8 9 bubble grid

4 TODAY'S DATE

MONTH	DAY	YEAR
○ Jan		
○ Feb		
○ Mar	0	0 0
○ Apr	1	1 1
○ May	2	2 2
○ June	3	3 3
○ July		4 4
○ Aug		5 5
○ Sept		6 6
○ Oct		7 7
○ Nov		8 8
○ Dec		9 9

5 RACIAL/ETHNIC DESCRIPTION

6 GENDER

7 DOMINANT LANGUAGE

8 ENGLISH FLUENCY

9 TEST BOOK SERIAL NO.

10 TEST FORM

11 TEST DATE

12 CENTER NUMBER

0 1 2 3 4 5 6 7 8 9 bubble grid

13 TEST FORM CODE

0 1 2 3 4 5 6 7 8 9 bubble grid

=== Law School Admission Test* ===

Mark one and only one answer to each question. Be sure to fill in completely the space for your intended answer choice. If you erase, do so completely. Make no stray marks.

SECTION 1 / SECTION 2 / SECTION 3 / SECTION 4 / SECTION 5

Questions 1–30, each with answer bubbles Ⓐ Ⓑ Ⓒ Ⓓ Ⓔ

14 PLEASE PRINT ALL INFORMATION

LAST NAME   FIRST

EMAIL

PHONE NUMBER

MAILING ADDRESS

CLASS CODE

KAPLAN

TEST PREP

www.kaptest.com/lsat

1-800-KAP-TEST

SCANTRON Mark Reflex® EM-284925-1:654321   LL3225A

General Directions for the LSAT* Answer Sheet

The actual testing time for this portion of the test will be 2 hours 55 minutes. There are five sections, each with a time limit of 35 minutes. The supervisor will tell you when to begin and end each section. If you finish a section before time is called, you may check your work on that section only; do not turn to any other section of the test book and do not work on any other section either in the test book or on the answer sheet.

There are several different types of questions on the test, and each question type has its own directions. Be sure you understand the directions for each question type before attempting to answer any questions in that section.

Not everyone will finish all the questions in the time allowed. Do not hurry, but work steadily and as quickly as you can without sacrificing accuracy. You are advised to use your time effectively. If a question seems too difficult, go on to the next one and return to the difficult question after completing the section. MARK THE BEST ANSWER YOU CAN FOR EVERY QUESTION. NO DEDUCTIONS WILL BE MADE FOR WRONG ANSWERS. YOUR SCORE WILL BE BASED ONLY ON THE NUMBER OF QUESTIONS YOU ANSWER CORRECTLY.

ALL YOUR ANSWERS MUST BE MARKED ON THE ANSWER SHEET. Answer spaces for each question are lettered to correspond with the letters of the potential answers to each question in the test book. After you have decided which of the answers is correct, blacken the corresponding space on the answer sheet. BE SURE THAT EACH MARK IS BLACK AND COMPLETELY FILLS THE ANSWER SPACE. Give only one answer to each question. If you change an answer, be sure that all previous marks are erased completely. Since the answer sheet is machine scored, incomplete erasures may be interpreted as intended answers. ANSWERS RECORDED IN THE TEST BOOK WILL NOT BE SCORED.

There may be more questions noted on this answer sheet than there are questions in a section. Do not be concerned but be certain that the section and number of the question you are answering matches the answer sheet section and question number. Additional answer spaces in any answer sheet section should be left blank. Begin your next section in the number one answer space for that section.

Kaplan takes various steps to ensure that answer sheets are returned from test centers in a timely manner for processing. In the unlikely event that an answer sheet(s) is not received, Kaplan will permit the examinee to either retest at no additional fee or to receive a refund of his or her test fee. THESE REMEDIES ARE THE EXCLUSIVE REMEDIES AVAILABLE IN THE UNLIKELY EVENT THAT AN ANSWER SHEET IS NOT RECEIVED BY KAPLAN.

Score Cancellation

Complete this section only if you are absolutely certain you want to cancel your score. A CANCELLATION REQUEST CANNOT BE RESCINDED. IF YOU ARE AT ALL UNCERTAIN, YOU SHOULD NOT COMPLETE THIS SECTION.

To cancel your score from this administration, you must:

A. fill in both ovals here..... ⚪⚪

B. read the following statement. Then sign your name and enter the date. YOUR SIGNATURE ALONE IS NOT SUFFICIENT FOR SCORE CANCELLATION. BOTH OVALS MUST BE FILLED IN FOR SCANNING EQUIPMENT TO RECOGNIZE YOUR REQUEST FOR SCORE CANCELLATION.

I certify that I wish to cancel my test score from this administration. I understand that my request is irreversible and that my score will not be sent to me or to the law schools to which I apply.

_____
Sign your name in full

_____
Date

HOW DID YOU PREPARE FOR THE LSAT*?
(Select all that apply.)

Responses to this item are voluntary and will be used for statistical research purposes only.

- ⚪ By attending a Kaplan LSAT* prep course or tutoring program
- ⚪ By attending a non-Kaplan prep course or tutoring program (Please specify:_____)
- ⚪ By using a Kaplan LSAT* prep book
- ⚪ By using a non-Kaplan prep book (Please specify: _____)
- ⚪ By working through the sample questions and free sample tests provided by the LSAC
- ⚪ By working through official LSAT* PrepTests and/or other LSAC test prep products
- ⚪ Other preparation (Please specify: _____)
- ⚪ No preparation

CERTIFYING STATEMENT

Please write (DO NOT PRINT) the following statement. Sign and date.

I certify that I am the examinee whose name appears on this answer sheet and that I am here to take the LSAT for the sole purpose of being considered for application to law school. I further certify that I will neither assist nor receive assistance from any other candidate, and I agree not to copy or retain examination questions or to transmit them to or discuss them with any other person in any form.

_____
_____
_____
_____
_____
_____
_____
_____
_____
_____

SIGNATURE: _____   TODAY'S DATE: ___/___/___
                                                            MONTH DAY YEAR

*LSAT is a registered trademark of the Law School Admissions Council, Inc.

USE ONLY A NO 2. OR HB PENCIL TO COMPLETE THIS ANSWER SHEET. DO NOT USE INK.

● Right Mark Ø ⊗ ⊙ Wrong Marks

1 LAST NAME FIRST NAME MI

2 SOCIAL SECURITY/ SOCIAL INSURANCE NO.

3 KAPLAN ENROLLMENT ID

4 TODAY'S DATE
MONTH DAY YEAR
Jan Feb Mar Apr May June July Aug Sept Oct Nov Dec

5 RACIAL/ETHNIC DESCRIPTION

6 GENDER

7 DOMINANT LANGUAGE

8 ENGLISH FLUENCY

9 TEST BOOK SERIAL NO.

10 TEST FORM

11 TEST DATE

12 CENTER NUMBER

13 TEST FORM CODE

Law School Admission Test*

Mark one and only one answer to each question. Be sure to fill in completely the space for your intended answer choice. If you erase, do so completely. Make no stray marks.

SECTION 1 SECTION 2 SECTION 3 SECTION 4 SECTION 5

(Answer bubbles 1–30, each A B C D E, for all five sections)

14 PLEASE PRINT ALL INFORMATION

LAST NAME FIRST
EMAIL
PHONE NUMBER
MAILING ADDRESS
CLASS CODE

KAPLAN
TEST PREP
www.kaptest.com/lsat
1-800-KAP-TEST

LSAT is a registered trademark Law School Admissions Counc

SCANTRON Mark Reflex® EM-284925-1:654321 LL3225A

General Directions for the LSAT* Answer Sheet

The actual testing time for this portion of the test will be 2 hours 55 minutes. There are five sections, each with a time limit of 35 minutes. The supervisor will tell you when to begin and end each section. If you finish a section before time is called, you may check your work on that section only; do not turn to any other section of the test book and do not work on any other section either in the test book or on the answer sheet.

There are several different types of questions on the test, and each question type has its own directions. Be sure you understand the directions for each question type before attempting to answer any questions in that section.

Not everyone will finish all the questions in the time allowed. Do not hurry, but work steadily and as quickly as you can without sacrificing accuracy. You are advised to use your time effectively. If a question seems too difficult, go on to the next one and return to the difficult question after completing the section. MARK THE BEST ANSWER YOU CAN FOR EVERY QUESTION. NO DEDUCTIONS WILL BE MADE FOR WRONG ANSWERS. YOUR SCORE WILL BE BASED ONLY ON THE NUMBER OF QUESTIONS YOU ANSWER CORRECTLY.

ALL YOUR ANSWERS MUST BE MARKED ON THE ANSWER SHEET. Answer spaces for each question are lettered to correspond with the letters of the potential answers to each question in the test book. After you have decided which of the answers is correct, blacken the corresponding space on the answer sheet. BE SURE THAT EACH MARK IS BLACK AND COMPLETELY FILLS THE ANSWER SPACE. Give only one answer to each question. If you change an answer, be sure that all previous marks are erased completely. Since the answer sheet is machine scored, incomplete erasures may be interpreted as intended answers. ANSWERS RECORDED IN THE TEST BOOK WILL NOT BE SCORED.

There may be more questions noted on this answer sheet than there are questions in a section. Do not be concerned but be certain that the section and number of the question you are answering matches the answer sheet section and question number. Additional answer spaces in any answer sheet section should be left blank. Begin your next section in the number one answer space for that section.

Kaplan takes various steps to ensure that answer sheets are returned from test centers in a timely manner for processing. In the unlikely event that an answer sheet(s) is not received, Kaplan will permit the examinee to either retest at no additional fee or to receive a refund of his or her test fee. THESE REMEDIES ARE THE EXCLUSIVE REMEDIES AVAILABLE IN THE UNLIKELY EVENT THAT AN ANSWER SHEET IS NOT RECEIVED BY KAPLAN.

Score Cancellation

Complete this section only if you are absolutely certain you want to cancel your score. A CANCELLATION REQUEST CANNOT BE RESCINDED. IF YOU ARE AT ALL UNCERTAIN, YOU SHOULD NOT COMPLETE THIS SECTION.

To cancel your score from this administration, you must:

A. fill in both ovals here..... ○ ○

B. read the following statement. Then sign your name and enter the date. **YOUR SIGNATURE ALONE IS NOT SUFFICIENT FOR SCORE CANCELLATION. BOTH OVALS MUST BE FILLED IN FOR SCANNING EQUIPMENT TO RECOGNIZE YOUR REQUEST FOR SCORE CANCELLATION.**

I certify that I wish to cancel my test score from this administration. I understand that my request is irreversible and that my score will not [be s]ent to me or to the law schools to [whic]h I apply.

_____
[N]ame in full

HOW DID YOU PREPARE FOR THE LSAT*?
(Select all that apply.)

Responses to this item are voluntary and will be used for statistical research purposes only.

○ By attending a Kaplan LSAT* prep course or tutoring program
○ By attending a non-Kaplan prep course or tutoring program (Please specify:_____)
○ By using a Kaplan LSAT* prep book
○ By using a non-Kaplan prep book (Please specify: _____)
○ By working through the sample questions and free sample tests provided by the LSAC
○ By working through official LSAT* PrepTests and/or other LSAC test prep products
○ Other preparation (Please specify: _____)
○ No preparation

CERTIFYING STATEMENT

Please write (DO NOT PRINT) the following statement. Sign and date.

I certify that I am the examinee whose name appears on this answer sheet and that I am here to take the LSAT for the sole purpose of being considered for application to law school. I further certify that I will neither assist nor receive assistance from any other candidate, and I agree not to copy or retain examination questions or to transmit them to or discuss them with any other person in any form.

_____
_____
_____
_____
_____
_____
_____
_____
_____
_____

SIGNATURE: _____   TODAY'S DATE: ____/____/____
                                                                                        MONTH DAY   YEAR

*LSAT is a registered trademark of the Law School Admissions Council, Inc.

USE ONLY A NO 2. OR HB PENCIL TO COMPLETE THIS ANSWER SHEET. DO NOT USE INK.

● Right Mark   ⊘ ⊗ ⊙ Wrong Marks

1 LAST NAME / FIRST NAME / MI

2 SOCIAL SECURITY/ SOCIAL INSURANCE NO.

3 KAPLAN ENROLLMENT ID

4 TODAY'S DATE

5 RACIAL/ETHNIC DESCRIPTION

6 GENDER

7 DOMINANT LANGUAGE

8 ENGLISH FLUENCY

9 TEST BOOK SERIAL NO.

10 TEST FORM

11 TEST DATE

12 CENTER NUMBER

13 TEST FORM CODE

Law School Admission Test*

Mark one and only one answer to each question. Be sure to fill in completely the space for your intended answer choice. If you erase, do so completely. Make no stray marks.

SECTION 1 | SECTION 2 | SECTION 3 | SECTION 4 | SECTION 5 (each 1–30, A B C D E)

14 PLEASE PRINT ALL INFORMATION

LAST NAME FIRST
EMAIL
PHONE NUMBER
MAILING ADDRESS
CLASS CODE

KAPLAN
TEST PREP
www.kaptest.com/lsat
1-800-KAP-TEST

LSAT is a registered trademark of the Law School Admissions Council, Inc.

SCANTRON Mark Reflex® EM-284925-1:654321   LL3225A

General Directions for the LSAT* Answer Sheet

The actual testing time for this portion of the test will be 2 hours 55 minutes. There are five sections, each with a time limit of 35 minutes. The supervisor will tell you when to begin and end each section. If you finish a section before time is called, you may check your work on that section only; do not turn to any other section of the test book and do not work on any other section either in the test book or on the answer sheet.

There are several different types of questions on the test, and each question type has its own directions. Be sure you understand the directions for each question type before attempting to answer any questions in that section.

Not everyone will finish all the questions in the time allowed. Do not hurry, but work steadily and as quickly as you can without sacrificing accuracy. You are advised to use your time effectively. If a question seems too difficult, go on to the next one and return to the difficult question after completing the section. MARK THE BEST ANSWER YOU CAN FOR EVERY QUESTION. NO DEDUCTIONS WILL BE MADE FOR WRONG ANSWERS. YOUR SCORE WILL BE BASED ONLY ON THE NUMBER OF QUESTIONS YOU ANSWER CORRECTLY.

ALL YOUR ANSWERS MUST BE MARKED ON THE ANSWER SHEET. Answer spaces for each question are lettered to correspond with the letters of the potential answers to each question in the test book. After you have decided which of the answers is correct, blacken the corresponding space on the answer sheet. BE SURE THAT EACH MARK IS BLACK AND COMPLETELY FILLS THE ANSWER SPACE. Give only one answer to each question. If you change an answer, be sure that all previous marks are erased completely. Since the answer sheet is machine scored, incomplete erasures may be interpreted as intended answers. ANSWERS RECORDED IN THE TEST BOOK WILL NOT BE SCORED.

There may be more questions noted on this answer sheet than there are questions in a section. Do not be concerned but be certain that the section and number of the question you are answering matches the answer sheet section and question number. Additional answer spaces in any answer sheet section should be left blank. Begin your next section in the number one answer space for that section.

Kaplan takes various steps to ensure that answer sheets are returned from test centers in a timely manner for processing. In the unlikely event that an answer sheet(s) is not received, Kaplan will permit the examinee to either retest at no additional fee or to receive a refund of his or her test fee. THESE REMEDIES ARE THE EXCLUSIVE REMEDIES AVAILABLE IN THE UNLIKELY EVENT THAT AN ANSWER SHEET IS NOT RECEIVED BY KAPLAN.

Score Cancellation

Complete this section only if you are absolutely certain you want to cancel your score. A CANCELLATION REQUEST CANNOT BE RESCINDED. IF YOU ARE AT ALL UNCERTAIN, YOU SHOULD NOT COMPLETE THIS SECTION.

To cancel your score from this administration, you must:

A. fill in both ovals here..... ◯ ◯

B. read the following statement. Then sign your name and enter the date. YOUR SIGNATURE ALONE IS NOT SUFFICIENT FOR SCORE CANCELLATION. BOTH OVALS MUST BE FILLED IN FOR SCANNING EQUIPMENT TO RECOGNIZE YOUR REQUEST FOR SCORE CANCELLATION.

I certify that I wish to cancel my test score from this administration. I understand that my request is irreversible and that my score will not be sent to me or to the law schools to which I apply.

_____
Sign your name in full

_____
Date

HOW DID YOU PREPARE FOR THE LSAT*?
(Select all that apply.)

Responses to this item are voluntary and will be used for statistical research purposes only.

- ◯ By attending a Kaplan LSAT* prep course or tutoring program
- ◯ By attending a non-Kaplan prep course or tutoring program (Please specify:_____)
- ◯ By using a Kaplan LSAT* prep book
- ◯ By using a non-Kaplan prep book (Please specify: _____)
- ◯ By working through the sample questions and free sample tests provided by the LSAC
- ◯ By working through official LSAT* PrepTests and/or other LSAC test prep products
- ◯ Other preparation (Please specify: _____)
- ◯ No preparation

CERTIFYING STATEMENT

Please write (DO NOT PRINT) the following statement. Sign and date.

I certify that I am the examinee whose name appears on this answer sheet and that I am here to take the LSAT for the sole purpose of being considered for application to law school. I further certify that I will neither assist nor receive assistance from any other candidate, and I agree not to copy or retain examination questions or to transmit them to or discuss them with any other person in any form.

_____
_____
_____
_____
_____
_____
_____
_____
_____

SIGNATURE:_____ TODAY'S DATE: _____/_____/_____
                                                                    MONTH DAY YEAR

*LSAT is a registered trademark of the Law School Admissions Council, Inc.

USE ONLY A NO 2. OR HB PENCIL TO COMPLETE THIS ANSWER SHEET. DO NOT USE INK.

● Right Mark   ⊘ ⊗ ⊙ Wrong Marks

1 LAST NAME | FIRST NAME | MI

2 SOCIAL SECURITY/ SOCIAL INSURANCE NO.

3 KAPLAN ENROLLMENT ID

4 TODAY'S DATE

MONTH	DAY	YEAR
○ Jan		
○ Feb		
○ Mar	⓪ ⓪ ⓪ ⓪
○ Apr	① ① ① ①
○ May	② ② ② ②
○ June	③ ③ ③ ③
○ July	④ ④ ④
○ Aug	⑤ ⑤ ⑤
○ Sept	⑥ ⑥ ⑥
○ Oct	⑦ ⑦ ⑦
○ Nov	⑧ ⑧ ⑧
○ Dec	⑨ ⑨ ⑨

5 RACIAL/ETHNIC DESCRIPTION

6 GENDER

7 DOMINANT LANGUAGE

8 ENGLISH FLUENCY

9 TEST BOOK SERIAL NO.

10 TEST FORM

11 TEST DATE

12 CENTER NUMBER

13 TEST FORM CODE

=== Law School Admission Test* ===

Mark one and only one answer to each question. Be sure to fill in completely the space for your intended answer choice. If you erase, do so completely. Make no stray marks.

SECTION 1 / SECTION 2 / SECTION 3 / SECTION 4 / SECTION 5

Each section: questions 1–30, answer choices Ⓐ Ⓑ Ⓒ Ⓓ Ⓔ

14 PLEASE PRINT ALL INFORMATION

LAST NAME   FIRST

EMAIL

PHONE NUMBER

MAILING ADDRESS

CLASS CODE

TEST PREP
www.kaptest.com/lsat
1-800-KAP-TEST

LSAT is a registered trademark of the Law School Admissions Council, Inc.

SCANTRON Mark Reflex® EM-284925-1:654321   LL3225A

General Directions for the LSAT* Answer Sheet

The actual testing time for this portion of the test will be 2 hours 55 minutes. There are five sections, each with a time limit of 35 minutes. The supervisor will tell you when to begin and end each section. If you finish a section before time is called, you may check your work on that section only; do not turn to any other section of the test book and do not work on any other section either in the test book or on the answer sheet.

There are several different types of questions on the test, and each question type has its own directions. Be sure you understand the directions for each question type before attempting to answer any questions in that section.

Not everyone will finish all the questions in the time allowed. Do not hurry, but work steadily and as quickly as you can without sacrificing accuracy. You are advised to use your time effectively. If a question seems too difficult, go on to the next one and return to the difficult question after completing the section. MARK THE BEST ANSWER YOU CAN FOR EVERY QUESTION. NO DEDUCTIONS WILL BE MADE FOR WRONG ANSWERS. YOUR SCORE WILL BE BASED ONLY ON THE NUMBER OF QUESTIONS YOU ANSWER CORRECTLY.

ALL YOUR ANSWERS MUST BE MARKED ON THE ANSWER SHEET. Answer spaces for each question are lettered to correspond with the letters of the potential answers to each question in the test book. After you have decided which of the answers is correct, blacken the corresponding space on the answer sheet. BE SURE THAT EACH MARK IS BLACK AND COMPLETELY FILLS THE ANSWER SPACE. Give only one answer to each question. If you change an answer, be sure that all previous marks are erased completely. Since the answer sheet is machine scored, incomplete erasures may be interpreted as intended answers. ANSWERS RECORDED IN THE TEST BOOK WILL NOT BE SCORED.

There may be more questions noted on this answer sheet than there are questions in a section. Do not be concerned but be certain that the section and number of the question you are answering matches the answer sheet section and question number. Additional answer spaces in any answer sheet section should be left blank. Begin your next section in the number one answer space for that section.

Kaplan takes various steps to ensure that answer sheets are returned from test centers in a timely manner for processing. In the unlikely event that an answer sheet(s) is not received, Kaplan will permit the examinee to either retest at no additional fee or to receive a refund of his or her test fee. THESE REMEDIES ARE THE EXCLUSIVE REMEDIES AVAILABLE IN THE UNLIKELY EVENT THAT AN ANSWER SHEET IS NOT RECEIVED BY KAPLAN.

Score Cancellation

Complete this section only if you are absolutely certain you want to cancel your score. A CANCELLATION REQUEST CANNOT BE RESCINDED. IF YOU ARE AT ALL UNCERTAIN, YOU SHOULD NOT COMPLETE THIS SECTION.

To cancel your score from this administration, you must:

A. fill in both ovals here..... ○ ○

B. read the following statement. Then sign your name and enter the date. YOUR SIGNATURE ALONE IS NOT SUFFICIENT FOR SCORE CANCELLATION. BOTH OVALS MUST BE FILLED IN FOR SCANNING EQUIPMENT TO RECOGNIZE YOUR REQUEST FOR SCORE CANCELLATION.

I certify that I wish to cancel my test score from this administration. I understand that my request is irreversible and that my score will not be sent to me or to the law schools to which I apply.

_____
Sign your name in full

_____
Date

HOW DID YOU PREPARE FOR THE LSAT*?
(Select all that apply.)

Responses to this item are voluntary and will be used for statistical research purposes only.

- ○ By attending a Kaplan LSAT* prep course or tutoring program
- ○ By attending a non-Kaplan prep course or tutoring program (Please specify:_____)
- ○ By using a Kaplan LSAT* prep book
- ○ By using a non-Kaplan prep book (Please specify:_____)
- ○ By working through the sample questions and free sample tests provided by the LSAC
- ○ By working through official LSAT* PrepTests and/or other LSAC test prep products
- ○ Other preparation (Please specify: _____)
- ○ No preparation

CERTIFYING STATEMENT

Please write (DO NOT PRINT) the following statement. Sign and date.

I certify that I am the examinee whose name appears on this answer sheet and that I am here to take the LSAT for the sole purpose of being considered for application to law school. I further certify that I will neither assist nor receive assistance from any other candidate, and I agree not to copy or retain examination questions or to transmit them to or discuss them with any other person in any form.

_____
_____
_____
_____
_____
_____
_____
_____
_____
_____

SIGNATURE:_____   TODAY'S DATE: ____ / ____ / ____
                                                                 MONTH DAY   YEAR

*LSAT is a registered trademark of the Law School Admissions Council, Inc.

USE ONLY A NO 2. OR HB PENCIL TO COMPLETE THIS ANSWER SHEET. DO NOT USE INK.

● Right Mark   ⌀ ⊗ ⊙ Wrong Marks

1 LAST NAME | FIRST NAME | MI

2 SOCIAL SECURITY/ SOCIAL INSURANCE NO.

3 KAPLAN ENROLLMENT ID

(A–Z bubble grid for name fields)

4 TODAY'S DATE

MONTH	DAY	YEAR
○ Jan		
○ Feb		
○ Mar	⓪ ⓪ ⓪
○ Apr	① ① ① ①
○ May	② ② ② ②
○ June	③ ③ ③ ③
○ July	④ ④ ④
○ Aug	⑤ ⑤ ⑤
○ Sept	⑥ ⑥ ⑥
○ Oct	⑦ ⑦ ⑦
○ Nov	⑧ ⑧ ⑧
○ Dec	⑨ ⑨ ⑨

5 RACIAL/ETHNIC DESCRIPTION

6 GENDER

7 DOMINANT LANGUAGE

8 ENGLISH FLUENCY

9 TEST BOOK SERIAL NO.

10 TEST FORM

11 TEST DATE

12 CENTER NUMBER

13 TEST FORM CODE

Law School Admission Test*

Mark one and only one answer to each question. Be sure to fill in completely the space for your intended answer choice. If you erase, do so completely. Make no stray marks.

SECTION 1	SECTION 2	SECTION 3	SECTION 4	SECTION 5
1 Ⓐ Ⓑ Ⓒ Ⓓ Ⓔ	1 Ⓐ Ⓑ Ⓒ Ⓓ Ⓔ	1 Ⓐ Ⓑ Ⓒ Ⓓ Ⓔ	1 Ⓐ Ⓑ Ⓒ Ⓓ Ⓔ	1 Ⓐ Ⓑ Ⓒ Ⓓ Ⓔ
2 Ⓐ Ⓑ Ⓒ Ⓓ Ⓔ	2 Ⓐ Ⓑ Ⓒ Ⓓ Ⓔ	2 Ⓐ Ⓑ Ⓒ Ⓓ Ⓔ	2 Ⓐ Ⓑ Ⓒ Ⓓ Ⓔ	2 Ⓐ Ⓑ Ⓒ Ⓓ Ⓔ
3 Ⓐ Ⓑ Ⓒ Ⓓ Ⓔ	3 Ⓐ Ⓑ Ⓒ Ⓓ Ⓔ	3 Ⓐ Ⓑ Ⓒ Ⓓ Ⓔ	3 Ⓐ Ⓑ Ⓒ Ⓓ Ⓔ	3 Ⓐ Ⓑ Ⓒ Ⓓ Ⓔ
4 Ⓐ Ⓑ Ⓒ Ⓓ Ⓔ	4 Ⓐ Ⓑ Ⓒ Ⓓ Ⓔ	4 Ⓐ Ⓑ Ⓒ Ⓓ Ⓔ	4 Ⓐ Ⓑ Ⓒ Ⓓ Ⓔ	4 Ⓐ Ⓑ Ⓒ Ⓓ Ⓔ
5 Ⓐ Ⓑ Ⓒ Ⓓ Ⓔ	5 Ⓐ Ⓑ Ⓒ Ⓓ Ⓔ	5 Ⓐ Ⓑ Ⓒ Ⓓ Ⓔ	5 Ⓐ Ⓑ Ⓒ Ⓓ Ⓔ	5 Ⓐ Ⓑ Ⓒ Ⓓ Ⓔ
6 Ⓐ Ⓑ Ⓒ Ⓓ Ⓔ	6 Ⓐ Ⓑ Ⓒ Ⓓ Ⓔ	6 Ⓐ Ⓑ Ⓒ Ⓓ Ⓔ	6 Ⓐ Ⓑ Ⓒ Ⓓ Ⓔ	6 Ⓐ Ⓑ Ⓒ Ⓓ Ⓔ
7 Ⓐ Ⓑ Ⓒ Ⓓ Ⓔ	7 Ⓐ Ⓑ Ⓒ Ⓓ Ⓔ	7 Ⓐ Ⓑ Ⓒ Ⓓ Ⓔ	7 Ⓐ Ⓑ Ⓒ Ⓓ Ⓔ	7 Ⓐ Ⓑ Ⓒ Ⓓ Ⓔ
8 Ⓐ Ⓑ Ⓒ Ⓓ Ⓔ	8 Ⓐ Ⓑ Ⓒ Ⓓ Ⓔ	8 Ⓐ Ⓑ Ⓒ Ⓓ Ⓔ	8 Ⓐ Ⓑ Ⓒ Ⓓ Ⓔ	8 Ⓐ Ⓑ Ⓒ Ⓓ Ⓔ
9 Ⓐ Ⓑ Ⓒ Ⓓ Ⓔ	9 Ⓐ Ⓑ Ⓒ Ⓓ Ⓔ	9 Ⓐ Ⓑ Ⓒ Ⓓ Ⓔ	9 Ⓐ Ⓑ Ⓒ Ⓓ Ⓔ	9 Ⓐ Ⓑ Ⓒ Ⓓ Ⓔ
10 Ⓐ Ⓑ Ⓒ Ⓓ Ⓔ	10 Ⓐ Ⓑ Ⓒ Ⓓ Ⓔ	10 Ⓐ Ⓑ Ⓒ Ⓓ Ⓔ	10 Ⓐ Ⓑ Ⓒ Ⓓ Ⓔ	10 Ⓐ Ⓑ Ⓒ Ⓓ Ⓔ
11 Ⓐ Ⓑ Ⓒ Ⓓ Ⓔ	11 Ⓐ Ⓑ Ⓒ Ⓓ Ⓔ	11 Ⓐ Ⓑ Ⓒ Ⓓ Ⓔ	11 Ⓐ Ⓑ Ⓒ Ⓓ Ⓔ	11 Ⓐ Ⓑ Ⓒ Ⓓ Ⓔ
12 Ⓐ Ⓑ Ⓒ Ⓓ Ⓔ	12 Ⓐ Ⓑ Ⓒ Ⓓ Ⓔ	12 Ⓐ Ⓑ Ⓒ Ⓓ Ⓔ	12 Ⓐ Ⓑ Ⓒ Ⓓ Ⓔ	12 Ⓐ Ⓑ Ⓒ Ⓓ Ⓔ
13 Ⓐ Ⓑ Ⓒ Ⓓ Ⓔ	13 Ⓐ Ⓑ Ⓒ Ⓓ Ⓔ	13 Ⓐ Ⓑ Ⓒ Ⓓ Ⓔ	13 Ⓐ Ⓑ Ⓒ Ⓓ Ⓔ	13 Ⓐ Ⓑ Ⓒ Ⓓ Ⓔ
14 Ⓐ Ⓑ Ⓒ Ⓓ Ⓔ	14 Ⓐ Ⓑ Ⓒ Ⓓ Ⓔ	14 Ⓐ Ⓑ Ⓒ Ⓓ Ⓔ	14 Ⓐ Ⓑ Ⓒ Ⓓ Ⓔ	14 Ⓐ Ⓑ Ⓒ Ⓓ Ⓔ
15 Ⓐ Ⓑ Ⓒ Ⓓ Ⓔ	15 Ⓐ Ⓑ Ⓒ Ⓓ Ⓔ	15 Ⓐ Ⓑ Ⓒ Ⓓ Ⓔ	15 Ⓐ Ⓑ Ⓒ Ⓓ Ⓔ	15 Ⓐ Ⓑ Ⓒ Ⓓ Ⓔ
16 Ⓐ Ⓑ Ⓒ Ⓓ Ⓔ	16 Ⓐ Ⓑ Ⓒ Ⓓ Ⓔ	16 Ⓐ Ⓑ Ⓒ Ⓓ Ⓔ	16 Ⓐ Ⓑ Ⓒ Ⓓ Ⓔ	16 Ⓐ Ⓑ Ⓒ Ⓓ Ⓔ
17 Ⓐ Ⓑ Ⓒ Ⓓ Ⓔ	17 Ⓐ Ⓑ Ⓒ Ⓓ Ⓔ	17 Ⓐ Ⓑ Ⓒ Ⓓ Ⓔ	17 Ⓐ Ⓑ Ⓒ Ⓓ Ⓔ	17 Ⓐ Ⓑ Ⓒ Ⓓ Ⓔ
18 Ⓐ Ⓑ Ⓒ Ⓓ Ⓔ	18 Ⓐ Ⓑ Ⓒ Ⓓ Ⓔ	18 Ⓐ Ⓑ Ⓒ Ⓓ Ⓔ	18 Ⓐ Ⓑ Ⓒ Ⓓ Ⓔ	18 Ⓐ Ⓑ Ⓒ Ⓓ Ⓔ
19 Ⓐ Ⓑ Ⓒ Ⓓ Ⓔ	19 Ⓐ Ⓑ Ⓒ Ⓓ Ⓔ	19 Ⓐ Ⓑ Ⓒ Ⓓ Ⓔ	19 Ⓐ Ⓑ Ⓒ Ⓓ Ⓔ	19 Ⓐ Ⓑ Ⓒ Ⓓ Ⓔ
20 Ⓐ Ⓑ Ⓒ Ⓓ Ⓔ	20 Ⓐ Ⓑ Ⓒ Ⓓ Ⓔ	20 Ⓐ Ⓑ Ⓒ Ⓓ Ⓔ	20 Ⓐ Ⓑ Ⓒ Ⓓ Ⓔ	20 Ⓐ Ⓑ Ⓒ Ⓓ Ⓔ
21 Ⓐ Ⓑ Ⓒ Ⓓ Ⓔ	21 Ⓐ Ⓑ Ⓒ Ⓓ Ⓔ	21 Ⓐ Ⓑ Ⓒ Ⓓ Ⓔ	21 Ⓐ Ⓑ Ⓒ Ⓓ Ⓔ	21 Ⓐ Ⓑ Ⓒ Ⓓ Ⓔ
22 Ⓐ Ⓑ Ⓒ Ⓓ Ⓔ	22 Ⓐ Ⓑ Ⓒ Ⓓ Ⓔ	22 Ⓐ Ⓑ Ⓒ Ⓓ Ⓔ	22 Ⓐ Ⓑ Ⓒ Ⓓ Ⓔ	22 Ⓐ Ⓑ Ⓒ Ⓓ Ⓔ
23 Ⓐ Ⓑ Ⓒ Ⓓ Ⓔ	23 Ⓐ Ⓑ Ⓒ Ⓓ Ⓔ	23 Ⓐ Ⓑ Ⓒ Ⓓ Ⓔ	23 Ⓐ Ⓑ Ⓒ Ⓓ Ⓔ	23 Ⓐ Ⓑ Ⓒ Ⓓ Ⓔ
24 Ⓐ Ⓑ Ⓒ Ⓓ Ⓔ	24 Ⓐ Ⓑ Ⓒ Ⓓ Ⓔ	24 Ⓐ Ⓑ Ⓒ Ⓓ Ⓔ	24 Ⓐ Ⓑ Ⓒ Ⓓ Ⓔ	24 Ⓐ Ⓑ Ⓒ Ⓓ Ⓔ
25 Ⓐ Ⓑ Ⓒ Ⓓ Ⓔ	25 Ⓐ Ⓑ Ⓒ Ⓓ Ⓔ	25 Ⓐ Ⓑ Ⓒ Ⓓ Ⓔ	25 Ⓐ Ⓑ Ⓒ Ⓓ Ⓔ	25 Ⓐ Ⓑ Ⓒ Ⓓ Ⓔ
26 Ⓐ Ⓑ Ⓒ Ⓓ Ⓔ	26 Ⓐ Ⓑ Ⓒ Ⓓ Ⓔ	26 Ⓐ Ⓑ Ⓒ Ⓓ Ⓔ	26 Ⓐ Ⓑ Ⓒ Ⓓ Ⓔ	26 Ⓐ Ⓑ Ⓒ Ⓓ Ⓔ
27 Ⓐ Ⓑ Ⓒ Ⓓ Ⓔ	27 Ⓐ Ⓑ Ⓒ Ⓓ Ⓔ	27 Ⓐ Ⓑ Ⓒ Ⓓ Ⓔ	27 Ⓐ Ⓑ Ⓒ Ⓓ Ⓔ	27 Ⓐ Ⓑ Ⓒ Ⓓ Ⓔ
28 Ⓐ Ⓑ Ⓒ Ⓓ Ⓔ	28 Ⓐ Ⓑ Ⓒ Ⓓ Ⓔ	28 Ⓐ Ⓑ Ⓒ Ⓓ Ⓔ	28 Ⓐ Ⓑ Ⓒ Ⓓ Ⓔ	28 Ⓐ Ⓑ Ⓒ Ⓓ Ⓔ
29 Ⓐ Ⓑ Ⓒ Ⓓ Ⓔ	29 Ⓐ Ⓑ Ⓒ Ⓓ Ⓔ	29 Ⓐ Ⓑ Ⓒ Ⓓ Ⓔ	29 Ⓐ Ⓑ Ⓒ Ⓓ Ⓔ	29 Ⓐ Ⓑ Ⓒ Ⓓ Ⓔ
30 Ⓐ Ⓑ Ⓒ Ⓓ Ⓔ	30 Ⓐ Ⓑ Ⓒ Ⓓ Ⓔ	30 Ⓐ Ⓑ Ⓒ Ⓓ Ⓔ	30 Ⓐ Ⓑ Ⓒ Ⓓ Ⓔ	30 Ⓐ Ⓑ Ⓒ Ⓓ Ⓔ

14 PLEASE PRINT ALL INFORMATION

LAST NAME   FIRST

EMAIL

PHONE NUMBER

MAILING ADDRESS

CLASS CODE

KAPLAN)

TEST PREP

www.kaptest.com/lsat

1-800-KAP-TEST

LSAT is a registered trademark of the Law School Admissions Council, Inc.

General Directions for the LSAT* Answer Sheet

The actual testing time for this portion of the test will be 2 hours 55 minutes. There are five sections, each with a time limit of 35 minutes. The supervisor will tell you when to begin and end each section. If you finish a section before time is called, you may check your work on that section only; do not turn to any other section of the test book and do not work on any other section either in the test book or on the answer sheet.

There are several different types of questions on the test, and each question type has its own directions. Be sure you understand the directions for each question type before attempting to answer any questions in that section.

Not everyone will finish all the questions in the time allowed. Do not hurry, but work steadily and as quickly as you can without sacrificing accuracy. You are advised to use your time effectively. If a question seems too difficult, go on to the next one and return to the difficult question after completing the section. MARK THE BEST ANSWER YOU CAN FOR EVERY QUESTION. NO DEDUCTIONS WILL BE MADE FOR WRONG ANSWERS. YOUR SCORE WILL BE BASED ONLY ON THE NUMBER OF QUESTIONS YOU ANSWER CORRECTLY.

ALL YOUR ANSWERS MUST BE MARKED ON THE ANSWER SHEET. Answer spaces for each question are lettered to correspond with the letters of the potential answers to each question in the test book. After you have decided which of the answers is correct, blacken the corresponding space on the answer sheet. BE SURE THAT EACH MARK IS BLACK AND COMPLETELY FILLS THE ANSWER SPACE. Give only one answer to each question. If you change an answer, be sure that all previous marks are erased completely. Since the answer sheet is machine scored, incomplete erasures may be interpreted as intended answers. ANSWERS RECORDED IN THE TEST BOOK WILL NOT BE SCORED.

There may be more questions noted on this answer sheet than there are questions in a section. Do not be concerned but be certain that the section and number of the question you are answering matches the answer sheet section and question number. Additional answer spaces in any answer sheet section should be left blank. Begin your next section in the number one answer space for that section.

Kaplan takes various steps to ensure that answer sheets are returned from test centers in a timely manner for processing. In the unlikely event that an answer sheet(s) is not received, Kaplan will permit the examinee to either retest at no additional fee or to receive a refund of his or her test fee. THESE REMEDIES ARE THE EXCLUSIVE REMEDIES AVAILABLE IN THE UNLIKELY EVENT THAT AN ANSWER SHEET IS NOT RECEIVED BY KAPLAN.

Score Cancellation

Complete this section only if you are absolutely certain you want to cancel your score. A CANCELLATION REQUEST CANNOT BE RESCINDED. IF YOU ARE AT ALL UNCERTAIN, YOU SHOULD NOT COMPLETE THIS SECTION.

To cancel your score from this administration, you must:

A. fill in both ovals here..... ○○

B. read the following statement. Then sign your name and enter the date.
YOUR SIGNATURE ALONE IS NOT SUFFICIENT FOR SCORE CANCELLATION. BOTH OVALS MUST BE FILLED IN FOR SCANNING EQUIPMENT TO RECOGNIZE YOUR REQUEST FOR SCORE CANCELLATION.

I certify that I wish to cancel my test score from this administration. I understand that my request is irreversible and that my score will not be sent to me or to the law schools to which I apply.

_____
Sign your name in full

_____
Date

HOW DID YOU PREPARE FOR THE LSAT*?
(Select all that apply.)

Responses to this item are voluntary and will be used for statistical research purposes only.

○ By attending a Kaplan LSAT* prep course or tutoring program
○ By attending a non-Kaplan prep course or tutoring program (Please specify:_____)
○ By using a Kaplan LSAT* prep book
○ By using a non-Kaplan prep book (Please specify: _____)
○ By working through the sample questions and free sample tests provided by the LSAC
○ By working through official LSAT* PrepTests and/or other LSAC test prep products
○ Other preparation (Please specify: _____)
○ No preparation

CERTIFYING STATEMENT

Please write (DO NOT PRINT) the following statement. Sign and date.

I certify that I am the examinee whose name appears on this answer sheet and that I am here to take the LSAT for the sole purpose of being considered for application to law school. I further certify that I will neither assist nor receive assistance from any other candidate, and I agree not to copy or retain examination questions or to transmit them to or discuss them with any other person in any form.

_____
_____
_____
_____
_____
_____
_____
_____
_____
_____

SIGNATURE: _____ TODAY'S DATE: ____/____/____
                                                          MONTH DAY YEAR

*LSAT is a registered trademark of the Law School Admissions Council, Inc.

USE ONLY A NO 2. OR HB PENCIL TO COMPLETE THIS ANSWER SHEET. DO NOT USE INK.

● Right Mark   ⦸ ⊗ ⊙ Wrong Marks

1 LAST NAME | FIRST NAME | MI

2 SOCIAL SECURITY/ SOCIAL INSURANCE NO.

3 KAPLAN ENROLLMENT ID

4 TODAY'S DATE

MONTH	DAY	YEAR
Jan		
Feb		
Mar		
Apr		
May		
June		
July		
Aug		
Sept		
Oct		
Nov		
Dec		

5 RACIAL/ETHNIC DESCRIPTION

6 GENDER

7 DOMINANT LANGUAGE

8 ENGLISH FLUENCY

9 TEST BOOK SERIAL NO.

10 TEST FORM

11 TEST DATE

12 CENTER NUMBER

13 TEST FORM CODE

Law School Admission Test*

Mark one and only one answer to each question. Be sure to fill in completely the space for your intended answer choice. If you erase, do so completely. Make no stray marks.

SECTION 1 | SECTION 2 | SECTION 3 | SECTION 4 | SECTION 5

(Each section contains questions 1–30, each with answer choices A B C D E)

14 PLEASE PRINT ALL INFORMATION

LAST NAME   FIRST

EMAIL

PHONE NUMBER

MAILING ADDRESS

CLASS CODE

TEST PREP
www.kaptest.com/lsat
1-800-KAP-TEST

LSAT is a registered trademark of the Law School Admissions Council, Inc.

SCANTRON   Mark Reflex® EM-284925-1:654321   LL3225A

General Directions for the LSAT* Answer Sheet

The actual testing time for this portion of the test will be 2 hours 55 minutes. There are five sections, each with a time limit of 35 minutes. The supervisor will tell you when to begin and end each section. If you finish a section before time is called, you may check your work on that section only; do not turn to any other section of the test book and do not work on any other section either in the test book or on the answer sheet.

There are several different types of questions on the test, and each question type has its own directions. Be sure you understand the directions for each question type before attempting to answer any questions in that section.

Not everyone will finish all the questions in the time allowed. Do not hurry, but work steadily and as quickly as you can without sacrificing accuracy. You are advised to use your time effectively. If a question seems too difficult, go on to the next one and return to the difficult question after completing the section. MARK THE BEST ANSWER YOU CAN FOR EVERY QUESTION. NO DEDUCTIONS WILL BE MADE FOR WRONG ANSWERS. YOUR SCORE WILL BE BASED ONLY ON THE NUMBER OF QUESTIONS YOU ANSWER CORRECTLY.

ALL YOUR ANSWERS MUST BE MARKED ON THE ANSWER SHEET. Answer spaces for each question are lettered to correspond with the letters of the potential answers to each question in the test book. After you have decided which of the answers is correct, blacken the corresponding space on the answer sheet. BE SURE THAT EACH MARK IS BLACK AND COMPLETELY FILLS THE ANSWER SPACE. Give only one answer to each question. If you change an answer, be sure that all previous marks are erased completely. Since the answer sheet is machine scored, incomplete erasures may be interpreted as intended answers. ANSWERS RECORDED IN THE TEST BOOK WILL NOT BE SCORED.

There may be more questions noted on this answer sheet than there are questions in a section. Do not be concerned but be certain that the section and number of the question you are answering matches the answer sheet section and question number. Additional answer spaces in any answer sheet section should be left blank. Begin your next section in the number one answer space for that section.

Kaplan takes various steps to ensure that answer sheets are returned from test centers in a timely manner for processing. In the unlikely event that an answer sheet(s) is not received, Kaplan will permit the examinee to either retest at no additional fee or to receive a refund of his or her test fee. THESE REMEDIES ARE THE EXCLUSIVE REMEDIES AVAILABLE IN THE UNLIKELY EVENT THAT AN ANSWER SHEET IS NOT RECEIVED BY KAPLAN.

Score Cancellation

Complete this section only if you are absolutely certain you want to cancel your score. A CANCELLATION REQUEST CANNOT BE RESCINDED. IF YOU ARE AT ALL UNCERTAIN, YOU SHOULD NOT COMPLETE THIS SECTION.

To cancel your score from this administration, you must:

A. fill in both ovals here..... ◯ ◯

B. read the following statement. Then sign your name and enter the date. YOUR SIGNATURE ALONE IS NOT SUFFICIENT FOR SCORE CANCELLATION. BOTH OVALS MUST BE FILLED IN FOR SCANNING EQUIPMENT TO RECOGNIZE YOUR REQUEST FOR SCORE CANCELLATION.

I certify that I wish to cancel my test score from this administration. I understand that my request is irreversible and that my score will not be sent to me or to the law schools to which I apply.

_____
Sign your name in full

_____
Date

HOW DID YOU PREPARE FOR THE LSAT*?
(Select all that apply.)

Responses to this item are voluntary and will be used for statistical research purposes only.

◯ By attending a Kaplan LSAT* prep course or tutoring program
◯ By attending a non-Kaplan prep course or tutoring program (Please specify:_____)
◯ By using a Kaplan LSAT* prep book
◯ By using a non-Kaplan prep book (Please specify:_____)
◯ By working through the sample questions and free sample tests provided by the LSAC
◯ By working through official LSAT* PrepTests and/or other LSAC test prep products
◯ Other preparation (Please specify:_____)
◯ No preparation

CERTIFYING STATEMENT

Please write (DO NOT PRINT) the following statement. Sign and date.

I certify that I am the examinee whose name appears on this answer sheet and that I am here to take the LSAT for the sole purpose of being considered for application to law school. I further certify that I will neither assist nor receive assistance from any other candidate, and I agree not to copy or retain examination questions or to transmit them to or discuss them with any other person in any form.

_____
_____
_____
_____
_____
_____
_____
_____
_____
_____

SIGNATURE: _____   TODAY'S DATE: _____/_____/_____
                                                        MONTH DAY   YEAR

*LSAT is a registered trademark of the Law School Admissions Council, Inc.

USE ONLY A NO 2. OR HB PENCIL TO COMPLETE THIS ANSWER SHEET. DO NOT USE INK.

● Right Mark   ⊘ ⊗ ⊙ Wrong Marks

1 LAST NAME | FIRST NAME | MI

2 SOCIAL SECURITY/ SOCIAL INSURANCE NO.

3 KAPLAN ENROLLMENT ID

4 TODAY'S DATE

MONTH	DAY	YEAR
○ Jan		
○ Feb		
○ Mar		
○ Apr		
○ May		
○ June		
○ July		
○ Aug		
○ Sept		
○ Oct		
○ Nov		
○ Dec		

5 RACIAL/ETHNIC DESCRIPTION

6 GENDER

7 DOMINANT LANGUAGE

8 ENGLISH FLUENCY

9 TEST BOOK SERIAL NO.

10 TEST FORM

11 TEST DATE

12 CENTER NUMBER

13 TEST FORM CODE

Law School Admission Test*

Mark one and only one answer to each question. Be sure to fill in completely the space for your intended answer choice. If you erase, do so completely. Make no stray marks.

SECTION 1 | **SECTION 2** | **SECTION 3** | **SECTION 4** | **SECTION 5**

(Answer bubbles 1–30, each with choices A B C D E, for all five sections)

14 PLEASE PRINT ALL INFORMATION

LAST NAME   FIRST

EMAIL

PHONE NUMBER

MAILING ADDRESS

CLASS CODE

KAPLAN

TEST PREP

www.kaptest.com/lsat
1-800-KAP-TEST

LSAT is a registered trademark of the Law School Admissions Council, Inc.

SCANTRON   Mark Reflex® EM-284925-1:654321   LL3225A

General Directions for the LSAT* Answer Sheet

The actual testing time for this portion of the test will be 2 hours 55 minutes. There are five sections, each with a time limit of 35 minutes. The supervisor will tell you when to begin and end each section. If you finish a section before time is called, you may check your work on that section only; do not turn to any other section of the test book and do not work on any other section either in the test book or on the answer sheet.

There are several different types of questions on the test, and each question type has its own directions. Be sure you understand the directions for each question type before attempting to answer any questions in that section.

Not everyone will finish all the questions in the time allowed. Do not hurry, but work steadily and as quickly as you can without sacrificing accuracy. You are advised to use your time effectively. If a question seems too difficult, go on to the next one and return to the difficult question after completing the section. MARK THE BEST ANSWER YOU CAN FOR EVERY QUESTION. NO DEDUCTIONS WILL BE MADE FOR WRONG ANSWERS. YOUR SCORE WILL BE BASED ONLY ON THE NUMBER OF QUESTIONS YOU ANSWER CORRECTLY.

ALL YOUR ANSWERS MUST BE MARKED ON THE ANSWER SHEET. Answer spaces for each question are lettered to correspond with the letters of the potential answers to each question in the test book. After you have decided which of the answers is correct, blacken the corresponding space on the answer sheet. BE SURE THAT EACH MARK IS BLACK AND COMPLETELY FILLS THE ANSWER SPACE. Give only one answer to each question. If you change an answer, be sure that all previous marks are erased completely. Since the answer sheet is machine scored, incomplete erasures may be interpreted as intended answers. ANSWERS RECORDED IN THE TEST BOOK WILL NOT BE SCORED.

There may be more questions noted on this answer sheet than there are questions in a section. Do not be concerned but be certain that the section and number of the question you are answering matches the answer sheet section and question number. Additional answer spaces in any answer sheet section should be left blank. Begin your next section in the number one answer space for that section.

Kaplan takes various steps to ensure that answer sheets are returned from test centers in a timely manner for processing. In the unlikely event that an answer sheet(s) is not received, Kaplan will permit the examinee to either retest at no additional fee or to receive a refund of his or her test fee. THESE REMEDIES ARE THE EXCLUSIVE REMEDIES AVAILABLE IN THE UNLIKELY EVENT THAT AN ANSWER SHEET IS NOT RECEIVED BY KAPLAN.

Score Cancellation

Complete this section only if you are absolutely certain you want to cancel your score. A CANCELLATION REQUEST CANNOT BE RESCINDED. IF YOU ARE AT ALL UNCERTAIN, YOU SHOULD NOT COMPLETE THIS SECTION.

To cancel your score from this administration, you must:

A. fill in both ovals here..... ⃝ ⃝

B. read the following statement. Then sign your name and enter the date.
YOUR SIGNATURE ALONE IS NOT SUFFICIENT FOR SCORE CANCELLATION. BOTH OVALS MUST BE FILLED IN FOR SCANNING EQUIPMENT TO RECOGNIZE YOUR REQUEST FOR SCORE CANCELLATION.

I certify that I wish to cancel my test score from this administration. I understand that my request is irreversible and that my score will not be sent to me or to the law schools to which I apply.

_____
Sign your name in full

_____
Date

HOW DID YOU PREPARE FOR THE LSAT*?
(Select all that apply.)

Responses to this item are voluntary and will be used for statistical research purposes only.

- ⃝ By attending a Kaplan LSAT* prep course or tutoring program
- ⃝ By attending a non-Kaplan prep course or tutoring program (Please specify:_____)
- ⃝ By using a Kaplan LSAT* prep book
- ⃝ By using a non-Kaplan prep book (Please specify: _____)
- ⃝ By working through the sample questions and free sample tests provided by the LSAC
- ⃝ By working through official LSAT* PrepTests and/or other LSAC test prep products
- ⃝ Other preparation (Please specify: _____)
- ⃝ No preparation

CERTIFYING STATEMENT

Please write (DO NOT PRINT) the following statement. Sign and date.

I certify that I am the examinee whose name appears on this answer sheet and that I am here to take the LSAT for the sole purpose of being considered for application to law school. I further certify that I will neither assist nor receive assistance from any other candidate, and I agree not to copy or retain examination questions or to transmit them to or discuss them with any other person in any form.

_____
_____
_____
_____
_____
_____
_____
_____
_____
_____

SIGNATURE: _____   TODAY'S DATE: _____/_____/_____
                                                                                  MONTH DAY YEAR

*LSAT is a registered trademark of the Law School Admissions Council, Inc.

Index